Honda Civic & Acura Integra Automotive Repair Manual

by Larry Warren, Alan Ahlstrand, and John H Haynes

Member of the Guild of Motoring Writers

Models covered:
Honda Civic - 1996 through 1998
Acura Integra - 1994 through 1998

ABCDE
FGHIJ
KLMNO
PQRST

Haynes Publishing Group
Sparkford Nr Yeovil
Somerset BA22 7JJ England

Haynes North America, Inc
861 Lawrence Drive
Newbury Park
California 91320 USA

About this manual

Its purpose

The purpose of this manual is to help you get the best value from your vehicle. It can do so in several ways. It can help you decide what work must be done, even if you choose to have it done by a dealer service department or a repair shop; it provides information and procedures for routine maintenance and servicing; and it offers diagnostic and repair procedures to follow when trouble occurs.

We hope you use the manual to tackle the work yourself. For many simpler jobs, doing it yourself may be quicker than arranging an appointment to get the vehicle into a shop and making the trips to leave it and pick it up. More importantly, a lot of money can be saved by avoiding the expense the shop must pass on to you to cover its labor and overhead costs. An added benefit is the sense of satisfaction and accomplishment that you feel after doing the job yourself.

Using the manual

The manual is divided into Chapters. Each Chapter is divided into numbered Sections, which are headed in bold type between horizontal lines. Each Section consists of consecutively numbered paragraphs.

At the beginning of each numbered Section you will be referred to any illustrations which apply to the procedures in that Section. The reference numbers used in illustration captions pinpoint the pertinent Section and the Step within that Section. That is, illustration 3.2 means the illustration refers to Section 3 and Step (or paragraph) 2 within that Section.

Procedures, once described in the text, are not normally repeated. When it's necessary to refer to another Chapter, the reference will be given as Chapter and Section number. Cross references given without use of the word "Chapter" apply to Sections and/or paragraphs in the same Chapter. For example, "see Section 8" means in the same Chapter.

References to the left or right side of the vehicle assume you are sitting in the driver's seat, facing forward.

Even though we have prepared this manual with extreme care, neither the publisher nor the author can accept responsibility for any errors in, or omissions from, the information given.

NOTE

A **Note** provides information necessary to properly complete a procedure or information which will make the procedure easier to understand.

CAUTION

A **Caution** provides a special procedure or special steps which must be taken while completing the procedure where the Caution is found. Not heeding a Caution can result in damage to the assembly being worked on.

WARNING

A **Warning** provides a special procedure or special steps which must be taken while completing the procedure where the Warning is found. Not heeding a Warning can result in personal injury.

Acknowledgements
Wiring diagrams provided exclusively for Haynes North America, Inc. by Valley Forge Technical Communications

© **Haynes North America, Inc. 1999**

With permission from J.H. Haynes & Co. Ltd.

A book in the Haynes Automotive Repair Manual Series

Printed in the U.S.A.

ISBN 1 56392 330 0

Library of Congress Catalog Card Number 98-88165

While every attempt is made to ensure that the information in this manual is correct, no liability can be accepted by the authors or publishers for loss, damage or injury caused by any errors in, or omissions from, the information given.

Contents

Haynes mechanic, author and photographer with 1995 Acura Integra

Introduction to the Honda Civic and Acura Integra

These models are available in two-door coupe, hatchback and four-door sedan body styles.

The transversely mounted inline four-cylinder engine used in these models is equipped with electronic fuel injection.

The engine drives the front wheels through either a five-speed manual transaxle, four-speed automatic transaxle or a Continuously Variable Transaxle (CVT) via independent driveaxles.

Independent suspension, featuring coil spring/shock absorber units, is used on all four wheels. The power-assisted rack-and-pinion steering unit is mounted behind the engine.

The brakes are disc at the front and either discs or drums at the rear, with power assist standard. An Anti-lock Braking System (ABS) is available on most models.

Vehicle identification numbers

Modifications are a continuing and unpublicized process in vehicle manufacturing. Since spare parts manuals and lists are compiled on a numerical basis, the individual vehicle numbers are essential to correctly identify the component required.

Vehicle identification number (VIN)

This very important number is stamped on the firewall in the engine compartment and on a plate attached to the dashboard inside the windshield on the driver's side of the vehicle. The VIN also appears on the Vehicle Certificate of Title and Registration. It contains information such as where and when the vehicle was manufactured, the model year and the body style (see illustration).

Engine and models year codes

Two particularly important pieces of information found in the VIN are the model year code and the line/body/engine type code. Counting from the left, the line/body/engine code are the 4th, 5th and 6th digits. The model year code letter designation is the 10th digit.

Line/body/engine codes

Civic

    EJ6 = 3 door/D16Y7
    EJ7 = 2 door/D16Y5
    EJ8 = 4 door/D16Y8

Integra

    DB7 = 4 door/B18B1
    DB8 = 4 door/B18C1
    DC2 = 3 door/B18C1, B18C5
    DC4 = 3 door/B18B1

Model year codes

    R = 1994
    S = 1995
    T = 1996
    V = 1997
    W = 1998

Engine number

The engine code number, which is commonly needed when ordering engine parts, can be found near the right (passenger side) end of the engine, near the exhaust manifold. The engine code is the first five digits of the number. The four engines covered by this manual are:

Civic

    D16Y5 - 1.6L SOHC 16-valve VTEC-E
    D16Y7 - 1.6L SOHC 16-valve
    D16Y8 - 1.6L SOHC 16-valve VTEC

Integra

    B18B1 - 1.8L DOHC 16-valve
    B18C1 - 1.8L SOHC 16-valve VTEC
    B18C5 - 1.8L DOHC 16-valve VTEC

Transaxle number

The transaxle number is commonly needed when ordering transaxle parts. On manual transaxles it's located on the bellhousing, near the starter motor. On automatic transaxles, it's located on the right front of the transaxle case, above the dipstick. On Continuously Variable Transaxles, the number is found on the vertical surface near the fluid dipstick.

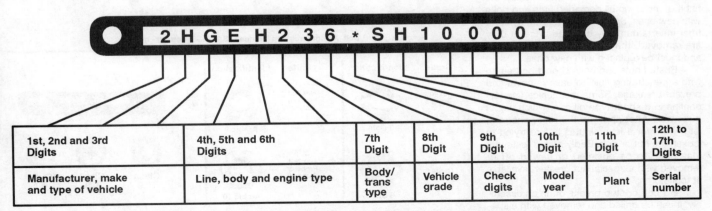

1st, 2nd and 3rd Digits	4th, 5th and 6th Digits	7th Digit	8th Digit	9th Digit	10th Digit	11th Digit	12th to 17th Digits
Manufacturer, make and type of vehicle	Line, body and engine type	Body/trans type	Vehicle grade	Check digits	Model year	Plant	Serial number

The Vehicle Identification Number (VIN) contains important information on the vehicle

Buying parts

Replacement parts are available from many sources, which generally fall into one of two categories - authorized dealer parts departments and independent retail auto parts stores. Our advice concerning these parts is as follows:

Retail auto parts stores: Good auto parts stores will stock frequently needed components which wear out relatively fast, such as clutch components, exhaust systems, brake parts, tune-up parts, etc. These stores often supply new or reconditioned parts on an exchange basis, which can save a considerable amount of money. Discount auto parts stores are often very good places to buy materials and parts needed for general vehicle maintenance such as oil, grease, filters, spark plugs, belts, touch-up paint, bulbs, etc. They also usually sell tools and general accessories, have convenient hours, charge lower prices and can often be found not far from home.

Authorized dealer parts department: This is the best source for parts which are unique to the vehicle and not generally available elsewhere (such as major engine parts, transmission parts, trim pieces, etc.).

Warranty information: If the vehicle is still covered under warranty, be sure that any replacement parts purchased - regardless of the source - do not invalidate the warranty!

To be sure of obtaining the correct parts, have engine and chassis numbers available and, if possible, take the old parts along for positive identification.

Maintenance techniques, tools and working facilities

Maintenance techniques

There are a number of techniques involved in maintenance and repair that will be referred to throughout this manual. Application of these techniques will enable the home mechanic to be more efficient, better organized and capable of performing the various tasks properly, which will ensure that the repair job is thorough and complete.

Fasteners

Fasteners are nuts, bolts, studs and screws used to hold two or more parts together. There are a few things to keep in mind when working with fasteners. Almost all of them use a locking device of some type, either a lockwasher, locknut, locking tab or thread adhesive. All threaded fasteners should be clean and straight, with undamaged threads and undamaged corners on the hex head where the wrench fits. Develop the habit of replacing all damaged nuts and bolts with new ones. Special locknuts with nylon or fiber inserts can only be used once. If they are removed, they lose their locking ability and must be replaced with new ones.

Rusted nuts and bolts should be treated with a penetrating fluid to ease removal and prevent breakage. Some mechanics use turpentine in a spout-type oil can, which works quite well. After applying the rust penetrant, let it work for a few minutes before trying to loosen the nut or bolt. Badly rusted fasteners may have to be chiseled or sawed off or removed with a special nut breaker, available at tool stores.

If a bolt or stud breaks off in an assembly, it can be drilled and removed with a special tool commonly available for this purpose. Most automotive machine shops can perform this task, as well as other repair procedures, such as the repair of threaded holes that have been stripped out.

Flat washers and lockwashers, when removed from an assembly, should always be replaced exactly as removed. Replace any damaged washers with new ones. Never use a lockwasher on any soft metal surface (such as aluminum), thin sheet metal or plastic.

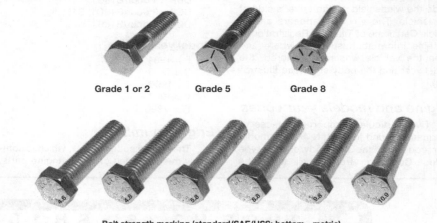

Grade 1 or 2   Grade 5   Grade 8

Bolt strength marking (standard/SAE/USS; bottom - metric)

Grade	Identification	Grade	Identification
Hex Nut Grade 5	3 Dots	Hex Nut Property Class 9	Arabic 9
Hex Nut Grade 8	6 Dots	Hex Nut Property Class 10	Arabic 10

Standard hex nut strength markings

Metric hex nut strength markings

Class 10.9   Class 9.8   Class 8.8

Metric stud strength markings

00-1 HAYNES

Fastener sizes

For a number of reasons, automobile manufacturers are making wider and wider use of metric fasteners. Therefore, it is important to be able to tell the difference between standard (sometimes called U.S. or SAE) and metric hardware, since they cannot be interchanged.

All bolts, whether standard or metric, are sized according to diameter, thread pitch and length. For example, a standard 1/2 - 13 x 1 bolt is 1/2 inch in diameter, has 13 threads per inch and is 1 inch long. An M12 - 1.75 x 25 metric bolt is 12 mm in diameter, has a thread pitch of 1.75 mm (the distance between threads) and is 25 mm long. The two bolts are nearly identical, and easily confused, but they are not interchangeable.

In addition to the differences in diameter, thread pitch and length, metric and standard bolts can also be distinguished by examining the bolt heads. To begin with, the distance across the flats on a standard bolt head is measured in inches, while the same dimension on a metric bolt is sized in millimeters (the same is true for nuts). As a result, a standard wrench should not be used on a metric bolt and a metric wrench should not be used on a standard bolt. Also, most standard bolts have slashes radiating out from the center of the head to denote the grade or strength of the bolt, which is an indication of the amount of torque that can be applied to it. The greater the number of slashes, the greater the strength of the bolt. Grades 0 through 5 are commonly used on automobiles. Metric bolts have a property class (grade) number, rather than a slash, molded into their heads to indicate bolt strength. In this case, the higher the number, the stronger the bolt. Property class numbers 8.8, 9.8 and 10.9 are commonly used on automobiles.

Strength markings can also be used to distinguish standard hex nuts from metric hex nuts. Many standard nuts have dots stamped into one side, while metric nuts are marked with a number. The greater the number of dots, or the higher the number, the greater the strength of the nut.

Metric studs are also marked on their ends according to property class (grade). Larger studs are numbered (the same as metric bolts), while smaller studs carry a geometric code to denote grade.

It should be noted that many fasteners, especially Grades 0 through 2, have no distinguishing marks on them. When such is the case, the only way to determine whether it is standard or metric is to measure the thread pitch or compare it to a known fastener of the same size.

Standard fasteners are often referred to as SAE, as opposed to metric. However, it should be noted that SAE technically refers to a non-metric fine thread fastener only. Coarse thread non-metric fasteners are referred to as USS sizes.

Since fasteners of the same size (both standard and metric) may have different

Metric thread sizes	Ft-lbs	Nm
M-6	6 to 9	9 to 12
M-8	14 to 21	19 to 28
M-10	28 to 40	38 to 54
M-12	50 to 71	68 to 96
M-14	80 to 140	109 to 154

Pipe thread sizes		
1/8	5 to 8	7 to 10
1/4	12 to 18	17 to 24
3/8	22 to 33	30 to 44
1/2	25 to 35	34 to 47

U.S. thread sizes		
1/4 - 20	6 to 9	9 to 12
5/16 - 18	12 to 18	17 to 24
5/16 - 24	14 to 20	19 to 27
3/8 - 16	22 to 32	30 to 43
3/8 - 24	27 to 38	37 to 51
7/16 - 14	40 to 55	55 to 74
7/16 - 20	40 to 60	55 to 81
1/2 - 13	55 to 80	75 to 108

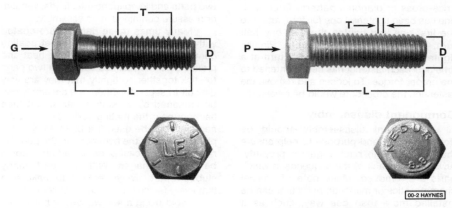

Standard (SAE and USS) bolt dimensions/grade marks

G — Grade marks (bolt strength)
L — Length (in inches)
T — Thread pitch (number of threads per inch)
D — Nominal diameter (in inches)

Metric bolt dimensions/grade marks

P — Property class (bolt strength)
L — Length (in millimeters)
T — Thread pitch (distance between threads in millimeters)
D — Diameter

strength ratings, be sure to reinstall any bolts, studs or nuts removed from your vehicle in their original locations. Also, when replacing a fastener with a new one, make sure that the new one has a strength rating equal to or greater than the original.

Tightening sequences and procedures

Most threaded fasteners should be tightened to a specific torque value (torque is the twisting force applied to a threaded component such as a nut or bolt). Overtightening the fastener can weaken it and cause it to break, while undertightening can cause it to eventually come loose. Bolts, screws and studs, depending on the material they are made of and their thread diameters, have specific torque values, many of which are noted in the Specifications at the beginning of each Chapter. Be sure to follow the torque recommendations closely. For fasteners not assigned a specific torque, a general torque value chart is presented here as a guide. These torque values are for dry (unlubricated) fasteners threaded into steel or cast iron (not aluminum). As was previously mentioned, the size and grade of a fastener determine the amount of torque that can safely be applied to it. The figures listed here are approximate for Grade 2 and Grade 3 fasteners. Higher grades can tolerate higher torque values.

Fasteners laid out in a pattern, such as cylinder head bolts, oil pan bolts, differential cover bolts, etc., must be loosened or tightened in sequence to avoid warping the com-

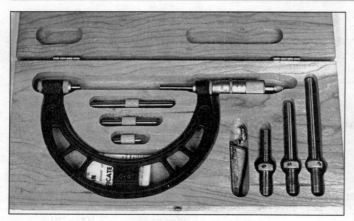

Micrometer set

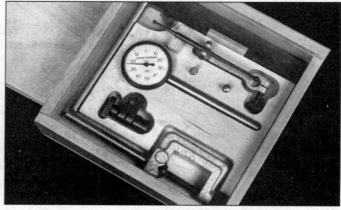

Dial indicator set

ponent. This sequence will normally be shown in the appropriate Chapter. If a specific pattern is not given, the following procedures can be used to prevent warping.

Initially, the bolts or nuts should be assembled finger-tight only. Next, they should be tightened one full turn each, in a criss-cross or diagonal pattern. After each one has been tightened one full turn, return to the first one and tighten them all one-half turn, following the same pattern. Finally, tighten each of them one-quarter turn at a time until each fastener has been tightened to the proper torque. To loosen and remove the fasteners, the procedure would be reversed.

Component disassembly

Component disassembly should be done with care and purpose to help ensure that the parts go back together properly. Always keep track of the sequence in which parts are removed. Make note of special characteristics or marks on parts that can be installed more than one way, such as a grooved thrust washer on a shaft. It is a good idea to lay the disassembled parts out on a clean surface in the order that they were removed. It may also be helpful to make sketches or take instant photos of components before removal.

When removing fasteners from a component, keep track of their locations. Sometimes threading a bolt back in a part, or putting the washers and nut back on a stud, can prevent mix-ups later. If nuts and bolts cannot be returned to their original locations, they should be kept in a compartmented box or a series of small boxes. A cupcake or muffin tin is ideal for this purpose, since each cavity can hold the bolts and nuts from a particular area (i.e. oil pan bolts, valve cover bolts, engine mount bolts, etc.). A pan of this type is especially helpful when working on assemblies with very small parts, such as the carburetor, alternator, valve train or interior dash and trim pieces. The cavities can be marked with paint or tape to identify the contents.

Whenever wiring looms, harnesses or connectors are separated, it is a good idea to

identify the two halves with numbered pieces of masking tape so they can be easily reconnected.

Gasket sealing surfaces

Throughout any vehicle, gaskets are used to seal the mating surfaces between two parts and keep lubricants, fluids, vacuum or pressure contained in an assembly.

Many times these gaskets are coated with a liquid or paste-type gasket sealing compound before assembly. Age, heat and pressure can sometimes cause the two parts to stick together so tightly that they are very difficult to separate. Often, the assembly can be loosened by striking it with a soft-face hammer near the mating surfaces. A regular hammer can be used if a block of wood is placed between the hammer and the part. Do not hammer on cast parts or parts that could be easily damaged. With any particularly stubborn part, always recheck to make sure that every fastener has been removed.

Avoid using a screwdriver or bar to pry apart an assembly, as they can easily mar the gasket sealing surfaces of the parts, which must remain smooth. If prying is absolutely necessary, use an old broom handle, but keep in mind that extra clean up will be necessary if the wood splinters.

After the parts are separated, the old gasket must be carefully scraped off and the gasket surfaces cleaned. Stubborn gasket material can be soaked with rust penetrant or treated with a special chemical to soften it so it can be easily scraped off. A scraper can be fashioned from a piece of copper tubing by flattening and sharpening one end. Copper is recommended because it is usually softer than the surfaces to be scraped, which reduces the chance of gouging the part. Some gaskets can be removed with a wire brush, but regardless of the method used, the mating surfaces must be left clean and smooth. If for some reason the gasket surface is gouged, then a gasket sealer thick enough to fill scratches will have to be used during reassembly of the components. For most applications, a non-drying (or semi-drying) gasket sealer should be used.

Hose removal tips

Warning: *If the vehicle is equipped with air conditioning, do not disconnect any of the A/C hoses without first having the system depressurized by a dealer service department or a service station.*

Hose removal precautions closely parallel gasket removal precautions. Avoid scratching or gouging the surface that the hose mates against or the connection may leak. This is especially true for radiator hoses. Because of various chemical reactions, the rubber in hoses can bond itself to the metal spigot that the hose fits over. To remove a hose, first loosen the hose clamps that secure it to the spigot. Then, with slip-joint pliers, grab the hose at the clamp and rotate it around the spigot. Work it back and forth until it is completely free, then pull it off. Silicone or other lubricants will ease removal if they can be applied between the hose and the outside of the spigot. Apply the same lubricant to the inside of the hose and the outside of the spigot to simplify installation.

As a last resort (and if the hose is to be replaced with a new one anyway), the rubber can be slit with a knife and the hose peeled from the spigot. If this must be done, be careful that the metal connection is not damaged.

If a hose clamp is broken or damaged, do not reuse it. Wire-type clamps usually weaken with age, so it is a good idea to replace them with screw-type clamps whenever a hose is removed.

Tools

A selection of good tools is a basic requirement for anyone who plans to maintain and repair his or her own vehicle. For the owner who has few tools, the initial investment might seem high, but when compared to the spiraling costs of professional auto maintenance and repair, it is a wise one.

To help the owner decide which tools are needed to perform the tasks detailed in this manual, the following tool lists are offered: *Maintenance and minor repair, Repair/overhaul* and *Special*.

The newcomer to practical mechanics

Dial caliper

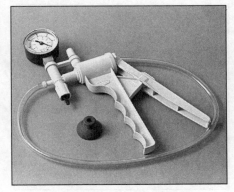

Hand-operated vacuum pump

Timing light

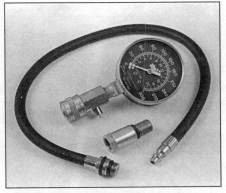

Compression gauge with spark plug hole adapter

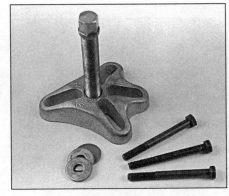

Damper/steering wheel puller

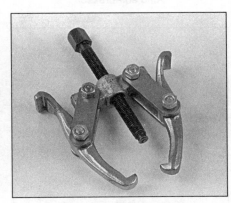

General purpose puller

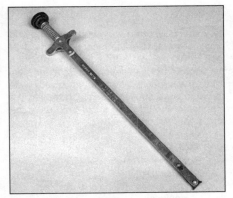

Hydraulic lifter removal tool

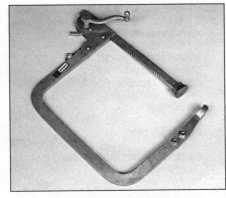

Valve spring compressor

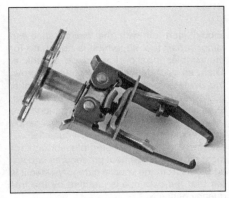

Valve spring compressor

Ridge reamer

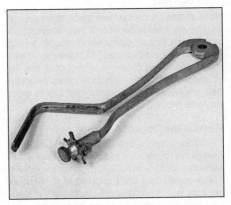

Piston ring groove cleaning tool

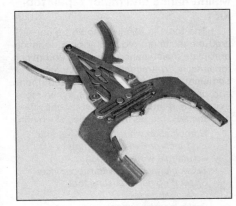

Ring removal/installation tool

Ring compressor

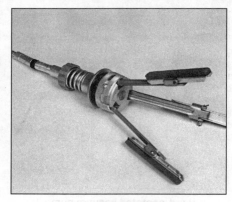
Cylinder hone

Brake hold-down spring tool

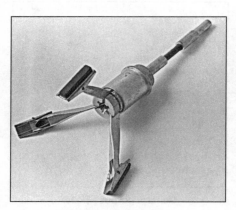
Brake cylinder hone

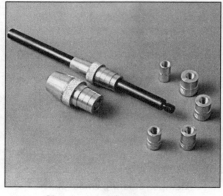
Clutch plate alignment tool

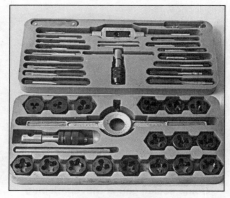
Tap and die set

should start off with the *maintenance and minor repair* tool kit, which is adequate for the simpler jobs performed on a vehicle. Then, as confidence and experience grow, the owner can tackle more difficult tasks, buying additional tools as they are needed. Eventually the basic kit will be expanded into the *repair and overhaul* tool set. Over a period of time, the experienced do-it-yourselfer will assemble a tool set complete enough for most repair and overhaul procedures and will add tools from the special category when it is felt that the expense is justified by the frequency of use.

Maintenance and minor repair tool kit

The tools in this list should be considered the minimum required for performance of routine maintenance, servicing and minor repair work. We recommend the purchase of combination wrenches (box-end and open-end combined in one wrench). While more expensive than open end wrenches, they offer the advantages of both types of wrench.

Combination wrench set (1/4-inch to 1 inch or 6 mm to 19 mm)
Adjustable wrench, 8 inch
Spark plug wrench with rubber insert
Spark plug gap adjusting tool
Feeler gauge set
Brake bleeder wrench

Standard screwdriver (5/16-inch x 6 inch)
Phillips screwdriver (No. 2 x 6 inch)
Combination pliers - 6 inch
Hacksaw and assortment of blades
Tire pressure gauge
Grease gun
Oil can
Fine emery cloth
Wire brush
Battery post and cable cleaning tool
Oil filter wrench
Funnel (medium size)
Safety goggles
Jackstands (2)
Drain pan

Note: *If basic tune-ups are going to be part of routine maintenance, it will be necessary to purchase a good quality stroboscopic timing light and combination tachometer/dwell meter. Although they are included in the list of special tools, it is mentioned here because they are absolutely necessary for tuning most vehicles properly.*

Repair and overhaul tool set

These tools are essential for anyone who plans to perform major repairs and are in addition to those in the maintenance and minor repair tool kit. Included is a comprehensive set of sockets which, though expensive, are invaluable because of their versatil-

ity, especially when various extensions and drives are available. We recommend the 1/2-inch drive over the 3/8-inch drive. Although the larger drive is bulky and more expensive, it has the capacity of accepting a very wide range of large sockets. Ideally, however, the mechanic should have a 3/8-inch drive set and a 1/2-inch drive set.

Socket set(s)
Reversible ratchet
Extension - 10 inch
Universal joint
Torque wrench (same size drive as sockets)
Ball peen hammer - 8 ounce
Soft-face hammer (plastic/rubber)
Standard screwdriver (1/4-inch x 6 inch)
Standard screwdriver (stubby - 5/16-inch)
Phillips screwdriver (No. 3 x 8 inch)
Phillips screwdriver (stubby - No. 2)
Pliers - vise grip
Pliers - lineman's
Pliers - needle nose
Pliers - snap-ring (internal and external)
Cold chisel - 1/2-inch
Scribe
Scraper (made from flattened copper tubing)
Centerpunch
Pin punches (1/16, 1/8, 3/16-inch)
Steel rule/straightedge - 12 inch

Allen wrench set (1/8 to 3/8-inch or
    4 mm to 10 mm)
A selection of files
Wire brush (large)
Jackstands (second set)
Jack (scissor or hydraulic type)

Note: Another tool which is often useful is an electric drill with a chuck capacity of 3/8-inch and a set of good quality drill bits.

Special tools

The tools in this list include those which are not used regularly, are expensive to buy, or which need to be used in accordance with their manufacturer's instructions. Unless these tools will be used frequently, it is not very economical to purchase many of them. A consideration would be to split the cost and use between yourself and a friend or friends. In addition, most of these tools can be obtained from a tool rental shop on a temporary basis.

This list primarily contains only those tools and instruments widely available to the public, and not those special tools produced by the vehicle manufacturer for distribution to dealer service departments. Occasionally, references to the manufacturer's special tools are included in the text of this manual. Generally, an alternative method of doing the job without the special tool is offered. However, sometimes there is no alternative to their use. Where this is the case, and the tool cannot be purchased or borrowed, the work should be turned over to the dealer service department or an automotive repair shop.

Valve spring compressor
Piston ring groove cleaning tool
Piston ring compressor
Piston ring installation tool
Cylinder compression gauge
Cylinder ridge reamer
Cylinder surfacing hone
Cylinder bore gauge
Micrometers and/or dial calipers
Hydraulic lifter removal tool
Balljoint separator
Universal-type puller
Impact screwdriver
Dial indicator set
Stroboscopic timing light (inductive
    pick-up)
Hand operated vacuum/pressure pump
Tachometer/dwell meter
Universal electrical multimeter
Cable hoist
Brake spring removal and installation
    tools
Floor jack

Buying tools

For the do-it-yourselfer who is just starting to get involved in vehicle maintenance and repair, there are a number of options available when purchasing tools. If maintenance and minor repair is the extent of the work to be done, the purchase of individual tools is satisfactory. If, on the other hand, extensive work is planned, it would be a good idea to purchase a modest tool set from one

of the large retail chain stores. A set can usually be bought at a substantial savings over the individual tool prices, and they often come with a tool box. As additional tools are needed, add-on sets, individual tools and a larger tool box can be purchased to expand the tool selection. Building a tool set gradually allows the cost of the tools to be spread over a longer period of time and gives the mechanic the freedom to choose only those tools that will actually be used.

Tool stores will often be the only source of some of the special tools that are needed, but regardless of where tools are bought, try to avoid cheap ones, especially when buying screwdrivers and sockets, because they won't last very long. The expense involved in replacing cheap tools will eventually be greater than the initial cost of quality tools.

Care and maintenance of tools

Good tools are expensive, so it makes sense to treat them with respect. Keep them clean and in usable condition and store them properly when not in use. Always wipe off any dirt, grease or metal chips before putting them away. Never leave tools lying around in the work area. Upon completion of a job, always check closely under the hood for tools that may have been left there so they won't get lost during a test drive.

Some tools, such as screwdrivers, pliers, wrenches and sockets, can be hung on a panel mounted on the garage or workshop wall, while others should be kept in a tool box or tray. Measuring instruments, gauges, meters, etc. must be carefully stored where they cannot be damaged by weather or impact from other tools.

When tools are used with care and stored properly, they will last a very long time. Even with the best of care, though, tools will wear out if used frequently. When a tool is damaged or worn out, replace it. Subsequent jobs will be safer and more enjoyable if you do.

How to repair damaged threads

Sometimes, the internal threads of a nut or bolt hole can become stripped, usually from overtightening. Stripping threads is an all-too-common occurrence, especially when working with aluminum parts, because aluminum is so soft that it easily strips out.

Usually, external or internal threads are only partially stripped. After they've been cleaned up with a tap or die, they'll still work. Sometimes, however, threads are badly damaged. When this happens, you've got three choices:

1) Drill and tap the hole to the next suitable oversize and install a larger diameter bolt, screw or stud.
2) Drill and tap the hole to accept a threaded plug, then drill and tap the plug to the original screw size. You can also buy a plug already threaded to the original size. Then you simply drill a hole to

the specified size, then run the threaded plug into the hole with a bolt and jam nut. Once the plug is fully seated, remove the jam nut and bolt.
3) The third method uses a patented thread repair kit like Heli-Coil or Slimsert. These easy-to-use kits are designed to repair damaged threads in straight-through holes and blind holes. Both are available as kits which can handle a variety of sizes and thread patterns. Drill the hole, then tap it with the special included tap. Install the Heli-Coil and the hole is back to its original diameter and thread pitch.

Regardless of which method you use, be sure to proceed calmly and carefully. A little impatience or carelessness during one of these relatively simple procedures can ruin your whole day's work and cost you a bundle if you wreck an expensive part.

Working facilities

Not to be overlooked when discussing tools is the workshop. If anything more than routine maintenance is to be carried out, some sort of suitable work area is essential.

It is understood, and appreciated, that many home mechanics do not have a good workshop or garage available, and end up removing an engine or doing major repairs outside. It is recommended, however, that the overhaul or repair be completed under the cover of a roof.

A clean, flat workbench or table of comfortable working height is an absolute necessity. The workbench should be equipped with a vise that has a jaw opening of at least four inches.

As mentioned previously, some clean, dry storage space is also required for tools, as well as the lubricants, fluids, cleaning solvents, etc. which soon become necessary.

Sometimes waste oil and fluids, drained from the engine or cooling system during normal maintenance or repairs, present a disposal problem. To avoid pouring them on the ground or into a sewage system, pour the used fluids into large containers, seal them with caps and take them to an authorized disposal site or recycling center. Plastic jugs, such as old antifreeze containers, are ideal for this purpose.

Always keep a supply of old newspapers and clean rags available. Old towels are excellent for mopping up spills. Many mechanics use rolls of paper towels for most work because they are readily available and disposable. To help keep the area under the vehicle clean, a large cardboard box can be cut open and flattened to protect the garage or shop floor.

Whenever working over a painted surface, such as when leaning over a fender to service something under the hood, always cover it with an old blanket or bedspread to protect the finish. Vinyl covered pads, made especially for this purpose, are available at auto parts stores.

Jacking and towing

Jacking

Warning: *The jack supplied with the vehicle should only be used for changing a tire or placing jackstands under the frame. Never work under the vehicle or start the engine while this jack is being used as the only means of support.*

The vehicle should be on level ground. Place the shift lever in Park, if you have an automatic, or Reverse if you have a manual transaxle. Block the wheel diagonally opposite the wheel being changed. Set the parking brake.

Remove the spare tire and jack from stowage. Remove the wheel cover and trim ring (if so equipped) with the tapered end of the lug nut wrench by inserting and twisting the handle and then prying against the back of the wheel cover. **Caution:** *On some models the wheel cover can't be removed by prying; the wheel nuts must be removed first. Loosen, but do not remove, the lug nuts (one-half turn is sufficient).*

Place the scissors-type jack under the side of the vehicle and adjust the jack height until the slot in the jack head engages with the raised portion of the ridge on the vertical rocker panel flange nearest the wheel to be changed. There is a front and rear jacking point on each side of the vehicle **(see illustration)**.

Turn the jack handle clockwise until the tire clears the ground. Remove the lug nuts and pull the wheel off. Replace it with the spare.

Install the lug nuts with the beveled edges facing in. Tighten them snugly. Don't attempt to tighten them completely until the vehicle is lowered or it could slip off the jack. Turn the jack handle counterclockwise to lower the vehicle. Remove the jack and tighten the lug nuts in a criss-cross pattern.

Install the cover (and trim ring, if used) and be sure it's snapped into place all the way around.

Stow the tire, jack and wrench. Unblock the wheels.

Towing

As a general rule, the vehicle should be towed with the front (drive) wheels off the ground (the best method is to have the vehicle placed on a flat-bed tow truck). If they can't be raised, place them on a dolly. The ignition key must be in the OFF position, since the steering lock mechanism isn't strong enough to hold the front wheels straight while towing.

Vehicles equipped with an automatic transaxle can be towed from the front with all four wheels on the ground, provided that speeds don't exceed 35 mph and the distance is not over 50 miles. Before towing, check the transmission fluid level (see Chapter 1). If the level is below the HOT line on the dipstick, add fluid or use a towing dolly. Additionally, perform the following steps:

a) *Release the parking brake*
b) *Start the engine*
c) *Move the transaxle gear selector into D4, then to Neutral*
d) *Turn off the engine*
e) *Place the ignition key in the OFF (not the LOCK position).*

Caution: *Never tow a vehicle with an automatic transaxle from the rear with the front wheels on the ground.*

When towing a vehicle equipped with a manual transaxle or Continuously Variable Transaxle with all four wheels on the ground, be sure to place the shift lever in neutral and release the parking brake.

Equipment specifically designed for towing should be used. It should be attached to the main structural members of the vehicle, not the bumpers or brackets.

Safety is a major consideration when towing and all applicable state and local laws must be obeyed. A safety chain system must be used at all times. Remember that power steering and power brakes will not work with the engine off.

The jacking points are located near the front and rear wheel on each side of the vehicle

Booster battery (jump) starting

Observe these precautions when using a booster battery to start a vehicle:

a) *Before connecting the booster battery, make sure the ignition switch is in the Off position.*
b) *Turn off the lights, heater and other electrical loads.*
c) *Your eyes should be shielded. Safety goggles are a good idea.*
d) *Make sure the booster battery is the same voltage as the dead one in the vehicle.*
e) *The two vehicles MUST NOT TOUCH each other!*
f) *Make sure the transaxle is in Neutral (manual) or Park (automatic).*
g) *If the booster battery is not a maintenance-free type, remove the vent caps and lay a cloth over the vent holes.*

Connect the red jumper cable to the positive (+) terminals of each battery **(see illustration)**.

Connect one end of the black jumper cable to the negative (-) terminal of the booster battery. The other end of this cable should be connected to a good ground on the vehicle to be started, such as a bolt or bracket on the body.

Start the engine using the booster battery, then, with the engine running at idle speed, disconnect the jumper cables in the reverse order of connection.

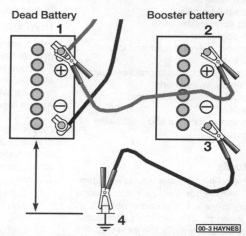

Make the booster battery cable connections in the numerical order shown (note that the negative cable of the booster battery is NOT attached to the negative terminal of the dead battery)

Automotive chemicals and lubricants

A number of automotive chemicals and lubricants are available for use during vehicle maintenance and repair. They include a wide variety of products ranging from cleaning solvents and degreasers to lubricants and protective sprays for rubber, plastic and vinyl.

Cleaners

Carburetor cleaner and choke cleaner is a strong solvent for gum, varnish and carbon. Most carburetor cleaners leave a dry-type lubricant film which will not harden or gum up. Because of this film it is not recommended for use on electrical components.

Brake system cleaner is used to remove grease and brake fluid from the brake system, where clean surfaces are absolutely necessary. It leaves no residue and often eliminates brake squeal caused by contaminants.

Electrical cleaner removes oxidation, corrosion and carbon deposits from electrical contacts, restoring full current flow. It can also be used to clean spark plugs, carburetor jets, voltage regulators and other parts where an oil-free surface is desired.

Demoisturants remove water and moisture from electrical components such as alternators, voltage regulators, electrical connectors and fuse blocks. They are non-conductive, non-corrosive and non-flammable.

Degreasers are heavy-duty solvents used to remove grease from the outside of the engine and from chassis components. They can be sprayed or brushed on and, depending on the type, are rinsed off either with water or solvent.

Lubricants

Motor oil is the lubricant formulated for use in engines. It normally contains a wide variety of additives to prevent corrosion and reduce foaming and wear. Motor oil comes in various weights (viscosity ratings) from 5 to 80. The recommended weight of the oil depends on the season, temperature and the demands on the engine. Light oil is used in cold climates and under light load conditions. Heavy oil is used in hot climates and where high loads are encountered. Multi-viscosity oils are designed to have characteristics of both light and heavy oils and are available in a number of weights from 5W-20 to 20W-50.

Gear oil is designed to be used in differentials, manual transmissions and other areas where high-temperature lubrication is required.

Chassis and wheel bearing grease is a heavy grease used where increased loads and friction are encountered, such as for wheel bearings, balljoints, tie-rod ends and universal joints.

High-temperature wheel bearing grease is designed to withstand the extreme temperatures encountered by wheel bearings in disc brake equipped vehicles. It usually contains molybdenum disulfide (moly), which is a dry-type lubricant.

White grease is a heavy grease for metal-to-metal applications where water is a problem. White grease stays soft under both low and high temperatures (usually from -100 to +190-degrees F), and will not wash off or dilute in the presence of water.

Assembly lube is a special extreme pressure lubricant, usually containing moly, used to lubricate high-load parts (such as main and rod bearings and cam lobes) for initial start-up of a new engine. The assembly lube lubricates the parts without being squeezed out or washed away until the engine oiling system begins to function.

Silicone lubricants are used to protect rubber, plastic, vinyl and nylon parts.

Graphite lubricants are used where oils cannot be used due to contamination problems, such as in locks. The dry graphite will lubricate metal parts while remaining uncontaminated by dirt, water, oil or acids. It is electrically conductive and will not foul electrical contacts in locks such as the ignition switch.

Moly penetrants loosen and lubricate frozen, rusted and corroded fasteners and prevent future rusting or freezing.

Heat-sink grease is a special electrically non-conductive grease that is used for mounting electronic ignition modules where it is essential that heat is transferred away from the module.

Sealants

RTV sealant is one of the most widely used gasket compounds. Made from silicone, RTV is air curing, it seals, bonds, waterproofs, fills surface irregularities, remains flexible, doesn't shrink, is relatively easy to remove, and is used as a supplementary sealer with almost all low and medium temperature gaskets.

Anaerobic sealant is much like RTV in that it can be used either to seal gaskets or to form gaskets by itself. It remains flexible, is solvent resistant and fills surface imperfections. The difference between an anaerobic sealant and an RTV-type sealant is in the curing. RTV cures when exposed to air, while an anaerobic sealant cures only in the absence of air. This means that an anaerobic sealant cures only after the assembly of parts, sealing them together.

Thread and pipe sealant is used for sealing hydraulic and pneumatic fittings and vacuum lines. It is usually made from a Teflon compound, and comes in a spray, a paint-on liquid and as a wrap-around tape.

Chemicals

Anti-seize compound prevents seizing, galling, cold welding, rust and corrosion in fasteners. High-temperature ant-seize, usually made with copper and graphite lubricants, is used for exhaust system and exhaust manifold bolts.

Anaerobic locking compounds are used to keep fasteners from vibrating or working loose and cure only after installation, in the absence of air. Medium strength locking compound is used for small nuts, bolts and screws that may be removed later. High-strength locking compound is for large nuts, bolts and studs which aren't removed on a regular basis.

Oil additives range from viscosity index improvers to chemical treatments that claim to reduce internal engine friction. It should be noted that most oil manufacturers caution against using additives with their oils.

Gas additives perform several functions, depending on their chemical makeup. They usually contain solvents that help dissolve gum and varnish that build up on carburetor, fuel injection and intake parts. They also serve to break down carbon deposits that form on the inside surfaces of the combustion chambers. Some additives contain upper cylinder lubricants for valves and piston rings, and others contain chemicals to remove condensation from the gas tank.

Miscellaneous

Brake fluid is specially formulated hydraulic fluid that can withstand the heat and pressure encountered in brake systems. Care must be taken so this fluid does not come in contact with painted surfaces or plastics. An opened container should always be resealed to prevent contamination by water or dirt.

Weatherstrip adhesive is used to bond weatherstripping around doors, windows and trunk lids. It is sometimes used to attach trim pieces.

Undercoating is a petroleum-based, tar-like substance that is designed to protect metal surfaces on the underside of the vehicle from corrosion. It also acts as a sound-deadening agent by insulating the bottom of the vehicle.

Waxes and polishes are used to help protect painted and plated surfaces from the weather. Different types of paint may require the use of different types of wax and polish. Some polishes utilize a chemical or abrasive cleaner to help remove the top layer of oxidized (dull) paint on older vehicles. In recent years many non-wax polishes that contain a wide variety of chemicals such as polymers and silicones have been introduced. These non-wax polishes are usually easier to apply and last longer than conventional waxes and polishes.

Conversion factors

Length (distance)
Inches (in)	X 25.4	= Millimetres (mm)	X 0.0394	= Inches (in)
Feet (ft)	X 0.305	= Metres (m)	X 3.281	= Feet (ft)
Miles	X 1.609	= Kilometres (km)	X 0.621	= Miles

Volume (capacity)
Cubic inches (cu in; in³)	X 16.387	= Cubic centimetres (cc; cm³)	X 0.061	= Cubic inches (cu in; in³)
Imperial pints (Imp pt)	X 0.568	= Litres (l)	X 1.76	= Imperial pints (Imp pt)
Imperial quarts (Imp qt)	X 1.137	= Litres (l)	X 0.88	= Imperial quarts (Imp qt)
Imperial quarts (Imp qt)	X 1.201	= US quarts (US qt)	X 0.833	= Imperial quarts (Imp qt)
US quarts (US qt)	X 0.946	= Litres (l)	X 1.057	= US quarts (US qt)
Imperial gallons (Imp gal)	X 4.546	= Litres (l)	X 0.22	= Imperial gallons (Imp gal)
Imperial gallons (Imp gal)	X 1.201	= US gallons (US gal)	X 0.833	= Imperial gallons (Imp gal)
US gallons (US gal)	X 3.785	= Litres (l)	X 0.264	= US gallons (US gal)

Mass (weight)
Ounces (oz)	X 28.35	= Grams (g)	X 0.035	= Ounces (oz)
Pounds (lb)	X 0.454	= Kilograms (kg)	X 2.205	= Pounds (lb)

Force
Ounces-force (ozf; oz)	X 0.278	= Newtons (N)	X 3.6	= Ounces-force (ozf; oz)
Pounds-force (lbf; lb)	X 4.448	= Newtons (N)	X 0.225	= Pounds-force (lbf; lb)
Newtons (N)	X 0.1	= Kilograms-force (kgf; kg)	X 9.81	= Newtons (N)

Pressure
Pounds-force per square inch (psi; lbf/in²; lb/in²)	X 0.070	= Kilograms-force per square centimetre (kgf/cm²; kg/cm²)	X 14.223	= Pounds-force per square inch (psi; lbf/in²; lb/in²)
Pounds-force per square inch (psi; lbf/in²; lb/in²)	X 0.068	= Atmospheres (atm)	X 14.696	= Pounds-force per square inch (psi; lbf/in²; lb/in²)
Pounds-force per square inch (psi; lbf/in²; lb/in²)	X 0.069	= Bars	X 14.5	= Pounds-force per square inch (psi; lbf/in²; lb/in²)
Pounds-force per square inch (psi; lbf/in²; lb/in²)	X 6.895	= Kilopascals (kPa)	X 0.145	= Pounds-force per square inch (psi; lbf/in²; lb/in²)
Kilopascals (kPa)	X 0.01	= Kilograms-force per square centimetre (kgf/cm²; kg/cm²)	X 98.1	= Kilopascals (kPa)

Torque (moment of force)
Pounds-force inches (lbf in; lb in)	X 1.152	= Kilograms-force centimetre (kgf cm; kg cm)	X 0.868	= Pounds-force inches (lbf in; lb in)
Pounds-force inches (lbf in; lb in)	X 0.113	= Newton metres (Nm)	X 8.85	= Pounds-force inches (lbf in; lb in)
Pounds-force inches (lbf in; lb in)	X 0.083	= Pounds-force feet (lbf ft; lb ft)	X 12	= Pounds-force inches (lbf in; lb in)
Pounds-force feet (lbf ft; lb ft)	X 0.138	= Kilograms-force metres (kgf m; kg m)	X 7.233	= Pounds-force feet (lbf ft; lb ft)
Pounds-force feet (lbf ft; lb ft)	X 1.356	= Newton metres (Nm)	X 0.738	= Pounds-force feet (lbf ft; lb ft)
Newton metres (Nm)	X 0.102	= Kilograms-force metres (kgf m; kg m)	X 9.804	= Newton metres (Nm)

Vacuum
Inches mercury (in. Hg)	X 3.377	= Kilopascals (kPa)	X 0.2961	= Inches mercury
Inches mercury (in. Hg)	X 25.4	= Millimeters mercury (mm Hg)	X 0.0394	= Inches mercury

Power
Horsepower (hp)	X 745.7	= Watts (W)	X 0.0013	= Horsepower (hp)

Velocity (speed)
Miles per hour (miles/hr; mph)	X 1.609	= Kilometres per hour (km/hr; kph)	X 0.621	= Miles per hour (miles/hr; mph)

Fuel consumption*
Miles per gallon, Imperial (mpg)	X 0.354	= Kilometres per litre (km/l)	X 2.825	= Miles per gallon, Imperial (mpg)
Miles per gallon, US (mpg)	X 0.425	= Kilometres per litre (km/l)	X 2.352	= Miles per gallon, US (mpg)

Temperature

Degrees Fahrenheit = (°C x 1.8) + 32

Degrees Celsius (Degrees Centigrade; °C) = (°F - 32) x 0.56

*It is common practice to convert from miles per gallon (mpg) to litres/100 kilometres (l/100km), where mpg (Imperial) x l/100 km = 282 and mpg (US) x l/100 km = 235

Safety first!

Regardless of how enthusiastic you may be about getting on with the job at hand, take the time to ensure that your safety is not jeopardized. A moment's lack of attention can result in an accident, as can failure to observe certain simple safety precautions. The possibility of an accident will always exist, and the following points should not be considered a comprehensive list of all dangers. Rather, they are intended to make you aware of the risks and to encourage a safety conscious approach to all work you carry out on your vehicle.

Essential DOs and DON'Ts

DON'T rely on a jack when working under the vehicle. Always use approved jackstands to support the weight of the vehicle and place them under the recommended lift or support points.

DON'T attempt to loosen extremely tight fasteners (i.e. wheel lug nuts) while the vehicle is on a jack - it may fall.

DON'T start the engine without first making sure that the transmission is in Neutral (or Park where applicable) and the parking brake is set.

DON'T remove the radiator cap from a hot cooling system - let it cool or cover it with a cloth and release the pressure gradually.

DON'T attempt to drain the engine oil until you are sure it has cooled to the point that it will not burn you.

DON'T touch any part of the engine or exhaust system until it has cooled sufficiently to avoid burns.

DON'T siphon toxic liquids such as gasoline, antifreeze and brake fluid by mouth, or allow them to remain on your skin.

DON'T inhale brake lining dust - it is potentially hazardous (see *Asbestos* below).

DON'T allow spilled oil or grease to remain on the floor - wipe it up before someone slips on it.

DON'T use loose fitting wrenches or other tools which may slip and cause injury.

DON'T push on wrenches when loosening or tightening nuts or bolts. Always try to pull the wrench toward you. If the situation calls for pushing the wrench away, push with an open hand to avoid scraped knuckles if the wrench should slip.

DON'T attempt to lift a heavy component alone - get someone to help you.

DON'T rush or take unsafe shortcuts to finish a job.

DON'T allow children or animals in or around the vehicle while you are working on it.

DO wear eye protection when using power tools such as a drill, sander, bench grinder, etc. and when working under a vehicle.

DO keep loose clothing and long hair well out of the way of moving parts.

DO make sure that any hoist used has a safe working load rating adequate for the job.

DO get someone to check on you periodically when working alone on a vehicle.

DO carry out work in a logical sequence and make sure that everything is correctly assembled and tightened.

DO keep chemicals and fluids tightly capped and out of the reach of children and pets.

DO remember that your vehicle's safety affects that of yourself and others. If in doubt on any point, get professional advice.

Asbestos

Certain friction, insulating, sealing, and other products - such as brake linings, brake bands, clutch linings, torque converters, gaskets, etc. - may contain asbestos. Extreme care must be taken to avoid inhalation of dust from such products, since it is hazardous to health. If in doubt, assume that they do contain asbestos.

Fire

Remember at all times that gasoline is highly flammable. Never smoke or have any kind of open flame around when working on a vehicle. But the risk does not end there. A spark caused by an electrical short circuit, by two metal surfaces contacting each other, or even by static electricity built up in your body under certain conditions, can ignite gasoline vapors, which in a confined space are highly explosive. Do not, under any circumstances, use gasoline for cleaning parts. Use an approved safety solvent.

Always disconnect the battery ground (-) cable at the battery before working on any part of the fuel system or electrical system. Never risk spilling fuel on a hot engine or exhaust component. It is strongly recommended that a fire extinguisher suitable for use on fuel and electrical fires be kept handy in the garage or workshop at all times. Never try to extinguish a fuel or electrical fire with water.

Fumes

Certain fumes are highly toxic and can quickly cause unconsciousness and even death if inhaled to any extent. Gasoline vapor falls into this category, as do the vapors from some cleaning solvents. Any draining or pouring of such volatile fluids should be done in a well ventilated area.

When using cleaning fluids and solvents, read the instructions on the container carefully. Never use materials from unmarked containers.

Never run the engine in an enclosed space, such as a garage. Exhaust fumes contain carbon monoxide, which is extremely poisonous. If you need to run the engine, always do so in the open air, or at least have the rear of the vehicle outside the work area.

If you are fortunate enough to have the use of an inspection pit, never drain or pour gasoline and never run the engine while the vehicle is over the pit. The fumes, being heavier than air, will concentrate in the pit with possibly lethal results.

The battery

Never create a spark or allow a bare light bulb near a battery. They normally give off a certain amount of hydrogen gas, which is highly explosive.

Always disconnect the battery ground (-) cable at the battery before working on the fuel or electrical systems.

If possible, loosen the filler caps or cover when charging the battery from an external source (this does not apply to sealed or maintenance-free batteries). Do not charge at an excessive rate or the battery may burst.

Take care when adding water to a non maintenance-free battery and when carrying a battery. The electrolyte, even when diluted, is very corrosive and should not be allowed to contact clothing or skin.

Always wear eye protection when cleaning the battery to prevent the caustic deposits from entering your eyes.

Household current

When using an electric power tool, inspection light, etc., which operates on household current, always make sure that the tool is correctly connected to its plug and that, where necessary, it is properly grounded. Do not use such items in damp conditions and, again, do not create a spark or apply excessive heat in the vicinity of fuel or fuel vapor.

Secondary ignition system voltage

A severe electric shock can result from touching certain parts of the ignition system (such as the spark plug wires) when the engine is running or being cranked, particularly if components are damp or the insulation is defective. In the case of an electronic ignition system, the secondary system voltage is much higher and could prove fatal.

Troubleshooting

Contents

This section provides an easy reference guide to the more common problems which may occur during the operation of your vehicle. These problems and their possible causes are grouped under headings denoting various components or systems, such as Engine, Cooling system, etc. They also refer you to the chapter and/or section which deals with the problem.

Remember that successful troubleshooting is not a mysterious art practiced only by professional mechanics. It is simply the result of the right knowledge combined with an intelligent, systematic approach to the problem. Always work by a process of elimination, starting with the simplest solution and working through to the most complex - and never overlook the obvious. Anyone can run the gas tank dry or leave the lights on overnight, so don't assume that you are exempt from such oversights.

Finally, always establish a clear idea of why a problem has occurred and take steps to ensure that it doesn't happen again. If the electrical system fails because of a poor connection, check the other connections in the system to make sure that they don't fail as well. If a particular fuse continues to blow, find out why - don't just replace one fuse after another. Remember, failure of a small component can often be indicative of potential failure or incorrect functioning of a more important component or system.

Engine

1 Engine will not rotate when attempting to start

1 Battery terminal connections loose or corroded (Chapter 1).
2 Battery discharged or faulty (Chapter 1).
3 Automatic transaxle/Continuously Variable Transaxle (CVT) not completely engaged in Park (Chapter 7) or clutch not completely depressed (Chapter 8).
4 Broken, loose or disconnected wiring in the starting circuit (Chapters 5 and 12).
5 Starter motor pinion jammed in flywheel ring gear (Chapter 5).
6 Starter solenoid faulty (Chapter 5).
7 Starter motor faulty (Chapter 5).
8 Ignition switch faulty (Chapter 12).
9 Starter pinion or flywheel teeth worn or broken (Chapter 5).

2 Engine rotates but will not start

1 Fuel tank empty.
2 Battery discharged (engine rotates slowly) (Chapter 5).
3 Battery terminal connections loose or corroded (Chapter 1).
4 Leaking fuel injector(s), faulty fuel pump, pressure regulator, etc. (Chapter 4).

5 Fuel not reaching fuel rail (Chapter 4).
6 Ignition components damp or damaged (Chapter 5).
7 Worn, faulty or incorrectly gapped spark plugs (Chapter 1).
8 Broken, loose or disconnected wiring in the starting circuit (Chapter 5).
9 Loose distributor is changing ignition timing (Chapter 5).
10 Broken, loose or disconnected wires at the ignition coil or faulty coil (Chapter 5).

3 Engine hard to start when cold

1 Battery discharged or low (Chapter 1).
2 Malfunctioning fuel system (Chapter 4).
3 Injector(s) leaking (Chapter 4).
4 Distributor rotor carbon tracked (Chapter 5).

4 Engine hard to start when hot

1 Air filter clogged (Chapter 1).
2 Fuel not reaching the fuel injection system (Chapter 4).
3 Corroded battery connections, especially ground (Chapter 1).

5 Starter motor noisy or excessively rough in engagement

1 Pinion or flywheel gear teeth worn or broken (Chapter 5).
2 Starter motor mounting bolts loose or missing (Chapter 5).

6 Engine starts but stops immediately

1 Loose or faulty electrical connections at distributor, coil or alternator (Chapter 5).
2 Insufficient fuel reaching the fuel injector(s) (Chapters 1 and 4).
3 Vacuum leak at the gasket between the intake manifold and throttle body (Chapters 1 and 4).

7 Oil puddle under engine

1 Oil pan gasket and/or oil pan drain bolt washer leaking (Chapter 2).
2 Oil pressure sending unit leaking (Chapter 2).
3 Cylinder head covers leaking (Chapter 2).
4 Engine oil seals leaking (Chapter 2).

8 Engine lopes while idling or idles erratically

1 Vacuum leakage (Chapters 2 and 4).

2 Leaking EGR valve (Chapter 6).
3 Air filter clogged (Chapter 1).
4 Fuel pump not delivering sufficient fuel to the fuel injection system (Chapter 4).
5 Leaking head gasket (Chapter 2).
6 Timing belt and/or pulleys worn (Chapter 2).
7 Camshaft lobes worn (Chapter 2).

9 Engine misses at idle speed

1 Spark plugs worn or not gapped properly (Chapter 1).
2 Faulty spark plug wires (Chapter 1).
3 Vacuum leaks (Chapter 1).
4 Incorrect ignition timing (Chapter 1).
5 Uneven or low compression (Chapter 2).
6 Fault in the fuel injection or engine control system (Chapters 4 and 6).

10 Engine misses throughout driving speed range

1 Fuel filter clogged and/or impurities in the fuel system (Chapter 1).
2 Low fuel pressure (Chapter 4).
3 Faulty or incorrectly gapped spark plugs (Chapter 1).
4 Incorrect ignition timing (Chapter 5).
5 Cracked distributor cap, disconnected distributor wires or damaged distributor components (Chapters 1 and 5).
6 Leaking spark plug wires (Chapters 1 or 5).
7 Faulty emission system components (Chapter 6).
8 Low or uneven cylinder compression pressures (Chapter 2).
9 Weak or faulty ignition system (Chapter 5).
10 Vacuum leak in fuel injection system, intake manifold, air control valve or vacuum hoses (Chapter 4).

11 Engine stumbles on acceleration

1 Spark plugs fouled (Chapter 1).
2 Fuel injection system faulty (Chapter 4).
3 Fuel filter clogged (Chapters 1 and 4).
4 Incorrect ignition timing (Chapter 5).
5 Intake manifold air leak (Chapters 2 and 4).

12 Engine surges while holding accelerator steady

1 Intake air leak (Chapter 4).
2 Fuel pump faulty (Chapter 4).
3 Loose fuel injector wire harness connectors (Chapter 4).
4 Defective ECU or information sensor (Chapter 6).

13 Engine stalls

1   Idle speed incorrect (Chapter 1).
2   Fuel filter clogged and/or water and impurities in the fuel system (Chapters 1 and 4).
3   Distributor components damp or damaged (Chapter 5).
4   Faulty emissions system components (Chapter 6).
5   Faulty or incorrectly gapped spark plugs (Chapter 1).
6   Faulty spark plug wires (Chapter 1).
7   Vacuum leak in the fuel injection system, intake manifold or vacuum hoses (Chapters 2 and 4).
8   Valve clearances incorrectly set (Chapter 1).

14 Engine lacks power

1   Incorrect ignition timing (Chapter 5).
2   Excessive play in distributor shaft (Chapter 5).
3   Worn rotor, distributor cap or wires (Chapters 1 and 5).
4   Faulty or incorrectly gapped spark plugs (Chapter 1).
5   Faulty fuel injection system (Chapter 4).
6   Faulty coil (Chapter 5).
7   Brakes binding (Chapter 9).
8   Automatic transaxle/Continuously Variable Transaxle (CVT) fluid level incorrect (Chapter 1).
9   Clutch slipping (Chapter 8).
10 Fuel filter clogged and/or impurities in the fuel system (Chapters 1 and 4).
11 Emission control system not functioning properly (Chapter 6).
12 Catalytic converter plugged (Chapter 6).
13 Low or uneven cylinder compression pressures (Chapter 2).
14 Obstructed exhaust system (Chapter 4).

15 Engine backfires

1   Emission control system not functioning properly (Chapter 6).
2   Ignition timing incorrect (Chapter 5).
3   Faulty secondary ignition system (cracked spark plug insulator, faulty plug wires, distributor cap and/or rotor) (Chapters 1 and 5).
4   Fuel injection system malfunctioning (Chapter 4).
5   Vacuum leak at fuel injector(s), intake manifold, air control valve or vacuum hoses (Chapters 2 and 4).
6   Valve clearances incorrectly set and/or valves sticking (Chapter 1).

16 Pinging or knocking engine sounds during acceleration or uphill

1   Incorrect grade of fuel.

2   Ignition timing incorrect (Chapter 5).
3   Fuel injection system faulty (Chapter 4).
4   Improper or damaged spark plugs or wires (Chapter 1).
5   Worn or damaged distributor components (Chapter 5).
6   EGR valve not functioning (Chapter 6).
7   Vacuum leak (Chapters 2 and 4).

17 Engine runs with oil pressure light on

1   Low oil level (Chapter 1).
2   Short in wiring circuit (Chapter 12).
3   Faulty oil pressure sender (Chapter 2).
4   Worn engine bearings and/or oil pump (Chapter 2).

18 Engine diesels (continues to run) after switching off

1   Idle speed too high (Chapter 5)
2   Excessive engine operating temperature (Chapter 3).
3   Ignition timing in need of adjustment (Chapter 5).

Engine electrical system

19 Battery will not hold a charge

1   Alternator drivebelt defective or not adjusted properly (Chapter 1).
2   Battery electrolyte level low (Chapter 1).
3   Battery terminals loose or corroded (Chapter 1).
4   Alternator not charging properly (Chapter 5).
5   Loose, broken or faulty wiring in the charging circuit (Chapter 5).
6   Short in vehicle wiring (Chapter 12).
7   Internally defective battery (Chapters 1 and 5).

20 Alternator light fails to go out

1   Faulty alternator or charging circuit (Chapter 5).
2   Alternator drivebelt defective or out of adjustment (Chapter 1).
3   Alternator voltage regulator inoperative (Chapter 5).

21 Alternator light fails to come on when key is turned on

1   Warning light bulb defective (Chapter 12).
2   Fault in the printed circuit, dash wiring or bulb holder (Chapter 12).

Fuel system

22 Excessive fuel consumption

1   Dirty or clogged air filter element (Chapter 1).
2   Incorrectly set ignition timing (Chapter 5).
3   Emissions system not functioning properly (Chapter 6).
4   Faulty fuel injection system (Chapter 4).
5   Low tire pressure or incorrect tire size (Chapter 1).

23 Fuel leakage and/or fuel odor

1   Leaking fuel feed or return line (Chapters 1 and 4).
2   Tank overfilled.
3   Evaporative canister filter clogged (Chapters 1 and 6).
4   Faulty fuel injection system (Chapter 4).

Cooling system

24 Overheating

1   Insufficient coolant in system (Chapter 1).
2   Radiator core blocked or grille restricted (Chapter 3).
3   Thermostat faulty (Chapter 3).
4   Electric coolant fan blades broken or cracked (Chapter 3).
5   Radiator cap not maintaining proper pressure (Chapter 3).
6   Ignition timing incorrect (Chapter 5).

25 Overcooling

1   Faulty thermostat (Chapter 3).
2   Inaccurate temperature gauge sending unit (Chapter 3)

26 External coolant leakage

1   Deteriorated/damaged hoses; loose clamps (Chapters 1 and 3).
2   Water pump defective (Chapter 3).
3   Leakage from radiator core or coolant reservoir bottle (Chapter 3).
4   Engine drain or water jacket core plugs leaking (Chapter 2).

27 Internal coolant leakage

1   Leaking cylinder head gasket (Chapter 2).
2   Cracked cylinder bore or cylinder head (Chapter 2).

28 Coolant loss

1   Too much coolant in system (Chapter 1).
2   Coolant boiling away because of over-heating (Chapter 3).
3   Internal or external leakage (Chapter 3).
4   Faulty radiator cap (Chapter 3).

29 Poor coolant circulation

1   Inoperative water pump (Chapter 3).
2   Restriction in cooling system (Chapters 1 and 3).
3   Thermostat sticking (Chapter 3).

Clutch

30 Pedal travels to floor - no pressure or very little resistance

1   No fluid in reservoir (Chapter 1).
2   Faulty clutch master cylinder, release cylinder or hydraulic line (Chapter 8).
3   Broken release bearing or fork (Chapter 8).

31 Unable to select gears

1   Faulty transaxle (Chapter 7).
2   Faulty clutch disc (Chapter 8).
3   Release lever and bearing not assembled properly (Chapter 8).
4   Faulty pressure plate (Chapter 8).
5   Pressure plate-to-flywheel bolts loose (Chapter 8).

32 Clutch slips (engine speed increases with no increase in vehicle speed)

1   Clutch plate worn (Chapter 8).
2   Clutch plate is oil soaked by leaking rear main seal (Chapter 8).
3   Clutch plate not seated. It may take 30 or 40 normal starts for a new one to seat.
4   Warped pressure plate or flywheel (Chapter 8).
5   Weak diaphragm spring (Chapter 8).
6   Clutch plate overheated. Allow to cool.

33 Grabbing (chattering) as clutch is engaged

1   Oil on clutch plate lining, burned or glazed facings (Chapter 8).
2   Worn or loose engine or transaxle mounts (Chapters 2 and 7).
3   Worn splines on clutch plate hub (Chapter 8).

4   Warped pressure plate or flywheel (Chapter 8).
5   Burned or smeared resin on flywheel or pressure plate (Chapter 8).

34 Transaxle rattling (clicking)

1   Release lever loose (Chapter 8).
2   Clutch plate damper spring failure (Chapter 8).
3   Low engine idle speed (Chapter 1).

35 Noise in clutch area

1   Fork shaft improperly installed (Chapter 8).
2   Faulty bearing (Chapter 8).

36 Clutch pedal stays on floor

1   Faulty clutch master or release cylinder (Chapter 8).
2   Broken release bearing or fork (Chapter 8).

37 High pedal effort

1   Piston binding in bore of clutch master or release cylinder (Chapter 8).
2   Pressure plate faulty (Chapter 8).

Manual transaxle

38 Knocking noise at low speeds

1   Worn driveaxle constant velocity (CV) joints (Chapter 8).
2   Worn driveaxle bore in differential case (Chapter 7A).*

39 Noise most pronounced when turning

Differential gear noise (Chapter 7A).*

40 Clunk on acceleration or deceleration

1   Loose engine or transaxle mounts (Chapters 2 and 7A).
2   Worn differential pinion shaft in case.*
3   Worn driveaxle bore in differential case (Chapter 7A).*
4   Worn or damaged driveaxle inboard CV joints (Chapter 8).

41 Clicking noise in turns

Worn or damaged outboard CV joint (Chapter 8).

42 Vibration

1   Rough wheel bearing (Chapters 1 and 10).
2   Damaged driveaxle (Chapter 8).
3   Out of round tires (Chapter 1).
4   Tire out of balance (Chapters 1 and 10).
5   Worn CV joint (Chapter 8).

43 Noisy in neutral with engine running

1   Damaged input gear bearing (Chapter 7A).*
2   Damaged clutch release bearing (Chapter 8).

44 Noisy in one particular gear

1   Damaged or worn constant mesh gears (Chapter 7A).*
2   Damaged or worn synchronizers (Chapter 7A).*
3   Bent reverse fork (Chapter 7A).*
4   Damaged fourth speed gear or output gear (Chapter 7A).*
5   Worn or damaged reverse idler gear or idler bushing (Chapter 7A).*

45 Noisy in all gears

1   Insufficient lubricant (Chapter 7A).
2   Damaged or worn bearings (Chapter 7A).*
3   Worn or damaged input gear shaft and/or output gear shaft (Chapter 7A).*

46 Slips out of gear

1   Worn or improperly adjusted linkage (Chapter 7A).
2   Transaxle loose on engine (Chapter 7A).
3   Shift linkage does not work freely, binds (Chapter 7A).
4   Input gear bearing retainer broken or loose (Chapter 7A).*
5   Dirt between clutch cover and engine block (Chapter 7A).
6   Worn shift fork (Chapter 7A).*

47 Leaks lubricant

1   Driveaxle oil seals worn (Chapter 7).
2   Excessive amount of lubricant in transaxle (Chapters 1 and 7A).

3   Loose or broken input gear shaft bearing retainer (Chapter 7A).*
4   Input gear bearing retainer O-ring and/or lip seal damaged (Chapter 7A).*

48   Locked in gear

Lock pin or interlock pin missing (Chapter 7A).*

Although the corrective action necessary to remedy the symptoms described is beyond the scope of the home mechanic, the above information should be helpful in isolating the cause of the condition so that the owner can communicate clearly with a professional mechanic.

Automatic transaxle/Continuously Variable Transaxle (CVT)

Note: *Due to the complexity of the automatic transaxle/Continuously Variable Transaxle (CVT), it is difficult for the home mechanic to properly diagnose and service this component. For problems other than the following, the vehicle should be taken to a dealer or transmission shop.*

49   Fluid leakage

1   Automatic transmission fluid is a deep red color. Fluid leaks should not be confused with engine oil, which can easily be blown onto the transaxle by air flow.
2   To pinpoint a leak, first remove all built-up dirt and grime from the transaxle housing with degreasing agents and/or steam cleaning. Then drive the vehicle at low speeds so air flow will not blow the leak far from its source. Raise the vehicle and determine where the leak is coming from. Common areas of leakage are:
  a) *Pan (Chapters 1 and 7)*
  b) *Dipstick tube (Chapters 1 and 7)*
  c) *Transaxle oil lines (Chapter 7)*
  d) *Speed sensor (Chapter 7)*

50   Transaxle fluid brown or has a burned smell

Transaxle fluid burned (Chapter 1).

51   General shift mechanism problems

1   Chapter 7, Part B, deals with checking and adjusting the shift linkage on automatic transaxles. Common problems which may be attributed to poorly adjusted linkage are:
  a) *Engine starting in gears other than Park or Neutral.*

  b) *Indicator on shifter pointing to a gear other than the one actually being used.*
  c) *Vehicle moves when in Park.*
2   Refer to Chapter 7B for the shift linkage adjustment procedure.

52   Engine will start in gears other than Park or Neutral

Neutral start switch malfunctioning (Chapter 7B).

53   Transaxle will not downshift with accelerator pressed to the floor

Throttle valve cable out of adjustment (Integra only) (Chapter 7B).

54   Transaxle slips, shifts roughly, is noisy or has no drive in forward or reverse gears

There are many probable causes for the above problems, but the home mechanic should be concerned with only one possibility - fluid level. Before taking the vehicle to a repair shop, check the level and condition of the fluid as described in Chapter 1. Correct the fluid level as necessary or change the fluid and filter if needed. If the problem persists, have a professional diagnose the cause.

Driveaxles

55   Clicking noise in turns

Worn or damaged outboard CV joint (Chapter 8).

56   Shudder or vibration during acceleration

1   Excessive toe-in (Chapter 10).
2   Incorrect spring heights (Chapter 10).
3   Worn or damaged inboard or outboard CV joints (Chapter 8).
4   Sticking inboard CV joint assembly (Chapter 8).

57   Vibration at highway speeds

1   Out of balance front wheels and/or tires (Chapters 1 and 10).
2   Out of round front tires (Chapters 1 and 10).
3   Worn CV joint(s) (Chapter 8).

Brakes

Note: *Before assuming that a brake problem exists, make sure that:*
  a) *The tires are in good condition and properly inflated (Chapter 1).*
  b) *The front end alignment is correct (Chapter 10).*
  c) *The vehicle is not loaded with weight in an unequal manner.*

58   Vehicle pulls to one side during braking

1   Incorrect tire pressures (Chapter 1).
2   Front end out of alignment (have the front end aligned).
3   Front, or rear, tires not matched to one another.
4   Restricted brake lines or hoses (Chapter 9).
5   Malfunctioning drum brake or caliper assembly (Chapter 9).
6   Loose suspension parts (Chapter 10).
7   Loose calipers (Chapter 9).
8   Excessive wear of brake shoe or pad material or disc/drum on one side.

59   Noise (high-pitched squeal when the brakes are applied)

Front disc brake pads worn out. The noise comes from the wear sensor rubbing against the disc (does not apply to all vehicles). Replace pads with new ones immediately (Chapter 9).

60   Brake roughness or chatter (pedal pulsates)

1   Excessive lateral runout (Chapter 9).
2   Uneven pad wear (Chapter 9).
3   Defective disc (Chapter 9).

61   Excessive brake pedal effort required to stop vehicle

1   Malfunctioning power brake booster (Chapter 9).
2   Partial system failure (Chapter 9).
3   Excessively worn pads or shoes (Chapter 9).
4   Piston in caliper or wheel cylinder stuck or sluggish (Chapter 9).
5   Brake pads or shoes contaminated with oil or grease (Chapter 9).
6   New pads or shoes installed and not yet seated. It will take a while for the new material to seat against the disc or drum.

62   Excessive brake pedal travel

1   Partial brake system failure (Chapter 9).

2 Insufficient fluid in master cylinder (Chapters 1 and 9).
3 Air trapped in system (Chapters 1 and 9).

63 Dragging brakes

1 Incorrect adjustment of brake light switch (Chapter 9).
2 Master cylinder pistons not returning correctly (Chapter 9).
3 Restricted brakes lines or hoses (Chapters 1 and 9).
4 Incorrect parking brake adjustment (Chapter 9).

64 Grabbing or uneven braking action

1 Malfunction of proportioning valve (Chapter 9).
2 Malfunction of power brake booster unit (Chapter 9).
3 Binding brake pedal mechanism (Chapter 9).

65 Brake pedal feels spongy when depressed

1 Air in hydraulic lines (Chapter 9).
2 Master cylinder mounting bolts loose (Chapter 9).
3 Master cylinder defective (Chapter 9).

66 Brake pedal travels to the floor with little resistance

1 Little or no fluid in the master cylinder reservoir caused by leaking caliper piston(s) (Chapter 9).
2 Loose, damaged or disconnected brake lines (Chapter 9).

67 Parking brake does not hold

Parking brake linkage improperly adjusted (Chapters 1 and 9).

Suspension and steering systems

Note: *Before attempting to diagnose the suspension and steering systems, perform the following preliminary checks:*

a) Tires for wrong pressure and uneven wear.
b) Steering universal joints from the column to the steering gear for loose connectors or wear.
c) Front and rear suspension and the steering gear assembly for loose or damaged parts.

d) Out-of-round or out-of-balance tires, bent rims and loose and/or rough wheel bearings.

68 Vehicle pulls to one side

1 Mismatched or uneven tires (Chapter 10).
2 Broken or sagging springs (Chapter 10).
3 Wheel alignment (Chapter 10).
4 Front brake dragging (Chapter 9).

69 Abnormal or excessive tire wear

1 Wheel alignment (Chapter 10).
2 Sagging or broken springs (Chapter 10).
3 Tire out of balance (Chapter 10).
4 Worn shock absorber (Chapter 10).
5 Overloaded vehicle.
6 Tires not rotated regularly.

70 Wheel makes a thumping noise

1 Blister or bump on tire (Chapter 10).
2 Improper shock absorber/coil spring action (Chapter 10).

71 Shimmy, shake or vibration

1 Tire or wheel out-of-balance or out-of-round (Chapter 10).
2 Loose or worn front hub or wheel bearings (Chapters 1, 8 and 10).
3 Worn tie-rod ends (Chapter 10).
4 Worn lower balljoints (Chapters 1 and 10).
5 Excessive wheel runout (Chapter 10).
6 Blister or bump on tire (Chapter 10).

72 Hard steering

1 Lack of lubrication at balljoints and tie-rod ends (Chapters 1 and 10).
2 Front wheel alignment (Chapter 10).
3 Low tire pressure(s) (Chapters 1 and 10).

73 Poor returnability of steering to center

1 Lack of lubrication at balljoints and tie-rod ends (Chapters 1 and 10).
2 Binding in balljoints (Chapter 10).
3 Binding in steering column (Chapter 10).
4 Lack of lubricant in steering gear assembly (Chapter 10).
5 Front wheel alignment (Chapter 10).

74 Abnormal noise at the front end

1 Lack of lubrication at balljoints and tie-

rod ends (Chapters 1 and 10).
2 Damaged shock absorber/coil spring mount (Chapter 10).
3 Worn control arm bushings or tie-rod ends (Chapter 10).
4 Loose stabilizer bar (Chapter 10).
5 Loose wheel nuts (Chapters 1 and 10).
6 Loose suspension bolts (Chapter 10)

75 Wander or poor steering stability

1 Mismatched or uneven tires (Chapter 10).
2 Lack of lubrication at balljoints and tie-rod ends (Chapters 1 and 10).
3 Worn shock absorber/coil spring assemblies (Chapter 10).
4 Loose stabilizer bar (Chapter 10).
5 Broken or sagging springs (Chapter 10).
6 Wheels out of alignment (Chapter 10).

76 Erratic steering when braking

1 Front hub bearings worn (Chapter 10).
2 Broken or sagging springs (Chapter 10).
3 Leaking wheel cylinder or caliper (Chapter 10).
4 Warped discs or drums (Chapter 10).

77 Excessive pitching and/or rolling around corners or during braking

1 Loose stabilizer bar (Chapter 10).
2 Worn shock absorbers or mounts (Chapter 10).
3 Broken or sagging springs (Chapter 10).
4 Overloaded vehicle.

78 Suspension bottoms

1 Overloaded vehicle.
2 Worn shock absorbers (Chapter 10).
3 Incorrect, broken or sagging springs (Chapter 10).

79 Cupped tires

1 Front wheel or rear wheel alignment (Chapter 10).
2 Worn shock absorbers (Chapter 10).
3 Wheel bearings worn (Chapter 10).
4 Excessive tire or wheel runout (Chapter 10).
5 Worn balljoints (Chapter 10).

80 Excessive tire wear on outside edge

1 Inflation pressures incorrect (Chapter 1).
2 Excessive speed in turns.
3 Front end alignment incorrect (excessive

toe-in). Have professionally aligned.
4   Suspension arm bent or twisted (Chapter 10).

81 Excessive tire wear on inside edge

1   Inflation pressures incorrect (Chapter 1).
2   Front end alignment incorrect (toe-out). Have professionally aligned.
3   Loose or damaged steering or suspension components (Chapter 10).

82 Tire tread worn in one place

1   Tires out of balance.
2   Damaged or buckled wheel. Inspect and replace if necessary.
3   Defective tire (Chapter 1).

83 Excessive play or looseness in steering system

1   Front hub bearing(s) worn (Chapter 10).

2   Tie-rod end loose (Chapter 10).
3   Steering gear loose or worn (Chapter 10).
4   Worn or loose steering intermediate shaft (Chapter 10).

84 Rattling or clicking noise in steering gear

1   Steering gear loose (Chapter 10).
2   Steering gear defective.

Chapter 1
Tune-up and routine maintenance

Contents

Specifications

Recommended lubricants and fluids

Note: *The fluids and lubricants listed here are those recommended by the manufacturer at the time this manual was printed. Vehicle manufacturers occasionally upgrade their fluid and lubricant specifications. Check with your local auto parts store for the most current fluid and lubricant recommendations for your vehicle.*

Engine oil
Type .... API grade SG, SH or SJ multigrade and fuel efficient oil
Viscosity .... See accompanying chart

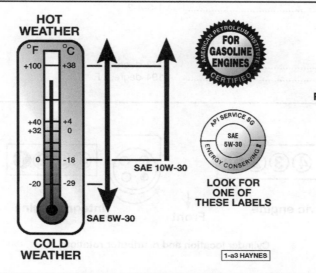

Recommended engine oil viscosity

1-a3 HAYNES

Recommended lubricants and fluids (continued)

Automatic transaxle fluid type .... Honda Premium Formula automatic transmission fluid or equivalent
Continuously Variable Transaxle fluid type.................................... Honda CVT fluid
Manual transaxle lubricant type... Honda Manual Transmission Fluid (MTF) or equivalent
Brake fluid type.. DOT 3 brake fluid
Power steering system fluid .... Honda power steering fluid or equivalent
Fuel .... Unleaded gasoline, 87 octane or higher

Capacities*

Engine oil
  Civic
    D16Y5 engine .... 3.5 quarts
    D16Y7 engine .... 3.8 quarts
    D16Y8 engine .... 3.5 quarts
  Integra
    B18B1 engine .... 4.0 quarts
    B18C1and B18C5 engine .... 4.2 quarts
Automatic transaxle (drain and refill) .... 2.9 quarts
Continuously Variable Transaxle (drain and refill)......................... 4.1 quarts
Manual transaxle
  Civic... 1.9 quarts
  Integra .... 2.3 quarts
Coolant
  Civic... 3.2 quarts
  Integra
    B18B1 engine .... 4.6 quarts
    B18C1and B18C5 engine .... 5.0 quarts

*All capacities approximate. Add as necessary to bring to appropriate level.

Ignition system

Spark plug type and gap
  Civic
    D16Y5
      Type... NGK ZFR4F-11 or equivalent
      Gap.. 0.039 to 0.043 inch
    D16Y7 and D16Y8 engine
      Type... NGK ZFR5F-11 or equivalent
      Gap.. 0.039 to 0.043 inch
  Integra
    Conventional
      Type... NGK ZFR5F-11 or equivalent
      Gap.. 0.039 to 0.043 inch
    Platinum
      Type... NGK PFR6G-13 or equivalent
      Gap.. 0.047 to 0.051 inch
Spark plug wire resistance .... Less than 25,000 ohms
Engine firing order 1-3-4-2

Cooling system

Thermostat rating
  Starts to open.. 173-degrees F
  Fully open .... 194-degrees F

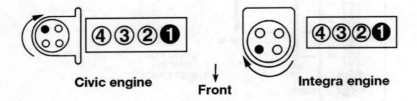

Civic engine   **Front**   **Integra engine**

Cylinder location and distributor rotation

Accessory drivebelt deflection
Power steering pump
    New belt .... 3/8 to 1/2-inch
    Old belt .... 1/2 to 5/8-inch
Alternator
    Without air-conditioning
        New belt .... 3/8 to 1/2-inch
        Old belt .... 1/4 to 7/16-inch
    With air-conditioning
        New belt .... 3/16 to 5/16-inch
        Old belt .... 3/8 to 1/2-inch

Brakes
Disc brake pad lining thickness (minimum) 1/16-inch
Drum brake shoe lining thickness (minimum) 3/32-inch
Parking brake adjustment .... 6 to 10 clicks

Idle Speed
Civic
    D16Y5
        Manual transaxle .... 670 +/- 50 rpm
        Automatic or CVT transaxle .... 700 +/- 50 rpm
    D16Y7 and D16Y8
        USA
            Manual transaxle .... 670 +/- 50 rpm
            Automatic or CVT transaxle..................................... 700 +/- 50 rpm
        Canada .... 750 +/- 50 rpm
Integra
    B18B1 and B18C1 .... 750 +/- 50 rpm
    B18C5 .... 800 +/- 50 rpm

General
Valve clearance (engine cold)
Civic
    Intake .... 0.007 to 0.009-inch
    Exhaust... 0.009 to 0.0011-inch
Integra
    B18B1 engine
        Intake .... 0.003 to 0.005-inch
        Exhaust... 0.006 to 0.008-inch
    B18C1 and B18C5 engine
        Intake .... 0.006 to 0.007-inch
        Exhaust .... 0.007 to 0.008-inch

Torque specifications   **Ft-lbs** (unless otherwise indicated)
Automatic and CVT transaxle drain plug................................ 36
Manual transaxle drain plug 29
Manual transaxle filler plug.. 33
Fuel filter
    Banjo bolt .... 132 in-lbs
    Banjo nut 16
Spark plugs.. 156 in-lbs
Wheel lug nuts 80

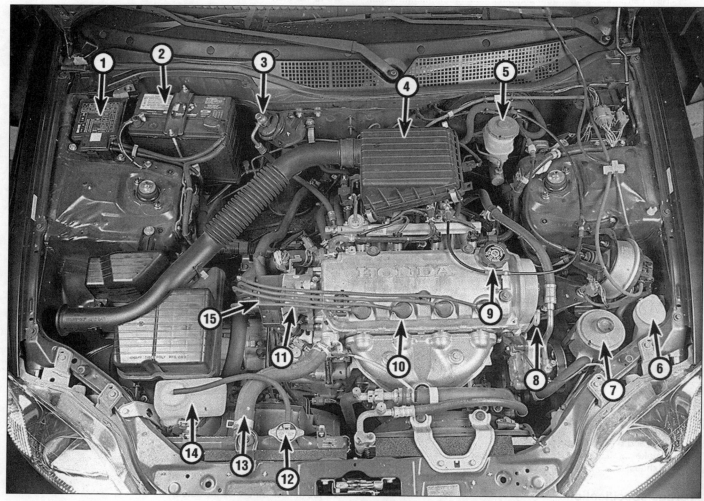

Typical Honda Civic engine compartment layout

1	Fuse block	6	Windshield washer fluid reservoir	11	Spark plug wires
2	Battery	7	Power steering fluid reservoir	12	Radiator cap
3	Fuel filter	8	Engine oil dipstick	13	Radiator hose
4	Air filter housing	9	Engine oil filler cap	14	Engine coolant reservoir
5	Brake master cylinder reservoir	10	Spark plug	15	Distributor cap

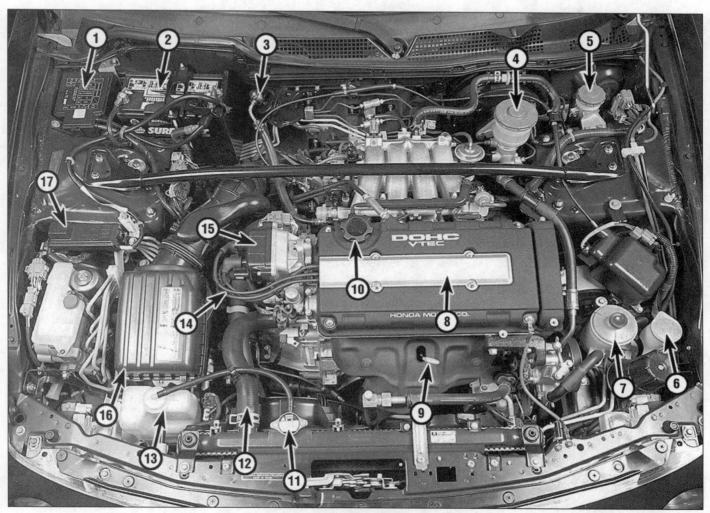

Typical Acura Integra engine compartment layout

1	Fuse block	7	Power steering fluid reservoir	13	Engine coolant reservoir
2	Battery	8	Spark plugs (under the cover)	14	Spark plug wires
3	Fuel filter	9	Engine oil dipstick	15	Distributor cap
4	Brake master cylinder reservoir	10	Engine oil filler cap	16	Air filter housing
5	Clutch master cylinder reservoir	11	Radiator cap	17	Anti-lock Braking System (ABS) fuse
6	Windshield washer fluid reservoir	12	Radiator hose		block

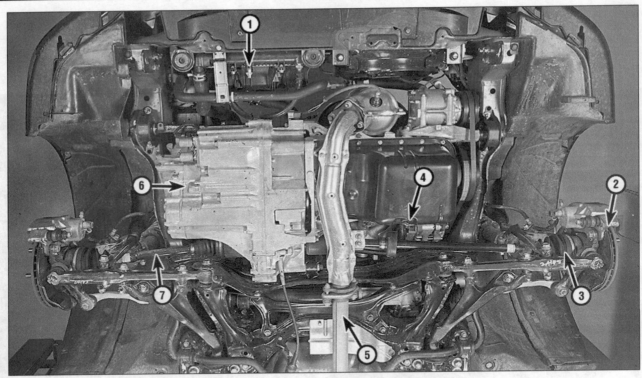

Typical engine compartment underside components

1	Radiator drain	4	Engine oil drain plug	6	Transaxle drain plug (automatic)
2	Front brake caliper	5	Exhaust pipe	7	Driveaxle
3	Outer driveaxle boot				

Typical rear underside components

1	Exhaust pipe	4	Rear disc brake caliper	6	Brake hose
2	Fuel tank	5	Muffler	7	Shock and spring assembly
3	Parking brake cable				

1   Maintenance schedule

The maintenance intervals in this manual are provided with the assumption that you, not the dealer, will be doing the work. These are the minimum maintenance intervals recommended by the factory for vehicles that are driven daily. If you wish to keep your vehicle in peak condition at all times, you may wish to perform some of these procedures even more often. Because frequent maintenance enhances the efficiency, performance and resale value of your car, we encourage you to do so. If you drive in dusty areas, tow a trailer, idle or drive at low speeds for extended periods or drive for short distances (less than four miles) in below freezing temperatures, shorter intervals are also recommended.

When your vehicle is new, it should be serviced by a factory authorized dealer service department to protect the factory warranty. In many cases, the initial maintenance check is done at no cost to the owner.

Every 250 miles or weekly, whichever comes first

Check the engine oil level (Section 4)
Check the engine coolant level (Section 4)
Check the windshield washer fluid level (Section 4)
Check the brake fluid level (Section 4)
Check the tires and tire pressures (Section 5)

Every 3000 miles or 3 months, whichever comes first

All items listed above plus:
Check the power steering fluid level (Section 6)
Check the automatic and Continuously Variable transaxle fluid level (Section 7)
Change the engine oil and oil filter (Section 8)

Every 7500 miles or 6 months, whichever comes first

All items listed above plus:
Inspect and replace, if necessary, the windshield wiper blades (Section 9)
Check and service the battery (Section 10)
Check and adjust, if necessary, the engine drivebelts (Section 11)
Inspect and replace, if necessary, all underhood hoses (Section 12)
Check the cooling system (Section 13)
Rotate the tires (Section 14)
Check the front disc brake pads (Section 15)

Every 15,000 miles or 12 months, whichever comes first

All items listed above plus:
Inspect the brake system (Section 15)*
Inspect the seatbelts (Section 16)
Adjust the valve clearances (Section 17)
Replace the air filter (Section 18)*
Inspect the fuel system (Section 19)
Adjust the valve clearances (Section 17)
Check the manual transaxle lubricant level (Section 20)*
Inspect the suspension and steering components and driveaxle boots (Section 21)*
Inspect the exhaust system (Section 22)

Every 30,000 miles or 24 months, whichever comes first

All items listed above plus:
Replace the spark plugs (conventional non -platinum] (Section 23)
Inspect and replace, if necessary, the spark plug wires, distributor cap and rotor (Section 24)
Check and replace, if necessary, the PCV valve (Section 25)
Service the cooling system (drain, flush and refill) (Section 25)
Replace the fuel filter (Section 26)
Check and adjust, if necessary, the engine idle speed (Section 27)
Service the cooling system (drain, flush and refill) (Section 28)
Change the brake fluid (Section 29)
Change the automatic and Continuously Variable transaxle fluid (Section 30)**
Change the manual transaxle lubricant (Section 31)

Every 60,000 miles or 24 months, whichever comes first

All items listed above plus:
Replace the spark plugs (platinum-tipped spark plugs) (Section 24)

Every 90,000 miles or 72 months, whichever comes first

Replace timing belt (Chapter 2A)

*This item is affected by "severe" operating conditions as described below. If your vehicle is operated under "severe" conditions, perform all maintenance indicated with a * at 3000 mile/3 month intervals. Severe conditions are indicated if you mainly operate your vehicle under one or more of the following conditions:
Operating in dusty areas
Towing a trailer
Idling for extended periods and/or low speed operation
Operating when outside temperatures remain below freezing and when most trips are less than four miles

**If operated under one or more of the following conditions, change the automatic transaxle fluid every 15,000 miles (12,000 for CVT):
In heavy city traffic where the outside temperature regularly reaches 90-degrees F (32-degrees C) or higher
In hilly or mountainous terrain

2   Introduction

This chapter is designed to help the home mechanic maintain his/her vehicle for peak performance, economy, safety and long life.

The following sections deal specifically with each item on the maintenance schedule. Visual checks, adjustments, component replacement and other helpful items are included. Refer to the accompanying photos of the engine compartment and the underside of the vehicle for the location of various components.

Servicing your vehicle in accordance with the mileage/time maintenance schedule and the following Sections will provide it with a planned maintenance program that should result in a long and reliable service life. This is a comprehensive plan, so maintaining some items but not others at the specified service intervals will not produce the same results.

As you service your car, you will discover that many of the procedures can - and should - be grouped together because of the nature of the particular procedure you're performing or because of the close proximity of two otherwise unrelated components to one another. For example, if the vehicle is raised for chassis lubrication, you should inspect the exhaust, suspension, steering and fuel systems while you're under the vehicle. When you're rotating the tires, it makes good sense to check the brakes and wheel bearings since the wheels are already removed.

Finally, let's suppose you have to borrow or rent a torque wrench. Even if you only need to tighten the spark plugs, you might as well check the torque of as many critical fasteners as time allows.

The first step of this maintenance program is to prepare yourself before the actual work begins. Read through all sections pertinent to the procedures you're planning to do, then make a list of and gather together all the parts and tools you will need to do the job. If it looks as if you might run into problems during a particular segment of some procedure, seek advice from your local parts distributor or dealer service department.

3   Tune-up general information

The term tune-up is used in this manual to represent a combination of individual operations rather than one specific procedure.

As suggested throughout this manual, the engine will be kept in relatively good running condition and the need for additional work will be minimized if the routine maintenance schedule is followed closely

More likely than not, however, there will be times when the engine is running poorly due to lack of regular maintenance. This is even more likely if a used vehicle, which has not received regular and frequent maintenance checks, is purchased. In such cases, an engine tune-up will be needed outside of

4.2a The Integra oil dipstick (arrow) extends through the exhaust manifold heat shield

4.2b The Civic engine oil dipstick (arrow) is located at left (drivers) end of the engine

the regular routine maintenance intervals.

The first step in any tune-up or engine diagnosis to help correct a poor running engine would be a cylinder compression check. A check of the engine compression (see Chapter 2 Part B) will give valuable information regarding the overall performance of many internal components and should be used as a basis for tune-up and repair procedures. If, for instance, a compression check indicates serious internal engine wear, a conventional tune-up will not help the running condition of the engine and would be a waste of time and money. Because of its importance, the compression check should be performed by someone with the proper compression testing gauge and the knowledge to use it properly.

The following series of operations are those most often needed to bring a generally poor running engine back into a proper state of tune.

Minor tune-up

Check all engine related fluids (Section 4)
Clean, inspect and test the battery (Section 10)
Check and adjust the drivebelts (Section 11)
Check all underhood hoses (Section 12)
Check the cooling system (Section 13)
Check the air filter (Section 18)
Inspect the distributor cap and rotor (Section 18)
Check and adjust the idle speed (Section 30)

Major tune-up

All items listed under minor tune-up, plus . . .
Replace the air filter (Section 16)
Replace the spark plugs (Section 23)
Replace the distributor cap and rotor (Section 24)
Inspect the spark plug and coil wires (Section 24)
Replace the spark plug wires (Section 24)
Check the fuel system (Section 19)
Check the charging system (Chapter 5)

4   Fluid level checks (every 250 miles or weekly)

1   Fluids are an essential part of the lubrication, cooling, brake, clutch and other systems. Because these fluids gradually become depleted and/or contaminated during normal operation of the vehicle, they must be periodically replenished. See *Recommended lubricants, fluids and capacities* at the beginning of this Chapter before adding fluid to any of the following components. **Note:** *The vehicle must be on level ground before fluid levels can be checked.*

Engine oil

Refer to illustrations 4.2a, 4.2b, 4.4 and 4.6
2   The engine oil level is checked with a dipstick located at the front side of the engine **(see illustration)**. The dipstick extends through a metal tube from which it protrudes down into the engine oil pan **(see illustration)**.
3   The oil level should be checked before the vehicle has been driven, or about 15 minutes after the engine has been shut off. If the oil is checked immediately after driving the vehicle, some of the oil will remain in the upper engine components, producing an inaccurate reading on the dipstick.
4   Pull the dipstick from the tube and wipe all the oil from the end with a clean rag or paper towel. Insert the clean dipstick all the way back into its metal tube and pull it out again. Observe the oil at the end of the dipstick. At its highest point, the level should be between the upper and lower holes **(see illustration)**.
5   It takes one quart of oil to raise the level from the lower hole to the upper hole on the dipstick. Do not allow the level to drop below the lower hole or oil starvation may cause engine damage. Conversely, overfilling the engine (adding oil above the upper hole) may cause oil fouled spark plugs, oil leaks or oil seal failures.

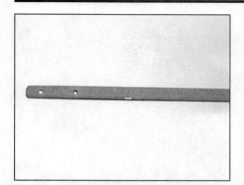

4.4 The oil level should be between the two holes in the dipstick - if it isn't, add enough oil to bring the level to or near the upper hole (it takes one quart to raise the level from the lower hole to the upper hole)

4.6 The threaded oil filler cap is located on the valve cover - to prevent dirt from contaminating the engine, always make sure the area around this opening is clean before unscrewing the cap

4.9 Make sure the coolant level is between the MAX and MIN lines - if it's below the MIN line, add a sufficient quantity of the specified mixture of antifreeze and water

1

6   Remove the threaded cap from the valve cover to add oil **(see illustration)**. Use an oil can spout or funnel to prevent spills. After adding the oil, install the filler cap hand tight. Start the engine and look carefully for any small leaks around the oil filter or drain plug. Stop the engine and check the oil level again after it has had sufficient time to drain from the upper block and cylinder head galleys.

7   Checking the oil level is an important preventive maintenance step. A continually dropping oil level indicates oil leakage through damaged seals, from loose connections, or past worn rings or valve guides. If the oil looks milky in color or has water droplets in it, a cylinder head gasket may be blown or the oil cooler could be leaking. The engine should be checked immediately. The condition of the oil should also be checked. Each time you check the oil level, slide your thumb and index finger up the dipstick before wiping off the oil. If you see small dirt or metal particles clinging to the dipstick, the oil should be changed (see Section 8).

Engine coolant

Refer to illustration 4.9

Warning: *Do not allow antifreeze to come in contact with your skin or painted surfaces of the vehicle. Rinse off spills immediately with plenty of water. Antifreeze is highly toxic if ingested. Never leave antifreeze lying around in an open container or in puddles on the floor; children and pets are attracted by it's sweet smell and may drink it. Check with local authorities about disposing of used antifreeze. Many communities have collection centers which will see that antifreeze is disposed of safely.* **Note:** *Non-toxic antifreeze is now manufactured and available at auto parts stores, but even this should be disposed of properly.*

8   All vehicles covered by this manual are equipped with a pressurized coolant recovery system. A coolant reservoir, located on the right side of the engine compartment, is connected by a hose to the base of the radiator

filler neck. If the coolant heats up during engine operation, coolant can escape through the pressurized filler cap, then through the connecting hose into the reservoir. As the engine cools, the coolant is automatically drawn back into the cooling system to maintain the correct level.

9   The coolant level in the reservoir should be checked regularly. It must be between the MAX and MIN lines on the tank. The level will vary with the temperature of the engine. When the engine is cold, the coolant level should be at or slightly above the MIN mark on the tank. Once the engine has warmed up, the level should be at or near the MAX mark. If it isn't, allow the fluid in the tank to cool, then remove the cap from the reservoir **(see illustration)** and add coolant to bring the level up to the MAX line. **Warning:** *Do not remove the radiator cap to check the coolant level when the engine is warm! Use only ethylene glycol type coolant and water in the mixture ratio recommended by your owner's manual. Do not use supplemental inhibitors or additives. If only a small amount of coolant is required to bring the system up to the proper level, water can be used. However, repeated additions of water will dilute the recommended antifreeze and water solution. In order to maintain the proper ratio of antifreeze and water, it is advisable to top up the coolant level with the correct mixture. Refer to your owner's manual for the recommended ratio.*

10   If the coolant level drops within a short time after replenishment, there may be a leak in the system. Inspect the radiator, hoses, engine coolant filler cap, drain plugs, air bleeder bolt and water pump. If no leak is evident, have the radiator cap pressure tested. **Warning:** *Never remove the radiator cap or the coolant recovery reservoir cap when the engine is running or has just been shut down, because the cooling system is hot. Escaping steam and scalding liquid could cause serious injury.*

11   If it is necessary to open the radiator cap, wait until the system has cooled completely, then wrap a thick cloth around the cap and turn it to the first stop. If any steam escapes, wait until the system has cooled further, then remove the cap.

12   When checking the coolant level, always note its condition. It should be relatively clear. If it is brown or rust colored, the system should be drained, flushed and refilled. Even if the coolant appears to be normal, the corrosion inhibitors wear out with use, so it must be replaced at the specified intervals.

13   Do not allow antifreeze to come in contact with your skin or painted surfaces of the vehicle. Flush contacted areas immediately with plenty of water.

Windshield washer fluid

Refer to illustration 4.14

14   Fluid for the windshield washer system is stored in a plastic reservoir located at the left front corner of the engine compartment **(see illustration)**. In milder climates, plain water can be used to top up the reservoir, but

4.14 The windshield washer fluid reservoir (arrow) is located at the left front corner of the engine compartment

4.16a The brake fluid should be kept between the MIN and MAX marks on the reservoir - turn and lift up the cap to add fluid

4.16b Keep the level between the MIN and MAX lines on the clutch fluid reservoir

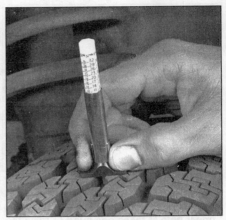

5.2 Use a tire tread depth gauge to monitor tire wear - they are available at auto parts stores and service stations and cost very little

the reservoir should be kept no more than 2/3 full to allow for expansion should the water freeze. In colder climates, the use of a specially designed windshield washer fluid, available at your dealer and any auto parts store, will help lower the freezing point of the fluid. Mix the solution with water in accordance with the manufacturer's directions on the container. Do not use regular antifreeze. It will damage the vehicle's paint.

Brake and clutch fluid

Refer to illustrations 4.16a and 4.16b

15   The brake master cylinder is mounted on the front of the power booster unit and the clutch master cylinder next to it on the firewall within the engine compartment. Models with an Anti-lock Brake System (ABS) also have a reservoir for the ABS modulator located on the right side of the engine compartment. ABS-equipped vehicles should be driven for a few minutes to equalize the fluid in the system before checking the fluid level in the reservoirs. If the level rises significantly above the MAX mark, have the system checked by a dealer because this could indicate a malfunction in the ABS system.

16   To check the fluid level of the brake or clutch master cylinder, simply look at the MAX and MIN marks on the reservoir **(see illustrations)**. The level should be between the two marks. If the vehicle is equipped with an Anti-lock Brake System (ABS), the fluid level in the ABS unit reservoir must also be checked. It's located on the right (passenger) side of the engine compartment.

17   If the level is low, wipe the top of the reservoir cover with a clean rag to prevent contamination of the brake system before lifting the cap.

18   Add only the specified brake fluid to the brake, clutch or ABS reservoir (refer to *Recommended lubricants and fluids* at the front of this chapter or to your owner's manual). Mixing different types of brake fluid can damage the system. Fill the brake master cylinder reservoir only to about 3/4-inch below the

MAX line - this brings the fluid to the correct level when you put the cap back on. **Warning:** *Use caution when filling the reservoir - brake fluid can harm your eyes and damage painted surfaces. Do not use brake fluid that has been opened for more than one year or has been left open. Brake fluid absorbs moisture from the air. Excess moisture can cause a dangerous loss of braking.*

19   While the reservoir cap is removed, inspect the master cylinder reservoir for contamination. If deposits, dirt particles or water droplets are present, the system should be drained and refilled (see Chapters 8 and 9).

20   After filling the reservoir to the proper level, make sure the lid is properly seated to prevent fluid leakage and/or system pressure loss.

21   The brake fluid in the master cylinder will drop slightly as the brake pads at each wheel wear down during normal operation. If the master cylinder requires repeated replenishing to keep it at the proper level, this is an indication of leakage in the brake system, which should be corrected immediately. Check all brake lines and connections, along with the wheel cylinders and booster (see Section 15 for more information). A drop in the clutch reservoir level indicates a leak in the clutch hydraulic system (Chapter 8).

22   If, upon checking the brake master cylinder fluid level, you discover an empty or nearly empty reservoir, the brake system should be bled (see Chapter 9).

---

5   Tire and tire pressure checks (every 250 miles or weekly)

Refer to illustrations 5.2, 5.3, 5.4a, 5.4b and 5.8

1   Periodic inspection of the tires may spare you from the inconvenience of being stranded with a flat tire. It can also provide you with vital information regarding possible problems in the steering and suspension systems before major damage occurs.

2   Normal tread wear can be monitored

with a simple, inexpensive device known as a tread depth indicator **(see illustration)**. When the tread depth reaches the specified minimum, replace the tire(s).

3   Note any abnormal tread wear **(see illustration)**. Tread pattern irregularities such as cupping, flat spots and more wear on one side than the other are indications of front end alignment and/or balance problems. If any of these conditions are noted, take the vehicle to a tire shop or service station to correct the problem.

4   Look closely for cuts, punctures and embedded nails or tacks. Sometimes a tire will hold its air pressure for a short time or leak down very slowly even after a nail has embedded itself into the tread. If a slow leak persists, check the valve core to make sure it is tight **(see illustration)**. Examine the tread for an object that may have embedded itself into the tire or for a "plug" that may have begun to leak (radial tire punctures are repaired with a plug that is installed in a puncture). If a puncture is suspected, it can be easily verified by spraying a solution of soapy water onto the puncture area **(see illustration)**. The soapy solution will bubble if there is a leak. Unless the puncture is inordinately large, a tire shop or gas station can usually repair the punctured tire.

5   Carefully inspect the inner side of each tire for evidence of brake fluid leakage. If you see any, inspect the brakes immediately.

6   Correct tire air pressure adds miles to the lifespan of the tires, improves mileage and enhances overall ride quality. Tire pressure cannot be accurately estimated by looking at a tire, particularly if it is a radial. A tire pressure gauge is therefore essential. Keep an accurate gauge in the glovebox. The pressure gauges fitted to the nozzles of air hoses at gas stations are often inaccurate.

7   Always check tire pressure when the tires are cold. "Cold," in this case, means the vehicle has not been driven over a mile in the three hours preceding a tire pressure check. A pressure rise of four to eight pounds is not

UNDERINFLATION

CUPPING

Cupping may be caused by:
- Underinflation and/or mechanical irregularities such as out-of-balance condition of wheel and/or tire, and bent or damaged wheel.
- Loose or worn steering tie-rod or steering idler arm.
- Loose, damaged or worn front suspension parts.

OVERINFLATION

1

INCORRECT TOE-IN OR EXTREME CAMBER

FEATHERING DUE TO MISALIGNMENT

5.3 This chart will help you determine the condition of the tires, the probable cause(s) of abnormal wear and the corrective action necessary

5.4a If a tire looses air on a steady basis, check the valve core first to make sure it's snug (special inexpensive wrenches are commonly available at auto parts stores)

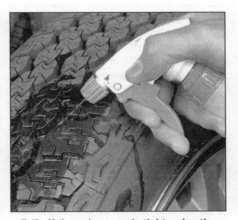

5.4b If the valve core is tight, raise the corner of the vehicle with the low tire and spray a soapy water solution onto the tread as the tire is turned slowly - leaks will cause small bubbles to appear

5.8 To extend the life of the tires, check the air pressure at least once a week with an accurate gauge (don't forget the spare)

uncommon once the tires are warm.

8   Unscrew the valve cap protruding from the wheel or hubcap and push the gauge firmly onto the valve **(see illustration)**. Note the reading on the gauge and compare this figure to the recommended tire pressure shown on the tire placard on the left door jamb. Be sure to reinstall the valve cap to keep dirt and moisture out of the valve stem mechanism. Check all four tires and, if neces-

sary, add enough air to bring them up to the recommended pressure levels.

9   Don't forget to keep the spare tire inflated to the specified pressure (consult your owner's manual). Note that the air pressure specified for the compact spare is significantly higher than the pressure of the regular tires.

6   Power steering fluid level check (every 3000 miles or 3 months)

Refer to illustration 6.4

1   The power steering system relies on fluid which may, over a period of time, require replenishing.

2   The fluid reservoir for the power steering pump is located on the inner fender panel

6.4 The power steering fluid reservoir is translucent so the fluid level can be checked without removing the cap - keep the fluid between the two lines

near the left front of the engine compartment.
3   For the check, the front wheels should be pointed straight ahead and the engine should be off. The fluid should be cold when checking the level.
4   On all models, the reservoir is translucent plastic and the fluid level can be checked visually **(see illustration)**.
5   If additional fluid is required, pour the specified type directly into the reservoir, using a funnel to prevent spills.
6   If the reservoir requires frequent fluid additions, all power steering hoses, hose connections, the power steering pump and the steering gear should be carefully checked for leaks.

7   Automatic transaxle and Continuously Variable Transaxle fluid level check (every 3000 miles or 3 months)

Refer to illustrations 7.5a and 7.5b
1   The level of the automatic or Continuously Variable transaxle fluid should be carefully maintained. Low fluid level can lead to slipping or loss of drive, while overfilling can cause foaming, loss of fluid and transaxle damage.
2   The transaxle fluid level should only be checked on level ground within one minute of the engine being shut off.
3   Remove the dipstick - it's located down low on the front of the transaxle (in the passenger's side of the engine compartment). Check the level of the fluid on the dipstick and note its condition.
4   Wipe the fluid from the dipstick with a clean rag and reinsert it.
5   Pull the dipstick out again and note the fluid level **(see illustration)**. The level should be between the upper and lower marks on the dipstick **(see illustration)**. If the level is low, add the specified automatic transmission fluid through the dipstick opening with a funnel.

7.5a The automatic transaxle fluid dipstick (arrow) is located on the right side of the engine compartment

6   Add just enough of the specified fluid to fill the transaxle to the proper level. It takes about one pint to raise the level from the lower mark to the upper mark, so add the fluid a little at a time and keep checking the level until it is correct.
7   The condition of the fluid should also be checked along with the level. If the fluid at the end of the dipstick is black or a dark reddish brown color, or if it emits a burned smell, the fluid should be changed (see Section 27). If you are in doubt about the condition of the fluid, purchase some new fluid and compare the two for color and smell.

8   Engine oil and oil filter change (every 3000 miles or 3 months)

Refer to illustrations 8.2, 8.7, 8.12 and 8.14
1   Frequent oil changes are the best preventive maintenance the home mechanic can give the engine, because aging oil becomes diluted and contaminated, which leads to premature engine wear.
2   Make sure you have all the necessary tools before you begin this procedure **(see illustration)**. You should also have plenty of rags or newspapers handy for mopping up any spills.
3   Access to the underside of the vehicle is greatly improved if the vehicle can be lifted on a hoist, driven onto ramps or supported by jackstands. **Warning:** *Do not work under a vehicle which is supported only by a bumper, hydraulic or scissors-type jack.*
4   If this is your first oil change, get under the vehicle and familiarize yourself with the locations of the oil drain plug and the oil filter. The engine and exhaust components will be warm during the actual work, so try to anticipate any potential problems before the engine and accessories are hot.
5   Park the vehicle on a level spot. Start the engine and allow it to reach its normal operating temperature. Warm oil and sludge will flow out more easily. Turn off the engine

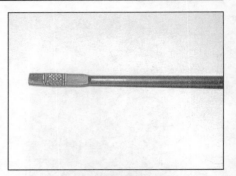

7.5b The automatic transaxle fluid level should be in the cross-hatched area on the dipstick

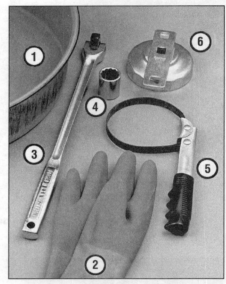

8.2 These tools are required when changing the engine oil and filter

1   **Drain pan** - *It should be fairly shallow in depth, but wide to prevent spills*
2   **Rubber gloves** - *When removing the drain plug and filter, you will get oil on your hands (the gloves will prevent burns)*
3   **Breaker bar** - *Sometimes the oil drain plug is tight, and a long breaker bar is needed to loosen it*
4   **Socket** - *To be used with the breaker bar or a ratchet (must be the correct size to fit the drain plug)*
5   **Filter wrench** - *This is a metal band-type wrench, which requires clearance around the filter to be effective*
6   **Filter wrench** - *This type fits on the bottom of the filter and can be turned with a ratchet or breaker bar (different-size wrenches are available for different types of filters)*

when it's warmed up. Remove the filler cap from the valve cover.
6   Raise the vehicle and support it securely on jackstands. **Warning:** *Never get beneath the vehicle when it is supported only by a jack. The jack provided with your vehicle is*

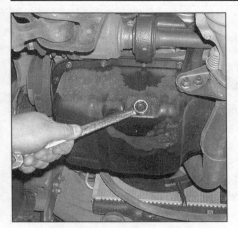

8.7 Use the proper size box-end wrench or socket to remove the oil drain plug without rounding off the corners

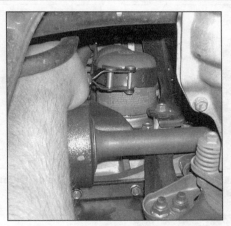

8.12 The oil filter is usually on very tight and will require a special wrench for removal - DO NOT use the wrench to tighten the new filter

8.14 Lubricate the oil filter gasket with clean engine oil before installing the filter on the engine

1

designed solely for raising the vehicle to remove and replace the wheels. Always use jackstands to support the vehicle when it becomes necessary to place your body underneath the vehicle.

7   Being careful not to touch the hot exhaust components, place the drain pan under the drain plug in the bottom of the pan and remove the plug **(see illustration)**. You may want to wear gloves while unscrewing the plug the final few turns if the engine is hot.

8   Allow the old oil to drain into the pan. It may be necessary to move the pan farther under the engine as the oil flow slows to a trickle. Inspect the old oil for the presence of metal shavings and chips.

9   After all the oil has drained, wipe off the drain plug with a clean rag. Even minute metal particles clinging to the plug would immediately contaminate the new oil.

10   Clean the area around the drain plug opening, reinstall the plug and tighten it securely, but do not strip the threads.

11   Move the drain pan into position under the oil filter.

12   Loosen the oil filter **(see illustration)** by turning it counterclockwise with the filter wrench. Any standard filter wrench will work. Sometimes the oil filter is screwed on so tightly that it cannot be loosened. If this situation occurs, punch a metal bar or long screwdriver directly through the side of the canister and use it as a T-bar to turn the filter. Be prepared for oil to spurt out of the canister as it is punctured. Once the filter is loose, use your hands to unscrew it from the block. Just as the filter is detached from the block, immediately tilt the open end up to prevent the oil inside the filter from spilling out. **Warning:** *The exhaust system may still be hot, so be careful.*

13   With a clean rag, wipe off the mounting surface on the block. If a residue of old oil is allowed to remain, it will smoke when the block is heated up. Also make sure that none of the old gasket remains stuck to the mounting surface. It can be removed with a scraper if necessary.

14   Compare the old filter with the new one to make sure they are the same type. Smear some clean engine oil on the rubber gasket of the new filter and screw it into place **(see illustration)**. Because overtightening the filter will damage the gasket, do not use a filter wrench to tighten the filter. Tighten it by hand until the gasket contacts the seating surface. Then seat the filter by giving it an additional 3/4-turn.

15   Remove all tools, rags, etc. from under the vehicle, being careful not to spill the oil in the drain pan, then lower the vehicle.

16   Add new oil to the engine through the oil filler cap in the valve cover. Use a funnel, if necessary, to prevent it from spilling onto the top of the engine. Pour three quarts of fresh oil into the engine. Wait a few minutes to allow the oil to drain into the pan, then check the level on the oil dipstick (see Section 4 if necessary). If the oil level is at or near the upper hole on the dipstick, install the filler cap hand tight, start the engine and allow the new oil to circulate.

17   Allow the engine to run for about a minute. While the engine is running, look under the vehicle and check for leaks at the oil pan drain plug and around the oil filter. If either is leaking, stop the engine and tighten the plug or filter.

18   Wait a few minutes to allow the oil to trickle down into the pan, then recheck the level on the dipstick and, if necessary, add enough oil to bring the level to the upper hole.

19   During the first few trips after an oil change, make it a point to check frequently for leaks and proper oil level.

20   The old oil drained from the engine cannot be re-used in its present state and should be discarded. Oil reclamation centers, auto repair shops and gas stations will normally accept the oil, which can be refined and used again. After the oil has cooled, it can be drained into a suitable container (capped plastic jugs, topped bottles, milk cartons, etc.) for transport to one of these disposal sites.

9   Windshield wiper blade inspection and replacement (every 7500 miles or 6 months)

Refer to illustrations 9.6, 9.7 and 9.8

1   The windshield wiper and blade assembly should be inspected periodically for damage, loose components and cracked or worn blade elements.

2   Road film can build up on the wiper blades and affect their efficiency, so they should be washed regularly with a mild detergent solution.

3   The action of the wiping mechanism can loosen bolts, nuts and fasteners, so they should be checked and tightened, as necessary, at the same time the wiper blades are checked.

4   If the wiper blade elements are cracked, worn or warped, or no longer clean adequately, they should be replaced with new ones.

5   Lift the arm assembly away from the glass for clearance.

6   Press in on the lock tab and push the blade assembly down the wiper arm, out of the hook at the end **(see illustration)**.

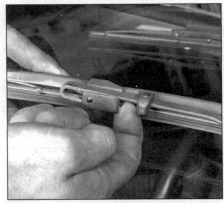

9.6 Press in on the tab and push the blade assembly out of the hook at the end to remove it

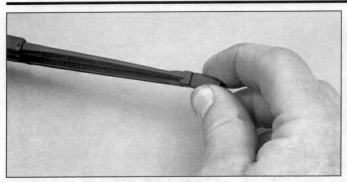

9.7 Squeeze the blade element tabs, then pull the element out of the metal frame and remove it

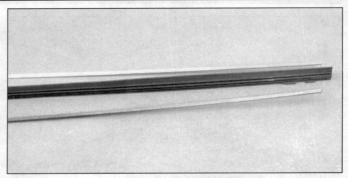

9.8 The metal retainers must be inserted into the slots in the rubber before installation

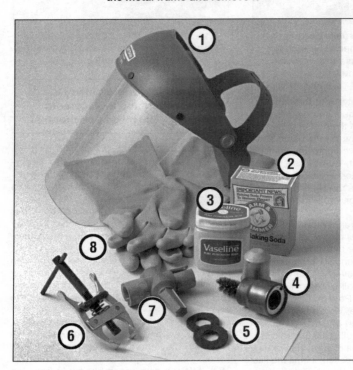

10.1 Tools and materials required for battery maintenance

1 **Face shield/safety goggles** - *When removing corrosion with a brush, the acidic particles can easily fly up into your eyes*
2 **Baking soda** - *A solution of baking soda and water can be used to neutralize corrosion*
3 **Petroleum jelly** - *A layer of this on the battery posts will help prevent corrosion*
4 **Battery post/cable cleaner** - *This wire brush cleaning tool will remove all traces of corrosion from the battery posts and cable clamps*
5 **Treated felt washers** - *Placing one of these on each post, directly under the cable clamps, will help prevent corrosion*
6 **Puller** - *Sometimes the cable clamps are very difficult to pull off the posts, even after the nut/bolt has been completely loosened. This tool pulls the clamp straight up and off the post without damage*
7 **Battery post/cable cleaner** - *Here is another cleaning tool which is a slightly different version of Number 4 above, but it does the same thing*
8 **Rubber gloves** - *Another safety item to consider when servicing the battery; remember that's acid inside the battery!*

7   Squeeze the blade element tabs tightly and pull the element out of the metal frame **(see illustration)**.
8   Remove the metal retainers from the element and install them in the new element **(see illustration)**.
9   Insert the element into the frame and push it until the element tabs lock.
10   Place the metal arm assembly in the hook on the wiper arm and press it into place until the lock tab snaps into place.

10   Battery check, maintenance and charging (every 7500 miles or 6 months)

Refer to illustrations 10.1, 10.6, 10.7a, 10.7b, 10.8a, 10.8b and 10.13
Warning: *Certain precautions must be followed when checking and servicing the battery. Hydrogen gas, which is highly flammable, is always present in the battery cells, so keep lighted tobacco and all other open*

flames and sparks away from the battery. The electrolyte inside the battery is actually dilute sulfuric acid, which will cause injury if splashed on your skin or in your eyes. It will also ruin clothes and painted surfaces. When removing the battery cables, always detach the negative cable first and hook it up last!

Check

1   A routine preventive maintenance program for the battery in your vehicle is the only way to ensure quick and reliable starts. But before performing any battery maintenance, make sure that you have the proper equipment necessary to work safely around the battery **(see illustration)**.
2   There are also several precautions that should be taken whenever battery maintenance is performed. Before servicing the battery, always turn the engine and all accessories off and disconnect the cable from the negative terminal of the battery.
3   The battery produces hydrogen gas, which is both flammable and explosive.

Never create a spark, smoke or light a match around the battery. Always charge the battery in a ventilated area.
4   Electrolyte contains poisonous and corrosive sulfuric acid. Do not allow it to get in your eyes, on your skin on your clothes. Never ingest it. Wear protective safety glasses when working near the battery. Keep children away from the battery.
5   Note the external condition of the battery. If the positive terminal and cable clamp on your vehicle's battery is equipped with a rubber protector, make sure that it's not torn or damaged. It should completely cover the terminal. Look for any corroded or loose connections, cracks in the case or cover or loose hold-down clamps. Also check the entire length of each cable for cracks and frayed conductors.
6   Some models with sealed batteries have a battery condition indicator on top of the battery **(see illustration)**. Compare the color showing in the window to the condition color chart on the battery. You may catch a low-

10.6 The indicator "eye" can tell you a lot about your battery condition at a glance

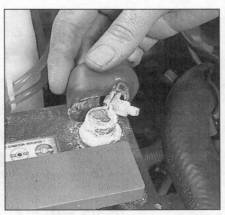

10.7a Battery terminal corrosion usually appears as light, fluffy powder

10.7b Removing the cable from a battery post with a wrench - sometimes special battery pliers are required for this procedure if corrosion has caused deterioration of the nut hex (always remove the ground cable first and hook it up last!)

10.8a When cleaning the cable clamps, all corrosion must be removed (the inside of the clamp is tapered to match the taper on the post, so don't remove too much material)

10.8b Regardless of the type of tool used on the battery posts, a clean, shiny surface should be the result

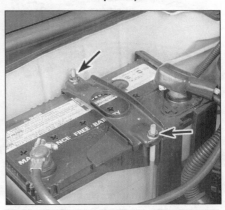

10.13 Make sure the battery hold-down nuts are tight

charge battery condition before it strands you on the roadside. If the color indicate a low state of charge, charge the battery and examine the charging system (see Chapter 5 and this Section).

Maintenance

7   If corrosion, which looks like white, fluffy deposits **(see illustration)** is evident, particularly around the terminals, the battery should be removed for cleaning. Loosen the cable clamp bolts with a wrench, being careful to remove the ground cable first, and slide them off the terminals **(see illustration)**. Then disconnect the hold-down clamp bolt and nut, remove the clamp and lift the battery from the engine compartment.

8   Clean the cable clamps thoroughly with a battery brush or a terminal cleaner and a solution of warm water and baking soda **(see illustration)**. Wash the terminals and the top of the battery case with the same solution but make sure that the solution doesn't get into the battery. When cleaning the cables, terminals and battery top, wear safety goggles and rubber gloves to prevent any solution from coming in contact with your eyes or hands.

Wear old clothes too - even diluted, sulfuric acid splashed onto clothes will burn holes in them. If the terminals have been extensively corroded, clean them up with a terminal cleaner **(see illustration)**. Thoroughly wash all cleaned areas with plain water.

9   Whenever the battery is removed for cleaning or charging, inspect the battery carrier before reinstalling the battery in the engine compartment. If the carrier is dirty or covered with corrosion, clean it in the same solution of warm water and baking soda. Inspect the metal brackets which support the carrier to make sure that they are not covered with corrosion. If they are, wash them off. If corrosion is extensive, sand the brackets down to bare metal and spray them with a zinc-based primer (available in spray cans at auto paint and body supply stores).

10   Reinstall the battery back into the engine compartment. Make sure that no parts or wires are laying on the carrier during installation of the battery. Information on removing and installing the battery can be found in Chapter 5. Information on jump starting can be found at the front of this manual. For more detailed battery checking procedures, refer to the *Haynes Automotive Electrical Manual*.

11   Install a pair of specially-treated felt washers around the terminals (available at auto parts stores), then coat the terminals and the cable clamps with petroleum jelly or grease to prevent further corrosion. Install the cable clamps and tighten the nuts, being careful to install the negative cable last.

12   Install the hold-down clamp and nuts. Tighten the nuts only enough to hold the battery firmly in place. Overtightening these nuts can crack the battery case.

13   Make sure that the battery tray is in good condition and the hold-down clamp bolts are tight **(see illustration)**. If the battery is removed from the tray, make sure no parts remain in the bottom of the tray when the battery is reinstalled. When reinstalling the hold-down clamp bolts, do not overtighten them.

Charging

Warning: *When batteries are being charged, hydrogen gas, which is very explosive and flammable, is produced. Do not smoke or allow open flames near a charging or a recently charged battery. Wear eye protection when near the battery during charging. Also,*

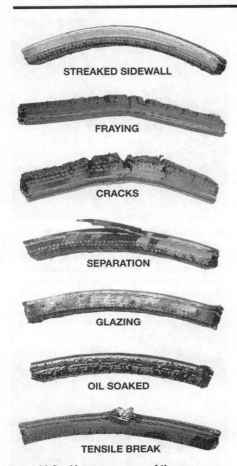

11.3a Here are some of the more common problems associated with drivebelts (check the belts very carefully to prevent an untimely breakdown)

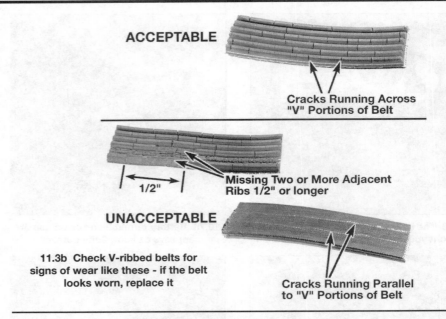

11.3b Check V-ribbed belts for signs of wear like these - if the belt looks worn, replace it

make sure the charger is unplugged before connecting or disconnecting the battery from the charger.

14 Slow-rate charging is the best way to restore a battery that's discharged to the point where it will not start the engine. It's also a good way to maintain the battery charge in a vehicle that's only driven a few miles between starts. Maintaining the battery charge is particularly important in the winter when the battery must work harder to start the engine and electrical accessories that drain the battery are in greater use.

15 It's best to use a one or two-amp battery charger (sometimes called a "trickle" charger). They are the safest and put the least strain on the battery. They are also the least expensive. For a faster charge, you can use a higher amperage charger, but don't use one rated more than 1/10th the amp/hour rating of the battery. Rapid boost charges that claim to restore the power of the battery in one to two hours are hardest on the battery and can damage batteries not in good condition. This type of charging should only be used in emergency situations.

16 The average time necessary to charge a battery should be listed in the instructions

that come with the charger. As a general rule, a trickle charger will charge a battery in 12 to 16 hours.

11 Drivebelt check, adjustment and replacement (every 7500 miles or 6 months)

Refer to illustrations 11.3a, 11.3b and 11.4

Check

1 The drivebelts or V-belts as they are sometimes called, are located at the front of the engine and play an important role in the overall operation of the vehicle and its components. Due to their function and material make-up, the belts are prone to failure after a period of time and should be inspected and adjusted periodically to prevent major engine damage.

2 The number of belts used on a particular vehicle depends on the accessories installed. Drivebelts are used to turn the alternator, power steering pump, water pump and air conditioning compressor. Depending on the

pulley arrangement, more than one of these components may be driven by a single belt.

3 With the engine off, open the hood and locate the drivebelts at the front of the engine. Using your fingers (and a flashlight if necessary), move along the belts chuckling for cracks and separation of the belt plies. Also check for fraying and glazing, which gives the belt a shiny appearance **(see illustrations)**. Both sides of the belt should be inspected, which means you will have to twist the belt to check the underside.

4 The tension of each belt is checked by pushing the belt at a distance halfway between the pulleys. Push firmly with your thumb and see how much the belt moves (deflects) **(see illustration)**. As a rule of thumb, if the distance from pulley center-to-pulley center is between 7 and 11 inches, the belt should deflect 1/4-inch. If the belt travels between pulleys spaced 12 to 16-inches apart, the belt should deflect 1/2-inch for a V-belt and 1/4-inch for a ribbed belt.

Adjustment

Refer to illustrations 11.6a, 11.6b and 11.6c

5 If it is necessary to adjust the belt ten-

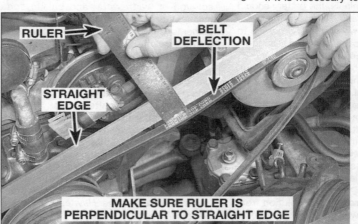

11.4 Measuring drivebelt deflection with a straightedge and ruler

11.6a Loosen the pivot bolt and lockbolt (arrows), then move the alternator in-or-out to adjust the drivebelt tension

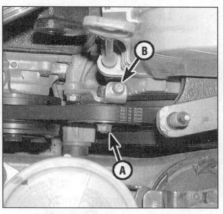

11.6b The air conditioning compressor uses an adjustable idler pulley to adjust belt tension - loosen the idler pulley bolt (A), then turn the adjusting bolt (B) to loosen or tighten the belt

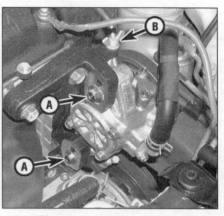

11.6c The power steering pump requires loosening the adjusting bolts (A) and turning the wingnut (B) (some models) or moving the pump in-or-out to tighten or loosen the belt

sion, either to make the belt tighter or looser, it is done by moving the belt-driven accessory on the bracket.

6   The alternator drivebelt is adjusted by loosening the pivot and adjusting bolts and moving the alternator to tension the drivebelt **(see illustration)**. After adjustment, tighten the pivot and adjusting bolts. The air conditioning compressor is rigidly mounted and uses an adjustable idler pulley which is mounted between the components to tension the belt **(see illustration)**. The power steering pump is adjusted by loosening the adjusting bolt(s) and moving the pump upward to tension the belt **(see illustration)**.

7   After the bolts have been loosened, move the component away from the engine to tighten the belt or toward the engine to loosen the belt. Measure the belt tension in accordance with the above methods. Repeat this step until the drivebelt is adjusted.

Replacement

8   To replace a belt, follow the above procedures for drivebelt adjustment but slip the belt off the crankshaft pulley and remove it. Since belts tend to wear out more or less at the same time, its a good idea to replace them all at the same time. Mark each belt and the corresponding pulley groove so the replacement belts can be installed properly.

9   Take the old belts with you when purchasing new ones in order to make a direct comparison for length, width and design.

10   Adjust the belts as described earlier in this Section.

12   Underhood hose check and replacement (every 7500 miles or 6 months)

Caution: *Replacement of air conditioning hoses must be left to a dealer service department or air conditioning shop that has the equipment to depressurize the system safely. Never remove air conditioning components or hoses until the system has been depressurized.*

General

1   High temperatures in the engine compartment can cause the deterioration of the rubber and plastic hoses used for engine, accessory and emission systems operation. Periodic inspection should be made for cracks, loose clamps, material hardening and leaks.

2   Information specific to the cooling system hoses can be found in Section 13.

3   Some, but not all, hoses are secured to the fittings with clamps. Where clamps are used, check to be sure they haven't lost their tension, allowing the hose to leak. If clamps aren't used, make sure the hose has not expanded and/or hardened where it slips over the fitting, allowing it to leak.

Vacuum hoses

4   It's quite common for vacuum hoses, especially those in the emissions system, to be color coded or identified by colored stripes molded into them. Various systems require hoses with different wall thicknesses, collapse resistance and temperature resistance. When replacing hoses, be sure the new ones are made of the same material.

5   Often the only effective way to check a hose is to remove it completely from the vehicle. If more than one hose is removed, be sure to label the hoses and fittings to ensure correct installation.

6   When checking vacuum hoses, be sure to include any plastic T-fittings in the check. Inspect the fittings for cracks and the hose where it fits over the fitting for distortion, which could cause leakage.

7   A small piece of vacuum hose (1/4-inch inside diameter) can be used as a stethoscope to detect vacuum leaks. Hold one end of the hose to your ear and probe around vacuum hoses and fittings, listening for the "hissing" sound characteristic of a vacuum leak.

Warning: *When probing with the vacuum hose stethoscope, be very careful not to come into contact with moving engine components such as the drivebelts, cooling fan, etc.*

Fuel hose

Warning: *Gasoline is extremely flammable, so take extra precautions when you work on any part of the fuel system. Don't smoke or allow open flames or bare light bulbs near the work area, and don't work in a garage where a natural gas-type appliance (such as a water heater or clothes dryer) with a pilot light is present. Since gasoline is carcinogenic, wear latex gloves when there's a possibility of being exposed to fuel, and, if you spill any fuel on your skin, rinse it off immediately with soap and water. Mop up any spills immediately and do not store fuel-soaked rags where they could ignite. The fuel system is under constant pressure, so, if any fuel lines are to be disconnected, the fuel pressure in the system must be relieved first (see Chapter 4 for more information). When you perform any kind of work on the fuel system, wear safety glasses and have a Class B type fire extinguisher on hand.*

8   Check all rubber fuel lines for deterioration and chafing. Check especially for cracks in areas where the hose bends and just before fittings, such as where a hose attaches to the fuel filter.

9   When replacing hose, use only hose that is specifically designed for your fuel injection system.

Metal lines

10   Sections of metal line are often used for fuel line between the fuel pump and fuel injection unit. Check carefully to be sure the line has not been bent or crimped and that cracks have not started in the line.

11   If a section of metal fuel line must be replaced, only seamless steel tubing should be used, since copper and aluminum tubing don't have the strength necessary to withstand normal engine vibration.

12   Check the metal brake lines where they enter the master cylinder and brake proportioning unit (if used) for cracks in the lines or loose fittings. Any sign of brake fluid leakage calls for an immediate thorough inspection of the brake system.

1

Check for a chafed area that could fail prematurely.

Check for a soft area indicating the hose has deteriorated inside.

Overtightening the clamp on a hardened hose will damage the hose and cause a leak.

Check each hose for swelling and oil-soaked ends. Cracks and breaks can be located by squeezing the hose.

13.4 Hoses, like drivebelts, have a habit of failing at the worst possible time - to prevent the inconvenience of a blown radiator or heater hose, inspect them carefully as shown here

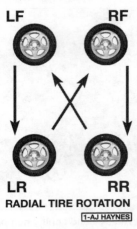

14.2a The recommended tire rotation pattern for models with NON-DIRECTIONAL tires

14.2b The recommended tire rotation pattern for models with DIRECTIONAL tires

13　Cooling system check (every 7500 miles or 6 months)

Refer to illustration 13.4

1　Many major engine failures can be attributed to a faulty cooling system. If the vehicle is equipped with an automatic transaxle, the cooling system also cools the transaxle fluid and thus plays an important role in prolonging transaxle life.

2　The cooling system should be checked with the engine cold. Do this before the vehicle is driven for the day or after the engine has been shut off for at least three hours.

3　Remove the radiator cap by turning it to the left until it reaches a stop. If you hear a hissing sound (indicating there is still pressure in the system), wait until it stops. Now press down on the cap with the palm of your hand and continue turning to the left until the cap can be removed. Thoroughly clean the cap, inside and out, with clean water. Also clean the filler neck on the radiator. All traces of corrosion should be removed. The coolant inside

the radiator should be relatively transparent. If it's rust colored, the system should be drained and refilled (see Section 28). If the coolant level isn't up to the top, add additional antifreeze/coolant mixture (see Sec-tion 4).

4　Carefully check the large upper and lower radiator hoses along with the smaller diameter heater hoses which run from the engine to the firewall. Inspect each hose along its entire length, replacing any hose which is cracked, swollen or shows signs of deterioration. Cracks may become more apparent if the hose is squeezed **(see illustration)**. Regardless of condition, it's a good idea to replace hoses with new ones every two years.

5　Make sure that all hose connections are tight. A leak in the cooling system will usually show up as white or rust colored deposits on the areas adjoining the leak. If wire-type clamps are used at the ends of the hoses, it may be a good idea to replace them with more secure screw-type clamps.

6　Use compressed air or a soft brush to remove bugs, leaves, etc. from the front of the radiator or air conditioning condenser. Be careful not to damage the delicate cooling fins or cut yourself on them.

7　Every other inspection, or at the first indication of cooling system problems, have the cap and system pressure tested. If you don't have a pressure tester, most gas stations and repair shops will do this for a minimal charge.

14　Tire rotation (every 7500 miles or 6 months)

Refer to illustrations 14.2a and 14.2b

1　The tires should be rotated at the specified intervals and whenever uneven wear is noticed. Since the vehicle will be raised and the tires removed anyway, check the brakes (see Section 15) at this time.

2　Radial tires must be rotated in a specific pattern **(see illustrations)**. Most models are

equipped with non-directional tires, but some models may have directional tires, which have a different rotation pattern. When choosing replacement tires, examine the sidewalls. Directional tires have arrows on the sidewall that indicate the direction they must turn, and a set of these tires includes two left-side tires and two right-side tires. The left and right side tires must not be rotated to the other side.

3　Refer to the information in *Jacking and towing* at the front of this manual for the proper procedures to follow when raising the vehicle and changing a tire. If the brakes are to be checked, do not apply the parking brake as stated. Make sure the tires are blocked to prevent the vehicle from rolling.

4　Preferably, the entire vehicle should be raised at the same time. This can be done on a hoist or by jacking up each corner and then lowering the vehicle onto jackstands placed under the frame rails. Always use four jackstands and make sure the vehicle is firmly supported.

5　After rotation, check and adjust the tire pressures as necessary and be sure to check the lug nut tightness. Ideally, lug nuts should be torqued to Specifications with a torque wrench, and rechecked after 25 miles of driving.

6　For further information on the wheels and tires, refer to Chapter 10.

15　Brake check (every 7500 miles or 6 months)

Warning: *The dust created by the brake system may contain asbestos, which is harmful to your health. Never blow it out with compressed air and don't inhale any of it. An approved filtering mask should be worn when working on the brakes. Do not, under any circumstances, use petroleum-based solvents to clean brake parts. Use brake system cleaner only! Try to use non-asbestos replacement parts whenever possible.*

15.6 You'll find an inspection hole like this in each caliper - placing a ruler across the hole should enable you to determine the thickness of the remaining material on the inner pad

15.7 The amount of brake pad material remaining on the outer pad can be checked by looking at the end of the pad

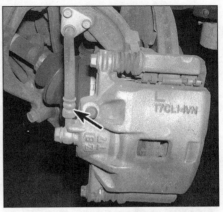

15.11 Check all brake lines and hoses for damage, wear and deformation, especially in the vicinity of the rubber hose at the caliper (arrow)

1

Note: *For detailed photographs of the brake system, refer to Chapter 9.*

1   In addition to the specified intervals, the brakes should be inspected every time the wheels are removed or whenever a defect is suspected.

2   Any of the following symptoms could indicate a potential brake system defect:

a) *The vehicle pulls to one side when the brake pedal is depressed.*
b) *The brakes make squealing or dragging noises when applied.*
c) *Brake pedal travel is excessive.*
d) *The brake pedal pulsates when applied.*
e) *Brake fluid leaks, usually onto the inside of the tire or wheel.*

3   Loosen the wheel lug nuts.

4   Raise the vehicle and place it securely on jackstands.

5   Remove the wheels (see *Jacking and towing* at the front of this book, or your owner's manual, if necessary).

Disc brakes

Refer to illustrations 15.6, 15.7 and 15.11

6   There are two pads (an outer and an inner) in each caliper. The pads are visible through inspection holes in each caliper **(see illustration).**

7   Check the pad thickness by looking at each end of the caliper and through the inspection hole in the caliper body **(see illustration).** If the lining material is less than the thickness listed in this Chapter's Specifications, replace the pads. **Note:** *Keep in mind that the lining material is riveted or bonded to a metal backing plate and the metal portion is not included in this measurement.*

8   If it is difficult to determine the exact thickness of the remaining pad material by the above method, or if you are at all concerned about the condition of the pads, remove the caliper(s), then remove the pads from the calipers for further inspection (refer to Chapter 9).

9   Once the pads are removed from the

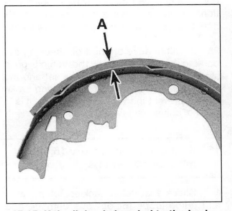

15.15 If the lining is bonded to the brake shoe, measure the lining thickness from the outer surface to the metal shoe, as shown here; if the lining is riveted to the shoe, measure from the lining outer surface to the rivet head

calipers, clean them with brake cleaner and re-measure them with a ruler or a vernier caliper.

10   Measure the disc thickness with a micrometer to make sure that it still has service life remaining. If any disc is thinner than the specified minimum thickness, replace it (refer to Chapter 9). Even if the disc has service life remaining, check its condition. Look for scoring, gouging and burned spots. If these conditions exist, remove the disc and have it resurfaced (see Chapter 9).

11   Before installing the wheels, check all brake lines and hoses for damage, wear, deformation, cracks, corrosion, leakage, bends and twists, particularly in the vicinity of the rubber hoses at the calipers **(see illustration).** Check the clamps for tightness and the connections for leakage. Make sure that all hoses and lines are clear of sharp edges, moving parts and the exhaust system. If any of the above conditions are noted, repair, reroute or replace the lines and/or fittings as necessary (see Chapter 9).

15.16 Typical assembled view of a rear drum brake (right side shown)

Drum brakes

Refer to illustrations 15.15, 15.16 and 15.17

12   On rear drum brakes, make sure the parking brake is off then proceed to tap on the outside of the drum with a rubber mallet to loosen it.

13   Remove the brake drums.

14   With the drums removed, carefully clean the brake assembly with brake system cleaner. **Warning:** *Don't blow the dust out with compressed air and don't inhale any of it (it may contain asbestos, which is harmful to your health).*

15   Note the thickness of the lining material on both front and rear brake shoes. If the material has worn away to within 1/16-inch of the recessed rivets or 1/8- inch of the metal backing on bonded type shoes, the shoes should be replaced **(see illustration).** The shoes should also be replaced if they're cracked, glazed (shiny areas), or covered with brake fluid.

16   Make sure all the brake assembly springs are connected and in good condition **(see illustration).**

17   Check the brake components for signs of fluid leakage. With your finger or a small

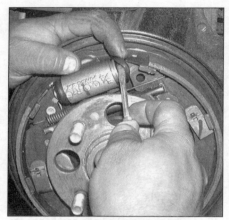

15.17 Check the wheel cylinders for leaking fluid indicating that the cylinder must be replaced

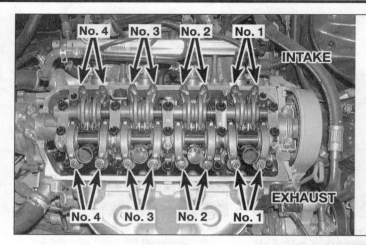

17.6 Valve layout (Civic shown, Integra similar)

screwdriver, carefully pry back the rubber cups on the wheel cylinder located at the top of the brake shoes **(see illustration)**. Any leakage here is an indication that the wheel cylinders should be replaced immediately (see Chapter 9). Also, check all hoses and connections for signs of leakage.
18   Wipe the inside of the drum with a clean rag and brake system cleaner. Again, be careful not to breathe the dangerous asbestos dust.
19   Check the inside of the drum for cracks, score marks, deep scratches and "hard spots" which will appear as small discolored areas. If imperfections cannot be removed with fine emery cloth, the drum must be taken to an automotive machine shop for resurfacing.
20   Repeat the procedure for the remaining wheel. If the inspection reveals that all parts are in good condition, reinstall the brake drums, install the wheels and lower the vehicle to the ground.

Brake booster check

21   Sit in the driver's seat and perform the following sequence of tests.
22   With the brake fully depressed, start the engine - the pedal should move down a little when the engine starts.
23   With the engine running, depress the brake pedal several times - the travel distance should not change.
24   Depress the brake, stop the engine and hold the pedal in for about 30 seconds - the pedal should neither sink nor rise.
25   Restart the engine, run it for about a minute and turn it off. Then firmly depress the brake several times - the pedal travel should decrease with each application.
26   If your brakes do not operate as described, the brake booster has failed. Refer to Chapter 9 for the replacement procedure.

Parking brake

27   Slowly pull up on the parking brake and count the number of clicks you hear until the

handle is up as far as it will go. The adjustment is correct if you hear the specified number of clicks (see this Chapter's Specifications). If you hear more or fewer clicks, it's time to adjust the parking brake (see Chapter 9).
28   An alternative method of checking the parking brake is to park the vehicle on a steep hill with the parking brake set and the transmission in Neutral. If the parking brake cannot prevent the vehicle from rolling, it is in need of adjustment (see Chapter 9).

16   Seat belt check (every 15,000 miles or 12 months)

1   Check seat belts, buckles, latch plates and guide loops for obvious damage and signs of wear.
2   See if the seat belt reminder light comes on when the key is turned to the Run or Start position. A chime should also sound. On passive restraint systems, the shoulder belt should move into position in the A-pillar.
3   The seat belts are designed to lock up during a sudden stop or impact, yet allow free movement during normal driving. Make sure the retractors return the belt against your chest while driving and rewind the belt fully when the buckle is unlatched.
4   If any of the above checks reveal problems with the seat belt system, replace parts as necessary.

17   Valve clearance check and adjustment (every 15,000 miles or 12 months)

Check

1   Valve clearances generally do not need adjustment unless valvetrain components have been replaced, or a valve job has been performed.
2   The simplest check for proper valve adjustment is to listen carefully to the engine running with the hood open. If the valvetrain is noisy, adjustment is necessary.

17.7a To make sure the adjusting screw doesn't move when the locknut is tightened, use a box-end wrench and have a good grip on the screwdriver (Civic shown)

Adjustment

Refer to illustrations 17.6, 17.7a, 17.7b and 17.8
3   The valve clearance must be checked and adjusted with the engine cold.
4   Remove the valve cover (see Chapter 2A or 2B).
5   Place the number one piston (closest to the drivebelt end of the engine) at Top Dead Center (TDC) on the compression stroke. This is accomplished by rotating the crankshaft in the normal direction of rotation (which is counterclockwise on these models) until the white TDC mark on the crankshaft pulley aligns with the timing pointer on the lower timing belt cover and the UP mark on the camshaft sprocket(s) are at the twelve o'clock position.
6   With the engine in this position, the number one cylinder valve adjustment can be checked and adjusted **(see illustration)**.
7   Start with the intake valve clearance. Insert a feeler gauge of the correct thickness (see this Chapter's Specifications) between the valve stem and the rocker arm on a Civic and an intake camshaft lobe and the rocker arm and on an Integra **(see illustrations)**.

17.7b On Integra models, insert the feeler gauge between the camshaft lobe and the rocker arm

17.8 On Integra models, a special tool is required to tighten the locknuts while holding the adjusting screw

18.2a On Civic models, the air cleaner housing cover is secured by four clips (arrows)

18.2b On Integra models, remove the air cleaner cover screws with either a nut driver or screwdriver

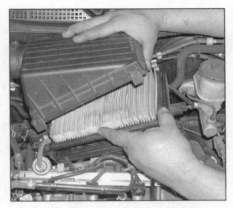

18.4a On Civic models, move the cover out of the way and remove the filter

18.4b On Integra models, remove the housing cover and detach the filter element from the air intake tube

Withdraw it; you should feel a slight drag. If there's no drag or a heavy drag, loosen the adjuster nut and back off the adjuster screw. Carefully tighten the adjuster screw until you can feel a slight drag on the feeler gauge as you withdraw it.

8   Hold the adjuster screw with a screwdriver (to keep it from turning) and tighten the locknut **(see illustration)**. Recheck the clearance to make sure it hasn't changed. Repeat the procedure in this Step and the previous Step on the other intake valve, then on the two exhaust valves.

9   Rotate the crankshaft pulley 180-degrees counterclockwise (the camshaft pulley will turn 90-degrees) until the number three cylinder is at TDC. With the number three cylinder at TDC, the UP mark on the camshaft sprocket(s) will be at the nine o'clock position. Check and adjust the number three cylinder valves.

10   Rotate the crankshaft pulley 180-degrees counterclockwise until the number four cylinder is at TDC. With the number four cylinder at TDC, the UP mark on the camshaft sprocket(s) will be pointed straight down. Check and adjust the number four cylinder valves.

11   Rotate the crankshaft pulley 180-degrees counterclockwise to bring the number two cylinder to TDC. The UP mark on the camshaft sprocket(s) should be at the three o'clock position. Check and adjust the number two cylinder valves.

12   Install the valve cover.

18   Air filter replacement (every 15,000 miles or 12 months)

Refer to illustrations 18.2a, 18.2b, 18.4a and 18.4b

1   At the specified intervals, the air filter should be replaced with a new one.

2   Detach the clips or loosen the air cleaner cover screws **(see illustrations)**.

3   Lift the cover up.

4   Lift the air filter element out of the housing and wipe out the inside of the air cleaner housing with a clean rag **(see illustrations)**.

5   While the air cleaner cover is off, be careful not to drop anything down into the air cleaner assembly.

6   Place the new filter in the air cleaner housing. Make sure it seats properly in the housing.

7   Install the air cleaner cover and tighten the screws securely.

19   Fuel system check (every 15,000 miles or 12 months)

Refer to illustration 19.6, 19.7 and 19.9

Warning : *Gasoline is extremely flammable, so take extra precautions when you work on any part of the fuel system. Don't smoke or allow open flames or bare light bulbs near the work area, and don't work in a garage where a natural gas-type appliance (such as a water heater or clothes dryer) with a pilot light is present. Since gasoline is carcinogenic, wear latex gloves when there's a possibility of being exposed to fuel, and, if you spill any fuel on your skin, rinse it off immediately with soap and water. Mop up any spills immediately and do not store fuel-soaked rags where they could ignite. When you perform any kind of work on the fuel system, wear safety glasses and have a Class B type fire extinguisher on hand. The fuel system is under constant pressure, so, before any lines are disconnected, the fuel system pressure must be relieved (see Chapter 4).*

1   If you smell gasoline while driving or after the vehicle has been sitting in the sun, inspect the fuel system immediately.

2   Remove the gas filler cap and inspect if

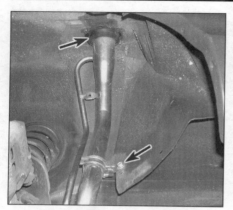

19.6 Inspect the fuel filler hoses for cracks and make sure the clamps (arrows) are tight

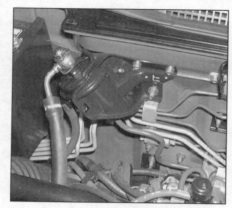

19.7 Carefully inspect fuel line couplings for damage

19.9 Inspect the evaporative system canister hoses (arrows) for damage and cracks

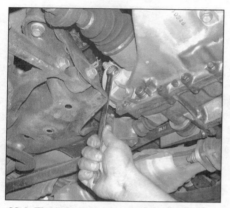

20.1 The manual transaxle check/fill plug is located on the passenger side of the transaxle - use a box end wrench to remove it

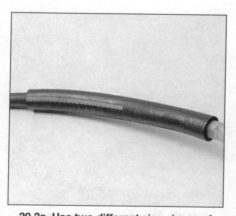

20.2a Use two different size pieces of hose to make an adapter on the funnel . . .

20.2b . . . so you can easily add lubricant to the transaxle from above

for damage and corrosion. The gasket should have an unbroken sealing imprint. If the gasket is damaged or corroded, install a new cap.

3   Inspect the fuel feed and return lines for cracks. Make sure that the connections between the fuel lines and the fuel injection system and between the fuel lines and the in-line fuel filter are tight. **Warning:** *Your vehicle is fuel injected, so you must relieve the fuel system pressure before servicing fuel system components. The fuel system pressure-relief procedure is outlined in Chapter 4.*

4   If the fuel injectors are visible, look for signs of fuel leakage (wet spots) around any of the injectors, they may need new O-rings (see Chapter 4).

5   Since some components of the fuel system - the fuel tank and part of the fuel feed and return lines, for example - are underneath the vehicle, they can be inspected more easily with the vehicle raised on a hoist. If that's not possible, raise the vehicle and support it on jackstands.

6   With the vehicle raised and safely supported, inspect the gas tank and filler neck for punctures, cracks and other damage. The connection between the filler neck and the tank is particularly critical. Sometimes a rub-

ber filler neck will leak because of loose clamps or deteriorated rubber **(see illustration)**. Inspect all fuel tank mounting brackets and straps to be sure that the tank is securely attached to the vehicle. **Warning:** *Do not, under any circumstances, try to repair a fuel tank (except rubber components). A welding torch or any open flame can easily cause fuel vapors inside the tank to explode.*

7   Carefully check all rubber hoses and metal lines leading away from the fuel tank **(see illustration)**. Check for loose connections, deteriorated hoses, crimped lines and other damage. Repair or replace damaged sections as necessary (see Chapter 4).

8   The evaporative emissions control system can also be a source of fuel odors. The function of the system is to store fuel vapors from the fuel tank in a charcoal canister until they can be routed to the intake manifold where they mix with incoming air before being burned in the combustion chambers.

9   The most common symptom of a faulty evaporative emissions system is a strong odor of fuel in the engine compartment. If a fuel odor has been detected, and you have already checked the areas described above, check the charcoal canister, located in the engine compartment, and the hoses connected to it **(see illustration)**.

20   Manual transaxle lubricant level check (every 15,000 miles or 12 months)

Refer to illustrations 20.1, 20.2a and 20.2b

1   The manual transaxle does not have a dipstick. To check the fluid level, raise the vehicle and support it securely on jackstands. The check/fill plug is on the right side of the transaxle housing **(see illustration)**. Remove the plug, if the lubricant level is correct, it should be up to the lower edge of the hole.

2   If the transaxle needs more lubricant (if the level is not up to the hole), use a funnel to add more **(see illustrations)**. Stop filling the transaxle when the lubricant begins to run out the hole.

3   Install the plug and tighten it securely. Drive the vehicle a short distance, then check for leaks.

21   Suspension, steering and driveaxle boot check (every 15,000 miles or 12 months)

Note: *The steering linkage and suspension components should be checked periodically.*

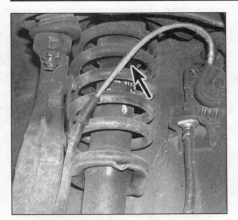

21.6 Check the front and rear shock absorbers for leakage where the rod enters the tube (arrow)

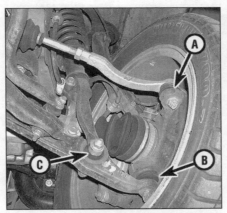

21.9a Inspect the tie rod ends (A) and the lower balljoints (B) for torn grease seals - inspect the lower shock fork bushings (C) for deteriorated bushings

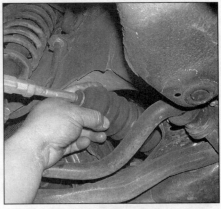

21.9b Check the steering gear boots for cracks and leaking steering fluid

Worn or damaged suspension and steering linkage components can result in excessive and abnormal tire wear, poor ride quality and vehicle handling and reduced fuel economy. For detailed illustrations of the steering and suspension components, refer to Chapter 10.

Shock absorber check

Refer to illustration 21.6

1 Park the vehicle on level ground, turn the engine off and set the parking brake. Check the tire pressures.

2 Push down at one corner of the vehicle, then release it while noting the movement of the body. It should stop moving and come to rest in a level position within one or two bounces.

3 If the vehicle continues to move up-and-down or if it fails to return to its original position, a worn or weak shock absorber is probably the reason.

4 Repeat the above check at each of the three remaining corners of the vehicle.

5 Raise the vehicle and support it securely on jackstands.

6 Check the shock absorbers for evidence of fluid leakage **(see illustration)**. A light film

of fluid is no cause for concern. Make sure that any fluid noted is from the shocks and not from some other source. If leakage is noted, replace the shocks as a set.

7 Check the shocks to be sure that they are securely mounted and undamaged. Check the upper mounts for damage and wear. If damage or wear is noted, replace the shocks as a set (front or rear).

8 If the shocks must be replaced, refer to Chapter 10 for the procedure.

Steering and suspension check

Refer to illustrations 21.9a, 21.9b and 21.9c

9 Visually inspect the steering and suspension components for damage and distortion. Look for damaged seals, boots and bushings and leaks of any kind **(see illustrations)**.

10 Clean the lower end of the steering knuckle. Have an assistant grasp the lower edge of the tire and move the wheel in-and-out while you look for movement at the steering knuckle-to-control arm balljoint. If there is any movement the suspension balljoint(s) must be replaced.

11 Grasp each front tire at the front and rear edges, push in at the front, pull out at the rear and feel for play in the steering system components If any freeplay is noted, check the idler arm and the tie-rod ends for looseness.

12 Additional steering and suspension system information and illustrations can be found in Chapter 10.

Driveaxle boot check

Refer to illustration 21.14

13 The driveaxle boots are very important because they prevent dirt, water and foreign material from entering and damaging the constant velocity (CV) joints. Oil and grease can cause the boot material to deteriorate prematurely, so it's a good idea to wash the boots with soap and water. Because it constantly pivots back and forth following the steering action of the front hub, the outer CV boot wears out sooner and should be inspected regularly.

14 Inspect the boots for tears and cracks as well as loose clamps **(see illustration)**. If there is any evidence of cracks or leaking lubricant, they must be replaced as described in Chapter 8.

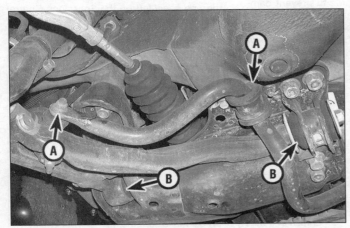

21.9c Check the stabilizer bar bushings and connectors (A) and the lower control arm bushings (B) for damage or distortion

21.14 Flex the driveaxle boots by hand to check for tears, cracks and leaking grease

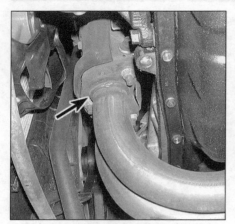

22.2a Check the exhaust pipe flange at the exhaust manifold (arrow) for leakage

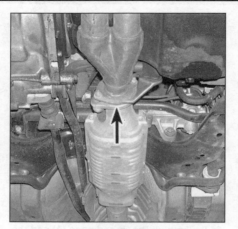

22.2b Inspect the exhaust pipe connection at the catalytic converter (arrow) for exhaust leaks - also check that the retaining nuts and bolts are securely tightened

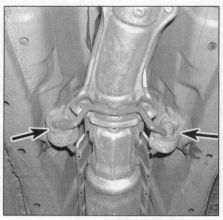

22.2c Check the exhaust system hangers (arrows) for damage or deterioration

22 Exhaust system check (every 6000 miles or 6 months)

Refer to illustrations 22.2a, 22.2b and 22.2c

1   With the engine cold (at least three hours after the vehicle has been driven), check the complete exhaust system from the engine to the end of the tailpipe. Ideally, the inspection should be done with the vehicle on a hoist to permit unrestricted access. If a hoist isn't available, raise the vehicle and support it securely on jackstands.

2   Check the exhaust pipes and connections for evidence of leaks, severe corrosion and damage. Make sure that all brackets and hangers are in good condition and tight **(see illustrations)**.

3   At the same time, inspect the underside of the body for holes, corrosion, open seams, etc. which may allow exhaust gases to enter the passenger compartment. Seal all body openings with silicone or body putty.

4   Rattles and other noises can often be traced to the exhaust system, especially the mounts and hangers. Try to move the pipes, muffler and catalytic converter. If the components can come in contact with the body or suspension parts, secure the exhaust system with new mounts.

5   Check the running condition of the engine by inspecting inside the end of the tailpipe. The exhaust deposits here are an

indication of engine state-of-tune. If the pipe is black and sooty or coated with white deposits, the engine may need a tune-up, including a thorough fuel system inspection and adjustment.

23 Spark plug check and replacement (see maintenance schedule)

Refer to illustrations 23.2, 23.5a, 23.5b, 23.6, 23.8, 23.9 and 23.10

Note: *If the original spark plugs are to be removed and reinstalled in the engine, the spark plugs must be marked and reinstalled in the original cylinder from which they were removed.*

1   All vehicles covered by this manual are equipped with transversely mounted engines which locate the spark plugs on the top.

2   In most cases, the tools necessary for spark plug replacement include a spark plug socket which fits onto a ratchet (spark plug sockets are padded inside to prevent damage to the porcelain insulators on the new plugs), various extensions and a gap gauge to check and adjust the gaps on the new plugs **(see illustration)**. A special plug wire

removal tool is available for separating the wire boots from the spark plugs, and is a good idea on these models because the boots fit very tightly. A torque wrench should be used to tighten the new plugs. It is a good idea to allow the engine to cool before removing or installing the spark plugs.

3   The best approach when replacing the spark plugs is to purchase the new ones in advance, adjust them to the proper gap and replace the plugs one at a time. When buying the new spark plugs, be sure to obtain the correct plug type for your particular engine. The plug type can be found in the Specifications at the front of this Chapter and on the Emission Control Information label located under the hood. If these two sources list different plug types, consider the emission control label correct.

4   Allow the engine to cool completely before attempting to remove any of the plugs. While you are waiting for the engine to cool, check the new plugs for defects and adjust the gaps.

5   Check the gap by inserting the proper thickness gauge between the electrodes at the tip of the plug **(see illustration)**. The gap between the electrodes should be the same as the one specified on the Emissions Control Information label or in Chapter 5. The wire should slide between the electrodes with a slight amount of drag. If the gap is incorrect, use the adjuster on the gauge body to bend

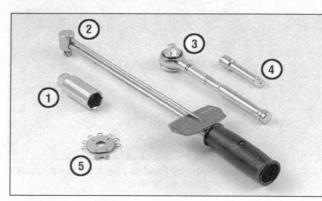

23.2 Tools required for changing spark plugs

1   *Spark plug socket* - This will have special padding inside to protect the spark plug's porcelain insulator
2   *Torque wrench* - Although not mandatory, using this tool is the best way to ensure the plugs are tightened properly
3   *Ratchet* - Standard hand tool to fit the spark plug socket
4   *Extension* - Depending on model and accessories, you may need special extensions and universal joints to reach one or more of the plugs
5   *Spark plug gap gauge* - This gauge for checking the gap comes in a variety of styles. Make sure the gap for your engine is included

23.5a Spark plug manufacturers recommend using a wire-type gauge when checking the gap - if the wire does not slide between the electrodes with a slight drag, adjustment is required

23.5b To change the gap, bend the side electrode only, as indicated by the arrows, and be very careful not to crack or chip the porcelain insulator surrounding the center electrode

23.6 On Integra models, remove the spark plug cover

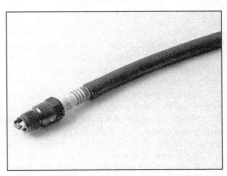

23.10 A piece of 3/8-inch rubber hose will aid in getting the spark plug started in the hole

23.8 Because they are deeply recessed, an extension will be required when removing or installing the spark plugs

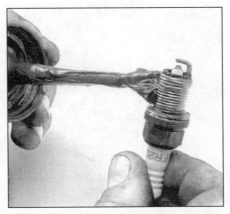

23.9 A light coat of anti-seize compound applied to the threads of the spark plugs will keep the threads in the cylinder head from being damaged the next time the plugs are removed

the curved side electrode slightly until the proper gap is obtained (see illustration). If the side electrode is not exactly over the center electrode, bend it with the adjuster until it is. Check for cracks in the porcelain insulator (if any are found, the plug should not be used).

6   On Integra models, remove the spark plug cover (see illustration). With the engine cool, remove the spark plug wire as described in Section 24 from one spark plug. Pull only on the boot at the end of the wire - do not pull on the wire. A plug wire removal tool should be used if available.

7   If compressed air is available, use it to blow any dirt or foreign material away from the spark plug hole. A common bicycle pump will also work. The idea here is to eliminate the possibility of debris falling into the cylinder as the spark plug is removed.

8   The spark plugs on these models are recessed so a spark plug socket incorporating a long extension will be necessary. Place the spark plug socket over the plug and remove it from the engine by turning it in a counterclockwise direction (see illustration).

9   Compare the spark plug with the chart

shown on the inside back cover of this manual to get an indication of the general running condition of the engine. Before installing the new plugs, it is a good idea to apply a thin coat of anti-seize compound to the threads (see illustration).

10   Thread one of the new plugs into the hole until you can no longer turn it with your fingers, then tighten it with a torque wrench (if available) or the ratchet. It's a good idea to slip a short length of rubber hose over the end of the plug to use as a tool to thread it into place (see illustration). The hose will grip the plug well enough to turn it, but will start to slip if the plug begins to cross-thread in the hole - this will prevent damaged threads and the accompanying repair costs.

11   Before pushing the spark plug wire onto the end of the plug, inspect it following the procedures outlined in the next Section.

12   Attach the plug wire to the new spark plug, again using a twisting motion on the boot until it's seated on the spark plug.

13   Repeat the procedure for the remaining

spark plugs, replacing them one at a time to prevent mixing up the spark plug wires.

24   Spark plug wire, distributor cap and rotor check and replacement (every 30,000 miles or 24 months)

Refer to illustration 24.11a, 24.11b, 24.11c, 24.12a and 24.12b

1   The spark plug wires should be checked whenever new spark plugs are installed (see the next Section).

2   Begin this procedure by making a visual check of the spark plug wires while the engine is running. In a darkened garage (make sure there is ventilation) start the engine and observe each plug wire. Be careful not to come into contact with any moving engine parts. If there is a break in the wire, you will see arcing or a small spark at the damaged area. If arcing is noticed, make a note to obtain new wires, then allow the engine to cool and check the distributor cap and rotor.

3   The spark plug wires should be inspected one at a time to prevent mixing up the order, which is essential for proper engine operation. Each original plug wire should be numbered to help identify its location. If the number is illegible, a piece of tape can be marked with the correct number and

24.11a Use a screwdriver or nut driver to remove the distributor cap screws

24.11b Inspect the outside of the distributor cap for carbon tracks, broken or cracked towers and damage (if in doubt about its condition, install a new one)

24.11c Check the inside of the distributor cap for carbon tracks, charred or eroded terminals and a worn or eroded button (if in doubt about its condition, install a new one)

wrapped around the plug wire.

4   Disconnect the plug wire from the spark plug. A removal tool can be used for this purpose or you can grasp the rubber boot, twist the boot half a turn and pull the boot free. Do not pull on the wire itself.

5   Check inside the boot for corrosion, which will look like a white crusty powder.

6   Push the wire and boot back onto the end of the spark plug. It should fit tightly onto the end of the plug. If it doesn't, remove the wire and use pliers to carefully crimp the metal connector inside the wire boot until the fit is snug.

7   Using a clean rag, wipe the entire length of the wire to remove built-up dirt and grease. Once the wire is clean, check for burns, cracks and other damage. Do not bend the wire sharply, because the conductor might break.

8   Disconnect the wire from the distributor. Again, pull only on the rubber boot. Check for corrosion and a tight fit. Replace the wire in the distributor.

9   Inspect the remaining spark plug wires, making sure that each one is securely fastened at the distributor and spark plug when the check is complete.

10   If new spark plug wires are required, purchase a set for your specific engine model. Pre-cut wire sets with the boots already installed are available. Remove and replace the wires one at a time to avoid mix-ups in the firing order.

11   Detach the distributor cap by removing the cap retaining screws **(see illustration)**. Check the outside for cracks and damage **(see illustration)**, then look inside it for cracks, carbon tracks and worn, burned or loose contacts **(see illustration)**.

12   Loosen the retaining screw and pull the rotor off the distributor shaft **(see illustration)**. It may be necessary to use a small screwdriver to gently pry off the rotor and examine it for cracks and carbon tracks **(see illustration)**. Replace the cap and rotor if any damage or defects are noted.

13   It is common practice to install a new cap and rotor whenever new spark plug wires are installed, but if you wish to continue using the old cap, check the resistance between

24.12a Loosen the retaining screw and remove the distributor rotor

the spark plug wires and the cap first. If the indicated resistance is more than the specified maximum value (see this Chapter's Specifications), replace the cap and/or wires.

14   When installing a new cap, remove the wires from the old cap one at a time and attach them to the new cap in the exact same location. **Note:** *If an accidental mix-up occurs, refer to the firing order at the beginning of this Chapter. On most models, the location of the number one plug wire tower is marked on the distributor cap.*

25   Positive Crankcase Ventilation (PCV) valve and hose check and replacement (every 30,000 miles or 24 months)

Refer to illustrations 25.2a, 25.2b and 25.4

1   The Positive Crankcase Ventilation (PCV) system directs blowby gases from the crankcase through the PCV valve and hose back into the intake manifold so they can be burned in the engine. The system consists of a hose leading from the valve cover to the intake manifold and a fresh air hose between

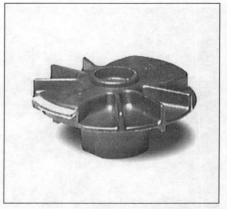

24.12b Check the inside of the distributor rotor for cracks, insufficient spring tension and an eroded or worn tip (if in doubt about its condition, buy a new one)

the air cleaner assembly and the valve cover.

2   The PCV valve and hose is located in the intake manifold below the fuel injector rail and at the rear of the engine, depending on model **(see illustrations)**.

25.2a The PCV valve is located on top of the engine in the intake manifold below the fuel rail (arrow) on some models, or . . .

25.2b . . . is accessible from below at the rear of the engine (arrow) on others

25.4 Pull the PCV valve out of the rubber grommet and check for vacuum at the opening

26.4a Unscrew the banjo bolt (it isn't necessary to remove the small service port bolt in the center of the banjo bolt) . . .

1

3   With the engine idling at normal operating temperature, pull the PCV valve (with hose attached) from the manifold or hose.

4   Place your finger over the valve opening or hose **(see illustration)**. If there is no vacuum, check for a plugged hose, manifold port, or the valve itself. Replace any plugged or deteriorated hoses.

5   Turn off the engine and shake the PCV valve, listening for a rattle. If the valve doesn't rattle, replace it with a new one.

6   To replace the valve, pull it out of the end of the hose, noting its installed position and direction.

7   When purchasing a replacement PCV valve, make sure it's for your particular vehicle, model vehicle and engine size. Compare the old valve with the new one to make sure they are the same.

8   Push the valve into the end of the hose until it's seated.

9   Inspect all the rubber hoses grommets for damage and hardening. Replace them, if necessary.

10   Press the PCV valve and hose securely into position. For further information on the PCV system refer to Chapter 6.

26 Fuel filter replacement (every 30,000 miles or 24 months)

Refer to illustrations 26.4a, 26.4b and 26.4c
Warning: *Gasoline is extremely flammable, so take extra precautions when you work on any part of the fuel system. Don't smoke or allow open flames or bare light bulbs near the work area, and don't work in a garage where a natural gas-type appliance (such as a water heater or clothes dryer) with a pilot light is present. Since gasoline is carcinogenic, wear latex gloves when there's a possibility of being exposed to fuel, and, if you spill any fuel on your skin, rinse it off immediately with soap and water. Mop up any spills immediately and do not store fuel-soaked rags where they could ignite. The fuel system is under constant pressure, so, if any fuel lines are to*

be disconnected, the fuel pressure in the system must be relieved first (see Chapter 4 for more information). When you perform any kind of work on the fuel system, wear safety glasses and have a Class B type fire extinguisher on hand.

1   This job should be done with the engine cold (after sitting at least three hours).

2   The fuel filter is located on the firewall in the engine compartment.

3   Relieve the fuel system pressure as described in Chapter 4.

4   Place shop towels around and under the filter. Remove the banjo bolt, unscrew the threaded fitting, remove the clamp bolt and lift the filter from the engine compartment **(see illustrations)**. **Note:** *If available, use a flare-nut wrench when disconnecting the fuel line fitting at the filter.*

5   Installation is the reverse of removal. Use new sealing washers on either side of the banjo fitting and tighten the banjo bolt to the torque listed in this Chapter's Specifications. Tighten the threaded line fitting securely. Start the engine and check for leaks.

27 Idle speed check and adjustment (every 30,000 miles or 24 months)

Refer to illustration 27.5

1   Engine idle speed is the speed at which the engine operates when no accelerator pedal pressure is applied, as when stopped at a traffic light. The speed is critical to the performance of the engine itself, as well as many subsystems. Before checking or adjusting the idle speed make sure the CHECK ENGINE light in not on, the air cleaner and spark plugs are in good condition, the PCV system is operating properly and the ignition timing is correct.

2   Connect a hand-held tachometer in accordance with the tool manufacturer's instructions.

3   Set the parking brake firmly and block the wheels to prevent the vehicle from rolling.

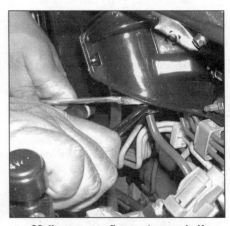

26.4b . . .use a flare nut wrench, if available, to disconnect the fuel line . . .

26.4c . . . then use a socket and extension to remove the filter clamp bolt

Place the transaxle in Neutral (manual transaxle) or Park (automatic transaxle).

4   Start the engine and run it at 3000 rpm until it warms up to normal operating temperature (the cooling fan comes on), then allow the engine to idle.

5   On all Integra models and all <u>except</u> the

27.5 Pry off the cap and turn the adjusting screw (A) until the idle speed is correct with the IAC valve connector (B) disconnected on most models

28.5 Remove the radiator cap with the engine cool to the touch

28.6 On most models you will have to remove a cover for access to the radiator drain fitting located at the bottom of the radiator (arrow)

following Civic models; 1996 and 1997 with D16Y5 with Continuously Variable Transaxle (CVT), 1996 through 1998 D16Y8 and automatic transaxle, all D16Y7 engines and 1998 D16Y5 with CVT; proceed as follows:

a) *Stop the engine and disconnect the electrical connector from the Idle Air Control (IAC) valve (see Chapter 4). On all 1998 Integra models and 1998 Civic models with D16Y8 engine and manual transaxle and D16Y5 engines with CVT, disconnect the EVAP purge control solenoid.*

b) *Start the engine with the accelerator slightly depressed and stabilize the idle at 1000 rpm. Slowly release the accelerator and allow the engine to idle. Make sure all accessories are turned off and the radiator fan and air conditioning are not operating.*

c) *The idle speed should be; Civic models - 450 (+/- 50 rpm), all Integra models except 1998 B18C5 - 480 (+/- 50 rpm), 1998 Integra B18C5 - 550 (+/- 50 rpm).*

d) *If the idle speed is too low or too high, remove the cap and turn the idle adjust screw to obtain the specified idle speed* **(see illustration)**. *Make changes slowly in 1/4-turn increments only.*

e) *Turn off the engine and connect the electrical connectors to the IAC valve and EVAP canister purge.*

f) *Remove the 7.5 amp BACK UP fuse from the underhood fuse block for ten seconds. This will clear any trouble codes from the ECM memory.*

g) *Start the engine and allow the idle to stabilize for one minute. Note the idle speed on the tachometer and compare it to that listed on the VECI label or in this Chapter's Specifications. If the idle speed listed on the VECI label is different than that listed in this Chapter's Specifications, use the specification shown on the VECI label.*

6   On the following Civic models; 1996 and 1997 with D16Y5 with Continuously Variable

Transaxle (CVT), 1996 through 1998 D16Y8 and automatic transaxle, all D16Y7 engines and 1998 D16Y5 with CVT; DO NOT disconnect the IAC valve and proceed as follows:

a) *Start the engine and allow the idle to stabilize for one minute. Note the idle speed on the tachometer and compare it to that listed on the VECI label or in this Chapter's Specifications. If the idle speed listed on the VECI label is different than that listed in this Chapter's Specifications, use the specification shown on the VECI label.*

b) *If the idle speed is too low or too high, remove the cap and turn the idle adjust screw to obtain the specified idle speed. Make changes slowly in 1/4-turn increments only.*

7   On all models, turn the air conditioning on and place the heater blower fan to the High position. The idle should increase 50 to 100 rpm. If it doesn't there could be a problem with the IAC valve or control system (see Chapter 6).

---

28   Cooling system servicing (draining, flushing and refilling) (every 30,000 miles or 24 months)

Warning: *Do not allow antifreeze to come in contact with your skin or painted surfaces of the vehicle. Rinse off spills immediately with plenty of water. Antifreeze is highly toxic if ingested. Never leave antifreeze lying around in an open container or in puddles on the floor; children and pets are attracted by it's sweet smell and may drink it. Check with local authorities about disposing of used antifreeze. Many communities have collection centers which will see that antifreeze is disposed of safely. Non-toxic antifreeze solutions are now widely available, but even these should be disposed of properly.*

1   Periodically, the cooling system should be drained, flushed and refilled to replenish the antifreeze mixture and prevent formation

of rust and corrosion, which can impair the performance of the cooling system and cause engine damage.

2   At the same time the cooling system is serviced, all hoses and the radiator cap should be inspected and replaced if defective (see Section 13).

3   Since antifreeze is a corrosive and poisonous solution, be careful not to spill any of the coolant mixture on the vehicle's paint or your skin. If this happens, rinse it off immediately with plenty of clean water. Consult local authorities about where to recycle or dispose of antifreeze before draining the cooling system. In many areas, reclamation centers have been set up to collect automobile oil and drained antifreeze/water mixtures, rather than allowing them to be added to the sewage system.

Draining

Refer to illustrations 28.5 and 28.6

4   Apply the parking brake and block the wheels. If the vehicle has just been driven, wait several hours to allow the engine to cool down before beginning this procedure.

5   Once the engine is completely cool, remove the radiator cap and the reservoir cap **(see illustration)**.

6   Drain the radiator by opening the drain plug at the bottom of the radiator **(see illustration)**. If the drain plug is corroded and can't be turned easily, or if the radiator isn't equipped with a plug, disconnect the lower radiator hose to allow the coolant to drain. Be careful not to get antifreeze on your skin or in your eyes.

7   After the coolant stops flowing out of the radiator, remove the lower radiator hose and allow the remaining fluid in the upper half of the engine block to drain.

8   While the coolant is draining from the engine block, disconnect the hose from the coolant reservoir and remove the reservoir (see Chapter 3 if necessary). Flush the reservoir out with water until it's clean, and if necessary, wash the inside with soapy water and a brush to make reading the fluid level easier.

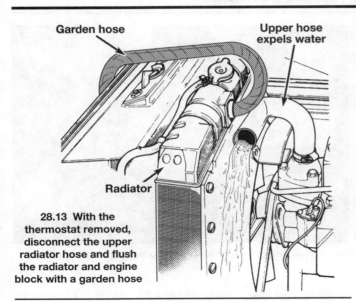

28.13 With the thermostat removed, disconnect the upper radiator hose and flush the radiator and engine block with a garden hose

28.18 The air bleed bolt is located on the thermostat housing - use a wrench to open it during the filling process to bleed air from the system

9   While the coolant is draining, check the condition of the radiator hoses, heater hoses and clamps (refer to Section 13 if necessary).

10   Replace any damaged clamps or hoses (refer to Chapter 3 for detailed replacement procedures).

Flushing

Refer to illustration 28.13

11   Once the system is completely drained, remove the thermostat from the engine (see Chapter 3). Then reinstall the thermostat housing without the thermostat. This will allow the system to be flushed.

12   Reinstall the lower radiator hose and tighten the radiator drain plug. Turn your heating system controls to Hot, so that the heater core will be flushed at the same time as the rest of the cooling system.

13   Disconnect the upper radiator hose, then place a garden hose in the upper radiator inlet and flush the system until the water runs clear at the upper radiator hose **(see illustration)**.

14   In severe cases of contamination or clogging of the radiator, remove the radiator (see Chapter 3) and have a radiator repair facility clean and repair it if necessary.

15   Many deposits can be removed by the chemical action of a cleaner available at auto parts stores. Follow the procedure outlined in the manufacturer's instructions. **Note:** *When the coolant is regularly drained and the system refilled with the correct antifreeze/water mixture, there should be no need to use chemical cleaners or descalers.*

Refilling

Refer to illustration 28.18

16   To refill the system, install the thermostat, reconnect any radiator hoses and install the reservoir and the overflow hose.

17   Place the heater temperature control in the maximum heat position.

18   Make sure to use the proper coolant listed in this Chapter's Specifications. Slowly fill the radiator with the recommended mixture of antifreeze and water to the base of the filler neck. On Integra models, loosen the air bleed bolt, located on the side of the thermostat housing and make sure a steady, bubble-free stream flows out, then tighten the bolt securely **(see illustration)**. Add coolant to the reservoir until it reaches the FULL COLD mark. Wait five minutes and recheck the coolant level in the radiator, adding if necessary.

19   Leave the radiator cap off and run the engine in a well-ventilated area until the thermostat opens (coolant will begin flowing through the radiator and the upper radiator hose will become hot).

20   Turn the engine off and let it cool. Add more coolant mixture to bring the level back up to the base of the filler neck.

21   Squeeze the upper radiator hose to expel air, then add more coolant mixture if necessary. Replace the radiator cap.

22   Place the heater temperature control and the blower motor speed control to their maximum setting.

23   Start the engine, allow it to reach normal operating temperature and check for leaks.

29 Brake fluid change (every 30,000 miles or 24 months)

Warning: *Brake fluid can harm your eyes and damage painted surfaces, so use extreme caution when handling or pouring it. Do not use brake fluid that has been standing open or is more than one year old. Brake fluid absorbs moisture from the air. Excess moisture can cause a dangerous loss of braking effectiveness.*

1   At the specified intervals, the brake fluid should be drained and replaced. Since the brake fluid may drip or splash when pouring it, place plenty of rags around the master cylinder to protect any surrounding painted surfaces.

2   Before beginning work, purchase the specified brake fluid (see *Recommended lubricants and fluids* at the beginning of this Chapter).

3   Remove the cap from the master cylinder reservoir.

4   Using a hand suction pump or similar device, withdraw the fluid from the master cylinder reservoir.

5   Add new fluid to the master cylinder until it rises to the base of the filler neck.

6   Bleed the brake system as described in Chapter 9 at all four brakes until new and uncontaminated fluid is expelled from the bleeder screw. Be sure to maintain the fluid level in the master cylinder as you perform the bleeding process. If you allow the master cylinder to run dry, air will enter the system.

7   Refill the master cylinder with fluid and check the operation of the brakes. The pedal should feel solid when depressed, with no sponginess. **Warning:** *Do not operate the vehicle if you are in doubt about the effectiveness of the brake system.*

30 Automatic transaxle and Continuously Variable Transaxle fluid change (every 30,000 miles or 24 months)

Refer to illustration 30.7

1   At the specified time intervals, the automatic transaxle fluid should be drained and replaced.

2   Before beginning work, purchase the specified transmission fluid (see *Recommended fluids and lubricants* at the front of this Chapter).

3   Other tools necessary for this job include jackstands to support the vehicle in a raised position, a 3/8-inch drive ratchet and extension, a drain pan capable of holding at least eight pints, newspapers and clean rags.

4   The fluid should be drained immediately after the vehicle has been driven. Hot fluid is

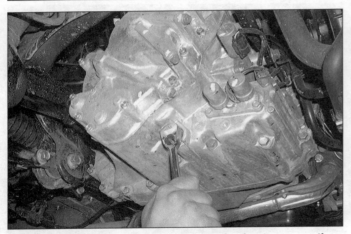

30.7 Use a 3/8-inch drive ratchet or breaker bar to remove the automatic transaxle drain plug

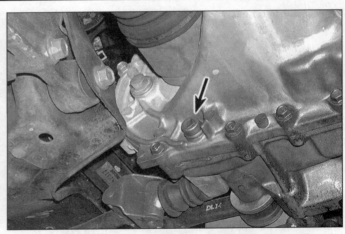

31.4 Remove the manual transaxle drain plug (arrow)

more effective than cold fluid at removing built-up sediment. **Warning:** *Fluid temperature can exceed 350-degrees F in a hot transaxle. Wear protective gloves.*

5   After the vehicle has been driven to warm up the fluid, raise it and place it on jackstands for access to the transaxle drain plug.

6   Move the necessary equipment under the vehicle, being careful not to touch any of the hot exhaust components.

7   Place the drain pan under the transaxle and remove the drain plug - it's located on the right (passenger's) side of the transaxle, near the bottom **(see illustration)**. Be sure the drain pan is in position, as fluid will come out with some force. Once the fluid is drained, clean the drain plug and reinstall it securely.

8   Lower the vehicle.

9   With the engine off pull out the dipstick, then add new fluid to the transaxle through the dipstick tube (see *Recommended fluids and lubricants* for the recommended fluid type and capacity). Use a funnel to prevent spills. It is best to add a little fluid at a time, continually checking the level with the dipstick (see Section 7).

10   Start the engine and slowly shift the selector into all positions, then shift into P and apply the parking brake.

11   Turn off the engine and check the fluid level. Add fluid to bring the level into the cross-hatched area on the dipstick.

31   Manual transaxle lubricant change (every 30,000 miles or 24 months)

Refer to illustration 31.4

1   At the specified time intervals, the manual transaxle lubricant should be drained and replaced.

2   Before beginning work, purchase the specified transaxle lubricant (see *Recommended fluids and lubricants and capacities* at the beginning of this Chapter).

3   Other tools necessary for this job include jackstands to support the vehicle in a raised position, 3/8-inch drive ratchet, a drain pan capable of holding at least four quarts, newspapers and clean rags.

4   After the vehicle has been driven to

warm up the fluid, raise it and place it on jackstands for access to the transaxle drain plug. Remove the drain plug and allow the old lubricant to drain into a drain pan **(see illustration)**.

5   Reinstall the drain plug securely.

6   Add new lubricant until it begins to run out of the filler hole (see Section 20).

7   Lower the vehicle.

32   Maintenance Required indicator - resetting

Refer to illustrations 32.1a and 32.1b

The Maintenance Required Indicator will glow yellow every 75,000 miles, reminding you its time for scheduled maintenance. If you exceed 7,500 miles between service, it will glow red. After performing the required maintenance (see maintenance schedule), reset the Maintenance Required Indicator by inserting the ignition key in the slot in the dash (Civic) or by pressing the reset button on the bottom of the dash to the right side of the steering column (Integra) **(see illustrations)**.

32.1a On Civic models insert the ignition key into the slot in the dash to reset the Maintenance Required indicator

32.1b Press the Maintenance Required reset button under the right side of the steering column on Integra models

Chapter 2 Part A
Civic engine

Contents

Specifications

General

Firing order	1-3-4-2
Cylinder numbers (front-to-rear)	1-2-3-4
Bore	2.95 inches
Stroke	3.54 inches
Displacement	97.0 cubic inches (1.6 liters)

Camshaft

Endplay	
Standard	0.002 to 0.006 inch
Maximum	0.020 inch
Lobe height	
D16Y5	
Intake	
Primary	1.5129 inches
Secondary	1.2674 inches
Exhaust	1.5269 inches
D16Y7	
Intake	1.3897 inches
Exhaust	1.4678 inches
D16Y8	
Intake	
Primary	1.4479 inches
Mid	1.5068 inches
Secondary	1.4592 inches
Exhaust	1.4964 inches
Runout	
Standard	0.001 inch
Service limit	0.002 inch maximum
Journal oil clearance	
Standard	0.0020 to 0.004 inch
Service limit	0.006 inch maximum

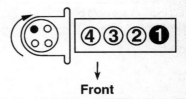

Front

Cylinder locations and distributor rotation

Oil pump

Rotor-to-cover clearance
    Standard .... 0.001 to 0.003 inch
    Service limit.. 0.006 inch maximum
Tooth tip clearance
    Standard... 0.001 to 0.006 inch
    Service limit.. 0.008 inch maximum
Outer rotor-to-pump body clearance
    Standard... 0.004 to 0.007 inch
    Service limit.. 0.008 inch maximum

Torque specifications

Ft-lbs (unless otherwise indicated)

Camshaft bearing cap bolts
    6 mm bolts .... 108 in-lbs
    8 mm bolts 14
Camshaft sprocket bolt 27
Crankshaft fluctuation sensor mounting bolt .... 104 in-lbs
Crankshaft pulley bolt... 134
Cylinder head bolts
    Step 1 14
    Step 2 36
    Step 3 49
    Step 4 49
Driveplate-to-crankshaft bolts 54
Intake manifold nuts 17
Exhaust manifold-to-cylinder head nuts............................. 23
Exhaust pipe-to-manifold nuts
    D16Y5, D16Y7 25
    D16Y8 40
Exhaust manifold upper cover bolts 17
Exhaust manifold lower cover bolts (D16Y5, D16Y7)........ 96 in-lbs
Flywheel-to-crankshaft bolts 87
Oxygen sensor.. 33
Oil pressure switch .... 156 in-lbs
Oil pan drain plug 29
Oil pan-to-engine bolts... 104 in-lbs
Oil pump pick-up tube to pump housing nuts..................... 96 in-lbs
Oil pump screen-to-main bearing cap................................. 96 in-lbs
Oil pump housing-to-block bolts... 96 in-lbs
Oil pump cover-to-housing.. 60 in-lbs
Rear main oil seal housing bolts .... 96 in-lbs
Timing belt cover bolts .... 86 in-lbs
Timing belt tensioner bolt 33
Valve cover bolts .... 86 in-lbs
VTEC lock-up solenoid bolts .... 104 in-lbs
Water pump bolts .... 108 in-lbs

1   General information

This Part of Chapter 2 is devoted to in-vehicle repair procedures for the 1.6 liter, fuel injected, four cylinder engine. All information concerning engine removal and installation and engine block and cylinder head overhaul can be found in Part C of this Chapter.

There are three different versions of the engine covered in this Part of Chapter 2. All versions are Single Overhead Camshaft (SOHC), with 4 valves per cylinder (16V). There are two versions of the VTEC (Variable Valve Timing and Lift Electronic Control) system available in models covered by this manual. For more information on the VTEC system, see Section 7 of this Chapter.

Engine designations include:

D16Y7............. 1.6L, 16V, SOHC
D16Y8............. 1.6L, 16V, SOHC VTEC
D16Y5............. 1.6L, 16V, SOHC VTEC-E*

* VTEC-E - The "E" is Honda's designation for "Enhanced Performance".

The following repair procedures are based on the assumption that the engine is installed in the vehicle. If the engine has been removed from the vehicle and mounted on a stand, many of the steps outlined in this Part of Chapter 2 will not apply.

The Specifications included in this Part of Chapter 2 apply only to the procedures contained in this chapter. Chapter 2C contains the Specifications necessary for cylinder head and engine block rebuilding.

It is a compact and lightweight engine with an aluminum alloy block (with steel cylinder liners) and an aluminum alloy cylinder head. The crankshaft rides in a single carriage unit that houses the renewable insert-type main bearings, with separate thrust bearings at the number four position assigned the task of controlling crankshaft endplay.

The pistons have two compression rings and one oil control ring. The semi-floating piston pins are press fitted into the small end of the connecting rod. The connecting rod big ends are also equipped with renewable insert-type plain bearings.

The engine is liquid-cooled, utilizing a centrifugal impeller-type pump, driven by the timing belt, to circulate coolant around the

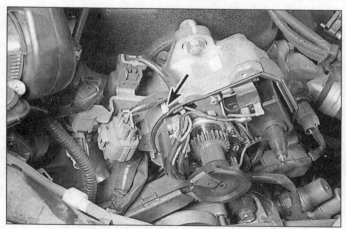

3.10 Mark the distributor housing directly beneath the number one spark plug wire terminal (check the distributor cap to verify that the rotor points to the number 1 spark plug wire)

3.11 Align the mark on the crankshaft pulley with the notch in the pointer then check to see if the distributor rotor is pointing to number 1 cylinder's terminal in the distributor cap (if not, number 4 is at TDC - the crankshaft will have to be rotated 360-degrees)

cylinders and combustion chambers and through the intake manifold.

Lubrication is handled by a rotor-type oil pump mounted on the front of the engine under the timing belt cover. It is driven directly by the crankshaft. The oil is filtered continuously by a cartridge-type filter mounted on the firewall side of the engine.

2 Repair operations possible with the engine in the vehicle

Clean the engine compartment and the exterior of the engine with some type of degreaser before any work is done. It will make the job easier and help keep dirt out of the internal areas of the engine.

Depending on the components involved, it may be helpful to remove the hood to improve access to the engine as repairs are performed (refer to Chapter 11 if necessary). Cover the fenders to prevent damage to the paint. Special pads are available, but an old bedspread or blanket will also work.

If vacuum, exhaust, oil or coolant leaks develop, indicating a need for gasket or seal replacement, the repairs can generally be made with the engine in the vehicle. The intake and exhaust manifold gaskets, oil pan gasket, crankshaft oil seals and cylinder head gasket are all accessible with the engine in place.

Exterior engine components, such as the intake and exhaust manifolds, the oil pan, the water pump, the starter motor, the alternator, the distributor and the fuel system components can be removed for repair with the engine in place.

Since the cylinder head can be removed without pulling the engine, camshaft and valve component servicing can also be accomplished with the engine in the vehicle. Replacement of the timing belt and sprockets is also possible with the engine in the vehicle.

In extreme cases caused by a lack of necessary equipment, repair or replacement

of piston rings, pistons, connecting rods and rod bearings is possible with the engine in the vehicle. However, this practice is not recommended because of the cleaning and preparation work that must be done to the components involved.

3 Top Dead Center (TDC) - locating

Refer to illustrations 3.10 and 3.11
Note: *The following procedure is based on the assumption that the spark plug wires and distributor are correctly installed. If you are trying to locate TDC to install the distributor correctly, piston position must be determined by feeling for compression at the number one spark plug hole, then aligning the ignition timing marks as described in Step 11.*

1   Top Dead Center (TDC) is the highest point in the cylinder that each piston reaches as it travels up-and-down when the crankshaft turns. Each piston reaches TDC on the compression stroke and again on the exhaust stroke, but TDC generally refers to piston position on the compression stroke.

2   Positioning the piston(s) at TDC is an essential part of many procedures such as camshaft and timing belt/sprocket removal and distributor removal.

3   Before beginning this procedure, be sure to place the transaxle in Neutral and apply the parking brake or block the rear wheels.

4   Disable the ignition system by detaching the electrical connectors at the distributor (see Chapter 5).

5   Disable the fuel system (see Chapter 4).

6   Remove the spark plugs (see Chapter 1).

7   In order to bring any piston to TDC, the crankshaft must be turned using one of the methods outlined below. When looking at the front (drive belt end) of the engine, normal crankshaft rotation is counterclockwise. Always rotate the engine counterclockwise; clockwise rotation may cause incorrect

adjustment of the timing belt.

a) *The preferred method is to turn the crankshaft with a socket and ratchet attached to the bolt threaded into the front of the crankshaft.*

b) *A remote starter switch, which may save some time, can also be used. Follow the instructions included with the switch. Once the piston is close to TDC, use a socket and ratchet as described in the previous paragraph.*

c) *If an assistant is available to turn the ignition switch to the Start position in short bursts, you can get the piston close to TDC without a remote starter switch. Make sure your assistant is out of the vehicle, away from the ignition switch, then use a socket and ratchet as described in Paragraph a) to complete the procedure.*

8   Note the position of the terminal for the number one spark plug wire on the distributor cap. If the terminal isn't marked, follow the plug wire from the number one cylinder spark plug to the cap.

9   Detach the cap from the distributor and set it aside (see Chapter 1 if necessary).

10   Mark the distributor housing directly under the rotor terminal **(see illustration)** for the number 1 cylinder.

11   Locate the timing marks on the crankshaft pulley. You'll see the timing increments directly next to the timing pointer. Turn the crankshaft (see Step 7 above) until the TDC mark (zero) on the flywheel/driveplate is aligned with the groove in the pointer **(see illustration)**.

12   Look at the distributor rotor - it should be pointing directly at the mark you made on the distributor body. If the rotor is 180-degrees off, the number one piston is at TDC on the exhaust stroke.

13   To get the piston to TDC on the compression stroke, turn the crankshaft one complete turn (360-degrees) counterclockwise. The rotor should now be pointing at the mark on the distributor.

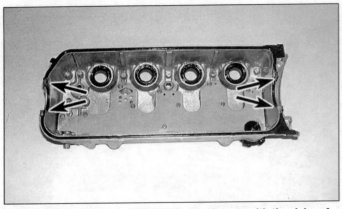

4.8 The corners of the gaskets (arrows) mate with the dabs of sealant on the cylinder head

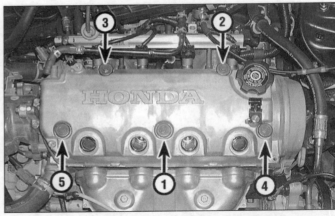

4.9 Valve cover bolt TIGHTENING sequence

14   When the rotor is pointing at the number one spark plug wire terminal in the distributor cap and the ignition timing marks are aligned, the number one piston is at TDC on the compression stroke.

15   After the number one piston has been positioned at TDC on the compression stroke, TDC for any of the remaining pistons can be located by turning the crankshaft and following the firing order. Mark the remaining spark plug wire terminal locations on the distributor body just like you did for the number one terminal, then number the marks to correspond with the cylinder numbers. As you turn the crankshaft, the rotor will also turn. When it's pointing directly at one of the marks on the distributor, the piston for that particular cylinder is at TDC on the compression stroke.

4   Valve cover - removal and installation

Removal

1   Detach the cable from the negative battery terminal. **Caution:** *If the radio in your vehicle is equipped with an anti-theft system, make sure you have the correct activation code before disconnecting the battery.*

2   Remove the distributor cap and wires from their cylinder head and valve cover connections (see Chapter 1). Be sure to mark each wire for correct installation.

3   Mark and detach any hoses or wires from the throttle body or valve cover that will interfere with the removal of the valve cover.

4   Wipe off the valve cover thoroughly to prevent debris from falling onto the exposed cylinder head or camshaft/valve train assembly.

5   Remove the valve cover bolts **(see illustration 4.9)**.

6   Carefully lift off the valve cover and gasket. If the gasket is stuck to the cylinder head, tap it with a rubber mallet to break the seal. Do not pry between the cover and cylinder head or you'll damage the gasket mating surfaces.

Installation

Refer to illustrations 4.8 and 4.9

7   Remove the old gasket and clean the mating surfaces of the cylinder head and the valve cover. Clean the surfaces with a rag soaked in lacquer thinner or acetone.

8   Apply beads of RTV sealant to the corners where the cylinder head mates with the rocker arm assembly **(see illustration)**. Wait five minutes or so and let the RTV set-up. **Note:** *Make sure the RTV sealant has slightly hardened before installing the valve cover. If the weather is damp and cold, the sealant will take some extra time to harden.*

9   Install a new molded rubber gasket into the groove around the valve cover perimeter. Install the valve cover sealing grommets, lubricate them with soapy water and tighten the bolts in the recommended sequence to the torque listed in this Chapter's Specifications **(see illustration)**.

10   The remainder of installation is the reverse of removal. Make sure the rubber spark plug seals are in position before connecting the spark plug wires.

5   Intake manifold - removal and installation

Warning: *Gasoline is extremely flammable, so take extra precautions when you work on any part of the fuel system. Don't smoke or allow open flames or bare light bulbs near the work area, and don't work in a garage where a natural gas-type appliance (such as a water heater or clothes dryer) with a pilot light is present. If you spill any fuel on your skin, rinse it off immediately with soap and water. When you perform any kind of work on the fuel system, wear safety glasses and have a Class B type fire extinguisher on hand.*

Removal

Refer to illustrations 5.4, 5.8, 5.9 and 5.10

1   Detach the cable from the negative battery terminal. **Caution:** *If the radio in your vehicle is equipped with an anti-theft system,*

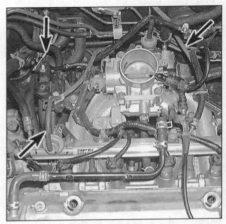

5.4 Disconnect the vacuum hoses (arrows)

make sure you have the correct activation code before disconnecting the battery.

2   Drain the cooling system (see Chapter 1).

3   Remove the intake air duct and air cleaner housing (see Chapter 4).

4   Clearly label and detach any vacuum lines and electrical connectors which will interfere with removal of the manifold **(see illustration)**.

5   Detach the accelerator cable from the throttle lever (see Chapter 4).

6   Remove the coolant hoses from the throttle body.

7   Relieve the fuel system pressure and disconnect the fuel feed and return lines at the fuel rail (see Chapter 4).

8   Working from underneath the engine compartment, remove the brace that supports the intake manifold **(see illustration)**.

9   Disconnect the coolant by-pass hose from the intake manifold **(see illustration)**.

10   Remove the intake manifold bolts and remove the manifold from the engine **(see illustration)**.

Installation

Refer to illustration 5.16

11   Clean the manifold nuts with solvent

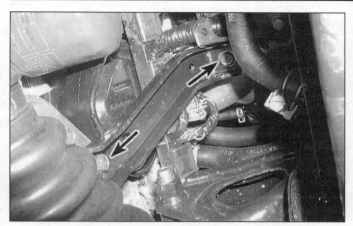

5.8 Remove the bolts (arrows) and remove the brace from the intake manifold

5.9 Disconnect the coolant bypass hose (arrow)

2A

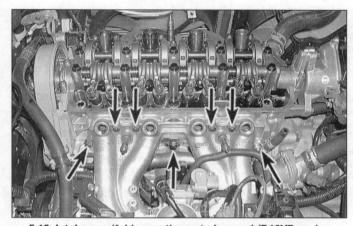

5.10 Intake manifold mounting nuts (arrows) (D16Y7 engine shown, others similar)

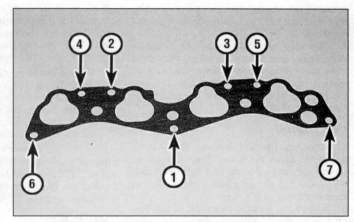

5.16 Intake manifold fastener TIGHTENING sequence

and dry them with compressed air, if available.

12 Check the mating surfaces of the manifold for flatness with a precision straightedge and feeler gauges.

13 Inspect the manifold for cracks and distortion. If the manifold is cracked or warped, replace it or see if it can be resurfaced at an automotive machine shop.

14 Check carefully for any stripped or broken intake manifold bolts/studs. Replace any defective bolts with new parts.

15 Using a scraper, remove all traces of old gasket material from the cylinder head and manifold mating surfaces. Clean the surfaces with lacquer thinner or acetone.

16 Install the intake manifold with a new gasket and tighten all the nuts finger-tight. Following the recommended sequence, tighten the nuts to the torque listed in this Chapter's Specifications **(see illustration)**.

17 The remainder of installation is the reverse of removal. Refer to Chapter 1 and refill the cooling system.

6 Exhaust manifold - removal and installation

Removal

Refer to illustrations 6.2, 6.3 and 6.4

1 Disconnect the battery cable from the negative battery terminal. **Caution:** *If the radio in your vehicle is equipped with an anti-theft system, make sure you have the correct activation code before disconnecting the battery.*

2 Raise the front of the vehicle and support it securely on jackstands. Disconnect the oxygen sensor electrical connector (two connectors on D16Y5 and D16Y7 models). Detach the exhaust pipe from the exhaust manifold **(see illustration)**. Apply penetrating oil to the fastener threads if they are difficult to remove.

3 Remove the heat shield from the exhaust manifold **(see illustration)**. Be sure

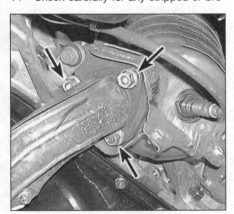

6.2 Remove the exhaust pipe flange nuts (arrows)

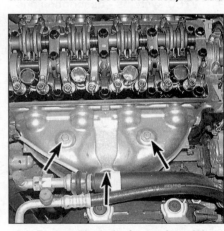

6.3 Remove the bolts (arrows) retaining the heat shield to the exhaust manifold

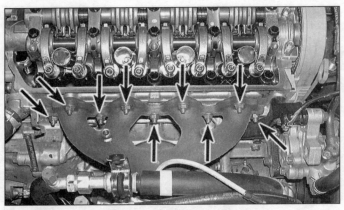

6.4 Exhaust manifold mounting nuts

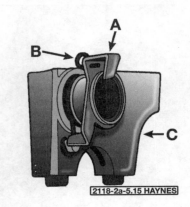

7.15 Timing plate synchronizing assembly (D16Y5 VTEC-E only)

A)   *Timing plate*
B)   *Return spring*
C)   *Cam holder*

to soak the bolts and nuts with penetrating oil before attempting to remove them from the manifold.

4   Remove the exhaust manifold nuts **(see illustration)** and detach the exhaust manifold from the cylinder head. **Note:** *Be sure to remove the bolts from the lower brace located near the flange of the exhaust manifold on D16Y8 models.*

Installation

5   Discard the old gasket and use a scraper to clean the gasket mating surfaces on the exhaust manifold and cylinder head, then clean the surfaces with a rag soaked in lacquer thinner or acetone.
6   Place the exhaust manifold in position on the cylinder head and install the nuts. Starting at the center and working out to the ends, tighten the nuts to the torque listed in this Chapter's Specifications.
7   The remainder of installation is the reverse of removal.
8   Start the engine and check for exhaust leaks between the manifold and the cylinder head and between the manifold and the exhaust pipe.

7   VTEC systems - description and component check

Description

1   The **VTEC** system (**V**ariable Valve **T**iming and Lift **E**lectronic **C**ontrol) is used on several models throughout the Honda vehicle line. Civic models may be equipped with either one of two different VTEC systems.
2   The difference between a non-VTEC engine and the VTEC counterpart is strictly in the components and operation of the valve train. The engine block, oiling and cooling systems are identical, as are all attached components. Models equipped with VTEC systems can be distinguished by the letters "VTEC" molded into the top of the valve cover.
3   The engine management computer has the ability to alter valve lift and timing through

the use of different camshaft intake valve lobes. The computer turns the system ON or OFF, depending on sensor input.
4   The following are used on both systems to determine VTEC operation:

   Engine speed (rpm)
   Vehicle speed (mph)
   Throttle position sensor output
   Engine load measured by the manifold
      absolute pressure sensor
   Coolant temperature

5   The components and method of operation are slightly different between the VTEC and VTEC-E systems. The following describes the differences in the way the two systems operate.

VTEC-E (D16Y5)

6   The camshaft has different primary and secondary intake valve lobe profiles (lift and duration specifications).
7   At low speeds, the secondary valve operates on its own camshaft lobe, which has very low lift and duration (compared to the primary valve). The opening is intended to be just enough to keep atomized fuel from puddling, at the valve head. This limited valve operation provides good low end torque and responsiveness.
8   When performance is needed, the secondary rocker arm is locked together (through the use of an electrically controlled, hydraulic system), with the primary rocker arm. **Note:** *The secondary rocker arm no longer contacts its own camshaft lobe, until the system is disengaged.* When activated, both valves open to the full lift and duration of the primary camshaft lobe, increasing performance at higher engine speeds.

VTEC (D16Y8)

9   The camshaft used in this system has identical primary and secondary intake lobes and has a additional third lobe and rocker arm placed between the primary and secondary. This third, or "Mid", lobe has larger lift and longer duration than the primary and secondary camshaft lobes.
10   During low speed operation both intake valves operate on their own camshaft lobes.

Both camshaft lobes have the same specifications for lift and duration (unlike the VTEC-E). As performance is required, the primary and secondary rocker arms are locked to the Mid rocker arm through the use of an electrically controlled, hydraulic system. Both intake valves now operate on the Mid intake camshaft lobe. **Note:** *The primary and secondary rocker arms no longer contact their respective camshaft lobes until the Mid rocker arm is disengaged.* This provides good torque at both low and high speeds by using the camshaft lobe profile that most matches driving needs at any given speed and load.

Component check

Lost motion assembly (VTEC only)

11   The lost motion assemblies (4 required) are held in place by the assembly holder. They resemble hydraulic lifters.
12   Unbolt and remove the lost motion assembly holder.
13   Remove the individual lost motion assemblies from the holder.
14   Test each motion assembly by pushing the plunger with your finger. If the assembly doesn't move smoothly, replace it.

Timing plate, collar and return spring (VTEC-E only)

Refer to illustration 7.15

15   The timing plate and return spring **(see illustration)** are assembled to the camshaft holder on the intake rocker shaft (4 required). **Note:** *As shown in the illustration, the collar used with the return spring and timing plate has a shoulder to hold the spring.*
16   Inspect the spring, making sure the spring is connected to the camshaft holder and timing plate.
17   Look for signs of scoring, broken parts or overheating (discoloration, bluish color).
18   Replace parts as necessary.
19   Reassemble as shown **(see illustration 7.15)**.

Synchronizing assembly

Refer to illustrations 7.20a and 7.20b

20   Once the rocker arm assemblies have been removed and disassembled (see Sec-

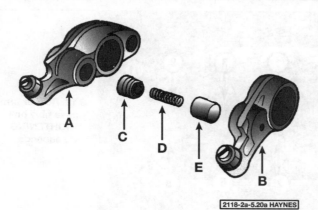

7.20a Rocker arms and synchronizing assembly
(D16Y5 VTEC-E only)

A) Primary rocker arm
B) Secondary rocker arm
C) Timing piston
D) Timing spring
E) Synchronizing piston

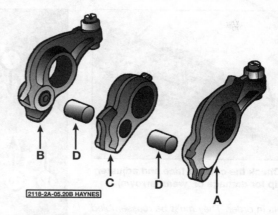

7.20b Rocker arms and synchronizing assembly
(D16Y8 VTEC only)

A) Primary rocker arm
B) Secondary rocker arm
C) Mid rocker arm
D) Synchronizing piston

2A

tion 8), separate the rocker arms and synchronizing components **(see illustrations)**.

VTEC-E components:

a) Primary rocker arm
b) Secondary rocker arm
c) Timing piston
d) Timing spring
e) Synchronizing piston

VTEC components:

a) Primary rocker arm
b) Secondary rocker arm
c) Mid rocker arm
d) Synchronizing piston

21 Inspect the timing spring (VTEC-E only). Be sure it's not broken or collapsed. Replace if necessary.

22 Inspect all other parts (rocker arms and synchronizing pistons) for wear, galling, scoring or signs of overheating (bluish in color). Replace any parts necessary.

23 Reassembly is the reverse of removal.
Note: *Reassemble and hold together (rubber bands work well) each cylinder's components before trying to assemble them on the rocker arm shaft (see Section 8).*

VTEC lock-up control solenoid valve

24 A problem in the VTEC solenoid valve circuit will turn on the CHECK ENGINE light and set a diagnostic trouble code (DTC) P1259. The lock-up control solenoid and its integral pressure switch are basically the same as for Integra VTEC models. For tests of the solenoid and oil pressure switch, refer to Part B of this Chapter.

Oil control orifice

Refer to Section 8 this Chapter for inspection details.

Primary rocker arm

Refer to Section 8 this Chapter for inspection details.

Secondary rocker arm

Refer to Section 8 of this Chapter for inspection details.

Mid rocker arm (VTEC only)

Refer to Section 8 of this Chapter for inspection details.

Mid camshaft lobe (VTEC only)

Refer to Section 12 of this Chapter for inspection details.

---

8 Rocker arm assembly - removal, inspection and installation

Note 1: *The camshaft bearing caps are removed together with the rocker arm assembly. To prevent the transaxle end of the camshaft from popping up from timing belt tension after the assembly is removed, have an assistant hold the camshaft down, then reinstall the bearing cap on that end to hold it in place until reassembly (assuming the timing belt remains installed).*

Note 2: *While the camshaft bearing caps are off, inspect them, as well as the camshaft bearing journals, as described in Section 12.*

Removal

Refer to illustration 8.4

1 Remove the valve cover (see Section 4).
2 Position the number one piston at Top Dead Center (see Section 3).
3 Have an assistant hold down the transaxle end of the camshaft, then loosen the camshaft bearing cap bolts 1/4-turn at a time, in the correct order, until the spring pressure is relieved **(see illustration 8.12)**.
4 Lift the rocker arm and shaft assembly from the cylinder head **(see illustration)**.

Oil control orifice (VTEC engines only)

5 Pull the orifice from the cylinder head.

Inspection

Refer to illustration 8.7

6 If you wish to disassemble and inspect the rocker arm assembly, (a good idea as long as you have them off), remove the retaining bolts and slip the rocker arms, springs and bearing caps off the shafts. **Caution:** *On VTEC engines, it is a good idea to bundle the intake rocker arms together with rubber bands. Mark the relationship of the shafts to the bearing caps and keep the com-*

8.4 Remove the camshaft bearing caps, bolts and rocker arm assembly

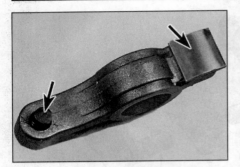

8.7 Check the contact face and adjuster tip for damage or wear (arrows)

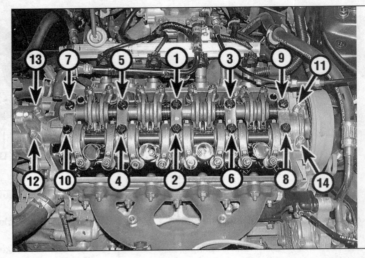

8.12 Rocker arm assembly bolt TIGHTENING sequence

ponents in order. They must be reassembled in the same positions they were removed from.

7   Thoroughly clean the components and inspect them for wear and damage. Check the rocker arm faces that contact the camshaft and the rocker arm tips **(see illustration)**. Check the surfaces of the shafts that the rocker arms ride on, as well as the bearing surfaces inside the rocker arms, for scoring and excessive wear. Replace any parts that are damaged or excessively worn. Also, make sure the oil holes in the shafts are not plugged.

8   Clean the orifice so there are no obstructions and oil flows freely through the orifice.

Installation

Refer to illustration 8.12

9   Lubricate all components with engine assembly lubricant or engine oil and reassemble the shafts. When installing the rocker arms, shafts and springs, note the markings and the difference between the left and right side components.

10   On VTEC engines, replace the O-ring on the oil control orifice, then install the orifice in the cylinder head.

11   Coat the camshaft lobes and journals with camshaft installation lubricant. Apply anaerobic-type sealant to the cylinder head contact surfaces of bearing caps 1 and 6 and install the rocker arm assembly.

12   Tighten the camshaft bearing cap bolts a little at a time, in the proper sequence **(see illustration)** to the torque listed in this Chapter's Specifications.

13   The remainder of installation is the reverse of removal. Adjust the valve clearance, if necessary (see Chapter 1).

14   Run the engine and check for oil leaks and proper operation.

9   Valve springs, retainers and seals - replacement

Refer to illustrations 9.5, 9.8 and 9.17
Note: *Broken valve springs and defective valve stem seals can be replaced without removing the cylinder heads. Two special tools and a compressed air source are nor-*

9.5 This is what the air hose adapter that threads into the spark plug hole looks like - they're commonly available from auto parts stores

mally required to perform this operation, so read through this Section carefully and rent or buy the tools before beginning the job.

1   Refer to Section 4 and remove the valve cover.

2   Remove the spark plug from the cylinder that has the defective component. If all of the valve stem seals are being replaced, all of the spark plugs should be removed.

3   Turn the crankshaft until the piston in the affected cylinder is at top dead center on the compression stroke (refer to Section 3 for instructions). If you're replacing all of the valve stem seals, begin with cylinder number one and work on the valves for one cylinder at a time. Move from cylinder-to-cylinder following the firing order sequence (see this Chapter's Specifications).

4   Remove the rocker arms and shafts (see Section 8).

5   Thread an adapter into the spark plug hole and connect an air hose from a compressed air source to it **(see illustration)**. Most auto parts stores can supply the air hose adapter. **Note:** *Many cylinder compression gauges utilize a screw-in fitting that may work with your air hose quick-disconnect fitting.*

9.8 Use a valve spring compressor to compress the springs, then remove the keepers from the valve stem with a magnet or small needle-nose pliers

6   Apply compressed air to the cylinder. **Warning:** *The piston may be forced down by compressed air, causing the crankshaft to turn suddenly. If the wrench used when positioning the number one piston at TDC is still attached to the bolt in the crankshaft nose, it could cause damage or injury when the crankshaft moves.*

7   The valves should be held in place by the air pressure.

8   Stuff shop rags into the cylinder head holes around the valves to prevent parts and tools from falling into the engine, then use a valve spring compressor to compress the spring **(see illustration)**.

9   Remove the keepers with small needle-nose pliers or a magnet.

10   Remove the spring retainer, shield and valve spring, then remove the valve guide seal. **Note:** *If air pressure fails to hold the valve in the closed position during this operation, the valve face or seat is probably damaged. If so, the cylinder head will have to be removed for additional repair operations.*

11   Wrap a rubber band or tape around the top of the valve stem so the valve won't fall

9.17 Apply a small dab of grease to each keeper as shown here before installation - it'll hold them in place on the valve stem as the spring is released

into the combustion chamber, then release the air pressure.

12 Inspect the valve stem for damage. Rotate the valve in the guide and check the end for eccentric movement, which would indicate that the valve is bent.

13 Move the valve up-and-down in the guide and make sure it doesn't bind. If the valve stem binds, either the valve is bent or the guide is damaged. In either case, the head will have to be removed for repair.

14 Reapply air pressure to the cylinder to retain the valve in the closed position, then remove the tape or rubber band from the valve stem.

15 Lubricate the valve stem with clean engine oil and install a new guide seal. **Note:** *The springs on the valve stem seals are color coded; white for the intake valves and black for the exhaust valves.*

16 Install the spring in position over the valve. Place the end of the spring with the closely wound coils toward the cylinder head.

17 Install the valve spring retainer. Compress the valve spring and carefully position

the keepers in the groove. Apply a small dab of grease to the inside of each keeper to hold it in place **(see illustration)**.

18 Remove the pressure from the spring tool and make sure the keepers are seated.

19 Disconnect the air hose and remove the adapter from the spark plug hole.

20 Refer to Section 8 and install the rocker arm assembly.

21 Refer to Section 4 and install the valve cover.

22 Install the spark plug(s) and hook up the wire(s).

23 Start and run the engine, then check for oil leaks and unusual sounds coming from the valve cover area.

---

10 Timing belt and sprockets - removal, inspection and installation

Removal

Refer to illustrations 10.11, 10.13, 10.17 and 10.18

1 Disconnect the negative cable from the battery. **Caution:** *If the radio in your vehicle is equipped with an anti-theft system, make sure you have the correct activation code before disconnecting the battery.*

2 Place blocks behind the rear wheels and set the parking brake.

3 Loosen the lug nuts on the front wheels and raise the front of the vehicle. Support the front of the vehicle securely on jackstands (see Chapter 1).

4 Remove the front wheels and remove the splash shield from under the engine.

5 Support the engine with a floor jack. Place a wood block between the jack pad and the oil pan to avoid damaging the pan.

6 Remove the upper engine mounting bracket (see Section 18).

7 Remove the spark plugs and drivebelts (see Chapter 1).

8 Unbolt the power steering pump without

10.11 Timing belt upper cover bolts (arrows)

disconnecting the hoses and set it aside (see Chapter 10).

9 Remove the engine oil dipstick.

10 Position the number one piston at Top Dead Center (see Section 3). **Caution:** *Always rotate the crankshaft counterclockwise (viewed from the pulley end of the engine). Clockwise rotation may cause incorrect adjustment of the timing belt.*

11 Remove the upper timing belt cover **(see illustration)**.

12 Remove the drivebelt idler pulley and bracket from the front of the engine.

13 Using a strap wrench to hold the crankshaft pulley stationary, loosen the crankshaft pulley bolt with a socket and breaker bar **(see illustration)**.

14 Slip the pulley off the crankshaft.

15 Remove the dipstick tube from the front of the engine.

16 Remove the lower timing belt cover.

17 If you intend to reuse the timing belt, use white paint or chalk to make match marks to align the sprockets with the belt and an arrow to indicate the direction of rotation **(see illustration)**.

2A

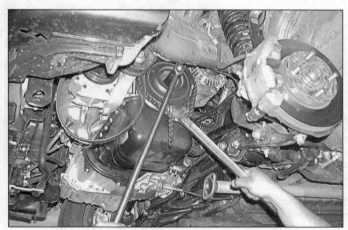

10.13 Hold the crankshaft pulley with a strap wrench while you loosen the crankshaft pulley bolt

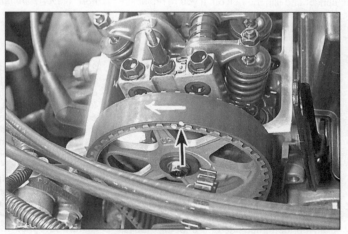

10.17 If you intend to reuse the belt, make an arrow to indicate direction of rotation and match marks (arrow) to align the sprockets with the belt

10.18 Location of the timing belt tensioner bolt (upper arrow) and crankshaft fluctuation sensor (lower arrow)

10.20 Check the belt tensioner pulley for rough operation, bearing play and freedom of movement

10.21 Carefully inspect the timing belt for wear or damage

10.23 Alignment marks for the camshaft sprocket - be sure the word UP is at the twelve o'clock position. It may be necessary to use a straight-edge or ruler to align the two timing marks (arrows) with the cylinder head surface

10.24 Align the mark on the crankshaft sprocket with the pointer on the oil pump (arrows)

18   Loosen the timing belt tensioner bolt **(see illustration)**. Push on the tensioner to release the tension on the belt, then retighten the bolt. Remove the crankshaft fluctuation sensor and slip the belt off. If you're replacing the crankshaft oil seal, slip the sprocket and inner belt guide off the crankshaft (see Section 11).

19   If you're replacing the camshaft or camshaft oil seal, slip a large screwdriver through the camshaft sprocket to keep it from rotating and remove the bolt, then pull off the sprocket. Also remove the Woodruff key.

Inspection

Refer to illustrations 10.20 and 10.21

20   Rotate the belt tensioner pulley by hand and move it from side-to-side, checking for play and rough rotation **(see illustration)**. Replace it if roughness or play is detected.

21   Check the timing belt for wear (especially on the thrust side of the teeth), cracks, splits, fraying and oil contamination **(see illustration)**. Replace the belt if any of these conditions are noted. **Note:** *Unless the*

engine has very low mileage, it's common practice to replace the timing belt with a new one every time it's removed. Don't reinstall the original belt unless it's in like-new condition. Never reinstall a belt in questionable condition.

Installation

Refer to illustrations 10.23, 10.24 and 10.25

22   If you removed the sprockets, reinstall them. Don't forget the Woodruff key for the camshaft sprocket and the inner belt guide for the crankshaft sprocket. Tighten the camshaft sprocket bolt to the torque listed in this Chapter's specifications.

23   Before installing the timing belt, make sure the dot or "UP" mark on the camshaft sprocket is at the top and the two index marks are in line with the cylinder head surface **(see illustration)**.

24   Temporarily reinstall the crankshaft pulley and bolt and turn the crankshaft (if it was disturbed) until the timing mark on the crankshaft sprocket and the pointer on the oil pump are aligned **(see illustration)**.

25   Install the timing belt tightly around the

10.25 Routing of timing belt around the belt tensioner and water pump

crankshaft sprocket, then around the tensioner pulley, water pump pulley and camshaft sprocket in sequence **(see illustration)**.

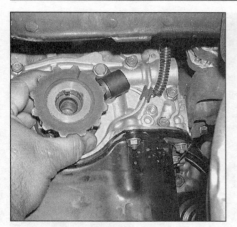

11.4a It's not necessary to remove the crankshaft sprocket unless you intend to replace the oil seal

11.4b After removing the sprocket, slide off the inner belt guide; note that the curved edge faces away from the timing belt

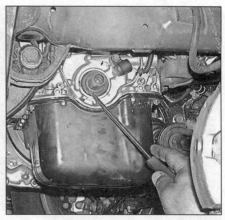

11.5 Carefully pry the oil seal out with a removal tool or a screwdriver - don't nick or scratch the crankshaft or oil pump housing or the new seal will leak

2A

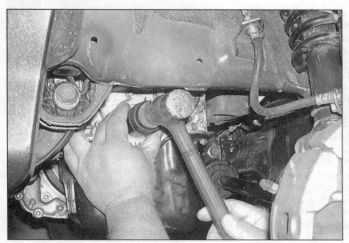

11.6 Drive in a new seal with a socket the same diameter as the seal

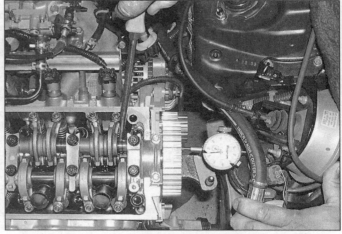

12.1 To check camshaft endplay, set a dial indicator like this, with the gauge plunger touching the nose of the camshaft

26   Loosen the belt tensioner bolt, allowing the tensioner to tension the belt, then temporarily tighten the bolt.

27   Carefully turn the crankshaft counterclockwise six revolutions and recheck the timing marks and camshaft sprocket index marks for proper alignment. If the crankshaft binds or seems to hit something, do not force it, as the valves may be hitting the pistons. If this happens, valve timing is incorrect. Remove the belt and repeat the installation procedure and verify that the installation is correct.

28   To properly tension the timing belt, loosen the tensioner bolt 1/2 turn (180-degrees), rotate the crankshaft counterclockwise three teeth past TDC and tighten the tensioner bolt to the torque listed in this Chapter's Specifications.

29   Reinstall the remaining parts in the reverse order of removal.

30   Refer to Chapter 1 and adjust the drivebelts.

31   Run the engine and check for proper operation.

11   Crankshaft front oil seal - replacement

Refer to illustrations 11.4a, 11.4b, 11.5 and 11.6

1   Remove the drivebelts (see Chapter 1).

2   Remove the crankshaft pulley.

3   Remove the timing belt (see Section 10).

4   Remove the crankshaft sprocket from the crankshaft, then remove the inner belt guide **(see illustrations)**.

5   Carefully pry the seal out of the oil pump housing with a seal removal tool or a screwdriver **(see illustration)**. Don't scratch the seal bore or damage the crankshaft in the process (if the crankshaft is damaged, the new seal will end up leaking).

6   Clean the bore in the oil pump housing and coat the outer edge of the new seal with engine oil or multi-purpose grease. Using a socket with an outside diameter slightly smaller than the outside diameter of the seal, carefully drive the seal into place with a hammer **(see illustration)**. If a socket is not avail-

able, a short section of a large diameter pipe will work. Check the seal after installation to be sure the spring did not pop out.

7   Install the inner belt guide and the crankshaft sprocket. Install the timing belt (see Section 10).

8   Lubricate the sleeve of the crankshaft pulley with engine oil or multi-purpose grease, then install the crankshaft pulley. The remainder of installation is the reverse of removal.

9   Run the engine and check for leaks.

12   Camshaft - removal, inspection and installation

Endplay and runout check

Refer to illustration 12.1

1   To check camshaft endplay:

a) Install the camshaft and secure it with the caps.

b) Mount a dial indicator on the cylinder

12.8 Lift the camshaft from the cylinder head

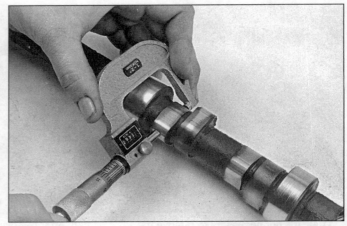

12.10 Measure the camshaft lobe heights with a micrometer

head with the pointer resting on the camshaft nose **(see illustration)**.

c) Using a large screwdriver as a lever at the opposite end, move the camshaft forward-and-backward and note the dial indicator reading.

d) Compare the reading with the endplay listed in this Chapter's Specifications.

e) If the indicated reading is excessive, either the camshaft or the cylinder head is worn. Replace parts as necessary.

2   To check camshaft runout:

a) Support the camshaft with a pair of V-blocks and set up a dial indicator with the plunger resting against the center bearing journal on the camshaft.

b) Rotate the camshaft and note the indicated runout.

c) Compare the results to the camshaft runout listed in this Chapter's Specifications.

d) If the indicated runout exceeds the specified runout limit, replace the camshaft.

Removal

Refer to illustration 12.8

3   Remove the valve cover (see Section 4).

4   Set the engine at TDC for cylinder number one (see Section 3) and remove the timing belt (see Section 10).

5   Remove the distributor (see Chapter 5).

6   If it necessary to separate the sprocket from the camshaft, remove the camshaft sprocket bolt. **Note:** *Prevent the camshaft from turning by inserting a screwdriver through one of the holes in the sprocket.*

7   Remove the rocker arm assembly (see Section 8). If the camshaft bearing caps must be removed from the assembly and they don't have numbers on them, number them before removal. Be sure to put the marks on the same ends of all the caps to prevent incorrect orientation of the caps during installation.

8   Lift out the camshaft **(see illustration)**, wipe it off with a clean shop towel, remove the camshaft seal and set the camshaft aside.

Inspection

Refer to illustration 12.10

9   Check the camshaft bearing journals and caps for scoring and signs of wear. If they are worn, replace the cylinder head with a new or rebuilt assembly. Check the oil clearance of each camshaft journal with Plastigage, comparing your readings with this Chapter's Specifications. **Note:** *For instructions on the use of Plastigage, see Chapter 2, Part C Sections 23 or 25.* If the oil clearance of any of the journals is out of specification, replace the camshaft.

10   Check the cam lobes for wear:

a) Check the toe and ramp areas of each cam lobe for score marks and uneven wear. Also check for flaking and pitting.

b) If there's wear on the toe or the ramp, replace the camshaft, but first try to find the cause of the wear. Look for abrasive substances in the oil and inspect the oil pump and oil passages for blockage. Lobe wear is usually caused by inadequate lubrication or dirty oil.

c) Using a micrometer, measure the cam lobe height **(see illustration)**. If the lobe wear is indicated, replace the camshaft.

11   Inspect the rocker arms for wear, galling and pitting of the contact surfaces.

12   If any of the conditions described above are noted, the cylinder head is probably getting insufficient lubrication or dirty oil. Make sure you track down the cause of this problem (low oil level, low oil pump capacity, clogged oil passage, etc.) before installing a new cylinder head, camshaft or rocker arm assembly.

Installation

Refer to illustration 12.14

13   Thoroughly clean the camshaft, the bearing surfaces in the head and caps and the rocker arms. Remove all sludge and dirt. Wipe off all components with a clean, lint-free cloth.

14   Lubricate the camshaft bearing surfaces in the head and the bearing journals and lobes on the camshaft with camshaft assem-

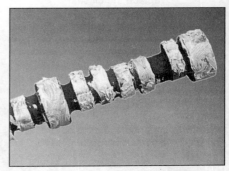

12.14 Be sure to apply camshaft assembly lubricant to the lobes and bearing journals before installing the camshaft

bly lubricant **(see illustration)**. **Caution:** *Failure to adequately lubricate the camshaft and related components can cause serious damage to bearing and friction surfaces during the first few seconds after engine start-up, when the oil pressure is low or nonexistent.*

15   Carefully lower the camshaft into position. Using an appropriate sized driver, deep socket or section of pipe, install a new camshaft seal with the open (spring) side facing in.

16   Install the rocker arm assembly (see Section 8).

17   Rotate the camshaft as necessary and install the camshaft sprocket with the **"UP"** mark stamped on the camshaft sprocket at the twelve o'clock position **(see illustration 10.23)**.

18   Install the timing belt and related components as described in Section 10. **Caution:** *if the crankshaft position was disturbed, be sure to realign the crankshaft sprocket before installing the timing belt* **(see illustration 10.27)**.

19   Remove the spark plugs and rotate the crankshaft by hand to make sure the valve timing is correct. After two revolutions, the timing marks on the sprockets should still be aligned. If they're not, remove the timing belt and set all the timing marks again. **Caution:** *If you feel resistance while rotating the*

crankshaft, stop immediately!

20 The remainder of installation is the reverse of removal.

13 Cylinder head - removal and installation

Caution: *Allow the engine to cool completely before beginning this procedure.*

Removal

1 Position the number one piston at Top Dead Center (see Section 3).

2 Disconnect the negative cable from the battery. **Caution:** *If the radio in your vehicle is equipped with an anti-theft system, make sure you have the correct activation code before disconnecting the battery.*

3 Drain the cooling system and remove the spark plugs (see Chapter 1).

4 Remove the air cleaner duct and housing (see Chapter 4).

5 Remove the drivebelts (see Chapter 1). Unbolt the power steering pump and set it aside with out disconnecting any hoses, then remove the power steering pump bracket (see Chapter 10).

6 Disconnect the throttle cable and relieve the fuel system pressure (see Chapter 4).

7 Disconnect the following hoses and lines (Chapters 4 and 6):

a) *Fuel feed hose*
b) *Evaporative emission control hose*
c) *Breather hose*
d) *PCV hose*

8 Disconnect the coolant bypass hose, heater hose and upper radiator hose (see Chapter 3).

9 Disconnect the following electrical connectors:

a) *Fuel injectors*
b) *Engine coolant temperature sensor*
c) *Engine coolant temperature switch*
d) *Temperature sender*
e) *Throttle position sensor*
f) *Manifold absolute pressure sensor*
g) *Oxygen sensor (and secondary oxygen sensor on D16Y7 engines)*
h) *EGR valve lift sensor (D16Y5 engine)*
i) *VTEC solenoid (D16Y5 and D16Y8 engines)*
j) *VTEC pressure switch (D16Y5 and D16Y8 engines)*
k) *Idle air control valve*

10 Support the engine with a floor jack. Place a wood block between the jack pad and the oil pan to avoid damaging the pan. Remove the upper engine mounting bracket (see Section 18).

11 Remove the intake manifold brace and exhaust manifold flange bolts. **Note:** *You may wish to detach the intake manifold (see Section 5) and/or exhaust manifold (see Section 6), rather than removing it with the cylinder head, to make the cylinder head easier to handle.*

12 Remove the valve cover (see Section 4).

13 Remove the distributor (see Chapter 5), including the cap and wires.

14 Remove the timing belt (see Section 10), rocker arm assembly (see Section 8) and the camshaft (see Section 12).

15 Loosen the cylinder head bolts in 1/4-turn increments until they can be removed by hand. Work in a pattern that's the reverse of the tightening sequence to avoid warping the cylinder head **(see illustration 13.23)**. Note where each bolt goes so it can be returned to the same location on installation.

16 Lift the cylinder head off the engine. If resistance is felt, don't pry between the head and block gasket mating surfaces - damage to the mating surfaces will result. Instead, pry between the power steering pump bracket and the engine block. Set the head on blocks of wood to prevent damage to the gasket sealing surfaces.

17 Cylinder head disassembly and inspection procedures are covered in detail in Chapter 2, Part C. Check the cylinder head for warpage.

Installation

Refer to illustration 13.23

18 The mating surfaces of the cylinder head and block must be perfectly clean when the head is installed.

19 Use a gasket scraper to remove all traces of carbon and old gasket material, then clean the mating surfaces with lacquer thinner or acetone. If there's oil on the mating surfaces when the cylinder head is installed, the gasket may not seal correctly and leaks may develop. When working on the engine block, stuff the cylinders with clean shop rags to keep out debris. Use a vacuum cleaner to remove material that falls into the cylinders. Since the cylinder head and engine block are made of aluminum, aggressive scraping can cause damage. Be extra careful not to nick or gouge the mating surfaces with the scraper.

20 Check the block and cylinder head mating surfaces for nicks, deep scratches and other damage. If damage is slight, it can be removed with a file; if it's excessive, machining may be the only alternative.

21 Use a tap of the correct size to chase the threads in the cylinder head bolt holes. Mount each head bolt in a vise and run a die down the threads to remove corrosion and restore the threads. Dirt, corrosion, sealant and damaged threads will affect torque readings.

22 Place a new gasket on the engine block. Check to see if there are any markings (such as "TOP") on the gasket to indicate how it is to be installed. Those identification marks must face UP. Also, apply sealant to the edges of the timing chain cover where it mates with the engine block. Set the cylinder head in position.

23 Lubricate the threads and the seats of the cylinder head bolts with clean engine oil, then install them. Tighten the bolts in the recommended sequence, in four stages, to the torque listed in this Chapter's Specifications **(see illustration)**. Because of the critical function of cylinder head bolts, the manufacturer specifies the following conditions for tightening them:

a) *A beam-type torque wrench is preferable to a pre-set (click-stop) torque wrench. If you use a pre-set torque wrench, tighten slowly and be careful not to overtighten the bolts.*

b) *If a bolt makes any sound while you're tightening it (squeaking, clicking, etc.), loosen it completely and tighten it again in the four specified steps.*

24 Attach the camshaft sprocket to the camshaft and install the timing belt (see Section 10).

25 Reinstall the remaining parts in the reverse order of removal.

26 Be sure to refill the cooling system and check all fluid levels.

27 Rotate the crankshaft counterclockwise slowly by hand through two complete revolutions. **Caution:** *If you feel any resistance while turning the engine over, stop and re-check the camshaft timing. The valves may be hitting the pistons.*

28 Start the engine and check the ignition timing (see Chapter 1).

29 Run the engine until normal operating temperature is reached. Check for leaks and proper operation.

2A

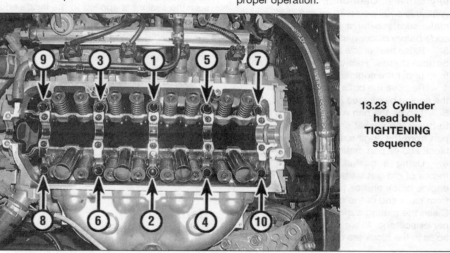

13.23 Cylinder head bolt TIGHTENING sequence

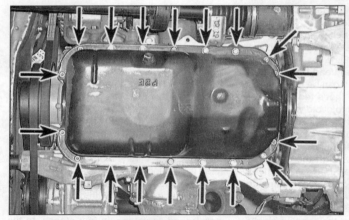

14.4 Remove the oil pan bolts (arrows) from the oil pan

15.3 Remove the oil pick-up tube bolts (arrows) from the oil pump and main bearing cap bridge

15.4 Remove the oil pump-to-block bolts (circled) and remove the oil pump

15.5 Remove the oil pump cover screws (arrows)

14 Oil pan - removal and installation

Removal

Refer to illustration 14.4

1   Warm up the engine, then drain the oil and replace the oil filter (see Chapter 1).

2   Detach the cable from the negative battery terminal. **Caution:** *If the radio in your vehicle is equipped with an anti-theft system, make sure you have the correct activation code before disconnecting the battery.*

3   Raise the vehicle and support it securely on jackstands. Remove the splash shield from under the engine.

4   Remove the bolts securing the oil pan to the engine block **(see illustration)**.

5   Tap on the pan with a soft-face hammer to break the gasket seal, then detach the oil pan from the engine. Don't pry between the block and oil pan mating surfaces.

6   Using a gasket scraper, remove all traces of old gasket and/or sealant from the engine block and oil pan. Remove the seals from each end of the engine block or oil pan. Clean the mating surfaces with lacquer thinner or acetone. Make sure the threaded bolt holes in the block are clean.

Installation

7   Clean the oil pan with solvent and dry it thoroughly. Check the gasket flanges for distortion, particularly around the bolt holes. If necessary, place the pan on a wood block and use a hammer to flatten and restore the gasket surface.

8   Apply a 1/8-inch wide bead of RTV sealant to the oil pan gasket surface. Make sure the sealant is applied to the inside edge of the bolt holes.

9   Carefully place the oil pan in position.

10   Install the bolts and tighten them in small increments to the torque listed in this Chapter's Specifications. Start with the bolts closest to the center of the pan and work out in a spiral pattern. Don't overtighten them or leakage may occur.

11   Add oil (see Chapter 1), run the engine and check for oil leaks.

15 Oil pump - removal, inspection and installation

Removal

Refer to illustrations 15.3, 15.4 and 15.5

1   Remove the timing belt (see Section 10).

2   Remove the oil pan (see Section 14).

3   Remove the oil pick-up tube and screen from the pump housing and the main bearing cap bridge **(see illustration)**.

4   Remove the bolts from the oil pump housing and separate the assembly from the engine **(see illustration)**.

5   Remove the screws and disassemble the oil pump **(see illustration)**. You may need to use an impact screwdriver to loosen the pump cover screws without stripping the heads.

Inspection

Refer to illustrations 15.6a, 15.6b and 15.6c

6   Check the oil pump rotor-to-cover-clearance, tooth tip clearance and rotor-to-body clearance **(see illustrations)**. Compare your measurements to the figures listed in this Chapter's Specifications. Replace the pump if any of the measurements exceed the specified limits.

7   Remove the pressure relief valve plug and extract the spring and pressure relief valve plunger from the pump housing. Check the spring for distortion and the relief valve plunger for scoring. Replace parts as necessary.

8   Install the pump rotors. Pack the spaces

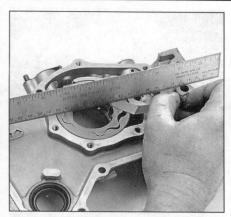

15.6a Use a feeler gauge and straight-edge to check the clearance between the rotors and the cover

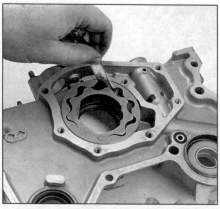

15.6b Use a feeler gauge to check the tooth-tip clearance between the inner and outer rotors

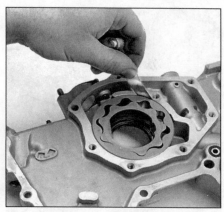

15.6c Use a feeler gauge to check the outer rotor-to-pump body clearance

2A

between the rotors with petroleum jelly (this will prime the pump).

9   Apply thread-locking compound the pump cover screws, install the cover and tighten the screws to the torque listed in this Chapter's Specifications. Install the oil pressure relief valve and spring assembly. Use a new sealing washer on the plug and tighten the plug securely.

Installation

10   Apply a thin coat of anaerobic sealant to the pump housing-to-block sealing surface and a new O-ring in the pump housing. Install the pump housing to the engine block and tighten the bolts to the torque listed in this Chapter's Specifications.

11   Install the oil pick-up tube and screen, using a new gasket. Tighten the bolts to the torque listed in this Chapter's Specifications.

12   Install the oil pan (see Section 14).

13   The remainder of installation is the reverse of removal. Add the specified type and quantity of oil and coolant (see Chapter 1), run the engine and check for leaks.

16 Flywheel/driveplate - removal and installation

Removal

Refer to illustration 16.3

1   Raise the vehicle and support it securely on jackstands, then refer to Chapter 7 and remove the transaxle.

2   Remove the pressure plate and clutch disc (see Chapter 8) (manual transaxle equipped vehicles). Now is a good time to check/replace the clutch components and pilot bearing.

3   Remove the bolts that secure the flywheel/driveplate to the crankshaft **(see illustration)**. If the crankshaft turns, remove the starter (see Chapter 5) and wedge a screwdriver in the ring gear teeth (manual transaxle models), or insert a long punch through one of the holes in the driveplate and allow it to rest against a projection on the engine block

16.3 Remove the flywheel/driveplate bolts (arrows) from the crankshaft

(automatic transaxle models).

4   Remove the flywheel/driveplate from the crankshaft. Since the flywheel is fairly heavy, be sure to support it while removing the last bolt.

5   Clean the flywheel to remove grease and oil. Inspect the surface for cracks, rivet grooves, burned areas and score marks. Light scoring can be removed with emery cloth. Check for cracked and broken ring gear teeth. Lay the flywheel on a flat surface and use a straightedge to check for warpage.

6   Clean and inspect the mating surfaces of the flywheel/driveplate and the crankshaft. If the rear main oil seal is leaking, replace it before reinstalling the flywheel/driveplate (see Section 17).

Installation

7   Position the flywheel/driveplate against the crankshaft. Note that some engines have an alignment dowel or staggered bolt holes to ensure correct installation. Before installing the bolts, apply thread-locking compound to the threads.

8   Prevent the flywheel/driveplate from turning by using one of the methods described in Step 3. Using a crossing pattern, tighten the bolts to the torque listed in

17.4a Carefully pry the oil seal out with a removal tool or a screwdriver - don't nick or scratch the crankshaft or the new seal will be damaged and leaks will develop

this Chapter's Specifications.

9   The remainder of installation is the reverse of the removal procedure.

17 Rear main oil seal - replacement

Refer to illustrations 17.4a and 17.4b

1   The transaxle must be removed from the vehicle for this procedure (see Chapter 7).

2   Remove the flywheel/driveplate (see Section 16).

3   Before removing the seal, it is very important that the clearance between the seal and the outside edge of the retainer is checked. Use a small ruler or caliper and record the distance. The new seal must not be driven in past this measurement (see Chapter 2C).

4   The seal can be replaced without removing the oil pan or seal retainer. Use a screwdriver and a rag to carefully pry the seal out of the housing **(see illustration)**. Use the rag to be sure no nicks are made in the crankshaft seal surface. Apply a film of clean oil to the crankshaft seal journal and the lip of

17.4b Because the seal lip is stiff, it won't slide over the end of the crankshaft easily - if you lubricate the journal and the seal lip with multi-purpose grease and carefully work the seal over the journal with a smooth, blunt object, it should go on without damage

18.9a Left side engine mount (arrow)

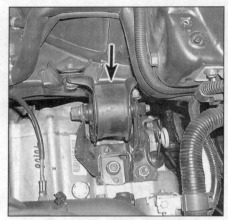

18.9b Right side transaxle mount (arrow)

18.9c Rear engine mount at firewall (arrow)

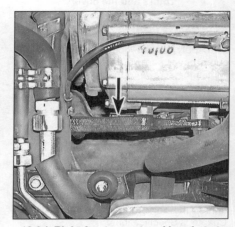

18.9d Right front mount and bracket at transaxle (arrow)

the new seal and carefully tap the seal into place **(see illustration)**. The lip is stiff so carefully work it onto the seal journal of the crankshaft with a smooth object like the end of a socket extension. Tap the seal into the retainer with a seal driver. If a seal driver isn't available, a large socket or piece of pipe, with an outside diameter slightly smaller than that of the seal, can be used. Don't rush it or you may damage the seal. **Note:** *Removal of the oil seal retainer and replacement of the seal are covered in Chapter 2, Part C.*
5   The remaining steps are the reverse of removal.
6   Run the engine and check for oil leaks.

18 Engine mounts - check and replacement

1   Engine mounts seldom require attention, but broken or deteriorated mounts should be replaced immediately or the added strain placed on the driveline components may cause damage or wear.

Check

2   During the check, the engine must be raised slightly to remove the weight from the mounts.
3   Raise the vehicle and support it securely on jackstands, then position a jack under the

engine oil pan. Place a large wood block between the jack head and the oil pan, then carefully raise the engine just enough to take the weight off the mounts. **Warning:** *DO NOT place any part of your body under the engine when it's supported only by a jack!*
4   Check the mount insulators to see if the rubber is cracked, hardened or separated from the metal plates. Sometimes the rubber will split right down the center.
5   Check for relative movement between the mount plates and the engine or frame (use a large screwdriver or pry bar to attempt to move the mounts). If movement is noted, lower the engine and tighten the mount fasteners.
6   Rubber preservative should be applied to the insulators to slow deterioration.

Replacement

Refer to illustrations 18.9a, 18.9b, 18.9c and 18.9d
7   Disconnect the battery cable from the negative battery terminal. **Caution:** *If the radio in your vehicle is equipped with an anti-theft system, make sure you have the correct activation code before disconnecting the battery.* Raise the vehicle and support it securely on jackstands (if not already done). Support the engine as described in Step 3.
8   Remove the fasteners, raise the engine with the jack and detach the mount from the frame bracket and engine.
9   Install the new mount, making sure it is correctly positioned in its bracket **(see illustrations)**. Install the fasteners and tighten them securely.

Chapter 2 Part B
Integra engine

Contents

2B

Specifications

General

Firing order	1-3-4-2
Cylinder numbers (left-to-right)	1-2-3-4
Bore	3.19 inches
Stroke	
B18B1	3.50 inches
B18C1, B18C5	3.43 inches
Displacement	
B18B1	112 cubic inches (1.8 liters)
B18C1, B18C5	110 cubic inches (1.8 liters)

 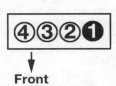

Front

Cylinder locations and distributor rotation

Camshaft

Endplay	
Standard	0.002 to 0.006 inch
Maximum	0.020 inch
Lobe height	
B18B1	
Intake	1.3274 inches
Exhaust	1.3200 inches
B18C1	
Intake	
Primary	1.3154 inches
Mid	1.4322 inches
Secondary	1.3601 inches
Exhaust	
Primary	1.3036 inches
Mid	1.4063 inches
Secondary	1.3536 inches

Camshaft (continued)

Lobe height (continued)

  B18C5

    Intake

      Primary .... 1.3027 inches

      Mid... 1.4138 inches

      Secondary .... 1.3674 inches

    Exhaust

      Primary .... 1.2907 inches

      Mid... 1.4304 inches

      Secondary .... 1.3658 inches

Runout

  Standard... 0.001 inch

  Service limit.. 0.002 inch maximum

Journal oil clearance

  B18B1

    Standard .... 0.0012 to 0.0027 inch

    Maximum .... 0.006 inch

  B18C1, B18C5

    Standard .... 0.0020 to 0.0035 inch

    Maximum .... 0.006 inch

Oil pump

Rotor-to-cover clearance

  Standard .... 0.001 to 0.003 inch

  Service limit.. 0.006 inch

Tooth tip clearance

  Standard... 0.002 to 0.006 inch

  Service limit.. 0.008 inch

Outer rotor-to-pump body clearance

  Standard... 0.001 to 0.003 inch

  Service limit.. 0.006 inch

Torque specifications   **Ft-lbs** (unless otherwise indicated)

Camshaft bearing cap bolts (B18B1)............................ 108 in-lb

Camshaft holder bolts (B18C1, B18C5)

  6 mm bolts .... 108 in-lbs

  8 mm bolts 20

Camshaft sprocket bolts

  B18B1 27

  B18C1, B18C5 41

Crankshaft fluctuation sensor bolts............................. 96 in-lbs

Crankshaft pulley bolt.. 130

Cylinder head bolts

  Step 1 22

  Step 2

    B18B1 61

    B18C1, B18C5 63

Driveplate-to-crankshaft bolts 54

Intake manifold bolts/nuts 17

Intake manifold air chamber nuts (B18C1) 17

Exhaust manifold-to-cylinder head nuts...................... 23

Exhaust pipe-to-manifold nuts 40

Exhaust manifold upper cover bolts............................. 17

Flywheel-to-crankshaft bolts 76

Oxygen sensor... 33

Oil jet bolts... 156 in-lbs

Oil pressure switch .... 156 in-lbs

Oil pan baffle plate bolts

  B18B1, B18C1 .... 96 in-lbs

  B18C5 .... 86 in-lbs

Oil pan drain plug 33

Oil pan-to-engine bolts.. 96 in-lbs

Oil pump pick-up tube to pump housing nuts

  B18B1, B18C1 .... 96 in-lbs

  B18C5 .... 86 in-lbs

Oil pump screen-to-main bearing cap

  B18B1, B18C1 .... 96 in-lbs

  B18C5 .... 86 in-lbs

Oil pump housing-to-block bolts	
6 mm bolts	
B18B1, B18C1	96 in-lbs
B18C5	86 in-lbs
8 mm bolts	17
Oil pump cover-to-housing	
1994 and 1995	48 in-lbs
1996-on	60 in-lbs
Oil pump relief valve plug	29
Rear main oil seal housing bolts..................................	96 in-lbs
Timing belt cover bolts	86 in-lbs
Timing belt tensioner bolt	40
Valve cover nuts	86 in-lbs
VTEC lock-up solenoid bolts	104 in-lbs
Water pump bolts	104 in-lbs

1 General information

This Part of Chapter 2 is devoted to in-vehicle repair procedures for the 1.8 liter, fuel injected, four cylinder engine. All information concerning engine removal and installation and engine block and cylinder head overhaul can be found in Part C of this Chapter.

There are three different versions of the engine covered in this Part of Chapter 2. All versions are Dual Overhead Camshaft (DOHC), with 4 valves per cylinder (16V).

There are two versions of the VTEC (Variable Valve Timing and Lift Electronic Control) system available in models covered by this manual. For more information on VTEC systems see Section 9 of this Chapter.

Engine designations include:

B18B1..............1.8L, 16V, DOHC
B18C1..............1.8L, 16V, DOHC VTEC
B18C5..............1.8L, 16V, DOHC VTEC

The following repair procedures are based on the assumption that the engine is installed in the vehicle. If the engine has been removed from the vehicle and mounted on a stand, many of the steps outlined in this Part of Chapter 2 will not apply.

The Specifications included in this Part of Chapter 2 apply only to the procedures contained in this chapter. Chapter 2C contains the Specifications necessary for cylinder head and engine block rebuilding.

It is a compact and lightweight engine with an aluminum alloy block (with steel cylinder liners) and an aluminum alloy cylinder head. The crankshaft rides in a single carriage unit that houses the renewable insert-type main bearings, with separate thrust bearings at the number four bearing position assigned the task of controlling crankshaft endplay.

The pistons have two compression rings and one oil control ring. The semi-floating piston pins are press fitted into the small end of the connecting rod. The connecting rod big ends are also equipped with renewable insert-type plain bearings.

The engine is liquid-cooled, utilizing a centrifugal impeller-type pump, driven by the timing belt, to circulate coolant around the cylinders and combustion chambers and through the intake manifold.

Lubrication is handled by a rotor-type oil pump mounted on the front of the engine under the timing belt cover. It is driven directly by the crankshaft. The oil is filtered continuously by a cartridge-type filter mounted on the firewall side of the engine.

2 Repair operations possible with the engine in the vehicle

Clean the engine compartment and the exterior of the engine with some type of degreaser before any work is done. It will make the job easier and help keep dirt out of the internal areas of the engine.

Depending on the components involved, it may be helpful to remove the hood to improve access to the engine as repairs are performed (refer to Chapter 11 if necessary). Cover the fenders to prevent damage to the paint. Special pads are available, but an old bedspread or blanket will also work.

If vacuum, exhaust, oil or coolant leaks develop, indicating a need for gasket or seal replacement, the repairs can generally be made with the engine in the vehicle. The intake and exhaust manifold gaskets, oil pan gasket, crankshaft oil seals and cylinder head gasket are all accessible with the engine in place.

Exterior engine components, such as the intake and exhaust manifolds, the oil pan, the water pump, the starter motor, the alternator, the distributor and the fuel system components can be removed for repair with the engine in place.

Since the cylinder head can be removed without pulling the engine, camshaft and valve component servicing can also be accomplished with the engine in the vehicle. Replacement of the timing belt and sprockets is also possible with the engine in the vehicle.

In extreme cases caused by a lack of necessary equipment, repair or replacement of piston rings, pistons, connecting rods and rod bearings is possible with the engine in the vehicle. However, this practice is not recommended because of the cleaning and preparation work that must be done to the components involved.

3 Top Dead Center (TDC) for number one piston - locating

Refer to illustrations 3.10 and 3.11
Note: *The following procedure is based on the assumption that the spark plug wires and distributor are correctly installed. If you are trying to locate TDC to install the distributor correctly, piston position must be determined by feeling for compression at the number one spark plug hole, then aligning the ignition timing marks as described in Step 11.*

1 Top Dead Center (TDC) is the highest point in the cylinder that each piston reaches as it travels up-and-down when the crankshaft turns. Each piston reaches TDC on the compression stroke and again on the exhaust stroke, but TDC generally refers to piston position on the compression stroke.

2 Positioning the piston(s) at TDC is an essential part of many procedures such as camshaft and timing belt/sprocket removal and distributor removal.

3 Before beginning this procedure, be sure to place the transaxle in Neutral and apply the parking brake or block the rear wheels.

3.10 Mark the distributor housing (arrow) directly beneath the number one spark plug wire terminal (check the distributor cap to verify that the rotor points to the number 1 spark plug wire)

3.11 Align the white notch in the crankshaft pulley with the pointer on the lower cover (arrow,) then check to see if the distributor rotor is pointing to number 1 cylinder's terminal in the distributor cap (if not, number 4 is at TDC - the crankshaft will have to be rotated 360-degrees)

4   Disable the ignition system by detaching the electrical connectors at the distributor (see Chapter 5).

5   Disable the fuel system (see Chapter 4).

6   Remove the spark plugs (see Chapter 1).

7   In order to bring any piston to TDC, the crankshaft must be turned using one of the methods outlined below. When looking at the front (drive belt end) of the engine, normal crankshaft rotation is counterclockwise. Always rotate the engine counterclockwise; clockwise rotation may cause incorrect adjustment of the timing belt.

  a) *The preferred method is to turn the crankshaft with a socket and ratchet attached to the bolt threaded into the front of the crankshaft.*

  b) *A remote starter switch, which may save some time, can also be used. Follow the instructions included with the switch. Once the piston is close to TDC, use a socket and ratchet as described in the previous paragraph.*

  c) *If an assistant is available to turn the ignition switch to the Start position in short bursts, you can get the piston close to TDC without a remote starter switch. Make sure your assistant is out of the vehicle, away from the ignition switch, then use a socket and ratchet as described in Paragraph a) to complete the procedure.*

8   Note the position of the terminal for the number one spark plug wire on the distributor cap. If the terminal isn't marked, follow the plug wire from the number one cylinder spark plug to the cap.

9   Detach the cap from the distributor and set it aside (see Chapter 1 if necessary).

10   Mark the distributor cover directly under the rotor terminal **(see illustration)** for the number 1 cylinder.

11   Locate the timing marks on the crankshaft pulley. The notch painted white is

the TDC mark. Turn the crankshaft (see Step 7 above) until the TDC mark on the crankshaft pulley is aligned with the pointer on the lower cover **(see illustration)**.

12   Look at the distributor rotor - it should be pointing directly at the mark you made on the distributor body (cover). If the rotor is 180-degrees off, the number one piston is at TDC on the exhaust stroke.

13   To get the piston to TDC on the compression stroke, turn the crankshaft one complete turn (360-degrees) counterclockwise. The rotor should now be pointing at the mark on the distributor.

14   When the rotor is pointing at the number one spark plug wire terminal in the distributor cap and the ignition timing marks are aligned, the number one piston is at TDC on the compression stroke.

15   After the number one piston has been positioned at TDC on the compression stroke, TDC for any of the remaining pistons can be located by turning the crankshaft and following the firing order. Mark the remaining spark plug wire terminal locations on the distributor body just like you did for the number one terminal, then number the marks to correspond with the cylinder numbers. As you turn the crankshaft, the rotor will also turn. When it's pointing directly at one of the marks on the distributor, the piston for that particular cylinder is at TDC on the compression stroke.

---

4   Valve cover - removal and installation

Removal

1   Detach the cable from the negative battery terminal. **Caution:** *If the radio in your vehicle is equipped with an anti-theft system, make sure you have the correct activation code before disconnecting the battery.*

2   Remove the distributor cap and wires from their cylinder head and valve cover connections (see Chapter 1). Be sure to mark each wire for correct installation.

3   Mark and detach any hoses or wires from the throttle body or valve cover that will interfere with the removal of the valve cover.

4   Wipe off the valve cover thoroughly to prevent debris from falling onto the exposed cylinder head or camshaft/valve train assembly.

5   Remove the valve cover nuts and washers **(see illustration 4.10)**.

6   Carefully lift off the valve cover and gasket. If the gasket is stuck to the cylinder head, tap it with a rubber mallet to break the seal. Do not pry between the cover and cylinder head or you'll damage the gasket mating surfaces.

Installation

Refer to illustration 4.10

7   Remove the old gasket and clean the mating surfaces of the cylinder head and the valve cover. Clean the surfaces with a rag soaked in lacquer thinner or acetone.

8   Inspect the sealing grommets and the rubber seals that fit at the bottoms of the spark plug wells. Replace them if they're cracked or flattened, or if the rubber has hardened. Make sure the rubber spark plug seals are in position before installing the valve cover.

9   Apply a bead of RTV sealant to the corners where the cylinder head mates with the rocker arm assembly. Wait five minutes or so and let the RTV set-up. **Note:** *Make sure the RTV sealant has slightly hardened before installing the valve cover. If the weather is damp and cold, the sealant will take some extra time to harden.*

10   Install a new molded rubber gasket into the groove around the perimeter of the valve cover and install the valve cover. Install the

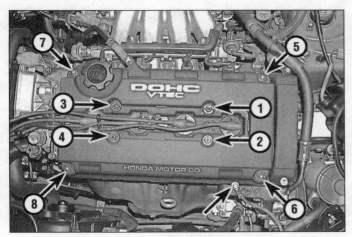

4.10 Valve cover bolt TIGHTENING sequence

5.4 Disconnect the vacuum hoses (arrows)

valve cover sealing grommets and nuts. Following the recommended sequence, tighten the nuts to the torque listed in this Chapter's Specifications (see illustration).

11 The remainder of installation is the reverse of removal.

5 Intake manifold - removal and installation

Warning: Gasoline is extremely flammable, so take extra precautions when you work on any part of the fuel system. Don't smoke or allow open flames or bare light bulbs near the work area, and don't work in a garage where a natural gas-type appliance (such as a water heater or clothes dryer) with a pilot light is present. If you spill any fuel on your skin, rinse it off immediately with soap and water. When you perform any kind of work on the fuel system, wear safety glasses and have a Class B type fire extinguisher on hand.

Removal

Refer to illustrations 5.4, 5.8, 5.9 and 5.11

1 Detach the cable from the negative battery terminal. Caution: If the radio in your vehicle is equipped with an anti-theft system, make sure you have the correct activation code before disconnecting the battery.

2 Drain the cooling system (see Chapter 1).

3 Remove the intake air duct and air cleaner housing (see Chapter 4).

4 Clearly label and detach any vacuum lines and electrical connectors which will interfere with removal of the manifold (see illustration). Note: On B18C1 engines, the intake air bypass solenoid connector is under the manifold and may be hard to reach. If you can't get at it, disconnect the connector after the manifold is detached and partly removed.

5 Detach the accelerator cable from the throttle lever (see Chapter 4).

6 Remove the coolant hoses from the throttle body. On B18B1 and B18C1 engines, disconnect the coolant hoses from the idle air control IAC) valve.

7 Relieve the fuel system pressure and disconnect the fuel feed and return lines at the fuel rail (see Chapter 4).

8 Working from underneath the engine compartment, remove the brace that supports the intake manifold (see illustration).

9 Disconnect the coolant by-pass hose from the timing belt end of the intake mani-

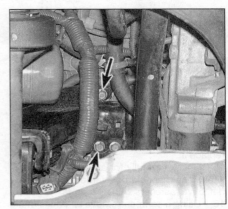

5.8 Remove the bolts (arrows) and remove the brace from the intake manifold

fold (see illustration).

10 Remove the intake manifold nuts and remove the manifold from the engine (see illustration 5.9).

11 If you're working on a manifold with a removable air chamber (B18C1 engine), remove the nuts and separate it from the manifold, if necessary (see illustration). Remove the gasket, intake air bypass (IAB) air chamber and second gasket.

5.9 Disconnect the coolant bypass hose and remove the intake manifold mounting nuts (arrows)

5.11 On B18C1 engines, remove the nuts (arrows), air chamber, gasket, intake air bypass (IAB) air chamber and second gasket

2B

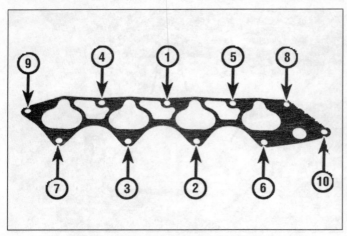

5.17 Intake manifold fastener TIGHTENING sequence

6.2 Remove the exhaust pipe flange nuts and bracket bolts (arrows), then lower the exhaust pipe

Installation

Refer to illustration 5.17

12   Clean the manifold nuts with solvent and dry them with compressed air, if available.

13   Check the mating surfaces of the manifold for flatness with a precision straightedge and feeler gauge.

14   Inspect the manifold for cracks and distortion. If the manifold is cracked or warped, replace it.

15   Check carefully for any stripped or broken intake manifold bolts/studs. Replace any defective fasteners with new parts.

16   Using a scraper, remove all traces of old gasket material from the cylinder head and manifold mating surfaces. Clean the surfaces with lacquer thinner or acetone.

17   Install the intake manifold with a new gasket and tighten the nuts finger-tight. Following the recommended sequence, tighten the nuts to the torque listed in this Chapter's Specifications **(see illustration)**.

18   The remainder of the installation procedure is the reverse of removal. Refer to Chapter 1 and refill the cooling system.

6   Exhaust manifold - removal and installation

Removal

Refer to illustrations 6.2, 6.3 and 6.4

1   Disconnect the battery cable from the negative battery terminal. **Caution:** *If the radio in your vehicle is equipped with an anti-theft system, make sure you have the correct activation code before disconnecting the battery.*

2   Raise the front of the vehicle and support it securely on jackstands. Unbolt the brace and detach the exhaust pipe from the exhaust manifold **(see illustration)**. Apply penetrating oil to the fastener threads if they are difficult to remove.

3   Remove the heat shield from the exhaust manifold **(see illustration)**. Be sure to soak the bolts and nuts with penetrating oil before attempting to remove them from the manifold.

4   Remove the exhaust manifold nuts **(see illustration)** and detach the exhaust manifold from the cylinder head.

Installation

5   Discard the old gasket and use a scraper to clean the gasket mating surfaces on the manifold and cylinder head, then clean the surfaces with a rag soaked in lacquer thinner or acetone.

6   Place the exhaust manifold in position on the cylinder head and install the nuts. Starting at the center, tighten the nuts in a criss-cross pattern to the torque listed in this Chapter's Specifications.

7   The remainder of installation is the reverse of removal.

8   Start the engine and check for exhaust leaks between the manifold and the cylinder head and between the manifold and the exhaust pipe.

7   Timing belt and sprockets - removal, inspection and installation

Removal

Refer to illustrations 7.12a, 7.12b, 7.13, 7.14 and 7.16

1   Disconnect the negative cable from the battery.

2   Place blocks behind the rear wheels and

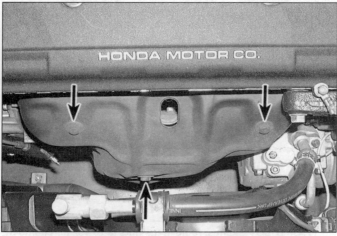

6.3 Remove the bolts (arrows) and lift off the heat shield

6.4 Exhaust manifold mounting nuts (arrows)

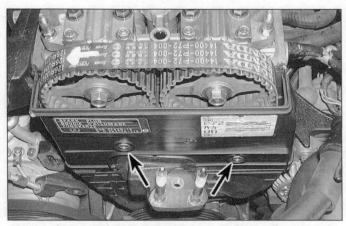

7.12a Center timing cover bolts (arrows)

7.12b Lower timing cover bolts (arrows)

set the parking brake.

3   Loosen the lug nuts on the front wheels and raise the front of the vehicle. Support the front of the vehicle securely on jackstands (see Chapter 1).

4   Remove the front wheels and remove the splash shield from under the engine.

5   Support the engine with a floor jack. Place a wood block between the jack pad and the oil pan to avoid damaging the pan.

6   Remove the upper engine mounting bracket (see Section 17).

7   Remove the spark plugs and drivebelts (see Chapter 1).

8   Unbolt the power steering pump without disconnecting the hoses and set it aside (see Chapter 10).

9   Remove the cruise control actuator (see Chapter 12).

10   Position the number one piston at Top Dead Center (see Section 3). **Caution:** *Always rotate the crankshaft counterclockwise (viewed from the pulley end of the engine). Clockwise rotation may cause incorrect adjustment of the timing belt.*

11   Remove the valve cover (see Section 4).

12   Remove the center and lower timing belt covers **(see illustrations)**. The upper cover is an integral part of the valve cover.

13   Loosen the belt tensioner bolt 1/2 turn **(see illustration)**. Push the tensioner away from the belt to loosen it, then tighten the bolt to hold the tensioner and maintain the belt slack.

14   Hold the crankshaft pulley stationary with a strap wrench while loosening the pulley-to-crankshaft bolt with a socket and breaker bar **(see illustration)**.

15   Slip the pulley off the crankshaft.

16   If you intend to reuse the timing belt, use white paint or chalk to make match marks to align the sprockets with the belt and an arrow to indicate the direction of rotation **(see illustration)**.

17   Loosen the timing belt tensioner bolt. Push on the tensioner to release the tension on the belt, then retighten the bolt. Slip the belt off. If you're replacing the crankshaft oil seal, slip the outer belt guide, sprocket and inner belt guide off the crankshaft (see Section 7).

18   If you're replacing the camshafts or camshaft oil seals, slip a large screwdriver through the camshaft sprocket to keep it from rotating and remove the bolt, then pull off the sprocket. Also remove the Woodruff key.

Inspection

Caution: *Do not rotate the camshaft or crankshaft sprockets with the timing belt off or valve damage may result from valves hitting the tops of pistons.*

19   Rotate the belt tensioner pulley by hand and move it from side-to-side, checking for play and rough rotation **(see illustration 7.13)**. Replace it if roughness or play is detected.

20   Check the timing belt for wear (especially on the thrust side of the teeth), cracks, splits, fraying and oil contamination **(see illustration 10.21 in Chapter 2 Part A)**. Replace the belt if any of these conditions are noted. **Note:** *Unless the engine has very low mileage, it's common practice to replace the timing belt with a new one every time it's removed. Don't reinstall the original belt unless it's in like-new condition. Never reinstall a belt in questionable condition.*

Installation

Refer to illustrations 7.22 and 7.23

21   If you removed the sprockets, reinstall them. Don't forget the Woodruff keys for the camshaft sprockets and the inner belt guide

2B

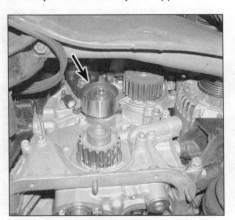

7.13 Timing belt tensioner (arrow)

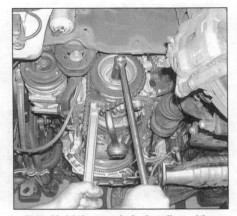

7.14 Hold the crankshaft pulley with a strap wrench and remove the bolt

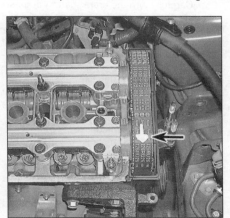

7.16 If you intend to reuse the belt, make an arrow to indicate direction of rotation and match marks to align the sprockets with the belt

7.22 Alignment marks for the camshaft sprockets - be sure the word UP is at the twelve o'clock position and the two timing marks (arrows) are aligned with the pointer on the rear cover

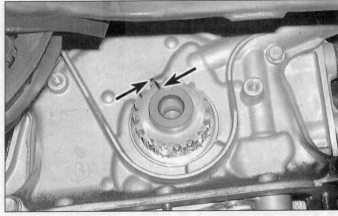

7.23 Align the mark on the crankshaft sprocket with the pointer on the oil pump housing (arrows)

for the crankshaft sprocket. Tighten the camshaft sprocket bolts to the torque listed in this Chapter's specifications.

22   Before installing the timing belt, make sure the "UP" marks on the camshaft sprockets are at the top and the two timing marks are aligned with the pointer on the rear cover **(see illustration)**.

23   Temporarily reinstall the crankshaft pulley and bolt and turn the crankshaft (if it was disturbed) until the timing mark on the crankshaft sprocket and the pointer on the oil pump housing are aligned **(see illustration)**. **Caution:** *If you feel resistance, stop turning the crankshaft. The pistons may be contacting open valves, and continued turning may bend the valves. Carefully re-position the camshaft sprockets and try rotating the crankshaft again.*

24   Install the timing belt, making sure there is no slack, first on the crankshaft sprocket, then around the tensioner pulley, water pump pulley, exhaust camshaft sprocket and intake camshaft sprocket in sequence. Loosen the belt tensioner bolt, allowing the tensioner to tension the belt and temporarily tighten the bolt.

25   Carefully turn the crankshaft through six revolutions and recheck the timing marks and camshaft sprocket index marks for proper alignment **(see illustrations 7.22 and 7.23)**. If the crankshaft binds or seems to hit something, do not force it, as the valves may be hitting the pistons. If this happens, valve timing is incorrect. Remove the belt and repeat the installation procedure and verify that the installation is correct.

26   To properly tension the timing belt, loosen the tensioner bolt 1/2 turn (180-degrees), rotate the crankshaft counterclockwise three teeth past TDC and tighten the tensioner bolt to the torque listed in this Chapter's Specifications.

27   Reinstall the remaining parts in the reverse order of removal.

28   Refer to Chapter 1 and adjust the drivebelts.

29   Run the engine and check for proper operation.

8   Crankshaft front oil seal - replacement

Refer to illustrations 8.4a, 8.4b, 8.4c and 8.5

1   Remove the drivebelts (see Chapter 1).

8.4a Remove the outer belt guide - note that the curved outer edge faces away from the belt (belt removed for clarity)

8.4c After removing the sprocket, slide off the inner belt guide (if equipped); the curved edge faces away from the timing belt

2   Remove the crankshaft pulley.

3   Remove the timing belt (see Section 7).

4   Remove the outer belt guide and crankshaft sprocket from the crankshaft. On models without a crankshaft fluctuation sensor, remove the inner belt guide **(see illustra-**

8.4b It's not necessary to remove the crankshaft sprocket unless you intend to replace the oil seal

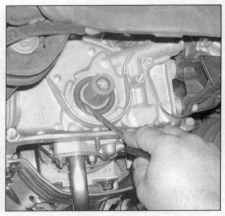

8.5 Carefully pry the oil seal out with a removal tool or a screwdriver - don't nick or scratch the crankshaft or oil pump or the new seal will leak

tions). **Note:** *If the engine is equipped with a crankshaft fluctuation sensor, the inner belt guide is an integral part of the sprocket,*

5   Carefully pry the seal out of the oil pump housing with a seal removal tool or a screwdriver **(see illustration)**. Don't scratch the seal bore or damage the crankshaft in the process (if the crankshaft is damaged, the new seal will end up leaking).

6   Clean the bore in the oil pump housing and coat the outer edge of the new seal with engine oil or multi-purpose grease. Using a socket with an outside diameter slightly smaller than the outside diameter of the seal, carefully drive the seal into place with a hammer **(see illustration 10.6 in Chapter 2, Part A)**. If a socket is not available, a short section of a large diameter pipe will work. Check the seal after installation to be sure the spring did not pop out.

7   Install the inner belt guide, crankshaft sprocket and outer belt guide. Install the timing belt (see Section 7).

8   Lubricate the sleeve of the crankshaft pulley with engine oil or multi-purpose grease, then install the crankshaft pulley. The remainder of installation is the reverse of removal.

9   Run the engine and check for leaks.

9   VTEC system - general description and component checks

Refer to illustrations 9.11 and 9.16

1   The **VTEC** system (**V**ariable Valve **Ti**ming and Lift **E**lectronic **C**ontrol) is used on various models throughout the Honda vehicle line.

2   The differences between the base engines and their VTEC counterparts is strictly in the components and operation of the valve train. The engine block, oiling and cooling systems are identical, as are all attached components. Models equipped with VTEC systems can be distinguished by the letters "VTEC" molded into the top of the valve cover.

3   The intake camshaft has three lobes for each intake valve. The Powertrain Control Module (PCM) has the ability to decide which set of lobes will be used for a given set of engine operating conditions. The PCM turns the system ON or OFF, depending on sensor input.

4   The following are used to determine VTEC operation:

a) *Engine speed (rpm)*
b) *Vehicle speed (mph)*
c) *Throttle position sensor output*
d) *Engine load measured by manifold absolute pressure sensor*
e) *Coolant temperature*

5   At low speeds, the primary and secondary intake valves operate on their own camshaft lobes. This limited valve operation is designed to provide good low end torque

and responsiveness.

6   When performance is needed, the primary and secondary rocker arms are locked together through the use of an electrically controlled hydraulic system. Hydraulically operated synchronizing pistons lock all three rocker arms together. When activated, both intake valves open to the higher lift and duration of the middle rocker arm, which has its own camshaft lobe. **Note:** *The secondary rocker arm no longer contacts its own camshaft lobe until the system is disengaged.*

VTEC lock-up control solenoid valve/pressure switch

7   The lock-up VTEC solenoid valve, which includes an oil pressure switch, is located on the left rear of the cylinder head (firewall side of head).

1994 and 1995 models

8   A problem in the VTEC solenoid valve circuit will set a diagnostic trouble code (DTC) 21, and turn on the CHECK ENGINE light on the dash. Refer to Chapter 6 for accessing trouble codes.

9   A problem in the VTEC pressure switch circuit will set a diagnostic trouble code (DTC) 22, and turn on the CHECK ENGINE light on the dash.

1996 and later models

10   A problem in either the VTEC solenoid valve circuit or VTEC pressure switch circuit will turn on the CHECK ENGINE light and set diagnostic trouble code (DTC) P1259. Accessing this trouble code requires an OBD II SCAN tool. Refer to Chapter 6 for more information.

All models

11   Disconnect the round electrical connector from the pressure switch **(see illustration)**.

12   Connect an ohmmeter between the terminals of the switch. There should be continuity. If there is no continuity, replace the switch.

13   Connect a voltmeter between body

ground and the blue-black wire terminal in the harness side of the connector. With the ignition key ON (engine not running), there should be approximately 12 volts. If not, look for a break or bad connection in the blue-black wire between the connector and its terminal at the PCM.

14   Once you've got the correct voltage at the blue-black wire terminal in the connector, connect the voltmeter between both of the terminals in the harness side of the connector (blue-black and black wires). With the key ON, there should still be approximately 12 volts. If not, check the black wire (which supplies the ground for this circuit) for a break or bad connection between the connector and body ground.

15   With the ignition key OFF, disconnect the single-pin connector from the VTEC solenoid **(see illustration 9.11)**. Connect an ohmmeter between the terminal pin in the solenoid (not in the harness) and body ground. If the ohmmeter doesn't indicate 14 to 30 ohms, replace the solenoid as described below.

16   Remove the 10 mm bolt from the oil pressure test port on the solenoid. Attach a mechanical oil pressure gauge, using an appropriate adapter **(see illustration)**.

17   Warm the engine to normal operating temperature (until the electric cooling fan comes on).

18   Briefly run the engine at 1000 rpm, 3000 rpm and 5000 rpm, noting the oil pressure reading at each engine speed. **Caution:** *Don't run the engine for more than one minute at no-load.*

19   The oil pressure should be less than 7 psi. If it isn't, inspect the VTEC solenoid.

20   Connect a length of wire between the battery positive terminal and the VTEC solenoid terminal **(see illustration 9.11)**. Briefly run the engine at 5,000 rpm (no more than one minute) and check the oil pressure reading. It should now be 60 psi or more. If not, inspect the VTEC solenoid.

21   Remove the solenoid assembly, separate the pressure switch from the solenoid

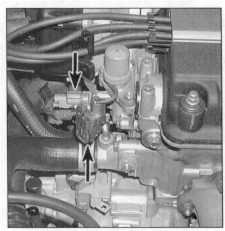

9.11 VTEC switch connector (upper arrow) and solenoid connector (lower arrow)

9.16 Connect an oil pressure gauge to the VTEC solenoid port (arrow)

2B

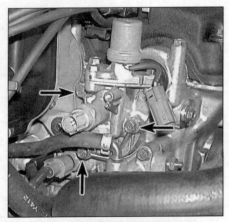

9.21a   VTEC solenoid mounting bolts (arrows)

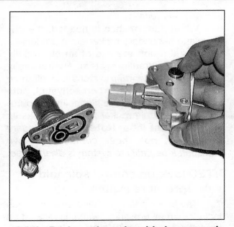

9.21b   Push on the solenoid plunger and check for free movement

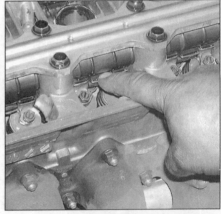

9.24   Press the mid rocker arm with a finger; it should move independently of the others

9.25   Rocker arms and synchronizing assembly (VTEC)

A)   *Primary rocker arm*
B)   *Secondary rocker arm*
C)   *Mid rocker arm*
D)   *Short piston*
E)   *Long piston*

and push the plunger to check for free movement **(see illustrations)**. Use a new O-ring when reinstalling the solenoid.
22   Check the filter/O-ring for clogging. Clean and reinstall with a new O-ring. If the filter was clogged, change the engine oil and filter to keep it from clogging again.

Rocker arms and oil control orifices

Refer to illustrations 9.24, 9.25 and 9.26
23   Remove the valve cover (see Section 4)

and place the no. 1 cylinder at TDC (see Section 3).
24   Press on the mid rocker arm with a finger **(see illustration)**. It should move separately from the primary and secondary rocker arms. If it doesn't, remove and disassemble the rocker arms for inspection (see Section 10).
25   Once the rocker arm assemblies have been removed and disassembled (see Section 10), separate the rocker arms and synchronizing pistons **(see illustration)**.
26   Inspect all other parts (rocker arms and

synchronizing pistons) for wear, galling, scoring or signs of overheating (bluish in color). Replace any parts necessary. Remove the oil control orifice from the intake and exhaust sides of the cylinder head **(see illustration)**, clean and reinstall them.
27   Reassembly is the reverse of removal. **Note:** *Reassemble and secure with a rubber band each cylinder's components before trying to assemble on the rocker shaft (see Section 10).*

Lost motion assemblies

Refer to illustration 9.30
28   The four lost motion assemblies sit in pockets in the cylinder head.
29   Remove the individual lost motion assemblies from the cylinder head (see Section 10).
30   Test each lost motion assembly by pushing the plunger with your finger **(see illustration)**. A light pressure should move the plunger slightly, and firmer pressure will move it further. If the assembly doesn't move smoothly, replace it.

---

10   Camshafts and rocker arms - removal, inspection and installation

Endplay and runout check

Refer to illustration 10.1
1   To check camshaft endplay:
  a) *Install the camshaft and secure it with the caps.*
  b) *Mount a dial indicator on the cylinder head with the gauge plunger touching the nose of the camshaft* **(see illustration)**.
  c) *Using a large screwdriver as a lever at the opposite end, move the camshaft forward-and-backward and note the dial indicator reading.*
  d) *Compare the reading with the endplay listed in this Chapter's Specifications.*
  e) *If the indicated reading is higher, either the camshaft or the head is worn. Replace parts as necessary.*

9.26 Pull out the intake oil orifice (shown) and the exhaust orifice (arrow); don't get the two mixed up

9.30   Check the lost motion sensors for free movement

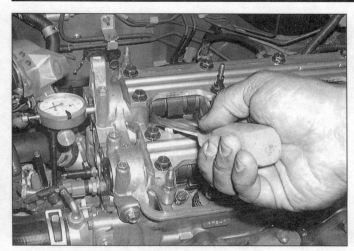

10.1 To check camshaft endplay, set a dial indicator like this, with the gauge plunger touching the nose of the camshaft

10.13a Lay a strip of Plastigage along each camshaft journal

2   To check camshaft runout:

a) *Support the camshaft with a pair of V-blocks and set up a dial indicator with the plunger resting against the center bearing journal on the camshaft.*

b) *Rotate the camshaft and note the indicated runout.*

c) *Compare the results to the camshaft runout listed in this Chapter's Specifications.*

d) *If the indicated runout exceeds the specified runout, replace the camshaft.*

B18B1 (non-VTEC) engine

Removal

3   Remove the distributor (see Chapter 5).

4   Remove the valve cover (see Section 4). Loosen the valve adjusting screws all the way (see Chapter 1).

5   Position the number one piston at Top Dead Center (see Section 3).

6   Remove the timing belt and camshaft sprockets (see Section 7).

7   Check the camshaft bearing caps for arrow marks pointing to the timing belt end of the engine. If you can't see them, make your own marks with a sharp scribe. Also number the bearing caps (1 through 6, starting at the timing belt end of the engine) and label them with an I for intake or E for exhaust. **Caution:** *Reinstalling the camshaft holders in the wrong positions (or turned around backwards) may cause the camshaft to seize.*

8   Loosen the camshaft bearing cap bolts 1/4-turn at a time, starting from the center and working outward, until the spring pressure is relieved.

9   Lift the camshafts from the cylinder head, then lift out the rocker arms. Label the rocker arms so they can be returned to their original locations.

Inspection

Refer to illustrations 10.13a and 10.13b

10   Thoroughly clean the parts and inspect them for wear and damage. Check the rocker arm faces that contact the camshaft and the rocker arm tips. Check the surfaces of the shafts that the rocker arms ride on, as well as the bearing surfaces inside the rocker arms, for scoring and excessive wear. Replace any parts that are damaged or excessively worn. Also, make sure the oil holes in the shafts are not plugged.

11   Check the camshaft lobes for wear:

a) *Check the toe and ramp areas of each cam lobe for score marks or uneven wear. Also check for flaking and pitting.*

b) *If there's wear on the toe or the ramp, replace the camshaft, but first try to find the cause of the wear. Look for abrasive substances in the oil and inspect the oil pump and oil passages for blockage. Lobe wear is usually caused by inadequate lubrication or dirty oil.*

c) *Using a micrometer, measure the cam lobe height* **(see illustration 12.10 in Chapter 2 Part A).**

12   Check the camshaft bearing journals and caps for signs of scoring and wear. If they are worn, replace the cylinder head with a new or rebuilt unit.

13   Check the oil clearance of each camshaft journal with Plastigage as follows.

a) *Clean the bearing caps and camshaft journals with lacquer thinner or acetone and a clean cloth.*

b) *Carefully lay the camshafts in place in the head. Don't use any lubricant.* **Note:** *Do not turn the camshaft during this procedure.*

c) *Lay a strip of Plastigage on each journal* **(see illustration)***.*

d) *Install the camshaft bearing caps and tighten the bolts in stages to the torque listed in this Chapter's Specifications, working from the center bolts outward.*

e) *Loosen the cam bearing cap bolts and lift the caps off.*

f) *Compare the width of the crushed Plastigage at its widest point to the scale on the Plastigage envelope* **(see illustration)***.*

g) *If the clearance is greater than that listed in this Chapter's Specifications, replace the worn parts as necessary.*

h) *Scrape off the Plastigage with your fingernail or the edge of a credit card - don't nick or scratch the journals or bearing caps.*

Installation

14   Lubricate all components with assembly lube or engine oil and reinstall the rocker arms. When installing the rocker arms, note the labels.

15   Coat the cam lobes and journals with camshaft installation lubricant. Lay the camshafts in their bearings, making sure the intake and exhaust camshafts are installed in the correct side of the head. Apply anaerobic-type sealant to the cylinder head contact surfaces of bearing caps 1 and 6 and install the bearing caps. Tighten the caps evenly in stages, working from the center outward, to the torque listed in this Chapter's Specifications.

16   The remainder of installation is the reverse of removal. Adjust the valve clearance, if necessary (see Chapter 1).

17   Run the engine and check for oil leaks and proper operation.

2B

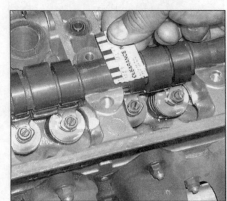

10.13b Measure the width of the flattened Plastigage

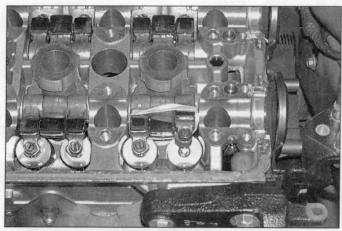

10.25 Wrap a rubber band around each rocker arm set to hold the components together

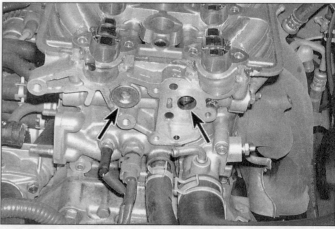

10.27a One of the rocker shafts (arrows) is secured by a threaded plug

B18C1 and B18C5 (VTEC) engines

Removal

Refer to illustrations 10.25, 10.27a, 10.27b and 10.28

18   Remove the timing belt and sprockets (see Section 7).

19   Remove the valve cover (see Section 4).

20   Remove the distributor and crankshaft fluctuation sensor (Chapters 5 and 6).

21   Loosen the valve adjustment locknuts and back off the screws all the way.

22   Check the camshaft bearing caps for arrow marks pointing to the timing belt end of the engine. If you can't see them, make your own marks with a sharp scribe. Also number the bearing caps (1 through 6, starting at the timing belt end of the engine) and label them with an I for intake or E for exhaust. **Caution:** *Reinstalling the camshaft holders in the wrong positions (or turned around backwards) may cause the camshaft to seize.*

23   Loosen the camshaft holder plate and bearing cap bolts 1/4-turn at a time, starting from the center and working outward, until the spring pressure is relieved **(see illustration 10.37)**. Lift off the holder plates and

bearing caps. There's a dowel with an O-ring in the underside of the no. 3 (center) bearing cap. Locate these so they won't be lost.

24   Lift the camshafts from the cylinder head.

25   Wrap each set of rocker arms with a rubber band before you remove them so the sets can be kept together **(see illustration)**.

26   Since the cylinder head bolts pass through the rocker shafts, you'll need to remove them to get the shafts out (See Section 12). You'll also need to remove the oil control orifice from each rocker shaft (see Section 10).

27   Thread a 12 mm bolt into the end of each rocker shaft and use it to pull the rocker shafts from the head **(see illustrations)**.

28   Remove the lost motion assemblies from the head **(see illustration)**. Inspect them as described in Section 9.

Inspection

29   Inspect the camshaft and rocker arms as described in Steps 10 through 13 above.

30   Disassemble each set of rocker arms and check the rocker arms and synchronizing pistons as described in Section 9. Be sure to keep the components from each set

together. Reassemble the sets after inspection if you're going to reinstall them, then secure each set together with a rubber band.

Installation

Refer to illustrations 10.35 and 10.27

31   Install the lost motion assemblies **(see illustration 10.28)**.

32   Lubricate all components with engine assembly lubricant or engine oil. Loosen the valve adjusting screws all the way. Lay the assembled rocker arms in their original locations, then install the shafts. There's a bore in each rocker shaft that accepts the oil control orifice. If the bores aren't aligned after the rocker shafts are installed, insert a 12 mm bolt into the end of the rocker shaft and use it as a handle to move the rocker shaft around until they align.

33   Replace the O-ring on each oil control orifice, then install the orifices in the cylinder head (see Section 9). Be sure to install the intake and exhaust orifices in the correct locations. Also make sure the orifices fit into their bores in the rocker shafts. They should prevent the rocker shafts from turning when correctly installed.

34   Coat the cam lobes and journals with camshaft installation lubricant. Lay the camshafts in their bearings, making sure the intake and exhaust camshafts are installed in the correct side of the head.

35   Make sure the oil seal contact surfaces of the cylinder head are clean and dry and install new oil seals **(see illustration)**. The oil seal springs face toward the cylinder head.

36   Apply anaerobic-type sealant to the cylinder head contact surfaces of bearing caps 1 and 5 and install the bearing caps.

37   Install the holders on the bearing caps. Tighten the caps evenly in stages, in the correct sequence, to the torque listed in this Chapter's Specifications **(see illustration)**.

38   The remainder of installation is the reverse of removal. Adjust the valve clearance (see Chapter 1).

39   Run the engine and check for oil leaks and proper operation.

10.27b Thread a bolt into each rocker shaft and use it to pull the shaft out

10.28 Remove the lost motion assemblies (arrow) from their bores in the cylinder head

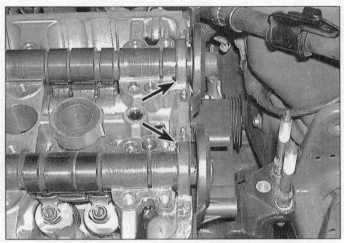

10.35 Install new oil seals (arrows) on the camshafts at the timing belt end of the engine

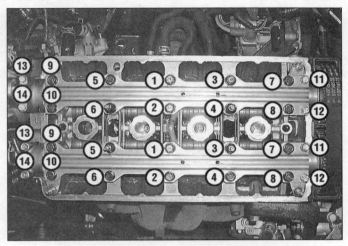

10.37 Camshaft holder TIGHTENING sequence

11 Valve springs, retainers and seals - replacement

Replacing broken valve springs and defective valve stem seals requires removing the head from the engine on VTEC models. Remove the camshafts and cylinder head, then refer to Chapter 2 Part C to remove the valves, valve springs and stem seals.

On non-VTEC models, they can be replaced without removing the cylinder head, but a special type of valve spring compressor is required. Refer to Chapter 2 Part A for the procedure.

12 Cylinder head - removal and installation

Caution: *Allow the engine to cool completely before beginning this procedure.*

Removal

Refer to illustration 12.2

1   Position the number one piston at Top Dead Center (see Section 3).

2   Disconnect the negative cable from the battery and disconnect the ground cable from the engine **(see illustration)**. **Caution:** *If the radio in your vehicle is equipped with an anti-theft system, make sure you have the correct activation code before disconnecting the battery.*

3   Drain the cooling system and remove the spark plugs (see Chapter 1).

4   Remove the air cleaner duct and housing (see Chapter 4).

5   Remove the drivebelts (see Chapter 1). Unbolt the power steering pump and set it aside with out disconnecting any hoses, then remove the power steering pump bracket (see Chapter 10).

6   Disconnect the throttle cable and relieve the fuel system pressure (see Chapter 4).

2B

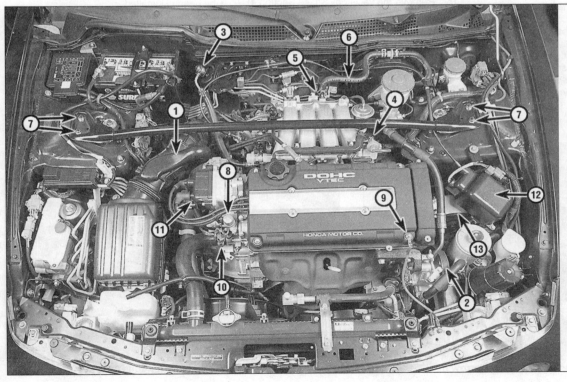

12.2 Cylinder head removal points (VTEC shown)

1   Air intake duct
2   Power steering pump
3   Fuel feed line
4   Fuel return line
5   PCV hose
6   Brake booster vacuum hose
7   Strut brace fasteners
8   VTEC solenoid/pressure switch
9   Engine ground cable
10   Coolant hose
11   Distributor
12   Cruise control actuator
13   Upper engine mount

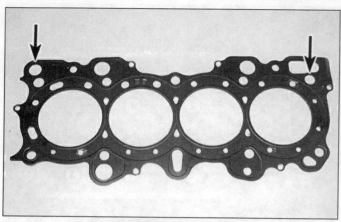

12.25 Cylinder head dowel locations (arrows)

12.26 Cylinder head TIGHTENING sequence

7   Disconnect the following hoses and lines (Chapters 4 and 6):

a) *Fuel feed and return hoses*
b) *Evaporative emission control hose*
c) *Breather hose*
d) *PCV hose*
e) *Brake booster vacuum hose*

8   Disconnect the coolant bypass hose, heater hose and upper radiator hose (see Chapter 3).

9   If you're working on a VTEC model, remove the strut brace that passes across the engine compartment (see Part C of this Chapter).

10   Disconnect the following electrical connectors:

a) *Fuel injectors*
b) *Engine coolant temperature sensor*
c) *Temperature gauge sender*
d) *TDC/crankshaft/camshaft position sensor*
e) *Crankshaft fluctuation sensor*
f) *Ignition coil*
g) *Throttle position sensor*
h) *Manifold absolute pressure sensor*
i) *Evap purge control solenoid*
j) *VTEC solenoid (18C1 and 18C5 engines)*
k) *VTEC pressure switch (18C1 and 18C5 engines)*

l) *Idle air control valve*
m) *Intake air bypass control solenoid (18C1 and 18C5 engines)*

11   Remove the cruise control actuator (see Chapter 12).
12   Remove the splash shield from under the engine compartment.
13   Support the engine with a floor jack. Place a wood block between the jack pad and the oil pan to avoid damaging the pan. Remove the upper engine mounting bracket (see Section 17).
14   Remove the intake manifold brace and exhaust manifold flange bolts. **Note:** *You may wish to detach the intake manifold (see Section 5) and/or exhaust manifold (see Section 6), rather than removing it with the cylinder head, to make the cylinder head easier to handle.*
15   Remove the valve cover (see Section 4).
16   Remove the distributor (see Chapter 5), including the cap and wires.
17   Remove the timing belt (see Section 7), camshafts and the rocker arm assembly (see Section 10).
18   Loosen the head bolts in 1/4-turn increments until they can be removed by hand. Work in a pattern that's the reverse of the tightening sequence **(see illustration 12.26)** to avoid warping the head. Note where each

bolt goes so it can be returned to the same location on installation.
19   Lift the head off the engine. If resistance is felt, don't pry between the head and block gasket mating surfaces - damage to the mating surfaces will result. Instead, pry between the power steering pump bracket and the engine block. Set the head on blocks of wood to prevent damage to the gasket sealing surfaces.
20   Cylinder head disassembly and inspection procedures are covered in detail in Chapter 2 Part C. Check the cylinder head for warpage.

Installation

Refer to illustrations 12.25 and 12.26

21   The mating surfaces of the cylinder head and block must be perfectly clean when the head is installed.
22   Use a gasket scraper to remove all traces of carbon and old gasket material, then clean the mating surfaces with lacquer thinner or acetone. If there's oil on the mating surfaces when the head is installed, the gasket may not seal correctly and leaks may develop. When working on the engine block, stuff the cylinders with clean shop rags to keep out debris. Use a vacuum cleaner to remove material that falls into the cylinders.

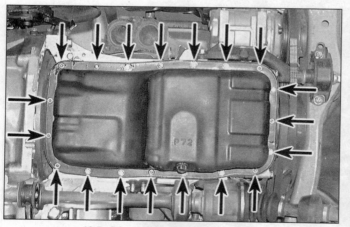

13.5 Oil pan bolt locations (arrows)

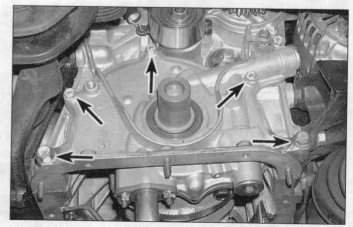

14.4 Oil pump bolt locations (arrows)

14.5 Remove the oil pump cover screws (arrows)

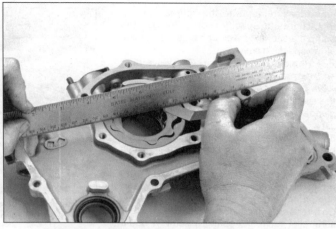

14.6a Use a feeler gauge and straight-edge to check the clearance between the rotors and the cover

Since the cylinder head and block are made of aluminum, aggressive scraping can cause damage. Be extra careful not to nick or gouge the mating surfaces with the scraper.

23 Check the engine block and cylinder head mating surfaces for nicks, deep scratches and other damage. If damage is slight, it can be removed with a file; if it's excessive, machining may be the only alternative.

24 Use a tap of the correct size to chase the threads in the head bolt holes. Mount each head bolt in a vise and run a die down the threads to remove corrosion and restore the threads. Dirt, corrosion, sealant and damaged threads will affect torque readings.

25 Place a new gasket on the engine block. Check to see if there are any markings (such as "TOP") on the gasket that say how it is to be installed. Those identification marks must face UP. Make sure the dowels are in the correct locations **(see illustration)**, and install the cylinder head oil orifice with a new O-ring. Set the cylinder head in position.

26 Lubricate the threads and the seats of the cylinder head bolts with clean engine oil, then install them. Following the recommended sequence, tighten the cylinder head bolts to the torque listed in this Chapter's Specifications **(see illustration)**.

27 Attach the camshaft sprockets to the camshafts and install the timing belt (see Section 10).

28 Reinstall the remaining parts in the reverse order of removal.

29 Be sure to refill the cooling system and check all fluid levels.

30 Rotate the crankshaft counterclockwise slowly by hand through two complete revolutions. **Caution:** *If you feel any resistance while turning the engine over, stop and recheck the camshaft timing. The valves may be hitting the pistons.*

31 Start the engine and check the ignition timing (see Chapter 1).

32 Run the engine until normal operating temperature is reached. Check for leaks and proper operation.

13 Oil pan - removal and installation

Removal

Refer to illustration 13.5

1 Warm up the engine, then drain the oil and replace the oil filter (see Chapter 1).

2 Detach the cable from the negative battery terminal. **Caution:** *If the radio in your vehicle is equipped with an anti-theft system, make sure you have the correct activation code before disconnecting the battery.*

3 Raise the vehicle and support it securely on jackstands. Remove the splash shield from under the engine.

4 Remove the front exhaust pipe (see Chapter 5).

5 Remove the bolts securing the oil pan to the engine block **(see illustration)**.

6 Tap on the pan with a soft-face hammer to break the gasket seal, then detach the oil pan from the engine. Don't pry between the block and oil pan mating surfaces.

7 Using a gasket scraper, remove all traces of old gasket and/or sealant from the engine block and oil pan. Remove the seals from each end of the engine block or oil pan. Clean the mating surfaces with lacquer thinner or acetone. Make sure the threaded bolt holes in the block are clean.

Installation

8 Clean the oil pan with solvent and dry it thoroughly. Check the gasket flanges for distortion, particularly around the bolt holes. If necessary, place the pan on a wood block and use a hammer to flatten and restore the gasket surfaces.

9 Apply a 1/8-inch wide bead of RTV sealant to the oil pan gasket surfaces. Make sure the sealant is applied to the inside edge of the bolt holes.

10 Carefully place the oil pan in position.

11 Install the bolts and tighten them in small increments to the torque listed in this Chapter's Specifications. Start with the bolts closest to the center of the pan and work out in a spiral pattern. Don't overtighten them or

leakage may occur.

12 Add oil (see Chapter 1), run the engine and check for oil leaks.

14 Oil pump - removal, inspection and installation

Removal

Refer to illustrations 14.4 and 14.5

1 Remove the timing belt (see Section 7).

2 Remove the oil pan (see Section 13).

3 Remove the oil pick-up tube and screen from the pump housing and the main bearing cap bridge.

4 Remove the bolts from the oil pump housing and separate the assembly from the engine **(see illustration)**.

5 Remove the screws and disassemble the oil pump **(see illustration)**. You may need to use an impact screwdriver to loosen the pump cover screws without stripping the heads.

Inspection

Refer to illustrations 14.6a, 14.6b and 14.6c

6 Check the oil pump rotor-to-cover-clearance, tooth tip clearance and rotor-to-body clearance **(see illustrations)**. Compare

14.6b Use a feeler gauge to check the tooth-tip clearance between the inner and outer rotors

your measurements to the figures listed in this Chapter's Specifications. Replace the pump if any of the measurements are outside of the specified limits.

7 Remove the pressure relief valve plug and extract the spring and pressure relief valve plunger from the pump housing. Check the spring for distortion and the relief valve plunger for scoring. Replace parts as necessary.

8 Install the pump rotors. Pack the spaces between the rotors with petroleum jelly (this will prime the pump).

9 Apply thread-locking compound to the pump cover screws, install the cover and tighten the screws to the torque listed in this Chapter's Specifications. Install the oil pressure relief valve and spring assembly. Use a new sealing washer on the plug and tighten the plug securely.

Installation

10 Apply a thin coat of RTV sealant to the pump housing-to-block sealing surface and a new O-ring in the pump housing. Install the pump housing to the engine block and tighten the bolts to the torque listed in this Chapter's Specifications.

11 Install the oil pick-up tube and screen, using a new gasket. Tighten the bolts to the torque listed in this Chapter's Specifications.

12 Install the oil pan (see Section 13).

13 The remainder of installation is the reverse of removal. Add the specified type and quantity of oil and coolant (see Chapter 1), run the engine and check for leaks.

---

15 Flywheel/driveplate - removal and installation

Refer to Chapter 2 Part A for this procedure.

---

16 Rear main oil seal - replacement

Refer to Chapter 2 Part A for this procedure.

---

17 Engine mounts - check and replacement

1 Engine mounts seldom require attention, but broken or deteriorated mounts should be replaced immediately or the added strain placed on the driveline components may cause damage or wear.

Check

2 During the check, the engine must be raised slightly to remove the weight from the mounts.

3 Raise the vehicle and support it securely on jackstands, then position a jack under the engine oil pan. Place a large wood block between the jack head and the oil pan, then

14.6c Use a feeler gauge to check the outer rotor-to-pump body clearance

carefully raise the engine just enough to take the weight off the mounts. **Warning:** *DO NOT place any part of your body under the engine when it's supported only by a jack!*

4 Check the mount insulators to see if the rubber is cracked, hardened or separated from the metal plates. Sometimes the rubber will split right down the center.

5 Check for relative movement between the mount plates and the engine or frame (use a large screwdriver or pry bar to attempt to move the mounts). If movement is noted, lower the engine and tighten the mount fasteners.

6 Rubber preservative should be applied to the insulators to slow deterioration.

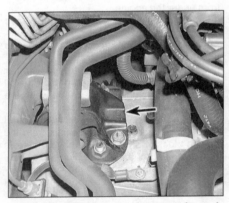

17.9b Right side transaxle mount (arrow)

17.9d Rear engine mount at engine (arrow)

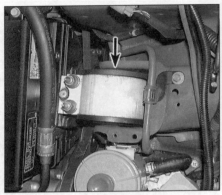

17.9a Upper engine mount (arrow)

Replacement

Refer to illustrations 17.9a through 17.9e

7 Disconnect the battery cable from the negative battery terminal. **Caution:** *If the radio in your vehicle is equipped with an anti-theft system, make sure you have the correct activation code before disconnecting the battery.* Raise the vehicle and support it securely on jackstands (if not already done). Support the engine as described in Step 3.

8 Remove the fasteners, raise the engine with the jack and detach the mount from the frame bracket and engine.

9 Install the new mount, making sure it is correctly positioned in its bracket **(see illustrations)**. Install the fasteners and tighten them securely.

17.9c Right front transaxle mount (arrow)

17.9e Right front mount at firewall (arrow)

Chapter 2 Part C
General engine overhaul procedures

Contents

2C

Specifications

Civic engine

General
Cylinder compression pressure
Standard	184 psi
Minimum	135 psi
Maximum variation between cylinders	28 psi

Oil pressure (hot)
At idle	10 psi
At 3000 rpm	50 psi

Engine block
Cylinder bore diameter
Standard	2.9528 to 2.9535 inches
Service limit	2.9555 inches maximum
Cylinder taper limit	0.002 inch maximum
Cylinder out-of-round limit	0.002 inch maximum
Cylinder overbore limit	0.020 inch maximum
Block deck warpage limit	0.004 inch maximum

Pistons and rings
Piston diameter
Standard	2.9520 to 2.9524 inches
Service limit	2.9516 inches minimum
Diameter measurement point (from bottom)	13/64 inch

Piston-to-cylinder wall clearance
Standard	0.0004 to 0.0016 inch
Service limit	0.002 inch maximum

Ring groove clearance
Top compression ring
Standard	0.0014 to 0.0024 inch
Service limit	0.005 inch maximum

Second compression ring
Standard	0.0012 to 0.0022 inch
Service limit	0.005 inch maximum

Civic engine (continued)

Pistons and rings

Ring end gap
   Top compression ring
      Standard .... 0.006 to 0.012 inch
      Service limit.. 0.024 inch maximum
   Second compression ring
      Standard .... 0.012 to 0.018 inch
      Service limit.. 0.028 inch maximum
   Oil control ring
      Standard .... 0.008 to 0.028 inch
      Service limit.. 0.031 inch maximum

Crankshaft and connecting rods

Endplay
   Standard.. 0.004 to 0.014 inch
   Service limit .... 0.018 inch maximum
Main bearing journals
   Diameter.. 2.1644 to 2.1654 inches
   Taper .... 0.0002 inch maximum
   Out-of-round .... 0.0002 inch maximum
   Runout .... 0.002 inch maximum
Main bearing oil clearance
   Journals no. 1 and 5
      Standard .... 0.0007 to 0.0014 inch
      Service limit.. 0.002 inch maximum
   Journals no. 2, 3 and 4
      Standard .... 0.0009 to 0.0017 inch
      Service limit.. 0.002 inch maximum
Connecting rod journal
   Diameter.. 1.7707 to 1.7717 inches
   Taper .... 0.0002 inch maximum
   Out-of-round .... 0.0002 inch maximum
   Runout .... 0.002 inch maximum
Connecting rod bearing oil clearance
   Standard.. 0.0008 to 0.0015 inch
   Service limit .... 0.002 inch maximum
Connecting rod side clearance (endplay)
   Standard.. 0.006 to 0.012 inch
   Service limit .... 0.016 inch maximum

Cylinder head and valves

Head warpage limits
   Maximum without resurfacing...................................... 0.002 inch
   Service limit .... 0.008 inch
Cylinder head height.. 3.659 to 3.663 inches
Valve seat angle... 45-degrees
Valve face angle... 45-degrees
Valve margin width
   Intake.. 0.026 inch minimum
   Exhaust... 0.037 inch minimum
Valve stem diameter
   Intake
      Standard .... 0.2157 to 0.2161 inch
      Service limit.. 0.2146 inch
   Exhaust
      Standard .... 0.2146 to 0.2150 inch
      Service limit.. 0.2134 inch
Valve guide inside diameter
   Standard.. 0.217 to 0.218 inch
   Service limit .... 0.219 inch maximum
Valve stem-to-guide clearance
   Intake
      Standard .... 0.001 to 0.002 inch
      Service limit.. 0.003 inch maximum
   Exhaust
      Standard .... 0.002 to 0.003 inch
      Service limit.. 0.004 inch maximum

Valve stem installed height
    Standard.. 2.093 to 2.112 inches
    Service limit... 2.122 inches maximum
Valve spring free length
    D16Y7.. 2.28 inches
    D16Y5
        Intake .... 2.22 inches
        Exhaust .... 2.28 inches
    D16Y8
        Intake .... 2.28 inches
        Exhaust .... 2.31 inches

Torque specifications*

                                                       Ft-lbs
Main bearing cap bolts
    Step 1.. 18
    Step 2.. 38
Connecting rod bearing cap nuts... 23

Refer to Part A or Part B for additional torque specifications.

Integra engine

General

Cylinder compression pressure
    B18B1
        Standard... 199 psi
        Minimum .... 140 psi
        Maximum variation between cylinders .... 28 psi
    B18C1, B18C5
        Standard... 270 psi
        Minimum .... 140 psi
        Maximum variation between cylinders .... 28 psi
Oil pressure (hot)
    At idle .... 10 psi
    At 3000 rpm.. 50 psi

Engine block

Cylinder bore diameter
    Standard.. 3.189 to 3.190 inches
    Service limit... 3.192 inches
Cylinder taper limit.. 0.002 inch maximum
Cylinder out-of-round limit .... 0.002 inch maximum
Cylinder overbore limit.. 0.010 inch maximum
Block deck warpage limit .... 0.004 inch maximum

Pistons and rings

Piston diameter
    Standard.. 3.188 to 3.189 inches
    Service limit... 3.188 inches minimum
Diameter measurement point (from bottom) .... 19/32 inch
Piston-to-cylinder wall clearance
    Standard.. 0.0004 to 0.0016 inch
    Service limit... 0.002 inch maximum
Ring groove clearance
    Top compression ring
        Standard... 0.0018 to 0.0028 inch
        Service limit.. 0.005 inch maximum
    Second compression ring
        B18B1 (Riken brand) .... 0.0016 to 0.0026 inch
        B18B1 (Teikoku brand) .... 0.0018 to 0.0028 inch
        B18C1, B18C5
            Standard... 0.0018 to 0.0028 inch
            Service limit (all) .... 0.005 inch maximum
Ring end gap
    Top compression ring
        B18B1 (Riken brand)... 0.008 to 0.014 inch
        B18B1 (Teikoku brand) .... 0.008 to 0.012 inch
        B18C1, B18C5
            Standard... 0.008 to 0.014 inch
            Service limit (all) .... 0.024 inch maximum

Integra engine (continued)

Pistons and rings

Second compression ring
    Standard .... 0.016 to 0.022 inch
    Service limit... 0.028 inch maximum
Oil control ring
    B18B1 (Riken brand)... 0.008 to 0.020 inch
    B18B1 (Teikoku brand) .... 0.008 to 0.018 inch
    B18C1, B18C5
        Standard .... 0.008 to 0.020 inch
        Service limit (all)... 0.028 inch maximum

Crankshaft and connecting rods

Endplay
    Standard.. 0.004 to 0.014 inch
    Service limit .... 0.018 inch maximum
Main bearing journals
    Diameter
        No. 1, 2, 4 and 5 journals... 2.1644 to 2.1654 inches
        No. 3 journal
            B18B1... 2.1642 to 2.1651 inches
            B18C1, B18C5.. 2.1643 to 2.1653 inches
        Taper .... 0.0004 inch maximum
        Out-of-round .... 0.0004 inch maximum
        Runout .... 0.002 inch maximum
Main bearing oil clearance
    Journals no. 1, 2, 4 and 5
        Standard .... 0.0009 to 0.0017 inch
        Service limit.. 0.002 inch maximum
    Journal no. 3
        Standard .... 0.0012 to 0.0019 inch
        Service limit.. 0.0024 inch maximum
Connecting rod journal
    Diameter.. 1.7707 to 1.7717 inches
    Taper .... 0.0004 inch maximum
    Out-of-round .... 0.0004 inch maximum
    Runout .... 0.002 inch maximum
Connecting rod bearing oil clearance
    B18B1
        Standard .... 0.0008 to 0.0015 inch
        Service limit.. 0.002 inch maximum
    B18C1, B18C5
        Standard .... 0.0013 to 0.0020 inch
        Service limit.. 0.0024 inch maximum
Connecting rod side clearance (endplay)
    Standard.. 0.006 to 0.012 inch
    Service limit .... 0.016 inch maximum

Cylinder head and valves

Head warpage limits
    Maximum without resurfacing.. 0.002 inch
    Service limit .... 0.008 inch
Valve seat angle... 45-degrees
Valve face angle... 45-degrees
Valve margin width
    Intake .... 0.045 inch minimum
    Exhaust.. 0.057 inch minimum
Valve stem diameter
    B18B1
        Intake
            Standard... 0.2591 to 0.2594 inch
            Service limit.. 0.258 inch minimum
        Exhaust
            Standard... 0.2579 to 0.2583 inch
            Service limit.. 0.257 inch minimum
    B18C1, B18C5
        Intake
            Standard... 0.2156 to 0.2159 inch
            Service limit.. 0.2144 inch minimum

2C

Exhaust
  Standard .... 0.2146 to 0.2150 inch
  Service limit .... 0.2134 inch minimum
Valve guide inside diameter
  B18B1
    Standard .... 0.260 to 0.261 inch
    Service limit .... 0.262 inch maximum
  B18C1, B18C5
    Standard .... 0.217 to 0.218 inch
    Service limit .... 0.219 inch maximum
Valve stem-to-guide clearance
  Intake
    Standard .... 0.001 to 0.002 inch
    Service limit .... 0.003 inch maximum
  Exhaust
    Standard .... 0.002 to 0.003 inch
    Service limit .... 0.004 inch maximum
Valve stem installed height
  B18B1
    Intake
      Standard .... 1.6049 to 1.6234 inches
      Service limit .... 1.6333 inches maximum
    Exhaust
      Standard .... 1.6837 to 1.7022 inches
      Service limit .... 1.7120 inches maximum
  B18C1, B18C5
    Intake
      Standard .... 1.4750 to 1.4935 inches
      Service limit .... 1.5033 inches maximum
    Exhaust
      Standard .... 1.4632 to 1.4817 inches
      Service limit .... 1.4915 inches maximum
Valve spring free length
  B18B1
    Intake .... 1.668 inches
    Exhaust .... 1.854 inches
  B18C1
    Intake
      Outer .... 1.616 inches
      Inner (Nihon Hatsujo brand) .... 1.424 inches
      Inner (Chuo Hatsujo brand) .... 1.425 inches
    Exhaust
      Nihon Hatsujo brand .... 1.652 inches
      Chuo Hatsujo brand .... 1.651 inches
  B18C5
    Intake
      Outer .... 1.700 inches
      Inner .... 1.450 inches
    Exhaust
      Outer .... 1.616 inches
      Inner .... 1.424 inches

Torque specifications*

Ft-lbs

Main bearing cap bolts
  Step 1 22
  Step 2
    B18B1 56
    B18C1, B18C5
      No. 1 and 5 caps 56
      No. 2, 3 and 4 caps 49
Connecting rod bearing cap nuts
  Step 1 14
  Step 2
    B18B1 23
    B18C1, B18C5 33

* Refer to Part A or Part B for additional torque specifications.

2.2a On the Civic engine, the oil pressure sending unit is located directly above the oil filter (filter removed for clarity)

2.2b The oil pressure sending unit on the Integra engine is located to the side of the oil filter

1   General information

Included in this portion of Chapter 2 are the general overhaul procedures for the cylinder head and internal engine components.

The information ranges from advice concerning preparation for an overhaul and the purchase of replacement parts to detailed, step-by-step procedures covering Removal and installation of internal engine components and the inspection of parts.

The following Sections have been written based on the assumption that the engine has been removed from the vehicle. For information concerning in-vehicle engine repair, as well as removal and installation of the external components necessary for the overhaul, see Chapter 2, Part A or part B.

The Specifications included in this Part are only those necessary for the inspection and overhaul procedures which follow. Refer to Chapter 2, Part A or Part B for additional Specifications.

It's not always easy to determine when, or if, an engine should be completely overhauled, as a number of factors must be considered.

High mileage is not necessarily an indication that an overhaul is needed, while low mileage doesn't preclude the need for an overhaul. Frequency of servicing is probably the most important consideration. An engine that's had regular and frequent oil and filter changes, as well as other required maintenance, will most likely give many thousands of miles of reliable service. Conversely, a neglected engine may require an overhaul very early in its life.

Excessive oil consumption is an indication that piston rings, valve seals and/or valve guides are in need of attention. Make sure that oil leaks aren't responsible before deciding that the rings and/or guides are bad. Perform a cylinder compression check to determine the extent of the work required (see Section 3). Also check the vacuum readings under various conditions (see Section 4).

Loss of power, rough running, knocking or metallic engine noises, excessive valve train noise and high fuel consumption rates may also point to the need for an overhaul, especially if they're all present at the same time. If a complete tune-up doesn't remedy the situation, major mechanical work is the only solution.

An engine overhaul involves restoring the internal parts to the specifications of a new engine. During an overhaul, the piston rings are replaced and the cylinder walls are reconditioned (re-bored and/or honed). If a re-bore is done by an automotive machine shop, new oversize pistons will also be installed. The main bearings, connecting rod bearings and camshaft bearings are generally replaced with new ones and, if necessary, the crankshaft may be reground to restore the journals. Generally, the valves are serviced as well, since they're usually in less-than-perfect condition at this point. While the engine is being overhauled, other components, such as the distributor, starter and alternator, can be rebuilt as well. The end result should be a like new engine that will give many trouble free miles. **Note:** *Critical cooling system components such as the hoses, drivebelts, thermostat and water pump should be replaced with new parts when an engine is overhauled. The radiator should be checked carefully to ensure that it isn't clogged or leaking (see Chapter 3). If you purchase a rebuilt engine or short block, some rebuilders will not warranty their engines unless the radiator has been professionally flushed. Also, be sure to check the oil pump carefully, as described in Chapter 2A or 2B.*

Before beginning the engine overhaul, read through the entire procedure to familiarize yourself with the scope and requirements of the job. Overhauling an engine isn't difficult, but it is time-consuming. Plan on the vehicle being tied up for a minimum of two weeks, especially if parts must be taken to an automotive machine shop for repair or reconditioning. Check on availability of parts and make sure that any necessary special tools and equipment are obtained in advance. Most work can be done with typical hand tools, although a number of precision measuring tools are required for inspecting parts to determine if they must be replaced. Often an automotive machine shop will handle the inspection of parts and offer advice concerning reconditioning and replacement. **Note:** *Always wait until the engine has been completely disassembled and all components, especially the engine block, have been inspected before deciding what service and repair operations must be performed by an automotive machine shop. Since the block's condition will be the major factor to consider when determining whether to overhaul the original engine or buy a rebuilt one, never purchase parts or have machine work done on other components until the block has been thoroughly inspected.* As a general rule, time is the primary cost of an overhaul, so it doesn't pay to install worn or substandard parts.

As a final note, to ensure maximum life and minimum trouble from a rebuilt engine, everything must be assembled with care in a spotlessly-clean environment.

2   Oil pressure check

Refer to illustrations 2.2a and 2.2b

1   Low engine oil pressure can be a sign of an engine in need of rebuilding. A "low oil pressure" indicator (often called an "idiot light") is not a test of the oiling system. Such indicators only come on when the oil pressure is dangerously low. Even a factory oil pressure gauge in the instrument panel is only a relative indication, although much better for driver information than a warning light. A better test is with a mechanical (not electrical) oil pressure gauge. When used in conjunction with an accurate tachometer, an engine's oil pressure performance can be compared to factory Specifications for that year and model.

2   Locate the oil pressure indicator sending unit **(see illustrations)**.

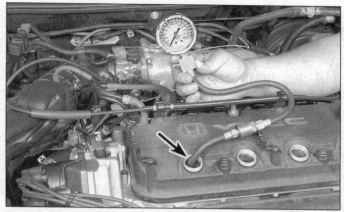

3.7 To use a compression gauge, you must have a gauge with an adapter long enough to reach down the spark plug tubes (arrow) - be sure to open the throttle as far as possible during the compression check

4.4 A simple vacuum gauge can be very handy in diagnosing engine condition and performance

3 Remove the oil pressure sending unit and install a fitting which will allow you to directly connect your hand-held, mechanical oil pressure gauge. Use Teflon tape or sealant on the threads of the adapter and the fitting on the end of your gauge's hose.

4 Connect an accurate tachometer to the engine, according to the tachometer manufacturer's instructions.

5 Check the oil pressure with the engine running (normal operating temperature) at the specified engine speed, and compare it to this Chapter's Specifications. If it's extremely low, the bearings and/or oil pump are probably worn out.

3 Cylinder compression check

Refer to illustration 3.7

1 A compression check will tell you what mechanical condition the upper end (pistons, rings, valves, head gaskets) of the engine is in. Specifically, it can tell you if the compression is down due to leakage caused by worn piston rings, defective valves and seats or a blown head gasket. **Note:** *The engine must be at normal operating temperature and the battery must be fully charged for this check.*

2 Begin by cleaning the area around the spark plugs before you remove them. Compressed air should be used, if available, otherwise a small brush or even a bicycle tire pump will work. The idea is to prevent dirt from getting into the cylinders as the compression check is being done.

3 Remove all of the spark plugs from the engine (see Chapter 1).

4 Block the throttle wide open.

5 Disable the fuel system by removing the PGM-FI main relay fuse (see Chapter 4).

6 Disable the ignition system by detaching the primary connectors at the distributor (see Chapter 5).

7 Install the compression gauge in the number one spark plug hole **(see illustration)**.

8 Crank the engine over at least seven compression strokes and watch the gauge. The compression should build up quickly in a healthy engine. Low compression on the first stroke, followed by gradually increasing pressure on successive strokes, indicates worn piston rings. A low compression reading on the first stroke, which doesn't build up during successive strokes, indicates leaking valves or a blown head gasket (a cracked head could also be the cause). Deposits on the undersides of the valve heads can also cause low compression. Record the highest gauge reading obtained.

9 Repeat the procedure for the remaining cylinders and compare the results to this Chapter's Specifications.

10 If the readings are below normal, add some engine oil (about three squirts from a plunger-type oil can) to each cylinder, through the spark plug hole, and repeat the test.

11 If the compression increases significantly after the oil is added, the piston rings are definitely worn. If the compression doesn't increase significantly, the leakage is occurring at the valves or head gasket. Leakage past the valves may be caused by burned valve seats and/or faces or warped, cracked or bent valves.

12 If two adjacent cylinders have equally low compression, there's a strong possibility the head gasket between them is blown. The appearance of coolant in the combustion chambers or the crankcase would verify this condition.

13 If one cylinder is about 20-percent lower than the others, and the engine has a slightly rough idle, a worn exhaust lobe on the camshaft could be the cause.

14 If the compression is unusually high, the combustion chambers are probably coated with carbon deposits. If that's the case, the cylinder head(s) should be removed and decarbonized.

15 If compression is way down or varies greatly between cylinders, it would be a good idea to have a leak-down test performed by

an automotive repair shop. This test will pinpoint exactly where the leakage is occurring and how severe it is.

4 Vacuum gauge diagnostic checks

Refer to illustrations 4.4 and 4.6

A vacuum gauge provides valuable information about what is going on in the engine at a low-cost. You can check for worn rings or cylinder walls, leaking head or intake manifold gaskets, incorrect carburetor adjustments, restricted exhaust, stuck or burned valves, weak valve springs, improper ignition or valve timing and ignition problems.

Unfortunately, vacuum gauge readings are easy to misinterpret, so they should be used in conjunction with other tests to confirm the diagnosis.

Both the absolute readings and the rate of needle movement are important for accurate interpretation. Most gauges measure vacuum in inches of mercury (in-Hg). The following references to vacuum assume the diagnosis is being performed at sea level. As elevation increases (or atmospheric pressure decreases), the reading will decrease. For every 1,000 foot increase in elevation above approximately 2000 feet, the gauge readings will decrease about one inch of mercury.

Connect the vacuum gauge directly to intake manifold vacuum, not to ported (throttle body) vacuum **(see illustration)**. Be sure no hoses are left disconnected during the test or false readings will result.

Before you begin the test, allow the engine to warm up completely. Block the wheels and set the parking brake. With the transmission in Park, start the engine and allow it to run at normal idle speed. **Warning:** *Keep your hands and the vacuum gauge clear of the fans.*

Read the vacuum gauge; an average, healthy engine should normally produce about 17 to 22 in-Hg with a fairly steady nee-

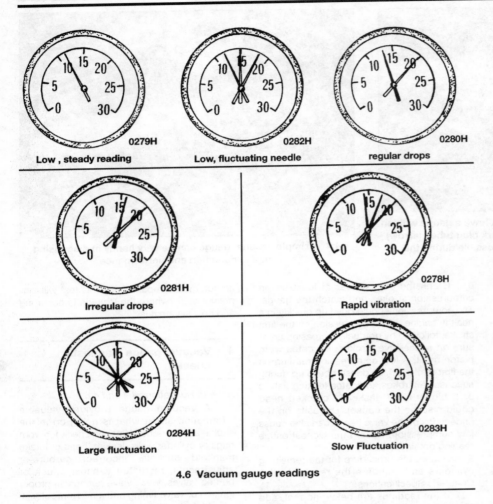

4.6 Vacuum gauge readings

5   Engine removal - methods and precautions

If you've decided the engine must be removed for overhaul or major repair work, several preliminary steps should be taken.

Locating a suitable place to work is extremely important. Adequate work space, along with storage space for the vehicle, will be needed. If a shop or garage isn't available, at the very least a flat, level, clean work surface made of concrete or asphalt is required.

Cleaning the engine compartment and engine before beginning the removal procedure will help keep tools clean and organized.

An engine hoist or A-frame will also be necessary. Make sure the equipment is rated in excess of the combined weight of the engine/transaxle and its accessories. Safety is of primary importance, considering the potential hazards involved in lifting the engine out of the vehicle.

If the engine is being removed by a novice, a helper should be available. Advice and aid from someone more experienced would also be helpful. There are many instances when one person cannot simultaneously perform all of the operations required when lifting the engine out of the vehicle.

Plan the operation ahead of time. Arrange for or obtain all of the tools and equipment you'll need prior to beginning the job. Some of the equipment necessary to perform engine removal and installation safely and with relative ease are (in addition to an engine hoist) a heavy duty floor jack, complete sets of wrenches and sockets as described in the front of this manual, wooden blocks and plenty of rags and cleaning solvent for mopping up spilled oil, coolant and gasoline. If the hoist must be rented, be sure to arrange for it in advance and perform all of the operations possible without it beforehand. This will save you money and time.

Plan for the vehicle to be out of use for quite a while. A machine shop will be required to perform some of the work the do-it-yourselfer can't accomplish without special equipment. These shops often have a busy schedule, so it would be a good idea to consult them before removing the engine in order to accurately estimate the amount of time required to rebuild or repair components that may need work.

Always be extremely careful when removing and installing the engine. Serious injury can result from careless actions. Plan ahead, take your time and a job of this nature, although major, can be accomplished successfully.

dle. Refer to the following vacuum gauge readings and what they indicate about the engine's condition **(see illustration)**:

1   A low steady reading usually indicates a leaking gasket between the intake manifold and cylinder head(s) or throttle body, a leaky vacuum hose, late ignition timing or incorrect camshaft timing. Check ignition timing with a timing light and eliminate all other possible causes, utilizing the tests provided in this Chapter before you remove the timing chain cover to check the timing marks.

2   If the reading is three to eight inches below normal and it fluctuates at that low reading, suspect an intake manifold gasket leak at an intake port or a faulty fuel injector.

3   If the needle has regular drops of about two-to-four inches at a steady rate, the valves are probably leaking. Perform a compression check or leak-down test to confirm this.

4   An irregular drop or down-flick of the needle can be caused by a sticking valve or an ignition misfire. Perform a compression check or leak-down test and read the spark plugs.

5   A rapid vibration of about four in-Hg vibration at idle combined with exhaust smoke indicates worn valve guides. Perform a leak-down test to confirm this. If the rapid

vibration occurs with an increase in engine speed, check for a leaking intake manifold gasket or head gasket, weak valve springs, burned valves or ignition misfire.

6   A slight fluctuation, say one inch up and down, may mean ignition problems. Check all the usual tune-up items and, if necessary, run the engine on an ignition analyzer.

7   If there is a large fluctuation, perform a compression or leak-down test to look for a weak or dead cylinder or a blown head gasket.

8   If the needle moves slowly through a wide range, check for a clogged PCV system, incorrect idle fuel mixture, carburetor/throttle body or intake manifold gasket leaks.

9   Check for a slow return after revving the engine by quickly snapping the throttle open until the engine reaches about 2,500 rpm and let it shut. Normally the reading should drop to near zero, rise above normal idle reading (about 5 in-Hg over) and then return to the previous idle reading. If the vacuum returns slowly and doesn't peak when the throttle is snapped shut, the rings may be worn. If there is a long delay, look for a restricted exhaust system (often the muffler or catalytic converter). An easy way to check this is to temporarily disconnect the exhaust ahead of the suspected part and redo the test.

6   Engine - removal and installation

Warning: *Gasoline is extremely flammable, so take extra precautions when you work on any part of the fuel system. Don't smoke or allow open flames or bare light bulbs near the*

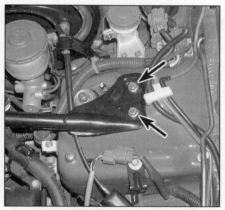

6.4 Remove the nuts at each end of the strut brace (arrows) and remove the brace (Integra models)

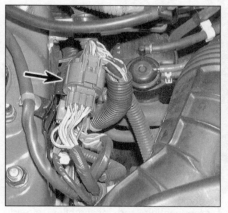

6.6a The Civic main wiring harness connector is at the right side of the engine compartment (arrow) . . .

6.6b . . . and the Integra main connectors are on the left side (arrow)

2C

6.24 Attach the hoist chain to fixtures (arrow) found mounted to the engine

work area, and don't work in a garage where a natural gas-type appliance (such as a water heater or clothes dryer) with a pilot light is present. If you spill any fuel on your skin, rinse it off immediately with soap and water. When you perform any kind of work on the fuel system, wear safety glasses and have a Class B type fire extinguisher on hand. Also, the air conditioning system is under high pressure - have a dealer service department or service station discharge the system before disconnecting any of the hoses or fittings.

Note: *The engine and transaxle must be removed together, as a single unit. Read through the following steps carefully and familiarize yourself with the procedure before beginning work. Also at this point it may be helpful to use a penetrating fluid or spray on nuts and bolts that may be difficult to remove, such as exhaust manifolds, engine mounts, etc.*

Removal

Refer to illustrations 6.4, 6.6a, 6.6b and 6.24

1   Refer to Chapter 4 and relieve the fuel system pressure.
2   Disconnect the negative battery cable. **Caution:** *If the radio in your vehicle is equipped with an anti-theft system, make sure you have the correct activation code before disconnecting the battery.* Disconnect the positive cable, then disconnect the other ends of the cables and remove them. If you're working on a Civic, remove the battery and battery tray from the engine compartment (see Chapter 5).
3   Cover the fenders and cowl. On Civic models, prop the hood open as wide as possible; on Integra models, remove the hood (see Chapter 11). Special pads are available to protect the fenders, but an old bedspread or blanket will also work.
4   If you're working on an Integra, remove the engine compartment strut brace **(see illustration)**.
5   Remove the air cleaner assembly (see Chapter 4), and the air intake duct.
6   Label the vacuum lines, emissions sys-

tem hoses, electrical connectors, ground straps and fuel lines to ensure correct reinstallation, then detach them **(see illustrations)**. If you're working on a Civic, disconnect the connectors from the PCM in the passenger compartment (see Chapter 6), then remove the wiring harness grommet at the firewall and push the main wiring harness through the firewall. Pieces of masking tape with numbers or letters written on them work well. If there's any possibility of confusion, make a sketch of the engine compartment and clearly label the lines, hoses and wires.
7   Label and detach all coolant hoses from the engine.
8   Remove the coolant reservoir, cooling fan, shroud and radiator (see Chapter 3).
9   Remove the drivebelt(s) and idler, if equipped (see Chapter 1).
10   Disconnect the fuel lines running from the engine to the chassis (see Chapter 4). Plug or cap all open fittings and lines.
11   Disconnect the accelerator linkage from the engine (see Chapter 4). Disconnect the cruise control cable and remove the cruise control actuator (if equipped).
12   Unbolt the power steering pump and set it aside (see Chapter 10). Leave the lines/hoses attached and make sure the pump is kept in an upright position in the engine compartment.
13   Unbolt the air conditioning compressor (see Chapter 3) and set it aside. Do not disconnect the hoses.
14   Unbolt the alternator and mounting strap and set it aside (see Chapter 5).
15   Raise the vehicle and support it securely on jackstands. Drain the cooling system (see Chapter 1).
16   Drain the engine oil and remove the filter (see Chapter 1).
17   Remove the starter (see Chapter 5).
18   Remove the splash shield from the underside of the engine compartment (see Chapter 11).
19   On automatic transaxle equipped models, disconnect the throttle control cable from the transaxle. Also, disconnect the electrical connectors and shift cable from the transaxle

(see Chapter 7B).
20   On automatic transaxle equipped models, disconnect the transaxle cooler lines from the transaxle.
21   Remove the crankshaft pulley and reinstall the bolt.
22   Disconnect the exhaust system from the engine (see Chapter 4).
23   Support the transaxle with a jack (preferably a transmission jack). If you're not using a transmission jack, position a wood block on the jack head to prevent damage to the transaxle.
24   Attach an engine sling or a length of chain to the lifting brackets on the engine **(see illustration)**.
25   Roll the hoist into position and connect the sling to it. Take up the slack in the sling or chain, but don't lift the engine. **Warning:** *DO NOT place any part of your body under the engine when it's supported only by a hoist or other lifting device.*
26   Remove the driveaxles (see Chapter 8).
27   If you're working on a model equipped with a manual transaxle, unbolt the clutch release cylinder (don't disconnect the hydraulic line) and position it out of the way (see Chapter 8). Disconnect the transaxle shift linkage (see Chapter 7A).
28   Remove the engine mount-to-chassis

bolts (see Chapter 2A or 2B).

29   Recheck to be sure nothing is still connecting the engine to the vehicle. Disconnect anything still remaining.

30   Raise the engine slightly to disengage the mounts. Also, slightly raise the jack supporting the transaxle. Slowly raise the engine/transaxle assembly out of the engine compartment, turning it sideways, as necessary, for clearance. Check carefully to make sure nothing is hanging up as the hoist is raised.

31   Lower the engine/transaxle assembly to the ground and support it with wood blocks. Remove the clutch and flywheel or driveplate and mount the engine on an engine stand.

32   Separate the transaxle from the engine at this time (see Chapter 7).

Installation

33   Check the engine and transaxle mounts. If they're worn or damaged, replace them.

34   If you're working on a manual transaxle equipped vehicle, install the clutch and pressure plate (see Chapter 8). Now is a good time to install a new clutch. Apply a dab of high-temperature grease to the input shaft.

35   Attach the transaxle to the engine. **Caution:** *DO NOT use the bolts to force the transaxle and engine together. If you're working on an automatic transaxle equipped vehicle, take great care when installing the torque converter, following the procedure outlined in Chapter 7B.* Line up the holes in the engine mounts with the frame and install the bolts, tightening them securely.

36   Attach a chain hoist to the engine/transaxle assembly and lower the assembly into the engine compartment.

37   The remainder of installation is the reverse of the removal steps.

38   Add coolant, oil, power steering and transmission fluid as needed (see Chapter 1).

39   Run the engine and check for leaks and proper operation of all accessories, then install the hood (if removed) and test drive the vehicle.

40   If the air conditioning system was discharged, have it evacuated, recharged and leak tested by the shop that discharged it.

7   Engine rebuilding alternatives

The home mechanic is faced with a number of options when performing an engine overhaul. The decision to replace the engine block, piston/connecting rod assemblies and crankshaft depends on a number of factors, with the number one consideration being the condition of the block. Other considerations are cost, access to machine shop facilities, parts availability, time required to complete the project and the extent of prior mechanical experience.

Some of the rebuilding alternatives include:

Note: *The costs of alternatives described in this Section can vary, depending upon quality of parts, machine work required and the necessary tools and equipment to correctly do*

the work. Many automotive parts stores carry complete (long and short block) assemblies in addition to individual repair parts. Consult the local parts store on price and availability to make the final repair/replace decision.

Individual parts - If the inspection procedures reveal the engine block and most engine components are in reusable condition, purchasing individual parts may be the most economical alternative. The block, crankshaft and piston/connecting rod assemblies should all be inspected carefully. Even if the block shows little wear, the cylinder bores should be surface honed.

Short block - A short block consists of an engine block with a crankshaft and piston/connecting rod assemblies already installed. All new bearings are incorporated and all clearances will be correct. The existing camshaft, valve train components, cylinder head(s) and external parts can be bolted to the short block with little or no machine shop work necessary.

Long block - A long block consists of a short block plus an oil pump, oil pan, cylinder head, valve cover, camshaft and valve train components, timing sprockets and belt. All components are installed with new bearings, seals and gaskets incorporated throughout. The installation of manifolds and external parts is all that's necessary.

Give careful thought to which alternative is best for you and discuss the situation with local automotive machine shops, auto parts dealers and experienced rebuilders before ordering or purchasing replacement parts.

8   Engine overhaul - disassembly sequence

1   It's much easier to disassemble and work on the engine if it's mounted on a portable engine stand. A stand can often be rented quite cheaply from an equipment rental yard. Before it's mounted on a stand, the flywheel/driveplate should be removed from the engine.

2   If a stand isn't available, it's possible to disassemble the engine with it blocked up on the floor. Be extra careful not to tip or drop the engine when working without a stand.

3   If you're going to obtain a rebuilt engine, all external components must come off first, to be transferred to the replacement engine, just as they will if you're doing a complete engine overhaul yourself. These include:

Alternator and brackets
Power steering pump and brackets
Emissions control components
Distributor, spark plug wires and spark plugs
Thermostat and housing cover
Water pump bypass pipe
Fuel injection components
Intake/exhaust manifolds
Oil filter
Engine mounts
Clutch and flywheel or driveplate

Note: *When removing the external components from the engine, pay close attention to details that may be helpful or important during installation. Note the installed position of gaskets, seals, spacers, pins, brackets, washers, bolts, wiring and other small items.*

4   If you're obtaining a short block, which consists of the engine block, crankshaft, pistons and connecting rods all assembled, then the cylinder head(s), oil pan and oil pump will have to be removed as well. See *Engine rebuilding alternatives* for additional information regarding the different possibilities to be considered.

5   If you're planning a complete overhaul, the engine must be disassembled and the internal components removed in the following general order:

Intake and exhaust manifolds
Valve cover
Timing belt covers and bolts
Timing belt and sprockets
Rocker arm assembly and camshaft(s)
Cylinder head
Water pump
Oil pan
Oil pump and pick-up tube
Oil jets (Integra models so equipped)
Piston/connecting rod assemblies
  (B18B1 engines)
Rear main oil seal retainer
Crankshaft and main bearings
Piston/connecting rod assemblies
  (B18C1, B18C5, D16Y5, D16Y7,
  and D16Y8 engines)

6   Before beginning the disassembly and overhaul procedures, make sure the following items are available. Also, refer to *Engine overhaul - reassembly sequence* for a list of tools and materials needed for engine reassembly.

Common hand tools
Small cardboard boxes or plastic bags for storing parts
Gasket scraper
Ridge reamer
Vibration damper puller
Micrometers
Telescoping gauges
Dial indicator set
Valve spring compressor
Cylinder surfacing hone
Piston ring groove cleaning tool
Electric drill motor
Tap and die set
Wire brushes
Oil gallery brushes
Cleaning solvent

9   Cylinder head - disassembly

Refer to illustrations 9.2, 9.3 and 9.4
Note: *New and rebuilt cylinder heads are commonly available for most engines at dealer parts departments and auto parts stores. Due to the fact that some specialized tools are necessary for the disassembly and inspection procedures, and replacement*

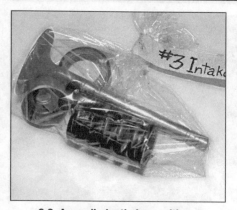

9.2 A small plastic bag, with an appropriate label, can be used to store the valve train components so they can be kept together and reinstalled in the original position

parts aren't always readily available, it may be more practical and economical for the home mechanic to purchase replacement head(s) rather than taking the time to disassemble, inspect and recondition the original(s).

1   Cylinder head disassembly involves removal of the intake and exhaust valves and related components. The rocker arm assemblies and camshaft(s) must be removed before beginning the cylinder head disassembly procedure (see Part A of this Chapter). Label the parts or store them separately so they can be reinstalled in their original locations.

2   Before the valves are removed, arrange to label and store them, along with their related components, so they can be kept separate and reinstalled in their original locations **(see illustration)**.

3   Compress the springs on the first valve with a spring compressor and remove the keepers **(see illustration)**. Carefully release the valve spring compressor and remove the retainer, the spring and the spring seat (if used). **Note:** On Integra models, use an adapter with the compressor to reach the recessed valve spring.

4   Pull the valve out of the head, then remove the oil seal from the guide. If the valve binds in the guide (won't pull through), push it back into the head and deburr the area around the stem and the keeper groove with a fine file or whetstone **(see illustration)**.

5   Repeat the procedure for the remaining valves. Remember to keep all the parts for each valve together so they can be reinstalled in the same locations. **Note:** On VTEC models only, remember to remove the oil control orifice and O-ring from the cylinder head (see Chapter 2A or 2B).

6   Once the valves and related components have been removed and stored in an organized manner, the head should be thoroughly cleaned and inspected. If a complete engine overhaul is being done, finish the engine disassembly procedures before beginning the cylinder head cleaning and inspection process.

10   Cylinder head - cleaning and inspection

1   Thorough cleaning of the cylinder head and related valve train components, followed by a detailed inspection, will enable you to decide how much valve service work must be done during the engine overhaul. **Note:** If the engine was severely overheated, the cylinder head is probably warped.

Cleaning

2   Scrape all traces of old gasket material and sealant off the head gasket, intake manifold and exhaust manifold mating surfaces. Be very careful not to gouge the cylinder head. Special gasket removal solvents that soften gaskets and make removal much easier are available at auto parts stores.

3   Remove all built-up scale from the coolant passages.

4   Run a stiff wire brush through the various holes to remove deposits that may have formed in them.

5   Run an appropriate size tap into each of

the threaded holes to remove corrosion and thread sealant that may be present. If compressed air is available, use it to clear the holes of debris produced by this operation. **Warning:** Wear eye protection when using compressed air!

6   Clean the camshaft bearing cap bolt threads with a wire brush.

7   Clean the cylinder head with solvent and dry it thoroughly. Compressed air will speed the drying process and ensure that all holes and recessed areas are clean. **Note:** Decarbonizing chemicals are available and may prove very useful when cleaning cylinder heads and valve train components. They're very caustic and should be used with caution. Be sure to follow the instructions on the container.

8   Clean the rocker arms and bearing caps with solvent and dry them thoroughly (don't mix them up during the cleaning process). Compressed air will speed the drying process and can be used to clean out the oil passages.

9   Clean all the valve springs, spring seats, keepers and retainers with solvent and dry them thoroughly. Do the components from one valve at a time to avoid mixing up the parts.

10   Scrape off any heavy deposits that may have formed on the valves, then use a motorized wire brush to remove deposits from the valve heads and stems. Again, make sure the valves don't get mixed up.

Inspection

Note: Be sure to perform all of the following inspection procedures before concluding machine shop work is required. Make a list of the items that need attention.

Cylinder head

Refer to illustrations 10.12 and 10.14

11   Inspect the head very carefully for cracks, evidence of coolant leakage and other damage. If cracks are found, check with an automotive machine shop concerning repair. If repair isn't possible, a new cylinder head should be obtained.

12   Using a straightedge and feeler gauge,

2C

9.3 Use a valve spring compressor to compress the springs then remove the keepers from the valve stem with a magnet or small needle-nose pliers

9.4 If the valve won't pull through the guide, deburr the edge of the stem end and the area around the top of the keeper groove with a file or whetstone

10.12 Check the cylinder head gasket surface for warpage by trying to slip a feeler gauge under the straightedge (see this Chapter's Specifications for the maximum warpage allowed and use a feeler gauge of that thickness)

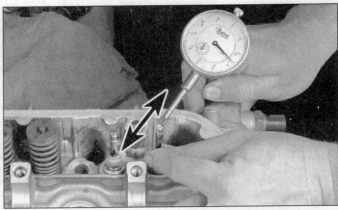

10.14 A dial indicator can be used to determine the valve stem-to-guide clearance (move the valve stem as indicated by the arrows)

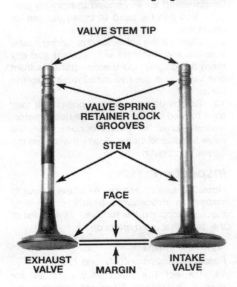

10.15 Check for valve wear at the points shown here

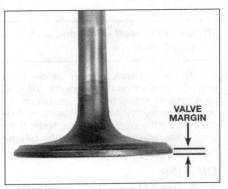

10.16 The margin width on each valve must be as specified (if no margin exists, the valve cannot be reused)

10.17 Measure the free length of each valve spring with a dial or vernier caliper

check the head gasket mating surface for warpage **(see illustration)**. If the warpage exceeds the limit in this Chapter's Specifications, it can be resurfaced at an automotive machine shop.

13   Examine the valve seats in each of the combustion chambers. If they're pitted, cracked or burned, the head will require valve service that's beyond the scope of the home mechanic.

14   Check the valve stem-to-guide clearance by measuring the lateral movement of the valve stem with a dial indicator attached securely to the head **(see illustration)**. The valve must be in the guide and approximately 1/16-inch off the seat. The total valve stem movement indicated by the gauge needle must be divided by two to obtain the actual clearance. After this is done, if there's still some doubt regarding the condition of the valve guides, they should be checked by an automotive machine shop (the cost should be minimal).

Valves

Refer to illustrations 10.15 and 10.16

15   Carefully inspect each valve face for uneven wear, deformation, cracks, pits and burned areas. Check the valve stem for scuffing and galling and the neck for cracks. Rotate the valve and check for any obvious indication that it's bent. Look for pits and excessive wear on the end of the stem **(see illustration)**. The presence of any of these conditions indicates the need for valve service by an automotive machine shop.

16   Check the margin width on each valve **(see illustration)**. Replace any valve with a margin less than the limit listed in this Chapter's Specifications.

Valve components

Refer to illustrations 10.17 and 10.18

17   Check each valve spring for wear (on the ends) and pits. Measure the free length and compare it to this Chapter's Specifications **(see illustration)**. Any springs that are shorter than specified have sagged and shouldn't be reused. The tension of all springs should be checked with a special fixture before deciding they're suitable for use in a rebuilt engine (take the springs to an automotive machine shop for this check).

18   Stand each spring on a flat surface and check it for squareness with a carpenters square **(see illustration)**. If any of the springs are distorted or sagged, replace all of them with new parts.

19   Check the spring retainers and keepers for obvious wear and cracks. Any questionable parts should be replaced with new ones, as extensive damage will occur if they fail during engine operation.

20   If the inspection process indicates the valve components are in generally poor condition and worn beyond the limits specified,

10.18 Check each valve spring for squareness

12.3 Install the spring seats over the valve guides

12.4a Gently tap the valve seals into place with a seal installation tool or a deep socket and hammer

12.4b The intake valve stem seals are color coded white and the exhaust seals are color coded black (arrows)

which is usually the case in an engine that's being overhauled, reassemble the valves in the cylinder head and refer to Section 11 for valve servicing recommendations.

11 Valves - servicing

1   Because of the complex nature of the job and the special tools and equipment needed, servicing of the valves, the valve seats and the valve guides, commonly known as a valve job, should be done by a professional.

2   The home mechanic can remove and disassemble the head, do the initial cleaning and inspection, then reassemble and deliver it to a dealer service department or an automotive machine shop for the actual service work. Doing the inspection will enable you to see what condition the head and valvetrain components are in and will ensure that you know what work and new parts are required when dealing with an automotive machine shop.

3   The dealer service department, or automotive machine shop, will remove the valves and springs, recondition or replace the valves and valve seats, recondition the valve guides, check and replace the valve springs, rotators, spring retainers and keepers (as necessary), replace the valve seals with new ones, reassemble the valve components and make sure the installed height is correct. The cylinder head gasket surface will also be resurfaced if it's warped.

4   After the valve job has been performed by a professional, the head will be in like new condition. When the head is returned, be sure to clean it again before installation on the engine to remove any metal particles and abrasive grit that may still be present from the valve service or head resurfacing operations. Use compressed air, if available, to blow out all the oil holes and passages.

12 Cylinder head - reassembly

Refer to illustrations 12.3, 12.4a, 12.4b, 12.6a, 12.6b and 12.8

1   Regardless of whether or not the head

12.6a Install the spring (closely-wound coils toward the head) and retainer over the valve stem

was sent to an automotive repair shop for valve servicing, make sure it's clean before beginning reassembly.

2   If the head was sent out for valve servicing, the valves and related components will already be in place. Begin the reassembly procedure with Step 8.

3   Install the spring seats before the valve seals **(see illustration)**.

4   Install new seals on each of the valve guides. Using a hammer and a deep socket or seal installation tool, gently tap each seal into place until it's completely seated on the guide **(see illustration)**. Don't twist or cock the seals during installation or they won't seal properly on the valve stems. **Note:** *The valve stem seals are color coded; white for the intake valves and black for the exhaust valves* **(see illustration)**.

5   Beginning at one end of the head, lubricate and install the first valve. Apply clean engine oil to the valve stem.

6   Position the valve springs (and shims, if used) over the valves **(see illustration)**. Place the end of the valve spring with the closely wound coils toward the cylinder head Compress the springs with a valve spring compressor and carefully install the keepers in the groove, then slowly release the compressor and make sure the keepers seat properly. Apply a small dab of grease to each keeper

12.6b Apply a small dab of grease to each keeper as shown here before installation - it'll hold them in place on the valve stem as the spring is released

to hold it in place if necessary **(see illustration)**.

7   Repeat the procedure for the remaining valves. Be sure to return the components to their original locations - don't mix them up!

8   Check the installed valve stem height (the distance from the spring seat to the top of the valve stem) with a vernier or dial caliper **(see illustration)**. If the head was sent out for service work, the installed height should be

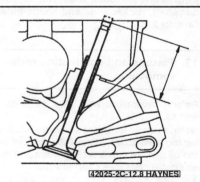

42025-2C-12.8 HAYNES

12.8 Be sure to check the valve stem installed height (the distance from the spring seat to the top of the valve stem)

2C

13.1 A ridge reamer is required to remove the ridge from the top of each cylinder - do this before removing the pistons!

13.4 Check the connecting rod side clearance (endplay) with a feeler gauge

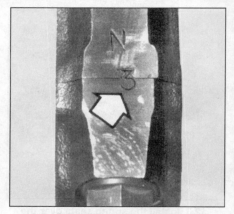

13.5a DO NOT confuse the stamped numbers on the parting surface, such as this 3 (arrow) with cylinder numbers - the numbers indicates big-end bore size

13.5b Mark the cylinder number on each connecting rod and cap with a center punch before removing them

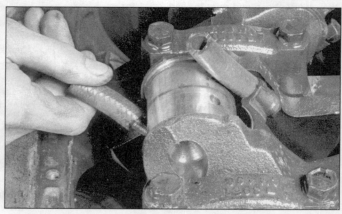

13.7 To prevent damage to the crankshaft journals and cylinder walls, slip sections of rubber or plastic hose over the rod bolts before removing the pistons

correct (but don't automatically assume it is). If the height is greater than listed in this Chapter's Specifications, replace the valve and recheck. If it's still over specification, replace the cylinder head, the valve seat has recessed into the cylinder head

9   Apply camshaft assembly lube to the rocker arm faces, the camshaft lobes and journals and the rocker shafts, then install the camshaft, rocker arms and shafts (refer to Chapter 2A).

13 Pistons and connecting rods - removal

Refer to illustrations 13.1, 13.4, 13.5a, 13.5b and 13.7
Note: *Prior to removing the piston/connecting rod assemblies, remove the cylinder head, the oil pan, oil pump pick-up tube and pump and baffle plate (see Chapter 2A or 2B).*

1   Use your fingernail to feel if a ridge has formed at the upper limit of ring travel (about 1/4-inch down from the top of each cylinder). If carbon deposits or cylinder wear have produced ridges, they must be completely

removed with a special tool **(see illustration)**. Follow the manufacturer's instructions provided with the tool. Failure to remove the ridges before attempting to remove the piston/connecting rod assemblies may result in piston breakage.

2   After the cylinder ridges (if any) have been removed, turn the engine upside-down so the crankshaft is facing up.

3   The bearing cap bridge must be removed first to access the connecting rods (except on B18B1 engines) (see Section 14).

4   Before the connecting rods are removed, check the side clearance (endplay) with feeler gauges. Slide them between the first connecting rod and the crankshaft throw until the play is removed **(see illustration)**. The endplay is equal to the thickness of the feeler gauge(s). If the endplay exceeds the service limit, new connecting rods will be required. If new rods (or a new crankshaft) are installed, the endplay may fall under the specified minimum (if it does, the rods will have to be machined to restore it - consult an automotive machine shop for advice if necessary). Repeat the procedure for the remaining connecting rods.

5   The existing numbers on the connecting

rods indicate the rod bore size, not the position in the engine **(see illustration)**. Use a small center punch to make the appropriate number of indentations on each rod and cap (1, 2, 3, etc., depending on the engine type and cylinder they're associated with) **(see illustration)**.

6   Loosen each of the connecting rod cap nuts 1/2-turn at a time until they can be removed by hand. Remove the number one connecting rod cap and bearing insert. Don't drop the bearing insert out of the cap.

7   Slip a short length of plastic or rubber hose over each connecting rod cap bolt to protect the crankshaft journal and cylinder wall as the piston is removed **(see illustration)**.

8   Remove the bearing insert and push the connecting rod/piston assembly out through the top of the engine. Use a wooden hammer handle to push on the upper bearing surface in the connecting rod. If resistance is felt, double-check to make sure that all of the ridge was removed from the cylinder.

9   Repeat the procedure for the remaining cylinders.

10   After removal, reassemble the connecting rod caps and bearing inserts in their

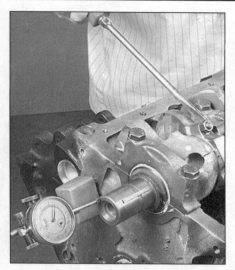

14.1 Place a dial indicator against the end of the crankshaft and pry the crankshaft back-and-forth to check endplay

14.3 The endplay can also be checked with a feeler gauge at the thrust bearing journal

14.4 The main bearing caps should have arrows pointing to the timing belt end and numbers indicating position - make your own marks if they aren't visible

15.2 Some Integra models are equipped with oil jets (arrows)

respective connecting rods and install the cap nuts finger tight. Leaving the old bearing inserts in place until reassembly will help prevent the connecting rod bearing surfaces from being accidentally nicked or gouged.

11   Don't separate the pistons from the connecting rods (see Section 18 for additional information).

14   Crankshaft - removal

Refer to illustrations 14.1, 14.3 and 14.4
Note: *The crankshaft can be removed only after the engine has been removed from the vehicle. It's assumed that the flywheel or driveplate, timing belt, oil pan, oil pick-up tube and oil pump, baffle plate and, on B18B1 engines, piston/connecting rod assemblies have already been removed. The rear main oil seal retainer must be unbolted and separated from the block before proceeding with crankshaft removal.*

1   Before the crankshaft is removed, check the endplay. Mount a dial indicator with the stem in line with the crankshaft and just touching the end **(see illustration)**. **Note:** *The main caps and main-cap bridge should be in place and torqued to Specifications.*
2   Push the crankshaft all the way to the rear and zero the dial indicator. Next, pry the crankshaft to the front as far as possible and check the reading on the dial indicator. The distance that it moves is the endplay. If it's greater than specified, check the crankshaft thrust surfaces for wear. If no wear is evident, new thrust washers should correct the endplay.
3   If a dial indicator isn't available, feeler gauges can be used. Gently pry or push the crankshaft all the way to the front of the engine. Slip feeler gauges between the crankshaft and the back face of the front thrust bearing to determine the clearance

(see illustration). The thrust bearing is journal number four.
4   If you're working on an Integra, check the main bearing caps to see if they're marked to indicate their locations. They should be numbered consecutively from the front of the engine to the rear **(see illustration)**. If they aren't, mark them with number-stamping dies or a center punch. Main bearing caps generally have a cast-in arrow, which points to the front of the engine. Loosen the main bearing cap and/or bridge assembly bolts 1/4-turn at a time each, working around the engine until they can be removed by hand **(see illustration 23.13a or 23.13b)**. Make sure all bolts are removed before trying to remove the caps and/or bridge assembly.
5   Remove the main bearing caps and or bridge assembly. If you're working on an Integra, gently tap the remaining caps with a soft-face hammer and separate them from the engine block. If necessary, use the bolts as levers to remove the caps. Try not to drop the bearing inserts if they come out with the caps.
6   Carefully lift the crankshaft out of the engine. It may be a good idea to have an assistant available, since the crankshaft is quite heavy. With the bearing inserts in place in the engine block, return the caps to their

respective locations on the engine block, install the main bearing cap bridge and tighten the bolts finger tight.

15   Engine block - cleaning

Refer to illustrations 15.2, 15.5a, 15.5b, 15.9 and 15.11

1   Remove the main bearing cap bridge (Civic) or caps and bridge (Integra) and separate the bearing inserts from the caps and the engine block. Tag the bearings, indicating which cylinder they were removed from and whether they were in the cap or the block, then set them aside.
2   If you're working on an Integra with a VTEC engine, unbolt the oil jets from the block and remove them **(see illustration)**. The spout holes in the oil jets are 0.050-inch in diameter and you should be able to fit a 0.040-inch drill into them. Insert the shank end of the drill bit into the oil inlet and push against the check ball. It should move freely and return with spring pressure. If the spring seems weak, test it with by blowing compressed air into the oil inlet. It should take at least 28 psi to push the check ball off its seat against the spring pressure. If the oil jet fails any of these tests, replace it.

15.5a A hammer and a large punch can be used to knock the core plugs sideways in their bores

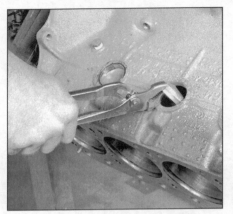

15.5b Pull the core plugs from the block with pliers

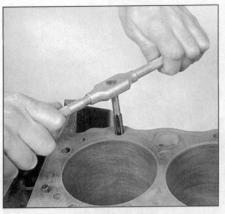

15.9 All bolt holes in the block - particularly the main bearing cap and head bolt holes - should be cleaned and restored with a tap (be sure to remove debris from the holes after this is done)

3   Using a gasket scraper, remove all traces of gasket material from the engine block. Be very careful not to nick or gouge the gasket sealing surfaces.

4   Remove all of the covers and threaded oil gallery plugs from the block. The plugs are usually very tight - they may have to be drilled out and the holes retapped. Use new plugs when the engine is reassembled.

5   Remove the core plugs from the engine block. To do this, knock one side of the plug into the block with a hammer and a punch, then grasp them with large pliers and pull them out **(see illustrations)**.

6   If the engine is extremely dirty, it should be taken to an automotive machine shop to be cleaned.

7   After the block is returned, clean all oil holes and oil galleries one more time. Brushes specifically designed for this purpose are available at most auto parts stores. Flush the passages with warm water until the water runs clear, dry the block thoroughly and wipe all machined surfaces with a light, rust preventive oil. If you have access to compressed air, use it to speed the drying process and blow out all the oil holes and galleries. **Warning:** *Wear eye protection when using compressed air!*

8   If the block isn't extremely dirty or sludged up, you can do an adequate cleaning job with hot soapy water and a stiff brush. Take plenty of time and do a thorough job. Regardless of the cleaning method used, be sure to clean all oil holes and galleries very thoroughly, dry the block completely and coat all machined surfaces with light oil.

9   The threaded holes in the block must be clean to ensure accurate torque readings during reassembly. Run the proper size tap into each of the holes to remove rust, corrosion, thread sealant or sludge and restore damaged threads **(see illustration)**. If possible, use compressed air to clear the holes of debris produced by this operation. Now is a good time to clean the threads on the head bolts and the main bearing cap bolts as well.

10   Reinstall the main bearing caps and tighten the bolts finger tight.

15.11 A large socket on an extension can be used to drive the new core plugs into the bores

11   After coating the sealing surfaces of the new core plugs with a hard-setting sealant (such as Permatex no. 1, or equivalent), install them in the engine block **(see illustration)**. Make sure they're driven in straight and seated properly or leakage could result. Special tools are available for this purpose, but a large socket, with an outside diameter that will just slip into the core plug, a 1/2-inch drive extension and a hammer will work just as well.

12   Apply a non-hardening sealant (such as Teflon pipe sealant) to the new oil gallery plugs and thread them into the holes in the block. Make sure they're tightened securely.

13   If the engine isn't going to be reassembled right away, cover it with a large plastic trash bag to keep it clean.

---

16   Engine block - inspection

Refer to illustrations 16.4a, 16.4b, 16.4c, 16.10a and 16.10b

1   Before the block is inspected, it should be cleaned as described in Section 15.

2   Visually check the block for cracks, rust and corrosion. Look for stripped threads in

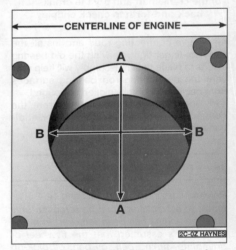

16.4a Measure the diameter of each cylinder at a right angle to the engine centerline (A), and parallel to engine centerline (B) - out-of-round is the difference between A and B; taper is the difference between A and B at the top of the cylinder and A and B and at the bottom of the cylinder

the threaded holes. It's also a good idea to have the block checked for hidden cracks by an automotive machine shop that has the special equipment to do this type of work. If defects are found, have the block repaired, if possible, or replaced.

3   Check the cylinder bores for scuffing and scoring.

4   Check the cylinders for taper and out-of-round conditions as follows **(see illustrations)**.

5   Measure the diameter of each cylinder at the top (just under the ridge area), center and bottom of the cylinder bore, parallel to the crankshaft axis.

6   Next measure each cylinder's diameter at the same three locations perpendicular to the crankshaft axis.

16.4b The ability to "feel" when the telescoping gauge is at the correct point will be developed over time, so work slowly and repeat the check until you're satisfied the bore measurement is accurate

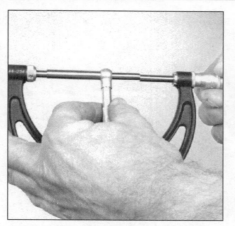

16.4c The gauge is then measured with a micrometer to determine the bore size

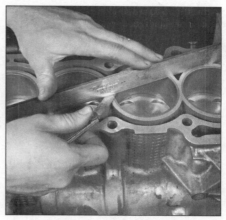

16.10a Check the block deck with a precision straightedge and feeler gauges

2C

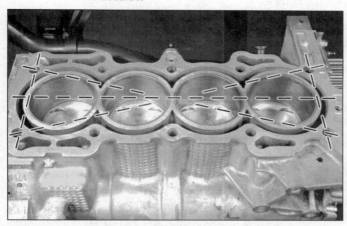

16.10b Lay the straightedge across the block, diagonally and from end-to-end when making the check

17.3a A spring-loaded, stone-edged hone is the most common type of cylinder hone but a bottle-brush hone is easier to use

7   The taper of the cylinder is the difference between the bore diameter at the top of the cylinder and the diameter at the bottom. The out-of-round specification of the cylinder bore is the difference between the parallel and perpendicular readings. Compare your results to those listed in this Chapter's Specifications.

8   Repeat the procedure for the remaining pistons and cylinders.

9   If the cylinder walls are badly scuffed or scored, or if they're out-of-round or tapered beyond the limits given in this Chapter's Specifications, have the engine block rebored and honed at an automotive machine shop. If a rebore is done, oversize pistons and rings will be required.

10   Using a precision straightedge and feeler gauge, check the block deck (the surface that mates with the cylinder head) for distortions **(see illustrations)**.

11   If the cylinders are in reasonably good condition and not worn to the outside of the limits, and if the piston-to-cylinder clearances can be maintained properly, then they don't have to be rebored. Honing is all that's necessary (see Section 17).

17   Cylinder honing

Refer to illustrations 17.3a and 17.3b

1   Prior to engine reassembly, the cylinder bores must be honed so the new piston rings will seat correctly and provide the best possible combustion chamber seal. **Note:** *If you don't have the tools or don't want to tackle the honing operation, most automotive machine shops will do it for a reasonable fee.*

2   Before honing the cylinders, install the main bearing caps and bridge and tighten the bolts to the specified torque.

3   Two types of cylinder hones are commonly available - the flex hone or "bottle-brush" type and the more traditional surfacing hone with spring-loaded stones. Both will do the job, but for the less experienced mechanic the "bottle brush" hone will probably be easier to use. You'll also need some honing oil (kerosene will work if honing oil isn't available), rags and an electric drill motor. Proceed as follows:

a)   *Mount the hone in the drill motor, compress the stones and slip it into the first*

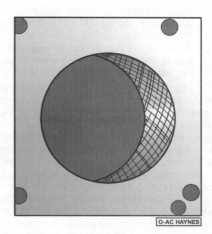

O-AC HAYNES

17.3b The cylinder hone should leave a smooth, crosshatch pattern with the lines intersecting at approximately a 60-degree angle

cylinder **(see illustration)**. *Be sure to wear safety goggles or a face shield!*

b)   *Lubricate the cylinder with plenty of honing oil, turn on the drill and move the*

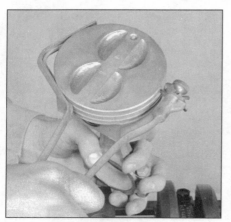

18.4a The piston ring grooves can be cleaned with a special tool, as shown here . . .

18.4b . . . or a section of a broken ring

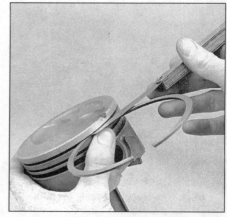

18.10 Check the ring side clearance with a feeler gauge at several points around the groove

hone up-and-down in the cylinder at a pace that will produce a fine crosshatch pattern on the cylinder walls. Ideally, the crosshatch lines should intersect at approximately a 60-degree angle **(see illustration)**. *Be sure to use plenty of lubricant and don't take off any more material than is absolutely necessary to produce the desired finish.* **Note:** *Piston ring manufacturers may specify a smaller crosshatch angle than the traditional 60-degrees - read and follow any instructions included with the new rings.*

c) *Don't withdraw the hone from the cylinder while it's running. Instead, shut off the drill and continue moving the hone up-and-down in the cylinder until it comes to a complete stop, then compress the stones and withdraw the hone. If you're using a "bottle brush" type hone, stop the drill motor, then turn the chuck in the normal direction of rotation while withdrawing the hone from the cylinder.*

d) *Wipe the oil out of the cylinder and repeat the procedure for the remaining cylinders.*

4   After the honing job is complete, chamfer the top edges of the cylinder bores with a small file so the rings won't catch when the pistons are installed. Be very careful not to nick the cylinder walls with the end of the file.

5   The entire engine block must be washed again very thoroughly with warm, soapy water to remove all traces of the abrasive grit produced during the honing operation. **Note:** *The bores can be considered clean when a lint-free white cloth - dampened with clean engine oil - used to wipe them out doesn't pick-up any more honing residue, which will show up as gray areas on the cloth. Be sure to run a brush through all oil holes and galleries and flush them with running water.*

6   After rinsing, dry the block and apply a coat of light rust preventive oil to all machined surfaces. Wrap the block in a plastic trash bag to keep it clean and set it aside until reassembly.

18   Pistons and connecting rods - inspection

Refer to illustrations 18.4a, 18,4b, 18.10 and 18.11

1   Before the inspection process can be carried out, the piston/connecting rod assemblies must be cleaned and the original piston rings removed from the pistons. **Note:** *Always use new piston rings when the engine is reassembled.*

2   Using a piston ring expander tool, carefully remove the rings from the pistons. Be careful not to nick or gouge the pistons in the process.

3   Scrape all traces of carbon from the top of the piston. A hand held wire brush or a piece of fine emery cloth can be used once the majority of the deposits have been scraped away. Do not, under any circumstances, use a wire brush mounted in a drill motor to remove deposits from the pistons. The piston material is soft and may be eroded away by the wire brush.

4   Use a piston ring groove cleaning tool to remove carbon deposits from the ring grooves. If a tool isn't available, a piece broken off the old ring will do the job. Be very careful to remove only the carbon deposits - don't remove any metal and do not nick or scratch the sides of the ring grooves **(see illustrations)**.

5   Once the deposits have been removed, clean the piston/rod assemblies with solvent and dry them with compressed air (if available). **Warning:** *Wear eye protection when using compressed air!* Make sure the oil return holes in the back sides of the ring grooves are clear.

6   If the pistons and cylinder walls aren't damaged or worn excessively, and if the engine block isn't rebored, new pistons won't be necessary. Normal piston wear appears as even vertical wear on the piston thrust surfaces and slight looseness of the top ring in its groove. New piston rings, however, should always be used when an engine is rebuilt.

7   Carefully inspect each piston for cracks

around the skirt, at the pin bosses and at the ring lands.

8   Look for scoring and scuffing on the thrust faces of the skirt, holes in the piston crown and burned areas at the edge of the crown. If the skirt is scored or scuffed, the engine may have been suffering from overheating and/or abnormal combustion, which caused excessively high operating temperatures. The cooling and lubrication systems should be checked thoroughly. A hole in the piston crown is an indication that abnormal combustion (pre-ignition) was occurring. Burned areas at the edge of the piston crown are usually evidence of spark knock (detonation). If any of the above problems exist, the causes must be corrected or the damage will occur again. The causes may include intake air leaks, incorrect fuel/air mixture, low octane fuel, ignition timing and EGR system malfunctions.

9   Corrosion of the piston, in the form of small pits, indicates coolant is leaking into the combustion chamber and/or the crankcase. Again, the cause must be corrected or the problem may persist in the rebuilt engine.

10   Measure the piston ring side clearance by laying a new piston ring in each ring groove and slipping a feeler gauge in beside it **(see illustration)**. Check the clearance at three or four locations around each groove. Be sure to use the correct ring for each groove - they are different. If the groove clearance is greater than specified in this Chapter's Specifications, new pistons will have to be used.

11   Check the piston-to-bore clearance by measuring the bore (see Section 16) and the piston diameter. Make sure the pistons and bores are correctly matched. Measure the piston across the skirt, at a 90-degree angle to the piston pin, at the height from the bottom of the skirt listed in this Chapter's Specifications **(see illustration)**.

12   Subtract the piston diameter from the bore diameter to obtain the clearance. If it's greater than listed in this Chapter's Specifications, the block will have to be rebored and

18.11 Measure the piston diameter at a 90-degree angle to the piston pin, at the specified distance from the bottom of the skirt

19.1 The oil holes should be chamfered so sharp edges don't gouge or scratch the new bearings

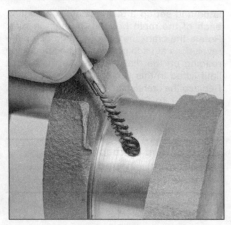

19.2 Use a wire or stiff plastic bristle brush to clean the oil passages in the crankshaft

2C

19.5 Measure the diameter of each crankshaft journal at several points to detect taper and out-of-round conditions

19.7 If the seals have worn grooves in the crankshaft journals, or if the seal contact surfaces are nicked or scratched, the new seals will leak

new pistons and rings installed.

13   Check the piston-to-rod clearance by twisting the piston and rod in opposite directions. Any noticeable play indicates excessive wear, which must be corrected. The piston/connecting rod assemblies should be taken to an automotive machine shop to have the pistons and rods re-sized and new pins installed.

14   If the pistons must be removed from the connecting rods for any reason, they should be taken to an automotive machine shop. While they are there have the connecting rods checked for bend and twist, since automotive machine shops have special equipment for this purpose. **Note:** *Unless new pistons and/or connecting rods must be installed, do not disassemble the pistons and connecting rods.*

15   Check the connecting rods for cracks and other damage. Temporarily remove the rod caps, lift out the old bearing inserts, wipe the rod and cap bearing surfaces clean and inspect them for nicks, gouges and scratches. After checking the rods, replace the old bearings, slip the caps into place and

tighten the nuts finger tight. **Note:** *If the engine is being rebuilt because of a connecting rod knock, be sure to install new rods.*

19 Crankshaft - inspection

Refer to illustrations 19.1, 19.2, 19.5 and 19.7

1   Remove all burrs from the crankshaft oil holes with a stone, file or scraper **(see illustration)**.

2   Clean the crankshaft with solvent and dry it with compressed air (if available). **Warning:** *Wear eye protection when using compressed air!* Be sure to clean the oil holes with a stiff brush **(see illustration)** and flush them with solvent.

3   Check the main and connecting rod bearing journals for uneven wear, scoring, pits and cracks.

4   Check the rest of the crankshaft for cracks and other damage. It should be magnafluxed to reveal hidden cracks - an automotive machine shop will handle the procedure.

5   Using a micrometer, measure the diameter of the main and connecting rod journals and compare the results to this Chapter's Specifications **(see illustration)**. By measuring the diameter at a number of points around each journal's circumference, you'll be able to determine whether or not the journal is out-of-round. Take the measurement at each end of the journal, near the crank throws, to determine if the journal is tapered.

6   If the crankshaft journals are damaged, tapered, out-of-round or worn beyond the limits given in the Specifications, the crankshaft will have to be replaced; it can't be reground.

7   Check the oil seal journals at each end of the crankshaft for wear and damage. If the seal has worn a groove in the journal, or if it's nicked or scratched **(see illustration)**, the new seal may leak when the engine is reassembled. In some cases, an automotive machine shop may be able to repair the journal by pressing on a thin sleeve. If repair isn't feasible, a new or different crankshaft should be installed.

8   Place the crankshaft in V-blocks or a

lathe and set up a dial indicator contacting each of the main bearing journals in turn. Rotate the crankshaft through two complete revolutions at each position and compare the reading on the dial indicator to the runout limit listed in this Chapter's Specifications. Replace the crankshaft if it's beyond the limit.

9   Refer to Section 20 and examine the main and rod bearing inserts.

20   Main and connecting rod bearings - inspection and selection

Inspection

Refer to illustration 20.1

1   Even though the main and connecting rod bearings should be replaced with new ones during the engine overhaul, the old bearings should be retained for close examination, as they may reveal valuable information about the condition of the engine **(see illustration)**.

2   Bearing failure occurs because of lack of lubrication, the presence of dirt or other foreign particles, overloading the engine and corrosion. Regardless of the cause of bearing failure, it must be corrected before the engine is reassembled to prevent it from happening again.

3   When examining the bearings, remove them from the engine block, the main bearing caps, the connecting rods and the rod caps and lay them out on a clean surface in the same general position as their location in the engine. This will enable you to match any bearing problems with the corresponding crankshaft journal.

4   Dirt and other foreign particles get into the engine in a variety of ways. It may be left in the engine during assembly, or it may pass through filters or the PCV system. It may get into the oil, and from there into the bearings. Metal chips from machining operations and normal engine wear are often present. Abrasives are sometimes left in engine components after reconditioning, especially when parts are not thoroughly cleaned using the proper cleaning methods. Whatever the source, these foreign objects often end up embedded in the soft bearing material and are easily recognized. Large particles will not embed in the bearing and will score or gouge the bearing and journal. The best prevention for this cause of bearing failure is to clean all parts thoroughly and keep everything spotlessly clean during engine assembly. Frequent and regular engine oil and filter changes are also recommended.

5   Lack of lubrication (or lubrication breakdown) has a number of interrelated causes. Excessive heat (which thins the oil), overloading (which squeezes the oil from the bearing face) and oil leakage or throw off (from excessive bearing clearances, worn oil pump or high engine speeds) all contribute to lubrication breakdown. Blocked oil passages,

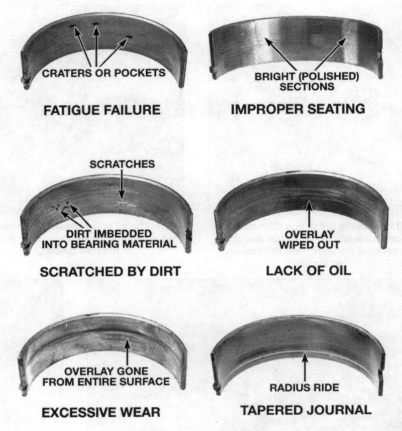

FATIGUE FAILURE — CRATERS OR POCKETS

IMPROPER SEATING — BRIGHT (POLISHED) SECTIONS

SCRATCHED BY DIRT — SCRATCHES / DIRT IMBEDDED INTO BEARING MATERIAL

LACK OF OIL — OVERLAY WIPED OUT

EXCESSIVE WEAR — OVERLAY GONE FROM ENTIRE SURFACE

TAPERED JOURNAL — RADIUS RIDE

20.1 Typical bearing failures

which usually are the result of misaligned oil holes in a bearing shell, will also oil starve a bearing and destroy it. When lack of lubrication is the cause of bearing failure, the bearing material is wiped or extruded from the steel backing of the bearing. Temperatures may increase to the point where the steel backing turns blue from overheating.

6   Driving habits can have a definite effect on bearing life. Full throttle, low speed operation (lugging the engine) puts very high loads on bearings, which tends to squeeze out the oil film. These loads cause the bearings to flex, which produces fine cracks in the bearing face (fatigue failure). Eventually the bearing material will loosen in pieces and tear away from the steel backing. Short-trip driving leads to corrosion of bearings because insufficient engine heat is produced to drive off the condensed water and corrosive gases. These products collect in the engine oil, forming acid and sludge. As the oil is carried to the engine bearings, the acid attacks and corrodes the bearing material.

7   Incorrect bearing installation during engine assembly will lead to bearing failure as well. Tight-fitting bearings leave insufficient bearing oil clearance and will result in oil starvation. Dirt or foreign particles trapped behind a bearing insert result in high spots on the bearing which lead to failure.

Selection

Refer to illustrations 20.10, 20.11, 20.12, 20.14, 20.15 and 20.16

8   If the original bearings are worn or damaged, or if the oil clearances are incorrect (see Section 23 or 25), the following procedures should be used to select the correct

20.10 The crankcase journal designations are stamped onto the engine block - on Civic engines they're at the end of the block near one of the transaxle mounting bolt holes; on Integra models they're near the oil pan rail

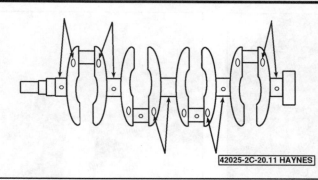

20.11 The crankshaft journal designations (numbers) are stamped onto the crankshaft

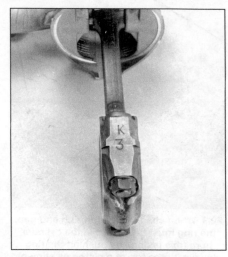

20.14 Connecting rod journal designation- half of the number is stamped on the connecting rod and half is stamped on the bearing cap

	A	B	C	D
1	RED	PINK	YELLOW	GREEN
2	PINK	YELLOW	GREEN	BROWN
3	YELLOW	GREEN	BROWN	BLACK
4	GREEN	BROWN	BLACK	BLUE

20.12 Main bearing selection chart for original crankshaft diameters - the numbers are stamped onto the crankshaft, the letters are stamped onto the engine block and the color code is on the edge of the bearing

new bearings for engine reassembly. Regardless of how the bearing sizes are determined, use the oil clearance, measured with Plastigage, as a guide to ensure the bearings are the right size. **Note:** *If the thickest bearings (smallest inside diameter) won't bring bearing clearance within the specified range, replace the crankshaft.*

Main bearings

9   If you need to use a STANDARD-size main bearing, install one that has the same color code as the original bearing.
10   If the color code on the original main bearing has been obscured, locate the codes stamped into the block for the corresponding cap location **(see illustration)**.

11   Locate the main journal grade numbers on the crankshaft as well **(see illustrations)**.
12   Use the accompanying chart to determine the correct bearings for each journal **(see illustration)**.

Connecting rod bearings

13   If you need to use a STANDARD-size rod bearing, install one that has the same color code as the original.
14   If the color code has been obscured, locate the number stamped on each connecting rod and cap **(see illustration)**. This code indicates the connecting rod big-end-bearing bore size, **not** the cylinder number it came from.
15   Locate the letters stamped on the

crankshaft **(see illustration)**. These denote the size of their respective connecting rod journals.
16   Use the accompanying chart **(see illustration)** to determine the correct bearings for each journal.

All bearings

17   Remember, the oil clearance is the final judge when selecting new bearing sizes. If you have any questions or are unsure which bearings to use, get help from your dealer parts or service department.

21 Engine overhaul - reassembly sequence

1   Before beginning engine reassembly, make sure you have all the necessary new parts, gaskets and seals as well as the following items on hand:

Common hand tools
Torque wrench (1/2-inch drive)
Piston ring installation tool
Piston ring compressor
Short lengths of rubber or plastic hose to fit over connecting rod bolts
Plastigage
Feeler gauges
Fine-tooth file
New engine oil
Engine assembly lubricant (with molybdenum disulfide)
Gasket sealant
Thread locking compound

2   To save time and avoid problems, engine reassembly must be done in the following general order:

Piston/connecting rod assemblies (B18C1, B18C5, D16Y5, D16Y7, and D16Y8 engines)
Crankshaft and main bearings

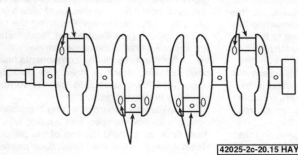

20.15 The connecting rod journal designations (letters) are also stamped onto the crankshaft

	1	2	3	4
A or I	RED	PINK	YELLOW	GREEN
B or II	PINK	YELLOW	GREEN	BROWN
C or III	YELLOW	GREEN	BROWN	BLACK
D or IIII	GREEN	BROWN	BLACK	BLUE

20.16 Connecting rod bearing selection chart for original sized crankshaft diameters - the numbers are stamped onto the connecting rod, the letters are stamped onto the crankshaft and the color code is on the edge of the bearing

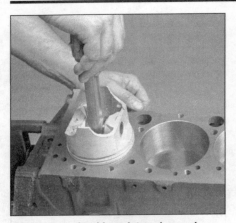

22.3 When checking piston ring end gap, the ring must be square in the cylinder bore (this is done by pushing the ring down with the top of a piston as shown)

Rear main oil seal and retainer
Piston/connecting rod assemblies
   (B18B1 engine)
Oil pan baffle
Oil pump and oil pump pick-up
Oil pan
Cylinder head
Camshaft(s) and rocker arm assembly
Water pump
Timing belt and sprockets
Intake and exhaust manifolds
Timing belt covers
Valve cover
Flywheel/driveplate

22 Piston rings - installation

Refer to illustrations 22.3, 22.4, 22.9a, 22.9b and 22.12

1   Before installing the new piston rings, the ring end gaps must be checked. It's assumed the piston ring side clearance has been checked and verified correct (see Section 18).

2   Lay out the piston/connecting rod assemblies and the new ring sets so the ring sets will be matched with the same piston and cylinder during the end gap measurement and engine assembly.

3   Insert the top (number one) ring into the first cylinder and square it up with the cylinder walls by pushing it in with the top of the piston **(see illustration)**. The ring should be near the bottom of the cylinder, at the lower limit of ring travel.

4   To measure the end gap, slip feeler gauges between the ends of the ring until a gauge equal to the gap width is found **(see illustration)**. The feeler gauge should slide between the ring ends with a slight amount of drag. Compare the measurement to this Chapter's Specifications. If the gap is larger or smaller than specified, double-check to make sure you have the correct rings before proceeding.

5   If the gap is too small, it must be enlarged or the ring ends may come in con-

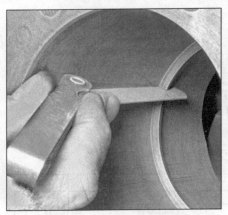

22.4 With the ring square in the cylinder, measure the end gap with a feeler gauge

22.9b DO NOT use a piston ring installation tool when installing the oil ring side rails

tact with each other during engine operation, which can cause serious engine damage. The end gap can be increased by filing the ring ends very carefully with a fine file. Mount the file in a vise equipped with soft jaws, slip the ring over the file with the ends contacting the file teeth and slowly move the ring to remove material from the ends. When performing this operation, file only from the outside in.

6   Excess end gap isn't critical unless it's greater than the service limit listed in this Chapter's Specifications. Again, double-check to make sure you have the correct rings for the engine.

7   Repeat the procedure for each ring that will be installed in the first cylinder and for each ring in the remaining cylinders. Remember to keep rings, pistons and cylinders matched up.

8   Once the ring end gaps have been checked/corrected, the rings can be installed on the pistons.

9   The oil control ring (lowest one on the piston) is usually installed first. It's composed of three separate components. Slip the spacer/expander into the groove **(see illustration)**. If an anti-rotation tang is used, make sure it's inserted into the drilled hole in the ring groove. Next, install the lower side rail.

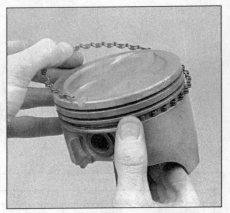

22.9a Installing the spacer/expander in the oil control ring groove

22.12 Installing the compression rings with a ring expander - the mark on the ring must face up

Don't use a piston ring installation tool on the oil ring side rails, as they may be damaged. Instead, place one end of the side rail into the groove between the spacer/expander and the ring land, hold it firmly in place and slide a finger around the piston while pushing the rail into the groove **(see illustration)**. Next, install the upper side rail in the same manner.

10   After the three oil ring components have been installed, check to make sure both the upper and lower side rails can be turned smoothly in the ring groove.

11   The number two (middle) ring is installed next. It's usually stamped with a mark, which must face up, toward the top of the piston. **Note:** *Always follow the instructions printed on the ring package or box - different manufacturers may require different approaches. Don't mix up the top and middle rings, as they have different cross-sections.*

12   Use a piston ring installation tool and make sure the identification mark is facing the top of the piston, then slip the ring into the middle groove on the piston **(see illustration)**. Don't expand the ring any more than necessary to slide it over the piston.

13   Install the number one (top) ring in the same manner. Make sure the mark is facing up. Be careful not to confuse the number one

23.6 Location of the number four thrust bearings (arrows) - the grooved sides face OUT

23.11 Lay the Plastigage strips on the main bearing journals, parallel to the crankshaft centerline

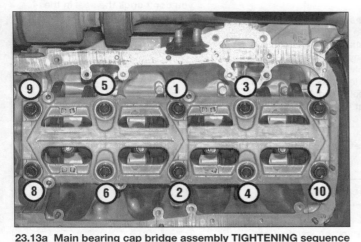

23.13a Main bearing cap bridge assembly TIGHTENING sequence (Civic engine)

23.13b Main bearing cap and bridge assembly TIGHTENING sequence (Integra engine); the bridge is used only on VTEC models only

and number two rings.

14   Repeat the procedure for the remaining pistons and rings.

23 Crankshaft - installation and main bearing oil clearance check

1   It's assumed at this point that the engine block and crankshaft have been cleaned, inspected and repaired or reconditioned.

2   Position the engine with the bottom facing up.

3   Remove the main bearing caps and/or bridge assembly.

4   Remove the original bearing inserts from the block and the main bearing caps. Wipe the bearing surfaces of the block and caps with a clean, lint-free cloth. They must be kept spotlessly clean.

Main bearing oil clearance check

Refer to illustrations 23.6, 23.11, 23.13a, 23.13b and 23.15

Note: *Don't touch the faces of the new bear-*

ing inserts with your fingers. Oil and acids from your skin can etch the bearings.

5   Clean the back sides of the new main bearing inserts and lay one in each main bearing saddle in the block. If one of the bearing inserts from each set has a large groove in it, make sure the grooved insert is installed in the block. Lay the other bearing from each set in the corresponding main bearing cap. Make sure the tab on the bearing insert fits into the recess in the block or cap.

6   The flanged thrust washers must be installed in the number four cap and saddle (counting from the front of the engine) **(see illustration)**.

7   Clean the faces of the bearings in the block and the crankshaft main bearing journals with a clean, lint-free cloth.

8   Check or clean the oil holes in the crankshaft, as any dirt here can go only one way - straight through the new bearings.

9   Once you're certain the crankshaft is clean, carefully lay it in position in the main bearings.

10   Before the crankshaft can be permanently installed, the main bearing oil clear-

ance must be checked.

11   Cut several pieces of the appropriate size Plastigage (they should be slightly shorter than the width of the main bearings) and place one piece on each crankshaft main bearing journal, parallel with the journal axis **(see illustration)**.

12   Clean the faces of the bearings in the main bearing caps and install the caps and/or bridge assembly. Don't disturb the Plastigage.

13   Working in the recommended sequence, tighten the main bearing caps and/or bridge assembly, in three steps, to the torque listed in this Chapter's Specifications **(see illustrations)**. Don't rotate the crankshaft at any time during this operation.

14   Remove the bolts and carefully lift off the main bearing caps and/or bridge assembly. Keep them in order. Don't disturb the Plastigage or rotate the crankshaft. If any of the main bearing caps are difficult to remove, tap them gently from side-to-side with a soft-face hammer to loosen them.

15   Compare the width of the crushed Plastigage on each journal to the scale printed on the Plastigage envelope to obtain the main

23.15 Compare the width of the crushed Plastigage to the scale on the envelope to determine the main bearing oil clearance (always take the measurement at the widest point of the Plastigage); be sure to use the correct scale - standard and metric ones are included

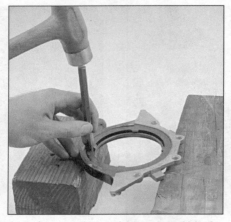

24.1 Support the retainer on wood blocks and drive out the old seal with a punch and hammer

24.2a Drive the new seal into the retainer with a wood block or a section of pipe, if you have one large enough - make sure you don't cock the seal in the retainer bore

bearing oil clearance **(see illustration)**. Check the Specifications at the beginning of this Chapter to make sure it's correct.

16   If the clearance is not as specified, the bearing inserts may be the wrong size (which means different ones will be required). Before deciding different inserts are needed, make sure no dirt or oil was between the bearing inserts and the caps or block when the clearance was measured. If the Plastigage was wider at one end than the other, the journal may be tapered (see Section 19).

17   Carefully scrape all traces of the Plastigage material off the main bearing journals and/or the bearing faces. Use your fingernail or the edge of a credit card - don't nick or scratch the bearing faces.

Final crankshaft installation

Note: *If you're working on an engine with a main bearing cap bridge (B18C1, B18C5, D16Y5, D16Y7 or D16Y8), install the piston/connecting rod assemblies first (see Section 25), placing then all at Top Dead Center so the connecting rods don't interfere with camshaft installation.*

18   Carefully lift the crankshaft out of the engine.

19   Clean the bearing faces in the block, then apply a thin, uniform layer of moly-base engine assembly lubricant to each of the bearing surfaces. Be sure to coat the thrust faces as well as the journal face of the thrust bearing.

20   Make sure the crankshaft journals are clean, then lay the crankshaft back in place in the block.

21   Clean the faces of the bearings in the caps, then apply lubricant to them.

22   Install the main bearing caps and/or bridge assembly.

23   Install the bolts.

24   Following the recommended sequence, tighten all main bearing cap bolts to the

torque listed in this Chapter's Specifications **(see illustration 23.13a or 23.13b)**.

25   Rotate the crankshaft a number of times by hand to check for any obvious binding.

26   Check the crankshaft endplay with feeler gauges or a dial indicator as described in Section 14. The endplay should be correct if the crankshaft thrust faces aren't worn or damaged and new bearings have been installed.

27   Refer to Section 24 and install the new rear main oil seal.

24   Rear main oil seal - installation

Refer to illustrations 24.1, 24.2a and 24.2b
Note: *The crankshaft must be installed and the main bearing caps bolted in place before the new seal and retainer assembly can be bolted to the block.*

1   Remove the old seal from the retainer with a hammer and punch by driving it out from the back side **(see illustration)**. Be sure to note how far it's recessed into the retainer bore before removing it; the new seal will have to be recessed an equal amount. Be very careful not to scratch or otherwise damage the bore in the retainer or oil leaks could develop.

2   Make sure the retainer is clean, then apply a thin coat of engine oil to the outer edge of the new seal. The seal must be pressed squarely into the retainer bore, so hammering it into place isn't recommended. If you don't have access to a press, sandwich the retainer and seal between two smooth pieces of wood and press the seal into place with the jaws of a large vise. If you don't have a vise big enough, lay the retainer on a workbench and drive the seal into place with a wood block and hammer **(see illustration)**. The piece of wood must be thick enough to distribute the force evenly around the entire circumference of the seal. Work slowly and make sure the seal enters the bore squarely.
Note: *Using a feeler gauge, confirm that the clearance between the seal and the retainer is*

24.2b Be sure to check the clearance between the seal and retainer using a feeler gauge

equal all the way around **(see illustration)**. *It should be 0.020 to 0.030-inch.*

3   Place a thin coat of RTV sealant to the entire edge of the retainer.

4   Lubricate the seal lips with multi-purpose grease or engine oil before you slip the seal/retainer over the crankshaft and bolt it to the block. Be sure to use a new gasket. **Note:** *Apply a film of RTV sealant to both sides of the gasket before installation.*

5   Tighten the retainer bolts, a little at a time, to the torque listed in the Chapter 2, Part A or Part B Specifications. Trim the gasket flush with the oil pan gasket surface, being careful not to scratch it.

25   Pistons and connecting rods - installation and rod bearing oil clearance check

1   Before installing the piston/connecting rod assemblies, the cylinder walls must be perfectly clean, the top edge of each cylinder

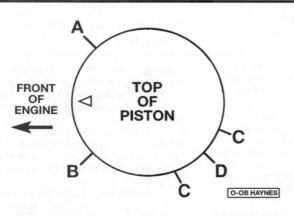

25.5 Ring end gap positions - align the oil ring spacer gap at D, the oil ring side rails at C, the second compression ring at A and the top compression ring at B

25.9 Using a piston ring compressor, install the pistons with the mark (arrow) toward the front of the engine (timing belt end)

must be chamfered, and the crankshaft must be in place.

2   Remove the cap from the end of the number one connecting rod (check the marks made during removal). Remove the original bearing inserts and wipe the bearing surfaces of the connecting rod and cap with a clean, lint-free cloth. They must be kept spotlessly clean.

Connecting rod bearing oil clearance check

Refer to illustrations 25.5, 25.9, 25.11, 25.13 and 25.17

Note: *Don't touch the faces of the new bearing inserts with your fingers. Oil and acids from your skin can etch the bearings.*

3   Clean the back side of the new upper bearing insert, then lay it in place in the connecting rod. Make sure the tab on the bearing fits into the recess in the rod. Don't hammer the bearing insert into place and be very careful not to nick or gouge the bearing face. Don't lubricate the bearing at this time.

4   Clean the back side of the other bearing insert and install it in the rod cap. Again, make sure the tab on the bearing fits into the

recess in the cap, and don't apply any lubricant. It's critically important that the mating surfaces of the bearing and connecting rod are perfectly clean and oil free when they're assembled.

5   Position the piston ring gaps at intervals around the piston **(see illustration)**. **Caution:** *DON'T position any ring gap inline with the piston pin hole or at piston thrust surfaces (90-degrees to piston pin).*

6   Slip a section of plastic or rubber hose over each connecting rod cap bolt.

7   Lubricate the piston and rings with clean engine oil and attach a piston ring compressor to the piston. Leave the skirt protruding about 1/4-inch to guide the piston into the cylinder. The rings must be compressed until they're flush with the piston.

8   Rotate the crankshaft until the number one connecting rod journal is at BDC (bottom dead center) and apply a coat of engine oil to the cylinder walls.

9   With the mark or notch on top of the piston facing the front of the engine **(see illustration)**, gently insert the piston/connecting rod assembly into the number one cylinder bore and rest the bottom edge of the ring compressor on the engine block.

10   Tap the top edge of the ring compressor to make sure it's contacting the block around its entire circumference.

11   Gently tap on the top of the piston with the end of a wooden or plastic hammer handle **(see illustration)** while guiding the end of the connecting rod into place on the crankshaft journal. The piston rings may try to pop out of the ring compressor just before entering the cylinder bore, so keep some pressure on the ring compressor. Work slowly, and if any resistance is felt as the piston enters the cylinder, stop immediately. Find out what's hanging up and fix it before proceeding. Do not, for any reason, force the piston into the cylinder - you might break a ring and/or the piston.

12   Once the piston/connecting rod assembly is installed, the connecting rod bearing oil clearance must be checked before the rod cap is permanently bolted in place.

13   Cut a piece of the appropriate size Plastigage slightly shorter than the width of the connecting rod bearing and lay it in place on the number one connecting rod journal, parallel with the journal axis **(see illustration)**.

14   Clean the connecting rod cap bearing face, remove the protective hoses from the

2C

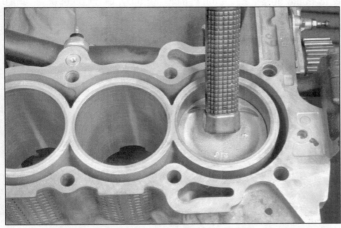

25.11 Drive the piston gently into the cylinder bore with the end of a wooden or plastic hammer handle

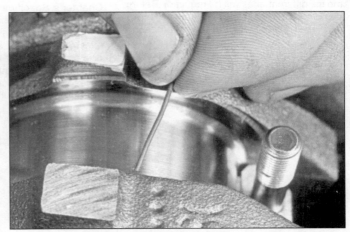

25.13 Lay the Plastigage strips on each rod bearing journal, parallel to the crankshaft centerline

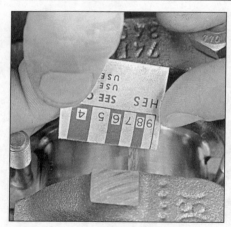

25.17 Measuring the width of the crushed Plastigage to determine the rod bearing oil clearance (be sure to use the correct scale - standard and metric ones are included)

connecting rod bolts and install the rod cap. Make sure the mating mark on the cap is on the same side as the mark on the connecting rod.

15   Install the nuts and tighten them to the torque listed in this Chapter's Specifications. Work up to it in two steps. **Note:** *Use a thinwall socket to avoid erroneous torque readings that can result if the socket is wedged between the rod cap and nut. If the socket tends to wedge itself between the nut and the cap, lift up on it slightly until it no longer contacts the cap. Do not rotate the crankshaft at any time during this operation.*

16   Remove the nuts and detach the rod cap, being very careful not to disturb the Plastigage.

17   Compare the width of the crushed Plastigage to the scale printed on the Plastigage envelope to obtain the oil clearance **(see illustration)**. Compare it to this Chapter's Specifications to make sure the clearance is correct.

18   If the clearance is not as specified, the bearing inserts may be the wrong size (which means different ones will be required). Before deciding different inserts are needed, make sure no dirt or oil was between the bearing inserts and the connecting rod or cap when the clearance was measured. Also, recheck the journal diameter. If the Plastigage was wider at one end than the other, the journal may be tapered.

Final connecting rod installation

19   Carefully scrape all traces of the Plastigage material off the rod journal and/or bearing face. Be very careful not to scratch the bearing - use your fingernail or the edge of a credit card.

20   Make sure the bearing faces are perfectly clean, then apply a uniform layer of clean moly-base engine assembly lube to both of them. You'll have to push the piston into the cylinder to expose the face of the bearing insert in the connecting rod - be sure to slip the protective hoses over the rod bolts first.

21   Slide the connecting rod back into place on the journal, remove the protective hoses from the rod cap bolts, install the rod cap and tighten the nuts to the torque listed in this Chapter's Specifications. Again, work up to the torque in two steps. **Note:** *Again, make sure the mating mark on the cap is on the same side as the mark on the connecting rod.*

22   Repeat the entire procedure for the remaining pistons/connecting rods.

23   The important points to remember are:

a) *Keep the back sides of the bearing inserts and the insides of the connecting rods and caps perfectly clean when assembling them.*

b) *Make sure you have the correct piston/rod assembly for each cylinder.*

c) *The arrow or mark on the piston must face the front (timing belt end) of the engine.*

d) *Lubricate the cylinder walls with clean oil.*

e) *Lubricate the bearing faces when installing the rod caps after the oil clearance has been checked.*

24   After all the piston/connecting rod assemblies have been properly installed, rotate the crankshaft a number of times by hand to check for any obvious binding.

25   As a final step, the connecting rod endplay must be checked. Refer to Section 13 for this procedure.

26   Compare the measured endplay to this Chapter's Specifications to make sure it's correct. If it was correct before disassembly and the original crankshaft and rods were reinstalled, it should still be right. If new rods or a new crankshaft were installed, the endplay may be inadequate. If so, the rods will have to be removed and taken to an automotive machine shop for re-sizing.

26   Initial start-up and break-in after overhaul

Warning: *Have a fire extinguisher handy when starting the engine for the first time.*

1   Once the engine has been installed in the vehicle, double-check the engine oil and coolant levels.

2   With the spark plugs out of the engine and the ignition system and fuel system disabled (see Section 3), crank the engine until oil pressure registers on the gauge or the light goes out.

3   Install the spark plugs, hook up the plug wires and restore the ignition and fuel system functions.

4   Start the engine. It may take a few moments for the fuel system to build up pressure, but the engine should start without a great deal of effort. **Note:** *If backfiring occurs through the throttle body, recheck the valve timing and ignition timing.*

5   After the engine starts, it should be allowed to warm up to normal operating temperature at idle speed, then allowed to idle for about 15 minutes. This is especially important after main or connecting rod bearings have been replaced. While the engine is warming up, make a thorough check for fuel, oil and coolant leaks.

6   Shut the engine off and recheck the engine oil and coolant levels.

7   Drive the vehicle to an area with minimum traffic, accelerate from 30 to 50 mph, then allow the vehicle to slow to 20 or 30 mph with the throttle closed. Repeat the procedure 10 or 12 times. This will load the piston rings and cause them to seat properly against the cylinder walls. Check again for oil and coolant leaks.

8   Drive the vehicle easily for the first 500 miles (no sustained high speeds or towing) and keep a constant check on the oil level. It isn't unusual for an engine to use oil during the break-in period.

9   At approximately 500 to 600 miles, change the oil **and** filter.

10   For the next few hundred miles, drive the vehicle normally. Don't pamper or abuse it.

11   After 2000 miles, change the oil and filter again and consider the engine broken in.

Chapter 3
Cooling, heating and air conditioning systems

Contents

3

Specifications

General

Coolant capacity	See Chapter 1
Drivebelt tension	See Chapter 1
Radiator pressure cap rating	14 to 18 psi
Thermostat rating	195 degrees F
Refrigerant type	R-134a
Refrigerant oil added for component replacement	
Compressor	4 to 4-2/3 ounces
Condenser	1 ounce
Evaporator	1-1/3 ounces
Receiver-drier	1/3 ounce
Line or hose	1/3 ounce

Torque specifications

	Ft-lbs (unless otherwise indicated)
Alternator adjustment bracket-to-water pump bolt	33
Thermostat housing cover bolts	108 in-lbs
Upper radiator hose fitting-to-block bolts	96 in-lbs
Water pump-to-block bolts	108 in-lbs

1   General information

Refer to illustrations 1.1a and 1.1b

Engine cooling system

All vehicles covered by this manual employ a pressurized engine cooling system with thermostatically controlled coolant circulation **(see illustrations)**. An impeller-type water pump mounted on the engine block pumps coolant through the engine. The coolant flows around each cylinder and toward the rear of the engine. Cast-in coolant passages direct coolant around the intake and exhaust ports, near the spark plug areas and in close proximity to the exhaust valve guides.

A wax pellet type thermostat controls engine coolant temperature. During warm up, the closed thermostat prevents coolant from circulating through the radiator. As the engine nears normal operating temperature, the thermostat opens and allows hot coolant to travel through the radiator, where it's cooled before returning to the engine.

The cooling system is sealed by a pressure type radiator cap, which raises the boiling point of the coolant and increases the cooling efficiency of the radiator. If the system pressure exceeds the cap pressure relief value, the excess pressure in the system forces the spring-loaded valve inside the cap off its seat and allows the coolant to escape through the overflow tube into a coolant reservoir. When the system cools the excess coolant is automatically drawn from the reservoir back into the radiator.

The coolant reservoir serves as both the point at which fresh coolant is added to the cooling system to maintain the proper fluid level and as a holding tank for overheated coolant.

This type of cooling system is known as a closed design because coolant that escapes past the pressure cap is saved and reused.

Heating system

The heating system consists of a blower fan and heater core located in the heater box, the hoses connecting the heater core to the engine cooling system and the heater/air conditioning control head on the dashboard. Hot engine coolant is circulated through the heater core. When the heater mode is activated, a flap door opens to expose the heater box to the passenger compartment. A fan switch on the control head activates the blower motor, which forces air through the core, heating the air.

Air conditioning system

The air conditioning system consists of a condenser mounted in front of the radiator, an evaporator mounted adjacent to the heater core, a compressor mounted on the engine, a receiver-drier which contains a high pressure relief valve and the plumbing connecting all of the above components.

A blower fan forces the warmer air of the passenger compartment through the evaporator core (sort of a radiator-in-reverse), transferring the heat from the air to the refrigerant. The liquid refrigerant boils off into low pressure vapor, taking the heat with it when it leaves the evaporator.

2   Antifreeze - general information

Warning: *Do not allow antifreeze to come in contact with your skin or painted surfaces of the vehicle. Rinse off spills immediately with plenty of water. Antifreeze is highly toxic if ingested. Never leave antifreeze lying around in an open container or in puddles on the floor; children and pets are attracted by it's sweet smell and may drink it. Check with local authorities about disposing of used antifreeze. Many communities have collection*

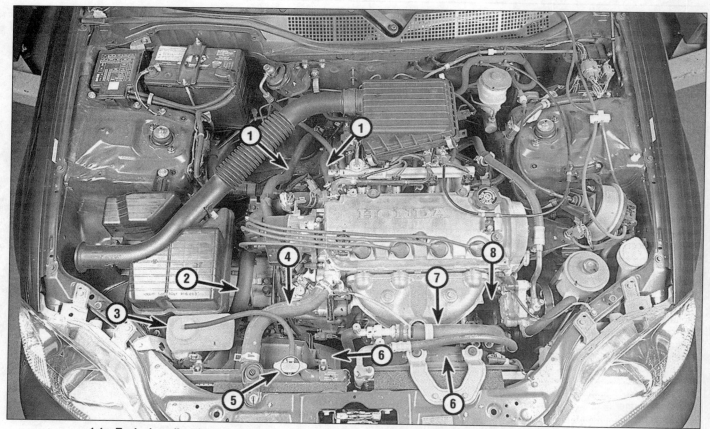

1.1a   Typical cooling, heater and air conditioning systems underhood component locations (Honda Civic)

1	Heater hoses	4	Upper radiator hose
2	Lower radiator hose	5	Radiator cap
3	Coolant reservoir	6	Cooling fans

7	Air conditioning refrigerant hose
8	Air conditioning compressor

1.1b Typical cooling, heater and air conditioning systems underhood component locations (Acura Integra)

1	Lower radiator hose	4	Radiator cap	6	Air conditioning refrigerant hose
2	Upper radiator hose	5	Cooling fans	7	Air conditioning compressor
3	Coolant reservoir				

centers which will see that antifreeze is disposed of safely.

Note: *Non-toxic antifreeze is now available at most auto parts stores, but even these types should be disposed of properly.*

The cooling system should be filled with a water/ethylene glycol based antifreeze solution, which will prevent freezing down to at least -20-degrees F, or lower if local climate requires it. It also provides protection against corrosion and increases the coolant boiling point.

The cooling system should be drained, flushed and refilled at the specified intervals (see Chapter 1). Old or contaminated antifreeze solutions are likely to cause damage and encourage the formation of rust and scale in the system.

Before adding antifreeze, check all hose connections, because antifreeze tends to leak through very minute openings. Engines don't normally consume coolant, so if the level goes down, find the cause and correct it.

The exact mixture of antifreeze-to-water which you should use depends on the relative weather conditions. The mixture should contain at least 50-percent antifreeze, but should never contain more than 70-percent antifreeze. Consult the mixture ratio chart on the antifreeze container before adding coolant. Hydrometers are available at most auto parts stores to test the coolant. Use

antifreeze which meets the vehicle manufacturer's specifications.

---

3   Thermostat - check and replacement

Warning: *Do not remove the radiator cap, drain the coolant or replace the thermostat until the engine has cooled completely. Read the* **Warning** *at the beginning of Section 2.*

Check

1   Before assuming the thermostat is to blame for a cooling system problem, check the coolant level, drivebelt tension (see Chapter 1) and temperature gauge operation.

2   If the engine seems to be taking a long time to warm up (based on heater output or temperature gauge operation), the thermostat is probably stuck open. Replace the thermostat with a new one.

3   If the engine runs hot, use your hand to check the temperature of the upper radiator hose. If the hose isn't hot, but the engine is, the thermostat is probably stuck closed, preventing the coolant inside the engine from escaping to the radiator. Replace the thermostat. **Caution:** *Don't drive the vehicle without a thermostat. The computer may stay in open loop and emissions and fuel economy will*

suffer.

4   If the upper radiator hose is hot, it means that the coolant is flowing and the thermostat is open. Consult the *Troubleshooting* section at the front of this manual for cooling system diagnosis.

Replacement

Refer to illustrations 3.10a, 3.10b, 3.13 and 3.14

5   Disconnect the cable from the negative battery terminal. **Caution:** *If the radio in your vehicle is equipped with an anti-theft system, make sure you have the correct activation code before disconnecting the battery.*

6   Drain the cooling system (see Chapter 1). If the coolant is relatively new or in good condition (see Chapter 1), save it and reuse it.

7   Follow the upper radiator hose to the engine to locate the thermostat housing cover.

8   Loosen the hose clamp, then detach the hose from the fitting. If it's stuck, grasp it near the end with a pair of adjustable pliers and twist it to break the seal, then pull it off. If the hose is old or deteriorated, cut it off and install a new one.

9   If the outer surface of the large fitting that mates with the hose is deteriorated (corroded, pitted, etc.) it may be damaged further by hose removal. If it is, the thermostat housing cover will have to be replaced.

3

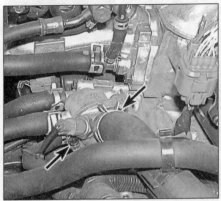

3.10a To replace the thermostat, pull off the hose, remove the two cover bolts (arrows), pull off the cover and remove the thermostat from the housing (Honda Civic)

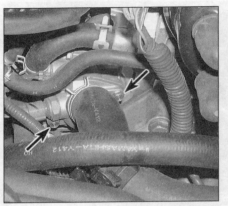

3.10b Acura Integra thermostat housing bolt locations (arrows)

3.13 Install a new rubber gasket over the thermostat

10   Disconnect the electrical connector from the engine coolant temperature (ECT) sensor, remove the thermostat cover bolts and detach the housing cover **(see illustrations)**. If the cover is stuck, tap it with a soft-face hammer to jar it loose. Be prepared for some coolant to spill as the gasket seal is broken.

11   Note how it's installed - with the jiggle pin up - then remove the thermostat.

12   Remove all traces of old gasket material and/or sealant from the housing and cover.

13   Install a new rubber gasket over the thermostat **(see illustration)**.

14   Install the new thermostat in the housing without using sealant. Make sure the jiggle pin, if equipped, is at the top and the spring end is directed into the engine **(see illustration)**.

15   Install the housing cover and bolts. Tighten the bolts to the torque listed in this Chapter's Specifications.

16   Reattach the hose and tighten the hose clamp securely. Install all components that were removed for access.

17   Refill the cooling system (see Chapter 1).

18   Start the engine and allow it to reach normal operating temperature, then check for leaks and proper thermostat operation (as described in Steps 2 through 4).

4   Engine cooling fan(s) and circuit - check and component replacement

Warning: *To avoid possible injury or damage, DO NOT operate the engine with a damaged fan. Do not attempt to repair fan blades - replace a damaged fan with a new one.*

Check

Refer to illustrations 4.1a, 4.1b, and 4.3
Note: *Models equipped with air conditioning have two complete fan circuits - one for the condenser and one for the radiator. The following procedures apply to both.*

1   To test a fan motor, disconnect the electrical connector at the motor **(see illustrations)** and use jumper wires to connect the fan directly to the battery. If the fan still doesn't work, replace the motor.

2   If the motor tests OK, check the fuse and relay (see Chapter 12), the fan switch, the condenser fan relay (mounted at the left front corner of the engine compartment), if equipped, or the wiring which connects the components.

3   To test the radiator fan switch, remove the switch electrical connector **(see illustration)** and, using an ohmmeter, check for continuity across the terminals of the switch with

3.14 Install the new thermostat in the housing with the spring towards the engine and the jiggle pin (arrow) at the top

the engine cold. The switch should not have continuity while the coolant is below 189 degrees F. Start the engine and allow the engine to reach normal operating temperature. Stop the engine and check for continuity again. The radiator fan switch should show continuity when the coolant temperature reaches 196 to 203-degrees F, and above. If the switch fails to show continuity above this temperature, replace it.

4   The air conditioning condenser fan is controlled by the ECM. If the fan fails to operate with the air conditioning On after all other

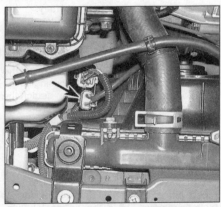

4.1a Location of the electrical connector for the radiator cooling fan motor (arrow)

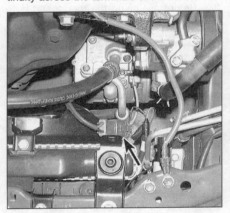

4.1b Location of the electrical connector for the condenser fan motor (arrow)

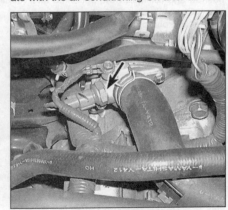

4.3 Location of the Engine coolant temperature switch (arrow)

4.8a The radiator fan shroud has two lower retaining bolts (right bolt shown, other bolt not visible in this photo) . . .

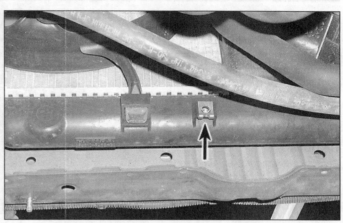

4.8b . . . but the condenser fan shroud doesn't have any bolts at the bottom; on Integra models it has a post that fits into a pocket on the radiator (arrow), and on Civic models there are two rubber mounts that fit into holes in two brackets

4.9 Upper condenser and radiator fan mounting bolts (arrows)

4.10 To remove the condenser fan, remove the air conditioning line bracket bolts, push the bracket aside, then carefully lift the fan out of the engine compartment; to remove the radiator fan assembly, simply unbolt it and pull it out

checks have been completed, check for a low refrigerant charge or have the ECM diagnosed by a dealership service department or other qualified repair facility.

Replacement

Refer to illustrations 4.8a, 4.8b, 4.9, 4.10, 4.11 and 4.12

Note: *This procedure applies to either fan.*

5   Disconnect the battery cable from the negative battery terminal. **Caution:** *If the radio in your vehicle is equipped with an anti-theft system, make sure you have the correct activation code before disconnecting the battery.*

6   Set the parking brake and block the rear wheels to prevent the vehicle from rolling. Raise the front of the vehicle and support it securely with jackstands. Remove the lower splash pan, if equipped, from under the radiator.

7   Insert a small screwdriver into the connector to lift the lock tab and disconnect the fan wiring.

8   Remove the fan lower mounting bolt(s) **(see illustrations)**.

9   Unbolt the fan upper brackets **(see illustration)** and the condenser top mountings.

10   Carefully lift the fan out of the engine compartment **(see illustration)**.

11   To detach the fan from the motor,

remove the motor shaft nut **(see illustration)**.

12   To detach the fan motor from the shroud, remove the mounting screws **(see illustration)**.

13   Installation is the reverse of removal.

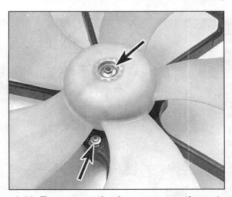

4.11 To remove the fan, unscrew the nut in the center (upper arrow), then pull the fan blade from the motor shaft (the lower arrow points to one of the motor mounting screws)

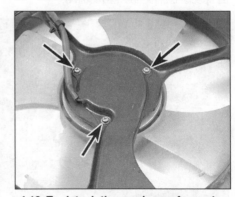

4.12 To detach the condenser fan motor from the shroud, remove these screws (arrows)

5   Radiator and coolant reservoir - removal and installation

Warning: *Wait until the engine is completely cool before beginning these procedures. Read the warning at the beginning of Section 2.*

Radiator

Removal

Refer to illustrations 5.6a, 5.6b and 5.8

1   Disconnect the cable from the negative battery terminal. **Caution:** *If the radio in your vehicle is equipped with an anti-theft system, make sure you have the correct activation code before disconnecting the battery.*
2   Set the parking brake and block the rear wheels. Raise the front of the vehicle and support it securely on jackstands. Remove the splash pan beneath the radiator.
3   Drain the cooling system (see Chapter 1). If the coolant is relatively new or in good condition, save it and reuse it.
4   If the vehicle is equipped with an automatic transaxle, disconnect the cooler lines from the radiator. Use a drip pan to catch spilled fluid and plug the lines and fittings.
5   Disconnect the electrical connector(s) for the cooling fan motor(s).
6   Loosen the hose clamps, then detach the radiator hoses from the fittings **(see illustrations)**. If they're stuck, grasp each hose near the end with a pair of slip joint pliers and twist it to break the seal, then pull it off - be careful not to damage the radiator fittings! If the hoses are old or deteriorated, cut them off and install new ones.
7   Remove the cooling fan(s) (see Section 4).
8   Unbolt and remove the small brackets that attach the upper end of the radiator to the radiator support **(see illustration)**.
9   Carefully lift out the radiator. Don't spill coolant on the vehicle or scratch the paint.
10   Inspect the radiator for leaks and damage. If it needs repair, have a radiator shop or dealer service department perform the work as special techniques are required.

5.6a   Loosen the hose clamp and detach the upper radiator hose (arrow) . . .

11   Bugs and dirt can be removed from the radiator by spraying with a garden hose from the back side.
12   Check the radiator mounts for deterioration and replace if necessary.

Installation

13   Installation is the reverse of the removal procedure. Guide the radiator into the mounts until they seat properly.
14   After installation, fill the cooling system with the proper mixture of antifreeze and water (see Chapter 1).
15   Start the engine and check for leaks. Allow the engine to reach normal operating temperature, indicated by the upper radiator hose becoming hot. Recheck the coolant level and add more if required.
16   If you're working on an automatic transaxle equipped vehicle, check and add fluid as needed.

Coolant reservoir

17   The coolant reservoir is mounted adjacent to the radiator in the right front corner of the engine compartment.
18   Trace the overflow hose from the radiator neck to the top of coolant reservoir. Remove the cap with the hose still attached. Lift the reservoir straight up out of the bracket.

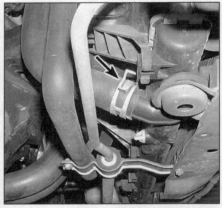

5.6b   . . . then loosen the hose clamp and detach the lower radiator hose (arrow)

19   Pour the coolant into a container.
20   Wash out and inspect the reservoir for cracks and chafing. Examine the reservoir closely. If it's damaged, replace it.
21   Installation is the reverse of removal.

6   Oil cooler - removal and installation

Refer to illustration 6.1

Warning: *Allow the engine to cool completely before beginning this procedure.*

1   The oil cooler used on some Integra models is mounted between the oil filter and engine block **(see illustration)**.
2   Remove the oil filter and drain the coolant (see Chapter 1).
3   Detach the two coolant lines from the oil cooler. Be prepared for coolant to escape from the open fittings. Cap or plug the open fittings.
4   Remove the large nut (actually part of the hollow retaining bolt) in the center of the oil cooler and separate the oil cooler from the engine.
5   Installation is the reverse of removal. Be sure to use a new O-ring between the block and oil cooler (lubricate the O-ring with clean engine oil before installation). Tighten the

5.8   Remove these bolts (arrows) and brackets that attach the radiator to the radiator support

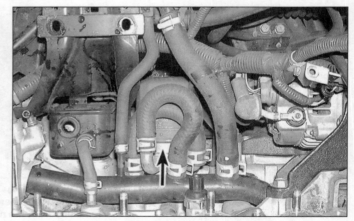

6.1   Oil cooler location (arrow)

7.3 The weep holes (arrows) are located on the rear side of the water pump

8.6 Remove the water pump bolts (arrows) and detach the water pump from the engine - be sure to note the location of the longer bolt (the same bolt that secures the timing belt spring tensioner)

coolant hoses securely at the fittings.

6   Install a new oil filter and change the engine oil (see Chapter 1).

7   Add coolant and oil as needed.

8   Start the engine and check for oil and coolant leaks.

9   Recheck the coolant and oil levels.

7   Water pump - check

Refer to illustration 7.3

1   A failure in the water pump can cause serious engine damage due to overheating.

2   There are two ways to check the operation of the water pump while it's installed on the engine. If the pump is defective, it should be replaced with a new or rebuilt unit.

3   Water pumps are equipped with weep (or vent) holes **(see illustration)**. If a failure occurs in the pump seal, coolant will leak from the hole. With the timing belt cover removed, you'll need a flashlight and small mirror to find the hole on the water pump from underneath to check for leaks.

4   If the water pump shaft bearings fail there may be a howling sound at the pump

while it's running. Shaft wear can be felt with the timing belt removed if the water pump pulley is rocked up and down (with the engine off). Don't mistake drivebelt slippage, which causes a squealing sound, for water pump bearing failure.

8   Water pump - replacement

Refer to illustrations 8.6 and 8.11

Warning: *Wait until the engine is completely cool before beginning this procedure. Read the warning at the beginning of Section 2.*

1   Disconnect the cable from the negative battery terminal. **Caution:** *If the radio in your vehicle is equipped with an anti-theft system, make sure you have the correct activation code before disconnecting the battery.*

2   Drain the cooling system (see Chapter 1). If the coolant is relatively new or in good condition, save it and reuse it.

3   Remove the drivebelts (see Chapter 1).

4   Remove the timing belt (see Chapter 2, Part A). On Integra models, remove the pulleys from the camshafts and the cover from the back of the engine.

5   Remove any accessory brackets from the water pump.

6   Remove the bolts **(see illustration)** and detach the water pump from the engine. Note the location of the longer bolt.

7   Clean the bolt threads and the threaded holes in the engine to remove corrosion and sealant.

8   Compare the new pump to the old one to make sure they're identical.

9   Remove all traces of old gasket sealant and O-ring from the engine.

10   Clean the engine and new water pump mating surfaces with lacquer thinner or acetone.

11   Apply a thin layer of RTV sealant to the O-ring groove of the new pump, then carefully set a new O-ring in the groove **(see illustration)**.

12   Carefully attach the pump to the engine and thread the bolts into the holes finger tight.

13   Install the remaining bolts (if they also hold an accessory bracket in place, be sure to reposition the bracket at this time). Tighten them to the torque listed in this Chapter's Specifications in 1/4-turn increments. Don't overtighten them or the pump may be distorted.

14   Reinstall all parts removed for access to the pump.

15   Refill and bleed the cooling system and check the drivebelt tension (see Chapter 1). Run the engine and check for leaks.

9   Coolant temperature gauge sending unit - check and replacement

Refer to illustration 9.1

Warning: *Wait until the engine is completely cool before beginning this procedure.*

1   The coolant temperature indicator system consists of a temperature gauge mounted in the instrument panel and a coolant temperature sending unit mounted

3

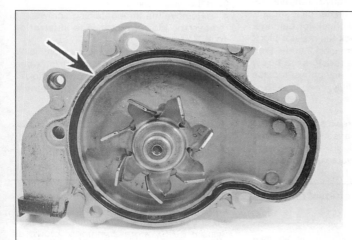

8.11 Apply a thin layer of RTV sealant to the O-ring groove of the new pump, then carefully set a new O-ring in the groove

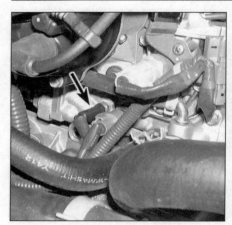

9.1 The coolant temperature sending unit (arrow) is located near the distributor (it's the one with the single wire)

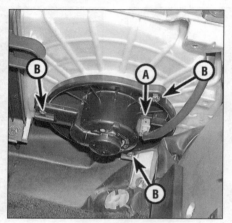

10.3 Insert a jumper wire into the backside of blue/black wire of the blower motor connector (A) and connect it to ground - the blower motor is retained by three bolts (B)

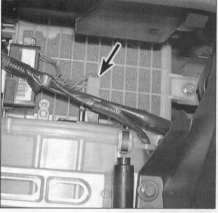

10.5 Remove the connector (arrow) from the blower motor resistor

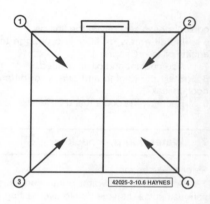

10.6 Blower motor resistor terminals - the resistance between terminals 2 and 4 should be 2 to 3 ohms

on the engine directly below the distributor **(see illustration)**.

2   If an overheating indication occurs even when the engine is cold, check the wiring between the dash and the sending unit for a short circuit to ground.

3   If the gauge is inoperative, test the circuit by briefly grounding the wire to the sending unit while the ignition is on (engine not running for safety). If the gauge deflects full scale, replace the sending unit. **Warning:** *This vehicle is equipped with electric cooling fans. Stay clear of the fan blades, which can come on even when the engine is not running.* If the gauge doesn't respond, check for an open circuit in the gauge wiring.

4   If the sending unit is suspect, check the resistance of the sensor with the engine cold and hot. The resistance should decrease as the temperature increases (when the engine is cool [130-degrees or cooler] the resistance should be approximately 140 ohms; when the engine is at normal operating temperature (186-degrees or warmer] the resistance should be approximately 30 to 46 ohms).

5   If the sending unit must be replaced, simply unscrew it from the engine and quickly install the replacement. Use sealant on the threads. **Warning:** *Make sure the engine is completely cool before removing the sending unit.* There will be some coolant loss as the unit is removed, so be prepared to catch it. Check the coolant level after the replacement part has been installed (see Chapter 1).

---

10   Blower motor and circuit - check and component replacement

Refer to illustrations 10.3, 10.5 and 10.6

Check

1   Check the fuse and all connections in the circuit for looseness and corrosion. Make sure the battery is fully charged.

2   With the transmission in Park, the parking brake securely set, turn the ignition switch On (engine not running).

3   Without disconnecting the blower motor, insert a jumper wire into the backside of the blower motor connector blue/black wire **(see illustration)** and connect the other end of the jumper wire to ground. If the blower motor runs the fault lies with the blower fan switch, the blower resistors or related wiring.

4   If the motor didn't run with the jumper connected to ground, remove the jumper, disconnect the electrical connector at the blower motor and with a voltmeter measure the voltage between the connector blue/white wire and ground **(see illustration 10.3)**. On all models, if there is battery voltage present and the motor didn't run at any speed, replace the blower motor (see Section 11). If no battery voltage is present, check the blower motor relay or related wiring (see Chapter 12).

5   The blower resistor assembly is located on the blower motor housing **(see illustration)**. There are several resistance elements mounted on the resistor board to provide low and medium blower speeds.

6   If the blower motor runs, but one or more speeds are inoperative, remove the blower resistor from the heater case mounting location and visually check for damage. Using an ohmmeter, check the resistor block for continuity between terminals 2 and 4 **(see illustration)**. If any of the resistors are below the minimum or there are any opens, replace the blower resistor assembly.

Replacement

7   Remove the two screws and detach the blower resistor board assembly from the heater case.

8   Installation is the reverse of removal.

---

11   Blower motor - removal and installation

1   Disconnect the cable from the negative

battery terminal. Disable the airbag (see Chapter 12). **Caution:** *If the radio in your vehicle is equipped with an anti-theft system, make sure you have the correct activation code before disconnecting the battery.*

2   The blower unit is located under the dash, behind the glovebox.

3   Disconnect the electrical connector from the blower motor.

4   Remove the three retaining screws and remove the blower motor **(see illustration 10.3)**.

5   If you're replacing the blower motor itself, separate the blower motor from the fan wheel and place the fan on the new blower motor.

6   Installation is the reverse of removal. Check for proper operation.

---

12   Heater and air conditioning control assembly - removal, installation and cable adjustment

Refer to illustrations 12.4 and 12.5
Warning: *The models covered by this manual are equipped with a Supplemental Restraint System (SRS), more commonly known as*

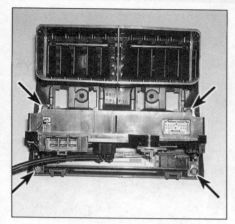

12.4 Remove the four mounting screws (arrows) retaining the heater/air conditioner control assembly to the center air vent

12.5 Detach the air mix cable from this clip (arrow) and disconnect it from the air mix control arm

13.3 Detach the control cable (arrow) from the heater valve using a small screwdriver to lift the cable end off the pin

airbags. *Always disable the airbag system before working in the vicinity of the SRS unit, steering column or instrument panel to avoid the possibility of accidental deployment of the airbag, which could cause personal injury* (see Chapter 12).

1 Disconnect the cable from the negative battery terminal. **Caution:** *If the radio in your vehicle is equipped with an anti-theft system, make sure you have the correct activation code before disconnecting the battery.*

2 Remove the center console lower trim (see Chapter 11).

3 Remove the stereo (see Chapter 12).

4 Remove the screws securing the center air vent, pull out the center air vent and remove the four control assembly mounting screws **(see illustration)**.

5 Pull out the heater/air conditioner control assembly and disconnect the electrical connector. Detach the air mix cable from the air mix control arm **(see illustration)**.

6 Installation is the reverse of removal.

7 Run the engine and check for proper functioning of the heater and air conditioning system.

Adjustment

Air mix control cable

Civic

8 To adjust the cable, disconnect the cable from the heater valve arm in the engine compartment. Disconnect the air mix control cable from the control arm under the dash.

9 Set the temperature control lever to MAX COOL, then carefully pull on the outer cable housing and close the door, making sure there is no slack in the cable.

10 With the air mix control arm held against the stop, snap the air mix cable into the cable clamp.

11 In the engine compartment, place the heater valve arm to fully closed and connect the cable. Hold the valve arm closed and remove any slack by pulling on the outer cable housing and connect the cable clamp.

Integra

12 Disconnect the cable from the control arm clamp.

13 Set the temperature control lever to MAX HEAT, then turn the air mix control arm to connect the cable.

14 Slide the cable housing back from the end to take up any slack, then secure the cable with the clamp.

Heater valve cable

15 Disconnect the cable from the valve arm in the engine compartment and the air mix control cable from the control arm under the dash.

16 Set the temperature control lever to MAX HEAT, then turn the heater control toward the cable and connect the cable into the cable and clamp. Hold the end of the cable against the stop and snap the air mix cable into the cable clamp.

17 In the engine compartment, place the heater valve arm to fully closed and connect the cable. Hold the valve arm closed and remove any slack by pulling on the outer cable housing and secure the cable with the clamp

13 Heater core - replacement

Refer to illustrations 13.3, 13.4a, 13.4b, 13.5 and 13.10

Warning 1: *The models covered by this manual are equipped with a Supplemental Restraint System (SRS), more commonly known as airbags. Always disable the airbag system before working in the vicinity of the SRS unit, steering column or instrument panel to avoid the possibility of accidental deployment of the airbag, which could cause personal injury* (see Chapter 12).

Warning 2: *The air conditioning system is under high pressure. Do not loosen any hose fittings or remove any components until after the system has been discharged. Air conditioning refrigerant should be properly discharged into an EPA-approved recov-*

ery/recycling unit at a dealer service department or an automotive air conditioning repair facility. Always wear eye protection when disconnecting air conditioning system fittings.

Warning 3: *Wait until the engine is completely cool before beginning this procedure.*

1 If the vehicle is equipped with air conditioning, have the system discharged by a dealer service department or automotive air conditioning repair facility. Disconnect the cable from the negative battery terminal. **Caution:** *If the radio in your vehicle is equipped with an anti-theft system, make sure you have the correct activation code before disconnecting the battery.* Disable the airbag, if equipped (see Chapter 12).

2 Drain the cooling system (see Chapter 1).

3 Disconnect the heater valve cable **(see illustration)**.

4 Working in the engine compartment, disconnect the heater hoses **(see illustration)** where they enter the firewall. Place a drain pan underneath the hoses to catch any coolant that runs out when the hoses are disconnected. Remove the heater unit mounting nut located above the heater hose inlet and

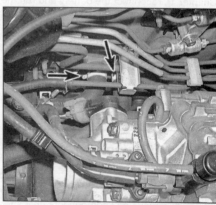

13.4a Loosen the two heater hose clamps and disconnect the heater hoses (arrows) from the heater core inlet and outlet pipes at the firewall

13.4b Remove the nut (arrow) retaining the heater unit to the firewall

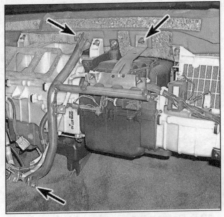

13.5 Integra model SRS beam retaining nuts (arrows)

13.10 Heater unit retaining nuts (arrows)

outlet tubes **(see illustration). Caution:** *Be careful not to damage or bend the fuel lines or brake pipes when removing the nut.*

5   On Integra models, remove the passenger side SRS beam **(see illustration)**.

6   Remove the heater/air conditioner control assembly (see Section 12).

7   Remove the instrument cluster trim panel, the console and the instrument panel (see Chapter 11).

8   On non-air conditioned models, remove the heater duct from between the heater unit and the blower unit. If equipped with air conditioning, remove the evaporator unit (see Section 19).

9   Remove the steering column bracket.

10   Remove the wire harness clip from the heater unit, the two nuts retaining the heater unit to the bulkhead and remove the heater unit from the vehicle **(see illustration)**.

11   Remove the screws from the heater core cover and the heater pipe clamp. Lift the heater core from the housing.

12   Installation is the reverse of removal. Be sure to check the operation of the air control flaps. If any parts bind, correct the problem before installation.

13   Refill and bleed the cooling system (see Chapter 1), reconnect the battery and run the engine. Check for coolant leaks and proper heater system operation. If equipped with air conditioning, have the system charged by a dealer service department or automotive air conditioning repair facility.

14 Air conditioning and heating system - check and maintenance

Air conditioning system

Refer to illustration 14.1

Warning: *The air conditioning system is under high pressure. Do not loosen any hose fittings or remove any components until after the system has been discharged. Air conditioning refrigerant should be properly discharged into an EPA-approved recovery/recycling unit at a dealer service department or*

an automotive air conditioning repair facility. Always wear eye protection when disconnecting air conditioning system fittings.

Caution: *When replacing entire components, additional refrigerant oil should be added equal to the amount that is removed with the component being replaced. Be sure to read the container before adding any oil to the system, to make sure it is compatible with the R-134a system.*

1   The following maintenance checks should be performed on a regular basis to ensure that the air conditioning continues to operate at peak efficiency.

   a) *Inspect the condition of the compressor drivebelt. If it is worn or deteriorated, replace it (see Chapter 1).*

   b) *Check the drivebelt tension and, if necessary, adjust it (see Chapter 1).*

   c) *Inspect the system hoses. Look for cracks, bubbles, hardening and deterioration. Inspect the hoses and all fittings for oil bubbles or seepage. If there is any evidence of wear, damage or leakage, replace the hose(s).*

   d) *Inspect the condenser fins for leaves, bugs and any other foreign material that may have embedded itself in the fins. Use a "fin comb" or compressed air to remove debris from the condenser.*

   e) *Make sure the system has the correct refrigerant charge.*

   f) *If you hear water sloshing around in the dash area or have water dripping on the carpet, slip off the evaporator housing condensation drain tube (located in the lower right forward corner of the housing) and insert a piece of wire into both openings to check for blockage* **(see illustration)**.

2   It's a good idea to operate the system for about ten minutes at least once a month. This is particularly important during the winter months because long term non-use can cause hardening, and subsequent failure, of the seals. Note that using the Defrost function operates the compressor.

3   If the air conditioning system is not working properly, first make sure the com-

14.1 Air conditioner condensation drain tube (arrow)

pressor clutch is operating (see Section 15).

4   Because of the complexity of the air conditioning system and the special equipment necessary to service it, in-depth troubleshooting and repairs are not included in this manual. However, simple checks and component replacement procedures are provided in this Chapter. For more complete information on the air conditioning system, refer to the *Haynes Automotive Heating and Air Conditioning Manual*. However, simple component replacement procedures are provided in this Chapter.

5   The most common cause of poor cooling is simply a low system refrigerant charge. If a noticeable drop in system cooling ability occurs, one of the following quick checks will help you determine whether the refrigerant level is low. Should the system lose its cooling ability, the following procedure will help you pinpoint the cause.

Check

Refer to illustration 14.8

6   Warm the engine up to normal operating temperature.

7   Place the air conditioning temperature selector at the coldest setting and put the

14.8 Insert a thermometer in the center vent while operating the air conditioning system - the output air should be 35 - 45 degrees F less than the ambient temperature, depending on humidity (but not lower than 40-degrees F)

14.10 A basic charging kit for 134A systems is available at most auto parts stores - it must say 134A (not R-12) and so should the can of refrigerant

14.13 Attach the charging kit to the low-side charging port (arrow)

blower at the highest setting. Open the doors (to make sure the air conditioning system doesn't cycle off as soon as it cools the passenger compartment).

8   Insert a thermometer in the center air distribution duct **(see illustration)** while operating the air conditioning system - the temperature of the output air should be 35 to 40 degrees F below the ambient air temperature (down to approximately 40 degrees F). If the ambient (outside) air temperature is very high, say 110 degrees F, the duct air temperature may be as high as 60 degrees F, but generally the air conditioning is 35 to 40 degrees F cooler than the ambient air.

9   If the air isn't as cold as it used to be, the system probably needs a charge. Further inspection or testing of the system is beyond the scope of the home mechanic and should be left to a professional.

Adding refrigerant

Refer to illustrations 14.10 and 14.13

Caution: *The vehicles covered by this manual use R-134a refrigerant. Make sure any refrigerant, refrigerant oil or replacement component your purchase is designated as compatible with environmentally friendly R-134a systems.*

10   Buy an R-134a automotive charging kit at an auto parts store. A charging kit includes a can of refrigerant, a tap valve and a short section of hose that can be attached between the tap valve and the system low side service valve **(see illustration)**. Because one can of refrigerant may not be sufficient to bring the system charge up to the proper level, it's a good idea to buy a couple of additional cans. Make sure that one of the cans contains red refrigerant dye. If the system is leaking, the red dye will leak out with the refrigerant and help you pinpoint the location of the leak. **Warning:** *Never add more than two cans of refrigerant to the system.*

11   Hook up the charging kit by following

the manufacturer's instructions. **Warning:** *DO NOT hook the charging kit hose to the system high side!* The fittings on the charging kit are designed to fit **only** on the low side of the system.

12   Back off the valve handle on the charging kit and screw the kit onto the refrigerant can, making sure first that the O-ring or rubber seal inside the threaded portion of the kit is in place. **Warning:** *Wear protective eyewear when dealing with pressurized refrigerant cans.*

13   Remove the dust cap from the low-side charging and attach the quick-connect fitting on the kit hose **(see illustration)**.

14   Warm up the engine and turn on the air conditioning. Keep the charging kit hose away from the fan and other moving parts. **Note:** *The charging process requires the compressor to be running. If the clutch cycles off, you can put the air conditioning switch on High and leave the car doors open to keep the clutch on and compressor working.* **Note:** *The compressor can be kept on during the charging by removing the connector from the low-pressure switch (combination high-limit and low-limit switch on some models) and bridging it with a paper clip or jumper wire during the procedure.*

15   Turn the valve handle on the kit until the stem pierces the can, then back the handle out to release the refrigerant. You should be able to hear the rush of gas. Add refrigerant to the low side of the system, keeping the can upright at all times, but shaking it occasionally. Allow stabilization time between each addition.

16   If you have an accurate thermometer, you can place it in the center air conditioning duct inside the vehicle and keep track of the output air temperature **(see illustration 14.9)**. A charged system that is working properly should cool down to approximately 40-degrees F. If the ambient (outside) air temperature is very high, say 110 degrees F, the duct air temperature may be as high as 60 degrees F, but generally the air conditioning is 30 to 40

degrees F cooler than the ambient air.

17   When the can is empty, turn the valve handle to the closed position and release the connection from the low-side port. Replace the dust cap.

18   Remove the charging kit from the can and store the kit for future use with the piercing valve in the UP position, to prevent inadvertently piercing the can on the next use.

Heating systems

19   If the carpet under the heater core is damp, or if antifreeze vapor or steam is coming through the vents, the heater core is leaking. Remove it (see Section 13) and install a new unit (most radiator shops will not repair a leaking heater core).

20   If the air coming out of the heater vents isn't hot, the problem could stem from any of the following causes:

a) *The thermostat is stuck open, preventing the engine coolant from warming up enough to carry heat to the heater core. Replace the thermostat (see Section 3).*

b) *There is a blockage in the system, preventing the flow of coolant through the heater core. Feel both heater hoses at the firewall. They should be hot. If one of them is cold, there is an obstruction in one of the hoses or in the heater core, or the heater control valve is shut. Detach the hoses and back flush the heater core with a water hose. If the heater core is clear but circulation is impeded, remove the two hoses and flush them out with a water hose.*

c) *If flushing fails to remove the blockage from the heater core, the core must be replaced (see Section 13).*

15   Air conditioning compressor clutch circuit - check

Refer to illustrations 15.1a, 15.1b, 15.1c, 15.4 and 15.5

1   If the compressor clutch does not engage, the relay may be faulty. Remove the

3

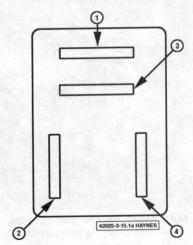

42025-3-15.1a HAYNES

15.1a Compressor clutch relay terminals (Civic) - there should be continuity between the terminals 1 and 3 with power and ground connected to terminals 2 and 4, and no continuity with power disconnected

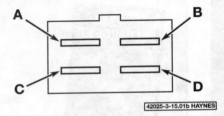

42025-3-15.01b HAYNES

15.1b Compressor clutch relay terminals (1997 and earlier Integra models) - there should be continuity between terminals A and C with power and ground connected to terminals B and D, and no continuity with power disconnected

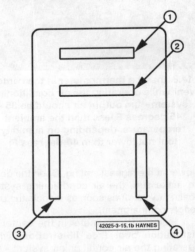

42025-3-15.1b HAYNES

15.1c Compressor clutch relay terminals (1998 Integra models) - there should be continuity between the terminals 1 and 2 with power and ground connected to terminals 3 and 4, and no continuity with power disconnected

relay and check it (see illustrations).

2   If the relay is ok, check the voltage between the terminals of the relay socket and a good ground to make sure the relay is receiving power. If it isn't receiving power, there is an open circuit that must be repaired.

3   After determining that the relay is receiving power, connect a jumper wire between relay socket terminals 1 and 3 on Civic models, socket terminals A and C on 1997 and earlier Integra models or socket terminals 1 and 2 on 1998 Integra models and listen for a clicking sound from the compressor clutch.

4   If the compressor clutch doesn't click, remove the jumper wire, unplug the compressor clutch connector and check for continuity between the red wire and the compressor (see illustration). If there is an open, repair it. If there is continuity, check the compressor clutch for damage.

5   Unplug the air conditioning low pressure

switch and, with the ignition switch on, check for battery voltage between the terminal 1 on Civic models (the one with the blue/white wire) or terminal 2 on Integra models (the one with the blue/red wire (Integra models) and a good ground (see illustration). If there is no voltage, there is an open. If there is voltage, turn off the ignition and check for continuity between the terminals of the pressure switch itself. If there is none, there is a problem with the switch or the system pressure.

16   Air conditioning receiver-drier - removal and installation

Refer to illustrations 16.3 and 16.4

Warning: *The air conditioning system is under high pressure. Do not loosen any hose fittings or remove any components until after the system has been discharged. Air conditioning refrigerant should be properly discharged into an EPA-approved recovery/recycling unit at a dealer service department or an automotive air conditioning repair facility. Always wear eye protection when disconnecting air conditioning system fittings.*

Caution: *When replacing entire components, additional refrigerant oil should be added equal to the amount that is removed with the component being replaced. Be sure to read the can before adding any oil to the system, to make sure it is compatible with the R-134a system.*

1   Have the refrigerant discharged and recycled by an air conditioning technician.

2   Disconnect the battery. **Caution:** *If the radio in your vehicle is equipped with an anti-theft system make sure you have the correct activation code before disconnecting the battery.*

3   Disconnect the refrigerant lines from the receiver and cap the open fittings to prevent dirt and moisture entry (see illustration).

4   Remove the inner fender panel (see

15.4 Unplug the connector (arrow) and check for continuity between the red wire and the compressor clutch - if there is an open, repair it

15.5 Unplug the air conditioning pressure switch (arrow) and check for voltage between the number 1 terminal and a good ground

16.3 In the engine compartment, remove the bolts (arrows) and disconnect both refrigerant line fittings

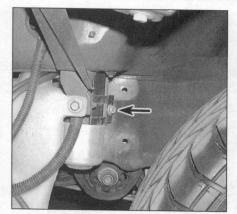

16.4 Working in the wheel well, remove the receiver-drier bracket pinch bolt (arrow)

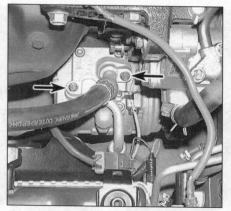

17.7 To remove the compressor, remove the bolts (arrows), disconnect the lines and plug the open fittings to prevent entry of dirt and moisture

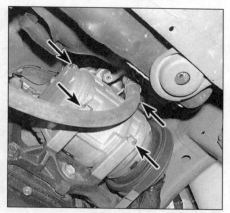

17.9 Remove the compressor mounting bolts (arrows) and lower the compressor out from under the vehicle

Chapter 11), loosen the receiver-drier bracket pinch bolt and lift the receiver-drier out of the vehicle **(see illustration)**.

5   Installation is the reverse of removal, using new O-rings where the lines connect to the receiver-drier.

6   Have the system evacuated, charged and leak tested by an air conditioning technician. If the receiver-drier was replaced, add 1/3 ounce of refrigerant oil.

17 Air conditioning compressor - removal and installation

Refer to illustrations 17.7 and 17.9
Warning: *The air conditioning system is under high pressure. Do not loosen any hose fittings or remove any components until after the system has been discharged. Air conditioning refrigerant should be properly discharged into an EPA-approved recovery/recycling unit at a dealer service department or an automotive air conditioning repair facility. Always wear eye protection when disconnecting air conditioning system fittings.*
Note: *The air conditioning compressor is a non-serviceable unit. It must be replaced with a complete unit or rebuilt by an authorized rebuild. The receiver-drier should be replaced whenever the compressor is replaced.*

1   Have the air conditioning system refrig-

erant discharged by dealer service department or air conditioning repair facility.

2   Disconnect the cable from the negative battery terminal. **Caution:** *If the radio in your vehicle is equipped with an anti-theft system, make sure you have the correct activation code before disconnecting the battery.*

3   Set the parking brake, block the rear wheels and raise the front of the vehicle, supporting it securely on jackstands.

4   Remove the drivebelt (see Chapter 1).

5   Remove the power steering pump (see Chapter 10).

6   Remove the cruise control actuator (if equipped).

7   Disconnect the refrigerant lines from the compressor **(see illustration)**. Plug the open fittings to prevent entry of dirt and moisture.

8   Disconnect the compressor clutch wiring harness.

9   Unbolt the compressor **(see illustration)** from the mounting bracket and remove it from the vehicle.

10   The clutch may have to be transferred from the old compressor to the new unit.

11   Here's how to calculate the amount of refrigerant oil for the new compressor:

a) *Drain the refrigerant oil from the old compressor through the suction fitting and measure it in ounces or cubic centimeters.*

b) *Subtract this volume from 4 fluid ounces (120 ml).*

c) *The difference between these two figures is equal to the amount you should drain from the new compressor.*

12   Installation is otherwise the reverse of removal.

13   Have the system evacuated, recharged and leak tested by a dealership service department or automotive air conditioning repair facility.

18 Air conditioning condenser - removal and installation

Refer to illustration 18.4
Warning: *The air conditioning system is under high pressure. Do not loosen any hose fittings or remove any components until after the system has been discharged. Air conditioning refrigerant should be properly discharged into an EPA-approved recovery/recycling unit at a dealer service department or an automotive air conditioning repair facility. Always wear eye protection when disconnecting air conditioning system fittings.*

1   Have the refrigerant discharged by a dealership service department or air conditioning repair facility.

2   Disconnect the cable from the negative battery terminal. **Caution:** *If the radio in your vehicle is equipped with an anti-theft system, make sure you have the correct activation code before disconnecting the battery.*

3   Disconnect the air conditioning pressure switch electrical connector and the condenser fan electrical connector.

4   Disconnect the condenser hose and discharge line from the condenser **(see illustration)**.

5   Remove the condenser brackets. On Integra models, also disconnect the upper radiator mounting brackets **(see illustration 4.9)**.

6   Lift the condenser from the vehicle. **Note:** *On Integra models it will be necessary*

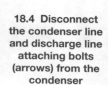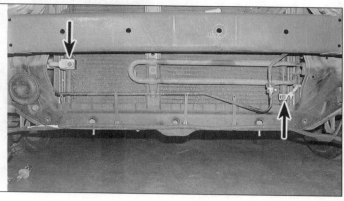

18.4 Disconnect the condenser line and discharge line attaching bolts (arrows) from the condenser

3

19.3 Disconnect the refrigerant lines (arrows) from the evaporator - plug both lines to prevent the entry of contaminants and moisture into the air conditioning system

19.6 Evaporator assembly retaining nuts and bolt locations (arrows)

to tilt the top of the radiator back to provide clearance. Be careful not to damage the condenser fins or the radiator when removing or installing the condenser.

7   Installation is the reverse of removal. **Note:** *Always replace all O-rings with new ones and lightly lubricate them with refrigerant oil before assembly.*

8   Have the system evacuated, charged and leak tested by a dealer service department or air conditioning repair facility. If a new condenser was installed, add one-ounce of refrigerant oil.

19   Air conditioning evaporator and expansion valve - removal and installation

Refer to illustrations 19.3, 19.6, 19.7a and 19.7b

Warning 1: *The air conditioning system is under high pressure. Do not loosen any hose fittings or remove any components until after the system has been discharged. Air conditioning refrigerant should be properly dis-*

charged into an EPA-approved recovery/recycling unit at a dealer service department or an automotive air conditioning repair facility. Always wear eye protection when disconnecting air conditioning system fittings.

Warning 2: *The models covered by this manual are equipped with a Supplemental Restraint System (SRS), more commonly known as airbags. Always disable the airbag system before working in the vicinity of the SRS unit, steering column or instrument panel to avoid the possibility of accidental deployment of the airbag, which could cause personal injury (see Chapter 12).*

1   Have the air conditioning system discharged by a dealer service department or automotive air conditioning repair facility.

2   Disconnect the cable from the negative battery terminal. Disable the airbag, if equipped (see Chapter 12). **Caution:** *If the radio in your vehicle is equipped with an antitheft system, make sure you have the correct activation code before disconnecting the battery.*

3   Disconnect the two lines from the evaporator **(see illustration)**. Plug both lines to

prevent the entry of contaminants and moisture into air conditioning system.

4   Remove the glovebox and the glovebox frame (see Chapter 11).

5   Disconnect the electrical connector from the air conditioning thermostat and remove the wiring harness clips from the evaporator housing.

6   Remove the evaporator unit retaining screws and nuts, pull the evaporator unit out far enough to disconnect the drain hose and remove the unit from the vehicle **(see illustration)**.

7   Remove the screws and clips retaining the evaporator case halves together, remove the air conditioning thermostat and separate the housing **(see illustrations)**.

8   Remove the evaporator core from the housing and remove the expansion valve, if necessary.

9   Installation is the reverse of removal.

10   Have the system evacuated, charged and leak tested by a dealer service department or automotive air conditioning repair facility. If a new evaporator was installed, add 1-1/3 ounces of refrigerant oil.

19.7a Remove the screws and detach the clips from the front . . .

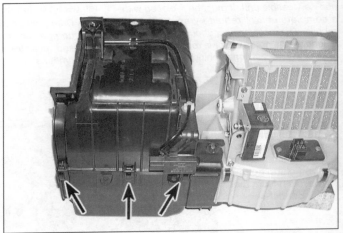

19.7b . . . and the back side of the evaporator housing

Chapter 4
Fuel and exhaust systems

Contents

Specifications

General

Fuel pressure (at idle)
  Civic
With regulator vacuum hose attached	28 to 36 psi
With regulator vacuum hose disconnected	38 to 46 psi

  Integra
    B18B1 engine
With regulator vacuum hose attached	31 to 36 psi
With regulator vacuum hose disconnected	40 to 47 psi

    B18C1 engines through 1997
With regulator vacuum hose attached	39 to 46 psi
With regulator vacuum hose disconnected	48 to 55 psi

    B18C1 and B18C5 engines, 1998
With regulator vacuum hose attached	38 to 46 psi
With regulator vacuum hose disconnected	47 to 54 psi

Fuel injector resistance
Civic	Not specified (but shouldn't be open or shorted)

  Integra
1994 and 1995	10 to 13 ohms
1996 on	Not specified (but shouldn't be open or shorted)

Fuel level sender resistance
  Civic (sender secured by nuts)
Full position	3.5 to 5 ohms
Half position	29.5 to 35.5 ohms
Empty position	105 to 108 ohms

  Civic (sender secured by locking ring)
Full position	2 to 5 ohms
Half position	25.5 to 39.5 ohms
Empty position	105 to 110 ohms

  Integra
Full position	2 to 5 ohms
Half position	29.5 to 35.5 ohms
Empty position	105 to 110 ohms

4

Torque specifications   **Ft-lbs** (unless otherwise indicated)

Fuel injection service bolt
   6 mm bolt
      1996 Civic .... 104 inch-lbs
      1994 through 1996 Integra .... 132 inch-lbs
   12 mm banjo bolt (all models) 25
Throttle body mounting nuts/bolts
   1994 and 1995 Integra .... 168 inch-lbs
   All other models 16
Fuel rail mounting nuts .... 108 in-lbs

1   General information

Refer to illustrations 1.1a and 1.1b

The fuel system consists of a fuel tank, an electric fuel pump (located in the fuel tank), a fuel pump relay, the fuel rail and fuel injectors, an air cleaner assembly and a throttle body unit. All models are equipped with a Sequential Electronic Fuel Injection (SEFI) system.

Sequential Electronic Fuel Injection (SEFI) system

Sequential Electronic Fuel Injection uses timed impulses to inject the fuel directly into the intake port of each cylinder according to its firing order. The injectors are controlled by the Powertrain Control Module (PCM). The PCM monitors various engine parameters and delivers the exact amount of fuel required into the intake ports. The throttle body serves only to control the amount of air passing into the system. Because each cylinder is equipped with its own injector, much better control of the fuel/air mixture ratio is possible.

Fuel pump and lines

Fuel is circulated from the fuel tank to the fuel injection system, and back to the fuel tank, through a pair of metal lines running along the underside of the vehicle. An electric fuel pump and fuel level sending unit is located inside the fuel tank. A vapor return system routes all vapors back to the fuel tank through a separate return line.

The PGM-FI main relay (fuel pump relay) is equipped with a primary and secondary voltage circuit. With the ignition switch ON, the primary circuit supplies current to the PCM, the fuel injectors and the secondary circuit. The secondary circuit supplies current to the fuel pump. The secondary circuit is energized for two seconds with the ignition switch ON and the engine not running, and constantly with the engine running.

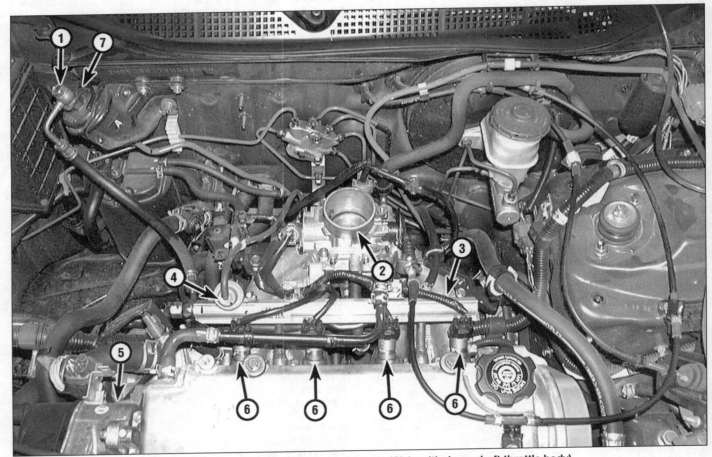

1.1a Typical fuel injection system components (Civic with down-draft throttle body)

1 Fuel filter banjo bolt	*4 Fuel pressure regulator*	*6 Fuel injectors*
2 Throttle body	*5 Distributor*	*7 Fuel filter*
3 Fuel rail		

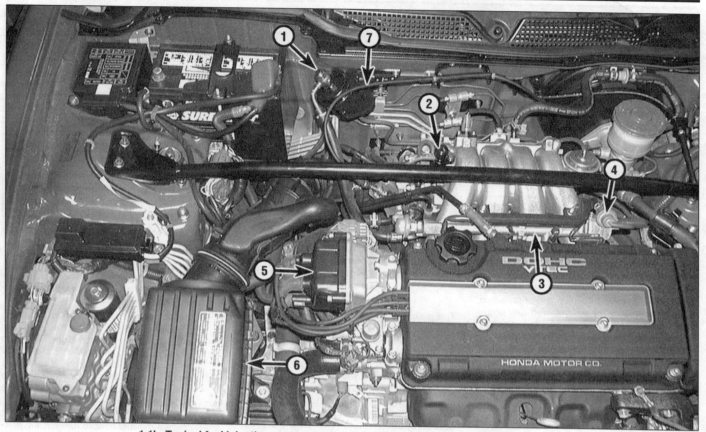

1.1b Typical fuel injection system components (Integra with side-draft throttle body)

1 Fuel filter banjo bolt	4 Fuel pressure regulator	6 Air cleaner housing
2 Throttle body (under cross brace)	5 Distributor	7 Fuel filter
3 Fuel rail		

Exhaust system

The exhaust system includes an exhaust manifold, an upstream (before catalytic converter) and downstream (after catalytic converter) oxygen sensor, a three-way (reduction) catalytic converter, a muffler and a tail pipe.

The catalytic converter is an emission control device added to the exhaust system to reduce pollutants. Refer to Chapter 6 for more information regarding the catalytic converter.

2 Fuel pressure relief procedure

Refer to illustration 2.4

Warning: *Gasoline is extremely flammable, so take extra precautions when you work on any part of the fuel system. Don't smoke or allow open flames or bare light bulbs near the work area, and don't work in a garage where a natural gas-type appliance (such as a water heater or a clothes dryer) with a pilot light is present. Since gasoline is carcinogenic, wear latex gloves when there's a possibility of being exposed to fuel, and, if you spill any fuel on your skin, rinse it off immediately with*

soap and water. Mop up any spills immediately and do not store fuel-soaked rags where they could ignite. The fuel system is under constant pressure, so, if any fuel lines are to be disconnected, the fuel pressure in the system must be relieved first. When you perform any kind of work on the fuel system, wear safety glasses and have a Class B type fire extinguisher on hand.*

1   Locate the fuel pump electrical connector (see Section 5). Disconnect it, then start the engine and let it run until it stalls. Detach the cable from the negative battery terminal. **Caution:** *If the stereo in your vehicle is equipped with an anti-theft system, make sure you have the correct activation code before disconnecting the battery. On all models, write down the preset radio stations.*
2   Unscrew the fuel filler cap to relieve pressure built up in the fuel tank.
3   Relieve residual pressure by opening the fuel line at the fuel filter. On models though 1996, this is done by loosening the service bolt that's threaded into the banjo bolt. On later models, loosen the banjo bolt (there is no separate service bolt).
4   You'll need two wrenches for this procedure. On models with a separate service bolt, one to loosen the service bolt and one to hold

the banjo bolt; on models with only a banjo bolt, one to loosen the banjo bolt and another to hold the fuel line fitting **(see illustration)**.
5   Place a shop rag around the fuel line fitting on top of the fuel filter.
6   While holding the banjo bolt or fuel line

2.4 Be sure to use a back-up wrench to prevent the fuel fitting from turning - before the bolt is loosened, cover the wrenches with a shop rag to catch the escaping fuel

4

fitting, *slowly* loosen the service bolt or banjo bolt one complete turn - fuel will begin to flow from the fitting. Allow the pressure to be relieved completely, then remove the bolt. If you're working on a vehicle with a separate service bolt, install a new service bolt sealing washer. If you're working on a vehicle with only a banjo bolt, install a new sealing washer on each side of the fuel line fitting.

7   After all work to the fuel system has been performed, install the service bolt or banjo bolt and tighten it to the torque listed in this Chapter's Specifications.

3   Fuel pump/fuel pressure - check

Warning: *Gasoline is extremely flammable, so take extra precautions when you work on any part of the fuel system. See the* **Warning** *in Section 2.*
Note: *In order to perform the fuel pressure test, you will need to obtain a fuel pressure gauge capable of measuring high fuel pressure and an adapter set for the fuel injection system being tested.*

General checks

1   Check that there is adequate fuel in the fuel tank.
2   Verify the fuel pump actually runs. Have an assistant turn the ignition switch to ON - you should hear a brief whirring noise (approximately two seconds) as the pump comes on and pressurizes the system. **Note:** *The fuel pump is easily heard through the gas tank filler neck.* If there is no response from the fuel pump (makes no sound) proceed to Step 9 and check the fuel pump electrical circuit.

Fuel pump output and pressure check

Refer to illustrations 3.3a, 3.b, 3.6 and 3.7
3   Connect a fuel pressure gauge to the test port on the fuel filter **(see illustrations)**.

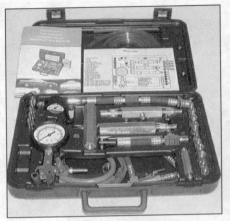

3.3a This aftermarket fuel pressure testing kit contains all the necessary fittings and adapters, along with a fuel pressure gauge, to test most automotive fuel systems

3.3b Connect a fuel pressure gauge to the service port

The gauge is connected in place of the service bolt (1996 and earlier) or banjo bolt (1997 and later) (see Section 2).

4   Turn the ignition switch ON (engine not running) with the air conditioning off. The fuel pump should run for about two seconds - pressure should register on the gauge and should hold steady.

5   Start the engine and let it idle at normal operating temperature. Compare the pressure reading with the value listed in this Chapter's Specifications. Now, disconnect the vacuum hose from the fuel pressure regulator - the pressure should increase immediately to the value listed in this Chapter's Specifications. If the pressures are correct, the system is operating properly.

6   If the pressure was too high with the vacuum hose connected, apply 12 to 14 inches of vacuum to the pressure regulator, using a hand-held vacuum pump **(see illustration)**. If the pressure drops, repair the vacuum source to the regulator. If the pressure

does not drop, replace the regulator.

7   If the fuel pressure is not within specifications, check the following:

a) *If the pressure is higher than specified, check for vacuum to the fuel pressure regulator* **(see illustration)**. *Vacuum must fluctuate with the increase or decrease in the engine rpm. If vacuum is present, check for a pinched or clogged fuel return hose or pipe. If the return line is OK, replace the regulator.*

b) *If the pressure is lower than specified, change the fuel filter to rule out the possibility of a clogged filter. If the pressure is still low, install a fuel line shut-off adapter between the pressure regulator and the return line (this can be fabricated from fuel line, a shut-off valve and the necessary fittings to mate with the pressure regulator and the return line, or, instead of a shut-off valve, use fuel hose that can be pinched with a pair of pliers). With the valve open (or the hose not pinched), start the engine (if possible) and slowly close the valve or pinch the hose (only pinch the hose on the*

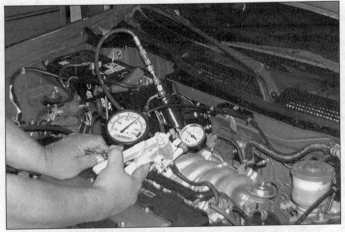

3.6 Connect a hand-held vacuum pump to the fuel pressure regulator and read fuel pressure with vacuum applied. Pressure should decrease as vacuum is increased

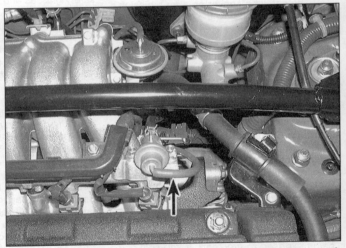

3.7 Check for vacuum at the fuel pressure regulator hose (arrow)

3.11a The Civic fuel injection main relay is on the right side of the cowl (arrow); lower the glove compartment for access

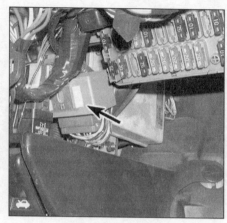

3.11b The Integra fuel injection main relay is on the left side of the cowl (arrow)

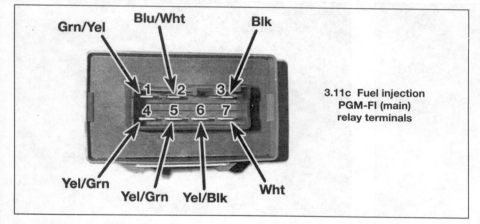

3.11c Fuel injection PGM-FI (main) relay terminals

nosing the fuel pump circuit.

12   If battery voltage exists, remove and check the relay. Using jumper wires, connect battery positive voltage to terminal 2 and ground terminal 1, then, using an ohmmeter, check for continuity between terminals 4 and 5. If there is no continuity, replace the relay.

13   If there is continuity, connect the positive jumper wire to terminal 5 and ground terminal 3, then check for continuity between terminals 6 and 7. If there is no continuity, replace the relay.

14   If there is continuity, connect the positive jumper wire to terminal 6 and ground terminal 1, then check for continuity between terminals 4 and 5. If there is no continuity, replace the relay.

***

4   Fuel lines and fittings - repair and replacement

Refer to illustrations 4.8, 4.12a and 4.12b
Warning: *Gasoline is extremely flammable, so take extra precautions when you work on any part of the fuel system. See the* **Warning** *in Section 2.*

1   Always relieve the fuel pressure before servicing fuel lines or fittings (see Section 2).

2   The fuel feed, return and vapor lines extend from the fuel tank to the engine compartment. The lines are secured to the underbody with clip and screw assemblies. These lines must be occasionally inspected for leaks, kinks and dents.

3   If evidence of dirt is found in the system or fuel filter during disassembly, the line should be disconnected and blown out. Check the fuel strainer on the fuel gauge sending unit (see Section 5) for damage and deterioration.

Steel tubing

4   If replacement of a fuel line or emission line is called for, use welded steel tubing meeting the manufacturer's specifications.

5   Don't use copper or aluminum tubing to replace steel tubing. These materials cannot withstand normal vehicle vibration.

6   Because fuel lines used on fuel-injected vehicles are under high pressure, they require special consideration.

7   Some fuel lines have threaded fittings with O-rings. Any time the fittings are loosened to service or replace components:

a) *Use a backup wrench while loosening and tightening the fittings.*

b) *Check all O-rings for cuts, cracks and deterioration. Replace any that appear hardened, worn or damaged.*

c) *If the lines are replaced, always use original equipment parts, or parts that meet the original equipment standards specified in this Section.*

Flexible hose

Warning: *Use only original equipment replacement hoses or their equivalent. Others*

adapter you fabricated). If the pressure rises above 46 psi, replace the regulator (see Section 13). **Warning:** *Don't allow the fuel pressure to exceed 60 psi. Also, don't attempt to restrict the vehicle's return line by pinching it, as the line will be damaged.*

c) *If the pressure is still low with the fuel return line restricted, an injector (or injectors) may be leaking (see Section 15) or the in-tank fuel pump may be faulty.*

8   After the testing is done, relieve the fuel pressure (see Section 2) and remove the fuel pressure gauge.

Fuel pump electrical circuit check

Refer to illustrations 3.11a, 3.11b and 3.11c
Note: *Refer to Chapter 12 for additional wiring schematics that detail the fuel pump relay and circuit.*

9   If the pump does not turn on (makes no sound) with the ignition switch in the ON position, check the fuel injection (PGM-FI) main relay fuse (see Chapter 12). If the fuse is blown, replace the fuse and see if the pump works. If the pump now works, check for a short in the circuit between the PGM-FI relay and the fuel pump.

10   If the fuel pump does not activate, check for power to the fuel pump at the fuel tank. Remove the rear seat and check for battery voltage at the electrical connector near the tank. If voltage (and ground) is present at the fuel pump connector, replace the fuel pump.

11   If no voltage is present at the pump, check the PGM-FI relay circuit. With the help of an assistant, cycle the ignition key ON and OFF (engine not running) while checking for battery voltage at the relay connector (terminals 5 and 7 should have voltage with the ignition key on) **(see illustrations)**. If battery voltage does not exist, trace the circuit for an open or shorted condition (see the Wiring Diagrams at the end of Chapter 12). **Note 1:** *On some vehicles, if oil pressure drops below the specified pressure level, the oil pressure switch will act as a fuel pressure cut-off device. Be sure to check the oil pressure switch and circuit in the event of a difficult problem diagnosing the fuel pump circuit (refer to the wiring diagrams at the end of Chapter 12).* **Note 2:** *The theft deterrent system (if equipped) is equipped with a fuel enable circuit. If this system is malfunctioning it will not allow the PCM to signal the fuel pump relay or the engine to crank over. Be sure to check the theft deterrent system and circuit in the event of a difficult problem diag-*

4

4.8 Be sure the fuel hoses (arrows) can't rub against anything

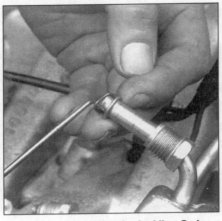

4.12a Always replace the fuel line O-rings (if equipped)

4.12b Use a new sealing washer on each side of the banjo fitting at the fuel filter

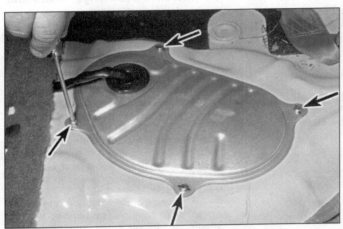

5.4a Remove the screws (arrows) from the fuel pump/fuel level sending unit access cover; this is the Civic cover . . .

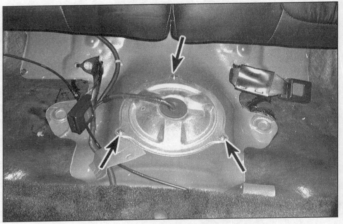

5.4b . . . and this is the Integra cover

may fail from the high pressures of this system.

8   Don't route fuel hose within four inches of any part of the exhaust system or within ten inches of the catalytic converter. Metal lines and rubber hoses must never be allowed to chafe against the frame **(see illustration)**. A minimum of 1/4-inch clearance must be maintained around a line or hose to prevent contact with the frame.

Removal and installation

9   Relieve the fuel pressure.
10   Remove all fasteners attaching the lines to the vehicle body.
11   Detach the clamp(s) that attach the fuel hoses to the metal lines, then pull the hoses off the fitting. Twisting the hoses back and forth will allow them to separate more easily.
12   Installation is the reverse of removal. Be sure to use new O-rings at the threaded fittings (if equipped) and new sealing washer(s) at the fuel filter **(see illustrations)**.

Repair

13   In the event of any fuel line damage (metal or flexible lines) it is necessary to replace the damaged lines with factory replacement parts. Others may fail from the high pressures of this system.

5   Fuel pump - removal and installation

Refer to illustrations 5.4a, 5.4b, 5.5, 5.6, 5.7, 5.8, 5.9 and 5.12
Warning: *Gasoline is extremely flammable, so take extra precautions when you work on any part of the fuel system. See the* **Warning** *in Section 2.*
1   Detach the cable from the negative battery terminal. **Caution:** *If the stereo in your vehicle is equipped with an anti-theft system, make sure you have the correct activation code before disconnecting the battery.*
2   Relieve the fuel system pressure (see Section 2).
3   On all except 1998 Integra hatchbacks, remove the rear seat (see Chapter 11). On 1998 Integra hatchbacks, remove the spare tire cover and protective cover.
4   Remove the bolts that retain the fuel pump access cover **(see illustrations)**.

5.5 Unplug the electrical connector and detach the fuel line

5   Unplug the electrical connector from the fuel pump and detach the fuel lines **(see illustration)**.
6   Remove the fuel pump assembly retaining nuts **(see illustration)**.
7   Remove the fuel pump from the tank **(see illustration)**.

5.6 Remove the nuts that retain the fuel pump to the fuel tank

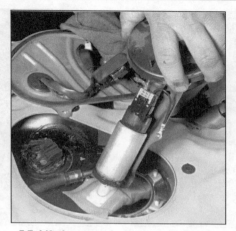

5.7 Lift the pump from the access hole. Be sure to angle it slightly to avoid damaging the pump screen attached to the bottom

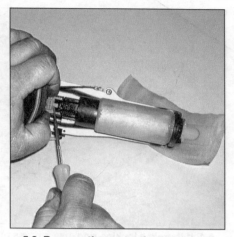

5.8 Remove the protective connector from the main electrical connector

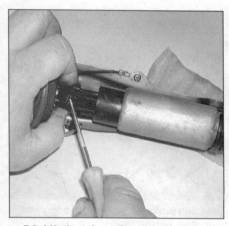

5.9 Lift the tab on the main electrical connector and disconnect it from the fuel pump

8 Remove the electrical connector protective cover **(see illustration)**.
9 Remove the electrical connector from the fuel pump **(see illustration)**.

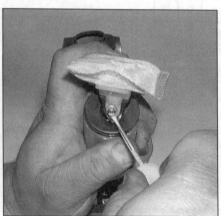

5.12 Pry off the retaining clip with a small screwdriver and detach the filter (sock) from the pump

10 Squeeze the hose clamps with a pair of pliers - remove the upper clamp from the hose and slide the lower clamp half-way up the hose, off the fuel pump inlet.

11 Separate the pump from the fuel pump bracket.
12 Remove the sock filter from the end of the pump **(see illustration)**.
13 Installation is the reverse of removal. Be sure to use a new gasket on the cover plate flange.

6 Fuel level sending unit - check and replacement

Refer to illustrations 6.2a, 6.2b, 6.3, 6.4, 6.6 and 6.7
Warning: *Gasoline is extremely flammable, so take extra precautions when you work on any part of the fuel system. See the* **Warning** *in Section 2.*
1 Remove the rear seat (see Chapter 11).
2 Remove the fuel level sending unit protective cover (if equipped) **(see illustration)**. Remove the access cover from the floor of the vehicle **(see illustration)**.
3 Disconnect the electrical connector from the sender **(see illustration)**.
4 If the sending unit is held in place by a

4

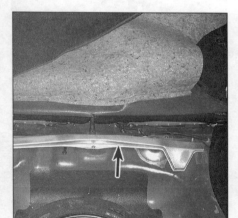

6.2a On Integras, remove the protective bar . . .

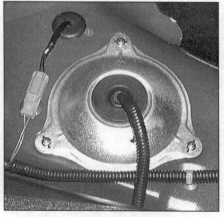

6.2b . . . and the sending unit access cover

6.3 Disconnect the electrical connector

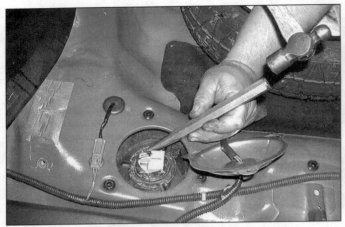

6.4 If there's a locking ring, use a brass punch to remove it; a steel punch may cause sparks

6.6 Lift the fuel level sending unit through the access hole

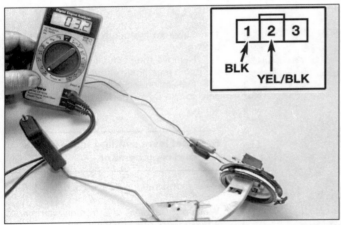

6.7 Measure the resistance of the fuel level sending unit with the float raised (full tank), halfway down and near the bottom (empty)

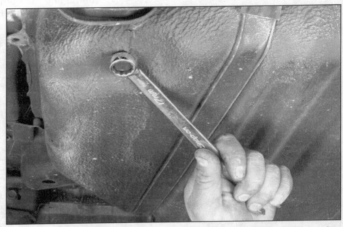

7.4 Loosen the drain plug and drain the fuel into an approved container for fuel storage

locking ring, use a brass punch and tap on the locking ring **(see illustration)** until the tabs line up with the recess in the housing. **Warning:** *A steel punch shouldn't be used, since a spark could cause an explosion.*

5   If the sending unit is held in place by nuts, remove them.

6   Lift the fuel level sending unit from the tank **(see illustration)**. Be careful not to damage the float arm.

7   Position the probes of an ohmmeter on the electrical connector terminals and check for resistance **(see illustration)**.

8   First, check the resistance of the sending unit with the float in the bottom (fuel tank empty) position. The resistance of the sending unit should be within the range listed in this Chapter's Specifications.

9   Now check the resistance of the unit with the float in the half-tank position and compare the reading to the value listed in this Chapter's Specifications.

10   Finally, lift the float to the full tank position and measure the resistance.

11   If the readings are incorrect or there is very little change in resistance as the float travels from full to empty, replace the sending unit.

12   Installation is the reverse of removal. Be sure to use a new gasket under the sealing flange.

7   Fuel tank - removal and installation

Refer to illustrations 7.4, 7.7a, 7.7b, 7.8 and 7.10

Warning: *Gasoline is extremely flammable, so take extra precautions when you work on any part of the fuel system. See the* **Warning** *in Section 2.*

Note: *The following procedure is much easier to perform if the fuel tank is empty.*

1   Remove the fuel tank filler cap to relieve fuel tank pressure.

2   Relieve the fuel system pressure (see Section 2).

3   Detach the cable from the negative terminal of the battery. **Caution:** *If the stereo in your vehicle is equipped with an anti-theft system, make sure you have the correct activation code before disconnecting the battery.*

4   Remove the tank drain plug and drain the fuel into an approved gasoline container

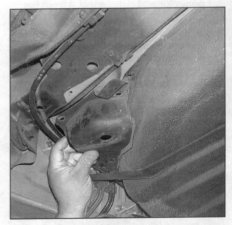

7.7a On Integras, remove the small covers . . .

(see illustration). If it doesn't have a drain plug, siphon the fuel into an approved gasoline container, using a siphoning kit (available at most auto parts stores). **Warning:** *Do not start the siphoning action by mouth!*

5   Remove the rear seat (see Chapter 11) and disconnect the fuel level sending unit,

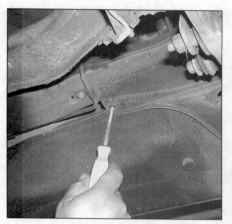

7.7b . . . there's one on each side

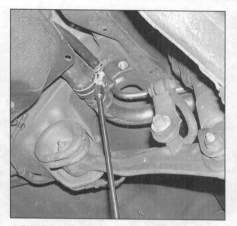

7.8 Remove the clamps that retain the rubber fuel lines to the inlet and vent pipes

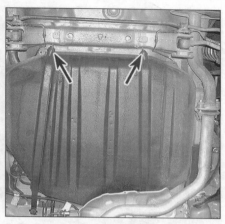

7.10 Support the fuel tank and remove the nuts from the strap bolts (arrows)

9.3a Remove the duct and resonator . . .

9.3b . . . and loosen the clamp (arrow) to remove the air cleaner

fuel pump electrical connectors and fuel hoses (see Sections 4 and 5).

6   Raise the rear of the vehicle and place it securely on jackstands.

7   Remove the splash panels that protect the fuel tank and the fuel lines. Civics use a single large panel; Integras use two small panels **(see illustrations)**.

8   Label and disconnect the fuel hoses and any brackets that may secure them **(see illustration)**.

9   Support the fuel tank with a floor jack. Position a wood block between the jack head and the fuel tank to protect the tank.

10   Disconnect both fuel tank retaining straps and pivot them down until they are hanging out of the way **(see illustration)**.

11   Remove the tank from the vehicle.

12   Installation is the reverse of removal.

8   Fuel tank cleaning and repair - general information

1   All repairs to the fuel tank or filler neck should be carried out by a professional who has experience in this critical and potentially dangerous work. Even after cleaning and flushing of the fuel system, explosive fumes can remain and ignite during repair of the tank.

2   If the fuel tank is removed from the vehicle, it should not be placed in an area where sparks or open flames could ignite the fumes coming out of the tank. Be especially careful inside garages where a natural gas-type appliance is located, because the pilot light could cause an explosion.

9   Air cleaner housing - removal and installation

Refer to illustrations 9.3a, 9.3b and 9.4

1   Detach the cable from the negative terminal of the battery.

2   Disconnect the IAT sensor wiring.

3   If you're working on a Civic with a D16Y7 engine, remove the air duct, then the air cleaner housing **(see illustrations)**.

4   If you're working on a Civic with a D16Y5 or D16Y8 engine, or on any Integra, remove the air intake duct and resonator, then remove the air cleaner housing **(see illustration)**.

5   Installation is the reverse of removal.

9.4 The air cleaner housing is secured by bolts (arrows)

10   Accelerator cable - removal, installation and adjustment

Replacement

Refer to illustrations 10.2, 10.3 and 10.4

1   Detach the cable from the negative battery terminal. **Caution:** *If the stereo in your*

4

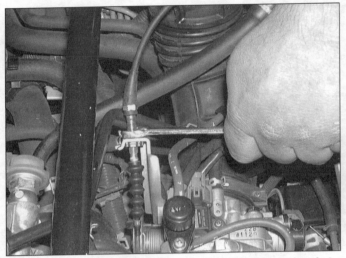

10.2 Loosen the locknut and detach the cable from its bracket

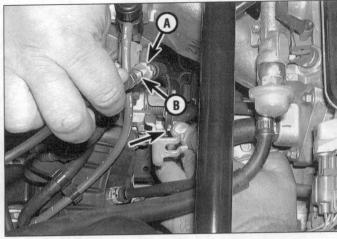

10.3 Remove the cable end from the throttle shaft bellcrank (arrow)

A   *Adjusting nut*   B   *Locknut*

vehicle is equipped with an anti-theft system, make sure you have the correct activation code before disconnecting the battery.

2   Loosen the locknut and remove the accelerator cable from its bracket **(see illustration)**.

3   Rotate the throttle shaft bellcrank until the cable is out of its guide groove in the bellcrank and detach the cable from the bellcrank **(see illustration)**.

4   Working underneath the dash, detach the cable from the accelerator pedal **(see illustration)**.

5   Pull the grommet from the firewall and pull the cable through the firewall from the engine compartment side.

6   Installation is the reverse of removal. Use the locknut and adjusting nut to get the throttle cable deflection as close as possible to the correct final setting, then adjust the cable as described below.

Adjustment

Refer to illustration 10.8

7   Start the engine and warm it up until the cooling fan comes on, then let it idle.

8   Check cable deflection (side-to-side slack) in the cable between the bellcrank and the cable bracket **(see illustration)**. Deflection should be 3/8 to 1/2-inch. If deflection is not within specifications, loosen the locknut and turn the adjusting nut until the deflection is as specified. Then tighten the locknut and shut the engine off.

9   After you have adjusted the throttle cable, have an assistant help you verify that the throttle valve opens all the way when you depress the accelerator pedal to the floor and that it returns to the idle position when you release the accelerator. Verify the cable operates smoothly. It must not bind or stick.

10   If the vehicle is equipped with an automatic transaxle, adjust the transaxle Throttle Valve (TV) cable (see Chapter 7B).

10.4 Working inside the driver's compartment, pull the accelerator cable end out and then lift the cable out of the recess in the pedal

11   Fuel injection system - general information

The Programmed Fuel Injection (PGM-FI) system **(see illustrations 1.1a and 1.1b)** consists of three sub-systems: air intake, electronic control and fuel delivery. The system uses a Powertrain Control Module (PCM) along with the sensors (coolant temperature sensor, Throttle Position Sensor (TPS), Manifold Absolute Pressure (MAP) sensor etc.) to determine the proper air/fuel ratio under all operating conditions.

The fuel injection system and the emissions control system are closely linked in function and design. For additional information, refer to Chapter 6.

Air intake system

The air intake system consists of the air cleaner, the air intake ducts, the throttle body, the idle control system and the intake

10.8 Measure the side-to-side cable deflection (arrows)

manifold. A resonator in the air intake tube provides silencing as air is drawn into the system.

The throttle body is a single barrel design; side-draft on Civics with D16Y5 and D16Y8 engines and down-draft on all other models. The lower portion of the throttle body is heated by engine coolant to prevent icing in cold weather. The idle adjusting screw is located on top of the throttle body. A throttle position sensor is attached to the throttle shaft to monitor changes in the throttle opening.

Electronic control system

The electronic control system and the Powertrain Control Module (PCM) are explained in detail in Chapter 6.

Fuel delivery system

The fuel delivery system consists of these components: The fuel pump, the pressure regulator, the fuel injectors, the fuel pulsation damper (some models) and the main relay.

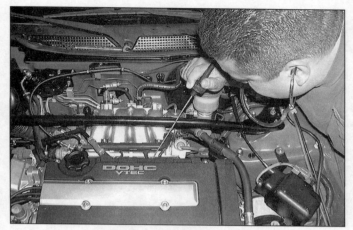

12.7 Use a stethoscope or screwdriver to determine if the injectors are working properly - they should make a steady clicking sound that rises and falls with engine speed changes

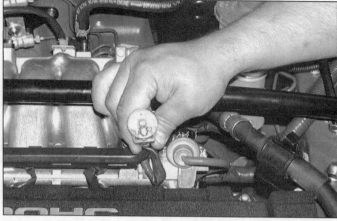

12.8 Install the "noid" light into each injector electrical connector and confirm that it blinks when the engine is cranking or running

The fuel pump is an in-tank type. Fuel is drawn through a filter into the pump, flows through the fuel delivery line, passes through another filter and is delivered to the injectors.

The pressure regulator maintains a constant fuel pressure to the injectors. Excess fuel is routed back to the fuel tank through the return line.

The injectors are solenoid-actuated, constant stroke, pintle types consisting of a solenoid, plunger, needle valve and housing. When current is applied to the solenoid coil, the needle valve raises and pressurized fuel fills the injector housing and squirts out the nozzle. The injection quantity is determined by the length of time the valve is open (the length of time during which current is supplied to the solenoid coils).

Injector open time is determined by the Powertrain Control Module (PCM). It contains a basic open time for various combinations of engine speed and air flow. This information is combined with inputs from the engine sensors to arrive at a final open time for a given set of conditions.

The main relay is installed in the left or right side of the cowl depending on model. It contains one relay for the Powertrain Control Module (PCM), fuel injectors and the other relay. The other relay supplies power to the fuel pump.

12 Fuel injection system - check

Refer to illustrations 12.7, 12.8 and 12.9
Warning: *Gasoline is extremely flammable, so take extra precautions when you work on any part of the fuel system. See the* **Warning** *in Section 2.*

1   Check all electrical connectors - especially ground connections - for the system. Loose connectors and poor grounds can cause at least half of all engine control system problems.
2   Verify that the battery is fully charged because the powertrain control module

(PCM) and sensors cannot operate properly without adequate supply voltage.
3   Refer to Chapter 1 and check the air filter element. A dirty or partially blocked filter will reduce performance and economy.
4   Check fuel pump operation (Section 3). If the fuel pump fuse is blown, replace it and see if it blows again. If it does, refer to Chapter 12 and the wiring diagrams and look for a grounded wire in the harness to the fuel pump.
5   Inspect the vacuum hoses connected to the intake manifold for damage, deterioration and leakage.
6   Remove the air intake duct from the throttle body and check for dirt, carbon, varnish, or other residue in the throttle body, particularly around the throttle plate. If it's dirty, refer to Chapter 6 and troubleshoot the PCV and EGR systems for the cause of excessive varnish buildup. An extremely dirty throttle body requires replacement. **Caution:** *The throttle bodies on these engines have a protective coating on their bores, throttle plates, and shafts. Do not try to clean the throttle body, since you might damage the coating and do more harm than good.*
7   With the engine running, place an automotive stethoscope against each injector, one at a time, and listen for a clicking sound that indicates operation **(see illustration)**. **Note:** *If you don't have a stethoscope, you can place the tip of a long screwdriver against the injector and listen through the handle.*
8   If an injector does not seem to be operating electrically (not clicking), purchase a special injector test light (sometimes called a "noid" light) and install it into the injector wiring harness connector **(see illustration)**. Start the engine and see if the noid light flashes. If it does, the injector is receiving proper voltage. If it doesn't flash, further diagnosis is necessary. You might want to have it checked by a dealership service department or other qualified repair shop.
9   With the engine off and the fuel injector electrical connectors disconnected, measure

12.9 Disconnect the fuel injector electrical connector and measure the resistance of each injector

the resistance of each injector with an ohmmeter **(see illustration)**. Check the specifications at the beginning of this Chapter for the correct resistance.
10   Refer to Chapter 6 for other system checks.

13 Throttle body - removal and installation

Refer to illustrations 13.6a and 13.6b
Warning: *Wait until the engine is completely cool before beginning this procedure.*

1   Detach the cable from the negative battery terminal. **Caution:** *If the stereo in your vehicle is equipped with an anti-theft system, make sure you have the correct activation code before disconnecting the battery.*
2   Remove the air duct that connects the air cleaner assembly to the throttle body.
3   Unplug the throttle position sensor and MAP sensor connectors from the throttle body. Also label and detach all vacuum hoses from the throttle body.

4

13.6a Remove the fasteners (arrows) and separate the throttle body from the air intake plenum; this is a side-draft throttle body . . .

13.6b . . . and this is a down-draft throttle body

4   Detach the accelerator cable (see Section 10) and, if equipped, the transaxle Throttle Valve (TV) cable (see Chapter 7B).

5   Detach the coolant hoses from the throttle body. Plug the lines to prevent coolant loss.

6   Unscrew the four mounting nuts (1994 Integra) or two mounting nuts and two mounting bolts (all other models) **(see illustrations)**. Remove the throttle body and gasket. Remove all traces of old gasket material from the throttle body and air intake plenum.

7   Installation is the reverse of removal. Be sure to use a new gasket. Tighten the mounting bolts or nuts to the torque listed in this Chapter's Specifications. Adjust the accelerator cable (see Section 10) and, if equipped, the Throttle Valve (TV) cable (see Chapter 7B). Check the coolant level and add some, if necessary (see Chapter 1).

14 Fuel pressure regulator - check and replacement

Refer to illustrations 14.3a and 14.3b
Warning: *Gasoline is extremely flammable, so take extra precautions when you work on any part of the fuel system. See the* **Warning** *in Section 2.*

1   Relieve the system fuel pressure (see Section 2).

2   Detach the cable from the negative battery terminal. **Caution:** *If the stereo in your vehicle is equipped with an anti-theft system, make sure you have the correct activation code before disconnecting the battery.*

3   Detach the vacuum hose and fuel hose from the pressure regulator, then unscrew the mounting bolts **(see illustrations)**.

4   Remove the pressure regulator.

5   Installation is the reverse of removal. Be sure to use a new O-ring. Lubricate the O-ring with a light coat of clean engine oil before installation.

6   Check for fuel leaks after installing the pressure regulator.

14.3a Remove the fuel pressure regulator bolts (arrows); this is a Civic . . .

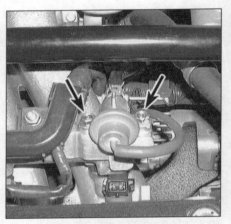

14.3b . . . and this is an Integra

15 Fuel injectors - check, removal and installation

Warning: *Gasoline is extremely flammable, so take extra precautions when you work on any part of the fuel system. See the* **Warning** *in Section 2.*

Removal

Refer to illustrations 15.3, 15.7a, 15.7b, 15.8a and 15.8b

1   Detach the cable from the negative battery terminal. **Caution:** *If the stereo in your vehicle is equipped with an anti-theft system, make sure you have the correct activation code before disconnecting the battery.*

2   Relieve the fuel pressure (see Section 2).

3   Unplug the injector connectors **(see illustration)**.

4   Detach the vacuum hose and fuel return hose from the fuel pressure regulator (see Section 14).

5   Detach any ground cables from the fuel rail.

6   Detach the fuel feed line from the fuel rail.

15.3 Use a small screwdriver or sharp pick to remove the bail from the fuel injector electrical connector

7   Remove the mounting nuts **(see illustrations)** and detach the fuel rail from the injectors.

8   Remove the injector(s) from the bores in the intake manifold and remove and discard the O-ring, cushion ring and seal ring **(see**

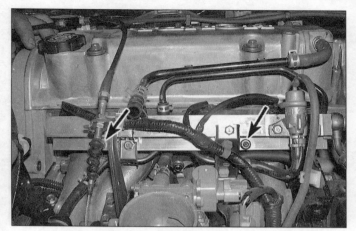

15.7a Remove the fuel rail mounting nuts (arrows); this is a Civic . . .

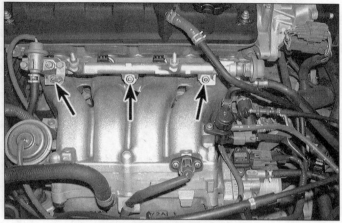

15.7b . . . and this is an Integra

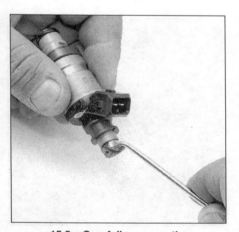

15.8a Carefully remove the injector O-rings

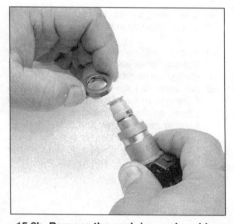

15.8b Remove the seal ring and cushion ring from the injector

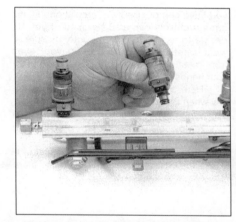

15.10 Install the injectors in the fuel rail, then install the assembly in the intake manifold

illustrations). **Note:** *Whether you're replacing an injector or a leaking O-ring, it's a good idea to remove all the injectors from the intake manifold and replace all the O-rings, seal rings and cushion rings.*

Installation

Refer to illustration 15.10
Caution: *To protect the injector seals, install all of the injectors in the fuel rail, then install the injector and fuel rail assembly in the intake manifold.*

9   Coat the new cushion rings with clean engine oil and slide them onto the injectors.
10   Coat the new O-rings with clean engine oil and install them on the injector(s), then insert each injector into its corresponding bore in the fuel rail **(see illustration)**.
11   Coat the new seal rings with clean engine oil and press them into the injector bore(s) in the intake manifold.
12   Install the injector and fuel rail assembly on the intake manifold. Tighten the fuel rail mounting nuts to the torque listed in this Chapter's Specifications.
13   The remainder of installation is the reverse of removal.
14   After the injector/fuel rail assembly

installation is complete, turn the ignition switch to ON, but don't operate the starter (this activates the fuel pump for about two seconds, which builds up fuel pressure in the fuel lines and the fuel rail). Repeat this about two or three times, then check the fuel lines, rail and injectors for fuel leakage.

16   Exhaust system servicing - general information

Refer to illustrations 16.4a, 16.4b and 16.4c
Warning 1: *Inspection and repair of exhaust system components should be done only after enough time has elapsed after driving the vehicle to allow the system components to cool completely. Also, when working under the vehicle, make sure it is securely supported on jackstands.*
Warning 2: *All models covered by this manual are equipped with an exhaust system flex tube which is extremely sensitive to sharp bends. Do not allow the flex tube to hang downward during servicing or damage will occur.*
1   The exhaust system consists of the

exhaust manifold(s), the catalytic converter, the muffler, the tailpipe and all connecting pipes, brackets, hangers and clamps. The exhaust system is attached to the body with mounting brackets and rubber hangers. If any of the parts are improperly installed, excessive noise and vibration will be transmitted to the body.
2   Conduct regular inspections of the exhaust system to keep it safe and quiet. Look for any damaged or bent parts, open seams, holes, loose connections, excessive corrosion or other defects which could allow exhaust fumes to enter the vehicle. Deteriorated exhaust system components should not be repaired; they should be replaced with new parts.
3   If the exhaust system components are extremely corroded or rusted together, welding equipment will probably be required to remove them. The convenient way to accomplish this is to have a muffler repair shop remove the corroded sections with a cutting torch. If, however, you want to save money by doing it yourself (and you don't have a welding outfit with a cutting torch), simply cut off the old components with a hacksaw. If

4

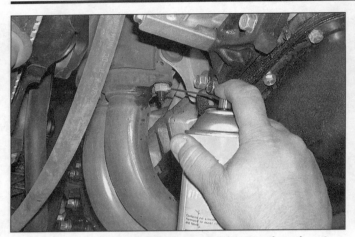

16.4a Be sure to apply penetrating lubricant to the exhaust system fasteners before attempting to remove them

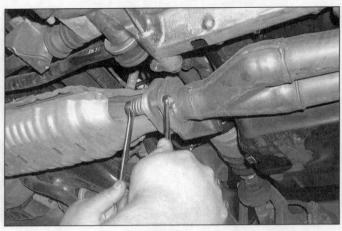

16.4b Unscrew the exhaust system fasteners with a pair of wrenches

you have compressed air, special pneumatic cutting chisels can also be used. If you do decide to tackle the job at home, be sure to wear safety goggles to protect your eyes from metal chips and work gloves to protect your hands.

4   Here are some simple guidelines to follow when repairing the exhaust system:

a) *Work from the back to the front when removing exhaust system components* **(see illustrations)**.

b) *Apply penetrating oil to the exhaust system component fasteners to make them easier to remove.*

c) *Use new gaskets, hangers and clamps when installing exhaust systems components.*

d) *Apply anti-seize compound to the threads of all exhaust system fasteners during reassembly.*

e) *Be sure to allow sufficient clearance between newly installed parts and all points on the underbody to avoid overheating the floor pan and possibly damaging the interior carpet and insulation. Pay particularly close attention to the catalytic converter and heat shield.*

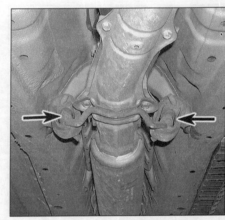

16.4c Check for any broken or missing rubber hangers

Chapter 5
Engine electrical systems

Contents

Specifications

Ignition coil

Civic (Hitachi distributor)
Primary resistance .... 0.45 to 0.55 ohms
Secondary resistance .... 22.4 to 33.6 K-ohms
Civic (TEC distributor)
Primary resistance .... 0.63 to 0.77 ohms
Secondary resistance .... 12.8 to 19.2 K-ohms
Integra
Primary resistance .... 0.6 to 0.8 ohms
Secondary resistance .... 12.8 to 19.2 K-ohms

Ignition timing

Civic
Manual transmission
D16Y5, D16Y8 .... 12+/-2 degrees BTDC (RED) at 450+/-50 rpm
D16Y7
US .... 12+/-2 degrees BTDC (RED) at 670+/-50 rpm
Canada .... 12+/-2 degrees BTDC (RED) at 750+/-50 rpm
CVT or automatic transmission
US .... 12+/-2 degrees BTDC (RED) at 700+/-50 rpm
Canada .... 12+/-2 degrees BTDC (RED) at 750+/-50 rpm
Integra
B18B1, B18C1 .... 16+/-2 degrees (RED) at 750+/-50 rpm
B18C5 .... 16+/-2 degrees (RED) at 800+/-50 rpm

Charging system
Alternator brush length (minimum) 1/16-inch

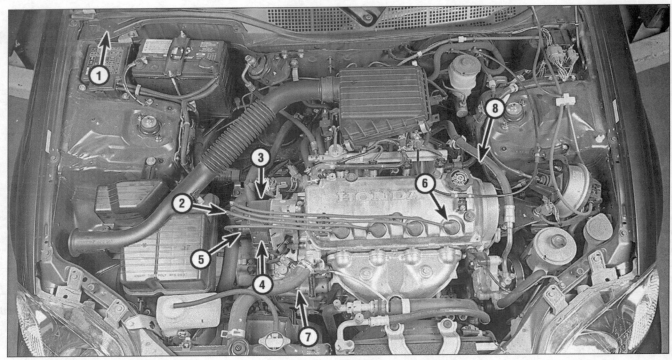

1.1a Engine electrical system components (Civic)

1	Powertrain control module (in passenger compartment)	
2	Spark plug wires	
3	TDC/CKP/CYP sensor (inside distributor)	
4	Ignition coil (inside distributor)	
5	Ignition control module (inside distributor)	
6	Spark plugs	
7	Starter motor	
8	Alternator (located at the front of the engine - out of view)	

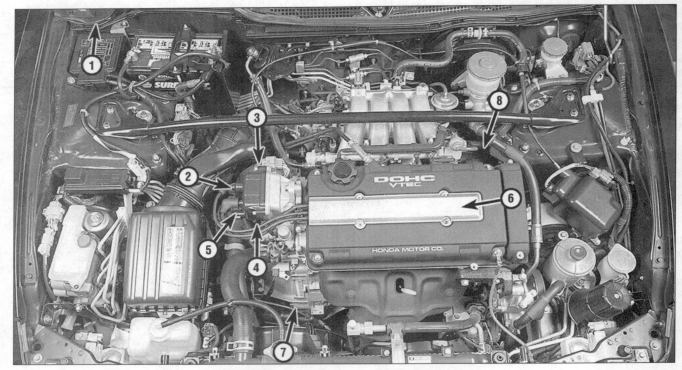

1.1b Engine electrical system components (Integra)

1	Powertrain control module (in passenger compartment)	
2	Spark plug wires	
3	TDC/CKP/CYP sensor (inside distributor)	
4	Ignition coil (inside distributor)	
5	Ignition control module (inside distributor)	
6	Spark plugs (beneath cover)	
7	Starter motor	
8	Alternator (located at the front of the engine - out of view)	

1 General information

The engine electrical systems include all ignition, charging and starting components **(see illustrations)**. Because of their engine-related functions, these components are considered separately from chassis electrical devices like the lights, instruments, etc.

Be very careful when working on the engine electrical components. They are easily damaged if checked, connected or handled improperly. The alternator is driven by an engine drivebelt which could cause serious injury if your hands, hair or clothes become entangled in it with the engine running. Both the starter and alternator are connected directly to the battery and could arc or even cause a fire if mishandled, overloaded or shorted out.

Never leave the ignition switch on for long periods of time with the engine off. Don't disconnect the battery cables while the engine is running. Correct polarity must be maintained when connecting battery cables from another source, such as another vehicle, during jump starting. Always disconnect

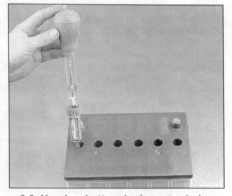

3.2 Here's a battery hydrometer being used to draw electrolyte from a battery cell - this hydrometer has a thermometer on it so it's easier to make temperature corrections

the negative cable first and hook it up last or the battery may be shorted by the tool being used to loosen the cable clamps.

Additional safety related information on the engine electrical systems can be found in *Safety first* near the front of this manual. It should be referred to before beginning any operation included in this Chapter.

2 Battery - emergency jump starting

Refer to the *Booster battery (jump) starting procedure* at the front of this manual.

3 Battery - check and replacement

Check

Refer to illustrations 3.2 and 3.3

1   Disconnect both cables from the battery terminals.

Warning: *Always disconnect the negative cable first and hook it up last or the battery may be shorted by the tool being used to loosen the cable clamps.*

Caution: *If the radio in your vehicle is equipped with an anti-theft system, make sure you have the correct activation code before disconnecting the battery.*

2   Check the battery electrolyte. This procedure is only possible on batteries with removable caps. The electrolyte level should be above the upper edge of the plates. If the level is low, add distilled water. DO NOT OVERFILL. The excess electrolyte may spill over during periods of heavy charging. Test the specific gravity of the electrolyte using a hydrometer **(see illustration)**. Remove the caps and extract a sample of the electrolyte and observe the float inside the barrel of the hydrometer. Follow the instructions from the tool manufacturer and determine the exact condition of the solution for each cell. A normal battery will indicate approximately 1.270 (green zone). If the electrolyte content is too

low (red zone), charge the battery (see Chapter 1). The battery voltage should be 12.6 volts or slightly above. Do not proceed with the battery test unless the battery charge is correct. **Note:** *Cold temperatures will cause the specific gravity requirements to vary. As temperature rises, the specific gravity decreases and vice versa. Follow the chart given in the manufacturer's instructions to compensate for cold climates.*

3   An accurate check of the battery condition can be performed with a load tester (available at most auto parts stores). This test evaluates the ability of the battery to operate the starter and other accessories during periods of heavy amperage draw (load). Install a special battery load testing tool onto the terminals **(see illustration)**. Load test the battery according to the manufacturer's instructions for the particular tool. This tool utilizes a carbon pile to increase the load demand (amperage draw) on the battery. Maintain the load on the battery for 15 seconds or less and observe that the battery voltage does not drop below 9.6 volts. If the battery is weak or defective, the tool will indicate this condition immediately. **Note:** *Cold temperatures will cause the minimum voltage requirements to drop slightly. Follow the chart given in the manufacturer's instructions to compensate for cold climates. Minimum load voltage for freezing temperatures (32-degrees F) should be approximately 9.1 volts.*

Replacement

Refer to illustrations 3.5 and 3.6

4   Disconnect both cables from the battery terminals. **Warning:** *Always disconnect the negative cable first and hook it up last or the battery may be shorted by the tool being used to loosen the cable clamps.* **Caution:** *If the radio in your vehicle is equipped with an anti-theft system, make sure you have the correct activation code before disconnecting the battery.*

5   Remove the battery hold-down clamp **(see illustration)**.

5

3.3 Here's a load tester in use - note that this one has an ammeter so the battery load can be precisely dialed in, as shown - less expensive testers have a load switch and a voltmeter only

3.5 Remove the hold-down strap (upper arrow) to detach the battery; the plastic cap on the positive cable terminal (lower arrow) prevents accidental shorts (make sure it's in place when you reinstall the battery)

3.6 If available, attach a battery strap and lift the battery straight up

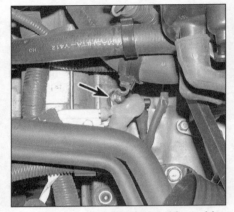

4.2a The lower end of the positive cable connects to the starter motor (arrow) . . .

4.2b . . . and the lower end of the negative cable is attached to the vehicle body (arrow)

6   Lift out the battery **(see illustration)**. Be careful - it's heavy. **Note:** *Battery straps and handles are available at most auto parts stores for a reasonable price. They make it easier to remove and carry the battery.*

7   While the battery is out, remove and inspect the carrier (tray) for corrosion.

8   If corrosion has leaked down to the battery support, remove the bolts and lift the support out. Clean the deposits from the metal to protect the support from further oxidation.

9   If you are replacing the battery, make sure you get one that's identical, with the same dimensions, amperage rating, cold cranking rating, etc.

10   Installation is the reverse of removal.

4   Battery cables - check and replacement

Refer to illustrations 4.2a, 4.2b, 4.2c and 4.2d

1   Periodically inspect the entire length of each battery cable for damage, cracked or burned insulation and corrosion. Poor battery cable connections can cause starting problems and decreased engine performance.

2   Check the cable-to-terminal connections at the ends of the cables for cracks, loose wire strands and corrosion **(see illustrations)**. The presence of white, fluffy deposits under the insulation at the cable terminal connection is a sign that the cable is corroded and should be replaced. Check the terminals for distortion, missing mounting bolts and corrosion.

3   When removing the cables, always disconnect the negative cable first and hook it up last or the battery may be shorted by the tool used to loosen the cable clamps. Even if only the positive cable is being replaced, be sure to disconnect the negative cable from the battery first (see Chapter 1 for further information regarding battery cable removal). **Caution:** *If the radio in your vehicle is equipped with an anti-theft system, make*

sure you have the correct activation code before disconnecting the battery.

4   Disconnect the old cables from the battery, then trace each of them to their opposite ends and detach them from the starter solenoid and ground terminals. Note the routing of each cable to ensure correct installation.

5   If you are replacing any of the cables, take the old cable(s) with you to the parts store. It is vitally important that you replace the cables with identical parts. Cables have characteristics that make them easy to identify: positive cables are usually red and larger in cross-section; ground cables are usually black and smaller in cross-section.

6   Clean the threads of the solenoid or ground connection with a wire brush to remove rust and corrosion. Apply a light coat of battery terminal corrosion inhibitor, or petroleum jelly, to the threads to prevent future corrosion.

7   Attach the cable to the solenoid or ground connection and tighten the mounting nut/bolt securely.

8   Before connecting a new cable to the battery, make sure that it reaches the battery post without having to be stretched.

9   Connect the positive cable first, followed by the negative cable.

5   Ignition system - general information

Warning: *The transistorized electronic ignition systems used on the models covered by this manual generate considerably higher voltage than conventional systems. Be extra careful when servicing these ignition systems.*

The Programmed Ignition (PGM-IG) system provides complete control of the ignition timing by determining the optimum timing using a micro computer in response to engine speed, coolant temperature, throttle position and vacuum pressure in the intake manifold. These parameters are relayed to the ECM by the TDC/CKP/CYP Sensor, Throttle Angle Sensor (TPS), Coolant Temperature Sensor and MAP Sensor. Ignition timing is altered during warm-up, idling and warm running conditions by the PGM-IG system. This electronic ignition system also consists of the ignition switch, battery, coil, distributor, spark plug wires and spark plugs **(see illustration 1.1a or 1.1b)**.

All distributors are driven by the camshaft (the intake camshaft on Integra models). Distributors are advanced and retarded by the Engine Control Module

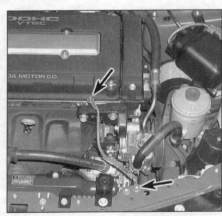

4.2c Integras have a ground cable attached to the engine and body (arrows)

4.2d Note the positions of the cable routing clamps (arrows)

6.2 To use a calibrated ignition tester, simply disconnect a spark plug wire, connect it to the tester, clip the tester to a convenient ground and operate the starter with the ignition on - if there's enough power to fire the plug, sparks will be visible between the electrode tip and the tester body

6.4 With the key ON, probe the positive terminal in the ignition coil connector to make sure voltage is getting to the coil

(ECM). All models employ a crank angle sensor which is located inside the distributor. Testing the TDC/CKP/CYP sensors is covered in Chapter 6.

6 Ignition system - check

Refer to illustrations 6.2 and 6.4

Warning: *Because of the high voltage generated by the ignition system, extreme care should be taken whenever an operation is performed involving ignition components. This not only includes the igniter, coil, distributor and spark plug wires, but related components such as plug connectors, tachometer and other test equipment also.*

1   If a malfunction occurs in the ignition system, do not immediately assume that the distributor is causing the problem. First, check the following items:

  a) *Make sure the battery cable clamps, where they connect to the battery, are clean and tight.*
  b) *Test the condition of the battery (see Section 3). If it does not pass all the tests, replace it with a new battery.*
  c) *Check the external distributor and ignition coil wiring and connections.*
  d) *Check the fusible links (if equipped) exiting the engine compartment fuse box (see Chapter 12). If they're burned, determine the cause and repair the circuit.*

2   Check the ignition spark at the plug. If the engine turns over but won't start, disconnect the spark plug wire from any spark plug and attach it to a calibrated tester (available at most auto parts stores) **(see illustration)**. Connect the clip on the tester to a bolt or metal bracket on the engine. If you're unable to obtain a calibrated ignition tester, remove the wire from one of the spark plugs and using an insulated tool, pull back the boot and hold the end of the wire about 1/4-inch

from a good ground. Crank the engine and watch the end of the tester or spark plug wire to see if a bright blue, well-defined sparks occur.

  a) *If sparks occur, sufficient voltage is reaching the plug to fire it (repeat the check at the remaining plug wires to verify that the distributor cap and rotor are OK). However, the plugs themselves may be fouled, so remove and check them as described in Chapter 1.*
  b) *If no sparks or intermittent sparks occur, remove the distributor cap (and leak cover if equipped) and check the cap and rotor as described in Chapter 1. If moisture is present, dry out the cap and rotor, then reinstall the cap and repeat the spark test.*
  c) *If there's still no spark, detach the coil secondary wire from the distributor cap and hook it up to the tester (reattach the plug wire to the spark plug), then repeat the spark check. Again, if you don't have a tester, hold the end of the wire about 1/4-inch from a good ground.* **Note:** *These models are equipped with an integral coil assembly mounted within the distributor. Check the condition of the spring and carbon button inside the distributor cap for burn marks or damage. Replace the cap if necessary.*

3   Check the condition of the distributor cap, rotor or plug wires. If there is an intermittent ignition misfire, the distributor cap, rotor or plug wire(s) may be defective. Refer to Chapter 1 for the component checks.

4   Check the coil primary circuit. If no sparks occur, check the primary wire connections at the coil to make sure they're clean and tight. Check for voltage to the coil on the primary circuit from the ignition switch **(see illustration)**. Check the ignition coil (see Section 7). Make any necessary repairs, then repeat the check again.

5   Check the ignition coil. Using an ohmmeter, check the primary and secondary

resistance of the ignition coil (see Section 7). If an open is found (verified by an infinite reading), replace the coil.

6   Check the ignition control module. Check the Ignition Control Module (ICM) for proper operation (see Section 8).

7 Ignition coil - check and replacement

Check

Refer to illustrations 7.4a, 7.4b, 7.5a and 7.5b

1   Make sure the ignition switch is turned OFF for the following checks.

2   Remove the distributor cap, rotor and the leak cover (if equipped).

3   Disconnect the primary electrical connectors from the ignition coil.

4   Using an ohmmeter, touch the probes to the primary terminals (A and B) of the coil, measure the primary resistance and compare your reading to the value listed in this Chapter's Specifications **(see illustrations)**.

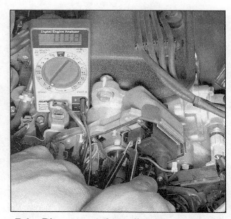

7.4a Disconnect the coil connectors and check resistance between the primary terminals; this is a Hitachi distributor . . .

5

7.4b . . . and this is a TEC distributor

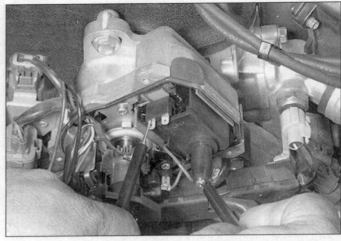

7.5a Check resistance between the coil primary and secondary terminals; this is a Hitachi distributor . . .

5   Touch the probes to the secondary winding terminal and the positive primary terminal (A) **(see illustrations)**, measure the secondary resistance and compare your reading to the resistance value listed in this Chapter's Specifications.

6   The figures in the specifications will vary somewhat with the temperature of the coil. The specified resistance values are for a coil temperature of about 70-degrees F.

7   If the coil fails either check, replace it with a new part.

Replacement

Refer to illustration 7.10

8   Detach the cable from the negative terminal of the battery. **Caution:** *If the radio in your vehicle is equipped with an anti-theft system, make sure you have the correct activation code before disconnecting the battery.*

9   Remove the distributor cap (see Chapter 1) and leak cover (if equipped). Remove the screws and detach the wires from the primary terminals.

10   Remove the two screws and slide the coil out **(see illustration)**.

11   Installation is the reverse of removal.

8   Ignition Control Module (ICM) - check and replacement

Check

Refer to illustrations 8.1 and 8.3

1   Check for battery voltage to the ignition module. Remove the distributor cap and the rotor and remove the black/yellow wire from the ICM **(see illustration)**. Check for battery voltage directly at the harness connector with the ignition key ON (engine not running).

2   Check the ignition circuit and related components. If there is no voltage to the ICM, check the circuit from the ICM to the battery (see Chapter 12). First check the ignition switch fuses number 41 (80 amp Civic/100 amp Integra) and 42 (40 amps) in the underhood fuse/relay box. Also check the number 9 (15 amp) fuse in the fuse/relay box in the passenger compartment. Follow the circuit carefully and make sure the ignition switch delivers battery voltage to the ICM with the key ON. Also check the yellow-green wire between the ICM and powertrain control module (PCM), and the blue wire that connects to the tachometer or tachometer ser-

vice connector. If there isn't continuity between the ends of each wire, there is a break in the wire. If there is continuity between either end of the wire and body ground, there is a short in the wire. Refer to the wiring schematics at the end of Chapter 12 for additional information.

3   Check for battery voltage from the ignition coil to the ignition module. With the ignition key turned ON (engine not running), check for voltage between the blue wire (Hitachi distributor) or white/blue wire (TEC distributor) and body ground **(see illustration)**. There should be battery voltage.

4   Check the circuit from the ignition coil to the ignition module. If there is no voltage, check the circuit between the corresponding wire and the ignition coil. Also check for an open circuit inside the ignition coil by checking for continuity between the primary terminals of the ignition coil (see Section 7).

5   If the ignition coil and circuits are good and there is still no spark, replace the ICM.

Replacement

Refer to illustration 8.9

6   Disconnect the negative battery cable from the battery terminal. **Caution:** *If the*

7.5b . . . and this is a TEC distributor

7.10 The coil is secured by two screws (arrows)

8.1 Check for battery voltage between the black/yellow wire and body ground

8.3 Check for battery voltage between the white/blue wire and body ground

8.9 Remove the screw(s) (arrow) and pull the ICM unit straight out from the distributor body

radio in your vehicle is equipped with an anti-theft system, make sure you have the correct activation code before disconnecting the battery.

7   Remove the distributor cap and cover from the distributor (see Chapter 1).

8   Remove all the electrical connectors from the ICM unit.

9   Remove the set screw(s) from the ICM body and pull the ICM unit straight out **(see illustration)**.

10   Installation is the reverse of removal.

9   Distributor - removal and installation

Removal

Refer to illustrations 9.5a and 9.5b

1   Detach the cable from the negative battery terminal. **Caution:** *If the radio in your vehicle is equipped with an anti-theft system, make sure you have the correct activation code before disconnecting the battery.*

2   Detach any clamps and electrical connectors on the distributor. Mark the wires and hoses so they can be returned to their original locations.

3   Look for a raised number or letter on the distributor cap. This marks the location for the number one cylinder spark plug wire terminal. If the cap does not have a mark for the number one terminal, locate the number one spark plug and trace the wire back to the terminal on the cap.

4   Remove the distributor cap (see Chapter 1) and turn the engine over until the rotor is pointing toward the number one spark plug terminal (see the locating TDC procedure in Chapter 2A or 2B).

5   Make a mark on the edge of the distributor base directly below the rotor tip and in line with it (if the rotor on your engine has more than one tip, use the center one for reference). Also, mark the distributor base and the cylinder head to ensure the distributor is installed correctly **(see illustrations)**.

6   Remove the distributor hold-down bolt(s) and pull out the distributor. **Caution:** *Do not turn the crankshaft while the distributor is out of the engine, or the alignment marks will be useless.*

Installation

Note: *If the crankshaft has been moved while the distributor is out, the number one piston must be repositioned at TDC. This can be done by feeling for compression pressure at the number one plug hole as the crankshaft is turned. Once compression is felt, align the ignition timing zero mark with the pointer.*

7   Install a new O-ring on the distributor housing.

8   Insert the distributor into the cylinder head in exactly the same relationship to the head that it was when removed. **Note:** *The lugs on the end of the distributor and the corresponding grooves in the camshaft end are offset to eliminate the possibility of installing the distributor 180-degrees out of phase.*

9   Recheck the alignment marks between the distributor base and the cylinder head to verify the distributor is in the same position it was in before removal. Also check the rotor to see if it's aligned with the mark you made on the distributor.

10   Loosely install the hold-down bolt(s).

11   The remainder of installation is the reverse of removal. Check the ignition timing and tighten the distributor hold-down bolt(s) securely.

5

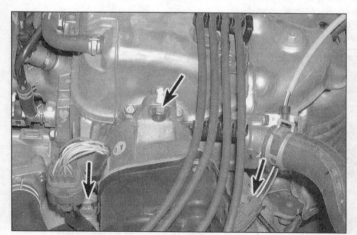

9.5a Mark the distributor position and remove the mounting bolts (arrows); this is a Civic distributor . . .

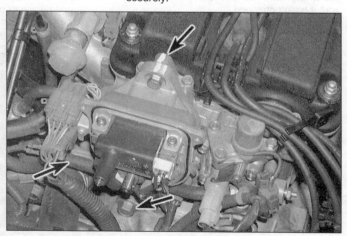

9.5b . . . this is an Integra distributor

10 Ignition timing - check and adjustment

Refer to illustrations 10.2, 10.4 and 10.5

Note: *It is imperative that the procedures included on the Vehicle Emissions Control Information (VECI) label be followed when adjusting the ignition timing. The label will include all information concerning preliminary steps to be performed before adjusting the timing, as well as the timing specifications.*

1   Start the engine and allow it to reach normal operating temperature.

2   With the ignition off, locate the VECI label under the hood and read through and perform all preliminary instructions concerning ignition timing. It's especially important to set idle speed correctly, because changes in engine speed will cause changes in timing. Several special tools will be needed for this procedure **(see illustration)**.

3   With the ignition off, hook up an inductive pick-up timing light in accordance with the manufacturer's instructions. Connect the inductive pick-up lead of the timing light to the number one spark plug wire. On all models, number one is the one closest to the drivebelt end of the engine.

4   Locate the timing marks on the front pulley **(see illustration)**.

5   Locate the service check connector **(see illustration)**. It's the two-terminal electrical connector behind the kick panel in the far right (passenger's side) corner. With the ignition off, connect the two terminals together with a jumper wire.

6   With the engine at normal operating temperature, start the engine and point the timing light at the timing pointer.

7   The appropriate mark on the flywheel (refer to the VECI label or this Chapter's Specifications) will appear stationary and be aligned with the pointer if the timing is correct.

8   If an adjustment is required, loosen the three mounting bolts and rotate the distributor slightly until the timing is correct.

9   Tighten the mounting bolts and recheck the timing. Also recheck idle speed to make sure it hasn't changed.

10   Turn off the engine and remove the timing light.

11   Replace inspection plug and remove the jumper wire from the service check connector.

11 Charging system - general information and precautions

The charging system includes the alternator, an internal voltage regulator, a charge indicator light, the battery, a fusible link and the wiring between all the components. The charging system supplies electrical power for the ignition system, the lights, the radio, etc. The alternator is driven by a drivebelt at the timing belt end of the engine.

The alternator control system within the ECU changes the voltage generated at the alternator in accordance with driving conditions. Depending upon electric load, vehicle speed, engine coolant temperature, accessories (air conditioning system, radio, cruise control etc.) and the intake air temperature, the system will adjust the amount of voltage generated, creating less load on the engine.

The purpose of the voltage regulator is to limit the alternator's voltage to a preset value. This prevents power surges, circuit overloads, etc., during peak voltage output.

The charging system doesn't ordinarily require periodic maintenance. However, the drivebelt, battery and wires and connections should be inspected at the intervals outlined in Chapter 1.

The dashboard warning light should come on when the ignition key is turned to On, but it should go off immediately after the engine is started. If it remains on, there is a malfunction in the charging system (see Section 11). Some vehicles are also equipped with a voltmeter. If the voltmeter indicates abnormally high or low voltage, check the charging system (see Section 11).

Be very careful when making electrical circuit connections to a vehicle equipped with an alternator and note the following:

a) *When reconnecting wires to the alternator from the battery, be sure to note the polarity.*

b) *Before using arc welding equipment to repair any part of the vehicle, disconnect the wires from the alternator and the battery terminals.*

10.2 Tools needed to check and adjust the ignition timing

1   ***Vacuum plugs*** *- Vacuum hoses will, in most cases, have to be disconnected and plugged. Molded plugs in various shapes and sizes are available for this*

2   ***Inductive pick-up timing light*** *- Flashes a bright, concentrated beam of light when the number one spark plug fires. Connect the leads according to the instructions supplied with the light*

3   ***Distributor wrench -*** *On some models, the hold-down bolt for the distributor is difficult to reach and turn with conventional wrenches or sockets. A special wrench like this must be used*

c) *Never start the engine with a battery charger connected.*

d) *Always disconnect both battery leads before using a battery charger.*

e) *The alternator is turned by an engine drivebelt which could cause serious injury it your hands, hair or clothes become entangled in it with the engine running.*

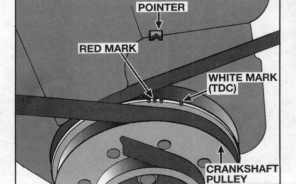

10.4 Be sure when viewing the timing mark on the pulley that you are directly above the pointer, aiming the timing light down so as not to create an extreme angle

POINTER

RED MARK

WHITE MARK (TDC)

CRANKSHAFT PULLEY

2118-5-10.04 HAYNES

10.5 The service check connector is located behind the kick-panel on the passenger side

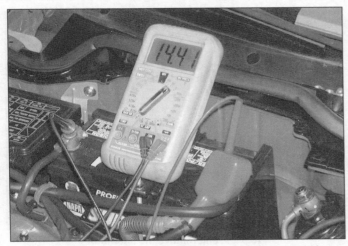

12.3 With the engine running, the battery voltage should be approximately 14 volts

13.3a Loosen the pivot bolt at the top of the alternator . . .

f) *Because the alternator is connected directly to the battery, it could arc or cause a fire if overloaded or shorted out.*

g) *Wrap a plastic bag over the alternator and secure it with rubber bands before steam cleaning the engine.*

12 Charging system - check

Refer to illustration 12.3

1   If a malfunction occurs in the charging circuit, do not immediately assume that the alternator is causing the problem. First, check the following items:

a) *Make sure the battery cable clamps, where they connect to the battery, are clean and tight.*

b) *Test the condition of the battery (see Section 3). If it does not pass all the tests, replace it with a new battery.*

c) *Check the external alternator wiring and connections.*

d) *Check the drivebelt condition and tension (see Chapter 1).*

e) *Check the alternator mounting bolts for tightness.*

f) *Run the engine and check the alternator for abnormal noise.*

g) *Check the fusible links (if equipped) exiting the engine compartment fuse box (see Chapter 12). If they're burned, determine the cause and repair the circuit.*

h) *Check the charge light on the dash. It should illuminate when the ignition key is turned ON (engine not running). If it does not, disconnect the 4 terminal connector from the back of the alternator and ground the white/blue wire's terminal. The charge light should illuminate. If it does not, check fuse number 15 (7.5 amp) and the charge light bulb. If they are blown, replace them. Also, check for battery voltage on terminal number 1. If battery voltage is available, replace the alternator.*

i) *Make sure the on board computer has not stored any trouble codes for the Electric Load Detector (ELD) system. Refer to Chapter 6 for the code extraction process and the diagnostic procedures.*

2   Check the battery voltage. With the ignition key off, check the battery voltage with no accessories (blower fan, radio, cigarette lighter, cooling fan, etc.) operating. It should be approximately 12.5 volts. It may be slightly higher if the engine had been operating within the last hour.

3   Check the charging voltage with the engine running. Start the engine, raise the engine rpm to 1500 and check the battery voltage again. It should now be approximately 13.8 to 14.8 volts **(see illustration)**.

4   Load the battery and observe the charging voltage. Turn on the high beam headlights, the A/C blower on HIGH, the windshield wipers and the radio. The voltage should drop and then come back up as each accessory is selected. If the charging system is working properly the voltage should stay above 13.5 volts. If the voltage drops below 13 volts, the charging system is weak or defective.

5   Lower the engine rpm back to idle and observe the charging voltage. The charging voltage should not drop below 13 volts with the decrease in engine rpm. Apply the brakes and observe the charging voltage at idle. It should remain above 13 volts. **Note:** *Some smaller amperage alternators may drop below 13 volts but, if they are in good condition, they will regulate the charging voltage to normal.*

6   Turn off all the electrical loads (high beam headlights, the A/C blower on HIGH, the windshield wipers and the radio), run the engine at 1600 rpm and watch the charging voltage rise. It should not rise above 15 volts. **Note:** *Cold temperatures will cause the voltage readings to increase slightly while hot temperatures will lower the charging system voltage readings.*

7   If the charging voltage does not exhibit

distinct changes when engine rpm increases and accessory loads are added, the voltage regulator is defective. If the charging voltages are low and the drivebelts and battery are all in good condition, the alternator is defective. In this situation, replace the alternator and voltage regulator as a single unit.

13 Alternator - removal and installation

Refer to illustrations 13.3a, 13.3b, 13.4 and 13.5

1   Detach the cable from the negative terminal of the battery. **Caution:** *If the radio in your vehicle is equipped with an anti-theft system, make sure you have the correct activation code before disconnecting the battery.*

2   Mark and detach the electrical connector and any ground straps from the alternator.

3   Loosen the alternator adjusting bolt and pivot bolt, then detach the drivebelt **(see illustrations)**.

4   To remove the alternator from the engine compartment, it will be necessary to partially remove the driveaxle beneath the alternator. Detach the lower end of the con-

13.3b . . . and the adjustment bolt located at the bottom of the alternator

5

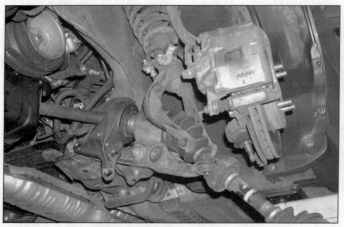

13.4 Remove the driveaxle partway, like this . . .

13.5 . . . and remove the alternator

trol arm from the suspension strut (see Chapter 10) and separate the outer end of the left driveaxle from the wheel hub. On Integra models it will also be necessary to unbolt the intermediate shaft support bearing from the engine block **(see illustration)**. Refer to Chapter 8 for more information.

5   Remove the adjusting and pivot bolts and lower the alternator from the engine **(see illustration)**.

6   If you are replacing the alternator, take the old one with you when purchasing a replacement unit. Make sure the new/rebuilt unit looks identical to the old alternator. Look at the terminals - they should be the same in number, size and location as the terminals on the old alternator. Finally, look at the identification numbers - they will be stamped into the housing or printed on a tag attached to the housing. Make sure the numbers are the same on both alternators.

7   Many new/rebuilt alternators DO NOT have a pulley installed, so you may have to switch the pulley from the old unit to the new/rebuilt one. When buying an alternator, find out the shop's policy regarding pulleys; some shops will perform this service free of charge.

8   Installation is the reverse of removal.

9   After the alternator is installed, adjust the drivebelt tension (see Chapter 1).
10   Check the charging voltage to verify proper operation of the alternator (see Section 11).

14   Voltage regulator and alternator brushes - replacement

Refer to illustrations 14.2, 14.3, 14.5 and 14.7
Note 1: *All Civic models and some 1998 Integra models use Mitsubishi alternators. Replacing the brushes and regulator on these alternators requires major disassembly and should be done by a qualified repair shop.*
Note 2: *It's practical to replace the brushes and regulator on a Nippondenso alternator, but don't attempt to completely overhaul the alternator. If replacing the brushes and regulator does not solve the alternator problem, take the alternator to a dealer service department or other repair shop and have it rebuilt or exchange it for a rebuilt unit.*
1   Remove the alternator (see Section 13) and place it on a clean workbench.
2   Remove the three rear cover nuts, the nut and terminal insulator and the rear cover

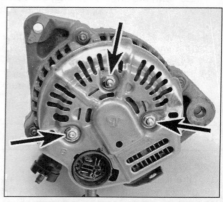

14.2 Remove the three nuts (arrows) and detach the rear cover from the alternator

(see Illustration).
3   Remove the two brush holder retaining screws **(see illustration)**.
4   Remove the brush holder from the rear end frame.
5   Measure the exposed length of the brush **(see illustration)** and compare it to the minimum length in this Chapter's Specifications. If the length of the brush is less than specified, replace the brush.

14.3 Once the rear cover is removed, remove the two screws (arrows) that retain the brush holder

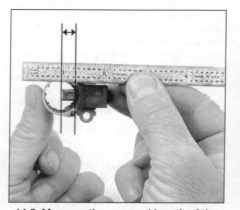

14.5 Measure the exposed length of the brushes and compare your measurements to the specified minimum length to determine if they should be replaced

14.7 Remove the voltage regulator screws (arrows) and remove the regulator from the alternator assembly

6   Make sure that each brush moves smoothly in the brush holder.

7   To remove the voltage regulator, remove the brushes as described above, then remove the mounting screws and take the regulator off **(see illustration)**.

8   Installation is the reverse of removal. Install the brush holder by depressing the brush with a small screwdriver to clear the shaft.

15   Starting system - general information and precautions

The starting system consists of the battery, the starter motor, the starter solenoid and the wires connecting them. The solenoid is mounted directly on the starter motor.

The solenoid/starter motor assembly is installed at the rear of the engine, next to the transaxle bellhousing.

When the ignition key is turned to the Start position, the starter solenoid is actuated through the starter control circuit. The starter solenoid then connects the battery to the starter. The battery supplies the electrical energy to the starter motor, which does the actual work of cranking the engine.

The starter motor on models equipped with manual transaxles can only be operated when the clutch pedal is depressed; the starter on models equipped with automatic transaxles can only be operated when the selector lever is in Park or Neutral.

Always observe the following precautions when working on the starting system:

a)   *Excessive cranking of the starter motor can overheat it and cause serious damage. Never operate the starter motor for more than 15 seconds at a time without pausing to allow it to cool for at least two minutes.*

b)   *The starter is connected directly to the battery and could arc or cause a fire if mishandled, overloaded or shorted out.*

c)   *Always detach the cable from the negative terminal of the battery before working on the starting system.*

16   Starter motor and circuit - in-vehicle check

Refer to illustration 16.4

1   If a malfunction occurs in the starting circuit, do not immediately assume that the starter is causing the problem. First, check the following items:

a)   *Make sure the battery cable clamps, where they connect to the battery, are clean and tight.*

b)   *Check the condition of the battery cables (see Section 4). Replace any defective battery cables with new parts.*

c)   *Test the condition of the battery (see Section 2). If it does not pass all the tests, replace it with a new battery.*

d)   *Check the starter solenoid wiring and*

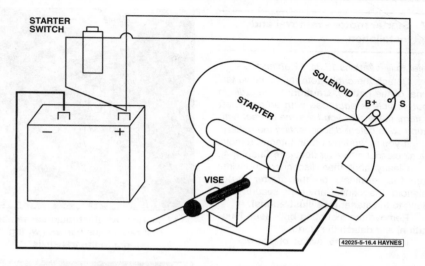

16.4 Connection diagram for testing the starter/solenoid assembly on the bench

connections. Refer to Chapter 12 wiring diagrams.

e)   *Check the starter mounting bolts for tightness.*

f)   *Check the fusible links (if equipped) exiting the engine compartment fuse box (see Chapter 12). If they're burned, determine the cause and repair the circuit. Also, check the ignition switch circuit for correct operation (see Chapter 12).*

g)   *Check the operation of the gear position switch (automatic transaxle) or clutch start circuit (manual transaxle) systems. Make sure the shift lever is in PARK or NEUTRAL (automatic transaxle) or the clutch pedal is pressed (manual transaxle). Refer to Chapter 7 for the gear position switch check and adjustment procedure. Refer to Chapter 12 wiring diagrams for the necessary circuit checks for the clutch activation system. These systems must operate correctly to provide battery voltage to the starter solenoid.*

2   If the starter does not actuate when the ignition switch is cranked, check for battery voltage to the solenoid. First determine if the solenoid is receiving the correct voltage signal from the ignition switch. Install a voltmeter to the starter solenoid terminal and while an assistant cranks the engine, observe the voltage. It should be approximately 12.6 volts. If voltage is not available, refer to the wiring diagrams in Chapter 12 and check all the fuses and relays in series with the starting system. On Integras, locate the fuse/relay panel in the driver's side dash area and check fuse number 31 (7.5 amp). Also, check the starter cut relay for correct operation. Refer to Chapter 12 for the location of the driver's side relay center along with the relay checks. If voltage is available but there is no movement from the starter motor, remove the starter from the engine compartment (see Section 17) and bench test the starter (see Step 4).

3   If the starter turns over slowly, check the starter cranking voltage and the current draw

from the battery. This test must be performed with the starter assembly on the engine. Crank the engine over (for 10 seconds or less) and observe the battery voltage. It should not drop below 8.5 volts on Civics or 8.0 volts on Integras. Also, observe the current draw using an ammeter. It should not exceed 350 amps on Civics; 360 amps on automatic transaxle Integras; or 270 amps on manual transaxle Integras. If the starter motor exceeds these values, replace it with a new unit. There are several conditions that may affect the starter cranking potential. The battery must be in good condition and the cold-cranking rating must not be under-rated for the particular application. Be sure to check the battery specifications carefully. The battery terminals and cables must be clean and not corroded. Also, in cases of extreme cold temperatures, make sure the battery and/or engine block is warmed before performing the tests.

4   If the starter is receiving voltage but does not activate, remove and check the starter/solenoid assembly on the bench. Most likely the solenoid is defective. In some rare cases, the engine may be seized so be sure to try and rotate the crankshaft pulley (see Chapter 2A or 2B) before proceeding. With the starter/solenoid assembly mounted in a vise on the bench, install one jumper cable from the negative terminal (—) to the body of the starter **(see illustration)**. Install the other jumper cable from the positive terminal (+) on the battery to the B+ terminal on the starter. Install a starter switch and apply battery voltage to the solenoid S terminal (for 10 seconds or less) and observe the solenoid plunger, shift lever and overrunning clutch extend and rotate the pinion drive. If the pinion drive extends but does not rotate, the solenoid is operating but the starter motor is defective. If there is no movement but the solenoid clicks, the solenoid and/or the starter motor is defective. If the solenoid plunger extends and rotates the pinion drive, the starter/solenoid assembly is working properly.

5

17 Starter motor - removal and installation

Refer to illustrations 17.3a, 17.3b and 17.4

1   Detach the cable from the negative terminal of the battery. **Caution:** *If the radio in your vehicle is equipped with an anti-theft system, make sure you have the correct activation code before disconnecting the battery.*
2   If you're working on an Integra, remove the air cleaner intake air duct (see Chapter 4).
3   Clearly label, then disconnect the wires from the terminals on the starter motor solenoid. Disconnect any clips securing the wiring to the starter **(see illustrations)**.
4   Remove the mounting bolts **(see illustration)** and detach the starter.
5   Installation is the reverse of removal.

18 Starter solenoid - removal and installation

Refer to illustrations 18.4, 18.5, 18.6 and 18.7
Note: *Integra models are equipped with Nippondenso starters, which have non-replaceable solenoids. If an Integra solenoid is defective, the entire starter should be replaced. This procedure applies to the Mitsuba starters used on Civics.*

1   Detach the cable from the negative terminal of the battery. **Caution:** *If the radio in your vehicle is equipped with an anti-theft system, make sure you have the correct activation code before disconnecting the battery.*
2   Remove the starter motor (see Section 17).
3   Disconnect the large wire from the solenoid to the starter motor terminal.
4   Remove the long bolts that secure the end cover to the gear housing **(see illustration)** and remove the armature housing from the assembly.
5   Remove the screws from the gear hous-

17.3a Remove the bracket assembly that retains the harness wiring loom to the transaxle

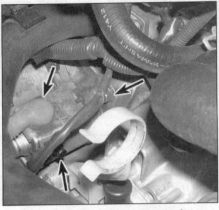

17.3b Disconnect the starter wires and remove the upper mounting bolt (arrows) . . .

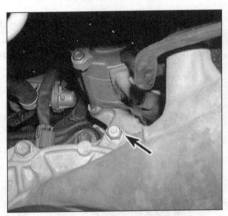

17.4 . . . and remove the lower bolt (arrow) to separate the starter from the transaxle

18.4 Remove the bolts that retain the end cover to the gear housing

ing **(see illustration)** and separate it from the gear housing cover.
6   Remove the screws from the gear housing **(see illustration)** and separate it from the solenoid.

7   Installation is the reverse of removal. Be sure to apply a slight amount of grease to the solenoid plunger and lever before installation **(see illustration)**.

18.5 Remove the screws (arrows) that retain the gear housing to the gear housing cover

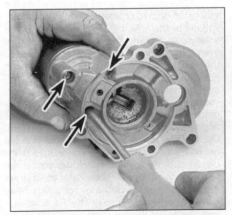

18.6 Remove the screws (arrows) that retain the solenoid to the gear housing

18.7 Apply grease to the lever and plunger (arrow) before assembly

Chapter 6
Emissions and engine control systems

Contents

Specifications

CKP circuit resistance	
Civic	350 to 700 ohms
Integra	0.5 to 1.0 k-ohms
CYP circuit resistance	
Civic	350 to 700 ohms
Integra	0.5 to 1.0 k-ohms
TDC circuit resistance	
Civic	350 to 700 ohms
Integra	0.5 to 1.0 k-ohms
Intake air temperature sensor resistance	1k to 4 k-ohms at room temperature

Torque specifications

Knock sensor	23 ft-lbs
Fast Idle Thermo (FIT) valve	84 in-lbs

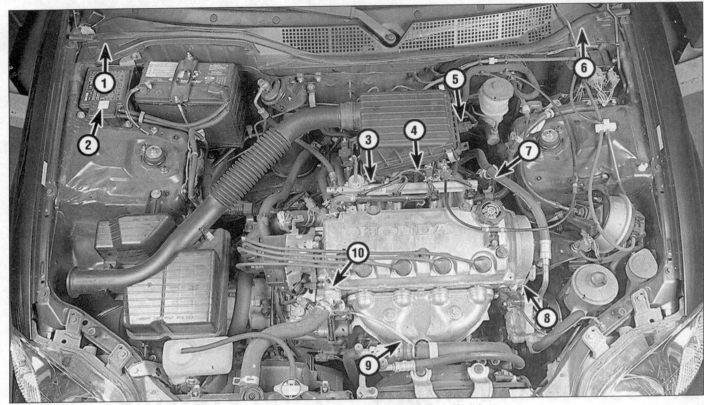

1.1a Typical emission control components (Civic)

1 ECM/PCM and check connector (under dash)	6 Diagnostic connector (under dash)
2 Electrical load detector (under fuse box)	7 Power steering pressure switch (in pressure line)
3 Throttle Position Sensor (TPS)	8 Crankshaft fluctuation (CKF) sensor
4 Manifold Absolute Pressure (MAP) sensor	9 Oxygen sensors (in manifold and catalytic converter)
5 Intake Air Temperature (IAT) sensor	10 Engine Coolant Temperature (ECT) sensor

1   General information

Refer to illustrations 1.1a, 1.1b and 1.6

To prevent pollution of the atmosphere from incompletely burned and evaporating gases, and to maintain good driveability and fuel economy, a number of emission control systems are incorporated **(see illustrations)**. They include the:

Self diagnosis system
Electronic engine controls (PGM-FI)
Electronic Load Detector (ELD)
Exhaust Gas Recirculation (EGR) system
Evaporative Emissions Control (EVAP) system
Positive Crankcase Ventilation (PCV) system
Catalytic converter

The Sections in this Chapter include general descriptions, checking procedures within the scope of the home mechanic and component replacement procedures (when possible) for each of the systems listed above.

Before assuming that an emissions control system is malfunctioning, check the fuel and ignition systems carefully. The diagnosis of some emission control devices requires specialized tools, equipment and training. If checking and servicing become too difficult

or if a procedure is beyond your ability, consult a dealer service department or other repair shop. Remember, the most frequent cause of emissions problems is simply a loose or broken wire or vacuum hose, so always check the hose and wiring connections first.

This doesn't mean, however, that emissions control systems are particularly difficult to maintain and repair. You can quickly and easily perform many checks and do most of the regular maintenance at home with common tune-up and hand tools. **Note**: *Because of a Federally mandated extended warranty which covers the emissions control system components, check with your dealer about warranty coverage before working on any emissions-related systems. Once the warranty has expired, you may wish to perform some of the component checks and/or replacement procedures in this Chapter to save money.*

Pay close attention to any special precautions outlined in this Chapter. It should be noted that the illustrations of the various systems may not exactly match the system installed on your vehicle because of changes made by the manufacturer during production or from year-to-year.

A Vehicle Emissions Control Information

(VECI) label is attached to the underside of the hood **(see illustration)**. This label contains important emissions specifications and adjustment information. Part of this label, the Vacuum Hose Routing Diagram, provides a vacuum hose schematic with emissions components identified. When servicing the engine or emissions systems, the VECI label and the vacuum hose routing diagram in your particular vehicle should always be checked for up-to-date information.

2   On-Board Diagnostic (OBD) system and trouble codes

Diagnostic tool information

Refer to illustrations 2.1 and 2.2

1   A digital multimeter is necessary for checking fuel injection and emission related components **(see illustration)**. A digital volt-ohmmeter is preferred over the older style analog multimeter for several reasons. The analog multimeter cannot display the volts-ohms or amps measurement in hundredths and thousandths increments. When working with electronic circuits which are often very low voltage, this accurate reading is most important. Another good reason for the digital

1.1b Typical emission and engine control components (Integra)

1   ECM/PCM and check connector (under dash)
2   Electrical load detector (under fuse box)
3   Throttle Position Sensor (TPS)
4   Manifold Absolute Pressure (MAP) sensor
5   Intake Air Temperature (IAT) sensor
6   Idle Air Control (IAC) valve

7   Power steering pressure switch (in pressure line)
8   Crankshaft fluctuation (CKF) sensor
9   Knock sensor
10 Oxygen sensors (in manifold and catalytic converter)
11 Engine Coolant Temperature (ECT) sensor
12 Diagnostic connector (under dash)

multimeter is the high impedance circuit. The digital multimeter is equipped with a high resistance internal circuitry (10 million ohms). Because a voltmeter is hooked up in parallel with the circuit when testing, it is vital that none of the voltage being measured should be allowed to travel the parallel path set up

by the meter itself. This dilemma does not show itself when measuring larger amounts of voltage (9 to 12 volt circuits) but if you are measuring a low voltage circuit such as the oxygen sensor signal voltage, a fraction of a volt may be a significant amount when diagnosing a problem.

2   Hand-held scanners are the most powerful and versatile tools for analyzing engine management systems used on later model vehicles **(see illustration)**. Early model scanners handle codes and some diagnostics for many OBD I systems. Each brand scan tool must be examined carefully to match the

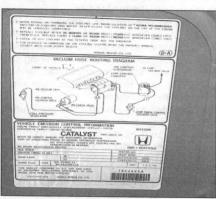

1.6 The Vehicle Emission Control Information and vacuum hose routing diagram decals are located under the hood

2.1 Digital multimeters can be used for testing all types of circuits; because of their high impedance, they are much more accurate than analog meters for measuring low-voltage computer circuits

2.2 Scanners like the Actron Scantool and the AutoXray XP240 are powerful diagnostic aids, programmed with comprehensive diagnostic information

6

year, make and model of the vehicle you are working on. Often, interchangeable cartridges are available to access the particular manufacturer (Ford, GM, Chrysler, etc.). Some manufacturers will specify by continent (Asia, Europe, USA, etc.).

3   With the arrival of the Federally mandated emission control system (OBD-II), a specially designed scanner has been developed. Several manufacturers have released OBD-II scan tools for the home mechanic. Ask the parts salesman at a local auto parts store for additional information concerning dates and costs.

OBD system general description

4   1994 and 1995 models use the first-generation On-Board Diagnostic (OBD) system. Beginning in 1996, Honda Motor Company began to manufacture a second generation self diagnosis system specified by the CARB and EPA regulations called On Board Diagnosis-II (OBD-II). This system incorporates a series of diagnostic monitors that detect and identify emissions systems faults and store the information in the computer memory. This updated system also tests sensors and output actuators, diagnoses drive cycles, freezes data and clears codes.

5   This powerful diagnostic computer can be accessed using an OBD-II compatible SCAN tool connected to the 16 pin Data Link Connector (DLC) located under the driver's dash area. All 1996 and later engines and powertrain combinations described in this manual are equipped with the On Board Diagnosis II (OBD-II) system. This system consists of an onboard computer, known as the Engine Control Module (ECM) or Powertrain Control Module (PCM), and information sensors, which monitor various functions of the engine and send data to the ECM/PCM. Based on the data and the information programmed into the computer's memory, the ECM/PCM generates output signals to control various engine functions via control relays, solenoids and other output actuators.

6   The ECM/PCM is the "brain" of the engine management system. It receives data from a number of sensors and other electronic components (switches, relays, etc.). Based on the information it receives, the ECM/PCM generates output signals to control various relays, solenoids and other actuators. The ECM/PCM is specifically calibrated to optimize the emissions, fuel economy and driveability of the vehicle.

7   Because of a Federally mandated extended warranty which covers the engine management system components and because any owner-induced damage to the ECM/PCM, the sensors and/or the control devices may void the warranty, it isn't a good idea to attempt diagnosis or replacement of the ECM/PCM at home while the vehicle is under warranty. Take the vehicle to a dealer service department if the ECM/PCM or a system component malfunctions.

Information sensors

8   **Heated Oxygen sensors (HO2S)** - The HO2S generates a voltage signal that varies with the difference between the oxygen content of the exhaust and the oxygen in the surrounding air.

9   **Crankshaft position (CKP) sensor** - The CKP sensor, used on OBD I models, provides information on crankshaft position and the engine speed signal to the ECM/PCM.

10   **Top dead center/crankshaft position/cylinder position (TDC/CKP/CYP) sensor** - This sensor, used on OBD II models, produces a signal which the ECM/PCM uses to identify number 1 cylinder and to time the sequential fuel injection and ignition.

11   **Crankshaft speed fluctuation (CKF) sensor** - The CKF sensor provides information on changes in the rotational speed of the crankshaft. If the rotational speed changes beyond a set limit, the ECM/PCM concludes that a misfire has occurred.

12   **Engine coolant temperature (ECT) sensor** - The ECT monitors engine coolant temperature and sends the ECM/PCM a voltage signal that affects ECM/PCM control of the fuel mixture, ignition timing, and EGR operation.

13   **Intake Air Temperature (IAT) sensor** - The IAT provides the ECM/PCM with intake air temperature information. The ECM/PCM uses this information to control fuel flow, ignition timing, and EGR system operation (if equipped).

14   **Throttle Position Sensor (TPS)** - The throttle position sensor (TPS) is located on the end of the throttle shaft on the throttle body. By monitoring the output voltage from the TPS, the ECM/PCM can determine fuel delivery based on throttle valve angle (driver demand). A broken or loose TPS can cause intermittent bursts of fuel from the injector and an unstable idle because the ECM/PCM thinks the throttle is moving.

15   **Manifold Absolute Pressure (MAP) sensor** - The Manifold Absolute Pressure (MAP) sensor monitors the intake manifold pressure changes resulting from changes in engine load and speed and converts the information into a voltage output. The ECM/PCM uses the MAP sensor to control fuel delivery and ignition timing. The ECM/PCM will receive information as a voltage signal that will vary from 1.0 to 1.5 volts at closed throttle (high vacuum) and 4.0 to 4.5 volts at wide open throttle (low vacuum). The MAP sensor is located on the throttle body.

16   **Vehicle Speed Sensor (VSS)** - The vehicle speed sensor provides information to the ECM/PCM to indicate vehicle speed.

17   **Fuel tank pressure sensor** - The fuel tank pressure sensor is part of the evaporative emission control system and is used to monitor vapor pressure in the fuel tank. The ECM/PCM uses this information to turn on and off the purge valves and solenoids of the evaporative emission system.

18   **Power Steering Pressure (PSP) switch** - The PSP switch is used to inform the ECM/PCM when the power steering load is high. The ECM/PCM can then compensate for the added load by raising the idle speed, via the IAC valve, as necessary.

19   **Knock sensor** - The knock sensor detects the vibrations of spark knock and signals the ECM/PCM to retard the ignition timing.

20   **Transaxle sensors** - In addition to the vehicle speed sensor, the ECM/PCM receives input signals from the following sensors inside the transaxle or connected to it: (a) the turbine shaft speed sensor, (b) the transmission fluid temperature sensor, and (c) the transmission range sensor.

21   **A/C clutch control switch** - When battery voltage is applied to the air conditioning compressor solenoid, a signal is sent to the ECM/PCM, which interprets the signal as an added load created by the compressor and increases engine idle speed accordingly to compensate.

Output actuators

22   **PGM-FI main (fuel pump) relay** - The fuel pump relay is activated by the ECM/PCM with the ignition switch in the Start or Run position. When the ignition switch is turned on, the relay is activated to supply initial line pressure to the system. The PGM-FI main relay is in the power distribution box in the engine compartment. For more information on fuel pump check and replacement, refer to Chapter 4.

23   **Fuel injectors** - The ECM/PCM opens the fuel injectors individually in firing order sequence. The ECM/PCM also controls the time the injector is open, called the "pulse width." The pulse width of the injector (measured in milliseconds) determines the amount of fuel delivered. For more information on the fuel delivery system and the fuel injectors, including injector replacement, refer to Chapter 4.

24   **Ignition Control Module (ICM)** - The ICM triggers the ignition coils and determines proper spark advance based on inputs from the ECM/PCM. All models use an ignition module which is incorporated into the distributor. Refer to Chapter 5 for more information on the Ignition Control Module.

25   **Idle air control (IAC) valve** - The IAC valve controls the amount of air to bypass the throttle plate when the throttle valve is closed or at idle position. The IAC valve opening and the resulting airflow is controlled by the ECM/PCM. Refer to Chapter 4 for more information on the IAC valve.

26   **Canister purge valve** - The evaporative emission canister purge valve is a solenoid valve, operated by the ECM/PCM to purge the fuel vapor canister and route fuel vapor to the intake manifold for combustion.

Obtaining trouble codes

Refer to illustrations 2.27a and 2.27b

27   The service check connector is located under the dashboard, on the passenger side **(see illustration)**. The codes can be read by jumping the service check connector and reading the CHECK engine light on the instru-

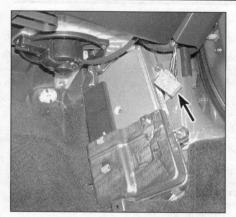

2.27a The service check connector, under the passenger side glove box behind the kick panel, can be used to read trouble codes with the CHECK engine light

2.27b The 16-pin diagnostic connector (for scan tool connection) is under the left side of the dash

ment panel (all models). If you have a scan tool, it can be connected to the data link connector under the dash on the left side **(see illustration)**.

28   To view any trouble codes stored in the ECM/PCM memory, install a jumper wire into the service check connector **(see illustration 2.27a)** located in the far right corner under the dash, then turn the ignition switch to the ON position. If any are present, they will blink a sequence on the CHECK light on the instrument panel to indicate a number or code that represents a system or component failure.

29   The CHECK light will blink a longer blink to represent the first digit of a two digit number and then will blink short for the second digit (for example, 1 long blink then 6 short blinks for the code 16). **Note:** *If the system has more than one problem, the codes will be displayed in sequence, then a there will be pause, then the codes will repeat.*

OBD-I trouble codes

Trouble code	Circuit or system	Corrective action
Code 0	Faulty ECM/PCM	Check the ECM/PCM electrical connector. If no loose connectors are found, have the ECM/PCM diagnosed by a dealer service department.
Code 1	Oxygen content	Check the oxygen sensor, heater and the oxygen sensor circuit (see Section 4).
Codes 3 and 5	Manifold Absolute Pressure	Check the MAP sensor and circuit (see Section 4).
Code 4	Crank angle sensor (CKP)	Check the crank angle sensor and circuit (see Section 4).
Code 6	Coolant temperature	Check the coolant temperature sensor and circuit (see Section 4).
Code 7	Throttle angle (TPS)	Check the Throttle Position Sensor (TPS) and the circuit (see Section 4).
Code 8	TDC Position	Check the TDC sensor and the circuit (see Section 4).
Code 9	No. 1 cylinder position (CYP)	Check the CYP sensor and the circuit (see Section 4).
Code 10	Intake Air Temperature (IAT)	Check the TA sensor and the circuit (see Section 4).
Code 12	Exhaust Gas Recirculation	Check the hoses, the EGR valve lift sensor and the System EGR valve (see Section 6).
Code 13	Barometric Pressure	Have the vehicle checked at a dealer service repair shop.
Code 14	Idle Air Control (IAC) valve	Check the IAC valve and system (see Chapter 4).
Code 15	Ignition output signal	Check the ignition system (see Chapter 5).
Code 16	Fuel injector	Check the fuel injection system and the fuel injectors (see Chapter 4).
Code 17	Vehicle speed sensor	Have the vehicle checked at a dealer service department or other repair shop.
Code 19	Lock-up Control Solenoid	On automatic transaxles, check the solenoid (see Chapter 7B).
Code 20	Electronic load detector (ELD)	Check the ELD system (see Section 8).
Code 21	Variable Valve Timing and	See Chapter 2A VTEC Solenoid checks. Valve Lift Solenoid
Code 22	Variable Valve Timing and	See Chapter 2A VTEC Pressure switch checks. control pressure switch
Code 30	A/T FI signal A (automatic	Have the vehicle checked at a dealer service department or other repair shop (automatic transaxle vehicles)
Code 41	Oxygen sensor heater	Check the heater for the proper voltage signal (see Section 4).
Code 43	Fuel supply system	Check the fuel pressure, fuel pressure regulator (see Chapter 4) Also, check for any oxygen sensor vacuum leaks (see Section 4).
Code 48	Heated Oxygen sensor	Check the heater for the proper voltage signal (see Section 4).

6

OBD-II Trouble Codes

Code (MIL flashes)	Probable cause
P0106 (5)	Manifold Absolute Pressure (MAP) circuit range/performance problem
P0107 (3)	Manifold Absolute Pressure (MAP) sensor circuit low input
P0108 (3)	Manifold Absolute Pressure (MAP) sensor circuit high input
P0111 (10)	Intake Air Temperature (IAT) sensor circuit range/performance problem
P0112 (10)	Intake Air Temperature (IAT) sensor circuit low input
P0113 (10)	Intake Air Temperature (IAT) sensor circuit high input
P0116 (86)	Engine Coolant Temperature (ECT) sensor circuit range/performance problem
P0117 (6)	Engine Coolant Temperature (ECT) sensor circuit low input
P0118 (6)	Engine Coolant Temperature (ECT) sensor circuit high input
P0122 (7)	Throttle Position Sensor (TPS) circuit low input
P0123 (7)	Throttle Position Sensor (TPS) circuit high input
P0131 (1)	Primary heated O2 sensor circuit low voltage (Sensor 1)
P0132 (1)	Primary heated O2 sensor circuit high voltage (Sensor 1)
P0133 (61)	Primary heated O2 sensor circuit slow response (Sensor 1)
P0135 (41)	Primary heated O2 sensor heater circuit fault (Sensor 1)
P0137 (63)	Secondary heated O2 sensor circuit low voltage (Sensor 2)
P0138 (63)	Secondary heated O2 sensor circuit high voltage (Sensor 2)
P0139 (63)	Secondary heated O2 sensor circuit slow response (Sensor 2)
P0141 (65)	Secondary heated O2 sensor heater circuit fault (Sensor 2)
P0171 (45)	System too lean
P0172 (45)	System too rich
P0300	Random misfire
P0301 (71)	Cylinder no. 1 misfire detected
P0302 (72)	Cylinder no. 2 misfire detected
P0303 (73)	Cylinder no. 3 misfire detected
P0304 (74)	Cylinder no. 4 misfire detected
P0325 (23)	Knock sensor circuit fault
P0335 (4)	Crankshaft position sensor circuit fault
P0336 (4)	Crankshaft position sensor range/performance
P0401 (80)	EGR insufficient flow detected
P0420 (67)	Catalyst system efficiency below threshold
P0441 (92)	EVAP system insufficient purge flow
P0452 (91)	EVAP fuel tank pressure sensor low input
P0453 (91)	EVAP fuel tank pressure sensor high input
P0500 (17)	Vehicle speed sensor circuit fault
P0501 (17)	Vehicle speed sensor range/performance
P0505 (14)	IAC valve system fault

Code (MIL flashes)	Probable cause
P0700 (70)	Automatic transaxle
P0715 (70)	Automatic transaxle
P0720 (70)	Automatic transaxle
P0725 (70)	Automatic transaxle
P0730 (70)	Automatic transaxle
P0740 (70)	Automatic transaxle
P0753 (70)	Automatic transaxle
P0758 (70)	Automatic transaxle
P1106 (13)	BARO sensor circuit range/performance fault
P1107 (13)	BARO sensor circuit low input
P1108 (13)	BARO sensor circuit high input
P1121 (7)	Throttle position higher than expected
P1122 (7)	Throttle position lower than expected
P1128 (5)	Manifold absolute pressure lower than expected
P1129 (5)	Manifold absolute pressure higher than expected
P1162 (48)	Primary heated oxygen sensor circuit malfunction (Sensor 1)
P1163 (61)	Primary heated oxygen sensor circuit slow response (Sensor 1)
P1164 (61)	Primary heated oxygen sensor circuit range/performance fault (Sensor 1)
P1165 (61)	Primary heated oxygen sensor circuit range/performance fault (Sensor 1)
P1166 (41)	Primary heated oxygen sensor circuit electrical fault (Sensor 1)
P1167 (41)	Primary heated oxygen sensor circuit heater system fault (Sensor 1)
P1168 (48)	Primary heated oxygen sensor circuit LABEL low input (Sensor 1)
P1169 (48)	Primary heated oxygen sensor circuit LABEL high input (Sensor 1)
P1259 (22)	VTEC system malfunction
P1297 (20)	Electrical Load Detector (ELD) circuit low input
P1298 (20)	Electrical Load Detector (ELD) circuit high input
P1300 (—)	Random misfire
P1301 (71)	Cylinder no. 1 misfire
P1302 (72)	Cylinder no. 2 misfire
P1303 (73)	Cylinder no. 3 misfire
P1304 (74)	Cylinder no. 4 misfire
P1336 (54)	Crankshaft fluctuation (CKF) sensor intermittent interruption
P1337 (54)	Crankshaft fluctuation (CKF) sensor no signal
P1359 (8)	Crankshaft position/TDC position sensor disconnected
P1361 (8)	Crankshaft position/TDC position intermittent interruption
P1362 (8)	TDC sensor no signal
P1381 (9)	Cylinder position sensor intermittent interruption
P1381 (9)	Cylinder position sensor no signal

6

OBD-II Trouble Codes (continued)

Code (MIL flashes)	Probable cause
P1456 (90)	EVAP system leak detected in fuel tank area
P1457 (90)	EVAP system leak detected in canister area
P1491 (12)	EGR valve insufficient lift
P1498 (12)	EGR valve lift sensor high voltage
P1508 (14)	Idle Air Control (IAC) valve circuit fault (1)
P1509 (14)	Idle Air Control (IAC) valve circuit fault (2)
P1607 (—)	ECM/PCM internal circuit failure
P1655 (30)	TMA/TMB signal line open or short
P1705 (70)	Automatic transaxle fault
P1706 (70)	Automatic transaxle fault
P1753 (70)	Automatic transaxle fault
P1758 (70)	Automatic transaxle fault
P1768 (70)	Automatic transaxle fault
P1785 (70)	Automatic transaxle fault
P1790 (70)	Automatic transaxle fault
P1791 (70)	Automatic transaxle fault
P1793 (70)	Automatic transaxle fault
P1870 (70)	Automatic transaxle fault
P1873 (70)	Automatic transaxle fault
P1879 (70)	Automatic transaxle fault
P1885 (70)	Automatic transaxle fault
P1886 (70)	Automatic transaxle fault
P1888 (70)	Automatic transaxle fault
P1890 (70)	Automatic transaxle fault
P1891 (70)	Automatic transaxle fault

Clearing codes

30   When the ECM/PCM sets a trouble code, the CHECK engine light will come on and a trouble code will be stored in the memory. The trouble code will stay in the ECM/PCM memory until the voltage to the ECM/PCM is interrupted. To clear the memory, remove the BACK-UP fuse from the fuse/relay box located in the right side of the engine compartment for at least ten seconds (see Chapter 12 for fuse box location). **Note:** *Unplugging the BACK-UP fuse also cancels the radio preset stations and the clock setting. Be sure to make a note of the various radio stations that are programmed into the memory before removing the fuse.*

3   Powertrain Control Module (ECM/PCM) - removal and installation

Refer to illustration 3.4

Warning: *Most models covered by this manual are equipped with a Supplemental Restraint System (SRS), more commonly known as an airbag(s). Always disable the airbag system before working in the vicinity of the SRS unit, steering column or instrument panel to avoid the possibility of accidental deployment of the airbag, which could cause personal injury (see Chapter 12).*

1   The Powertrain Control Module (ECM/PCM) is located inside the passenger compartment under the dashboard behind the kick panel (right side). **Caution:** *Avoid any static electricity damage to the computer by grounding yourself to the body before touching the ECM/PCM and using a special anti-static pad to store the ECM/PCM on once it is removed.*

2   Disable the airbag system (see Chapter 12). **Caution:** *If the stereo in your vehicle is equipped with an anti-theft system, make sure you have the correct activation code before disconnecting the battery.*

3   Remove the carpet from the lower panel assembly and the floor area (see Chapter 11) under the right end of the dash. Place the carpet sufficiently out of the way.

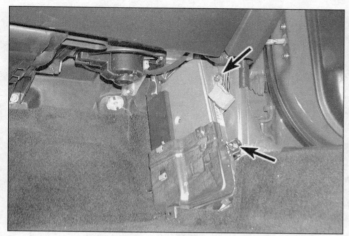

3.4 Remove the mounting nuts to detach the ECM/PCM from the side panel

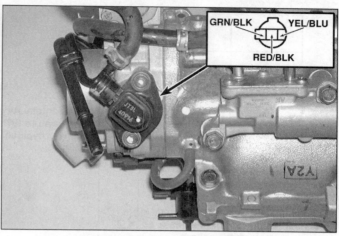

4.2a Civic Throttle Position Sensor

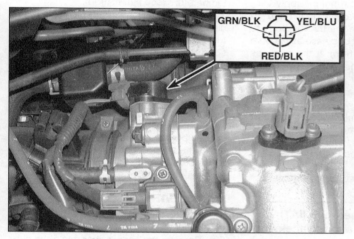

4.2b Integra Throttle Position Sensor

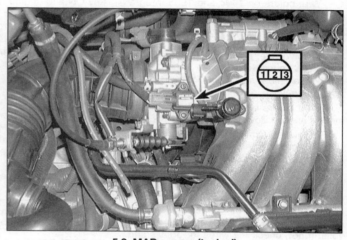

5.2 MAP sensor (typical)

| 1 | Power | 2 | Signal | 3 | Ground |

6

4   Remove the kick plate to expose the relay panel and the ECM/PCM **(see illustration)**.

5   Remove the retaining nuts from the ECM/PCM bracket.

6   Unplug the electrical connectors from the ECM/PCM. **Caution:** *The ignition switch must be turned OFF when pulling out or plugging in the electrical connectors to prevent damage to the ECM/PCM.*

7   Carefully remove the ECM/PCM.

8   Installation is the reverse of removal.

---

4   Throttle Position Sensor (TPS) - check and replacement

Check

Refer to illustrations 4.2a and 4.2b

1   Follow the wiring harness from the TPS to the back of the intake manifold and remove it from the firewall. This will give you more room to probe the electrical terminals. Check the electrical connector at the sensor for a snug fit. Check the terminals in the connector and the wires leading to it for loose-ness and breaks. Repair as required.

2   Using a voltmeter, check the reference voltage from the ECM/PCM. Connect the positive probe to the yellow/blue wire and the negative probe to ground **(see illustrations)**. It should read approximately 5.0 volts.

3   Next, check the TPS signal voltage. With the engine Off, throttle fully closed and TPS electrical connector connected, connect the probes of the voltmeter to the red/black wire (positive probe) and ground (negative probe) **(see illustrations 4.2a and 4.2b). Note:** *Use a straight pin to backprobe the connector terminal.* Gradually open the throttle valve and observe the TPS voltage. With the throttle valve fully closed, the voltage should read approximately 0.5 volts. Slowly move the throttle valve and see if the voltage changes as the sensor travels from idle to full throttle. The voltage should increase smoothly to approximately 4.5 volts. If the readings are incorrect, replace the TPS sensor.

4   A problem in any of the TPS circuits will set a code (see Section 2). Once a trouble code is set, the ECM/PCM will use an artificial default value for TPS and some vehicle performance will return.

Replacement

5   The TPS is an integral part of the throttle body and must be replaced with the throttle body as a unit (see Chapter 4).

---

5   Manifold Absolute Pressure (MAP) sensor - check and replacement

Refer to illustrations 5.2 and 5.8

Check

1   Check the electrical connector at the sensor for a snug fit. Check the terminals in the connector and the wires leading to it for looseness and breaks. Repair as required.

2   Identify the MAP sensor wires **(see illustration)**. There are three wires, with colors that vary from model to model.

3   Wire colors on Civic models are as follows:

a) *Yellow/red, power to MAP sensor*
b) *Green/white, ground*
c) *Red/green, signal to ECM/PCM*

Vacuum (in. HG)	Voltage
0	3.0
5	2.5
10	2.0
15	1.5
20	1.0
25	0.5

5.8 Manifold Absolute Pressure (MAP) sensor voltage should decrease as vacuum is applied

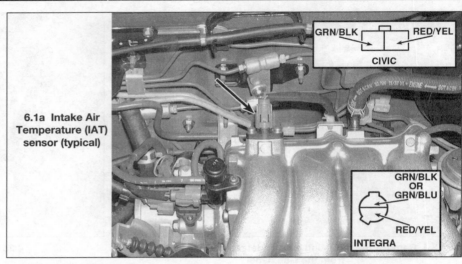

6.1a Intake Air Temperature (IAT) sensor (typical)

4   Wire colors on 1994 and 1995 Integra models are as follows:

a) *Yellow/red, power to MAP sensor on B18B1 engines*
b) *Yellow/white, power to MAP sensor on B18C1 engines*
c) *White/yellow, signal to ECM/PCM*
d) *Green/white, ground*

5   Wire colors on 1996 and later Integra models are as follows:

a) *Yellow/red, power to MAP sensor*
b) *Red/green, signal to ECM/PCM*
c) *Green/white, ground*

6   Disconnect the MAP sensor connector, turn the ignition key ON (engine not running) and check for voltage between the power and ground wires in the harness side of the connector. There should be approximately 5 volts. If not, check the wires for breaks and poor connections and repair as needed.

7   Remove the mounting screws and detach the sensor from the throttle body **(see illustration 5.2).** Leave the electrical connector attached to the sensor.

8   Connect a voltmeter between the signal wire and body ground (backprobe the connector terminal with a straight pin). With the

Temperature (degrees F)	Resistance (ohms)
-4	12
32	5
68	2
104	1
176	0.5
212	0.4
248	0.2

6.1b Intake Air Temperature (IAT) sensor resistance should decrease as temperature increases

key ON and engine not running, apply vacuum to the sensor base (you'll need to remove the sensor from the throttle body to do this). Voltage should decrease as vacuum increases **(see illustration).** If the readings are incorrect, replace the MAP sensor with a new part.

Replacement

9   Disconnect the electrical connector from the MAP sensor **(see illustration 5.2).**
10   Remove the screws that retain the MAP sensor to the throttle body and remove the sensor.
11   Installation is the reverse of removal.

---

6   Intake Air Temperature (IAT) sensor - check and replacement

Check

Refer to illustrations 6.1a and 6.1b

1   With the ignition switch ON, disconnect the electrical connector from the IAT sensor, which is located on the intake manifold **(see illustration).** Using an ohmmeter, measure the resistance between the two terminals on the sensor. There should be 0.4 to 4 k-ohms at room temperature, depending upon the

7.2 Engine Coolant Temperature (ECT) sensor (typical)

temperature **(see illustration).**
2   With the ignition key ON (engine not running), check for reference voltage at the electrical connector (red/yellow wire) to the sensor **(see illustration 6.1a).** It should be approximately 5.0 volts. If not, follow the red/yellow wire back to the ECM/PCM and check it for breaks or poor connections.
3   If the wiring is good and the test results are incorrect, replace the IAT sensor.
4   If the sensor checks out okay but there is still a problem, have the vehicle checked at a dealer service department or other qualified repair shop, as the ECM/PCM may be malfunctioning.

Replacement

5   Unplug the electrical connector from the IAT sensor **(see illustration 6.1a).**
6   Remove the screws that retain the sensor to the intake manifold and remove the IAT sensor.
7   Installation is the reverse of removal.

---

7   Engine Coolant Temperature (ECT) sensor - check and replacement

Check

Refer to illustration 7.2

1   The Engine Coolant Temperature (ECT) is a thermistor (a resistor which varies its resistance in accordance with temperature changes). The change in the resistance values will directly affect the voltage signal from the ECT to the ECM/PCM. As the sensor temperature DECREASES, the resistance values will INCREASE. As the sensor temperature INCREASES, the resistance values will DECREASE. A trouble code for this sensor indicates a failure in the thermosensor circuit, so in most cases the appropriate solution to the problem will be either repair of a wire or replacement of the sensor.
2   To check the sensor, check the resistance value **(see illustration 6.1b and the accompanying illustration)** of the coolant

8.2 The Crankshaft Position/Top Dead Center/Cylinder Position (CKP/TDC/CYP) sensor is mounted in the distributor; its connector (arrow) is accessible from outside

9.2 Location of the crankshaft fluctuation sensor (left arrow) (timing belt cover removed for clarity) - follow the harness (right arrow) to find the electrical connector

temperature sensor while it is completely cold (50 to 80 degrees F). Next, start the engine and warm it up until it reaches operating temperature. The resistance should be lower.

3   Check the supply voltage (red/white wire) with the ignition key ON (engine not running). It should be approximately 5.0 volts. If not, check for an open circuit in the red/white wire from the sensor to the ECM/PCM.

Replacement

Warning: *Wait until the engine has cooled completely before beginning this procedure.*

4   Before installing the new sensor, wrap the threads with Teflon sealing tape to prevent leakage and thread corrosion.

5   To remove the sensor, depress the locking tab, unplug the electrical connector, then carefully unscrew the sensor. Coolant will leak out when the sensor is removed, so install the new sensor as quickly as possible. **Caution:** *Handle the coolant sensor with care. Damage to this sensor will affect the operation of the entire fuel injection system.*

6   Installation is the reverse of removal. Check the coolant level, adding as necessary (see Chapter 1).

---

8   Crankshaft Position (CKP) sensor - check and replacement

Refer to illustration 8.2

1   On these models, the conventional crankshaft position sensor is a three-part sensor consisting of the CKP sensor, the TDC sensor and the CYP sensor. The CKP sensor determines the timing for the fuel injection and ignition on each cylinder. It also detects engine RPM. The TDC sensor determines the ignition timing at start-up (engine cranking) and the CYP sensor determines the

position of the cylinder for sequential fuel injection to each cylinder. All three sensors are built into the distributor. Diagnostics for all three sensors are performed by checking for trouble codes (see Section 2) and then checking for the proper resistance at the electrical connector.

CKP sensor

2   To check the CKP sensor, disconnect the electrical connector at the distributor and probe terminals 2 and 6 with an ohmmeter **(see illustration)**. Check the resistance listed in this Chapter's Specifications.

3   Check for continuity to ground on terminals 2 and 6. Continuity should NOT exist. If the test results are incorrect, replace the distributor unit (see Chapter 5).

4   If the test results are all correct, have the system diagnosed by a technician with a scan tool.

TDC sensor

5   To check the TDC sensor, disconnect the ignition harness connector at the distributor and probe terminals 3 and 7 with an ohmmeter **(see illustration 8.2)**. Check the resistance listed in this Chapter's Specifications.

6   Check for continuity to ground on terminals 3 and 7. Continuity should NOT exist. If the test results are incorrect, replace the distributor unit (see Chapter 5).

7   If the test results are all correct, have the system diagnosed by a technician with a scan tool.

CYP sensor

8   To check the CYP sensor, disconnect the ignition harness connector at the distributor and probe terminals 4 and 8 with an ohmmeter **(see illustration 8.2)**. Check the resistance listed in this Chapter's Specifications.

9   Check for continuity to ground on termi-

nals 4 and 8. Continuity should NOT exist. If the test results are incorrect, replace the distributor unit (see Chapter 5).

10   If the test results are all correct, have the system diagnosed by a technician with a scan tool.

---

9   Crankshaft Fluctuation Sensor (CKF) - check and replacement

1   The crankshaft fluctuation sensor consists of a pulse rotor on the front end of the crankshaft and a pickup sensor mounted on the engine next to the rotor. The ECM/PCM uses the signal to measure changes (fluctuations) in the rotational speed of the crankshaft. If the changes exceed a set limit, the ECM/PCM concludes that a misfire has occurred.

Check

2   Locate the electrical connector for the sensor at the timing belt end of the engine **(see illustration)**. Make sure the key is in the OFF position, then disconnect the electrical connector.

3   Connect an ohmmeter between the two outer terminals in the connector (not the center terminal). There should be 1.6 to 3.2 k-ohms. If not, replace the sensor.

4   Connect the ohmmeter between body ground and each of the sensor's outer terminals in turn (again, not to the center terminal). If the ohmmeter shows continuity, replace the sensor.

Replacement

5   Remove the valve cover, crankshaft pulley and timing belt cover (see Chapter 2A).

6   Disconnect the sensor's electrical connector and remove its mounting bolt.

7   Installation is the reverse of removal.

6

10   Electrical Load Detector (ELD) - check and replacement

Refer to illustration 10.2

1   The ELD system detects excess amperage draw (load) on the electrical circuits that govern the headlights, fuel injection, charging system etc. The prime symptom of an electrical overload is a driveability problem, usually occurring when the engine is idling. The ELD is mounted on the underside of the engine compartment fuse box.

Check

2   Disconnect the electrical connector from the ELD system **(see illustration)**.
3   Measure voltage between the power (black/white [Civic] or black/yellow [Integra]) and ground (black) wires with the ignition key ON (engine not running). There should be battery voltage. If no voltage is present, check the wiring harness back to the fuse box (under the dash) and the main fuse box (engine compartment).
4   Measure voltage with the ignition key ON (engine not running) between the green/red (+) terminal and the black terminal. There should be approximately 4.5 to 5 volts. If no voltage is present, check the ELD circuit between the fuse box and the ECM/PCM.
5   Switch the engine off and reconnect the three-pin connector to the ELD system. Start the engine and let it idle, then measure the voltage at the green/red terminal.
6   Now, turn on the low beam headlights and check the amount of voltage. It should be less than in Step 5. If not, replace the ELD unit.

Replacement

7   If the test results are not correct, replace the ELD unit. This requires changing the entire main fuse box. The ELD unit is not available separately.

11   Power Steering Pressure (PSP) switch - check and replacement

1   The power steering pressure (PSP) switch, used on US models, is a normally closed switch. It is mounted in the pressure line near the steering gear. When steering system pressure reaches a high-pressure setpoint, the PSP switch sends a signal to the ECM/PCM that the ECM/PCM uses to maintain engine idle speed during parking maneuvers. The OBD system can detect switch problems and set trouble codes to indicate specific faults.

Check

Refer to illustration 11.4

2   Check the operation of the PSP switch if the engine stalls during parking or if the engine runs continuously at high rpm.
3   Disconnect the PSP switch electrical

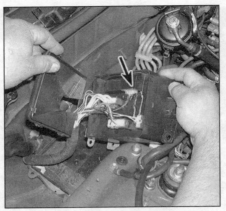

10.2 The Electrical Load Detector (ELD) is mounted under the engine compartment fuse box (arrow)

connector.
4   Connect an ohmmeter to the terminals of the switch **(see illustration)**.
5   Start the engine and let it idle.
6   With the front wheels pointing straight ahead, read the ohmmeter. It should indicate a continuity of close to zero ohms.
7   Turn the steering wheel to either side and watch the ohmmeter. The PSP should open as the wheel nears the steering stop on either side, and the meter should indicate an open circuit (infinite, or very high resistance).
8   If the switch fails either test, replace it. If the switch is OK, troubleshoot the engine idle control operation if high idle speed or stalling problems continue.

Replacement

9   Disconnect the cable from the negative terminal of the battery. *Caution: If the radio in your vehicle is equipped with an anti-theft system, make sure you have the correct activation code before disconnecting the battery.*
10   If necessary for access, raise the vehicle and support it securely on jackstands.
11   Disconnect the electrical connector from the switch and unscrew the switch from its fitting.
12   Install and connect the new switch. Lower the vehicle to the ground if it was raised.
13   Refer to Chapter 10 and bleed air from the power steering system. Add fluid as required (see Chapter 1).

12   Oxygen sensor (O2S) - check and replacement

1   The oxygen sensor, which is located in the exhaust manifold, monitors the oxygen content of the exhaust gas stream. The oxygen content in the exhaust reacts with the oxygen sensor to produce a voltage output which varies from 0.1-volt (high oxygen, lean mixture) to 0.9-volts (low oxygen, rich mixture). The ECM/PCM constantly monitors this variable voltage output to determine the ratio

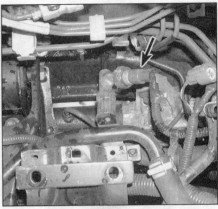

11.4 The Power Steering Pressure (PSP) switch is mounted in the power steering pressure line (arrow)

of oxygen-to-fuel in the mixture. The ECM/PCM alters the air/fuel mixture ratio by controlling the pulse width (open time) of the fuel injectors. A mixture ratio of 14.7 parts air to 1 part fuel is the ideal mixture ratio for minimizing exhaust emissions, thus allowing the catalytic converter to operate at maximum efficiency. It is this ratio of 14.7 to 1 which the ECM/PCM and the oxygen sensor attempt to maintain at all times.
2   The oxygen sensor produces no voltage when it is below its normal operating temperature of about 600-degrees F. During this initial period before warm-up, the ECM/PCM operates in OPEN LOOP mode.
3   If the engine reaches normal operating temperature and/or has been running for two or more minutes, and if the oxygen sensor is producing a steady signal voltage below 0.45-volts at 1,500 rpm or greater, the ECM/PCM will set a Code. The ECM/PCM will also set a code if it detects any problem with the heater circuit.
4   When there is a problem with the oxygen sensor or its circuit, the ECM/PCM operates in the open loop mode - that is, it controls fuel delivery in accordance with a programmed default value instead of feedback information from the oxygen sensor.
5   The proper operation of the oxygen sensor depends on four conditions:

  a)   *Electrical - The low voltages generated by the sensor depend upon good, clean connections which should be checked whenever a malfunction of the sensor is suspected or indicated.*

  b)   *Outside air supply - The sensor is designed to allow air circulation to the internal portion of the sensor. Whenever the sensor is removed and installed or replaced, make sure the air passages are not restricted.*

  c)   *Proper operating temperature - The ECM/PCM will not react to the sensor signal until the sensor reaches approximately 600-degrees F. This factor must be taken into consideration when evaluating the performance of the sensor.*

12.7 The oxygen sensor (arrow) is mounted in the catalytic converter - follow the harness to find the electrical connector

12.15 A special socket that allows clearance for the wiring harness is recommended for oxygen sensor removal (an open-end wrench may round-off the sensor hex)

13.3 The knock sensor is threaded into a coolant passage (arrow) (intake manifold removed for clarity)

d) **Unleaded fuel** - *The use of unleaded fuel is essential for proper operation of the sensor. Make sure the fuel you are using is of this type.*

6   In addition to observing the above conditions, special care must be taken whenever the sensor is serviced.

a) *The oxygen sensor has a permanently attached pigtail and electrical connector which should not be removed from the sensor. Damage or removal of the pigtail or electrical connector can adversely affect operation of the sensor.*

b) *Grease, dirt and other contaminants should be kept away from the electrical connector and the louvered end of the sensor.*

c) *Do not use cleaning solvents of any kind on the oxygen sensor.*

d) *Do not drop or roughly handle the sensor.*

e) *The silicone boot must be installed in the correct position to prevent the boot from being melted and to allow the sensor to operate properly.*

Check

Refer to illustration 12.7

7   Locate the oxygen sensor electrical connector and insert a long pin into the oxygen sensor connector containing the signal voltage wire, which is the white or white/red wire **(see illustration)**. **Note:** *Refer to the wiring diagrams at the end of Chapter 12 for the terminal designations, if necessary.* Connect the positive probe of a voltmeter to the pin and the negative probe to ground. **Note:** *Consult the wiring diagrams at the end of Chapter 12 for additional information on the oxygen sensor electrical connector wire color designations.*

8   Monitor the voltage signal (millivolts) as the engine goes from cold to warm.

9   The oxygen sensor will produce a steady voltage signal at first (open loop) of approximately 0.1 to 0.2 volts with the engine cold. After a period of approximately two

minutes, the engine will reach operating temperature and the oxygen sensor will start to fluctuate between 0.1 to 0.9 volts (closed loop). If the oxygen sensor fails to reach the closed loop mode or there is a very long period of time until it does switch into closed loop mode (lazy oxygen sensor), replace the oxygen sensor with a new part.

10   Also inspect the oxygen sensor heater. Disconnect the oxygen sensor electrical connector and connect an ohmmeter between the heater terminals (refer to the wiring diagrams at the end of Chapter 12 for the proper terminals to check). It should measure 10 to 40 ohms.

11   Check for proper supply voltage to the heater. Measure the voltage on the harness side of the oxygen sensor electrical connector, with the connector unplugged (again, refer to the wiring diagrams at the end of Chapter 12). There should be battery voltage with the ignition key ON (engine not running). If there is no voltage, check the circuit between the main relay, the ECM/PCM and the sensor.

12   If the oxygen sensor fails any of the tests described in Steps 7 through 10, replace it with a new part.

Replacement

Refer to illustration 12.15

Note: *Because it is installed in the exhaust manifold or pipe, which contracts when cool, the oxygen sensor may be very difficult to loosen when the engine is cold. Rather than risk damage to the sensor (assuming you are planning to reuse it in another manifold or pipe), start and run the engine for a minute or two, then shut it off. Be careful not to burn yourself during the following procedure.*

13   Disconnect the cable from the negative terminal of the battery. **Caution:** *If the stereo in your vehicle is equipped with an anti-theft system, make sure you have the correct activation code before disconnecting the battery.* Raise the vehicle and place it securely on jackstands.

14   Disconnect the sensor's electrical connector.

15   Carefully unscrew the sensor from the exhaust manifold **(see illustration)**.

16   Anti-seize compound must be used on the threads of the sensor to facilitate future removal. The threads of new sensors will already be coated with this compound, but if an old sensor is removed and reinstalled, recoat the threads.

17   Install the sensor and tighten it securely.

18   Reconnect the electrical connector of the pigtail lead to the main engine wiring harness.

19   Lower the vehicle, take it on a test drive and check to see that no trouble codes set.

13 Knock sensor - check and replacement

Warning: *Wait until the engine is completely cool before removing the knock sensor.*

1   Knock sensors detect abnormal vibration in the engine. The knock control system is designed to reduce spark knock during periods of heavy detonation. This allows the engine to use maximum spark advance to improve driveability. Knock sensors produce AC output voltage which increases with the severity of the knock. The signal is fed into the ECM/PCM and the timing is retarded to compensate for the detonation.

2   Knock sensors are used on the following models:

a) *Civic with the D16Y5 engine and CVT*
b) *Civic with the D16Y8 engine*
c) *Integra with the B18C1 and B18C5 engines*

Check

Refer to illustration 13.3

3   To check a knock sensor, disconnect the electrical connector and unscrew it from the engine **(see illustration)**. Reconnect the wiring harness to the sensor. This type of sensor must be checked by observing voltage fluctuations with a voltmeter. Simply

6

switch the voltmeter to the lowest AC voltage scale and connect the negative probe (-) to the sensor body and the positive (+) probe to the sensor terminal. With the voltmeter connected to the sensor, gently tap on the bottom of the knock sensor with a hammer or similar device (this simulates the knock from the engine) and observe voltage fluctuations on the meter. If no voltage fluctuations can be detected, the sensor is bad and should be replaced with a new part. Note: You may be able to perform this test without removing the sensor

Replacement

4   The knock sensor is threaded into the engine block coolant passage **(see illustration 13.3)**. When it is removed, coolant will drain from the block. Drain the cooling system (see Chapter 1). Place a drain pan under the sensor, disconnect the electrical connector and unscrew the sensor.
5   New sensors are pre-coated with thread sealant. Don't use any additional sealant or the operation of the sensor may be affected. Install the sensor and tighten it to the torque listed in this Chapter's Specifications. Don't overtighten the sensor or damage may occur. Plug in the electrical connector, refill the cooling system (see Chapter 1) and check for leaks.

14   Vehicle Speed Sensor (VSS) - check and replacement

Refer to illustration 14.2
1   The Vehicle Speed Sensor (VSS) is located on the transaxle. This sensor is a permanent magnetic variable reluctance sensor that produces a pulsing voltage whenever vehicle speed is over 3 mph. These pulses are used by the ECM/PCM to control fuel injector duration and transaxle shift control.

Check

2   To check the vehicle speed sensor, disconnect the electrical connector in the wiring harness at the sensor. Using a voltmeter,

check for voltage at the electrical connector to the sensor **(see illustration)**. You'll need to refer to the wiring diagrams at the end of Chapter 12 to identify the power wire. The circuit should have battery voltage available. If there is no voltage available, check for an open circuit between the VSS and the fuse box. Using an ohmmeter, check the black wire of the connector for continuity to body ground. If there's no continuity, check the black wire for breaks or poor connections.
3   Raise the front of the vehicle and place it securely on jackstands. Block the rear wheels and place the transaxle in Neutral. Connect the electrical connector to the VSS, turn the ignition to On and backprobe the VSS connector signal wire with a voltmeter positive lead. Connect the negative lead of the meter to body ground. While holding one wheel steady, rotate the other wheel by hand. The voltmeter should pulse between zero and 5 volts. If it doesn't, replace the sensor.

Replacement

4   To replace the VSS, disconnect the electrical connector from the VSS.
5   Remove the retaining bolt and lift the VSS from the transaxle.
6   Installation is the reverse of removal.

15   Idle Air Control (IAC) system

1   When the engine is idling, the air/fuel ratio is controlled by the Idle Air Control (IAC) system. On Civics, the system consists of the Powertrain Control Module and Idle Air Control (IAC) valve. On Integras, it consists of the Powertrain Control Module, the fast idle thermo valve and the IAC valve. The IAC valve is activated by the ECM/PCM depending upon the running conditions of the engine (air conditioning system, power steering, cold and warm running etc.). This valve regulates the amount of airflow past the throttle plate and into the intake manifold. The ECM/PCM receives information from the sensors (vehicle speed, coolant temperature, air conditioning, power steering pressure, etc.) and

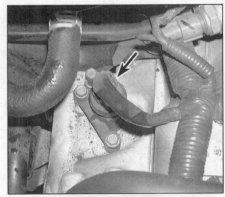

14.2 The Vehicle Speed Sensor (VSS) is mounted on the transaxle (arrow)

adjusts the idle according to the demands of the engine. Finally, to prevent rough running after the engine starts, the IAC valve is opened during cranking and immediately after starting to provide additional air into the intake manifold.

Check

Refer to illustrations 15.3a and 15.3b
2   Apply the parking brake, block the wheels and place the transaxle in Neutral (manual) or Park (automatic). Connect a tachometer, according to the manufacturer's instructions, to the engine. Start the engine and hold the accelerator steady at 3,000 rpm until the coolant fan comes on. Return the engine to idle and disconnect the electrical connector to the IAC valve. **Warning:** *Keep hands, loose clothing, etc. away from any moving engine parts while working on a running engine or personal injury may result.* There should be a noticeable reduction in idle speed with the IAC valve disconnected. If there isn't, the IAC valve is probably defective. If there was a drop in idle with the IAC valve disconnected and an intermittent idle problem still persists, check the wiring harness from the IAC valve to the ECM/PCM for poor connections or damaged wires.
3   Disconnect the electrical connector from

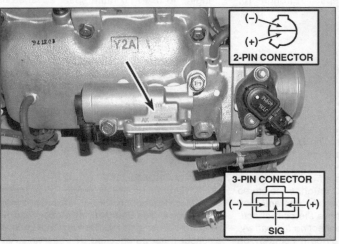

15.3a Idle Air Control (IAC) valve (typical Civic)

15.3b This is a typical Integra IAC valve

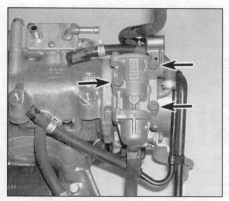

16.3 The Fast Idle Thermo (FIT) valve is mounted on the underside of the throttle body and is retained by three bolts (arrows)

the IAC valve, turn the ignition key ON (engine not running) and measure the voltage between the positive terminal of the wiring harness connector (yellow/black wire) and body ground **(see illustrations)**. There should be battery voltage. If no voltage is present, check for an open circuit in the yellow/black wire from the IAC valve to the PGM-FI main relay. In any case, leave the IAC valve connector disconnected for the next steps.

4   If the IAC valve has two wires in its harness, connect the IAC valve directly to battery voltage with a pair of jumper wires (positive to black/yellow; negative to black/blue). The valve should click each time voltage is applied. If not, replace it. **Caution:** *Don't connect power any longer than is necessary to make the valve click.*

5   If the IAC valve has three wires in its harness, connect the negative probe of an ohmmeter to the center terminal of the connector, then connect the ohmmeter positive probe to each of the other terminals in turn. There should be 16 to 28 ohms in each case.

6   If the IAC valve performs correctly in Step 4 or 5, have the ECM/PCM and the electrical circuit for the IAC valve diagnosed by a dealer service department or other qualified repair shop.

IAC valve replacement

7   Disconnect the electrical connector from the IAC valve.

8   Remove the two mounting screws from the valve and lift it from the air intake plenum **(see illustrations 15.3a and 15.3b)**.

9   Installation is the reverse of removal. Be sure to install a new O-ring.

16   Fast Idle Thermo (FIT) valve - check and replacement

1   The Fast Idle Thermo (FIT) valve, used on some models, allows extra air into the intake manifold when the engine is cold, causing the idle speed to increase.

Check

Refer to illustration 16.3

2   Start this procedure with the engine cold. Disconnect the air intake duct from the throttle body (see Chapter 4).

3   Start the engine and let it idle. Reach inside the throttle body and place a finger over the port that connects to the FIT valve **(see illustration)**. You should feel suction.

4   Warm the engine to normal operating temperature and check for suction at the FIT valve port again. There should not be any. If there is, the valve hasn't closed. This might be caused by a low coolant level or air bubbles in the coolant passages. Make sure the engine coolant is full and free of air bubbles.

5   If the test results weren't correct, replace the FIT valve.

Replacement

Warning: *Wait until the engine is completely cool before beginning this procedure.*

6   Disconnect the hose from the valve and unscrew the mounting bolts **(see illustration 16.3)**. Take off the valve and its O-rings. Plug the hose to prevent coolant loss.

7   Install the valve, using new O-rings, and tighten the mounting bolts to the torque listed in this Chapter's Specifications. Replace the hose clamp with a new one if it has lost its tension.

8   Check the coolant level and add some, if necessary (see Chapter 1).

17   Intake Air Bypass (IAB) system

1   Some models are equipped with the Intake Air Bypass (IAB) system. The IAB system allows the intake manifold to divert the path of intake air into the combustion chamber. Two air intake paths are provided in the intake manifold to allow the option of the intake volume most favorable for the particular engine speed. Optimum performance is achieved by switching the valves from either the closed position (for high torque at low RPM) or the open position (for maximum horsepower at high RPM).

Check

Refer to illustrations 17.2 and 17.5

2   With the engine off, disconnect the vacuum hose from the IAB diaphragm and connect a vacuum pump to it **(see illustration)**. If the diaphragm rod doesn't move when vacuum is applied, replace the diaphragm.

3   With the engine idling, check for vacuum at the disconnected end of the hose. There should be vacuum at idle, and no vacuum when engine speed is raised to 6000 rpm.

4   If there isn't any vacuum at idle, follow the vacuum hose from the diaphragm to the control valve under the intake manifold, and then to the vacuum tank. Disconnect the hose that leads from the tank to the intake manifold and check for vacuum. If there isn't any, look for a blocked or cracked vacuum hose.

5   Disconnect the electrical connector from the IAB solenoid **(see illustration)**. Connect a voltmeter positive probe to the red/blue wire and the negative probe to the black wire (in the harness side of the connector). With the ignition key ON, there should be battery voltage. If not, check the wiring harness for breaks or poor connections.

6   If there's battery voltage at the wiring harness terminals and the vacuum lines are good, but test results weren't correct in Step 3, replace the solenoid.

6

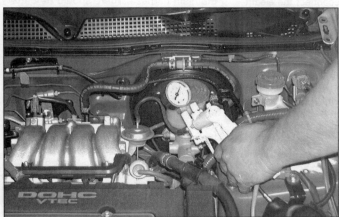

17.2 Apply vacuum to the IAB valve diaphragm; the rod should move

17.5 Intake Air Bypass (IAB) solenoid electrical connector

17.7 Unscrew the mounting screws (arrows) to remove the IAB diaphragm

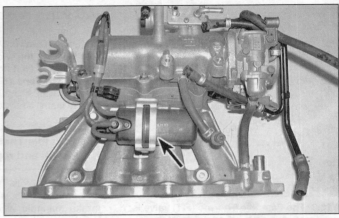

17.8 The IAB solenoid and vacuum tank assembly is mounted in a clamp on the underside of the intake manifold (intake manifold removed for clarity)

Replacement

Refer to illustrations 17.7 and 17.8
7   To replace the diaphragm, remove its mounting screws **(see illustration)**.
8   To replace the solenoid and vacuum tank assembly, detach it from its mounting clamp and remove it from the intake manifold **(see illustration)**.
9   Installation is the reverse of removal.

18   Positive Crankcase Ventilation (PCV) system

1   The Positive Crankcase Ventilation (PCV) system reduces hydrocarbon emissions by scavenging crankcase vapors. It does this by circulating fresh air from the air cleaner through the crankcase, where it mixes with blow-by gases and is then rerouted through a PCV valve to the intake manifold.
2   The main components of the PCV system are the PCV valve, a blow-by filter and the vacuum hoses connecting these two components with the engine.
3   To maintain idle quality, the PCV valve restricts the flow when the intake manifold vacuum is high. If abnormal operating conditions (such as piston ring problems) arise, the system is designed to allow excessive amounts of blow-by gases to flow back through the crankcase vent tube into the air cleaner to be consumed by normal combustion.
4   Checking and replacement of the PCV valve is covered in Chapter 1.

19   Exhaust Gas Recirculation (EGR) system

General description

1   To reduce oxides of nitrogen emissions, some of the exhaust gases are recirculated through the EGR valve to the intake manifold

to lower combustion temperatures.
2   The EGR system consists of the EGR valve, the EGR control solenoid valve (some models), an EGR valve lift sensor and the Powertrain Control Module (ECM/PCM). The ECM/PCM is programmed to produce the ideal EGR valve lift for each operating condition. The EGR valve lift sensor monitors the amount of EGR valve lift and sends this information to the ECM/PCM. The ECM/PCM then compares it with the ideal EGR valve lift, which is determined by data received from the other sensors. If necessary, the ECM/PCM adjusts the amount of vacuum available to the EGR valve via the EGR control solenoid valve.

Check

Continuously Variable Transaxle (CVT) models

3   Start the engine and warm it to its normal operating temperature (wait for the electric cooling fan to come on).
4   Detach the vacuum hose from the EGR valve and attach a vacuum gauge to the hose.
5   There should be NO vacuum. If there is no vacuum, proceed to Step 7.
6   If vacuum exists, disconnect the electrical connector from the EGR control solenoid valve and recheck for vacuum at the vacuum hose to the EGR valve. **Note:** *To find the EGR vacuum control solenoid valve, follow the vacuum hose from the EGR valve.* If vacuum does not exist, have the ECM/PCM diagnosed by a technician with a scan tool. If vacuum is present, check all the vacuum lines to make sure they are routed properly. If the hoses are OK, replace the control solenoid valve.
7   If there originally was no vacuum, install a hand-held vacuum pump to the EGR valve and apply 8 in-Hg of vacuum to the valve and confirm that the engine stalls. Also, does the EGR valve hold vacuum? If not, replace the EGR valve.
8   Check for battery voltage to the EGR control solenoid valve. Disconnect the two-

pin connector from the solenoid and check for battery voltage at the red wire (+) terminal on the main harness. There should be battery voltage.
9   Reconnect the vacuum gauge to the EGR vacuum hose, start the engine and allow it to idle. Connect battery positive voltage with a jumper wire to the red wire's terminal on the two-pin connector (the solenoid side, not the harness side). While observing the vacuum gauge, ground the other terminal with another jumper wire. Vacuum should increase within one second (and you should be able to hear the solenoid activate). If there is no vacuum, replace the EGR control solenoid valve.
10   Further checking of the EGR control system requires a scan tool. Take the vehicle to a dealer service department or other qualified repair shop for checking.

Manual transmission models

11   Start the engine and warm it to its normal operating temperature (wait for the electric cooling fan to come on).
12   Disconnect the six-pin connector from the EGR valve and check for battery voltage between the pink and black wire terminals on the main harness. There should be battery voltage. If there isn't, check the pink wire back to the ECM/PCM for breaks and poor connections. Also check the black wire for a good ground. If the wiring is OK, have the ECM/PCM diagnosed by a technician with a scan tool.
13   If there is battery voltage, shut the engine off. Using a jumper wire, connect battery positive voltage to the terminal on the EGR valve/lift sensor that corresponds with the pink wire terminal in the six-pin connector. Start the engine, and while it's idling, ground the terminal that corresponds with the black wire terminal in the connector with another jumper wire. The engine should run roughly or stall. If not, replace the EGR valve/lift sensor assembly. If it does run roughly or stall, check the wiring harness for breaks or poor connections.

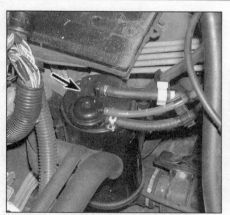

20.10 The EVAP canister is located in the right side of the engine compartment

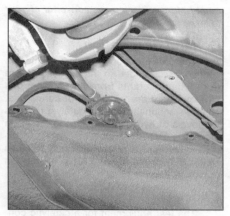

20.17 The two-way valve (models so equipped) is located near the fuel tank

14 Further checking of the EGR control system requires a scan tool. Take the vehicle to a dealer service department or other qualified repair shop for checking.

Component replacement

EGR valve

15 Unplug the electrical connector for the EGR valve lift sensor. Detach the vacuum hose.
16 Remove the two nuts that secure the EGR valve to the intake manifold and detach the EGR valve.
17 Clean the mating surfaces of the EGR valve and adapter.
18 Install the EGR valve, using a new gasket. Tighten the nuts securely.
19 Connect the electrical connector.

EGR control solenoid (CVT models only)

20 Locate the EGR control solenoid by following the vacuum hose from the EGR valve to the solenoid. Detach the vacuum hoses, unplug the electrical connector, remove the mounting screws and lift the solenoid off.
21 Installation is the reverse of removal.

20 Evaporative emissions control (EVAP) system

General description

1 The fuel evaporative emissions control system absorbs fuel vapors and, during engine operation, releases them into the engine intake where they mix with the incoming air-fuel mixture.
2 Every evaporative system employs a canister filled with activated charcoal to absorb fuel vapors. The means by which these vapors are controlled, however, varies considerably from one system to another. The following descriptions of a typical system for the models covered by this manual should provide you enough information to understand the system on your vehicle. **Note:** *The following descriptions are not intended as a*

specific description of the evaporative system on your particular vehicle. Rather, they are intended as a general description of a typical system used on fuel-injected vehicles. Although the following components are most likely all used on your particular system, there may also be other devices, not included here, which are unique to your system. Check with the VECI label and the Vacuum Hose Routing Diagram under the hood.
3 The fuel filler cap is fitted with a two-way valve as a safety device. The valve vents fuel vapors to the atmosphere if the evaporative control system fails.
4 Another fuel cut-off valve (two-way valve), mounted on the fuel tank, regulates fuel vapor flow from the fuel tank to the charcoal canister, based on the pressure or vacuum caused by temperature changes.
5 After passing through the two-way valve, fuel vapor is carried by vent hoses to the charcoal canister in the engine compartment. The activated charcoal in the canister absorbs and stores these vapors.
6 When the engine is running and warmed to a pre-set temperature, a purge cut-off solenoid valve near the canister closes, allowing a purge control diaphragm valve in the charcoal canister to be opened by intake manifold vacuum. Fuel vapors from the canister are then drawn through the purge control diaphragm valve by intake manifold vacuum.

Check

Note: *Complete checking of the evaporative emissions control system is beyond the scope of the average home mechanic. Fortunately, the evaporative control system, like all emission control systems, is protected by a Federally mandated extended warranty (5 years or 50,000 miles at the time this manual was written). The EVAP system probably won't fail during the service life of the vehicle; however, if it does, the hoses or charcoal canister are usually to blame.*
7 Always check the hoses first. A disconnected, damaged or missing hose is the most likely cause of a malfunctioning EVAP system. Refer to the Vacuum Hose Routing Diagram (attached to the underside of the hood)

to determine whether the hoses are correctly routed and attached. Repair any damaged hoses or replace any missing hoses as necessary.

Purge control solenoid

Refer to illustration 20.10
8 The purge control solenoid allows intake manifold vacuum to purge vapors from the canister when the engine is warm, and cuts off vacuum to the canister when the engine is cold.
9 Make sure the engine temperature is below the specified opening point of the solenoid:

1994 and 1995 models - 163-degrees F.
1996-on models - 154-degrees F

10 Locate the purge hose on top of the canister **(see illustration)**. Refer to the Vacuum Hose Routing Diagram and follow the vacuum hose from the purge control valve to the canister to make sure you've got the right hose.
11 Once you've found the hose, disconnect it from the canister and connect a vacuum gauge to the disconnected end of the hose. Start the engine and allow it to idle. There should be NO vacuum present.
12 Let the engine idle until it warms up. There should now be vacuum at the end of the hose.
13 If the vacuum test results weren't correct, locate the purge control solenoid on the intake manifold and disconnect its electrical connector. Disconnect its vacuum hoses and connect a piece of rubber hose to one of the fittings on the solenoid.
14 Connect the battery directly to the solenoid with jumper wires. Try to blow into the piece of hose (through the solenoid). The solenoid should open (allowing air to flow) and close (blocking the flow of air) as the jumper wires are connected and disconnected. (Some models will open when voltage is applied and close when it's removed; others will do the opposite. The important thing is that the solenoid opens and closes consistently as battery power is connected and disconnected.)
15 If the solenoid test results aren't correct, replace the solenoid.

Two-way valve

Refer to illustration 20.17
16 Remove the fuel filler cap.
17 Detach the vapor line from the fuel tank and connect a T-fitting into a vacuum pump and vacuum gauge **(see illustration)**.
18 Apply vacuum slowly and steadily and observe the gauge. Vacuum should stabilize momentarily at 0.2 to 0.6-inch Hg. If the valve opens (stabilizes) before the correct vacuum, replace it with a new part.
19 Move the hand-held vacuum pump over to the pressure fitting (same vacuum line arrangement). Pressurize the line and observe the gauge. Pressure should stabilize at 0.4 to 1.4 Hg (valve opens).
20 If the valve opens (stabilizes) before or after the correct vacuum, replace it with a new part.

6

Canister vent shutoff valve

21   To determine whether your vehicle has a canister vent shutoff valve, look at the top of the canister. If there's a two-wire electrical connector directly on top of the canister, it has a shutoff valve.

22   Follow the hose from the shutoff valve down to the three-way valve, which is alongside the canister. Disconnect the hose from the three-way valve and attach a vacuum pump to the end of the hose.

23   Remove the shutoff valve from the canister, leaving the electrical connector and vacuum pump connected to it.

24   Switch the ignition key to ON (but don't start the engine) and apply vacuum to the hose. If the valve holds vacuum, disconnect the electrical connector. If it still holds vacuum, replace the valve with a new one.

21   Catalytic converter

Note: *Because of a Federally mandated extended warranty which covers emissions-related components such as the catalytic converter, check with a dealer service depart-* *ment before replacing the converter at your own expense.*

General description

1   The catalytic converter is an emission control device added to the exhaust system to reduce pollutants from the exhaust gas stream. There are two types of converters. The conventional oxidation catalyst reduces the levels of hydrocarbon (HC) and carbon monoxide (CO). The three-way catalyst lowers the levels of oxides of nitrogen (NOx) as well as hydrocarbons (HC) and carbon monoxide (CO).

Check

2   The test equipment for a catalytic converter is expensive and highly sophisticated. If you suspect that the converter on your vehicle is malfunctioning, take it to an authorized emissions inspection facility for diagnosis and repair.

3   Whenever the vehicle is raised for servicing of underbody components, check the converter for leaks, corrosion, dents and other damage. Check the welds/flange bolts that attach the front and rear ends of the con- verter to the exhaust system. If damage is discovered, the converter should be replaced.

4   Although catalytic converters don't break too often, they can become plugged. The easiest way to check for a restricted converter is to use a vacuum gauge to diagnose the effect of a blocked exhaust on intake vacuum.

a) *Open the throttle until the engine speed is about 2000 rpm.*

b) *Release the throttle quickly.*

c) *If there is no restriction, the gauge will quickly drop to not more than 2 in-Hg or more above its normal reading.*

d) *If the gauge does not show 5 in-Hg or more above its normal reading, or seems to momentarily hover around its highest reading for a moment before it returns, the exhaust system, or the converter, is plugged (or an exhaust pipe is bent or dented, or the core inside the muffler has shifted).*

Component replacement

5   Refer to the exhaust system servicing section in Chapter 4.

Chapter 7 Part A
Manual transaxle

Contents

Specifications

Torque specifications

	Ft-lbs (unless otherwise indicated)
Lower rear engine-to-transaxle bolt	
Self-locking bolt	87
Non-self-locking bolts	47
Non-self-locking bolt with washer	61
Upper transaxle-to-engine bolts	47
Short bolt	47
Starter bolt	33
Right transaxle mount	
Mount bolt and nuts	47
Engine bracket-to-mount through-bolt	54
Engine stiffeners	
Short bolts	17
Long bolts	42
Splash shield bolts	84 in-lbs
Clutch cover bolts	
Civic	17
Integra	
Short bolts	144 in-lbs
Left lower bolt	42
Right lower bolt	17

1 General information

Vehicles covered by this manual are equipped with a five-speed manual transaxle, a four-speed automatic transaxle or a Continuously Variable Transaxle (CVT). Civic models are equipped with either of two types of five-speed manual transaxles for all years: S40 and S4C. Integra models use two five speed transaxles as well: the Y80 on 1994 models and the S80 on later models.

All information on the manual transaxle is included in this Part of Chapter 7. Service procedures for the four-speed automatic transaxle and Continuously Variable Transaxle can be found in Chapter 7, Part B. You'll also find certain procedures common to both transaxles - such as oil seal replacement - in this Chapter.

Depending on the expense involved in having a transaxle overhauled, it might be a better idea to consider replacing it with either a new or rebuilt unit. Your local dealer or transaxle shop should be able to supply information concerning cost, availability and exchange policy. Regardless of how you decide to remedy a transaxle problem, you can still save a lot of money by removing and installing the unit yourself.

1.1 An underside view of the manual transaxle and its related components

| 1 | *Transaxle* | 2 | *Shift rod* | 3 | *Shift extension rod* | 4 | *Driveaxle* |

2   Driveaxle oil seals - replacement

Refer to illustrations 2.4 and 2.6

1   Oil leaks frequently occur due to wear of the driveaxle oil seals. Replacement of these seals is relatively easy, since the repair can usually be performed without removing the transaxle from the vehicle.

2   Driveaxle oil seals are located at the sides of the transaxle, where the driveaxles are attached. If leakage at the seal is suspected, raise the vehicle and support it securely on jackstands. If the seal is leaking, lubricant will be found on the sides of the transaxle, below the seals.

3   Refer to Chapter 8 and remove the driveaxles.

4   Use a screwdriver or prybar to carefully pry the oil seal out of the transaxle bore **(see illustration)**.

5   If the oil seal cannot be removed with a screwdriver or prybar, a special oil seal removal tool (available at auto parts stores) will be required.

6   Using a large section of pipe or a large deep socket (slightly smaller than the outside

2.4 Insert the tip of a large screwdriver or prybar behind the oil seal and very carefully pry it out

2.6 Using a large socket or a section of pipe, drive the new seal squarely into the bore

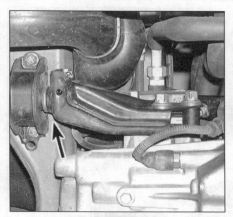

3.2 To check the transaxle mount, insert a large screwdriver at the point shown (arrow) and try to move the transaxle; if it moves appreciably, replace the mount

4.1 Remove this shift lever boot and the dust seal underneath

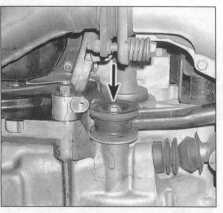

4.3 To disconnect the extension rod from its bracket on the transaxle, remove this bolt (arrow)

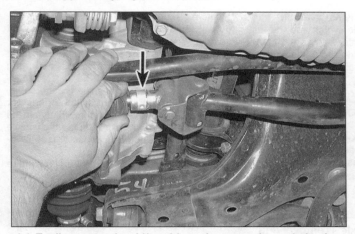

4.4 To disconnect the shift rod from the transaxle, push the dust boot forward, remove the clip and drive out the spring pin (arrow) - discard the old pin and install a new one when reassembling the linkage

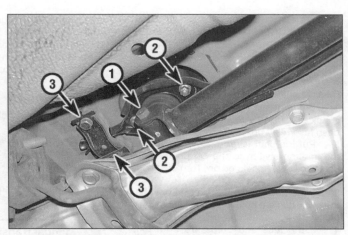

4.5 To disconnect the shift rod from the shift lever, remove the nut and bolt (1); to disconnect the extension rod from the shift lever, remove the nuts (2) and the two bolts (3) retaining the extension mounting bracket and cushion

diameter of the seal) as a drift, install the new oil seal **(see illustration)**. Drive it into the bore squarely and make sure it's completely seated. Coat the seal lip with transaxle lubricant.

7   Install the driveaxle(s). Be careful not to damage the lip of the new seal.

3   Transaxle mount - check and replacement

Refer to illustration 3.2

1   Raise the front of the vehicle and place it securely on jackstands.

2   Insert a large screwdriver or prybar between the mount support arm and the frame and try to lever the support arm **(see illustration)**.

3   The transaxle support arm should not move up more than about 1/2 to 3/4-inch within the mount. If it does, replace the mount.

4   To replace the mount, support the

transaxle with a jack, remove the nuts and bolts and remove the mount. **Warning:** *Do not place any part of your body under the transaxle when it's supported only by a jack.*

5   Installation is the reverse of removal.

4   Shift lever and linkage - removal and installation

Refer to illustrations 4.1, 4.3, 4.4 and 4.5

1   Unscrew the shift lever knob. Remove the center console (see Chapter 11). Remove the rubber shift lever boot and the dust seal underneath **(see illustration)**.

2   Raise the vehicle and place it securely on jackstands.

3   To disconnect the extension rod from the transaxle, simply remove the bolt that attaches it to the extension bracket **(see illustration)**.

4   To disconnect the shift rod from the transaxle, push the dust boot forward **(see**

illustration), remove the clip and drive out the spring pin with a pin punch. Discard the spring pin - do not re-use it.

5   To disconnect the rear end of the shift rod from the shift lever, remove the nuts and bolts **(see illustration)**.

6   Remove the two nuts and washers that retain the change ball holder to the underside of the extension rod **(see illustration 4.5)** and remove the change ball holder, lower shift lever dust seal, shift lever ball seat, shift lever and extension rod.

7   Inspect the bushing at the front end of the extension rod and replace it if it's cracked, torn or worn.

8   Replace the O-rings in the base of the shift lever.

9   Installation is the reverse of removal. Lubricate the new O-rings and the bushings with silicone grease. Use a new spring pin to attach the shift rod to the transaxle. Tighten all fasteners to the torque values listed in this Chapter's Specifications.

10   Check the operation of the shift lever.

5.4 The back-up light switch (arrow) is located on the side of the transaxle housing

6.4 Unplug the electrical connector (arrow) from the vehicle speed sensor

5   Back-up light switch - check and replacement

Check

Refer to illustration 5.4

1   Before testing the back-up light switch, check the No. 19 7.5-amp fuse in the under-dash fuse/relay box.

2   Put the shift lever in Reverse and turn the ignition switch to the On position. The back-up lights should go on. Turn off the ignition switch.

3   If the back-up lights don't go on, check the back-up light bulbs in the tail light assembly.

4   If the fuse and bulbs are both okay, locate the back-up light switch on top of the transaxle **(see illustration)**, trace the leads back to the electrical connector, unplug the connector and hook up an ohmmeter or continuity tester across the two terminals.

5   With the shift lever in Reverse, there should be continuity; with the shifter in any other gear, there should be no continuity.

6   If the switch fails this test, replace it (see below).

7   If the switch is OK, but the back-up lights aren't coming on, check for power to the switch. If voltage is not available, trace the circuit between the switch and the fuse block. If power is present, trace the circuit between the switch and the back-up lights for an open circuit condition.

Replacement

8   Unplug the back-up light switch electrical connector.

9   Unscrew the back-up light switch.

10   Discard the old washer.

11   Using a new washer, install the new switch.

12   Plug in the connector.

6   Manual transaxle - removal and installation

Removal

Refer to illustrations 6.4, 6.12, 6.17, 6.18, 6.19 and 6.21

1   Disconnect the negative, *then* the positive, cables from the battery and remove the battery. **Caution:** *If the radio in your vehicle is equipped with an anti-theft system, make sure you have the correct activation code*

before disconnecting the battery.

2   Remove the resonator, intake air duct and air cleaner housing (see Chapter 4).

3   Disconnect the starter motor cables and remove the upper starter motor mounting bolt (see Chapter 5).

4   Disconnect the transaxle ground cable, unplug the back-up light switch connector (see Section 5) and detach the wiring harness clamp from the transaxle. Unplug the vehicle speed sensor electrical connector **(see illustration)**.

5   Loosen the driveaxle/hub nut (see Chapter 8). Loosen the front wheel lug nuts, raise the vehicle and support it securely on jackstands. Remove the front wheels.

6   Remove the splash shield, if equipped.

7   Remove the elbow-shaped exhaust pipe section under the transaxle (see Chapter 4).

8   Drain the transaxle lubricant (see Chapter 1).

9   Disconnect the shift and extension rods from the transaxle (see Section 4).

10   Remove the clutch fluid hose-to-clutch fluid pressure line junction, the clutch fluid pressure line, the release cylinder and the release cylinder pushrod (see Chapter 8). **Caution:** *Be careful not to bend or kink the clutch fluid pressure line, and don't depress the clutch pedal while the clutch release cylinder is removed.*

11   Remove the driveaxles (see Chapter 8).

12   Remove the engine stiffener (if equipped) **(see illustration)**.

13   Remove the clutch access cover bolts and remove the cover.

14   Remove the distributor mounting bolt and attach an engine hoist to the cylinder head to support the engine, then lift the engine slightly to take the load off the engine and transaxle mounts.

15   Remove the splash guard (if equipped).

16   Support the transaxle with a jack; preferably one made for this purpose. Secure the transaxle to the jack with a safety chain. Transmission jacks or adapters that fit onto floor jacks are available at equipment rental yards and tool supply stores. Raise the

6.12 Remove the stiffener bolts (arrows)

6.17 Remove the transaxle mount retaining bolts and nuts (arrows)

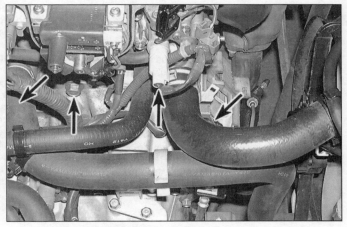

6.18 Remove the upper transaxle-to-engine mounting bolts (arrows)

transaxle just enough to take the weight off the mounts.

17 Remove the right side transaxle mounting bracket bolts and nuts **(see illustration)**.

18 Remove the four upper transaxle-to-engine mounting bolts **(see illustration)**.

19 Remove the clutch hydraulic line supporting bracket bolts **(see illustration)**.

20 Remove the rear lower transaxle-to-engine bolt immediately above the right driveaxle.

21 Remove the lower transaxle-to-engine bolt and transaxle mounting bracket bolts **(see illustration)**.

22 Make a final check that all wires and hoses have been disconnected from the transaxle, then carefully pull the transaxle and jack away from the engine.

23 Once the input shaft is clear, lower the transaxle and remove it from under the vehicle.

24 With the transaxle removed, the clutch components are now accessible and can be inspected. In most cases, new clutch components should be routinely installed when the transaxle is removed (see Chapter 8).

Installation

25 If removed, install the clutch components (see Chapter 8).

26 Make sure the two dowel pins are installed. With the transaxle secured to the jack with a chain, raise it into position behind the engine, then carefully slide it forward, engaging the two dowel pins on the transaxle with the corresponding holes in the block and the input shaft with the clutch plate hub splines. Do not use excessive force to install the transaxle - if the input shaft does not slide into place, readjust the angle of the transaxle so it is level and/or turn the input shaft so the splines engage properly with the clutch plate hub.

27 Install the transaxle housing-to-engine bolts and the transaxle rear mounting bracket bolts and tighten them to the torque listed in this Chapter's Specifications.

28 Install the three upper transaxle-to-engine bolts and the lower starter motor mounting bolt and tighten them to the torque listed in this Chapter's Specifications.

29 Raise the transaxle slightly, then install

the right transaxle mounting bracket and the bracket bolt and nuts. Tighten the bolts and nuts to the torque listed in this Chapter's Specifications.

30 Install the front stopper bracket and tighten the bolts to the torque listed in this Chapter's Specifications.

31 Install the splash shield and tighten the bolts to the torque listed in this Chapter's Specifications.

32 Remove the chain hoist and install the distributor mounting bolt.

33 Install the clutch cover and, on models so equipped, install the engine stiffeners. Tighten the clutch cover and engine stiffener bolts to the torque listed in this Chapter's Specifications.

34 The remainder of installation is the reverse of removal.

35 Refill the transaxle with the specified amount of lubricant (see Chapter 1).

36 Bleed the clutch hydraulic system (see Chapter 8).

37 Road test the vehicle for proper operation and check for leaks.

7A

6.19 Remove the clutch hydraulic line bracket bolts (arrows)

6.21 Remove the lower transaxle bolt and mounting bracket bolts (arrows)

7   Manual transaxle overhaul - general information

1   Overhauling a manual transaxle is a difficult job for the do-it-yourselfer. It involves the disassembly and reassembly of many small parts. Numerous clearances must be precisely measured and, if necessary, changed with select fit spacers and snap-rings. As a result, if transaxle problems arise, it can be removed and installed by a competent do-it-yourselfer, but overhaul should be left to a transaxle repair shop. Rebuilt transaxles may be available - check with your dealer parts department and auto parts stores. At any rate, the time and money involved in an overhaul is almost sure to exceed the cost of a rebuilt unit.

2   Nevertheless, it's not impossible for an inexperienced mechanic to rebuild a transaxle if the special tools are available and the job is done in a deliberate step-by-step manner so nothing is overlooked.

3   The tools necessary for an overhaul include internal and external snap-ring pliers, a bearing puller, a slide hammer, a set of pin punches, a dial indicator and possibly a hydraulic press. In addition, a large, sturdy workbench and a vise or transaxle stand will be required.

4   During disassembly of the transaxle, make careful notes of how each piece comes off, where it fits in relation to other pieces and what holds it in place. Noting how the parts are installed when you remove them will make it much easier to get the transaxle back together.

5   Before taking the transaxle apart for repair, it will help if you have some idea what area of the transaxle is malfunctioning. Certain problems can be closely tied to specific areas in the transaxle, which can make component examination and replacement easier. Refer to the *Troubleshooting* section at the front of this manual for information regarding possible sources of trouble.

Chapter 7 Part B
Automatic transaxle and Continuously Variable Transaxle (CVT)

Contents

Specifications

Shift lock solenoid clearance	3/32 ± 1/64-inch
Lock-up control solenoid resistance	12 to 25 ohms
Shift control solenoid resistance	12 to 25 ohms

Torque specifications — **Ft-lbs** (unless otherwise indicated)

Shift lock solenoid self-locking nuts	84 in-lbs
Lock-up control solenoid bolts	108 in-lbs
Transaxle-to-engine bolts	
Civic	47
Integra	
1996 and earlier	
Lower bolts	43
Upper bolts	54
1997 and later	47
Rear engine/transaxle mount bolts	
Civic	61
Integra	87
Transaxle mount nuts	47
Transaxle mount through-bolt	54
Engine stiffeners	
Bolts-to-transaxle	33
Bolt-to-engine	17
Right front mount bracket	
Short bolt	33
Long Bolt	47
Driveplate-to-torque converter bolts	108 in-lbs
Driveplate/torque converter cover	108 in-lbs

7B

1.1 An underside view of the automatic transaxle and its related components

1 Transaxle	*2 Shift cable*	*3 Driveaxle*	*4 Transaxle cooler lines*

1   General information

Refer to illustration 1.1

The vehicles covered by this manual are equipped with a five-speed manual, a four-speed automatic transaxle or a Continuously Variable Transaxle (CVT). Civics use three models of four-speed automatic transaxles: A4RA, B4RQ and A4RA, plus the Continuously Variable Transaxle (CVT), designated M4VA. Integra models use three four-speed automatic transaxles as well: the MP7A, S4XA and SP7A.

All information on automatic transaxles and the Continuously Variable Transaxle is included in this Part of Chapter 7. Information for the manual transaxle can be found in Part A of this Chapter.

Due to the complexity of the automatic transaxles and Continuously Variable Transaxles covered in this manual and to the specialized equipment necessary to perform most service operations, this Chapter contains only those procedures related to gen-eral diagnosis, routine maintenance, adjustment and removal and installation.

If the transaxle requires major repair work, this should be left to a dealer service department or an automotive or transmission repair shop. You can, however, remove and install the transaxle yourself and save the expense, even if a transmission shop does the repair work (but be sure a proper diagnosis has been made before removing the transaxle).

2   Diagnosis - general

Note: *Automatic transaxle or Continuously Variable Transaxle malfunctions may be caused by five general conditions: poor engine performance, improper adjustments, hydraulic malfunctions, mechanical malfunctions or malfunctions in the computer or its signal network. Diagnosis of these problems should always begin with a check of the easily repaired items: fluid level and condition (see Chapter 1), shift control cable adjustment and* *throttle control cable adjustment. Next, perform a road test to determine if the problem has been corrected or if more diagnosis is necessary. If the problem persists after the preliminary tests and corrections are completed, additional diagnosis should be done by a dealer service department or transmission repair shop. Refer to the Troubleshooting section at the front of this manual for information on symptoms of transaxle problems.*

Preliminary checks

1   Drive the vehicle to warm the transaxle to normal operating temperature.

2   Check the fluid level as described in Chapter 1:

 a) *If the fluid level is unusually low, add enough fluid to bring the level within the designated area of the dipstick, then check for external leaks (see below).*

 b) *If the fluid level is abnormally high, drain off the excess, then check the drained fluid for contamination by coolant. The presence of engine coolant in the automatic transmission fluid indicates that a failure has occurred in the internal radiator walls that separate the coolant from the transmission fluid (see Chapter 3).*

c) If the fluid is foaming, drain it and refill the transaxle, then check for coolant in the fluid, or a high fluid level.

3   Check the engine idle speed. **Note:** *If the engine is malfunctioning, do not proceed with the preliminary checks until it has been repaired and runs normally.*

4   Check the throttle control cable (Integra models) for freedom of movement. Adjust it if necessary (see Section 3). **Note:** *The cable may function properly when the engine is shut off and cold, but it may malfunction once the engine is hot. Check it cold and at normal engine operating temperature.*

5   Inspect the shift cable linkage (see Section 4). Make sure that it's properly adjusted and that the linkage operates smoothly.

Fluid leak diagnosis

6   Most fluid leaks are easy to locate visually. Repair usually consists of replacing a seal or gasket. If a leak is difficult to find, the following procedure may help.

7   Identify the fluid. Make sure it's transmission fluid and not engine oil or brake fluid (automatic transmission fluid is a deep red color).

8   Try to pinpoint the source of the leak. Drive the vehicle several miles, then park it over a large sheet of cardboard. After a minute or two, you should be able to locate the leak by determining the source of the fluid dripping onto the cardboard.

9   Make a careful visual inspection of the suspected component and the area immediately around it. Pay particular attention to gasket mating surfaces. A mirror is often helpful for finding leaks in areas that are hard to see.

10   If the leak still cannot be found, clean the suspected area thoroughly with a degreaser or solvent, then dry it.

11   Drive the vehicle for several miles at normal operating temperature and varying speeds. After driving the vehicle, visually inspect the suspected component again.

12   Once the leak has been located, the cause must be determined before it can be properly repaired. If a gasket is replaced but the sealing flange is bent, the new gasket will not stop the leak. The bent flange must be straightened.

13   Before attempting to repair a leak, check to make sure that the following conditions are corrected or they may cause another leak. **Note:** *Some of the following conditions cannot be fixed without highly specialized tools and expertise. Such problems must be referred to a transmission shop or a dealer service department.*

Gasket leaks

14   Check the right side cover periodically. Make sure the bolts are tight, no bolts are missing, the gasket is in good condition and the cover is not damaged.

15   If the leak is from the right side cover area, the bolts may be too tight, the sealing surface of the transaxle housing may be damaged, the gasket may be damaged or the transaxle casting may be cracked or porous. If sealant instead of gasket material has been used to form a seal between the cover and the transaxle housing, it may be the wrong sealant.

Seal leaks

16   If a transaxle seal is leaking, the fluid level or pressure may be too high, the vent may be plugged, the seal bore may be damaged, the seal itself may be damaged or improperly installed, the surface of the shaft protruding through the seal may be damaged or a loose bearing may be causing excessive shaft movement.

17   Make sure the dipstick tube seal is in good condition and the tube is properly seated. Periodically check the area around the speedometer gear or sensor for leakage. If transmission fluid is evident, check the O-ring for damage.

Case leaks

18   If the case itself appears to be leaking, the casting is porous and will have to be repaired or replaced.

19   Make sure the oil cooler hose fittings are tight and in good condition.

Fluid comes out vent pipe or fill tube

20   If this condition occurs, the transaxle is overfilled, there is coolant in the fluid, the case is porous, the dipstick is incorrect, the vent is plugged or the drain-back holes are plugged.

---

3   Throttle control cable (Integra models) - check and adjustment

Note: *The throttle control cable regulates the shift points of the automatic transaxle. Don't confuse it with the accelerator cable, which actuates the air intake throttle body for the fuel injection system.*

Check

1   Before you check the throttle control cable, make sure the accelerator cable freeplay (see Chapter 4) and the idle speed (see Chapter 1) are correct.

2   Warm up the engine to normal operating temperature.

3   Verify that the throttle control lever on the transaxle is synchronized with the accelerator linkage while depressing and releasing the accelerator pedal.

4   If the throttle control lever isn't synchronized with the accelerator linkage, adjust the throttle control cable (see below).

5   Have an assistant depress the accelerator pedal to the full-throttle position, then verify that there's a little freeplay in the throttle control lever (on the transaxle).

6   Disconnect the end of the throttle control cable from the throttle control lever at the transaxle.

7   Verify that the throttle control lever moves smoothly. If it doesn't, take the vehicle to a transmission specialist or other qualified repair shop.

8   Reconnect the throttle control cable to the throttle control lever.

Adjustment

9   Follow Steps 1 and 2 above.

10   Verify that the accelerator lever is in the fully closed position.

11   Loosen the throttle control cable locknut at the upper end, near the throttle body.

12   While pushing the throttle control lever to the fully closed position, remove all freeplay from the throttle control cable by tightening the adjusting nut.

13   Tighten the locknut.

14   After the locknut is tightened, check the synchronization and throttle control lever movement. Also, make sure there is a little freeplay in the throttle control lever at the transaxle when the accelerator pedal is fully depressed (if there isn't, the lever or the control mechanism in the transaxle may become damaged).

---

4   Shift cable - replacement and adjustment

Replacement

Refer to illustrations 4.2, 4.3, 4.4, 4.5 and 4.6

Warning: *The models covered by this manual are equipped with airbags. Always disable the airbag system before working in the vicinity of the impact sensors, steering column or instrument panel. See Chapter 12 for the airbag disarming procedure.*

1   Remove the center console (see Chapter 11).

2   Put the shift lever in the Neutral position, then remove the retaining clip from the cable adjuster (**see illustration**).

3   Raise the front of the vehicle and sup-

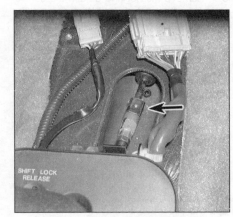

4.2 Detach the shift cable retaining clip (arrow)

4.3 Remove the shift cable bracket bolts (arrows)

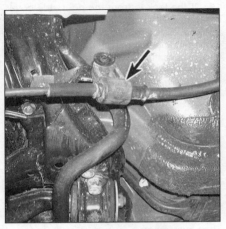

4.4 Detach the shift cable from the brace (arrow)

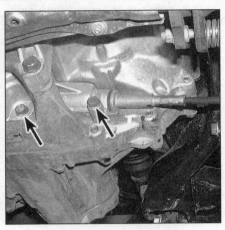

4.5 Remove the shift cable cover bolts (arrows)

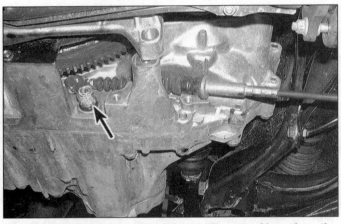

4.6 Remove the nut (arrow) and detach the control lever from the control shaft (arrow)

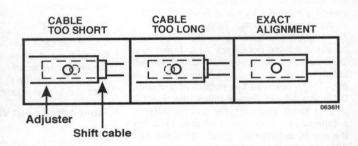

4.10 Make sure the hole in the adjuster is perfectly aligned with the hole in the shift cable

port it securely on jackstands. Unbolt the shift cable bracket **(see illustration)**.

4   Detach the shift cable holder from the floorpan and detach the cable from the brace **(see illustration)**.

5   Remove the shift cable cover **(see illustration)**.

6   Remove the nut and detach the control lever from the control shaft, then remove the shift cable **(see illustration)**. Be careful not to bend the cable when removing or installing it.

7   Installation is the reverse of removal. Be sure to adjust the shift cable when you're through.

Adjustment

Refer to illustrations 4.10 and 4.15

8   Remove the center console, if not already done (see Chapter 11).

9   Shift to the Neutral position, then remove the retaining clip from the cable adjuster **(see illustration 4.2)**.

10   There are two holes in the end of the shift cable. They're positioned 90-degrees apart to allow cable adjustments in 1/4-turn increments. Verify that the hole in the adjuster is perfectly aligned with the hole in the shift cable **(see illustration)**.

11   If the two holes aren't perfectly aligned, loosen the locknut on the shift cable and adjust it as required, then retighten the locknut.

12   Install the retaining clip on the adjuster.

4.15 Make sure the white index mark at the base of the shift lever lines up with the corresponding neutral mark on the shift indicator panel

If the clip feels as if it's binding as you reinstall it, the cable is still out of adjustment and must be readjusted.

13   Remove the shift indicator panel mounting screws and align the marks by moving the panel.

14   Install the panel screws and tighten them securely.

15   Verify that the index mark on the shift lever is aligned with the Neutral mark on the shift indicator panel when the transaxle is in Neutral **(see illustration)**. If they're not aligned, adjust the shift indicator panel.

16   Start the engine and check the shift lever in all gears. If any gear doesn't work properly, refer to Section 2.

---

5   Gear position switch - check, adjustment and replacement

Check

Refer to illustrations 5.2a, 5.2b, 5.3a, 5.3b and 5.3c

Warning: *The models covered by this manual are equipped with airbags. Always disable the airbag system before working in the vicinity of*

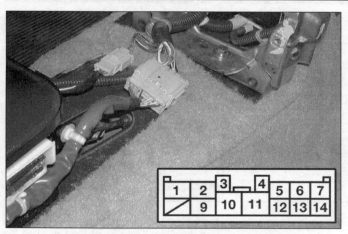

5.2a Terminal guide for the Civic 14-pin connector

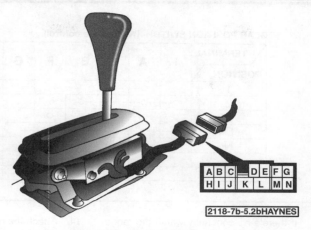

5.2b Terminal guide for the Integra 14-pin connector

GEAR POSITION SWITCH

TERMINAL / POSITION		1	2	5	6	7	9*	12	13	14	Back-up Light Switch 3	4	Neutral Safety Switch 10	11
NOT USED		O—O												
2	L	O		O			O							
D3	S	O			O		O							
D4	D	O				O	O							
N		O								O			O—O	
R		O							O		O—O			
P		O						O					O—O	

* CRUISE CONTROL

5.3a Continuity table for the gear position switch (Civic models)

GEAR POSITION SWITCH (Without cruise control)

TERMINAL ▶ / POSITION ▼	A	B	E	F	G	N	M	L	BACK-UP LIGHT SWITCH C	D	NEUTRAL SAFETY SWITCH J	K
1	O—O											
2	O		O									
D₃	O			O								
D₄	O				O							
N	O					O					O—O	
R	O						O		O—O			
P	O							O			O—O	

5.3b Continuity table for the gear position switch (Integra models without cruise control)

7B

the impact sensors, steering column or instrument panel. See Chapter 12 for the airbag disarming procedure.

1   Remove the console (see Chapter 11).

2   Unplug the 14-pin electrical connector from the gear position switch (see illustrations).

3   Check for continuity between the indicated terminals in each switch position in accordance with the accompanying tables (see illustrations). Move the shift lever back and forth at each switch position without touching the push-button and check for continuity within the range of shift lever freeplay (about 5/64-inch).

GEAR POSITION SWITCH (With cruise control)

| | | | | | | | | | | Back-up Light Switch | | Neutral Safety Switch | |
TERMINAL / POSITION	I	A	B	E	F	G	N	M	L	C	D	J	K
1		o	o										
2	o	o		o									
D3	o	o			o								
D4	o	o				o							
N		o					o					o	o
R		o						o		o	o		
P		o							o			o	o

5.3c Continuity table for the gear position switch (Integra models with cruise control)

42025-7b-5.3c HAYNES

4   If there's no continuity within the range of shift lever freeplay at each shift lever position, adjust the position of the switch.

Adjustment

5   Move the shift lever to the Park position and loosen the switch mounting nuts **(see illustration 5.11)**.
6   Slide the switch toward the Drive positions until there's continuity between terminals 2 and 14 (Civic) or A and L (Integra) within the range of shift lever freeplay (about 5/64-inch).
7   Recheck continuity as described above in Step 3. Make sure the engine starts when the shift lever is in the Neutral position.
8   If there's still no continuity at each shift lever position, inspect the shift lever detent and bracket for damage. If they're undamaged, replace the gear position switch.

Replacement

Refer to illustration 5.11
9   Remove the console (see Chapter 11).
10   Unplug the 14-pin connector **(see illustrations 5.2a and 5.2b)**.
11   Remove the two switch mounting nuts and washers **(see illustration)**.
12   Position the switch slider at the Neutral position.
13   Move the shift lever to the Neutral position, then install the new switch.

14   Attach the new switch with the two nuts and washers.
15   Test the new switch as described above in Step 3. Make sure the engine starts when the shift lever is in the Neutral position.
16   Reconnect the electrical connector. Clamp the harness.
17   Install the console (see Chapter 11).

---

6   Interlock system - description, check and solenoid replacement and adjustment

Warning: *The models covered by this manual are equipped with airbags. Always disable the airbag system before working in the vicinity of the impact sensors, steering column or instrument panel. See Chapter 12 for the airbag disarming procedure.*

Description

1   Vehicles equipped with an automatic transaxle have an interlock system to prevent unintentional shifting. The interlock system consists of two subsystems: a shift lock system and a key interlock system.

Key interlock system

2   The key interlock system prevents the ignition key from being removed from the ignition switch unless the shift lever is in the Park position. If you insert the key when the shift lever is in any position other than Park, a solenoid is activated, making it impossible for you to remove the key until the shift lever is moved to the Park position.

Shift lock system

3   The shift lock system prevents the shift lever from moving from the Park position into the Reverse or Drive positions unless the brake pedal is depressed. Nor can the shift lever be shifted when the brake pedal and the accelerator pedal are depressed at the same time. In the event of a system malfunction, you can release the shift lever by inserting a key into the release slot near the shift lever.

Check

4   The following checks are simple tests of the key interlock solenoid and the shift lock solenoid you can do at home. Further testing of the interlock system should be left to a dealer service department.

Key interlock solenoid

Refer to illustration 6.6
5   Remove the lower instrument panel and knee bolster (see Chapter 11).
6   Unplug the 7-pin connector **(see illustration)** from the main wire harness.
7   Check for continuity between the termi-

5.11 Remove the nuts (arrows) and detach the gear position switch (note the position in which the switch slider must be when installing the switch)

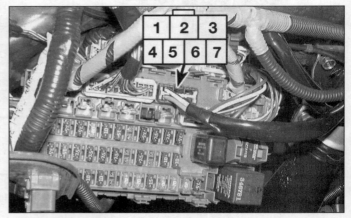

6.6 Terminal guide for the key interlock solenoid connector (as seen from the back side of the connector) (Civic shown, Integra similar)

6.11 Terminal guide for the shift lock solenoid connector

6.18 Energize the solenoid, check the clearance between the shift lock lever and the lock pin groove (arrows) and compare your measurement to the clearance listed in this Chapter's Specifications

6.19 When the shift lock solenoid is Off, make sure the lock pin (A) is blocked by the shift lock lever (B)

nals in each switch position. With the key pushed in, there should be continuity between terminals 5, 6 and 7; with the key released, there should be continuity only between terminals 5 and 6 (approximately 15 to 20 ohms between these two terminals).

8   Verify that the key can't be removed when the battery is connected to terminals 7 and 5.

9   If the key can't be removed, the key interlock solenoid is okay; if the key can be removed, the steering lock assembly needs to be replaced (the key interlock solenoid isn't available separately).

Shift lock solenoid

Refer to illustration 6.11

10   Remove the console (see Chapter 11).

11   Unplug the two-pin connector from the shift lock solenoid **(see illustration)**.

12   Using a pair of jumper wires, momentarily touch a *positive* battery lead *to the number 1 terminal* of the two-pin connector and a negative lead to the number 2 terminal and note whether the solenoid clicks on or not. **Caution:** *Make sure you don't connect the battery voltage leads to the wrong connector terminals. Reversing the polarity can damage or destroy the diode inside the solenoid.*

a) *If the solenoid doesn't operate, replace it.*

b) *If the solenoid does operate, but you have been having problems with the shift lock system, it may be necessary to adjust the solenoid at its Off and On positions (see below).*

13   While the solenoid is on, it's a good idea to check the clearance between the shift lock lever and the lock pin groove (see below).

14   With the solenoid turned off, note whether or not the lock pin is blocked by the shift lock lever. If it isn't, adjust the position of the shift lock solenoid until it is (see below).

Solenoid replacement and adjustment

Refer to illustrations 6.18 and 6.19
Note: *The following procedure pertains only*

to the shift lock solenoid. For information on how to replace the key interlock solenoid, refer to the "Ignition switch/key lock cylinder replacement" Section in Chapter 12. The key interlock solenoid isn't available separately.

15   Remove the shift lock collar and the solenoid pin.

16   Remove the self-locking nuts and the shift lock solenoid. Discard the old nuts.

17   Installation is the reverse of removal. Don't tighten the new nuts until you have adjusted the solenoid as follows.

18   To adjust the shift lock solenoid, energize the solenoid and check the clearance between the shift lock lever and the lock pin groove **(see illustration)** and compare your measurement to the clearance listed in this Chapter's Specifications. Position the solenoid so the clearance is correct, then tighten the new self-locking nuts to the torque listed in this Chapter's Specifications. **Note:** *Be sure to use new self-locking nuts.*

19   With the solenoid turned off, note whether or not the lock pin is blocked by the shift lock lever **(see illustration)**. If it isn't, readjust the position of the shift lock solenoid until it is.

7   Lock-up control solenoid and shift control solenoid - check and replacement

Check

Refer to illustration 7.1

Lock-up control solenoid

1   Unplug the connector from the lock-up control solenoid valve assembly **(see illustration)**.

2   Measure the resistance between each of the connector terminals (solenoid side) and ground and compare your measurements to the resistance listed in this Chapter's Specifications. If the resistance is out of specification for either terminal, replace the entire solenoid assembly.

3   Connect each of the connector terminals to the battery positive terminal with a jumper cable. You should hear a clicking sound as each solenoid valve is energized. If you don't, have the ECM and lock-up control solenoid valve circuits checked out by a transmission specialist or other qualified repair shop.

7B

7.1 Unplug the connector (A) from the lock-up control solenoid valve assembly (B) located on top of the transaxle

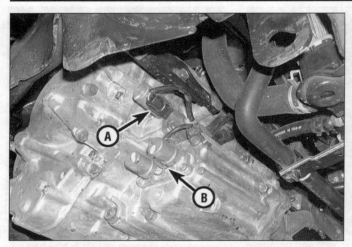

7.4 Unplug the electrical connector (A) from the shift control solenoid assembly (B)

7.8 The lock-up and shift control solenoid valve assemblies are retained by three bolts (arrows) - lock-up assembly shown

Shift control solenoid

Refer to illustration 7.4

4   Unplug the connector from the shift control solenoid valve assembly **(see illustration)**.

5   Measure the resistance between each of the connector terminals (solenoid side) and ground and compare your measurements to the resistance listed in this Chapter's Specifications. If the resistance is out of specification for either terminal, replace the entire solenoid assembly.

6   Connect each of the connector terminals to the battery positive terminal with a jumper cable. You should hear a clicking sound as each solenoid valve is energized. If you don't, take the vehicle to a dealer and have the ECM and lock-up control solenoid valve circuits checked out.

7   Connect each of the connector terminals to the battery positive terminal with a jumper cable. You should hear a clicking sound as each solenoid valve is energized. If you don't, have the ECM and lock-up control solenoid valve circuits checked out by a transmission specialist or other qualified repair shop.

Replacement

Note: *You cannot replace only one solenoid valve; both the lock-up and shift control solenoid valve assembly must be replaced as a single unit.*

Refer to illustration 7.8

8   Remove the mounting bolts and remove the lock-up solenoid control solenoid valve assembly **(see illustration)**

9   Clean the mounting surface and oil passages; make sure all dirt and dust is removed.

10   Install a new base gasket and install the new lock-up control solenoid valve assembly. Tighten the solenoid valve bolts to the torque listed in this Chapter's Specifications.

11   Check the electrical connector for dirt, corrosion and oil; clean it thoroughly if neces-

sary. Reconnect it.

12   Check the solenoid valves as described above and make sure the new unit is functioning properly.

8   Automatic transaxle and Continuously Variable Transaxle (CVT) - removal and installation

Refer to illustrations 8.7, 8.20, 8.22, 8.26 and 8.27

Removal

1   Disconnect the negative cable from the battery. **Caution:** *If the radio in your vehicle is equipped with an anti-theft system, make sure you have the correct activation code before disconnecting the battery.*

2   Remove the resonator, intake air duct and air cleaner housing (see Chapter 4).

3   Remove the starter motor cables and cable bracket from the starter (see Chapter 5).

4   Disconnect the transaxle ground cable from the transaxle.

5   Unplug the electrical connector from the lock-up control solenoid (see Section 7).

6   Unplug the speed sensor electrical connector (see Chapter 7A).

7   Remove the three upper transaxle-to-engine mounting bolts and the rear engine mounting bolt **(see illustration)**.

8   Raise the vehicle and support it securely on jackstands.

9   Drain the transmission fluid (see Chapter 1). Be sure to use a new sealing washer when you reinstall the drain plug.

10   Disconnect the lower arms from the steering knuckles (see Chapter 10).

11   Separate the driveaxles from the differential (see Chapter 8). Cover the inner CV joints with plastic bags to keep them clean.

12   Remove the right damper fork (see Chapter 10).

13   Remove the driveaxles (see Chapter 8).

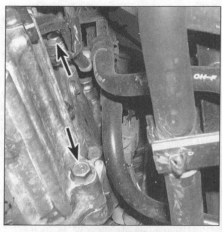

8.7 Remove the transaxle-to-engine mounting bolts (arrows)

14   Remove the splash shield.

15   Remove the elbow-shaped exhaust pipe section from underneath the engine (see Chapter 4).

16   Remove the shift cable cover, then remove the control lever and shift cable. It's not necessary to disconnect the shift cable from the control lever.

17   Remove the stopper mount (see Chapter 7A).

18   Disconnect the throttle control cable from the throttle control lever (see Section 3).

19   Disconnect the transaxle fluid cooler hoses from the cooler lines. Turn the hoses up to prevent fluid from flowing out, then plug the lines to prevent contamination.

20   Remove the engine stiffener(s) **(see illustration)**.

21   Remove the torque converter (conventional transaxle) or flywheel (CVT) access plate.

22   Mark the relationship of the torque converter (conventional transaxle) or flywheel (CVT) to the driveplate so that they can be reinstalled in the same relationship to one another **(see illustration)**.

8.20 Remove the engine stiffener bolts (arrows) - Civic model shown

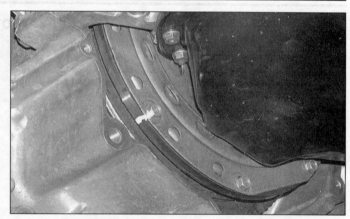

8.22 Before removing the driveplate-to-torque converter (or CVT driveplate and flywheel) bolts, mark the edge of the driveplate and torque converter or flywheel to ensure they're reattached in the same relationship when the transaxle is reinstalled

8.26 Transaxle side mount connection details (arrows) - Civic model shown

8.27 Remove the rear engine mount bolts (arrows)

23   Remove the torque converter- or flywheel-to-driveplate bolts one at a time by rotating the crankshaft pulley for access to each bolt.

24   Remove the distributor mounting bolt, then attach an engine hoist to the engine.

25   Place a transmission jack or a floor jack under the transaxle. Raise the transaxle assembly just enough to take the load off the transaxle mount.

26   Remove the transaxle side mount **(see illustration)**.

27   Remove the lower transaxle-to-engine bolt, the lower engine-to-transaxle bolt and the rear engine mount bolts **(see illustration)**.

28   Move the transaxle back to disengage it from the engine block dowel pins and make sure the torque converter is detached from the driveplate. Secure the torque converter to the transaxle so it will not fall out during removal. Lower the transaxle from the vehicle. **Note:** *It may be necessary to slowly lower the jack supporting the engine while the jack supporting the transaxle is being lowered. This will provide more clearance between the transaxle and the body.*

Installation

29   Honda recommends flushing the transaxle cooler and the cooler hoses and lines with solvent whenever the transaxle is removed from the vehicle. Flush the lines and fluid cooler thoroughly and make sure no solvent remains in the lines or cooler after flushing. It's a good idea to repeat the flushing procedure with clean automatic transmission fluid to ensure that no solvent remains in the lines or cooler.

30   Install the starter motor (see Chapter 5).

31   Prior to installation, make sure that the torque converter hub is securely engaged in the pump. With the transaxle secured to the jack, raise it into position. Be sure to keep it level so the torque converter does not slide out.

32   Turn the torque converter to line it up with the driveplate. The marks you made on the torque converter and the driveplate must line up.

33   Make sure the two dowel pins are still installed, then move the transaxle forward carefully until the dowel pins and the torque converter are engaged.

34   Install the lower transaxle-to-engine bolt and the lower engine-to-transaxle bolt. Tighten them to the torque listed in this Chapter's Specifications. **Caution:** *Don't use the bolts to force the transaxle and engine together. If the transaxle doesn't slide easily up against the engine, find out why before you tighten the bolts.*

35   The remainder of installation is the reverse of removal.

36   Refill the transaxle with fluid to the specified level (see Chapter 1). Note that the transaxle may require more fluid than in a normal fluid and filter change, since the torque converter may be empty (the converter is not drained during a fluid change).

37   Start the engine, set the parking brake and shift the transaxle through all gears three times. Make sure the shift cable is working properly (see Section 4).

38   Check and, if necessary, adjust the ignition timing (see Chapter 1).

39   Allow the engine to reach its proper operating temperature with the transaxle in Park or Neutral, then turn it off and check the fluid level.

40   Road test the vehicle and check for fluid leaks.

7B

Notes

Chapter 8
Clutch and driveaxles

Contents

Specifications

General

Clutch pedal standard height	6-1/2 inches
Clutch pedal freeplay	1/2 to 3/4 inch
Clutch pedal stroke	5-1/8 to 5-1/2 inches

Driveaxles

Driveaxle length
Civic
Left	30-1/2 to 30-11/16 inches
Right	19-11/16 to 19-29/32 inches
Integra	18-11/16 to 18-29/32 inches

Dynamic damper (distance from inner CV joint boot)
Civic
Left
With SR1 mark	3 inches
Without SR1 mark	3-11/16 +/- 7/64 inches
Right	2-13/64 +/- 7/64 inches
Integra	1 inch

Torque specifications

	Ft-lbs
Clutch pressure plate bolts	19
Driveaxle/hub nut	134
Intermediate shaft bearing support bolts	29

8

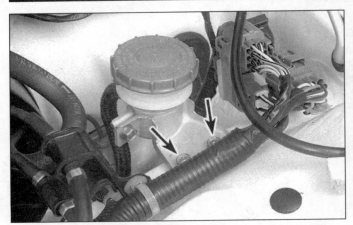

3.3a The remote reservoir for the clutch master cylinder is located in the left (driver's side) rear corner of the engine compartment, and the master cylinder is right below it; to get at the master cylinder, remove these two bolts (arrows) and lift the reservoir out of the way

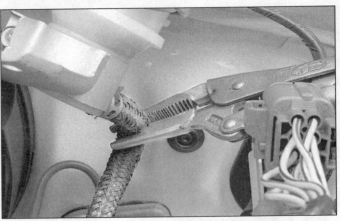

3.3b Pinch off the fluid feed hose between the reservoir and the clutch master cylinder with a pair of locking pliers to prevent the fluid from running out of the end of the hose when you disconnect it from the clutch master cylinder.

1   General information

The information in this Chapter deals with the components from the rear of the engine to the front wheels, except for the transaxle, which is dealt with in the previous Chapter. For the purposes of this Chapter, these components are grouped into two categories - clutch and driveaxles. Separate Sections within this Chapter offer general descriptions and checking procedures for components in each of the two groups.

Since nearly all the procedures covered in this Chapter involve working under the vehicle, make sure it's securely supported on sturdy jackstands or on a hoist where the vehicle can be easily raised and lowered.

2   Clutch - description and check

1   All vehicles with a manual transaxle use a single dry-plate, diaphragm-spring type clutch. The clutch disc has a splined hub which allows it to slide along the splines of the transaxle input shaft. The clutch and pressure plate are held in contact by spring pressure exerted by the diaphragm in the pressure plate.

2   The clutch release system is operated by hydraulic pressure. The hydraulic release system consists of the clutch pedal, a master cylinder and fluid reservoir, the hydraulic line, a release (or slave) cylinder which actuates the clutch release lever and the clutch release (or throwout) bearing.

3   When pressure is applied to the clutch pedal to release the clutch, hydraulic pressure is exerted against the outer end of the clutch release lever. As the lever pivots the shaft fingers push against the release bearing. The bearing pushes against the fingers of the diaphragm spring of the pressure plate assembly, which in turn releases the clutch plate.

4   Terminology can be a problem when

discussing the clutch components because common names are in some cases different from those used by the manufacturer. For example, the driven plate is also called the clutch plate or disc, the clutch release bearing is sometimes called a throwout bearing, the release cylinder is sometimes called the operating or slave cylinder.

5   Other than to replace components with obvious damage, some preliminary checks should be performed to diagnose clutch problems. These checks assume that the transaxle is in good working condition.

a)   *The first check should be of the fluid level in the clutch master cylinder (see Chapter 1). If the fluid level is low, add fluid as necessary and inspect the hydraulic system for leaks. If the master cylinder reservoir has run dry, bleed the system as described in Section 5 and retest the clutch operation.*

b)   *To check "clutch spin-down time," run the engine at normal idle speed with the transaxle in Neutral (clutch pedal up - engaged). Disengage the clutch (pedal down), wait several seconds and shift the transaxle into Reverse. No grinding noise should be heard. A grinding noise would most likely indicate a problem in the pressure plate or the clutch disc.*

c)   *To check for complete clutch release, run the engine (with the parking brake applied to prevent movement) and hold the clutch pedal approximately 1/2-inch from the floor. Shift the transaxle between 1st gear and Reverse several times. If the shift is rough, component failure is indicated. Check the release cylinder pushrod travel. With the clutch pedal depressed completely, the release cylinder pushrod should extend substantially. If it doesn't, check the fluid level in the clutch master cylinder.*

d)   *Visually inspect the pivot bushing at the top of the clutch pedal to make sure there is no binding or excessive play.*

3.4 To remove the clutch master cylinder, loosen the hose clamp (left arrow) on the feed line and use a flare-nut wrench to loosen the pressure line fitting (right arrow), then, working inside the vehicle, remove the two mounting bolts from under the dash

e)   *Crawl under the vehicle and make sure the clutch release lever is solidly mounted on the ball stud.*

3   Clutch master cylinder - removal and installation

Removal
Refer to illustrations 3.3a, 3.3b, 3.4 and 3.5

1   Disconnect the cable from the negative battery terminal. **Caution:** *If the radio in your vehicle is equipped with an anti-theft system, make sure you have the correct activation code before disconnecting the battery.*

2   Working under the dashboard, remove the cotter pin from the master cylinder pushrod clevis. Pull out the clevis pin to disconnect the pushrod from the pedal.

3   Detach the clutch master cylinder reservoir **(see illustration)**. Clamp a pair of locking pliers onto the clutch fluid feed hose, a cou-

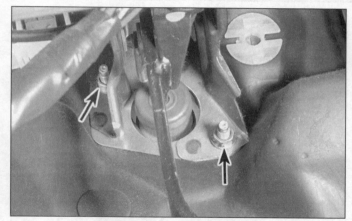

3.5 To disconnect the clutch master cylinder from the clutch pedal, remove the cotter pin and clevis pin that attach it to the top of the pedal; to detach the master cylinder from the firewall, remove the two mounting nuts (arrows)

4.3 Using a flare-nut wrench, loosen the clutch fluid line fitting (arrow) at the release cylinder

4.4 Remove the two mounting bolts (arrows) from the clutch release cylinder

5.4 The setup for bleeding the clutch hydraulic system is simple: a length of hose between the bleeder plug and a small container with about two inches of brake fluid in it; make sure the hose is submerged in the fluid

ple of inches downstream of the reservoir **(see illustration)**. The pliers should be just tight enough to prevent fluid flow when the hose is disconnected.

4 Disconnect the hydraulic lines at the cylinder **(see illustration)**. Loosen the fluid feed hose clamp and detach the hose from the cylinder. Have rags handy as some fluid will be lost as the line is removed. Cap or plug the ends of the lines (and/or hose) to prevent fluid leakage and the entry of contaminants. **Caution:** *Don't allow brake fluid to come into contact with the paint as it will damage the finish.*

5 Working under the dash, unscrew the two clutch master cylinder retaining nuts **(see illustration)** and remove the cylinder.

Installation

6 Place the master cylinder in position and install the mounting bolts finger tight.

7 Connect the hydraulic lines to the master cylinder. Move the cylinder slightly as necessary to thread the fitting into the cylinder (don't tighten the fitting yet). Attach the fluid feed hose to the cylinder and tighten the hose clamp.

8 Tighten the mounting bolts securely, then tighten the hydraulic line fitting securely.

9 Connect the pushrod to the clutch pedal. Use a new cotter pin to secure the clevis pin.

10 Remove the locking pliers from the feed hose. Fill the clutch master cylinder reservoir with brake fluid conforming to DOT 3 specifications and bleed the clutch system as outlined in Section 5.

4 Clutch release cylinder - removal and installation

Removal

Refer to illustrations 4.3 and 4.4

1 Disconnect the negative cable from the battery. **Caution:** *If the radio in your vehicle is equipped with an anti-theft system, make sure you have the correct activation code before disconnecting the battery.*

2 Raise the vehicle and support it securely on jackstands.

3 Disconnect the fluid hose at the release cylinder. Use a flare nut wrench so you don't strip the corners off the fitting **(see illustra-**

tion). Have a small can and rags handy - some fluid will be spilled as the line is removed. Plug the line to prevent excessive fluid loss.

4 Remove the two release cylinder mounting bolts **(see illustration)**.

5 Remove the release cylinder.

Installation

6 Install the release cylinder on the clutch housing, but don't completely tighten the bolts yet. Make sure the pushrod is seated in the release fork pocket.

7 Connect the hydraulic line to the release cylinder, then tighten the release cylinder mounting bolts securely. Using a flare-nut wrench, tighten the hydraulic fitting securely.

8 Fill the clutch master cylinder with brake fluid conforming to DOT 3 specifications.

9 Bleed the system as described in Section 5.

10 Lower the vehicle and connect the negative battery cable.

5 Clutch hydraulic system - bleeding

Refer to illustration 5.4

1 Bleed the hydraulic system whenever any part of the system has been removed or the fluid level has fallen so low that air has been drawn into the master cylinder. The bleeding procedure is very similar to bleeding a brake system.

2 Fill the master cylinder with new brake fluid conforming to DOT 3 specifications. **Caution:** *Do not re-use any of the fluid coming from the system during the bleeding operation or use fluid which has been inside an open container for an extended period of time.*

3 Raise the vehicle and place it securely on jackstands to gain access to the release cylinder, which is located on the front of the transaxle.

4 Remove the dust cap which fits over the bleeder valve and push a length of plastic hose over the valve **(see illustration)**. Place

8

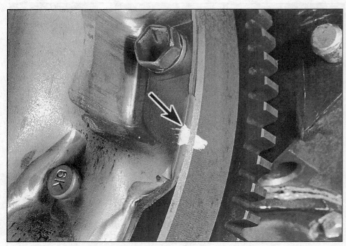

6.5   Mark the relationship of the pressure plate to the flywheel (just in case you're going to re-use the old pressure plate)

6.6   Remove the pressure plate bolts (arrows) gradually and evenly in a criss-cross pattern

the other end of the hose into a clear container with about two inches of brake fluid. The hose end must be in the fluid at the bottom of the container.

5   Have an assistant depress the clutch pedal and hold it. Open the bleeder valve on the release cylinder, allowing fluid to flow through the hose. Close the bleeder valve when the flow of fluid (and bubbles) ceases. Once closed, have your assistant release the pedal.

6   Continue this process until all air is evacuated from the system, indicated by a solid stream of fluid being ejected from the bleeder valve each time with no air bubbles in the hose or container. Keep a close watch on the fluid level inside the clutch master cylinder reservoir - if the level drops too far, air will get into the system and you'll have to start all over again.

7   Install the dust cap and lower the vehicle. Check carefully for proper operation before placing the vehicle into normal service.

6   Clutch components - removal, inspection and installation

Warning: *Dust produced by clutch wear and deposited on clutch components may contain asbestos, which is hazardous to your health. DO NOT blow it out with compressed air and DO NOT inhale it. DO NOT use gasoline or petroleum-based solvents to remove the dust. Brake system cleaner should be used to flush the dust into a drain pan. After the clutch components are wiped clean with a rag, dispose of the contaminated rags and cleaner in a covered, marked container.*

Removal

Refer to illustrations 6.5 and 6.6

1   Access to the clutch components is normally accomplished by removing the transaxle, leaving the engine in the vehicle. If

the engine is being removed for major overhaul, check the clutch for wear and replace worn components as necessary. However, the relatively low cost of the clutch components compared to the time and trouble spent gaining access to them warrants their replacement anytime the engine or transaxle is removed, unless they are new or in near-perfect condition. The following procedures are based on the assumption the engine will stay in place.

2   Remove the transaxle from the vehicle (see Chapter 7, Part A). Support the engine while the transaxle is out. Preferably, an engine hoist should be used to support it from above. However, if a jack is used underneath the engine, make sure a piece of wood is positioned between the jack and oil pan to spread the load. **Caution:** *The pick-up for the oil pump is very close to the bottom of the oil pan. If the pan is bent or distorted in any way, engine oil starvation could occur.*

3   The clutch fork and release bearing can remain attached to the transaxle housing for the time being.

4   To support the clutch disc during removal, install a clutch alignment tool through the clutch disc hub.

5   Carefully inspect the flywheel and pres-

sure plate for indexing marks. The marks are usually an X, an O or a white letter. If they cannot be found, scribe or paint marks yourself so the pressure plate and the flywheel will be in the same alignment during installation **(see illustration)**.

6   Turning each bolt a little at a time, loosen the pressure plate-to-flywheel bolts **(see illustration)**. Work in a criss-cross pattern until all spring pressure is relieved. Then hold the pressure plate securely and completely remove the bolts, followed by the pressure plate and clutch disc.

Inspection

Refer to illustrations 6.9, 6.11a and 6.11b

7   Ordinarily, when a problem occurs in the clutch, it can be attributed to wear of the clutch driven plate assembly (clutch disc). However, all components should be inspected at this time.

8   Inspect the flywheel for cracks, heat checking, grooves and other obvious defects. If the imperfections are slight, a machine shop can machine the surface flat and smooth, which is highly recommended regardless of the surface appearance. Refer to Chapter 2 for the flywheel removal and installation procedure.

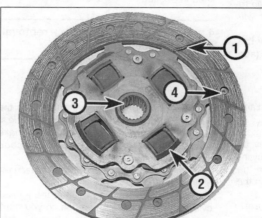

6.9   The clutch disc

1   *Lining* - this will wear down in use

2   *Springs or dampers* - check for cracking and deformation

3   *Splined hub* - the splines must not be worn and should slide smoothly on the transaxle input shaft splines

4   *Rivets* - these secure the lining and will damage the flywheel or pressure plate if allowed to contact the surfaces

NORMAL FINGER WEAR   EXCESSIVE FINGER WEAR   BROKEN OR BENT FINGERS

6.11a Replace the pressure plate if any of these conditions are noted

9   Inspect the lining on the clutch disc. There should be at least 1/16-inch of lining above the rivet heads. Check for loose rivets, distortion, cracks, broken springs and other obvious damage **(see illustration)**. As mentioned above, ordinarily the clutch disc is routinely replaced, so if in doubt about the condition, replace it with a new one.

10   The release bearing should also be replaced along with the clutch disc (see Section 8). This is also a good time to check the condition of the pilot bearing (see Section 7).

11   Check the machined surfaces and the diaphragm spring fingers of the pressure plate **(see illustrations)**. If the surface is grooved or otherwise damaged, replace the pressure plate. Also check for obvious damage, distortion, cracking, etc. Light glazing can be removed with emery cloth or sandpaper. If a new pressure plate is required, new and factory-rebuilt units are available.

Installation

Refer to illustration 6.13

12   Before installation, clean the flywheel and pressure plate machined surfaces with brake cleaner, lacquer thinner or acetone. It's important that no oil or grease is on these surfaces or the lining of the clutch disc. Handle the parts only with clean hands.

13   Position the clutch disc and pressure plate against the flywheel with the clutch held in place with an alignment tool **(see illustration)**. Make sure the disc is installed properly (most replacement clutch discs will be marked "flywheel side" or something similar - if not marked, install the clutch disc with the damper springs toward the transaxle).

14   Tighten the pressure plate-to-flywheel bolts only finger tight, working around the pressure plate.

15   Center the clutch disc by ensuring the alignment tool extends through the splined hub and into the pocket in the crankshaft. Wiggle the tool up, down or side-to-side as needed to center the disc. Tighten the pressure plate-to-flywheel bolts a little at a time, working in a criss-cross pattern to prevent distorting the cover. After all of the bolts are snug, tighten them to the torque listed in this Chapter's Specifications. Remove the alignment tool.

16   Using high-temperature grease, lubricate the inner groove of the release bearing (see Section 8). Also place grease on the release lever contact areas and the transaxle input shaft bearing retainer.

17   Install the clutch release bearing (see Section 7).

18   Install the transaxle and all components removed previously.

7   Pilot bearing - inspection and replacement

Refer to illustrations 7.5 and 7.7

1   The clutch pilot bearing is a ball bearing which is pressed into the flywheel. It's greased at the factory and doesn't require additional lubrication. Its primary purpose is to support the front of the transaxle input shaft. The pilot bearing should be inspected whenever the clutch components are removed from the engine. Because of its inaccessibility, replace it with a new one if you have any doubt about its condition. **Note:** *If the engine has been removed from the vehicle, disregard the following Steps which don't apply.*

2   Remove the transaxle (see Chapter 7A).

3   Remove the clutch components (see Section 6).

4   Using a flashlight, inspect the bearing for excessive wear, scoring, dryness, roughness and any other obvious damage. If any of these conditions are noted, replace the bearing.

5   Removal can be accomplished with a slide hammer and puller attachment **(see illustration)**, which are available at most auto parts stores or tool rental yards.

6.11b Inspect the pressure plate friction surface for score marks, cracks and signs of overheating

6.13 Center the clutch disc in the pressure plate with a clutch alignment tool

7.5 A small slide-hammer puller is handy for removing a pilot bearing

7.7 Tap the bearing into place with a bearing driver or a socket that is slightly smaller than the outside diameter of the bearing

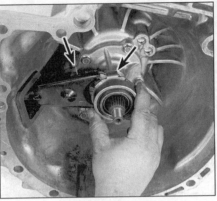

8.3 Reach behind the release lever and disengage the retention spring (left arrow), then remove the lever and slide the bearing tangs (right arrow) off the lever

6   If a slide hammer is not available, remove the flywheel (see Chapter 2 Part A). Using hammer and drift, drive the bearing out of the flywheel, from the rear to the front.

7   To install a new bearing, lightly lubricate the outside surface with grease, then drive it into the recess with a bearing driver or a socket **(see illustration)**.

8   Install the flywheel, if removed (see Chapter 2A). Install the clutch components, transaxle and other components removed previously. Tighten all fasteners to the recommended torque values.

8   Clutch release bearing and fork - removal, inspection and installation

Warning: *Dust produced by clutch wear and deposited on clutch components may contain asbestos, which is hazardous to your health. DO NOT blow it out with compressed air and DO NOT inhale it. DO NOT use gasoline or petroleum-based solvents to remove the dust. Brake system cleaner should be used to flush the dust into a drain pan. After the clutch components are wiped clean with a rag, dispose of the contaminated rags and cleaner in a labeled, covered container.*

Removal

Refer to illustration 8.3 and 8.4

1   Unbolt the clutch release cylinder (see Section 4), but don't disconnect the fluid line between the master cylinder and the release cylinder. Suspend the release cylinder out of the way with a piece of wire.

2   Remove the transaxle (see Chapter 7, Part A).

3   Slide the release bearing off the input shaft, disengage the clutch release fork retention spring from the ball stud and remove the fork **(see illustration)**.

Inspection

4   Hold the bearing by the outer race and rotate the inner race while applying pressure. If the bearing doesn't turn smoothly or if it's noisy, replace the bearing/hub assembly with

a new one **(see illustration)**.

5   Wipe the bearing with a clean rag and inspect it for damage, wear and cracks. It's common practice to replace the bearing with a new one whenever a clutch job is performed, to decrease the possibility of a bearing failure in the future. Don't immerse the bearing in solvent - it's sealed for life and to do so would ruin it. Also check the release lever for cracks and bends.

Installation

Refer to illustrations 8.6, 8.7a, 8.7b and 8.7c

6   Fill the inner groove of the release bearing with high temperature grease. Also apply a light coat of the same grease to the transaxle input shaft splines and the input shaft bearing retainer **(see illustration)**.

7   Lubricate the release fork ball socket, fork ends and release cylinder pushrod socket with high temperature grease **(see illustrations)**.

8   Attach the release bearing to the release fork.

8.4 To check the bearing, hold it by the outer race and rotate the inner race while applying pressure; if the bearing doesn't turn smoothly or if it's noisy, replace the bearing

9   Slide the release bearing onto the transaxle input shaft front bearing retainer while passing the end of the release fork

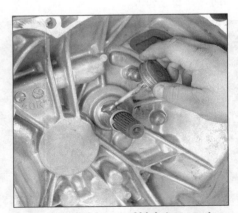

8.6 Apply a light coat of high-temperature grease to the bearing surface of the retainer (before installing the transaxle, apply the same grease to the input shaft splines to help the shaft slide through the clutch hub)

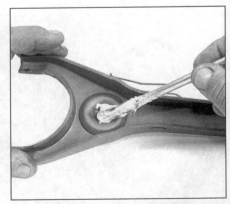

8.7a Using high-temperature grease, lubricate the ball stud socket in the back of the release lever . . .

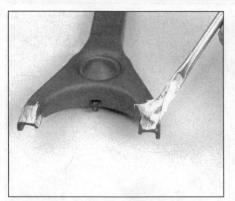

8.7b . . . the lever ends, the depression for the release cylinder pushrod . . .

8.7c . . . and the ball stud

9.1 Pedal height is the distance between the pedal pad and the floor

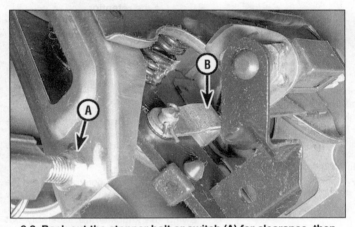

9.2 Back out the stopper bolt or switch (A) for clearance, then loosen the locknut on the pushrod (B). Turn the pushrod to adjust the pedal height

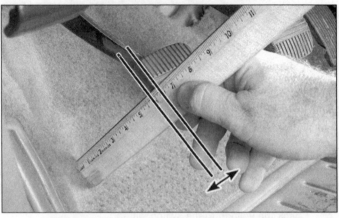

9.5 Pedal freeplay is the distance the pedal travels before resistance is felt

through the opening in the clutch housing. Push the clutch release fork onto the ball stud until it's firmly seated.

10　Apply a light coat of high temperature grease to the face of the release bearing where it contacts the pressure plate diaphragm fingers.

11　The remainder of installation is the reverse of the removal procedure.

9　Clutch pedal adjustment

Pedal height

Refer to illustrations 9.1 and 9.2

1　The height of the clutch pedal is the distance the pedal sits off the floor **(see illustration)**. If the pedal height is not within the specified range, it must be adjusted.

2　To adjust the clutch pedal, loosen the locknut on the clutch switch or adjusting bolt and back the switch out until it no longer touches the pedal, then loosen the locknut on the clutch pushrod **(see illustration)**. Turn the pushrod to adjust the pedal height, then tighten the locknut.

3　Turn the switch or bolt clockwise until it just contacts the pedal arm, then turn it in an additional 3/4 to 1 turn. Tighten the locknut.

4　Adjust the starter/clutch interlock switch as described in Section 10.

Pedal freeplay

Refer to illustration 9.5

5　The freeplay is the pedal slack, or the distance the pedal can be depressed before it begins to have any effect on the clutch system **(see illustration)**. If the pedal freeplay is not within the specified range, it must be adjusted.

6　To adjust the pedal freeplay, loosen the locknut on the clutch pushrod. Then back off the pushrod to adjust the pedal freeplay to the specified range and retighten the locknut.

7　Check and, if necessary, adjust the starter/interlock switch (see Section 10).

10　Starter/clutch interlock switch - check, replacement and adjustment

Refer to illustration 10.1

Check

1　The starter/clutch interlock switch is located near the upper end of the clutch pedal

10.1 The interlock switch (arrow) is located on a bracket near the top of the clutch pedal; it's secured to the bracket by a pair of nuts, one above the bracket, one below, which are also used to adjust the position of the switch plunger in relation to the stopper on the pedal

(see illustration). It has two wires - one coming from the starter relay and one going to ground. When the ignition switch key is turned to the Start position and the clutch pedal is depressed, the starter relay's path to ground is closed by the starter/clutch interlock switch and the starter motor is activated.

8

11.1 If the driveaxle nut is "staked", use a center punch to unstake it (wheel removed for clarity)

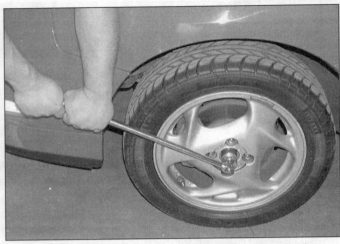

11.2 Loosen the driveaxle/hub nut with a long breaker bar

2   If the engine won't crank when the clutch pedal is depressed, adjust the switch (see Step 6) and try again. If it still won't turn over, check the switch (see Step 3) and, if necessary, replace it (see Step 5). If the engine rotates when the clutch pedal isn't depressed, adjust the switch and try again.

3   If the engine won't start when the clutch pedal is depressed, either there's no voltage from the starter relay to the switch, or there's no continuity between the two terminals on the switch.

4   Check the voltage to the switch with a voltmeter or test light. When you turn the ignition key to the Start position and depress the clutch pedal, there should be voltage in the wire from the starter relay. If there isn't, look for an open or short circuit condition somewhere between the starter relay and the switch. If there is voltage in this wire, check the other side of the switch for voltage (with the pedal depressed). If there's voltage on both sides of the switch, the switch should be operating correctly. Try adjusting it (see Step 6). If voltage isn't present on both sides, the switch is bad.

Replacement

5   Unplug the electrical connector, loosen the adjustment nut and unscrew the switch from its mounting bracket. Installation is the reverse of removal.

Adjustment

6   Loosen the locknut and turn the switch in or out, as necessary, to provide continuity through the switch when the clutch pedal is depressed.

11 Driveaxles - removal and installation

Removal

Refer to illustrations 11.1, 11.2, 11.6, 11.7a and 11.7b

1   Remove the wheel cover or hub cap. If the driveaxle/hub nut is staked, unstake it with a punch or chisel **(see illustration)**; if it's secured by locking tabs, bend the tabs out.

2   Break the hub nut loose with a socket and large breaker bar **(see illustration)**.

3   Loosen the wheel lug nuts, raise the vehicle and support it securely on jackstands. Remove the wheel. Drain the transaxle lubricant (see Chapter 1).

4   Disconnect the damper fork from the shock absorber assembly and the lower control arm (see Chapter 10).

5   Separate the lower control arm from the steering knuckle (see Chapter 10). Now remove the driveaxle/hub nut.

6   Swing the knuckle/hub assembly out (away from the vehicle) until the end of the driveaxle is free of the hub **(see illustration)**. **Note:** *If the driveaxle splines stick in the hub, tap on the end of the driveaxle with a plastic hammer.* Support the outer end of the driveaxle with a piece of wire to avoid unnecessary strain on the inner CV joint.

7   Carefully pry the inner end of the driveaxle from the transaxle - or, on Integra models, the intermediate shaft - using a large screwdriver or prybar positioned between the transaxle or bearing support and the CV joint housing **(see illustrations)**. Support the CV

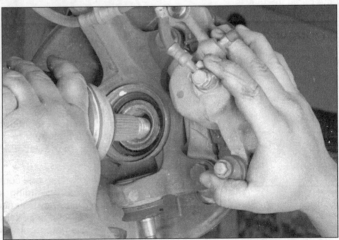

11.6 Swing the hub/knuckle out (away from the vehicle) and pull the driveaxle from the hub

11.7a Use a large screwdriver or a prybar to pop the inner end of the driveaxle from the transaxle, or . . .

11.7b . . . if you're removing the left driveaxle from an Integra model, insert the prybar between the intermediate shaft bearing and the driveaxle to pop it loose

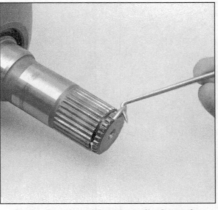

11.8a Pry the old spring clip from the inner end of the driveaxle with a small screwdriver or awl

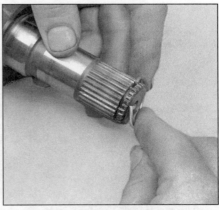

11.8b To install the new spring clip, start one end in the groove and work the clip over the shaft end, into the groove

joints and carefully remove the driveaxle from the vehicle. To prevent damage to the intermediate shaft seal or the differential seal, hold the inner CV joint horizontal until the driveaxle is clear of the intermediate shaft or transaxle.

Installation

Refer to illustrations 11.8a and 11.8b

8   Pry the old spring clip from the inner end of the driveaxle and install a new one **(see illustrations)**. Lubricate the differential or intermediate shaft seal with multi-purpose grease and raise the driveaxle into position while supporting the CV joints.

9   Insert the splined end of the inner CV joint into the differential side gear (or, on Integra models, the intermediate shaft) and make sure the spring clip locks in its groove.

10   Apply a light coat of multi-purpose grease to the outer CV joint splines, pull out on the strut/steering knuckle assembly and install the stub axle into the hub.

11   Insert the stud of the lower control arm balljoint into the steering knuckle and tighten the nut (see the torque specifications in Chapter 10). Be sure to use a new cotter pin. Install the damper fork (see Chapter 10).

12   Install the driveaxle/hub nut (and, if applicable, a new locking tab washer). Tighten the hub nut securely, but don't try to tighten it to the actual torque specification until you've lowered the vehicle to the ground.

13   Grasp the inner CV joint housing (not the driveaxle) and pull out to make sure the driveaxle has seated securely in the transaxle.

14   Install the wheel and lug nuts, then lower the vehicle.

15   Tighten the lug nuts to the torque listed in the Chapter 1 Specifications. Tighten the hub nut to the torque listed in this Chapter's Specifications. Using a hammer and punch, stake the nut to the groove in the driveaxle. If the hub nut uses a locking tab, be sure to bend the tabs up against the nut. Install the wheel cover (if applicable).

16   Refill the transaxle with the recommended type and amount of lubricant (see Chapter 1).

12   Intermediate shaft (Integra models) - removal and installation

Removal

Refer to illustration 12.5

1   Loosen the left (driver's side) front wheel lug nuts, raise the front of the vehicle and support it securely on jackstands. Remove the wheel.

2   Drain the transaxle lubricant (see Chapter 1).

3   Separate the left lower control arm from the steering knuckle (see Chapter 10).

4   Pry the inner CV joint housing from the intermediate shaft. Position the driveaxle out of the way and hang it with a piece of wire. Do not allow it to hang unsupported, as the outer CV joint may be damaged.

5   Remove the three bearing support-to-engine block bolts **(see illustration)** and slide the intermediate shaft out of the transaxle. Be careful not to damage the differential seal when pulling the shaft out.

6   Check the support bearing for smooth operation by turning the shaft while holding the bearing. If you feel any roughness, take the bearing support to a dealer service department or other repair shop to have a new bearing installed. To do the job at home, you'd need specialized tools.

Installation

7   Lubricate the lips of the differential seal with multi-purpose grease. Carefully guide the intermediate shaft into the differential side gear then install the mounting bolts through the bearing support. Tighten the bolts to the torque listed in this Chapter's Specifications.

8   Install a new spring clip on the inner CV joint **(see illustrations 11.8a and 11.8b)** and seat the driveaxle into the intermediate shaft splines.

9   Connect the lower control arm to the steering knuckle and tighten the balljoint stud nut to the torque listed in the Chapter 10 Specifications.

10   Install the wheel and lug nuts, lower the vehicle and tighten the lug nuts to the torque listed in the Chapter 1 Specifications.

11   Refill the transaxle with the proper type and amount of lubricant (see Chapter 1).

8

12.5 Location of the intermediate shaft bearing support bolts (arrows)

13.3a Cut off the boot clamps and discard them - don't try to re-use old clamps

13.3b Slide the boot down the driveaxle, out of the way

13 Driveaxle boot - replacement

Note 1: *If the CV joints are worn, indicating the need for an overhaul (usually due to torn boots), explore all options before beginning the job. Complete rebuilt driveaxles are available on an exchange basis, which eliminates much time and work. If you decide to rebuild a CV joint, check on the cost and availability of parts before disassembling the driveaxle.*

Note 2: *Some auto parts stores carry "split" type replacement boots, which can be installed without removing the driveaxle from the vehicle. This is a convenient alternative; however, the driveaxle should be removed and the CV joint disassembled and cleaned to ensure the joint is free from contaminants such as moisture and dirt which will accelerate CV joint wear.*

1   Remove the driveaxle from the vehicle (see Section 11).

2   Mount the driveaxle in a vise. The jaws of the vise should be lined with wood or rags to prevent damage to the driveaxle.

Inner CV joint and boot

Disassembly

Refer to illustrations 13.3a, 13.3b and 13.6

3   If you have any doubts about the condition of the outer boot this would be a good time to replace it as well. Cut off both boot clamps and slide the boot towards the center of the driveaxle **(see illustrations)**.

4   Scribe or paint alignment marks on the outer race and the tri-pot bearing assembly so they can be returned to their original position, then slide the outer race off the tri-pot bearing assembly.

5   Remove the snap-ring from the end of the axleshaft.

6   Secure the bearing rollers with tape, then remove the tri-pot bearing assembly from the axleshaft with a brass drift and a hammer **(see illustration)**. Remove the tape, but don't let the rollers fall off and get mixed up.

7   Remove the stop-ring, slide the old boot off the driveaxle and discard it.

Inspection

8   Clean the old grease from the outer race and the tri-pot bearing assembly. Carefully disassemble each section of the tri-pot assembly, one at a time so as not to mix up the parts, and clean the needle bearings with solvent.

9   Inspect the rollers, tri-pot, bearings and outer race for scoring, pitting or other signs of abnormal wear, which will warrant the replacement of the inner CV joint.

Reassembly

Refer to illustrations 13.10a, 13.10b, 13.12, 13.13, 13.14, 13.15, 13.16, 13.17a and 13.17b

10   Wrap the splines of the axleshaft with tape to avoid damaging the new boot, then slide the boot onto the axleshaft **(see illustration)**. Remove the tape and slide the inner stop-ring into place **(see illustration)**.

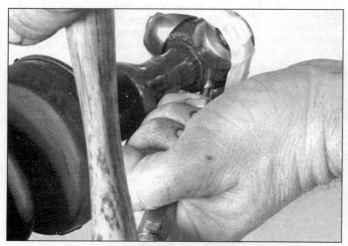

13.6 Secure the bearing rollers with tape and drive the tri-pot off the shaft with a hammer and brass drift, then remove the stop-ring

13.10a Wrap the splined area of the axleshaft with tape to prevent damage to the boot when installing it

13.10b Install the stop-ring on the axleshaft, making sure it seats in its groove

13.12 Install the tri-pot assembly on the axleshaft, then install the snap-ring

13.13 Use plenty of CV joint grease to hold the needle bearings in place when you install the roller assemblies on the tri-pot, and make sure you put each roller in its original position

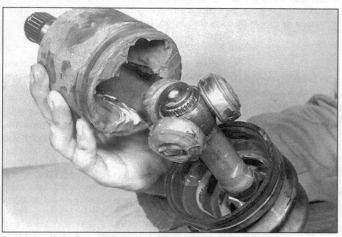

13.14 Pack the outer race with grease and slide it over the tri-pot assembly - make sure the match marks on the outer race and tri-pot line up

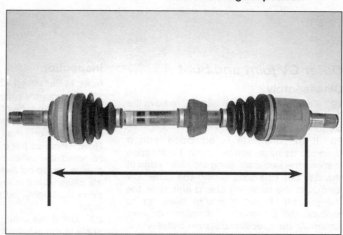

13.15 Before tightening the boot clamps, adjust the driveaxle length to the dimension listed in this Chapter's Specifications

11   Slide the tri-pot assembly onto the axle-shaft.
12   Install the outer snap-ring **(see illustration)**.

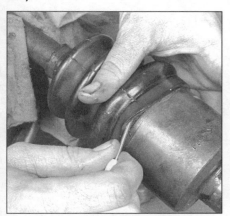

13.16 Equalize the pressure inside the boot by inserting a small, dull screwdriver between the boot and the outer race

13   Apply a coat of CV joint grease to the inner bearing surfaces to hold the needle bearings in place when reassembling the tri-pot assembly **(see illustration)**. Make sure

13.17a To install the new clamps, bend the tang down . . .

each roller is installed on the same post as before. **Note:** *If the rollers are equipped with a flat, rectangular shaped surface, make sure the flat sides are positioned closest to the driveaxle.*
14   Pack the outer race with half of the grease furnished with the new boot and place the remainder in the boot. Install the outer race **(see illustration)**. Make sure the marks you made on the tri-pot assembly and the outer race are aligned.
15   Seat the boot in the grooves in the outer race and the axleshaft, then adjust the driveaxle to the proper length **(see illustration)**.
16   With the driveaxle set to the proper length, equalize the pressure in the boot by inserting a blunt screwdriver between the boot and the outer race **(see illustration)**. Don't damage the boot with the tool.
17   Install and tighten the new boot clamps **(see illustrations)**.
18   Install the driveaxle assembly (see Section 11).

8

13.17b . . . and flatten the tabs to hold it in place

13.23 After the old grease has been rinsed away and the solvent has been blown out with compressed air, rotate the outer joint assembly through its full range of motion and inspect the bearing surfaces for wear and damage - if any of the ball bearings, the race or the cage look damaged, replace the driveaxle and outer joint assembly

Outer CV joint and boot

Disassembly

19   Following Steps 3 through 7, remove the inner CV joint from the driveaxle and disassemble it.

20   If the driveaxle is equipped with a dynamic damper, scribe or paint a location mark on the axleshaft along the outer edge of the damper (the side facing the outer CV joint), cut the retaining clamp and slide the damper off. **Note:** *If you're planning to replace the axleshaft and outer CV joint assembly, the specified distance between the inner CV joint boot and the dynamic damper is listed in this Chapter's Specifications.*

21   Cut the boot clamps from the outer CV joint. Slide the boot off the shaft. **Note:** *The outer CV joint can't be disassembled or removed from the shaft.*

Inspection

Refer to illustration 13.23

22   Thoroughly wash the inner and outer CV joints in clean solvent and blow them dry with compressed air, if available. **Warning:** *Wear eye protection when using compressed air.* **Note:** *Because the outer joint can't be disassembled, it is difficult to wash away all the old grease and to rid the bearing of solvent once it's clean. But it is imperative that the job be done thoroughly, so take your time and do it right.*

23   Bend the outer CV joint housing at an angle to the axleshaft to expose the bearings, inner race and cage **(see illustration)**. Inspect the bearing surfaces for signs of wear. If the bearings are damaged or worn, replace the driveaxle.

Reassembly

24   Slide the new outer boot onto the axle-

shaft. It's a good idea to wrap tape around the splines of the shaft to prevent damage to the boot **(see illustration 13.10a)**. When the boot is in position, add the specified amount of grease (included in the boot replacement kit) to the outer joint and the boot (pack the joint with as much grease as it will hold and put the rest into the boot). Slide the boot on the rest of the way and install the new clamps **(see illustrations 13.17a and 13.17b)**.

25   Slide the dynamic damper, if equipped, onto the shaft. Make sure its outer edge is aligned with the previously applied mark. **Note:** *If you're using a new axleshaft and outer CV joint assembly, the specified distance between the inner CV joint boot and the dynamic damper is listed in this Chapter's Specifications.* Install a new retaining clamp.

26   Clean and reassemble the inner CV joint by following Steps 8 through 17, then install the driveaxle as outlined in Section 11.

Chapter 9 Brakes

Contents

Specifications

General

Brake pedal
Freeplay
Civic ... 1/16 to 3/16 inch
Integra ... 1/16 to 13/64 inch
Height
Manual transaxle
Civic ... 6-1/32 inches
Integra ... 6-5/16 inches
Automatic transaxle/CVT
Civic ... 6-5/16 inches
Integra ... 6-1/2 inches
Parking brake lever travel ... See Chapter 1
Power brake booster pushrod-to-master cylinder piston
clearance (with a vacuum of 20 in-Hg applied to booster) ... 0.0 to 0.020 inch

Disc brakes

Brake pad minimum thickness ... See Chapter 1
Disc minimum thickness ... Refer to minimum thickness cast into disc
Thickness variation (parallelism) ... No more than 0.0006 inch
Runout limit ... 0.004 inch

Drum brakes

Brake lining minimum thickness ... See Chapter 1
Drum diameter ... Refer to maximum diameter cast into drum

Torque specifications

Ft-lbs (unless otherwise indicated)

Brake hose-to-caliper banjo bolt (front or rear) ... 25
Front caliper bolts
Civic (refer to the numbers on the caliper body for identification)
Type 5410 caliper ... 24
Type 2056 caliper
Upper bolt ... 25
Lower bolt ... 20
Integra
1994 through 1997 ... 23
1998 ... 24
Front caliper mounting bracket bolts ... 80
Rear caliper bolts ... 17
Rear caliper bracket bolts (Integra)
1994 through 1997 ... 28
1998 ... 41
Wheel cylinder nuts ... 84 in-lbs
Brake booster mounting nuts ... 108 in-lbs
Master cylinder mounting nuts ... 132 in-lbs

9

1   General information

General

All vehicles covered by this manual are equipped with hydraulically operated power assisted brake systems. All front brake systems are disc type (see illustration). Some models use drum type brakes at the rear, others are equipped with rear disc brakes (see illustration).

All brakes are self-adjusting. The front and rear disc brakes automatically compensate for pad wear, while the rear drum brakes incorporate an adjustment mechanism which is activated as the brakes are applied, either through the pedal or the parking brake lever.

The hydraulic system is a diagonally split design, meaning there are separate circuits for the left front/right rear and the right front/left rear brakes. If one circuit fails, the other circuit will remain functional and a warning indicator will light up on the dashboard when a substantial amount of brake fluid is lost, showing that a failure has occurred.

Master cylinder

The master cylinder is bolted to the power brake booster, which is mounted on the driver's side of the firewall. To locate the master cylinder, look for the large fluid reservoir on top. The fluid reservoir is a removable plastic cup, secured to the master cylinder by a clamp.

The master cylinder is designed for the "split system" mentioned earlier and has separate piston assemblies for each circuit.

Proportioning valve

The proportioning valve assembly is located on the firewall. On vehicles equipped with the Anti-lock Brake System (ABS), it's an integral part of the modulator/solenoid unit, which is located on the right (passenger's) side of the engine compartment.

The proportioning valve regulates the hydraulic pressure to the rear brakes during heavy braking to eliminate rear wheel lock-up. Under normal braking conditions, it allows full pressure to the rear brake system until a predetermined pedal pressure is reached. Above that point, the pressure to the rear brakes is limited.

The proportioning valve is not serviceable - if a problem develops with the valve, it must be replaced as an assembly.

Power brake booster

The power brake booster, which uses engine manifold vacuum and atmospheric pressure to provide assistance to the hydraulically operated brakes, is mounted on the firewall in the engine compartment.

Parking brake

A parking brake lever inside the vehicle operates a single front cable attached to a pair of rear cables, each of which is connected to its respective rear brake. When the parking brake lever is pulled up on drum brake models, each rear cable pulls on a lever attached to the brake shoe assembly, causing the shoes to expand against the drum. When the lever is pulled on models with rear disc brakes, the rear cables pull on levers that are attached to screw-type actuators in the caliper housings, which apply force to the caliper pistons, clamping the brake pads against the brake disc.

Precautions

There are some general cautions and warnings involving the brake system on these vehicles:

a) *Use only brake fluid conforming to DOT 3 specifications.*

b) *The brake pads and linings may contain asbestos fibers which are hazardous to your health if inhaled. Whenever you work on brake system components, clean all parts with brake system cleaner. Do not allow the fine dust to become airborne.*

c) *Safety should be paramount whenever any servicing of the brake components is performed. Do not use parts or fasteners which are not in perfect condition, and be sure that all clearances and torque specifications are adhered to. If you are at all unsure about a certain procedure, seek professional advice. Upon completion of any brake system work, test the brakes carefully in a controlled area before putting the vehicle into normal service.*

d) *No part of the brake hydraulic system on a vehicle equipped with an Anti-lock Brake System (ABS) should be disconnected, as special tools are required to properly bleed the system. Take the vehicle to a dealer service department or other qualified repair shop for repairs which require opening of the system.*

e) *If a problem is suspected in the brake system, don't drive the vehicle until it's fixed.*

2   Anti-lock Brake System (ABS) - general information and trouble codes

General information

In a conventional braking system, if you press the brake pedal too hard, the wheels can "lock up" (stop turning) and the vehicle can go into a skid. If the wheels lock up, you can lose control of the vehicle. The Anti-lock Brake System (ABS) prevents the wheels from locking up by modulating (pulsing on and off) the pressure of the brake fluid at each caliper.

The Anti-lock Brake System has two basic subsystems: One is an electrical system and the other is hydraulic. The electrical half has four "gear pulsers," four wheel sensors, a computer and an electrical circuit connecting all the components. The hydraulic part of the system consists of a

1.1   Typical front disc brake component layout

1	*Brake hose*	*3*	*Disc*
2	*Caliper*	*4*	*Caliper pin*

1.2   Typical rear disc brake component layout

1	*Caliper*	*3*	*Brake hose*
2	*Caliper bolts*	*4*	*Disc*

solenoid/modulator, the disc brake calipers and the hydraulic fluid lines between the solenoid/modulator and the calipers.

In principle, the system is pretty simple: Each wheel has a wheel sensor monitoring a gear pulser (a ring with evenly-spaced raised ridges cast into its circumference). The wheel sensor "counts" the ridges of the gear pulser as they pass by, converts this information into an electrical output and transmits it back to the computer. The computer constantly "samples" the voltage inputs from all four wheel sensors and compares them to each other. As long as the gear pulsers at all four wheels are rotating at the same speed, the Anti-lock Brake System is inactive. But when a wheel locks up, the voltage signal from that wheel sensor deviates from the signals coming from the other wheels. So the computer "knows" the wheel is locking up. It sends an electrical signal to the solenoid/modulator assembly, which releases the brake fluid pressure to the brake caliper at that wheel. As soon as the wheel unlocks and resumes turning at the same rate of speed as the other wheels, its wheel sensor voltage output once again matches the output of the other wheels and the computer deactivates the signal to the solenoid/modulator.

In reality, the Anti-lock Brake System is far more complex than it sounds, so we don't recommend that you attempt to diagnose or service it. If the Anti-lock Brake System on your vehicle develops problems, take it to a dealer service department or other qualified shop.

ABS trouble codes

1   Normally, the ABS indicator light should come on when the engine is started, then go off immediately. Under certain conditions, however, the indicator light may remain on. If this occurs, the ABS computer has stored a diagnostic trouble code because it has detected a problem in the ABS system. You can have the ABS indicator display the diagnostic trouble code as follows:

2   Unplug the service check connector from the connector cover located underneath the glove box (see Chapter 6).

3   Bridge the two terminals of the service check connector with a jumper wire.

Civic and 1998 Integra models

4   Turn the ignition switch to On, but don't start the engine. Two seconds after you turn on the ignition, the ABS computer will begin displaying any stored diagnostic trouble code(s) by blinking the ABS indicator light on and off. The sequence begins with a 3.6-second pause, followed by a series of blinks representing the code, followed by a one-second pause, followed by another series of blinks representing the sub-code (if any), followed by a five-second pause, then the next blinks, another five second pause, the next main code/sub-code combination, etc. The ABS computer can indicate any number of codes.

1997 and earlier Integra models

Refer to illustration 2.6

5   Turn the ignition switch to On, but don't start the engine. Two seconds after you turn on the ignition, the ABS computer will begin displaying any stored diagnostic trouble code(s) by blinking the ABS indicator light on and off. The sequence begins with a two-second pause, followed by a series of blinks representing the main code, followed by a one-second pause, followed by another series of blinks representing the sub-code (if any), followed by a five-second pause, then the next main code/sub-code blinks, another five second pause, the next main code/sub-code combination, etc. The ABS computer can indicate up to three codes.

6   If you miscount, turn the ignition switch to Off, then back to On, to recycle the ABS computer. Record the number of main code and sub-code blinks and compare them to the accompanying illustration (**see illustration**). Most ABS repairs must be performed by a dealer service department or other qualified automotive repair facility.

Civic and 1998 Integra models

7   Record the number of code blinks and refer to the following code chart.

8   The code chart lists the ABS codes for the most common Anti Lock Brake System problems.

Erasing diagnostic codes

10   Diagnostic codes must be cleared from the computer memory after the repairs have been performed.

TROUBLE CODE		MALFUNCTIONING COMPONENT/ SYSTEM	WHEELS-AFFECTED				OTHER COMPONENTS POSSIBLY INVOLVED
MAIN CODE	SUB-CODE		FRONT RIGHT	FRONT LEFT	REAR RIGHT	REAR LEFT	
1	—	Pump motor over-run	—	—	—	—	Pressure switch
	2	Pump motor circuit problem	—	—	—	—	Motor relay, Unit fuse, Motor fuse
	3	High pressure leakage	—	—	—	—	Solenoid
	4	Pressure switch	—	—	—	—	
	8	Accumulator gas leakage	—	—	—	—	
2	1	Parking brake switch-related problem	—	—	—	—	Brake fluid level switch BRAKE light
3	1	Pulser(s)	O				
	2			O			
	4				O	O	
	12	Different diameter tire					
4	1	Speed sensor	O				
	2			O			
	4				O		
	8					O	
5	—	Speed sensor(s)			O	O	Modulator
	4				O		
	8					O	
6	—	Fail-safe relay (Open, short)	—	—	—	—	Front or rear fail-safe relay
	1		—	—	—	—	Front fail-safe relay
	4		—	—	—	—	Rear fail-safe relay
7	1	Solenoid related problem (Open)	O				ABS B1 fuse
	2			O			Front fail-safe relay
	4				O	O	Rear fail-safe relay
8	1	ABS control unit problem	Faulty ABS unit				
	2						
	4						

2118-9-2.5 HAYNES

2.6 1997 and earlier model Integra ABS trouble codes

9

1997 and earlier Integra models

11   Clear the diagnostic codes by removing the jumper wire from the electrical connector, then remove the 15 amp ABS B2 fuse (located in the engine compartment fuse block) for at least three seconds. Reinstall the fuse and plug in the service check connector.

Civic and 1998 Integra models

12   With the jumper wire still installed and the ignition off, press on the brake pedal and then turn the ignition on. When the ABS indicator light goes out, release the brake pedal until the light comes on again and press on the brake pedal. Hold the pedal down until the indicator light goes out and release the pedal.
13   The indicator light should blink twice to indicate that the codes are erased. Turn off the ignition, remove the jumper wire and plug in the service check connector.

ABS Trouble Codes (Civic and 1998 Integra models)

Code	Probable cause
11	Right front wheel sensor (open/short to body ground or short to power)
12	Right front wheel sensor (electrical noise or intermittent interruption)
13	Left front wheel sensor (open/short to body ground or short to power)
14	Left front wheel sensor (electrical noise or intermittent interruption)
15	Right rear wheel sensor (open/short to body ground or short to power)
16	Right rear wheel sensor (electrical noise or intermittent interruption)
17	Left rear wheel sensor (open/short to body ground or short to power)
18	Left rear wheel sensor (electrical noise or intermittent interruption)
21	Right front pulser
22	Left front pulser
23	Right, rear pulser
24	Left rear pulser
31	Right front inlet solenoid
32	Right front outlet solenoid
33	Left front inlet solenoid
34	Left front outlet solenoid
35	Right rear inlet solenoid
36	Right rear outlet solenoid
37	Left rear inlet solenoid
38	Left, rear outlet solenoid
41	Right front wheel lock
42	Left front wheel lock
43	Right rear wheel lock
44	Left rear wheel lock
51	Motor lock
52	Motor remains OFF
53	Motor remains ON
54	Fail safe relay
61	Low ignition voltage
62	High ignition voltage
71	Different diameter tire
81	Central Processing Unit and ROM/RAM diagnostics

3   Disc brake pads - replacement

Warning: *Disc brake pads must be replaced on both front wheels at the same time - never replace the pads on only one wheel. Also, the dust created by the brake system may contain asbestos, which is harmful to your health. Never blow it out with compressed air and don't inhale any of it. An approved filtering mask should be worn when working on the brakes. Do not, under any circumstances, use petroleum-based solvents to clean brake parts. Use brake system cleaner only!*
Note: *This procedure applies to front and rear disc brakes.*

1   Remove the cap from the brake fluid reservoir.
2   Loosen the wheel lug nuts, raise the front, or rear, of the vehicle and support it securely on jackstands.
3   Remove the front, or rear, wheels. Work on one brake assembly at a time, using the assembled brake for reference if necessary.
4   Inspect the brake disc carefully as outlined in Section 5. If machining is necessary, follow the information in that Section to remove the disc, at which time the calipers and pads can be removed as well.

Front pads

Refer to illustrations 3.5 and 3.6a through 3.6p
5   Push the piston back into the bore to provide room for the new brake pads. A C-clamp can be used to accomplish this **(see illustration)**. As the piston is depressed to the bottom of the caliper bore, the fluid in the master cylinder will rise. Make sure it doesn't overflow. If necessary, siphon off some of the fluid.
6   Follow the accompanying illustrations, beginning with 3.6a, for the actual pad replacement procedure. Be sure to stay in order and read the caption under each illustration.

3.5 Using a large C-clamp, push the piston back into the caliper - note that one end of the clamp is on the back side of the caliper and the other end (screw end) is pressing on the outer brake pad

3.6a Before removing anything, spray the assembly with brake system cleaner to remove the dust produced by brake pad wear - DO NOT blow the dust off with compressed air!

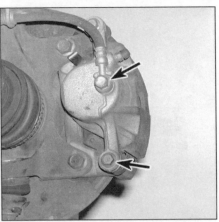

3.6b Remove the lower caliper bolt (lower arrow) (upper arrow points to banjo fitting for brake hose, which should not be disconnected unless you're removing the caliper from the vehicle)

3.6c Swing the caliper up . . .

3.6d . . . and support it in this position

3.6e Remove the outer brake pad and shim

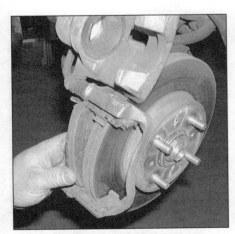

3.6f Remove the inner brake pad (some models don't have a shim on the inner pad)

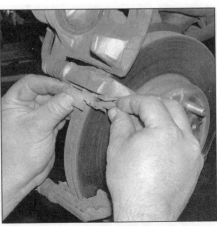

3.6g Remove and inspect the upper and lower brake pad retainer clips (upper clip shown); don't forget that the inner pad also has a pair of clips just like the two outer clips

3.6h The pad retainer clips should fit snugly into their respective grooves in the caliper mounting bracket; if they don't, replace them (lower outer clip shown)

9

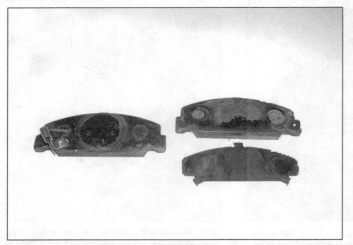

3.6i Inner pad (left) and outer pad and shim layout - some later Integra models have inner pad shims

3.6j Apply anti-squeal compound to the back of the pads, then install the shim(s)

3.6k Install the new inner pad; make sure the "ears" on the upper and lower ends of the pad are fully engaged with their respective grooves and the pad retainer clips

3.6l Install the new outer pad and shim (if the new pad has no shim, take the old shim off the old pad and install it on the new outer pad)

3.6m Before installing the caliper, remove the caliper pin dust boots and inspect them for tears and cracks; if they're damaged, replace them

3.6n Clean off the upper caliper pin and coat it with high-temperature grease; do the same thing with the lower caliper retaining bolt (Note: *This applies to Civic models with long shoulder bolts and fixed upper pins only [type 2056 caliper]*)

3.6o Slide the caliper onto the upper locating pin like this, then swing the caliper down over the disc and new pads (if the piston hits the inner pad, depress the piston further into the caliper bore with your C-clamp)

3.6p Install the lower bolt and tighten it to the torque listed in this Chapter's Specifications

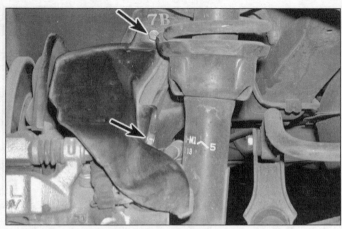

3.7a Remove the caliper shield bolts (arrows) and the shield

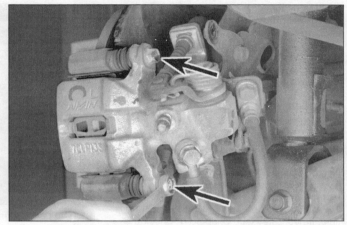

3.7b Remove the two caliper mounting bolts (arrows) . . .

3.7c . . . and lift the caliper from its mounting bracket; hang the caliper out of the way with a piece of wire (see illustration 3.6d) - don't let it hang by the brake hose

3.7d Remove the outer pad and shim

3.7e Remove the inner pad and shim

Rear pads

Refer to illustrations 3.7a through 3.7f, 3.8 and 3.12

7   Follow the accompanying illustrations, beginning with 3.7a, for the pad replacement procedure. Be sure to stay in order and read the caption under each illustration. When you have completed the Steps described in the accompanying photos, proceed to Step 8.

8   Apply a thin coat of disc brake anti-squeal compound, in accordance with the manufacturer's recommendations, on the backing plates of the new pads **(see illustration)**.

9   Install the shims onto their respective pads.

10   Install the pad retainers in the caliper mounting bracket. Lubricate the retainers with a thin film of silicone grease.

11   Install the new pads and shims to the caliper mounting bracket.

12   Retract the piston by engaging the tips of a pair of needle-nose pliers with two of the grooves in the top of the piston and turning it clockwise until it bottoms in the bore **(see illustration)**. Now, rotate the piston out until one of its grooves is aligned with the tab on the inner brake pad when you install the caliper. You may have to adjust the piston

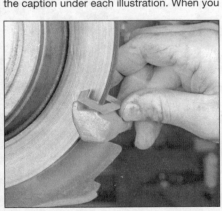

3.7f Remove the brake pad retainers from the caliper (lower retainer shown, upper retainer identical)

3.8 Before installing the brake pads, apply a coat of disc brake anti-squeal compound to the backing plates of the pads - follow the manufacturer's instructions on the label

3.12 To provide clearance for the new brake pads, back the piston into the caliper bore by rotating it with a pair of needle-nose pliers

9

position by turning it back and forth to fit the tab in the groove. If the piston dust boot becomes distorted when the piston is turned, turn the piston in the opposite direction to restore the shape of the boot, but make sure the groove is aligned properly.

13   Install the caliper protector.

Front or rear pads

14   Install the wheel and lug nuts, lower the vehicle and tighten the lug nuts to the torque specified in Chapter 1.

15   Apply and release the brake pedal and (if you replaced rear pads) the hand brake lever several times to bring the pads into contact with the brake discs.

16   Check the brake fluid level and add fluid, if necessary (see Chapter 1). Check the operation of the brakes in an isolated area before driving the vehicle in traffic.

---

4   Disc brake caliper - removal and installation

Warning: *Dust created by the brake system may contain asbestos, which is harmful to your health. Never blow it out with compressed air and don't inhale any of it. An approved filtering mask should be worn when working on the brakes. Do not, under any circumstances, use petroleum-based solvents to clean brake parts. Use brake system cleaner only!*

Removal

Refer to illustrations 4.2 and 4.3

1   Loosen - but don't remove - the lug nuts on the front, or rear wheels. Raise the front or rear of the vehicle and place it securely on jackstands. Remove the wheels.

2   If you're removing a rear caliper, remove the cotter pin from the clevis pin that connects the parking brake cable to the parking

4.2 The parking brake cable is attached to the rear caliper by a clevis pin that is secured by a cotter pin

brake lever **(see illustration)**. Pull out the pin and detach the cable.

3   Disconnect the brake line from the caliper **(see illustration 3.6b)** and plug it to keep contaminants out of the brake system and to prevent losing any more brake fluid than is necessary **(see illustration)**.

4   Refer to Section 3 and remove the caliper (it's part of the brake pad replacement procedure).

Installation

5   Install the caliper by reversing the removal procedure. Remember to replace the sealing washer on either side of the brake line fitting (they should be included with the rebuild kit).

6   Bleed the brake system (see Section 11).

7   Install the wheels, hand tighten the wheel lug nuts, remove the safety stands and lower the vehicle. Tighten the wheel lug nuts to the torque listed in the Chapter 1 Specifications.

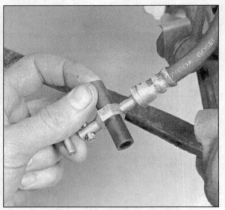

4.3 Using a short piece of rubber hose of the appropriate diameter, plug the brake line banjo fitting like this

5   Brake disc - inspection, removal and installation

Note: *This procedure applies to both the front and (on vehicles so equipped) rear brake discs.*

Inspection

Refer to illustrations 5.3, 5.4a, 5.4b, 5.5a and 5.5b

1   Loosen the wheel lugs nuts, raise the vehicle and support it securely on jackstands. Remove the wheel and install two lug nuts with 3 mm thick washers under them to hold the disc in place (if the two disc retaining screws are still in place, this will be unnecessary). If you're checking the rear disc, release the parking brake.

2   Remove the brake caliper (see Section 4). It's not necessary to disconnect the brake hose. After removing the caliper bolts, suspend the caliper out of the way with a piece of wire.

5.3 The brake pads on this vehicle were obviously neglected, as they wore down to the rivets; the rivets then cut deep grooves into the disc, and now the disc must be replaced

5.4a Make sure the disc retaining screws or lug nuts are tight, then rotate the disc and check the runout with a dial indicator - if the reading exceeds the maximum allowable runout limit, the disc will have to be machined or replaced

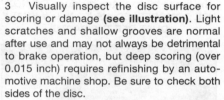

5.4b Using a swirling motion, remove the glaze from the disc with emery cloth or sandpaper

5.5a The minimum allowable thickness is stamped into the disc (typical)

5.5b A micrometer is used to measure disc thickness

3   Visually inspect the disc surface for scoring or damage **(see illustration)**. Light scratches and shallow grooves are normal after use and may not always be detrimental to brake operation, but deep scoring (over 0.015 inch) requires refinishing by an automotive machine shop. Be sure to check both sides of the disc.

4   If you've noted pulsation during braking, suspect disc runout. To check disc runout, place a dial indicator at a point about 1/2-inch from the outer edge of the disc **(see illustration)**. Set the indicator to zero and turn the disc. The indicator reading should not exceed the specified allowable runout limit. If it does, have the disc refinished by an automotive machine shop. **Note:** *Professionals recommend that the discs be resurfaced regardless of the dial indicator reading, as this will impart a smooth finish and ensure a perfectly flat surface, eliminating any brake pedal pulsation or other undesirable symptoms related to questionable discs. At the very least, if you elect not to have the discs resurfaced, remove the glazing from the surface with emery cloth or sandpaper using a swirling motion* **(see illustration)**.

5   It is absolutely critical that the disc not be machined to a thickness less than the minimum allowable thickness. The minimum wear (or discard) thickness is stamped on the disc **(see illustration)**. The disc thickness can be checked with a micrometer **(see illustration)**.

Removal

Refer to illustrations 5.6a, 5.6b, 5.7a, 5.7b and 5.7c

6   Remove the two caliper mounting bracket-to-steering knuckle bolts **(see illustration)** or, on rear calipers, the bracket-to-trailing arm bolts **(see illustration)**, and remove the mounting bracket.

7   Remove the two lug nuts which were installed to hold the disc in place, or the two disc retaining screws, if present **(see illustration)** and remove the disc from the hub. If the disc is stuck to the hub and won't come off, thread two bolts into the holes provided **(see illustration)** and tighten them. Alternate between the bolts, turning them a couple of turns at a time, until the disc is free **(see illustration)**.

5.6a Before you can remove the front disc, you'll have to remove these caliper mounting bracket-to-steering knuckle bolts (arrows) and the bracket

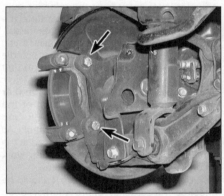

5.6b To remove the rear disc, remove the caliper-to-trailing arm bolts (arrows), then remove the caliper mounting bracket

5.7a If the disc retaining screws are stuck, use an impact screwdriver to loosen them

5.7b If the disc is stuck, thread two bolts into the disc and tighten them to force the disc off the hub

5.7c As you remove the disc, make sure you don't damage the threads on the studs for the wheel lug nuts

9

6.2 If the drum is hard to pull off, thread a pair of 8 mm bolts into the holes provided and press the drum off

6.4a Right rear drum brake assembly

6.4b Before removing anything, clean the brake assembly with brake cleaner and allow it to dry - position a drain pan under the brake to catch the residue - DO NOT USE COMPRESSED AIR TO BLOW BRAKE DUST OFF THE PARTS!

Installation

8   Place the disc in position over the threaded studs. Install the disc retaining screws.

9   Install the caliper mounting bracket, brake pads and caliper over the disc. Tighten the mounting bracket and caliper bolts to the torque listed in this Chapter's Specifications.

10   Install the wheel, then lower the vehicle to the ground. Depress the brake pedal a few times to bring the brake pads into contact with the disc. Bleeding of the system will not be necessary unless the fluid hose was disconnected from the caliper. Check the operation of the brakes carefully before placing the vehicle into normal service.

6   Drum brake shoes - replacement

Refer to illustrations 6.2, 6.4a through 6.4r and 6.5

Warning: *Drum brake shoes must be replaced on both wheels at the same time - never replace the shoes on only one wheel. Also, the dust created by the brake system may contain asbestos, which is harmful to your health. Never blow it out with compressed air and don't inhale any of it. An approved filtering mask should be worn when working on the brakes. Do not, under any circumstances, use petroleum-based solvents to clean brake parts. Use brake system cleaner only!*

Caution: *Whenever the brake shoes are replaced, the return and hold-down springs should also be replaced. Due to the continuous heating/cooling cycle that the springs are subjected to, they lose their tension over a period of time and may allow the shoes to drag on the drum and wear at a much faster rate than normal.*

1   Loosen the wheel lug nuts, raise the rear of the vehicle and support it securely on jackstands. Block the front wheels to keep the vehicle from rolling. Remove the rear wheels. Release the parking brake.

2   Remove the brake drum. It should sim-

ply pull straight off the hub. If the drum won't come off, tap it carefully with a soft-faced mallet, or screw a couple of 8.0 mm bolts into the tapped holes **(see illustration)**. If it still won't budge, the shoes have probably carved wear grooves into the drum. To get the drum off, you'll have to retract them. Remove the rubber plug in the backing plate. Use one screwdriver inserted through the hole in the backing plate to hold the self-adjuster lever away from the adjuster bolt, then use another screwdriver to rotate the adjuster bolt until the drum can be removed.

3   Replacing the shoes is a lot easier if you remove the rear wheel bearing cap, spindle nut and washer, and slide off the hub unit (see Chapter 10).

4   Follow **illustrations 6.4a through 6.4r** for the inspection and replacement of the brake shoes. Be sure to stay in order and read the caption under each illustration. All four rear brake shoes must be replaced at the same time, but to avoid mixing up parts, work on only one brake assembly at a time.

5   Before reinstalling the drum it should be checked for cracks, score marks, deep scratches and hard spots, which will appear as small discolored areas. If the hard spots

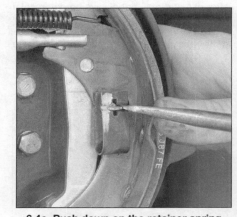

6.4c Push down on the retainer spring with a screwdriver, then turn the tension pin to align its blade with the slot in the retainer spring - the spring should pop off (repeat this on the other spring)

cannot be removed with sandpaper or emery cloth or if any of the other conditions listed above exist, the drum must be taken to an

6.4d Pull the shoe assembly away from the backing plate (hub removed for clarity) . . .

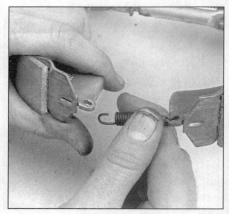

6.4e . . . and unhook the return spring

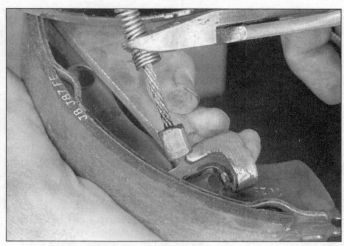

6.4f Pull back on the parking brake cable spring and squeeze the pliers just enough to grip the cable, holding the spring in the compressed position (diagonal cutting pliers are being used because they grip the cable well - be careful not to cut the cable); unhook the cable end from the parking brake lever

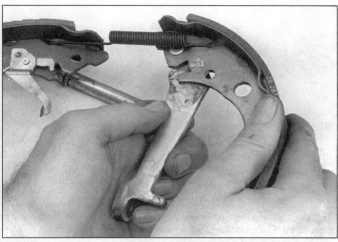

6.4g Swing the parking brake lever away from the trailing shoe, which will force the adjuster bolt clevis out of its groove in the shoe; the two shoes can now be separated

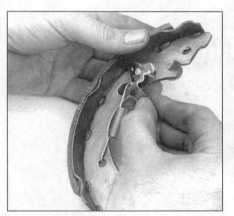

6.4h Remove the self-adjuster lever and spring from the leading shoe

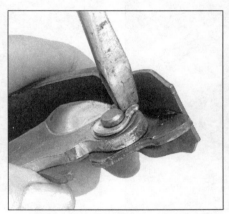

6.4i Pry open the parking brake lever retaining clip and separate the lever from the shoe; be careful not to lose the wave washer that is under the clip

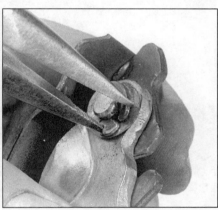

6.4j Put the new trailing shoe on the lever, place the wave washer over the pin, then install the retaining clip; crimp the ends of the clip together with a pair of needle-nose pliers

6.4k Clean the adjuster bolt and clevis, then lubricate the threads and ends with high-temperature grease

6.4l Connect the self-adjuster lever spring to the leading brake shoe, then insert the pin on the lever into its hole in the shoe

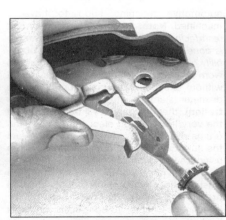

6.4m Insert the short clevis of the adjuster bolt into its slot in the leading shoe, making sure it catches the self-adjuster lever

9

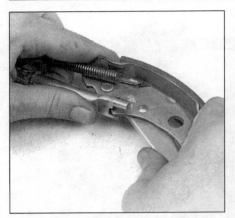

6.4n Connect the upper return spring between the two shoes, pry the lower ends of the shoes apart and insert the clevis at the other end of the adjuster bolt into the slot in the shoe; note the position of the stepped portion of the clevis opening

6.4o Lubricate the brake shoe contact areas on the backing plate with high-temperature grease

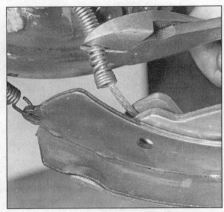

6.4p Compress the parking brake cable spring, hold it in position and connect the cable end to the parking brake lever (again, if you use diagonal cutting pliers, be careful not to cut or nick the cable)

6.4q Place the brake shoe assembly against the backing plate, engaging the upper ends of the shoes in the slots in the wheel cylinder pistons. Connect the lower return spring between the shoes

6.4r With the brake shoes in position on the backing plate, pass the tension pins through the holes in the backing plate and brake shoes, then install the retainer springs (see illustration 6.4c) - make sure the parking brake cable spring and the lower return spring are seated behind the anchor plate, as shown here

automotive machine shop to have it machined. **Note:** *Professionals recommend resurfacing the drums whenever a brake job is done. Resurfacing will eliminate the possibility of out-of-round drums.* If the drums are worn so much that they can't be resurfaced without exceeding the maximum allowable diameter (stamped into the drum) **(see illustration)**, then new ones will be required. At the very least, if you elect not to have the drums resurfaced, remove the glazing from the surface with sandpaper or emery cloth using a swirling motion.

6   Install the hub and bearing unit, the washer and a new spindle nut (if removed previously). Tighten the nut to the torque listed in the Chapter 10 Specifications. Install the brake drum.

7   Mount the wheel, install the lug nuts, then lower the vehicle. Tighten the lug nuts to the torque listed in the Chapter 1 Specifications.

8   Make a number of forward and reverse stops to adjust the brakes until satisfactory pedal action is obtained.

9   Check brake operation before driving the vehicle in traffic. **Warning:** *Do not operate the vehicle if you are in doubt about the effectiveness of the brake system.*

7   Wheel cylinder - removal and installation

Note: *If the wheel cylinders leak, they must be replaced with new ones - the manufacturer does not recommend rebuilding them.*

Removal

Refer to illustration 7.4

1   Raise the rear of the vehicle and support it securely on jackstands. Block the front wheels to keep the vehicle from rolling.

6.5 The maximum allowable diameter is cast into the drum (typical)

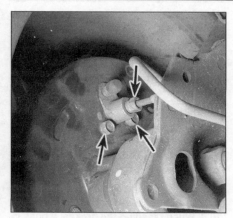

7.4 To remove the wheel cylinder, unscrew the brake line fitting (upper arrow), then remove the two wheel cylinder retaining bolts (lower arrows)

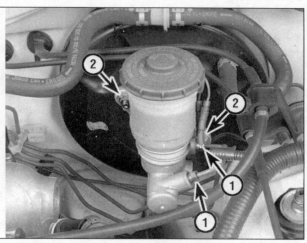

8.4 Use a flare-nut wrench to unscrew the threaded fittings (1) at the master cylinder - a regular wrench can round off the corners; to detach the master cylinder from the brake booster, unplug the electrical connector for the brake fluid warning switch, then remove the two nuts (2)

2   Remove the brake shoe assembly (see Section 6).
3   Remove all dirt and foreign material from around the wheel cylinder.
4   Unscrew the brake line fitting **(see illustration)**. Don't pull the brake line away from the wheel cylinder.
5   Remove the wheel cylinder mounting bolts.
6   Detach the wheel cylinder from the brake backing plate and place it on a clean workbench. Immediately plug the brake line to prevent fluid loss and contamination. Note: *If the brake shoe linings are contaminated with brake fluid, install new brake shoes and clean the drums with brake system cleaner.*

Installation

7   Apply RTV sealant to the mating surface of the wheel cylinder and the brake backing plate, place the cylinder in position and connect the brake line. Don't tighten the fitting completely yet.
8   Install the mounting bolts, tightening them securely. Tighten the brake line fitting. Install the brake shoe assembly.
9   Bleed the brakes (see Section 10).
10   Check brake operation before driving the vehicle in traffic. **Warning:** *Do not operate the vehicle if you are in doubt about the effectiveness of the brake system.*

---

8   **Master cylinder - removal and installation**

Note: *If the master cylinder is defective, it must be replaced with a new one - the manufacturer does not recommend rebuilding it.*

Removal

Refer to illustration 8.4

1   The master cylinder is located in the engine compartment, mounted to the power brake booster.

2   Remove as much fluid as you can from the reservoir with a syringe.
3   Place rags under the fluid fittings and prepare caps or plastic bags to cover the ends of the lines once they are disconnected. **Caution:** *Brake fluid will damage paint. Cover all painted surfaces and be careful not to spill fluid during this procedure.*
4   Loosen the tube nuts at the ends of the brake lines where they enter the master cylinder **(see illustration)**. To prevent rounding off the corners on these nuts, the use of a flare-nut wrench, which wraps around the nut, is preferred.
5   Pull the brake lines slightly away from the master cylinder and plug the ends to prevent contamination.
6   Disconnect the electrical connector at the master cylinder, then remove the nuts attaching the master cylinder to the power booster. Pull the master cylinder off the studs and out of the engine compartment. Again, be careful not to spill the fluid as this is done.

Installation

Refer to illustration 8.8

7   Bench bleed the new master cylinder before installing it. Because it will be necessary to apply pressure to the master cylinder piston and, at the same time, control flow from the brake line outlets, it is recommended that the master cylinder be mounted in a vise, with the jaws of the vise clamping on the mounting flange.
8   Attach a pair of master cylinder bleeder tubes (available at most auto parts stores) to the outlet ports of the master cylinder **(see illustration)**.
9   Fill the reservoir with brake fluid of the recommended type (see Chapter 1).
10   Slowly push the pistons into the master cylinder (a large Phillips screwdriver can be used for this) - air will be expelled from the pressure chambers and into the reservoir. Because the tubes are submerged in fluid, air can't be drawn back into the master cylinder when you release the pistons.
11   Repeat the procedure until no more air bubbles are present.
12   Remove the bleed tubes, one at a time,

and install plugs in the open ports to prevent fluid leakage and air from entering. Install the reservoir cover.
13   Install the master cylinder over the studs on the power brake booster and tighten the attaching nuts only finger tight at this time.
14   Thread the brake line fittings into the master cylinder. Since the master cylinder is still a bit loose, it can be moved slightly in order for the fittings to thread in easily. Do not strip the threads as the fittings are tightened.
15   Fully tighten the mounting nuts to the torque listed in this Chapter's Specifications, then the brake line fittings securely.
17   Fill the master cylinder reservoir with fluid, then bleed the master cylinder and the brake system as described in Section 10. To bleed the cylinder on the vehicle, have an assistant pump the brake pedal several times and then hold the pedal to the floor. Loosen the fitting nut to allow air and fluid to escape. Repeat this procedure on both fittings until the fluid is clear of air bubbles. Test the operation of the brake system carefully before placing the vehicle into normal service. **Warning:** *Do not operate the vehicle if you are in doubt about the effectiveness of the brake system.*

8.8 The best way to bleed air from the master cylinder before installing it on the vehicle is with a pair of bleed tubes

9

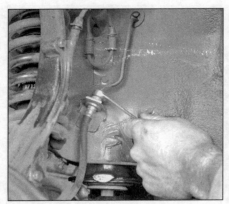

9.4a Use a flare-nut wrench to break loose the brake line-to-hose fitting . . .

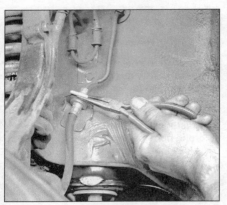

9.4b . . . then remove the clip and slide the hose out of the bracket

10.8 When bleeding the brakes, a hose is connected to the bleed screw at the caliper or wheel cylinder and then submerged in brake fluid - air will be seen as bubbles in the tube and container (all air must be expelled before moving to the next wheel)

9 Brake hoses and lines - inspection and replacement

Refer to illustrations 9.4a and 9.4b

1 About every six months the flexible hoses which connect the steel brake lines with the rear brakes and front calipers should be inspected for cracks, chafing of the outer cover, leaks, blisters, and other damage.

2 Replacement steel and flexible brake lines are commonly available from dealer parts departments and auto parts stores. **Warning:** *Do not, under any circumstances, use anything other than genuine steel brake lines or approved flexible brake hoses as replacement items.*

3 When installing the brake line, leave at least 3/4-inch clearance between the line and any moving or vibrating parts.

4 To disconnect a hose and line, use a flare-nut wrench **(see illustration)**. Then remove the clip and slide the hose out of the bracket **(see illustration)**.

5 When disconnecting two hoses, use normal wrenches on the hose fittings. When connecting two hoses, make sure they are not twisted or strained.

6 Steel brake lines are usually retained along their span with clips. Always remove these clips completely before removing a fixed brake line. Always reinstall these clips, or new ones if the old ones are damaged, when replacing a brake line, as they provide support and keep the lines from vibrating, which can eventually break them.

7 When replacing brake lines be sure to use the correct parts. NEVER use copper tubing! Purchase steel brake lines from a dealer or auto parts store.

8 When installing a steel line, make sure it's securely supported in the brackets and has plenty of clearance between moving or hot components.

9 After installation, check the fluid level in the master cylinder and add fluid as necessary. Bleed the brake system as described in Section 10 and test the brakes carefully before driving the vehicle in traffic. **Warning:** *Do not operate the vehicle if you are in doubt about the effectiveness of the brake system.*

10 Brake hydraulic system - bleeding

Refer to illustration 10.8

Warning: *Wear eye protection when bleeding the brake system. If the fluid comes in contact with your eyes, immediately rinse them with water and seek medical attention.*

1 Bleeding the hydraulic system is necessary to remove any air that manages to find its way into the system when it's been opened during removal and installation of a hose, line, caliper or master cylinder. It will probably be necessary to bleed the system at all four brakes if air has entered the system due to low fluid level, or if the brake lines have been disconnected at the master cylinder.

2 If a brake line was disconnected only at a wheel, then only that caliper or wheel cylinder must be bled. If a brake line is disconnected at a fitting located between the master cylinder and any of the brakes, that part of the system served by the disconnected line must be bled.

3 Remove any residual vacuum from the power brake booster by applying the brake several times with the engine off. Remove the master cylinder reservoir cover and fill the reservoir with brake fluid. Reinstall the cover. **Note:** *Check the fluid level often during the bleeding operation and add fluid as necessary to prevent the fluid level from falling low enough to allow air bubbles into the master cylinder.*

4 Have an assistant on hand, as well as a supply of new brake fluid, a clear container partially filled with clean brake fluid, a length of plastic, rubber or vinyl tubing to fit over the bleed screw and a wrench to open and close the bleed screw.

Models with ABS

5 If you're working on a vehicle equipped with an Anti-lock Brake System (ABS) and have removed and installed (or replaced) the master cylinder, or if the fluid level in the master cylinder became too low and allowed air into the system, begin the procedure by bleeding the lines at the master cylinder. Have an assistant slowly depress the brake pedal and hold it there, then loosen the brake line fittings (one at a time) at the master cylinder, allowing fluid and air to escape. Repeat this procedure until the fluid coming out is free of air, then proceed to the next step.

6 Also on models equipped with ABS, bleed the hydraulic modulator. Attach a snug-fitting bleed hose to the bleeder valve on the hydraulic modulator unit. Start the engine to build up pressure in the modulator, the slowly open the bleeder valve 1/8 to 1/4 turn to allow fluid and air to escape; do this in small increments, repeating the procedure until the fluid coming out of the modulator is free of air. **Warning:** *The fluid in the modulator is under high pressure. Don't open the bleeder valve rapidly or more than 1/4 of a turn, or the brake fluid may squirt out with great force.* Turn off the engine and proceed to bleed the remainder of the system. **Note:** *If the ABS light on the instrument panel comes on, repeat this step.*

All models

7 Beginning at the right rear wheel, loosen the bleed screw slightly, then tighten it to a point where it is snug but can still be loosened quickly and easily.

8 Place one end of the tubing over the bleed screw and submerge the other end in brake fluid in the container **(see illustration)**.

9 Have the assistant slowly depress the brake pedal and hold the pedal firmly depressed.

10 While the pedal is held depressed, open the bleed screw just enough to allow a flow of fluid to leave the screw. Watch for air bubbles to exit the submerged end of the tube. When the fluid flow slows after a couple of seconds, close the screw and have your assistant release the pedal.

11 Repeat Steps 9 and 10 until no more air is seen leaving the tube, then tighten the bleed screw and proceed to the left front wheel, the left rear wheel and the right front wheel, in that order, and perform the same

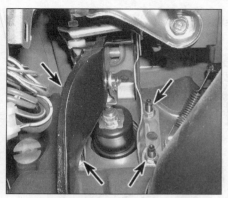

11.10 To remove the power brake booster, remove the cotter pin and clevis pin that connect the pushrod to the brake pedal, then remove the four mounting nuts (arrows)

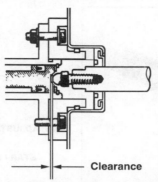

Clearance

11.13a The booster pushrod-to-master cylinder clearance must be as specified - if there is interference between the two, the brakes may drag; if there is too much clearance, there will be excessive brake pedal travel

procedure. Be sure to check the fluid in the master cylinder reservoir frequently.

12 Never use old brake fluid. It contains moisture which boils during (or after) heavy braking, rendering the brakes inoperative.

13 Refill the master cylinder with fluid at the end of the operation.

14 Check the operation of the brakes. The pedal should feel solid when depressed, with no sponginess. If necessary, repeat the entire process. **Warning:** *Do not operate the vehicle if you are in doubt about the effectiveness of the brake system.*

11 Power brake booster - check, removal and installation

Operating check

1 Depress the brake pedal several times with the engine off and make sure there is no change in the pedal reserve distance.

2 Depress the pedal and start the engine. If the pedal goes down slightly, operation is normal.

Airtightness check

3 Start the engine and turn it off after one or two minutes. Depress the brake pedal several times slowly. If the pedal goes down farther the first time but gradually rises after the second or third depression, the booster is airtight.

4 Depress the brake pedal while the engine is running, then stop the engine with the pedal depressed. If there is no change in the pedal reserve travel after holding the pedal for 30 seconds, the booster is airtight.

Removal

Refer to illustration 11.10

5 Power brake booster units should not be disassembled. They require special tools not normally found in most automotive repair stations or shops. They are fairly complex and because of their critical relationship to brake performance it is best to replace a defective booster unit with a new or rebuilt one.

6 To remove the booster, first remove the brake master cylinder as described in Section 8.

7 Disconnect the hose leading from the engine to the booster. Be careful not to damage the hose when removing it from the booster fitting.

8 Locate the pushrod clevis pin connecting the booster to the brake pedal. This is accessible from under the dash panel in front of the driver's seat.

9 Remove the cotter pin with pliers and pull out the clevis pin.

10 Remove the four nuts and washers **(see illustration)** holding the brake booster to the firewall. You may need a light to see them, because they're up under the dash area.

11 Slide the booster straight out from the firewall until the studs clear the holes and pull the booster, brackets and gaskets from the engine compartment area.

Installation

Refer to illustrations 11.13a 11.13b, 11.13c, 11.13d and 11.14

12 Installation procedures are basically the reverse of those for removal. Tighten the booster mounting nuts to the torque listed in this Chapter's Specifications. Also, be sure to use a new cotter pin on the clevis pin.

13 If a new power brake booster unit is being installed, check the pushrod clearance **(see illustration)** as follows:

a) *Using a hand-held vacuum pump, apply a vacuum of 20 in-Hg to the booster. Measure the distance that the pushrod protrudes from the master cylinder mounting surface on the front of the power brake booster, including the gasket (if used). Write down this measurement* **(see illustration)**. *This is "dimension A."*

b) *Measure the distance from the mounting flange to the end of the master cylinder* **(see illustration)**. *Write down this measurement. This is "dimension B."*

c) *Measure the distance from the end of the master cylinder to the bottom of the pocket in the piston* **(see illustration)**. *Write down this measurement. This is "dimension C."*

11.13b Measure the distance that the pushrod protrudes from the brake booster at the master cylinder mounting surface (including the gasket, if equipped

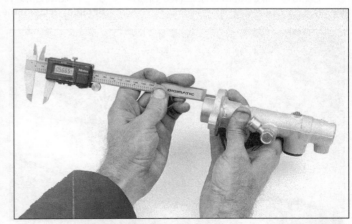

11.13c Measure the distance from the mounting flange to the end of the master cylinder

9

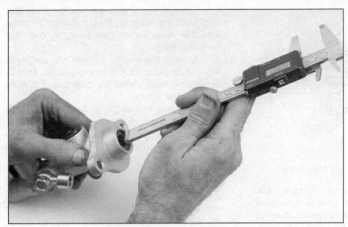

11.13d Measure the distance from the piston pocket to the end of
the master cylinder

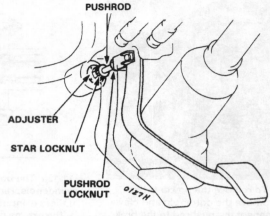

11.14 To adjust the length of the booster pushrod, loosen the
star locknut and turn the adjuster in or out, as necessary,
to achieve the desired setting

d) *Subtract measurement B from measurement C, then subtract measurement A from the difference between B and C. This the pushrod clearance.*

e) *Compare your calculated pushrod clearance to the pushrod clearance listed in this Chapter's Specifications. If necessary, adjust the pushrod length to achieve the correct clearance (see the next Step).*

14   If the clearance is more or less than specified, loosen the star locknut and turn the adjuster on the power booster pushrod until the clearance is within the specified limit **(see illustration)**. After adjustment, tighten the locknut. Recheck the clearance. Repeat this step as often as necessary until the clearance is correct.

15   After the final installation of the master cylinder and brake hoses and lines, bleed the brakes as described in Section 11.

12   Parking brake - adjustment

Refer to illustration 12.4

1   Remove the shift lever knob (see Chapter 7).

2   Remove the center console (see Chapter 11).

3   Block the front wheels, raise the rear of the vehicle and support it securely on jackstands. Apply the parking brake lever until you hear one click.

4   Turn the adjusting nut on the equalizer **(see illustration)** clockwise while rotating the rear wheels. Stop turning the nut when the brakes just start to drag on the rear wheels.

5   Release the parking brake lever and check to see that the brakes don't drag when the rear wheels are turned. The travel on the parking brake lever should be as listed in the Chapter 1 Specifications when properly adjusted.

6   Lower the vehicle and reinstall the console (see Chapter 11).

13   Parking brake cable(s) - replacement

Refer to illustration 13.4

1   Block the front wheels and loosen the rear wheel lug nuts. Raise the rear of the vehicle and support it securely on jackstands.

2   On vehicles with rear drum brakes, remove the brake drum(s) (see Section 6).

3   Following the procedure in the previous Section, loosen the cable adjusting nut.

Remove the cable clamps from the cable housing **(see illustration)**. Unhook the cable from the equalizer.

4   On models with rear drum brakes, remove the brake shoes (see Section 6) and disconnect the cable end from the lever on the trailing brake shoe **(see illustration 6.4f)**. Depress the tangs on the cable housing retainer and pass the cable through the backing plate. You can do this by passing an

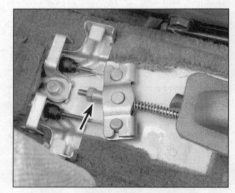

12.4 The parking brake adjusting nut
(arrow) is on the equalizer assembly

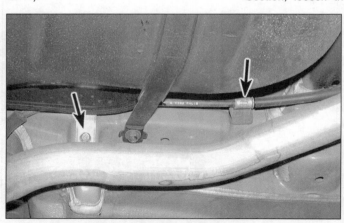

13.4 Loosen the bolts and detach the parking brake
cable from the clips (arrows)

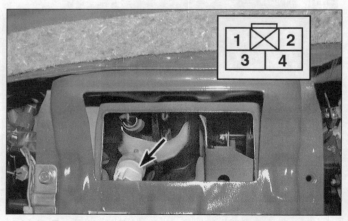

14.4a Terminal guide for the brake light switch (Honda Civic)

offset 12 mm box end wrench over the end of the cable and onto the retainer **(see illustration)**. This compresses all the tangs simultaneously.

5   On models with rear disc brakes, remove the clip and clevis to disconnect the cable end from the actuator lever on the caliper **(see illustration 4.2)**, then remove the spring clip to free the cable housing from the support bracket.

6   Unbolt the cable housing clamps from the underbody, noting how the cable is routed, then remove the cable from the vehicle. It may be necessary to remove the exhaust pipe heat shield bolts at the rear to allow cable removal.

7   If both cables are to be removed, repeat the above steps to remove the remaining cable.

8   Installation is the reverse of the removal procedure. After the cable(s) are installed, be sure to adjust them according to the procedure described in Section 12.

---

14   Brake light switch - check, replacement and adjustment

Check

Refer to illustrations 14.4a and 14.4b

1   To check the brake light switch, push on the brake pedal and verify that the brake lights come on.

2   If they don't, check the brake light fuse (see Chapter 12 or check your owner's manual for fuse locations). Also check the brake light bulbs in both tail light assemblies (don't forget to check the high-mount brake light).

3   If the fuse and the bulbs are okay, locate the brake light switch at the top of the brake pedal.

4   Unplug the switch electrical connector **(see illustrations)**.

5   On Civic models, check for continuity across terminals 1 and 2. When the brake pedal is depressed, there should be continuity; when it's released, there should be no continuity. If the switch doesn't operate as described, replace it. On Integra models, check for continuity across switch terminals B and C with an ohmmeter. When the brake pedal is depressed, there should be continuity; when it's released, there should be no continuity. If the switch doesn't operate as described, replace it.

Replacement

6   Disconnect the electrical connector from the switch, if you haven't already done so.

7   Remove the locknut on the pedal side of the switch and unscrew the switch from the bracket.

8   Installation of the brake light switch is the reverse of the removal procedure.

Adjustment

9   Loosen the brake light switch locknut and back off the brake light switch until

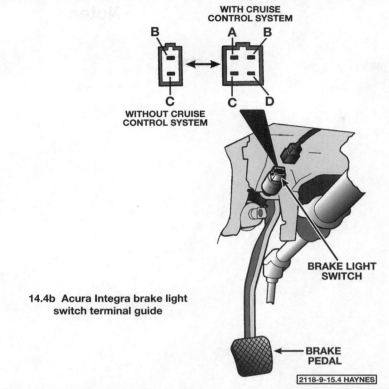

14.4b Acura Integra brake light switch terminal guide

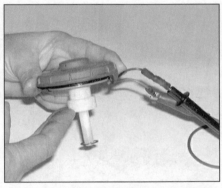

15.3a Raise the brake fluid level sensor float and make sure there is no continuity

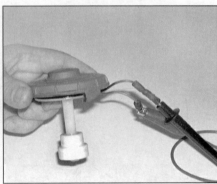

15.3b Make sure there is continuity with the float lowered

there's clearance between the switch plunger and the brake pedal.

10   Loosen the pushrod locknut and screw the pushrod in or out with pliers until the pedal height from the floor is correct (as listed in this Chapter's Specifications).

11   Tighten the locknut securely.

12   Screw in the brake light switch until the-plunger is fully depressed (threaded end touching the pad on the pedal arm), then back off the switch 1/2-turn and tighten the locknut securely.

13   Depress the pedal with your hand and measure the pedal freeplay. It should be within the dimensions listed in this Chapter's Specifications. Make sure the brake lights operate when the pedal is depressed and go off when the pedal is released.

---

15   Brake fluid level switch - check and replacement

Refer to illustrations 15.3a and 15.3b

1   Unplug the switch electrical connector and remove the brake fluid reservoir cap and switch assembly.

2   Make sure the fluid level float moves up and down easily, if it doesn't, replace the assembly.

3   Connect the leads of an ohmmeter to the electrical connectors of the fluid level switch. Raise and lower the float and check for continuity. When the float is raised, there should be no continuity; when it's lowered, there should be continuity **(see illustrations)**. If the float assembly doesn't operate as described, replace it.

9

Notes

Chapter 10
Suspension and steering systems

Contents

Specifications

General
Power steering fluid type .... See Chapter 1

Torque specifications **Ft-lbs** (unless otherwise indicated)

Front suspension
Shock absorber
Shock absorber-to-body mounting nuts	47
Shock absorber damper rod upper nut	22

Damper fork
Pinch bolt	32
Fork-to-lower arm through-bolt nut	47

Lower control arm
Front pivot bolt	
Integra	47
Civic	76
Rear pivot stud nut	61
Bushing clamp bolts	66

Stabilizer bar
Link nuts (upper and lower)	16
Bushing clamp nuts	16

Steering knuckle (lower) balljoint nut .... 36 to 43

Upper control arm
Balljoint nut	29 to 35
Civic	
Flange bolts	40
Integra	
Anchor bolt nuts	47
Pivot bolt nuts	22

10

Torque specifications

Ft-lbs (unless otherwise indicated)

Rear suspension

Compensator arm
  Compensator arm-to-body pivot bolt 47
  Compensator arm-to-trailing arm bolt 47
Hub-to-spindle nut 134
Lower arm
  Lower arm-to-body pivot bolt 40
  Lower arm-to-trailing arm bolt 40
Shock absorber
  Damper rod nut 22
  Shock-to-lower arm bolt 40
  Shock upper mounting nuts 36
Trailing arm bushing bracket-to-body bolts 47
Upper arm
  Bushing bracket-to-body bolts 29
  Upper arm-to-trailing arm bolt 40
Upper control arm inner mounting bolts 28
Stabilizer bar
  Link nuts (upper and lower) 16
  Bushing clamp nuts.. 16

Steering system

Steering wheel nut 36
Airbag module Torx bolts .... 84 in-lbs
Steering gear mounting bolts
  Left (driver's side) 32
  Right (passenger's) side 29
Tie-rod end-to-steering knuckle nut 33
Intermediate shaft pinch-bolt 16
Chassis stiffener bracket 28

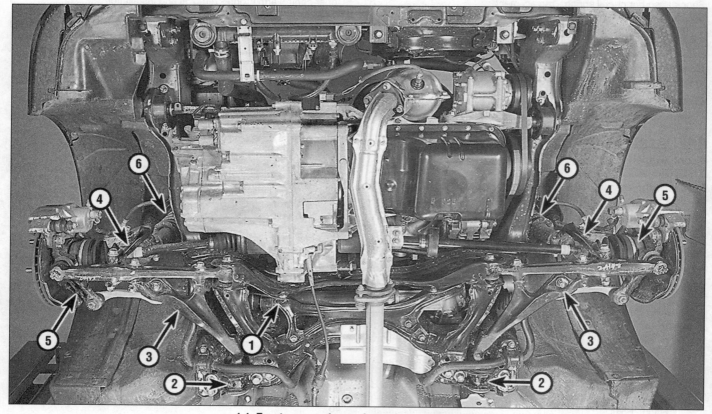

1.1 Front suspension and steering components

1	Steering gear	3	Lower control arm	5	Steering knuckle
2	Lower control arm bushing clamp	4	Damper fork	6	Shock absorber/coil spring assembly

1.2 Rear suspension components

1	Shock absorber/coil spring assembly	2	Upper arm	4	Compensator arm
		3	Lower arm	5	Trailing arm

1   General information

Refer to illustrations 1.1 and 1.2

The front suspension **(see illustration)** is a fully independent design with upper and lower control arms, shock absorber/coil spring assemblies and a stabilizer bar.

The rear suspension uses trailing arms, upper and lower control arms, "compensator" arms and shock absorber/coil spring units **(see illustration)**.

All models use rack-and-pinion steering. Some models are power-assisted. The power steering system employs an engine-driven pump connected by hoses to the steering gear.

Frequently, when working on the suspension or steering system components, you may come across fasteners which seem impossible to loosen. These fasteners on the underside of the vehicle are continually subjected to water, road grime, mud, etc., and can become rusted or "frozen," making them extremely difficult to remove. In order to unscrew these stubborn fasteners without damaging them (or other components), be sure to use lots of penetrating oil and allow it to soak in for a while. Using a wire brush to clean exposed threads will also ease removal of the nut or bolt and prevent damage to the threads. Sometimes a sharp blow with a hammer and punch is effective in breaking the bond between a nut and bolt threads, but care must be taken to prevent the punch from slipping off the fastener and ruining the threads. Heating the stuck fastener and surrounding area with a torch sometimes helps too, but isn't recommended because of the obvious dangers associated with fire. Long breaker bars and extension, or "cheater," pipes will increase leverage, but never use an extension pipe on a ratchet - the ratcheting mechanism could be damaged. Sometimes, turning the nut or bolt in the tightening (clockwise) direction first will help to break it loose. Fasteners that require drastic measures to loosen should always be replaced with new ones.

Since most of the procedures that are dealt with in this chapter involve jacking up the vehicle and working underneath it, a good pair of jackstands will be needed. A hydraulic floor jack is the preferred type of jack to lift the vehicle, and it can also be used to support certain components during various operations. **Warning:** *Never, under any circumstances, rely on a jack to support the vehicle while working on it. Whenever any of the suspension or steering fasteners are loosened or removed they must be inspected and, if necessary, be replaced with new ones of the same part number or of original equipment quality and design. Torque specifications must be followed for proper reassembly and component retention. Never attempt to heat or straighten any suspension or steering component. Instead, replace any bent or damaged part with a new one.*

2   Shock absorber/coil spring assembly (front) - removal and installation

Removal

Refer to illustrations 2.4, 2.5a, 2.5b and 2.6

1   Loosen the wheel lug nuts, raise the vehicle and support it securely on jackstands. Remove the wheel.
2   Unbolt the brake hose from the shock absorber assembly.
3   Disconnect the stabilizer bar from the

10

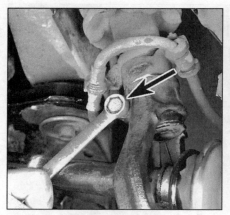

2.4 Remove the damper fork pinch bolt (arrow)

2.5a Remove the through-bolt that connects the damper fork to the lower control arm

2.5b Detach the damper fork from the shock absorber

2.6 Remove the nuts (arrows) from the shock absorber mounting studs

3.5 Install the spring compressor according to the tool manufacturer's instructions and compress the spring until all pressure is relieved from the mounting base

lower control arm (see Section 4).

4   Place a floor jack under the lower control arm to support it when the shock absorber assembly is removed. Remove the damper fork pinch bolt **(see illustration)**.

5   Remove the damper fork-to-lower control arm bolt and remove the fork **(see illustrations)**. It may be necessary to tap the fork from the shock absorber.

6   Support the shock absorber and coil spring assembly and remove the two upper mounting nuts **(see illustration)**. Remove the unit from the fenderwell.

Installation

7   Guide the shock absorber assembly up into the fenderwell and insert the upper mounting studs through the holes in the body. Once the studs protrude from the holes, install the nuts so the assembly won't fall back through, but don't tighten the nuts completely yet. The shock absorber is heavy and awkward, so get an assistant to help you, if possible.

8   Insert the lower end of the shock absorber into the damper fork. Make sure the aligning tab on the back of the shock body

enters the slot in the damper fork.

9   Connect the damper fork to the lower control arm, tightening the self-locking nut to the torque listed in this Chapter's Specifications. Now tighten the damper fork pinch bolt to the torque listed in this Chapter's Specifications.

10   Connect the stabilizer bar to the control arm (see Section 4). Attach the brake hose to its bracket and tighten the bolt securely.

11   Install the wheel and lug nuts, lower the vehicle and tighten the lug nuts to the torque listed in the Chapter 1 Specifications.

12   Tighten the upper mounting nuts to the torque listed in this Chapter's Specifications.

3   Shock absorber or coil spring - replacement

Refer to illustrations 3.5 and 3.6

1   Remove the shock absorber/coil spring assembly (see Section 2 or 10).

2   Check the shock absorber for leaking fluid, dents, cracks or other obvious damage. Check the coil spring for chips or cracks which could cause premature failure and

inspect the spring seats for hardness or general deterioration. The shock absorber assemblies, complete with the coil springs, are available on an exchange basis which eliminates much time and work. So, before disassembling your shock to replace individual components, check on the availability of parts and the price of a complete rebuilt unit. **Warning:** *Disassembling a shock absorber/coil spring assembly is potentially dangerous and utmost attention must be directed to the job, or serious injury may result. Use only a high-quality spring compressor and carefully follow the manufacturer's instructions furnished with the tool. After removing the coil spring from the shock absorber, set it aside in a safe, isolated area.*

3   Mount the shock absorber assembly in a vise. Line the vise jaws with wood or rags to prevent damage to the unit and don't tighten the vise excessively.

4   Mark the relationship of the damper mounting base to the spring (or if the spring is being replaced, put the mark on the damper unit). This will ensure correct positioning of the mounting base when the unit is reassembled.

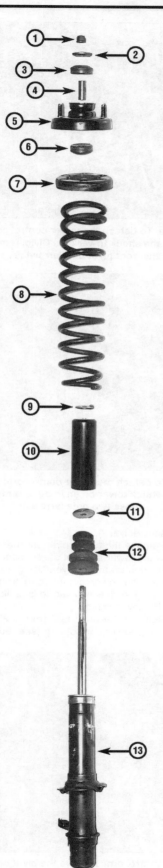

4.2 Remove the bolts (arrows) attaching the stabilizer bar bracket to the chassis

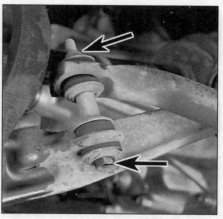

4.3 Remove the nut and bolt (arrows) and remove the stabilizer bar link assembly

5   Following the tool manufacturer's instructions, install the spring compressor (which can be obtained at most auto parts stores or equipment yards on a daily rental basis) on the spring and compress it sufficiently to relieve all pressure from the damper mounting base **(see illustration)**.

6   Remove the damper cap **(see illustration)**. Unscrew the self-locking nut while holding the damper shaft with an Allen wrench to prevent it from turning. Remove the parts from the upper part of the shock and lay them out in the exact order in which they're removed.

7   Carefully lift the compressed spring from the assembly and set it in a safe place. **Warning:** *Keep the ends of the spring facing away from your body!*

8   Slide the rest of the parts off of the damper shaft and lay them out in the exact order in which they're removed.

9   Install the bump stop, bump stop plate (if equipped), dust cover and dust cover plate onto the new damper unit. Extend the damper shaft as far as it will go and slide the components down to the damper body.

10   Carefully place the coil spring onto the shock absorber body, with the end of the spring resting in the lowest part of the seat.

11   Install the spring mounting rubber, lower

3.6 Exploded view of a typical front shock absorber/coil spring assembly

1   Self-locking nut
2   Damper mounting washer
3   Damper mounting rubber
4   Damper mounting collar
5   Damper mounting base
6   Damper mounting rubber
7   Spring mounting rubber
8   Spring
9   Dust cover plate
10   Dust cover
11   Bump stop plate
12   Bump stop
13   Damper unit

---

mounting rubber, damper mounting collar, damper mounting base, seal, upper mounting rubber, damper mounting washer and a new self-locking nut. Before tightening the nut, align the previously applied marks on the mounting base and the spring (or damper body).

12   Tighten the self-locking nut to the torque listed in this Chapter's Specifications, again using the Allen wrench to prevent the shaft from turning. Remove the spring compressor. Install the damper cap.

13   Install the shock absorber/coil spring assembly (see Section 2 or 10).

---

4   Stabilizer bar and bushings (front) - removal and installation

Refer to illustrations 4.2 and 4.3

1   Apply the parking brake. Loosen the front wheel lug nuts, raise the front of the vehicle and support it securely on jackstands. Remove the wheels.

2   Remove the bolts which attach the stabilizer bar brackets to the underside of the vehicle **(see illustration)**.

3   Detach the stabilizer bar link bolts from the lower control arms **(see illustration)**. Note the order in which the spacers, washers and bushings are arranged on the link bolt.

4   Remove the bar from under the vehicle.

5   Pull the brackets off the stabilizer bar and inspect the bushings for cracks, hardness and other signs of deterioration. If the bushings are damaged, replace them.

6   Installation is the reverse of removal.

---

5   Upper control arm (front) - removal and installation

Refer to illustrations 5.2, 5.3, 5.4a, 5.4b and 5.5

1   Loosen the front wheel lug nuts, raise the vehicle, place it securely on jackstands and remove the wheel. Support the lower

10

5.2 Loosen - but don't remove - the upper balljoint castle nut (arrow)

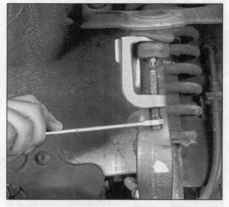

5.3 Install a puller and separate the upper control arm balljoint stud from the steering knuckle

5.4a To detach the upper control arm from the shock tower on a Civic, remove the front pivot bolt (arrow) . . .

control arm with a floor jack.

2   Remove the cotter pin and loosen, but do not remove, the castle nut **(see illustration)** from the upper balljoint stud. The nut will prevent the upper control arm and the steering knuckle from separating violently in the next step.

3   Separate the upper control arm from the steering knuckle with a puller **(see illustration)**. Remove the castle nut. Don't let the top of the steering knuckle fall out. If necessary, secure it to the shock absorber with a piece of wire.

4   If you're working on a Civic, remove the upper control arm pivot nuts and bolts from inside the engine compartment **(see illustrations)**, then remove the upper control arm.

5   If you're working on an Integra, remove the upper control arm-to-shock tower nuts **(see illustration)**, then guide the arm out around the coil spring.

6   Installation is the reverse of removal. Be sure to tighten all of the fasteners to the torque values listed in this Chapter's Specifications. **Note:** *If you're working on a Civic, raise the front suspension with a floor jack to simulate normal ride height before tightening the control arm pivot bolts.*

5.4b . . . and the rear pivot bolt

6   Lower control arm (front) - removal and installation

Refer to illustrations 6.4, 6.5 and 6.6

1   Loosen the front wheel lug nuts, raise the vehicle, place it securely on jackstands and remove the wheel.

2   Detach the stabilizer bar from the lower control arm (see Section 4).

3   Detach the damper fork from the control

5.5 To detach the upper control arm from the shock tower on an Integra, remove these two nuts (arrows)

arm (see Section 2).

4   Remove the cotter pin from the castle nut on the lower balljoint stud. Loosen the nut, but don't remove it yet. Using a puller, separate the lower control arm from the balljoint in the steering knuckle **(see illustration)**. Remove the nut.

5   Remove the pivot bolt from the inner end of the lower control arm **(see illustra-**

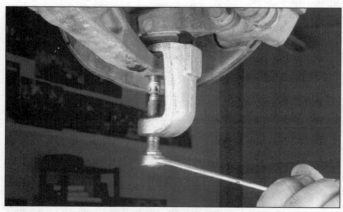

6.4 Separate the lower control arm from the steering knuckle balljoint with a puller

6.5 To remove the lower control arm, remove the pivot bolt (arrow) from the inner end of the arm

6.6 To detach the lower control arm's rear pivot stud from its bushing, remove this nut (arrow); it's not necessary to remove the three bushing clamp bolts (arrows) unless you need to replace the bushing itself

7.1 Loosen the driveaxle/hub nut with a socket and breaker bar

tion) and separate the arm from the chassis.
6   Remove the nut from the rear pivot stud **(see illustration)**, pull the stud out of the bushing and remove the arm. **Note:** *It's not necessary to remove the three bushing clamp retaining bolts unless the bushing is to be replaced.*
7   Installation is the reverse of removal.

7   Steering knuckle and hub assembly - removal and installation

Removal

Refer to illustration 7.1
1   Remove the wheel cover, if equipped. Loosen the driveaxle/hub nut **(see illustration)**. Loosen the wheel lug nuts, raise the front of the vehicle and support it securely on jackstands. Remove the wheel and the driveaxle/hub nut.
2   Unbolt the brake hose bracket from the steering knuckle. Unbolt the brake caliper, hang it out of the way with a piece of wire, remove the caliper mounting bracket and remove the brake disc (see Chapter 9).
3   Disconnect the tie-rod end from the steering knuckle (see Section 15).
4   Separate the lower control arm from the balljoint in the bottom of the steering knuckle (see Section 6).
5   Separate the upper end of the knuckle from the upper control arm balljoint.
6   Carefully pull the knuckle and hub assembly off of the driveaxle. Tap the end of the driveaxle with a soft-faced hammer to break the driveaxle loose from the hub. Support the driveaxle with a piece of wire to prevent damage to the inner CV joint.

Installation

7   Apply a light coat of chassis grease to the driveaxle splines. Insert the driveaxle through the splined bore of the hub while guiding the steering knuckle into position.
8   Connect the upper end of the knuckle to the upper control arm balljoint (see Sec-

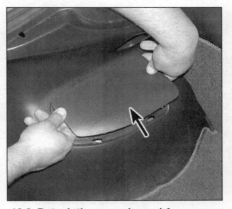

10.2 Detach the cover (arrow) for access to the upper shock absorber mounting nuts on models so equipped

tion 5). Tighten the balljoint stud nut to the torque listed in this Chapter's Specifications.
9   Connect the balljoint on the bottom of the knuckle to the lower control arm (see Section 6).
10   Install the brake disc, caliper mount and caliper (see Chapter 9). Attach the brake hose bracket.
11   Install the driveaxle/hub nut and tighten it securely.
12   Install the wheel and lug nuts, lower the vehicle and tighten the lug nuts to the torque listed in the Chapter 1 Specifications.
13   Tighten the driveaxle/hub nut to the torque specified in Chapter 8.

8   Hub and bearing assembly (front) - removal and illustration

1   Remove the steering knuckle assembly from the vehicle and separate the hub assembly from the brake disc (see Section 7).
2   Due to the special tools and expertise required to press the hub from the steering knuckle, the assembly should be taken to an automotive machine shop or other qualified shop to have the bearing replaced if it is worn.

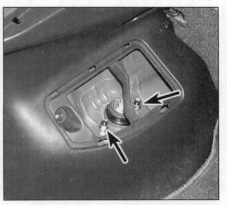

10.3 Remove the upper mounting nuts (arrows) - don't remove the larger center nut

9   Balljoints - replacement

1   The front suspension uses two balljoints. The upper balljoint, located in the upper control arm, can't be removed. If it's worn or damaged, replace the upper control arm (see Section 5).
2   The lower balljoint, located in the steering knuckle, can be removed, but special tools are needed. If it's worn or damaged, remove the knuckle (see Section 7) and take it to an automotive machine shop or other repair shop to have it replaced.

10   Shock absorber/coil spring assembly (rear) - removal and installation

Refer to illustrations 10.2, 10,3 and 10.4
1   Loosen the rear wheel lug nuts, raise the vehicle, place it securely on jackstands and remove the rear wheels.
2   Remove the damper upper cover (if equipped) **(see illustration)**.
3   Remove the shock absorber upper mounting nuts **(see illustration)**.
4   Remove the shock absorber lower

10

10.4 Remove the mounting bolt (right arrow) that attaches the lower end of the shock absorber to the lower arm; to disconnect the lower arm from the trailing arm (Section 13), remove the left bolt (left arrow)

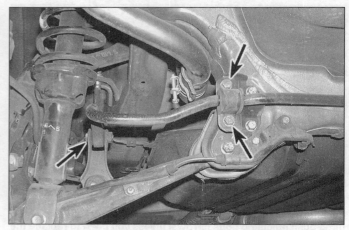

11.2 Remove the stabilizer bar-to-link bolts and the clamp bolts (arrows)

mounting bolt **(see illustration)**.
5   Pull down on the lower arm and remove the shock absorber/coil spring assembly.
6   To inspect or replace the shock absorber or coil spring, see Section 3.
7   Installation is the reverse of removal. Be sure to tighten all fasteners to the torque values listed in this Chapter's Specifications.

11   Stabilizer bar and bushings (rear) - removal and installation

Refer to illustration 11.2
Note: *This procedure applies to Integra models only.*
1   Loosen the rear wheel lug nuts, raise the vehicle, place it securely on jackstands and remove the rear wheels.
2   Remove the stabilizer bar-to-link bolts and the stabilizer bar-to-body clamp bolts and remove the stabilizer bar **(see illustration)**.
3   Pull the brackets off the stabilizer bar and inspect the bushings for cracks, hardness and other signs of deterioration. If the

bushings are damaged, replace them.
4   Installation is the reverse of removal.

12   Hub and bearing assembly (rear) - removal and installation

Refer to illustrations 12.3, 12.4a, 12.4b and 12.5
Note: *The rear hub and bearing are combined into a single assembly. The bearing is sealed for life and requires no lubrication or attention. If the bearing is worn or damaged, replace the entire hub and bearing assembly.*
1   Loosen the rear wheel lug nuts, raise the vehicle, place it securely on jackstands and remove the rear wheel.
2   Remove the brake drum or caliper and disc (see Chapter 9).
3   Remove the dust cover **(see illustration)**.
4   Unstake the hub retaining nut **(see illustration)**, unscrew the nut, then remove the thrust washer and the hub assembly **(see illustration)**.
5   Install the new hub assembly and thrust

12.3 Using a hammer and chisel, remove the dust cover

washer, tighten the new nut to the torque listed in this Chapter's Specifications, then stake its edge into the groove in the spindle **(see illustration)**.
6   Install the dust cover by tapping lightly around the edge until it is seated.

12.4a Unstake the hub nut

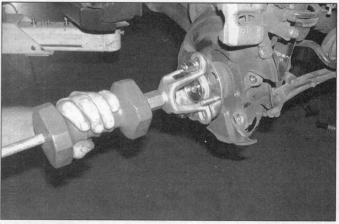

12.4b The hub assembly should come off easily, but if it's stuck, pull it from the rear knuckle with a slide hammer

12.5 Stake the hub nut back into place

13.2 To remove the upper arm, remove the bolt and nut (right arrows) that attach it to the trailing arm, then remove the two bolts (left arrows) that attach the inner end to the body

13.7 To disconnect the inner end of the lower arm from the chassis, remove the pivot bolt (arrow)

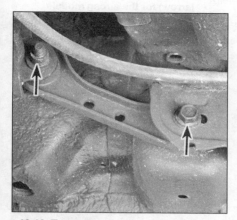

13.10 To remove the compensator arm, remove the bolt (right arrow) that attaches the arm to the body, then remove the bolt that attaches the compensator arm to the trailing arm (left arrow)

13.18a To disconnect the trailing arm from the body, remove the left bushing shaft bolt (arrow) . . .

13.18b . . . and the right bolt (right arrow); and don't forget to detach the bracket for the parking brake cable by removing the bolt indicated by the left arrow

7   The remainder of installation is the reverse of removal.

13 Rear suspension arms - removal and installation

1   Loosen the rear wheel lug nuts, raise the vehicle, place it securely on jackstands and remove the wheel.

Upper arm

Refer to illustration 13.2

2   Remove the upper arm-to-trailing arm bolt and nut **(see illustration)**.

3   Remove the mounting bolts from the upper arm inner bushing and remove the upper arm.

4   Inspect the bushing for cracking or deterioration. If it's worn, have it pressed out, and a new one installed, by an automotive machine shop or other repair shop.

5   Installation is the reverse of removal. Be sure to tighten all fasteners to the torque listed in this Chapter's Specifications.

Lower arm

Refer to illustration 13.7

6   Remove the lower arm-to-trailing arm bolt and the shock absorber-to-lower arm bolt (see Section 10).

7   Remove the inner pivot bolt and nut from the lower arm **(see illustration)**, then remove the lower arm.

8   Inspect the lower arm bushings for cracks and deterioration. If any of them are worn, have them pressed out, and new ones installed, by an automotive machine shop or other repair shop.

9   Installation is the reverse of removal. Be sure to tighten all fasteners to the torque listed in this Chapter's Specifications.

Compensator arm

Refer to illustration 13.10

10   Remove the compensator arm-to-trailing arm bolt **(see illustration)**.

11   Remove the compensator arm-to-body nut and bolt and remove the compensator arm.

12   Inspect the compensator arm bushings

for wear and deterioration. If either of them need to be replaced, have them pressed out, and new ones installed, by an automotive machine shop or other repair shop.

13   Installation is the reverse of removal. Be sure to tighten both fasteners to the torque listed in this Chapter's Specifications.

Trailing arm

Refer to illustrations 13.18a and 13.18b

14   Disconnect the brake hose from the wheel cylinder or rear caliper and plug the hose to prevent leakage or contamination. Remove the brake drum and brake shoes, or the rear caliper and disc. Disconnect the parking brake cable (see Chapter 9).

15   Remove the rear hub and bearing assembly (see Section 8).

16   Remove the brake backing plate.

17   Detach the upper, lower and compensator arms from the trailing arm (see above).

18   Disconnect the parking brake cable bracket from the trailing arm, then remove the bolts from the trailing arm bushing shaft **(see illustrations)** and remove the trailing arm.

10

14.2a Remove this screw and remove the access plate from the underside of the steering wheel

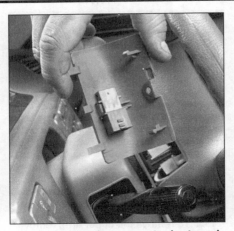

14.2b The shorting connector is stowed on the inside of the access plate

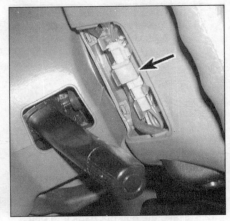

14.2c Unplug the yellow connector (arrow) for the airbag module

14.2d Plug the shorting connector into the airbag module connector to disable the airbag module

14.3a Remove the left Torx screw (arrow) that attaches the airbag module to the steering wheel

14.3b Rotate the steering wheel and remove the right Torx screw (arrow)

19 Inspect the trailing arm bushing for cracks and deterioration. If it needs to be replaced, have it pressed out, and a new one installed, by an automotive machine shop or other repair shop.

20 Installation is the reverse of removal. Be sure to tighten all fasteners to the torque listed in this Chapter's Specifications and bleed the brake hydraulic system (see Chapter 9).

14 Steering wheel - removal and installation

Removal

Refer to illustrations 14.2a, 14.2b, 14.c, 14.2d, 14.3a, 14.3b, 14.4 and 14.6

Warning: *Most models covered by this manual are equipped with a Supplemental Restraint System (SRS), more commonly known as an airbag(s). Always disable the airbag system before working in the vicinity of the airbag unit(s), steering column or instrument panel to avoid the possibility of accidental deployment of the airbag, which could*

cause personal injury (see Chapter 12).

1 Disconnect the cable from the negative battery terminal, then disconnect the positive battery cable. **Caution:** *If the stereo in your vehicle is equipped with an anti-theft system, make sure you have the correct activation code before disconnecting the battery.*

2 Rotate the wheel 180-degrees so the access panel is facing up. Remove the access plate and remove the shorting connector from the access plate **(see illustrations)**. Unplug the airbag module-to-cable reel connector and plug the shorting connector into the airbag module side of this connector to disable the airbag module **(see illustrations)**.

3 Remove both Torx screws from the side of the steering wheel facing toward the dash **(see illustrations)**. These screws retain the airbag module.

4 Pull off the module **(see illustration)** and carefully set the module in a safe location with the trim side facing up. **Warning:** *When carrying the airbag module, make sure the trim side is facing away from you. When you set it down, Place it in an isolated area with the trim side facing up. Also, don't set any*

objects on top of the airbag module.

5 Unplug the electrical connectors for the horn and, if equipped, the cruise control system.

6 Remove the steering wheel retaining

14.4 Remove the airbag module from the steering wheel and set it in a safe location (always store the airbag module with the trim side facing UP)

14.6 After removing the steering wheel nut, mark the relationship of the wheel to the shaft

nut. Paint or scribe a mark indicating the relationship of the steering wheel hub to the steering shaft **(see illustration)**.

7   Remove the steering wheel by pulling it straight off the shaft. If it sticks, use a rocking motion. **Warning:** *While the steering wheel is removed, DO NOT turn the steering shaft. If you do so, the airbag cable reel could be damaged.*

Installation

Refer to illustration 14.9

8   Make sure that the wheels are pointed straight ahead.

9   Make absolutely sure that the cable reel is centered with the arrow on the cable reel pointing up **(see illustration)**. This shouldn't be a problem as long as you have not turned the steering shaft while the wheel was removed. If for some reason the shaft was turned, center the cable reel as follows:

a) *Rotate the cable reel clockwise until it stops.*

b) *Rotate the cable reel counterclockwise about two turns until the yellow gear tooth lines up with the mark on the cover*

14.9 Before installing the steering wheel, make sure that the wheels are pointed straight ahead and the "Top" mark points straight up on the cable reel for the airbag system; also, note that on some models the yellow gear tooth at 7 o'clock is lined up with its mark on the cover

(some models) and the arrow on the cable reel points straight up.

10   Be sure to align the index mark on the steering wheel hub with the mark on the shaft when you slip the wheel onto the shaft. And make sure the locating pins on the steering column engage the holes in the backside of the steering wheel. Install the mounting nut and tighten it to the torque listed in this Chapter's Specifications.

11   Plug in the horn connector and, if equipped, the cruise control connector.

12   Reattach the airbag module with NEW Torx bolts and tighten the bolts to the torque listed in this Chapter's Specifications. Install the Torx bolt access panels.

13   Unplug the shorting connector from the airbag connector.

14   Plug the airbag and cable reel connector halves together.

15   Secure the shorting connector to the access plate and install the access plate.

15 Tie-rod ends - removal and installation

Removal

Refer to illustrations 15.2a, 15.2b and 15.4

1   Loosen the wheel lug nuts. Raise the front of the vehicle, support it securely on jackstands and remove the wheel.

2   Hold the tie-rod end with a back-up wrench and loosen the jam nut enough to mark the position of the tie-rod end in relation to the threads **(see illustrations)**.

3   Remove the cotter pin and loosen the nut on the tie-rod end stud. Don't completely remove the nut.

4   Separate the tie-rod from the steering knuckle arm with a puller **(see illustration)**. Remove the nut and detach the tie-rod.

5   Unscrew the tie-rod end from the tie-rod.

Installation

6   Thread the tie-rod end on to the marked position and insert the tie-rod stud into the steering knuckle arm. Don't tighten the jam nut yet.

7   Install the nut on the stud and tighten it to the torque listed in this Chapter's Specifications. Install a new cotter pin.

8   Tighten the jam nut securely.

9   Install the wheel and lug nuts. Lower the vehicle and tighten the lug nuts to the torque listed in the Chapter 1 Specifications.

10   Have the alignment checked by a dealer service department or an alignment shop.

16 Steering gear boots - replacement

Refer to illustration 16.3

1   Loosen the lug nuts, raise the front of the vehicle and support it securely on jackstands. Remove the wheel.

2   Remove the tie-rod end and jam nut

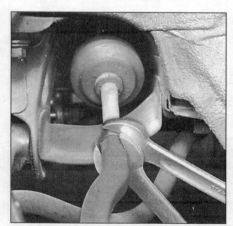

15.2a Using a back-up wrench to prevent the tie-rod end from turning, loosen the jam nut

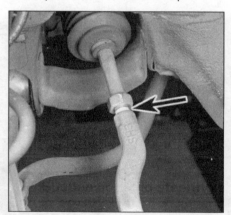

15.2b Make an alignment mark on the exposed threads, along the edge of the tie-rod end, so the new tie-rod end will be installed in the exact same position

15.4 Use a puller to separate the tie-rod end from the steering knuckle arm

10

16.3 Cut the steering gear boot clamps (arrows)

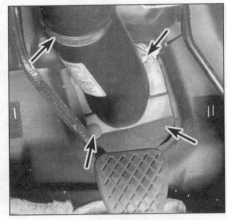

17.1 Pop off the upper and lower clamps (upper left arrow points to lower clamp; upper clamp not visible in this photo), pop out the single plastic retaining clip (lower left arrow) and slide off the cover; when you put it back on, make sure the two holes (right arrows) in the flange at the lower end of the shield engage with the locating pins in the firewall

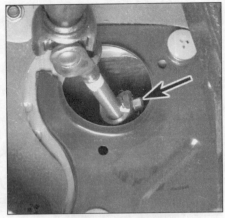

17.2 Mark the relationship of the intermediate shaft to the steering gear input shaft and remove the pinch bolt (arrow)

(see Section 15).

3   Remove the steering gear boot clamps and slide off the boot **(see illustration)**.

4   Before installing the new boot, wrap the threads and serrations on the end of the tie-rod with a layer of tape so the small end of the new boot isn't damaged.

5   Slide the new boot into position on the steering gear until it seats in the groove in the steering rod and install new clamps.

6   Remove the tape and install the tie-rod end (see Section 15).

7   Install the wheel and lug nuts. Lower the vehicle and tighten the lug nuts to the torque listed in the Chapter 1 Specifications.

17   Steering gear - removal and installation

Removal

Refer to illustrations 17.1, 17.2, 17.6a, 17.6b, 17.8a and 17.8b

1   Park the vehicle with the front wheels pointing straight ahead. Working under the dash, remove the steering joint cover **(see illustration)**.

2   Mark the relationship of the intermediate shaft universal joint to the steering gear input shaft **(see illustration)** and remove the pinch bolt.

3   Raise the front of the vehicle and support it securely on jackstands. Apply the parking brake. Lock the steering wheel with the ignition key. **Caution:** *DO NOT allow the steering wheel to rotate with the steering gear removed or damage to the SRS coil may result.*

4   Remove the shift and extension rods (manual transaxle) or shift control cable (automatic transaxle) from the transaxle (see Chapter 7).

5   Remove the catalytic converter (see Chapter 4).

6   Place a drain pan under the steering gear. Disconnect the power steering fluid lines **(see illustration)** and cap them to prevent contamination and loss of fluid. On models so equipped, remove the chassis stiffener bracket **(see illustration)**.

7   Separate the tie-rod ends from the steering knuckle arms (see Section 15). Remove the left tie-rod end.

8   Support the steering gear and remove the mounting bolts **(see illustrations)**. Lower the unit, separating the intermediate shaft from the steering gear input shaft. Move the steering gear as far as possible to the right. Rotate the steering gear so that the input shaft is facing forward. Lower the left end past the frame and remove the steering gear from the vehicle as you move it to the left side.

Installation

9   Raise the steering gear into position and

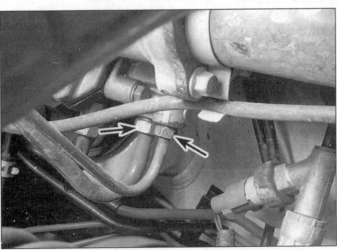

17.6a Loosen the power steering fluid line fittings (arrows), disconnect the lines and plug them to prevent leakage and contamination

17.6b On later models, remove the bolts (arrows) and detach the chassis stiffener bracket

17.8a Remove these bolts (arrows) from the left end (driver's side) of the steering gear

17.8b Remove these bolts (arrows) from the right (passenger side) steering gear mounting clamp and remove the clamp

connect the intermediate shaft, aligning the marks.

10 Install the steering gear mounting bolts and washers and tighten them to the torque listed in this Chapter's Specifications.

11 Install the left tie-rod end and connect the tie-rod ends to the steering knuckle arms (see Section 15).

12 Connect the power steering hoses/lines to the steering gear.

13 Install the transaxle control rods or cable and the catalytic converter.

14 Lower the vehicle, install the intermediate shaft pinch bolt and tighten it to the torque listed in this Chapter's Specifications. Install the steering joint cover and clamps. Make sure the two holes in the flange at the lower end of the shield are aligned with the locating pins in the floor.

15 Fill the power steering pump reservoir with the recommended fluid (see Chapter 1) and bleed the steering system (see Section 19).

18 Power steering pump - removal and installation

Refer to illustrations 18.2a and 18.2b

1 Disconnect the cable from the negative battery terminal, then disconnect the positive battery cable. **Caution:** *If the stereo in your vehicle is equipped with an anti-theft system, make sure you have the correct activation code before disconnecting the battery.*

2 Disconnect the fluid hoses at the pump **(see illustrations)**. Note the difference between the pressure and the return hoses; the return hose is held to the pump with a spring type clamp, and the pressure line has two bolts holding it to the pump body. Cap or plug both hoses to prevent leakage or contamination. Install a new O-ring on the end of the pressure line.

3 Remove the pump adjusting bolt.

4 Remove the pump mounting bolts and

remove the pump from the engine.

5 Installation is the reverse of removal. Be sure to bleed the power steering system (see Section 17) and adjust the drivebelt tension (see Chapter 1).

19 Power steering system - bleeding

1 Following any operation in which the power steering fluid lines have been disconnected, the power steering system must be bled to remove all air and obtain proper steering performance.

2 With the front wheels in the straight ahead position, check the power steering fluid level (see Chapter 1). If it's low, add fluid until it reaches the lower mark on the reservoir.

3 Start the engine and allow it to run at fast idle. Recheck the fluid level and add more if necessary to reach the Cold mark on the dipstick.

4 Bleed the system by turning the wheels from side-to-side, without hitting the stops. This will work the air out of the system. Keep the reservoir full of fluid as this is done.

5 When the air is worked out of the system, return the wheels to the straight ahead position and leave the vehicle running for several more minutes before shutting it off.

6 Road test the vehicle to be sure the steering system is functioning normally and noise free.

7 Recheck the fluid level to be sure it is up to the Hot mark on the reservoir while the engine is at normal operating temperature. Add fluid if necessary (see Chapter 1).

20 Wheels and tires - general information

Refer to illustration 20.1

All vehicles covered by this manual are

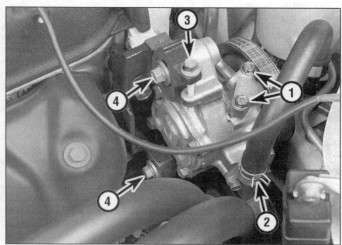

18.2a To remove the power steering pump on earlier models, disconnect the pressure line bolts (1) and the return line clamp (2), then remove the adjuster bolt (3) and the mounting bolts (4)

18.2b On later models, disconnect the pressure line bolts (1) and the return line clamp (2), then remove the mounting bolt (3) and the adjuster bolt (4)

10

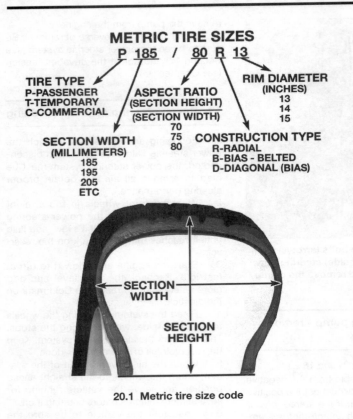

METRIC TIRE SIZES

P 185 / 80 R 13

TIRE TYPE
P-PASSENGER
T-TEMPORARY
C-COMMERCIAL

ASPECT RATIO
(SECTION HEIGHT)
—————————————
(SECTION WIDTH)
70
75
80

RIM DIAMETER
(INCHES)
13
14
15

SECTION WIDTH
(MILLIMETERS)
185
195
205
ETC

CONSTRUCTION TYPE
R-RADIAL
B-BIAS - BELTED
D-DIAGONAL (BIAS)

SECTION WIDTH

SECTION HEIGHT

20.1 Metric tire size code

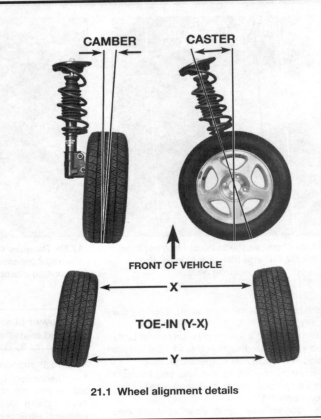

CAMBER   CASTER

FRONT OF VEHICLE

X

TOE-IN (Y-X)

Y

21.1 Wheel alignment details

equipped with metric-sized steel belted radial tires **(see illustration)**. Use of other size or type of tires may affect the ride and handling of the vehicle. Don't mix different types of tires, such as radials and bias belted, on the same vehicle as handling may be seriously affected. It's recommended that tires be replaced in pairs on the same axle, but if only one tire is being replaced, be sure it's the same size, structure and tread design as the other.

Because tire pressure has a substantial effect on handling and wear, the pressure on all tires should be checked at least once a month or before any extended trips (see Chapter 1).

Wheels must be replaced if they are bent, dented, leak air, have elongated bolt holes, are heavily rusted, out of vertical symmetry or if the lug nuts won't stay tight. Wheel repairs that use welding or peening are not recommended.

Tire and wheel balance is important to the overall handling, braking and performance of the vehicle. Unbalanced wheels can adversely affect handling and ride characteristics as well as tire life. Whenever a tire is installed on a wheel, the tire and wheel should be balanced by a shop with the proper equipment.

21   Wheel alignment - general information

Refer to illustration 21.1

A wheel alignment refers to the adjustments made to the wheels so they are in proper angular relationship to the suspension and the ground. Wheels that are out of proper alignment not only affect steering control, but also increase tire wear. Toe-in can be adjusted on the front and rear wheels. The front and rear camber and caster angles should be checked to determine if any of the suspension components are worn out or bent **(see illustration)**.

Getting the proper wheel alignment is a very exacting process, one in which complicated and expensive machines are necessary to perform the job properly. Because of this, you should have a technician with the proper equipment perform these tasks. We will, however, use this space to give you a basic idea of what is involved with wheel alignment so you can better understand the process and deal intelligently with the shop that does the work.

Toe-in is the turning in of the wheels. The purpose of a toe specification is to ensure parallel rolling of the wheels. In a vehi-cle with zero toe-in, the distance between the front edges of the wheels will be the same as the distance between the rear edges of the wheels. The actual amount of toe-in is normally only a fraction of an inch. At the front end, toe-in is controlled by the tie-rod end position on the tie-rod. At the rear it is adjusted by moving the compensating rod within its bracket on the body. Incorrect toe-in will cause the tires to wear improperly by making them scrub against the road surface.

Camber is the tilting of the wheels from the vertical when viewed from the front or rear of the vehicle. When the wheels tilt out at the top, the camber is said to be positive (+). When the wheels tilt in at the top the camber is negative (-). The amount of tilt is measured in degrees from the vertical and this measurement is called the camber angle. This angle affects the amount of tire tread which contacts the road and compensates for changes in the suspension geometry when the vehicle is cornering or traveling over an undulating surface. Camber isn't adjustable on these vehicles.

Caster is the tilting of the top of the steering axis from the vertical. A tilt toward the rear is positive caster and a tilt toward the front is negative caster. Caster isn't adjustable on these vehicles.

Chapter 11 Body

Contents

Specifications

Torque specification

Passenger's airbag module retaining nuts .... 86 in-lbs

1 General information

These models feature a "unibody" layout, using a floor pan with front and rear frame side rails which support the body components, front and rear suspension systems and other mechanical components.

Certain components are particularly vulnerable to accident damage and can be unbolted and repaired or replaced. Among these parts are the body moldings, bumpers, the hood and trunk lid (or liftgate) and all glass.

Only general body maintenance practices and body panel repair procedures within the scope of the do-it-yourselfer are included in this Chapter.

2 Body - maintenance

1   The condition of your vehicle's body is very important, because the resale value depends a great deal on it. It's much more difficult to repair a neglected or damaged body than it is to repair mechanical compo-

nents. The hidden areas of the body, such as the wheel wells, the frame and the engine compartment, are equally important, although they don't require as frequent attention as the rest of the body.
2   Once a year, or every 12,000 miles, it's a good idea to have the underside of the body steam cleaned. All traces of dirt and oil will be removed and the area can then be inspected carefully for rust, damaged brake lines, frayed electrical wires, damaged cables and other problems.
3   At the same time, clean the engine and the engine compartment with a steam cleaner or water soluble degreaser.
4   The wheel wells should be given close attention, since undercoating can peel away and stones and dirt thrown up by the tires can cause the paint to chip and flake, allowing rust to set in. If rust is found, clean down to the bare metal and apply an anti-rust paint.
5   The body should be washed about once a week. Wet the vehicle thoroughly to soften the dirt, then wash it down with a soft sponge and plenty of clean soapy water. If the surplus dirt is not washed off very carefully, it can wear down the paint.

6   Spots of tar or asphalt thrown up from the road should be removed with a cloth soaked in solvent.
7   Once every six months, wax the body and chrome trim. If a chrome cleaner is used to remove rust from any of the vehicle's plated parts, remember that the cleaner also removes part of the chrome, so use it sparingly.

3 Vinyl trim - maintenance

Don't clean vinyl trim with detergents, caustic soap or petroleum based cleaners. Plain soap and water works just fine, with a soft brush to clean dirt that may be ingrained. Wash the vinyl as frequently as the rest of the vehicle.

After cleaning, application of a high quality rubber and vinyl protectant will help prevent oxidation and cracks. The protectant can also be applied to weatherstripping, vacuum lines and rubber hoses, which often fail as a result of chemical degradation, and to the tires.

11

These photos illustrate a method of repairing simple dents. They are intended to supplement *Body repair - minor damage* in this Chapter and should not be used as the sole instructions for body repair on these vehicles.

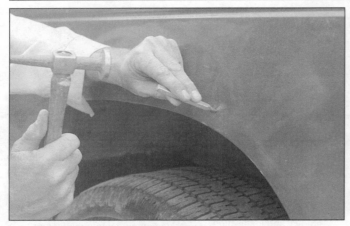

1   If you can't access the backside of the body panel to hammer out the dent, pull it out with a slide-hammer-type dent puller. In the deepest portion of the dent or along the crease line, drill or punch hole(s) at least one inch apart . . .

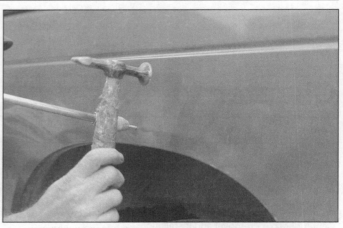

2   . . . then screw the slide-hammer into the hole and operate it. Tap with a hammer near the edge of the dent to help 'pop' the metal back to its original shape. When you're finished, the dent area should be close to its original contour and about 1/8-inch below the surface of the surrounding metal

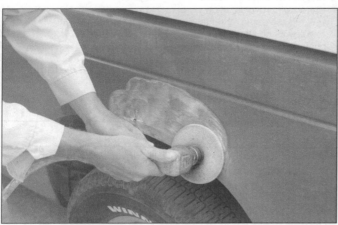

3   Using coarse-grit sandpaper, remove the paint down to the bare metal. Hand sanding works fine, but the disc sander shown here makes the job faster. Use finer (about 320-grit) sandpaper to feather-edge the paint at least one inch around the dent area

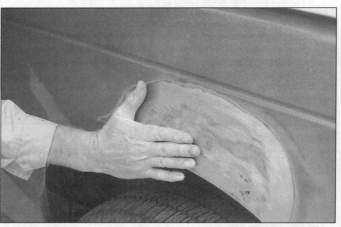

4   When the paint is removed, touch will probably be more helpful than sight for telling if the metal is straight. Hammer down the high spots or raise the low spots as necessary. Clean the repair area with wax/silicone remover

5   Following label instructions, mix up a batch of plastic filler and hardener. The ratio of filler to hardener is critical, and, if you mix it incorrectly, it will either not cure properly or cure too quickly (you won't have time to file and sand it into shape)

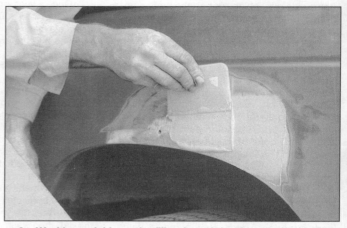

6   Working quickly so the filler doesn't harden, use a plastic applicator to press the body filler firmly into the metal, assuring it bonds completely. Work the filler until it matches the original contour and is slightly above the surrounding metal

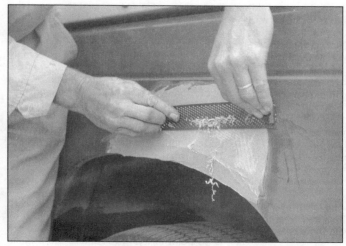

7   Let the filler harden until you can just dent it with your fingernail. Use a body file or Surform tool (shown here) to rough-shape the filler

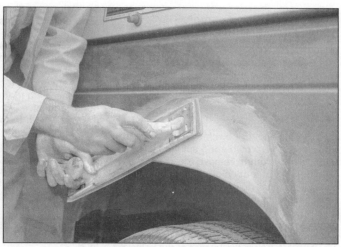

8   Use coarse-grit sandpaper and a sanding board or block to work the filler down until it's smooth and even. Work down to finer grits of sandpaper - always using a board or block - ending up with 360 or 400 grit

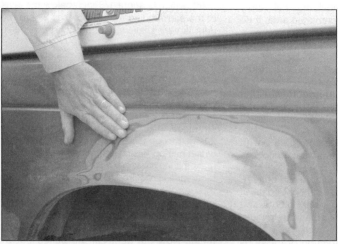

9   You shouldn't be able to feel any ridge at the transition from the filler to the bare metal or from the bare metal to the old paint. As soon as the repair is flat and uniform, remove the dust and mask off the adjacent panels or trim pieces

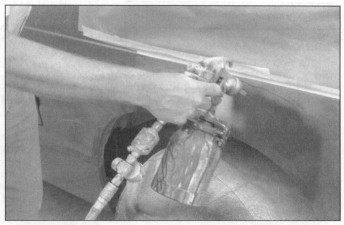

10   Apply several layers of primer to the area. Don't spray the primer on too heavy, so it sags or runs, and make sure each coat is dry before you spray on the next one. A professional-type spray gun is being used here, but aerosol spray primer is available inexpensively from auto parts stores

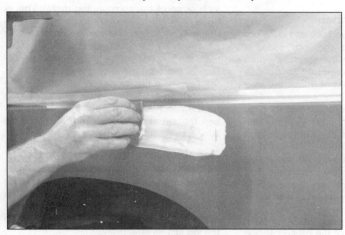

11   The primer will help reveal imperfections or scratches. Fill these with glazing compound. Follow the label instructions and sand it with 360 or 400-grit sandpaper until it's smooth. Repeat the glazing, sanding and respraying until the primer reveals a perfectly smooth surface

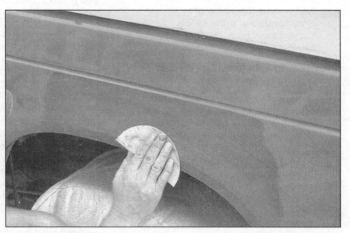

12   Finish sand the primer with very fine sandpaper (400 or 600-grit) to remove the primer overspray. Clean the area with water and allow it to dry. Use a tack rag to remove any dust, then apply the finish coat. Don't attempt to rub out or wax the repair area until the paint has dried completely (at least two weeks)

4   Upholstery and carpets - maintenance

1   Every three months remove the carpets or mats and clean the interior of the vehicle (more frequently if necessary). Vacuum the upholstery and carpets to remove loose dirt and dust.

2   Leather upholstery requires special care. Stains should be removed with warm water and a very mild soap solution. Use a clean, damp cloth to remove the soap, then wipe again with a dry cloth. Never use alcohol, gasoline, nail polish remover or thinner to clean leather upholstery.

3   After cleaning, regularly treat leather upholstery with a leather wax. Never use car wax on leather upholstery.

4   In areas where the interior of the vehicle is subject to bright sunlight, cover leather seats with a sheet if the vehicle is to be left out for any length of time.

5   Body repair - minor damage

Plastic body panels

The following repair procedures are for minor scratches and gouges. Repair of more serious damage should be left to a dealer service department or qualified auto body shop. Below is a list of the equipment and materials necessary to perform the following repair procedures on plastic body panels. Although a specific brand of material may be mentioned, it should be noted that equivalent products from other manufacturers may be used instead.

  Wax, grease and silicone removing solvent
  Cloth-backed body tape
  Sanding discs
  Drill motor with three-inch disc holder
  Hand sanding block
  Rubber squeegees
  Sandpaper
  Non-porous mixing palette
  Wood paddle or putty knife
  Curved tooth body file
  Flexible parts repair material

Flexible panels (front and rear bumper fascia)

1   Remove the damaged panel, if necessary or desirable. In most cases, repairs can be carried out with the panel installed.

2   Clean the area(s) to be repaired with a wax, grease and silicone removing solvent applied with a water-dampened cloth.

3   If the damage is structural, that is, if it extends through the panel, clean the backside of the panel area to be repaired as well. Wipe dry.

4   Sand the rear surface about 1-1/2 inches beyond the break.

5   Cut two pieces of fiberglass cloth large enough to overlap the break by about 1-1/2 inches. Cut only to the required length.

6   Mix the adhesive from the repair kit according to the instructions included with the kit, and apply a layer of the mixture approximately 1/8-inch thick on the backside of the panel. Overlap the break by at least 1-1/2 inches.

7   Apply one piece of fiberglass cloth to the adhesive and cover the cloth with additional adhesive. Apply a second piece of fiberglass cloth to the adhesive and immediately cover the cloth with additional adhesive insufficient quantity to fill the weave.

8   Allow the repair to cure for 20 to 30 minutes at 60-degrees to 80-degrees F.

9   If necessary, trim the excess repair material at the edge.

10   Remove all of the paint film over and around the area(s) to be repaired. The repair material should not overlap the painted surface.

11   With a drill motor and a sanding disc (or a rotary file), cut a "V" along the break line approximately 1/2-inch wide. Remove all dust and loose particles from the repair area.

12   Mix and apply the repair material. Apply a light coat first over the damaged area; then continue applying material until it reaches a level slightly higher than the surrounding finish.

13   Cure the mixture for 20 to 30 minutes at 60-degrees to 80-degrees F.

14   Roughly establish the contour of the area being repaired with a body file. If low areas or pits remain, mix and apply additional adhesive.

15   Block sand the damaged area with sandpaper to establish the actual contour of the surrounding surface.

16   If desired, the repaired area can be temporarily protected with several light coats of primer. Because of the special paints and techniques required for flexible body panels, it is recommended that the vehicle be taken to a paint shop for completion of the body repair.

Steel body panels

See photo sequence

Repair of minor scratches

17   If the scratch is superficial and does not penetrate to the metal of the body, repair is very simple. Lightly rub the scratched area with a fine rubbing compound to remove loose paint and built-up wax. Rinse the area with clean water.

18   Apply touch-up paint to the scratch, using a small brush. Continue to apply thin layers of paint until the surface of the paint in the scratch is level with the surrounding paint. Allow the new paint at least two weeks to harden, then blend it into the surrounding paint by rubbing with a very fine rubbing compound. Finally, apply a coat of wax to the scratch area.

19   If the scratch has penetrated the paint and exposed the metal of the body, causing the metal to rust, a different repair technique is required. Remove all loose rust from the bottom of the scratch with a pocket knife,

then apply rust inhibiting paint to prevent the formation of rust in the future. Using a rubber or nylon applicator, coat the scratched area with glaze-type filler. If required, the filler can be mixed with thinner to provide a very thin paste, which is ideal for filling narrow scratches. Before the glaze filler in the scratch hardens, wrap a piece of smooth cotton cloth around the tip of a finger. Dip the cloth in thinner and then quickly wipe it along the surface of the scratch. This will ensure that the surface of the filler is slightly hollow. The scratch can now be painted over as described earlier in this section.

Repair of dents

20   When repairing dents, the first job is to pull the dent out until the affected area is as close as possible to its original shape. There is no point in trying to restore the original shape completely as the metal in the damaged area will have stretched on impact and cannot be restored to its original contours. It is better to bring the level of the dent up to a point, which is about 1/8-inch below the level of the surrounding metal. In cases where the dent is very shallow, it is not worth trying to pull it out at all.

21   If the back side of the dent is accessible, it can be hammered out gently from behind using a soft-face hammer. While doing this, hold a block of wood firmly against the opposite side of the metal to absorb the hammer blows and prevent the metal from being stretched.

22   If the dent is in a section of the body which has double layers, or some other factor makes it inaccessible from behind, a different technique is required. Drill several small holes through the metal inside the damaged area, particularly in the deeper sections. Screw long, self-tapping screws into the holes just enough for them to get a good grip in the metal. Now the dent can be pulled out by pulling on the protruding heads of the screws with locking pliers.

23   The next stage of repair is the removal of paint from the damaged area and from an inch or so of the surrounding metal. This is done with a wire brush or sanding disk in a drill motor, although it can be done just as effectively by hand with sandpaper. To complete the preparation for filling, score the surface of the bare metal with a screwdriver or the tang of a file, or drill small holes in the affected area. This will provide a good grip for the filler material. To complete the repair, see the subsection on filling and painting later in this Section.

Repair of rust holes or gashes

24   Remove all paint from the affected area and from an inch or so of the surrounding metal using a sanding disk or wire brush mounted in a drill motor. If these are not available, a few sheets of sandpaper will do the job just as effectively.

25   With the paint removed, you will be able to determine the severity of the corrosion and decide whether to replace the whole panel, if

possible, or repair the affected area. New body panels are not as expensive as most people think and it is often quicker to install a new panel than to repair large areas of rust.

26   Remove all trim pieces from the affected area except those which will act as a guide to the original shape of the damaged body, such as headlight shells, etc. Using metal snips or a hacksaw blade, remove all loose metal and any other metal that is badly affected by rust. Hammer the edges of the hole in to create a slight depression for the filler material.

27   Wire brush the affected area to remove the powdery rust from the surface of the metal. If the back of the rusted area is accessible, treat it with rust inhibiting paint.

28   Before filling is done, block the hole in some way. This can be done with sheet metal riveted or screwed into place, or by stuffing the hole with wire mesh.

29   Once the hole is blocked off, the affected area can be filled and painted. See the following subsection on filling and painting.

Filling and painting

30   Many types of body fillers are available, but generally speaking, body repair kits which contain filler paste and a tube of resin hardener are best for this type of repair work. A wide, flexible plastic or nylon applicator will be necessary for imparting a smooth and contoured finish to the surface of the filler material. Mix up a small amount of filler on a clean piece of wood or cardboard (use the hardener sparingly). Follow the manufacturer's instructions on the package, otherwise the filler will set incorrectly.

31   Using the applicator, apply the filler paste to the prepared area. Draw the applicator across the surface of the filler to achieve the desired contour and to level the filler surface. As soon as a contour that approximates the original one is achieved, stop working the paste. If you continue, the paste will begin to stick to the applicator. Continue to add thin layers of paste at 20-minute intervals until the level of the filler is just above the surrounding metal.

32   Once the filler has hardened, the excess can be removed with a body file. From then on, progressively finer grades of sandpaper should be used, starting with a 180-grit paper and finishing with 600-grit wet-or-dry paper. Always wrap the sandpaper around a flat rubber or wooden block, otherwise the surface of the filler will not be completely flat. During the sanding of the filler surface, the wet-or-dry paper should be periodically rinsed in water. This will ensure that a very smooth finish is produced in the final stage.

33   At this point, the repair area should be surrounded by a ring of bare metal, which in turn should be encircled by the finely feathered edge of good paint. Rinse the repair area with clean water until all of the dust produced by the sanding operation is gone.

34   Spray the entire area with a light coat of primer. This will reveal any imperfections in the surface of the filler. Repair the imperfections with fresh filler paste or glaze filler and once more smooth the surface with sandpaper. Repeat this spray-and-repair procedure until you are satisfied that the surface of the filler and the feathered edge of the paint are perfect. Rinse the area with clean water and allow it to dry completely.

35   The repair area is now ready for painting. Spray painting must be carried out in a warm, dry, windless and dust free atmosphere. These conditions can be created if you have access to a large indoor work area, but if you are forced to work in the open, you will have to pick the day very carefully. If you are working indoors, dousing the floor in the work area with water will help settle the dust, which would otherwise be in the air. If the repair area is confined to one body panel, mask off the surrounding panels. This will help minimize the effects of a slight mismatch in paint color. Trim pieces such as chrome strips, door handles, etc., will also need to be masked off or removed. Use masking tape and several thickness of newspaper for the masking operations.

36   Before spraying, shake the paint can thoroughly, then spray a test area until the spray painting technique is mastered. Cover the repair area with a thick coat of primer. The thickness should be built up using several thin layers of primer rather than one thick one. Using 600-grit wet-or-dry sandpaper, rub down the surface of the primer until it is very smooth. While doing this, the work area should be thoroughly rinsed with water and the wet-or-dry sandpaper periodically rinsed as well. Allow the primer to dry before spraying additional coats.

37   Spray on the top coat, again building up the thickness by using several thin layers of paint. Begin spraying in the center of the repair area and then, using a circular motion, work out until the whole repair area and about two inches of the surrounding original paint is covered. Remove all masking material 10 to 15 minutes after spraying on the final coat of paint. Allow the new paint at least two weeks to harden, then use a very fine rubbing compound to blend the edges of the new paint into the existing paint. Finally, apply a coat of wax.

6   Body repair - major damage

1   Major damage must be repaired by an auto body shop specifically equipped to perform unibody repairs. These shops have the specialized equipment required to do the job properly.

2   If the damage is extensive, the body must be checked for proper alignment or the vehicle's handling characteristics may be adversely affected and other components may wear at an accelerated rate.

3   Due to the fact that all of the major body components (hood, fenders, etc.) are separate and replaceable units, any seriously damaged components should be replaced rather than repaired. Sometimes the components can be found in a wrecking yard that specializes in used vehicle components, often at considerable savings over the cost of new parts.

7   Hinges and locks - maintenance

Once every 3000 miles, or every three months, the hinges and latch assemblies on the doors, hood and trunk (or liftgate) should be given a few drops of light oil or lock lubricant. The door latch strikers should also be lubricated with a thin coat of grease to reduce wear and ensure free movement. Lubricate the door and trunk (or liftgate) locks with spray-on graphite lubricant.

8   Windshield and fixed glass - replacement

Replacement of the windshield and fixed glass requires the use of special fast-setting adhesive/caulk materials and some specialized tools and techniques. These operations should be left to a dealer service department or a shop specializing in glass work.

9   Hood - removal, installation and adjustment

Removal and installation

Refer to illustration 9.2

Note: *The hood is heavy and somewhat awkward to remove and install - at least two people should perform this procedure.*

1   Use blankets or pads to cover the fenders and cowl areas. This will protect the body and paint as the hood is lifted off.

2   Scribe or draw alignment marks around the bolt heads to ensure proper alignment during installation **(see illustration)**.

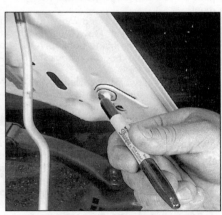

9.2 Scribe or draw alignment marks around the bolt heads (arrows) and the hood hinges to ensure proper alignment of the hood when it's reinstalled

11

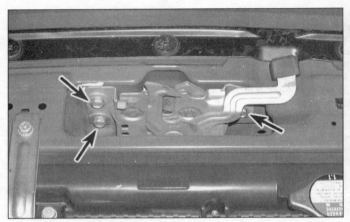

9.10 Scribe a line around the hood latch so you can judge the movement, then loosen the bolts (arrows) and adjust the latch position

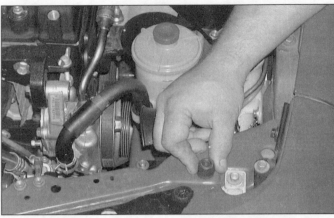

9.11 To adjust the vertical height of the leading edge of the hood so it's flush with the fenders, turn each edge cushion clockwise (to lower the hood) or counterclockwise (to raise the hood)

3   Disconnect any cables or wire harnesses, which will interfere with removal.

4   Have an assistant support the weight of the hood. Remove the hinge-to-hood bolts and any shims, if already installed. If there are any shims, make sure you keep the shims for each side with their respective bolts. Don't mix them up.

5   Lift off the hood.

6   Installation is the reverse of removal. If you fit the hood so that the hinges fit within the scribe marks you made before loosening the bolts and if you install the shims, if any, in the same number and location they were in prior to removal, then the hood should still be aligned. Of course, if you're installing a new hood, or forgot to scribe the hinge positions, or mixed up the shims, etc. then you'll need to readjust the hood position.

Adjustment

Refer to illustrations 9.10 and 9.11

7   You can adjust the hood fore-and-aft and right-and-left by means of the elongated holes in the hinges.

8   Scribe a line around the entire hinge plate so you can judge the amount of movement.

9   Loosen the bolts and move the hood into correct alignment. Move it only a little at a time. Tighten the hinge bolts or nuts and carefully lower the hood to check the alignment.

10   If necessary after installation, the entire hood latch assembly can be adjusted up-and-down as well as from side-to-side on the upper radiator support so the hood closes securely and is flush with the fenders **(see illustration)**. To do this, scribe a line around the hood latch mounting bolts to provide a reference point. Then loosen the bolts and reposition the latch assembly as necessary. Following adjustment, retighten the mounting bolts.

11   Adjust the vertical height of the leading edge of the hood by screwing the edge cushions in or out so that the hood, when closed, is flush with the fenders **(see illustration)**.

Finally, adjust the rear edge of the hood until it's flush with the fenders by using shims (available at a Honda dealer parts department) between the hood and the hinge plates.

12   The hood latch assembly, as well as the hinges, should be periodically lubricated with white lithium-base grease to prevent sticking and wear.

10   Hood release latch and cable - removal and installation

Warning: *Models covered by this manual are equipped with a Supplemental Restraint System (SRS), more commonly known as airbags. Always disable the airbag system before working in the vicinity of the SRS unit, steering column or instrument panel to avoid the possibility of accidental deployment of the airbag, which could cause personal injury (see Chapter 12).*

Latch

1   Remove the radiator grille opening cover, then scribe a line around the latch to aid alignment when installing, detach the latch retaining bolts from the radiator support **(see illustration 9.10)** and remove the latch.

10.4 Detach the cable and unhook the end from the latch

2   Disconnect the hood release cable by disengaging the cable from the latch assembly.

3   Installation is reverse of the removal. **Note:** *Adjust the latch so the hood engages securely when closed and the hood bumpers are slightly compressed.*

Cable

Refer to illustrations 10.4 and 10.5

4   Disconnect the hood release cable from the latch assembly as described above **(see illustration)**.

5   Working in the passenger's compartment, remove the driver's side kick panel. Then remove the two release lever mounting bolts and detach the hood release lever **(see illustration)**. Detach the cable from the lever.

6   Attach a piece of stiff wire to the latch end of the cable, then detach all the cable retaining clips.

7   Push the grommet through the firewall and pull the cable into the engine compartment. Ensure that the new cable has a grommet attached, then remove the old cable from the wire and replace it with the new cable.

8   Pull the wire back through the firewall.

9   Installation is the reverse of the removal **Note:** *Push on the grommet to seat it in the firewall completely.*

10.5 Remove the release lever bolts (arrows) and detach the cable

11.3a Remove the screws (arrows) on the lower splash panel

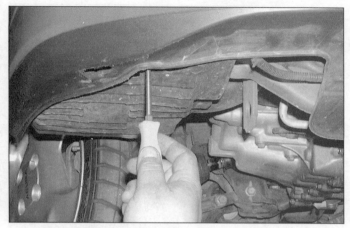

11.3b Remove the screws from the ends of the splash shield

11 Bumper covers and bumpers - removal and installation

Front

Refer to illustrations 11.3a, 11.3b, 11.4, 11.5 and 11.6

1 Apply the parking brake, raise the vehicle and support it securely on jackstands.

2 Disconnect the negative battery cable. **Caution:** *If the radio in your vehicle is equipped with an anti-theft system, make sure you have the correct activation code before disconnecting the battery.*

3 Working under the vehicle, detach the screws securing the lower edges of the bumper cover **(see illustrations)**.

4 Working in the front wheel opening, detach the plastic retaining screws securing the bumper cover to inner fenderwell splash shields **(see illustration)**.

5 Remove the bumper cover-to-chassis bolts **(see illustration)**.

6 Remove the screws (or the plastic retaining rivets on some models) securing the upper portion of the bumper cover **(see illustration)** and pull the bumper cover assembly

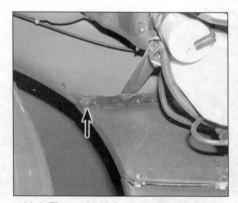

11.4 The ends of the bumper cover are retained by plastic screws (arrow)

out and away from the vehicle. **Note:** *To remove plastic retaining rivets, pull the center portion out, then pry the entire rivet out.*

7 Disconnect any electrical connections, which would interfere with removal. If necessary, remove the bumper beam gussets from each side of the bumper, then remove the four bolts and detach the bumper from the vehicle.

8 Installation is the reverse of removal.

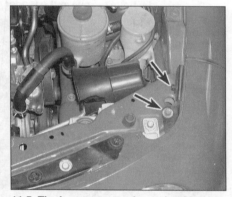

11.5 The bumper cover is retained by nuts and bolts at the top corners (arrows)

Rear

Refer to illustrations 11.10, 11.11, 11.12a and 11.12b

9 Apply the parking brake, raise the vehicle and support it securely on jackstands.

10 Working under the vehicle, detach the plastic clips and screws securing the lower edge of the bumper cover **(see illustration)**.

11 Remove the screws securing the

11.6 Remove the screws or rivets along the upper edge of the bumper cover (arrows)

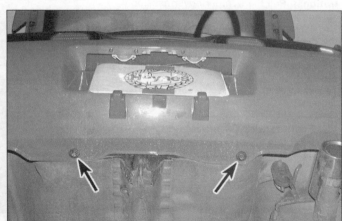

11.10 Remove the lower plastic rivets (arrows) from the rear bumper cover

11

11.11 The forward ends of the bumper cover are retained by bolts (arrow) in the fender opening

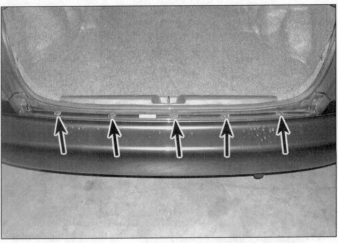

11.12a Remove the screws along the upper edge of the bumper cover

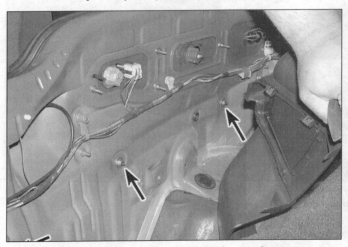

11.12b Pull the trim away for access to the rear bumper cover retaining nuts (arrows)

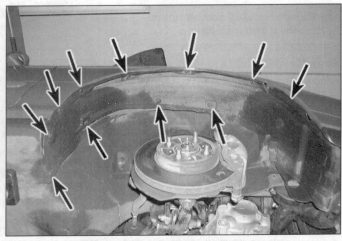

12.3 Remove the screws (arrows) retaining the inner panel to the fender

bumper cover in the rear wheel openings **(see illustration)**.

12   Open the trunk or rear liftgate and remove the screws and nuts securing the upper edge of the bumper cover **(see illustrations)**. Pull the bumper cover assembly out and away from the vehicle.

13   To remove the bumper beam, drill out the rivets securing the foam isolator, then remove the bumper retaining bolts and pull the bumper assembly out and away from the vehicle.

14   Installation is the reverse of removal.

12   Front fender - removal and installation

Refer to illustrations 12.3, 12.4a, 12.4b, 12.4c, 12.4d and 12.4e

1   Loosen the wheel lug nuts, raise the front of the vehicle and support it securely on jackstands. Remove the wheel.

2   Remove the front bumper cover (see Section 11).

3   Remove the retaining screws securing the inner fender housing panel and detach the panel **(see illustration)**.

4   Remove the remaining fender mounting bolts **(see illustrations)**.

5   Detach the fender. It's a good idea to have an assistant support the fender while it's being moved away from the vehicle to prevent damage to the surrounding body panels.

6   Installation is the reverse of removal.

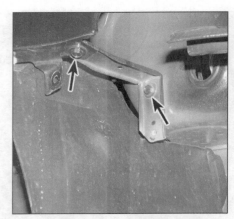

12.4a On Civic models, remove the bolts (arrows) and detach the bracket behind the headlight

12.4b Remove the lower bracket-to-fender bolt (arrow)

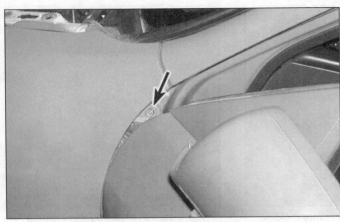

12.4c The upper rear corner of the fender is retained to the A-pillar with a bolt (arrow)

12.4d Remove the bolts (arrows) along the top of the fender

12.4e The lower rear corner of the fender is retained by two bolts (arrows)

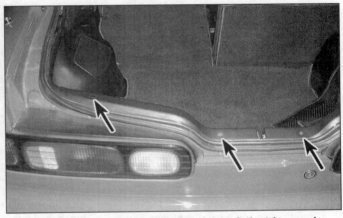

13.2a Remove the rivets (arrows) and detach the trim panel . . .

13 Liftgate latch, lock cylinder and support struts - removal and installation

Refer to illustrations 13.2a, 13.2b, 13.5, 13.9 and 13.10

1   Open the liftgate and remove the liftgate trim panel plastic clips.

Latch

2   Remove the trim cover and latch mounting screws **(see illustrations)**.
3   Disconnect the actuating rod, detach any electrical connectors, then remove the latch from the liftgate.
4   Installation is the reverse of removal.

Lock cylinder

5   Remove the bolt securing the lock cylinder to the liftgate **(see illustration)**.

6   Detach the actuating rod, rotate the lock cylinder and pull it out to remove it from the liftgate.
7   Installation is the reverse of removal.

Support struts

8   Open the liftgate and support it securely.
9   Use a small screwdriver to detach the retaining clips at upper end of the support strut. Then pry or pull sharply to detach it from the vehicle **(see illustration)**.

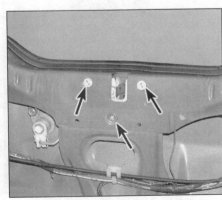

13.2b . . . then remove the latch screws (arrows)

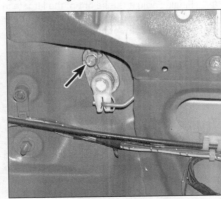

13.5 Remove the lock cylinder bolt (arrow)

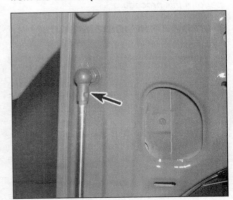

13.9 Use a small screwdriver to pry off the retaining clip (arrow)

11

13.10 Detach the lower strut cover and remove the bolt

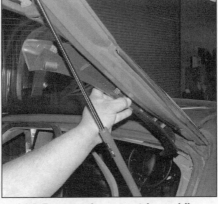

14.2 Remove the upper trim molding

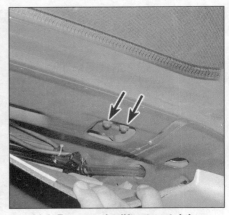

14.4 Remove the liftgate retaining nuts (arrows)

14.7 To adjust the liftgate striker, loosen the screws and move the striker as necessary

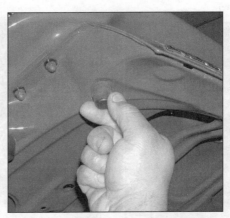

14.8 Screw the bumpers in-or-out to make final adjustments to the liftgate

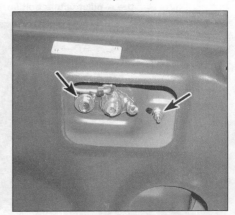

15.2 Trunk lid latch retaining screw and bolt (arrows)

10   Detach the cover and remove the retaining bolt at the lower end, then remove the strut **(see illustration)**.

11   Installation is the reverse of removal.

14   Liftgate - removal, installation and adjustment

Note: *The liftgate is heavy and somewhat awkward to hold - at least two people should perform this procedure.*

Removal and installation

Refer to illustrations 14.2 and 14.4

1   Open the liftgate and support it securely.

2   Remove the upper trim molding from the lift gate opening **(see illustration)** and disconnect all wiring harness connectors leading to the liftgate.

3   While an assistant supports the liftgate, detach both ends of the support struts. Then pry or pull sharply to remove them from the vehicle.

4   Detach the hinge-to-liftgate nuts **(see illustration)** and remove the liftgate from the vehicle.

5   Installation is the reverse of removal.

Adjustment

Refer to illustrations 14.7 and 14.8

6   Adjustments are made by loosening the hinge-to-liftgate bolts and moving the liftgate. Proper alignment is achieved when the edges of the liftgate are parallel with the rear quarter panels and the roof panel.

7   Adjust the latch striker assembly as necessary (up and down) to provide positive engagement with the latch mechanism **(see illustration)**.

8   Finally, adjust the height of the liftgate in relation to the body by screwing the rubber bumpers in-or-out **(see illustration)**.

15   Trunk lid latch, lock cylinder and support struts - removal and installation

Trunk lid latch

Refer to illustrations 15.2 and 15.3

1   Open the trunk and scribe a line around the trunk lid latch assembly for a reference point to aid the installation procedure.

2   Remove the bolt and nut retaining the trunk lid latch **(see illustration)**.

3   Remove the latch and disconnect the

cable and electrical connections **(see illustration)**.

4   Installation is the reverse of removal.

Trunk lock cylinder

5   Open the trunk. Look upward through the trunk lid access hole and detach the cable from the lock cylinder.

6   Grasp the lock cylinder twist it counterclockwise 90-degrees to align the tabs on the

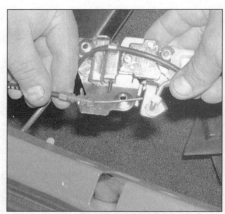

15.3 Detach the cable and unhook the end from the latch

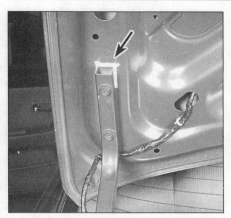

16.3 Draw around the hinge with a marking pen so the trunk can be installed in the same position

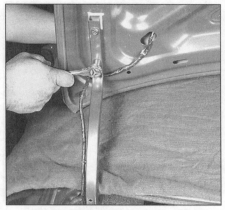

16.4 With an assistant holding the trunk lid, remove the four trunk lid retaining bolts

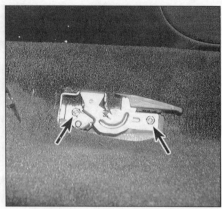

17.1 Remove the screws (arrows) and detach the release assembly

lock cylinder with the slots in the body and lower it from the trunk lid.

7   Installation is the reverse of removal.

Trunk support struts

8   Open the trunk and support it securely.

9   Remove the two bolts and detach the upper end of the support strut.

10   Use a small screwdriver to detach the cover and remove the retaining bolt at the lower end, then remove the strut.

11   Installation is the reverse of removal.

---

16   Trunk lid - removal, installation and adjustment

Note: *The trunk lid is heavy and somewhat awkward to remove and install - at least two people should perform this procedure.*

Removal and installation

Refer to illustrations 16.3 and 16.4

1   Open the trunk lid and cover the edges of the trunk compartment with pads or cloths to protect the painted surfaces when the lid is removed.

2   Disconnect any cables or wire harness connectors attached to the trunk lid that would interfere with removal.

3   Make alignment marks around the hinge **(see illustration)**.

4   While an assistant supports the trunk lid, remove the lid-to-hinge bolts on both sides and lift it off **(see illustration)**.

5   Installation is the reverse of removal.

Note: *When reinstalling the trunk lid, align the lid-to-hinge bolts with the marks made during removal.*

Adjustment

6   Fore-and-aft and side-to-side adjustment of the trunk lid is accomplished by moving the lid in relation to the hinge after loosening the bolts or nuts.

7   Scribe a line around the hinge plate as described earlier in this Section so you can

determine the amount of movement.

8   Loosen the bolts or nuts and move the trunk lid into correct alignment. Move it only a little at a time. Tighten the hinge bolts or nuts and carefully lower the trunk lid to check the alignment.

9   If necessary after installation, the entire trunk lid striker assembly can be adjusted up and down as well as from side to side on the trunk lid so the lid closes securely and is flush with the rear quarter panels. To do this, scribe a line around the trunk lid striker assembly to provide a reference point. Then loosen the bolts and reposition the striker as necessary. Following adjustment, retighten the mounting bolts.

10   The trunk lid latch assembly, as well as the hinges, should be periodically lubricated with white lithium-base grease to prevent sticking and wear.

11   Finally, adjust the height of the trunk lid in relation to the body by screwing the rubber bumpers in-or-out.

---

17   Trunk release and fuel door cable - removal and installation

Trunk release

Refer to illustrations 17.1 and 17.4

1   Working in the drivers side passenger compartment, remove the screw and detach the trim panel for access the release cable and lever retaining bolts. Then remove the lever retaining bolts **(see illustration)**. Detach the cable(s) from the release assembly.

2   Installation is the reverse of removal.

Fuel door cable

3   Working in the trunk or rear compartment, remove plastic clips securing the drivers side and rear inside finishing panels to allow access to the fuel door assembly.

4   Twist the cable 90-degrees to align the tabs on the striker assembly with the slots in the body and withdraw it into the rear compartment **(see illustration)**.

5   Detach all the cable retaining clips. Attach a piece of thin wire to the end of the cable.

6   Working in the trunk compartment, pull the cable assembly towards the rear of the vehicle until you can see the wire.

7   Installation is the reverse of removal.

---

18   Door trim panel - removal and installation

Refer to illustrations 18.1, 18.3a, 18.3b, 18.3c, 18.3d and 18.3e

Warning: *Models covered by this manual are equipped with a Supplemental Restraint System (SRS), more commonly known as airbags. Always disable the airbag system before working in the vicinity of the SRS unit, steering column or instrument panel to avoid the possibility of accidental deployment of the airbag, which could cause personal injury (see Chapter 12).*

Caution: *If the radio in your vehicle is equipped with an anti-theft system, make sure you have the correct activation code before disconnecting the battery.*

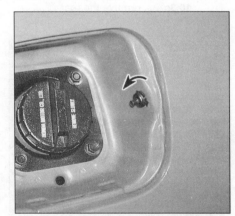

17.4 From inside the trunk or hatch area, rotate the fuel door release cable 90-degrees so the tabs line up with the slots in the body, then withdraw it

11

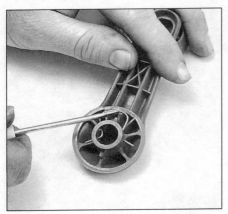

18.1 Remove the window crank by pulling this clip off with a wire hook or a special tool made for this purpose (handle removed for clarity)

1   On manual window regulator equipped models, remove the window crank **(see illustration)**.
2   Remove the inside door handle (see Section 20).
3   Remove the door trim panel retaining screws **(see illustrations),** then carefully pry loose the retaining clips with a trim pad remover or a putty knife between the trim panel and the door. Work slowly and carefully

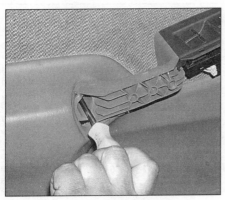

18.3c . . . remove the rear . . .

18.3d . . . and the front screws in the door pull

18.3a Remove the screw from the door handle

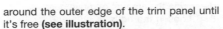

around the outer edge of the trim panel until it's free **(see illustration)**.
4   After all of the clips are disengaged, pull the trim panel up, unplug any wire harness connectors and remove the panel.
5   For access to the door inner panel, carefully pry out the retainers and detach the plastic shield.
6   Prior to installation of the door trim panel, be sure to reinstall any clips in the panel which may have come out when you removed the panel.
7   Plug in the wire harness connectors for the power door lock switch and the power window switch, if equipped, and place the panel in position in the door. Press the door panel into place until the clips are seated. Install the trim panel retaining screws and the armrest retaining screw. Install the power door lock switch assembly, if equipped. Install the manual regulator crank handle.

19 Door - removal, installation and adjustment

Note: *The door is heavy and somewhat awkward to remove and install - at least two people should perform this procedure.*

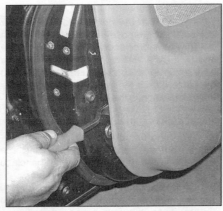

18.3e Carefully pry the clips free so the door trim panel can be removed

18.3b Remove the screw and detach the door pull trim panel screws, then . . .

Removal and installation

Refer to illustrations 19.6 and 19.8
1   Lower the window completely in the door and then disconnect the negative cable from the battery.
2   Open the door all the way and support it on jacks or blocks covered with rags to prevent damaging the paint.
3   Remove the door trim panel and water deflector as described in Section 18.
4   Disconnect all electrical connections, ground wires and harness retaining clips from the door. **Note:** *It is a good idea to label all connections to aid the reassembly process.*
5   From the door side, detach the rubber conduit between the body and the door. Then pull the wiring harness through conduit hole and remove from the door.
6   Remove the door stop strut center pin **(see illustration)**.
7   Mark around the door hinges with a pen or a scribe to facilitate realignment during reassembly.
8   With an assistant holding the door, remove the hinge to door bolts **(see illustration)** and lift the door off.
9   Installation is the reverse of removal.

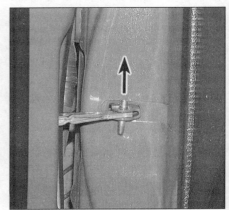

19.6 Use a small hammer to tap out the retaining pin (tap it upwards only)

19.8 Remove the door hinge
bolts (arrows)

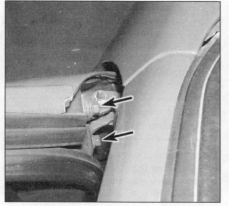

19.11 Loosen the hinge-to-body bolts
(arrows) to adjust the doors

19.13 Adjust the door lock striker by
loosening the mounting screws and
gently tapping the striker in the
desired direction (arrows)

Adjustment

Refer to illustrations 19.11 and 19.13

10   Having proper door to body alignment is a critical part of a well functioning door assembly. First check the door hinge pins for excessive play. Fully open the door and lift up and down on the door without lifting the body. If a door has 1/16-inch or more excessive play, the hinges should be replaced.

11   Door-to-body alignment adjustments are made by loosening the hinge-to-body bolts **(see illustration)** or hinge-to-door bolts and moving the door. Proper body alignment is achieved when the top of the doors are parallel with the roof section, the front door is flush with the fender, the rear door is flush with the rear quarter panel and the bottom of the doors are aligned with the lower rocker panel. If these goals can't be reached by adjusting the hinge-to-body or hinge-to-door bolts, body alignment shims may have to be purchased and inserted behind the hinges to achieve correct alignment.

12   To adjust the door closed position, scribe a line or mark around the striker plate to provide a reference point, then check that the door latch is contacting the center of the latch striker. If not adjust the up and down position first.

13   Finally adjust the latch striker sideways position, so that the door panel is flush with the center pillar or rear quarter panel and provides positive engagement with the latch mechanism **(see illustration)**.

---

20   Door latch, lock cylinder and handles - removal and installation

Door latch

Refer to illustrations 20.2 and 20.4

1   Raise the window then remove the door trim panel and watershield as described in Section 18.

2   Working through the large access hole, disengage the outside door handle-to-latch rod, outside door lock-to-latch rod, the inside lock-to-latch rod, the inside handle-to-latch rod and the lock solenoid-to-latch rod (if equipped) **(see illustration)**.

3   All door locking rods are attached by plastic clips. The plastic clips can be removed by unsnapping the portion engaging the connecting rod and then pulling the rod out of its locating hole.

4   Remove the screws securing the latch

to the door **(see illustration)**. Remove the latch assembly from the door.

5   Installation is the reverse of removal.

Outside handle and door lock cylinder

Refer to illustration 20.7

6   To remove the outside handle and lock cylinder assembly, raise the window and remove the door trim panel and watershield as described in Section 18.

7   Working through the access hole, disengage the plastic clips that secure the outside handle-to-latch rod and the outside door lock-to-latch rod **(see illustration)**.

8   Remove the outside handle retaining bolts **(see illustration 20.7)**.

9   Remove the handle and lock cylinder assembly from the vehicle.

10   Installation is the reverse of removal.

Inside handle

Refer to illustration 20.12

11   Remove the door trim panel as described in Section 14 and peel away the watershield.

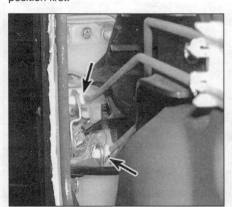

20.2 Detach the actuating rod links
(arrows) from the latch

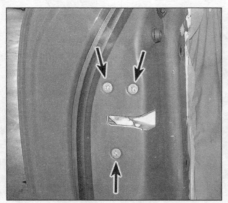

20.4 Remove the latch screws (arrows)
from the end of the door and pull the latch
assembly through the access hole

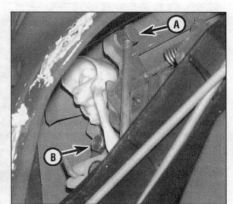

20.7 Detach the actuating rod (A) and
outside handle retaining fasteners (B) -
both items can be reached through the
access hole in the door

11

12 Unclip the door actuating rod guide, then remove the door handle retaining screws **(see illustration)**.

13 Pull the handle free from the door, then disconnect the actuating rod from the backside of the handle control and remove the handle from the door.

14 Installation is the reverse of removal.

21 Door window glass - removal and installation

Refer to illustrations 21.4 and 21.5

1 Remove the door trim panel and the plastic watershield (see Section 18).

2 Lower the window glass all the way down into the door.

3 Carefully pry the weatherstrip out of the door window opening.

4 Remove the bolt(s) and detach the glass run channel from the door **(see illustration)**.

5 Raise the window just enough to access the window retaining bolts through the hole in the door frame **(see illustration)**.

6 Place a rag over the glass to help prevent scratching the glass and remove the two glass mounting bolts.

7 Remove the glass by pulling it up and out.

8 Installation is the reverse of removal.

22 Door window glass regulator - removal and installation

Refer to illustrations 22.4a and 22.4b

1 Remove the door trim panel and the plastic watershield (see Section 14).

2 Remove the window glass assembly (see Section 16).

3 On power operated windows, disconnect the electrical connector from the window regulator motor.

4 On power operated windows, remove the equalizer arm bracket and the regulator mounting bolts **(see illustrations)**. On manually operated windows remove the regulator mounting bolts, then slide the regulator assembly out of the lower channel guide.

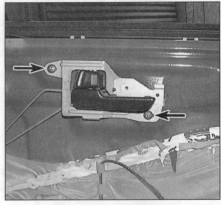

20.12 Remove the inside handle retaining screws (arrows) , then rotate the handle outward and detach the actuating rods from the backside

5 Pull the equalizer arm and regulator assemblies through the service hole in the door frame to remove it.

6 Installation is the reverse of removal.

21.4 Remove the window run channel bolt (arrow) from the end of the door (Civic shown, Integra similar)

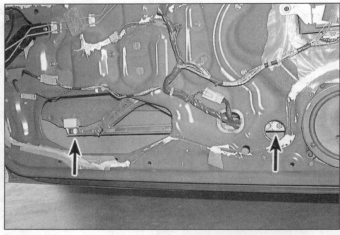

21.5 Raise the window just enough to access the glass retaining bolts (arrows) through the holes in the door frame - remove the bolts securing the glass to the equalizer arm

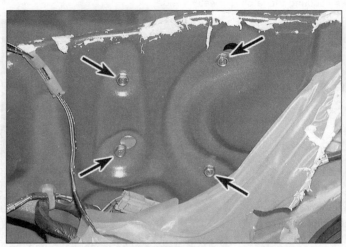

22.4a Detach the window equalizer arm channel retaining bolts (arrows) . . .

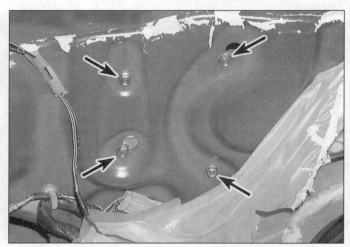

22.4b . . . then remove the window regulator bolts (arrows) (power window equipped model shown)

23.2 Use a small screwdriver to pry off
the mirror cover

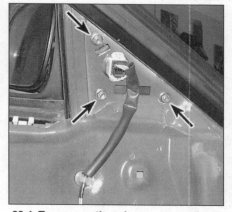

23.4 To remove the mirror, remove these
three nuts (arrows) - if the vehicle has
power mirrors, unplug the electrical
connector too

23.7 Remove the mirror cover

23   Rearview mirrors - removal and installation

Outside mirrors

Refer to illustration 23.2 and 23.4
1   Remove the door trim panel and the plastic watershield (see Section 18).
2   Pry off the mirror trim cover **(see illustration)**.
3   Disconnect the electrical connector from the mirror (if equipped).
4   Remove the three mirror retaining nuts and detach the mirror from the vehicle **(see illustration)**.
5   Installation is the reverse of removal.

Inside mirror

Refer to illustrations 23.7 and 23.8
6   Disconnect the electrical connector from the mirror (if equipped).
7   Detach the cover from the retaining bracket **(see illustration)**.
8   Remove the screws and lower the mirror **(see illustration)**.
9   Installation is the reverse of removal.

24   Center console - removal and installation

Warning: *Models covered by this manual are equipped with a Supplemental Restraint System (SRS), more commonly known as airbags. Always disable the airbag system before working in the vicinity of the SRS unit, steering column or instrument panel to avoid the possibility of accidental deployment of the airbag, which could cause personal injury (see Chapter 12).*
1   Disconnect the negative battery cable.
Caution: *If the radio in your vehicle is equipped with an anti-theft system, make sure you have the correct activation code before disconnecting the battery.*

Rear console

Refer to illustrations 24.2, 24.3a and 24.3b
2   Pry up the cover and remove the two rear console screws **(see illustration)**.
3   Remove the screws along both sides of console **(see illustrations)**.
4   Pull up on the parking brake handle. Remove the rear half of the console by lifting it up and toward the rear.

23.8 Remove the three screws (arrows)
and detach the mirror

Front console

Refer to illustrations 24.6a, 24.6b and 24.7
5   Remove the shift knob (see Chapter 7A or B).
6   Remove the console retaining screws **(see illustrations)**.

24.2 Remove the screws (arrows) from
the front edge of the rear console

24.3a Remove the screws (arrows) on
each side of the rear console

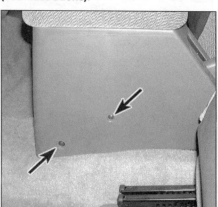

24.3b On some models, its easier to move
the front seat forward for access to the
rear console screw (arrows)

11

24.6a Remove the screws along the sides (arrow) . . .

7   Remove the front console screws and lift the console up and over the shift lever **(see illustration)**. Disconnect any electrical connections and remove the console from the vehicle.
8   Installation is the reverse of removal.

25 Dashboard trim panels - removal and installation

Warning: *Models covered by this manual are equipped with a Supplemental Restraint System (SRS), more commonly known as airbags. Always disable the airbag system before working in the vicinity of the SRS unit, steering column or instrument panel to avoid the possibility of accidental deployment of the airbag, which could cause personal injury (see Chapter 12).*
Caution: *If the radio in your vehicle is equipped with an anti-theft system, make sure you have the correct activation code before disconnecting the battery.*

Instrument cluster bezel

Refer to illustration 25.2
1   Tilt the steering wheel down to the lowest position.
2   Remove the Phillips screws **(see illustration)**, then grasp the bezel securely and pull back to detach the clips from the instrument panel.

3   Unplug any electrical connectors that interfere with removal.
4   Installation is the reverse of removal.

Lower instrument panel cover

Refer to illustration 25.5
5   Remove the lower screws securing the sound insulator panel to the lower steering cover, then remove the steering column cover retaining screws **(see illustration)**.
6   Lift the lower edge of the steering column cover upward and detach the clips or fasteners on the upper edge.
7   Unplug any electrical connectors, then lower the trim panel from the instrument panel.
8   Installation is the reverse of removal.

Knee bolster

Refer to illustration 25.10
9   Remove the lower steering column trim cover as described above.
10   Detach the knee bolster retaining bolts and remove it from the vehicle **(see illustration)**.
11   Installation is the reverse of removal.

24.6b . . . and (if equipped) along the front of the front edge of the console

24.7 Lift the rear of the console up, then pull it out

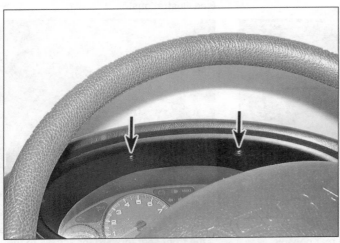

25.2 Remove the cluster retaining screws (arrows) with a Phillips screwdriver

25.5 Remove the screws (arrows) from the lower instrument panel cover

25.10 Remove the knee bolster retaining bolts (arrows)

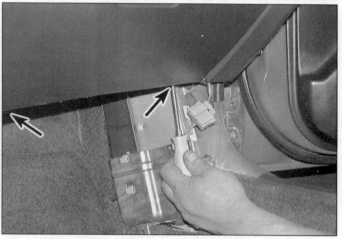

25.12 Remove the two glove box screws (arrows)

Glove box

Refer to illustration 25.12

12   To remove the glove box, simply remove the screws from the hinge **(see illustration)**. Open the glove box door, squeeze the plastic sides in and lower the glove box from the instrument panel.

13   Installation is the reverse of the removal.

Center lower cover

14   Remove the front center console (see Section 24).

15   Remove the screws and bolt and detach the cover from the instrument panel.

16   Installation is the reverse of the removal.

26 Steering column cover - removal and installation

Refer to illustration 26.3

Warning: *Models covered by this manual are equipped with a Supplemental Restraint System (SRS), more commonly known as airbags. Always disable the airbag system before working in the vicinity of the SRS unit,*

steering column or instrument panel to avoid the possibility of accidental deployment of the airbag, which could cause personal injury (see Chapter 12).

Caution: *If the radio in your vehicle is equipped with an anti-theft system, make sure you have the correct activation code before disconnecting the battery.*

1   Remove the instrument panel lower cover (see Section 25).

2   On tilt steering columns, move the column to the lowest position.

3   Remove the retaining screws, then separate the halves and remove the covers **(see illustration)**.

4   Installation is the reverse of the removal procedure.

27 Instrument panel - removal and installation

Refer to illustrations 27.8, 27.9a, 27.9b, 27.11 and 27.13

Warning: *Models covered by this manual are equipped with a Supplemental Restraint System (SRS), more commonly known as*

airbags. Always disable the airbag system before working in the vicinity of the SRS unit, steering column or instrument panel to avoid the possibility of accidental deployment of the airbag, which could cause personal injury (see Chapter 12).

1   Disconnect the negative battery cable.

Caution: *If the radio in your vehicle is equipped with an anti-theft system, make sure you have the correct activation code before disconnecting the battery.*

2   Remove the steering wheel (see Chapter 10).

3   Remove the center floor console (see Section 24).

4   Remove the instrument cluster bezel (see Section 25).

5   Remove the instrument cluster (see Chapter 12).

6   Remove all of the dashboard trim panels described in Section 25.

7   Detach the nuts and bolts securing the fuse box and the hood release handle (see Chapter 12 and Section 10).

8   Remove the nuts and lower the steering column **(see illustration)**.

9   Remove the screws and pry out the air

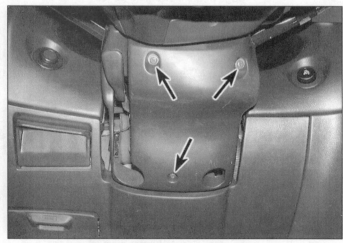

26.3 Steering column cover retaining screws

27.8 Steering column retaining nuts (arrows)

11

27.9a Remove the screw . . .

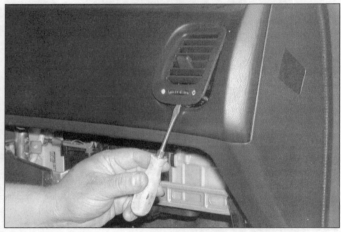

27.9b . . . pry the lower edge of the air vents out, then rotate them out of the instrument panel

vent grilles **(see illustrations)**

10   Pry out the driver's and passenger side lower kick panels.

11   Remove the screws from each end of the instrument panel **(see illustration)**.

12   Remove the radio (see Chapter 12) and the heater control assembly (see Chapter 3).

13   Remove the screws securing the lower center part of the instrument panel **(see illustration)**.

14   Remove the bolts retaining the upper front edge of instrument panel to the firewall.

15   Pull the instrument panel towards the rear of the vehicle and detach any electrical connectors interfering with removal.

16   Lift the instrument panel over the steering column and remove it from the vehicle.

17   Installation is the reverse of removal.

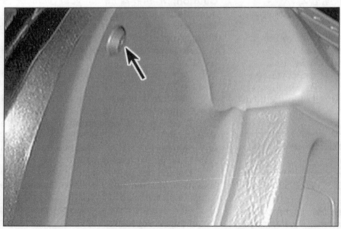

27.11 Remove the screw (arrow) at each end of the instrument panel

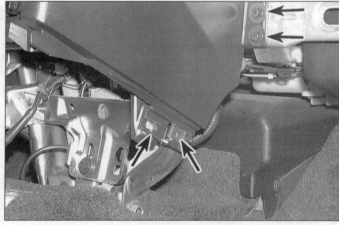

27.13 Remove the screws (arrows) along the lower edge of the instrument panel

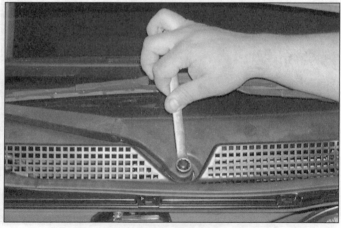

28.1 Remove the nuts and detach the wiper arms

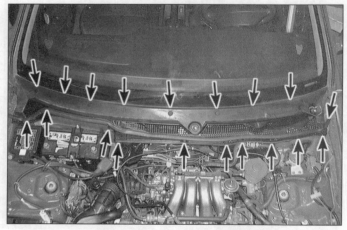

28.2 Remove the plastic rivets (upper arrows) and the clips (lower arrows), then detach the cowl

29.1a Move the front seat all the way forward to access the rear retaining bolts (arrows) . . .

29.1b . . . then move the seat all the way to the rear to access the front retaining bolts (arrows)

28 Cowl cover - removal and installation

Refer to illustrations 28.1 and 28.2

1   Mark the positions of the windshield wiper arms on the windshield with pieces of tape. Remove the windshield wiper arm retaining nuts and remove the wiper arms (see illustration).

2   Pull out the centers of the plastic rivets securing the rear of the cowl cover, then pry the rivets out **(see illustration)**.

3   Carefully remove the clips securing the hood seal **(see illustration 28.2)** and remove the cowl cover from the vehicle. Pry directly underneath the clips, being careful not to tear the hood seal.

4   Installation is the reverse of removal. Be sure to align the wiper arms with the tape marks on the windshield.

29 Seats - removal and installation

Front seat

Refer to illustrations 29.1a and 29.1b

1   Position the seat all the way forward, then all the way to the rear to access the seat retaining bolts **(see illustrations)**.

2   Detach any bolt trim covers and remove the retaining bolts.

3   Tilt the seat upward to access the underneath, then disconnect any electrical connectors and lift the seat from the vehicle.

4   Installation is the reverse of removal.

Rear seat

Refer to illustrations 29.5, 29.6b, 29.6b and 29.8

5   Remove the seat cushion bolts and remove the cushion **(see illustration)**.

6   Remove the seat back trim cover **(see illustrations)**.

7   Use pliers to pull off the pivot clips and remove the seat backs **(see illustration)**.

8   Installation is the reverse of removal.

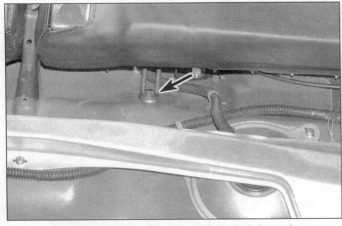

29.5 Remove the rear seat retaining bolt (arrow) - one on each side

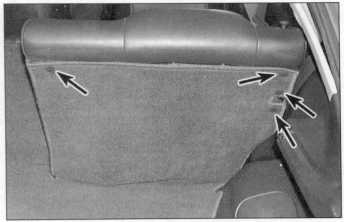

29.6a Pry out the trim (arrows) at the top . . .

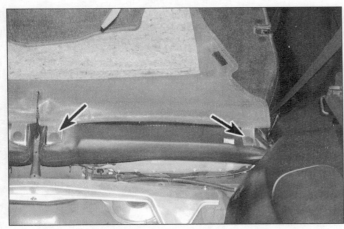

29.6b . . . and bottom (arrows) of the seat back

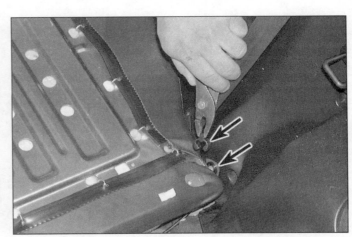

29.8 Use pliers to remove the clip from the pivot (arrows)

11

Notes

Chapter 12
Chassis electrical system

Contents

1 General information

The electrical system is a 12-volt, negative ground type. Power for the lights and all electrical accessories is supplied by a lead/acid-type battery charged by the alternator.

This Chapter covers repair and service procedures for the various electrical components not associated with the engine. Information on the battery, alternator, distributor and starter motor can be found in Chapter 5. It should be noted that when portions of the electrical system are serviced, the negative battery cable should be disconnected from the battery to prevent electrical shorts and/or fires. **Caution:** *The stereo in your vehicle may be equipped with an anti-theft system. Refer to the information at the front of this manual before detaching the battery cables.*

2 Electrical troubleshooting

Refer to illustration 2.15

A typical electrical circuit consists of an electrical component, any switches, relays, motors, fuses, fusible links or circuit breakers related to that component and the wiring and connectors that link the component to both the battery and the chassis. To help you pinpoint an electrical circuit problem, wiring diagrams are included at the end of this Chapter.

Before tackling any troublesome electrical circuit, first study the appropriate wiring diagrams to get a complete understanding of what makes up that individual circuit. Trouble spots, for instance, can often be narrowed down by noting if other components related to the circuit are operating properly. If several components or circuits fail at one time, chances are the problem is in a fuse or ground connection, because several circuits are often routed through the same fuse and ground connections.

Electrical problems usually stem from simple causes, such as loose or corroded connections, a blown fuse, a melted fusible link or a failed relay. Visually inspect the condition of all fuses, wires and connections in a problem circuit before troubleshooting the circuit.

If test equipment and instruments are going to be utilized, use the diagrams to plan ahead of time where you will make the necessary connections in order to accurately pinpoint the trouble spot.

The basic tools needed for electrical troubleshooting include a circuit tester or voltmeter (a 12-volt bulb with a set of test leads can also be used), a continuity tester, which includes a bulb, battery and set of test

12

leads, and a jumper wire, preferably with a circuit breaker incorporated, which can be used to bypass electrical components. Before attempting to locate a problem with test instruments, use the wiring diagram(s) to decide where to make the connections.

Voltage checks

Voltage checks should be performed if a circuit is not functioning properly. Connect one lead of a circuit tester to either the negative battery terminal or a known good ground. Connect the other lead to a connector in the circuit being tested, preferably nearest to the battery or fuse. If the bulb of the tester lights, voltage is present, which means that the part of the circuit between the connector and the battery is problem free. Continue checking the rest of the circuit in the same fashion. When you reach a point at which no voltage is present, the problem lies between that point and the last test point with voltage. Most of the time the problem can be traced to a loose connection. **Note:** *Keep in mind that some circuits receive voltage only when the ignition key is in the Accessory or Run position.*

Finding a short

One method of finding shorts in a circuit is to remove the fuse and connect a test light or voltmeter in place of the fuse terminals. There should be no voltage present in the circuit. Move the wiring harness from side-to-side while watching the test light. If the bulb goes on, there is a short to ground somewhere in that area, probably where the insulation has rubbed through. The same test can be performed on each component in the circuit, even a switch.

Ground check

Perform a ground test to check whether a component is properly grounded. Disconnect the battery and connect one lead of a self-powered test light, known as a continuity tester, to a known good ground. Connect the other lead to the wire or ground connection being tested. If the bulb goes on, the ground is good. If the bulb does not go on, the ground is not good.

Continuity check

A continuity check is done to determine if there are any breaks in a circuit - if it is passing electricity properly. With the circuit off (no power in the circuit), a self-powered continuity tester can be used to check the circuit. Connect the test leads to both ends of the circuit (or to the "power" end and a good ground), and if the test light comes on the circuit is passing current properly. If the light doesn't come on, there is a break somewhere in the circuit. The same procedure can be used to test a switch, by connecting the continuity tester to the switch terminals. With the switch turned On, the test light should come on.

2.15 To backprobe a connector, insert a small diameter probe with a sharp point (such as a straight pin) into the back of the connector along side the desired wire until the probe contacts the metal terminal; connect your meter leads to the probes - this allows you to test a functioning circuit

Finding an open circuit

When diagnosing for possible open circuits, it is often difficult to locate them by sight because oxidation or terminal misalignment are hidden by the connectors. Merely wiggling a connector on a sensor or in the wiring harness may correct the open circuit condition. Remember this when an open circuit is indicated when troubleshooting a circuit. Intermittent problems may also be caused by oxidized or loose connections.

Electrical troubleshooting is simple if you keep in mind that all electrical circuits are basically electricity running from the battery, through the wires, switches, relays, fuses and fusible links to each electrical component (light bulb, motor, etc.) and to ground, from which it is passed back to the battery. Any electrical problem is an interruption in the flow of electricity to and from the battery.

Connectors

Most electrical connections on these vehicles are made with multiwire plastic connectors. The mating halves of many connectors are secured with locking clips molded into the plastic connector shells. The mating halves of large connectors, such as some of those under the instrument panel, are held together by a bolt through the center of the connector.

To separate a connector with locking clips, use a small screwdriver to pry the clips apart carefully, then separate the connector halves. Pull only on the shell, never pull on the wiring harness as you may damage the individual wires and terminals inside the connectors. Look at the connector closely before trying to separate the halves. Often the locking clips are engaged in a way that is not immediately clear. Additionally, many connectors have more than one set of clips.

Each pair of connector terminals has a

3.1a The interior fuse box is located under the left (driver's side) of the instrument panel, under a cover

male half and a female half. When you look at the end view of a connector in a diagram, be sure to understand whether the view shows the harness side or the component side of the connector. Connector halves are mirror images of each other, and a terminal shown on the right side end view of one half will be on the left side end view of the other half.

It is often necessary to take circuit voltage measurements with a connector connected. Whenever possible, carefully insert the test probes of your meter into the rear of the connector shell to contact the terminal inside. This kind of connection is called "backprobing" **(see illustration)**. When inserting a test probe into a male terminal, be careful not to distort the terminal opening. Doing so can lead to a poor connection and corrosion at that terminal later. If the connector openings are too small for your meter's probes, insert small straight pins into the openings and attach the meter probes to them.

3   Fuses - general information

Refer to illustrations 3.1a, 3.1b, 3.1c and 3.3

1   The electrical circuits of the vehicle are protected by a combination of fuses and circuit breakers. The two fuse blocks (three fuse blocks on models equipped with ABS) are located under the instrument panel and on the right side of the engine compartment **(see illustrations)**.

2   Each of the fuses is designed to protect a specific circuit (or circuits), and the various circuits are identified on the fuse panel itself.

3   Miniaturized fuses are employed in the fuse blocks. These compact fuses, with blade terminal design, allow fingertip removal and replacement. If an electrical component fails, always check the fuse first. To check the fuses, turn the ignition key to the On position and, using a test light, probe each exposed terminal of each fuse. If the test light glows on both terminals of a fuse, the fuse is good. If power is available on one side of the

3.1b The engine compartment fuse box is located in the right rear corner of the engine compartment

3.1c The ABS fuse box is located in the engine compartment

fuse but not the other, the fuse is blown. When removed, a blown fuse is easily identified through the clear plastic body **(see illustration)**. Visually inspect the element for evidence of damage.

4   Be sure to replace blown fuses with the correct type. Fuses of different ratings are physically interchangeable, but only fuses of the proper rating should be used. Replacing a fuse with one of a higher or lower value than specified is not recommended. Each electrical circuit needs a specific amount of protection. The amperage value of each fuse is molded into the fuse body.

5   If the replacement fuse immediately fails, don't replace it again until the cause of the problem is isolated and corrected. In most cases, the cause will be a short circuit in the wiring caused by a broken or deteriorated wire.

6   All models are equipped with a main fuse (either an 80A or 100A) which protects all the circuits coming from the battery. If these circuits are overloaded, the main fuse blows, preventing damage to the main wiring harness. The main fuse consists of a metal strip which will be visibly melted when overloaded. Always disconnect the battery before

replacing a main fuse (available from your dealer). **Caution:** *If the stereo in your vehicle is equipped with an anti-theft system. Refer to the information at the front of this manual before detaching the battery cables.* The main fuse is located in the engine compartment fuse block. It's very similar in appearance to standard fuses and is replaced in the same way. If you have to replace a main fuse, make sure you install a replacement unit that's equivalent to the old fuse. In other words, if the old main fuse is an 80A unit, replace it with an 80A fuse; if it's a 100A unit, replace it with a 100A fuse. Don't switch amperage ratings on the main fuse!

4   Circuit breakers - general information

Circuit breakers protect components such as sunroof motors, power window motors and airbag inflator resistors.

On some models the circuit breaker resets itself automatically, so an electrical overload in a circuit breaker protected system will cause the circuit to fail momentarily, then come back on. If the circuit does not

come back on, check it immediately. Once the condition is corrected, the circuit breaker will resume its normal function. Some circuit breakers must be reset manually.

5   Relays - general information

General information

1   Several electrical accessories in the vehicle, such as the fuel injection system, horns, starter, and cooling fans use relays to transmit the electrical signal to the component. Relays use a low-current circuit (the control circuit) to open and close a high-current circuit (the power circuit). If the relay is defective, that component will not operate properly. The various relays are mounted in engine compartment fuse box **(see illustration 3.1b)** and several locations throughout the vehicle. If a faulty relay is suspected, it can be removed and tested using the procedure below. Defective relays must be replaced as a unit.

Testing

Refer to illustration 5.5

2   It's best to refer to the wiring diagram for the circuit to determine the proper hook-ups for the relay you're testing. However, if you're not able to determine the correct hook-up from the wiring diagrams, you may be able to determine the test hook-ups from the information that follows.

3   On most relays, two of the terminals are the relay's control circuit (they connect to the relay coil which, when energized, closes the large contacts to complete the circuit). The other terminals are the power circuit (they are connected together within the relay when the control-circuit coil is energized).

4   Most relays are marked as an aid to help you determine which terminals are the control circuit and which are the power circuit.

5   Connect an ohmmeter to the two terminals of the power circuit. Connect a fused jumper wire between one of the two control circuit terminals and the positive battery ter-

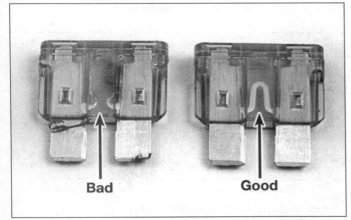

3.3 The fuses can easily be inspected visually to see if they are blown

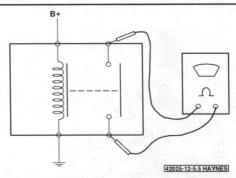

5.5 To test a typical four-terminal normally open relay, connect an ohmmeter to the two terminals of the power circuit - the meter will indicate no continuity until battery power and ground are connected to the two terminals of the control circuit, then the relay will click and continuity will be indicated

minal. Connect another jumper wire between the other control circuit terminal and ground. When the connections are made, the relay should click and continuity will be indicated on the meter **(see illustration)**. On some relays, polarity may be critical, so, if the relay doesn't click, try swapping the jumper wires on the control circuit terminals.

6   If the relay fails the above test, replace it.

6   Hazard/turn signal flashers - check and replacement

1   The hazard/turn signal flasher is a square relay located on the interior fuse block under the left side of the instrument panel **(see illustration)**.
2   If the flasher unit is functioning properly, you can hear an audible clicking sound when it's operating. If the turn signals fail on one side or the other and the flasher unit doesn't make its characteristic clicking sound, look for a faulty turn signal bulb.
3   If both turn signals fail to blink, the problem may be due to a blown fuse (in the engine compartment fuse box), a faulty flasher unit, a broken switch or a loose or open connection. If a quick check of the fuse box indicates that the turn signal fuse has

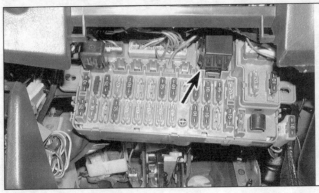

6.1 The turn signal/hazard flasher is located on the interior fuse box (arrow)

blown, check the wiring for a short before installing a new fuse.
4   To replace the flasher, simply pull it out of the fuse block.
5   Make sure that the replacement unit is identical to the original. Compare the old one to the new one before installing it.
6   Installation is the reverse of removal.

7   Steering column switches - check and replacement

Warning: *The models covered by this manual are equipped with a Supplemental Restraint system (SRS), more commonly known as airbags. Always disable the airbag system*

before working in the vicinity of the impact sensors, steering column or instrument panel to avoid the possibility of accidental deployment of the airbag, which could cause personal injury (see Section 26). Do not use electrical test equipment on any of the airbag system wiring or tamper with them in any way.

Combination light switch and windshield wiper/washer switch

Check

Refer to illustrations 7.3a, 7.3b, 7.3c and 7.3d

1   The exterior lighting and wiper switches are located on the steering column. The com-

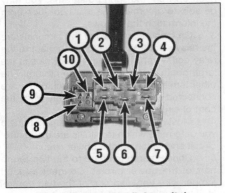

7.3a Combination light switch terminal identification

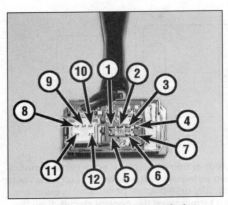

7.3c Windshield and rear window wiper/washer switch terminal identification

SWITCH POSITION	CONTINUITY BETWEEN
Parking lights	1 and 2
Headlights (low beam)	
Civic (USA)	1 and 2; 3 and 6
Civic (Canada)	1 and 2; 3, 4 and 6
Integra	1 and 2; 4 and 6
Headlights (high beam)	
Civic (USA)	1 and 2; 5 and 6
Civic (Canada)	1 and 2; 4, 5 and 6
Integra	1 and 2; 4, 5 and 6
Flash-to-pass	5 and 6
Right turn signal	8 and 10
Left turn signal	8 and 9

7.3b Combination light switch continuity table

SWITCH POSITION	CONTINUITY BETWEEN
Off	1 and 7
Intermittent	1 and 7; 3 and 4
Low	1 and 5
High	2 and 5
Wash	4 and 8
Mist	2 and 5

WINDSHIELD WIPER/WASHER SWITCH

SWITCH POSITION	CONTINUITY BETWEEN
Off	1 and 2
On	1 and 3
Wash	4 and 6

REAR WINDOW WIPER/WASHER SWITCH

7.3d Wiper/washer switch continuity table

7.4a To remove either of the steering column switches, remove the two retaining screws (arrows) (steering wheel removed for clarity only, position the spokes vertically to access the screws) . . .

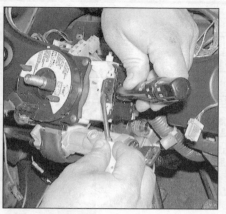

7.4b . . . and carefully pry the switch out of the steering column bracket

7.7 Cruise control set/resume switch terminal guide - with the switch in the Set position there should be continuity between terminals 1 and 3; with the switch in the Resume position there should be continuity between terminals 1 and 2

7.10 Remove the two mounting screws (arrows) and remove the switch

bination light switch incorporates the turn signal, headlight, dimmer and parking light switches into one switch on the left side of the column. The windshield wiper/washer functions are incorporated into another switch on the right side of the column.

2   Remove the switch(es) (see Step 4).

3   Using an ohmmeter or self-powered test light and the accompanying diagrams, check for continuity between the indicated switch terminals with the switch in each of the indicated positions **(see illustrations)**. If the continuity isn't as specified, replace the switch.

Replacement

Refer to illustrations 7.4a and 7.4b

4   Remove the steering column covers. Use a small screwdriver to carefully detach the electrical connectors from the switch. Remove the two retaining screws and detach the switch from the steering column **(see illustrations)**.

5   Installation is the reverse of removal.

Cruise control switch

Check

Refer to illustration 7.7

6   Remove the switch from the steering wheel (see Step 8).

7   Using an ohmmeter or self-powered test light and the accompanying diagram, check for continuity between the indicated terminals on the switch in each of the indicated positions **(see illustration)**. If the continuity isn't as specified, replace the switch.

Replacement

Refer to illustration 7.10

8   Disconnect the negative battery cable, then the positive battery cable and wait at least three minutes before proceeding any further (see **Warning** above). **Caution:** *If the radio in your vehicle is equipped with an anti-theft system, make sure you have the correct activation code before disconnecting the battery.*

9   Remove the cover over the cruise control switch.

10   Detach the switch retaining screws **(see illustration)**. Then disconnect the electrical connections and remove the switch from the steering wheel.

11   Installation is the reverse of removal.

8   Ignition switch and key lock cylinder - check and replacement

Warning: *The models covered by this manual are equipped with a Supplemental Restraint system (SRS), more commonly known as airbags. Always disable the airbag system before working in the vicinity of the impact sensors, steering column or instrument panel to avoid the possibility of accidental deployment of the airbag, which could cause personal injury (see Section 26). Do not use electrical test equipment on any of the airbag system wiring or tamper with them in any way.*

Ignition switch

Refer to illustrations 8.3, 8.4 and 8.9

1   Disconnect the negative battery cable, then the positive battery cable (see **Warning** above). **Caution:** *If the radio in your vehicle is equipped with an anti-theft system, make sure you have the correct activation code*

before disconnecting the battery.

2   Remove the lower instrument panel cover and the steering column covers (see Chapter 11).

3   Follow the wire harness for the ignition switch down the steering column and disconnect the connectors from the fuse box and

8.3 Disconnect the ignition switch connectors from the fuse box and wiring harness (arrow)

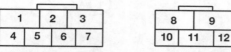

SWITCH POSITION	CONTINUITY BETWEEN
Accessory	
Civic	3 and 8
Integra	3 and 11
On	
Civic	3, 8, 10 and 12
Integra	3, 8, 9 and 11
Start	
Civic	1, 3 and 12
Integra	1, 3 and 8

42025 12-8.4 HAYNES

8.4 Ignition switch terminal guide and continuity table

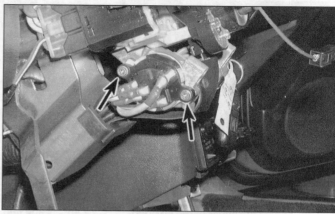

8.9 Remove the two ignition switch screws (arrows) and remove the switch

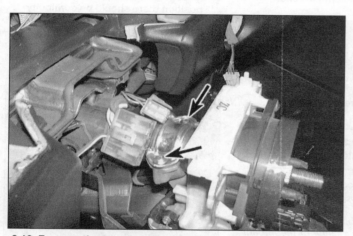

8.16 Remove the two shear-head screws (arrows) to remove the steering lock and key lock cylinder

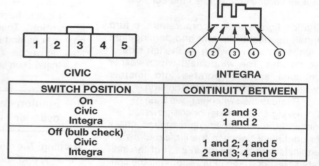

SWITCH POSITION	CONTINUITY BETWEEN
On	
Civic	2 and 3
Integra	1 and 2
Off (bulb check)	
Civic	1 and 2; 4 and 5
Integra	2 and 3; 4 and 5

42025 12-09.02 HAYNES

9.2 Cruise control on/off switch terminal guide and continuity table - if continuity is not indicated during a bulb check replace only the defective bulb

wiring harness **(see illustration)**.

4   Check the ignition switch for continuity between the indicated connector terminals with the ignition switch in each position **(see illustration)**.

5   If the continuity is not as specified, replace the switch.

6   Insert the key and turn it to the Lock position.

7   Remove the two retaining screws and detach the switch **(see illustration)**.

8   Installation is the reverse of removal.

Lock cylinder and steering column lock assembly

Refer to illustration 8.16

9   Check the lock cylinder in each position to make sure it isn't worn or loose and that the key position corresponds to the markings on the housing. If the lock cylinder is faulty, the entire steering column lock assembly will have to be replaced.

10   Disconnect the negative battery cable, then the positive battery cable (see **Warning** above). **Caution:** *If the radio in your vehicle is equipped with an anti-theft system, make sure you have the correct activation code before disconnecting the battery.*

11   Remove the steering column covers and lower instrument panel cover (see Chapter 11).

12   Remove the ignition switch (see above).

13   Remove the retaining nuts and lower the steering column.

14   The lock assembly is clamped to the steering column by two shear-head bolts **(see illustration)**. Use a center punch to make a dimple in the head of each bolt, then drill the head off the bolt with a 3/16-inch bit. Separate the clamp and remove the assembly from the steering column.

15   Place the new lock assembly in position without the key inserted and tighten the bolts until they are snug.

16   Insert the key and check the lock cylinder for proper operation.

17   Tighten the bolts until their heads break off.

18   Raise the steering column into position and install the nuts/bolts. Tighten the steering column-to-instrument panel flange nuts to 108 in-lbs. Tighten the retaining collar clamp bolts to 16 ft-lbs.

19   Install the ignition switch, instrument panel and steering column covers.

20   Connect the positive battery cable, followed by the negative cable.

9   Instrument panel switches - check and replacement

Warning: *The models covered by this manual are equipped with a Supplemental Restraint system (SRS), more commonly known as airbags. Always disable the airbag system before working in the vicinity of the impact sensors, steering column or instrument panel to avoid the possibility of accidental deployment of the airbag, which could cause personal injury (see Section 26). Do not use electrical test equipment on any of the airbag system wiring or tamper with them in any way.*

Cruise control on/off switch
Check

Refer to illustration 9.2

1   To check the switch it must first be removed (see Step 3).

2   Using an ohmmeter or self-powered test lamp and the accompanying diagram, check for continuity between each of the indicated switch terminals with the switch in each of the indicated positions **(see illustration)**. If the continuity isn't as specified, replace the switch.

9.3 Carefully pry the cruise on/off switch
out of the dash

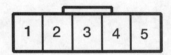

9.6 Rear defogger switch wiring harness
connector terminal identification -
Civic models

Replacement

Refer to illustration 9.3

3   To remove the switch, pry it out of the
dash and disconnect its electrical connector
(see illustration).

4   Installation is the reverse of removal.

Rear defogger switch

Check

Refer to illustrations 9.6 and 9.8

5   Remove the switch from the instrument
panel (see Step 9).

6   On Civic models, the timer circuitry is
contained within the switch, so the switch
can not be checked using conventional
methods. If the defogger does not operate

9.9 Carefully pry the defogger switch out
of the dash with a small screwdriver

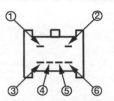

SWITCH POSITION	CONTINUITY BETWEEN
On	4 and 6
Off (bulb check)	1 and 3; 2 and 5

42025 12-9.8 HAYNES

9.8 Rear window defogger switch terminal identification and continuity table - Integra
models (if continuity is not indicated during a bulb check replace only the defective bulb)

Turn the ignition ON but don't start the
engine. Place the positive probe of a voltmeter at terminal no. 1 and the negative
probe at terminal no. 4 on the wiring harness
connector **(see illustration)**. Battery voltage
should be indicated. If there's no voltage,
check the wiring harness and fuse.

7   If there's battery voltage, connect a
jumper wire between terminal no. 1 and 4. If
the rear defogger now works, replace the
switch. If the defogger still doesn't work,
check the defogger relay (see section 5) and
related circuit.

8   If you're working on an Integra, use an
ohmmeter or self-powered test lamp and the
accompanying diagram to check for continuity between the indicated switch terminals
with the switch in the indicated positions **(see
illustration)**. If the continuity isn't as specified, replace the switch.

Replacement

Refer to illustration 9.9

9   To remove the switch, carefully pry it out
of the instrument panel and disconnect the
electrical connector **(see illustration)**.

10   Installation is the reverse of removal.

Instrument panel lights
dimmer switch

Check

Refer to illustration 9.13

11   Remove the switch from the instrument
panel (see Step 17).

12   The control circuitry is contained within
the switch, so the switch cannot be checked
using conventional methods. The following

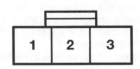

9.13 Instrument panel lights dimmer
switch wiring harness connector
terminal identification

check tests each individual circuit. If there is
a problem with the system and the circuits
are good, the switch is assumed defective.
Inspect the switch terminals, if they're corroded or bent, repair them if possible or
replace the switch.

13   Working on the wiring harness connector, connect an ohmmeter between terminal
no. 2 and a good chassis ground **(see illustration)**. There should be continuity. If not,
check the circuit for an open or bad connection.

14   With the headlight switch ON, connect a
voltmeter between terminal no. 1 and ground.
There should be battery voltage. If not, check
the circuit back to the under-dash fuse box
and combination switch.

15   With the headlight switch ON, connect a
jumper wire between terminal no. 3 and a
good chassis ground. The instrument panel
lights should come on at full brightness.

16   If the wiring test results were correct
and the switch doesn't work properly,
replace the switch.

Replacement

Refer to illustration 9.17

17   To remove the switch, carefully pry it out
of the instrument panel and disconnect the
electrical connector **(see illustration)**.

18   Installation is the reverse of removal.

9.17 Carefully pry the interior light
dimmer switch out of the dash with a
small screwdriver - Integra model shown

12

11.4a Remove the instrument cluster screws (arrows)

11.4b Pull the cluster out of the dash, turn it over and unplug the electrical connectors from the backside

10   Instrument panel gauges - check

Warning: *The models covered by this manual are equipped with a Supplemental Restraint system (SRS), more commonly known as airbags. Always disable the airbag system before working in the vicinity of the impact sensors, steering column or instrument panel to avoid the possibility of accidental deployment of the airbag, which could cause personal injury (see Section 26). Do not use electrical test equipment on any of the airbag system wiring or tamper with them in any way.*
Note: *This procedure applies to conventional analog type gauges (NON-digital) only.*

Fuel and temperature gauges

1   All tests below require the ignition switch to be turned to ON position when testing.
2   If the gauge pointer does not move from the empty or cold positions, check the fuse. If the fuse is OK, locate the particular sending unit for the circuit you're working on (see Chapter 4 for fuel sending unit location or Chapter 3 for the temperature sending unit location). Connect the sending unit connector to ground momentarily. If the pointer goes to the full or hot position replace the sending unit. If the pointer stays in the same position, use a jumper wire to ground the sending unit terminal on the back of the gauge. If necessary, refer to the wiring diagrams at the end of this Chapter. If the pointer moves, the problem lies in the wiring between the gauge and the sending unit. If the pointer does not move with the sending unit terminal on the back of the gauge grounded, check for voltage at the other terminal of the gauge. If voltage is present, replace the gauge.

11   Instrument cluster - removal and installation

Refer to illustrations 11.4a and 11.4b
Warning: *The models covered by this manual are equipped with a Supplemental Restraint system (SRS), more commonly known as*

12.4a Reach under the stereo and remove the retaining screws . . .

airbags. Always disable the airbag system before working in the vicinity of the impact sensors, steering column or instrument panel to avoid the possibility of accidental deployment of the airbag, which could cause personal injury (see Section 26). Do not use electrical test equipment on any of the airbag system wiring or tamper with them in any way.
1   Disconnect the negative battery cable, then the positive cable and wait three minutes before proceeding further (see **Warning** above). **Caution:** *If the radio in your vehicle is equipped with an anti-theft system, make sure you have the correct activation code before disconnecting the battery.*
2   Tilt the steering wheel to its lowest position and remove the instrument cluster bezel (see Chapter 11).
3   Pad the steering column to protect it.
4   Remove the cluster mounting screws, carefully pull it straight out of the instrument panel and disconnect the electrical connectors **(see illustrations).**
5   Installation is the reverse of removal.

12   Radio and speakers - removal and installation

Warning: *The models covered by this manual are equipped with a Supplemental Restraint*

12.4b . . . pull it out far enough to unplug the connectors and remove the unit

system (SRS), more commonly known as airbags. Always disable the airbag system before working in the vicinity of the impact sensors, steering column or instrument panel to avoid the possibility of accidental deployment of the airbag, which could cause personal injury (see Section 26). Do not use electrical test equipment on any of the airbag system wiring or tamper with them in any way.
1   The radio and cassette player are separate units on Civic models and a combined unit on Integra models.

Radio

Refer to illustrations 12.4a and 12.4b
2   Detach the cable from the negative terminal of the battery, then detach the positive cable (see **Warning** above). **Caution:** *If the radio in your vehicle is equipped with an anti-theft system, make sure you have the correct activation code before disconnecting the battery.*
3   Remove the center console (see Chapter 11).
4   Reach under the radio and remove the two retaining screws **(see illustration)**. Pull out the radio and unplug the electrical connector and antenna lead. If you're working on a Civic with a separate cassette player, disconnect the cassette player lead from the radio. Remove the radio **(see illustration)**.

12.8 Remove the screws, pull the speaker out and unplug it

13.3 Remove the antenna retaining screws

13.6 Tape the fender to protect it and remove the antenna nut with snap-ring pliers

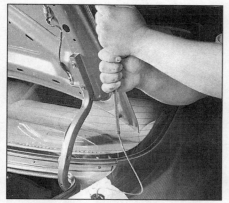

13.7 With the ignition key and the radio in the ON position, guide the antenna mast out of the motor assembly

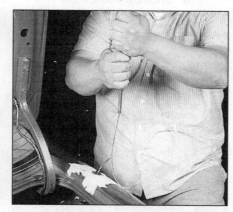

13.8 Insert the new antenna so that the antenna cable teeth face the rear of the vehicle

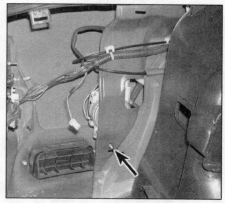

13.11 Remove the mounting nut (arrow) to detach the antenna motor

5   To remove the separate cassette player on Civic models, remove the mounting bolts (two on each side) and slide it out.
6   Installation is the reverse of removal.

Speakers

Front main speakers

Refer to illustration 12.8
7   Remove the speaker trim cover.
8   Remove the speaker mounting screws, pull out the speaker and unplug the electrical connector **(see illustration)**.
9   Installation is the reverse of removal.

Front tweeters

10   Remove the door trim panel.
11   Disconnect the tweeter electrical connector.
12   If you're working on a Civic, remove the side mirror trim.
13   Remove the tweeter mounting screws and take it out.
14   Installation is the reverse of removal.

Rear speakers

15   If you're working on a Civic, remove the rear side trim (hatchback) or rear shelf (coupe/sedan).
16   If you're working on an Integra hatchback, remove the speaker trim cover.

17   If you're working on an Integra sedan, remove three speaker cover screws from inside the trunk, then lift off the speaker cover.
18   Remove the speaker mounting screws and lift the speaker out.
19   Installation is the reverse of removal.

13   Antenna - removal and installation

Civic

Refer to illustration 13.3
1   Disconnect the antenna lead at the radio.
2   Connect a piece of string or wire to the antenna lead at the radio end.
3   Remove the mounting screws and pull the antenna out of the body pillar **(see illustration)**.
4   Fasten the wire or string to the lead of the new antenna. Lower the antenna into place while pulling the new lead into the pillar with the wire or string.
5   Disconnect the string or wire and connect the antenna lead to the radio. Install the antenna mounting screws and tighten them securely.

Integra

Power antenna mast

Refer to illustrations 13.6, 13.7 and 13.8
6   Tape the fender to protect it from scratches. Remove the nut and spacer **(see illustration)**.
7   Have an assistant switch the radio ON to extend the antenna. Guide the mast as it extends, then remove it from the vehicle **(see illustration)**.
8   Install the antenna with teeth facing the rear of the vehicle and engage the antenna teeth with the drive cable. Switch the radio ON and let the antenna motor pull the mast into the fender **(see illustration)**.
9   Install the spacer and antenna nut. **Note:** *If the spacer has a flat seal, it goes inside the collar, below the spacer. If the spacer has an O-ring, it goes on top of the spacer.*

Power antenna motor

Refer to illustration 13.11
10   If you're working on a sedan, remove the side trim panel from inside the trunk. If you're working on a hatchback, remove the quarter trim panel from the vehicle interior.
11   Remove the antenna nut and washer **(see illustration 13.6)**. Remove the antenna motor mounting nut **(see illustration)**. Dis-

12

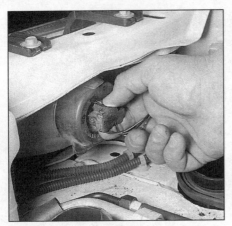

14.2 Unplug the electrical connector and remove the rubber boot

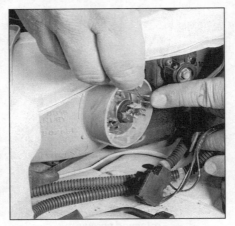

14.3a On Civic models, detach the wire clip . . .

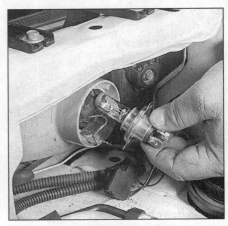

14.3b . . . then pull the assembly straight out of the housing

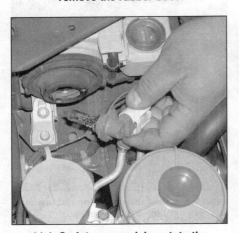

14.4 On Integra models, rotate the bulb/holder assembly counterclockwise and pull the assembly out of the housing (there are separate bulbs for the low beam and high beam headlights)

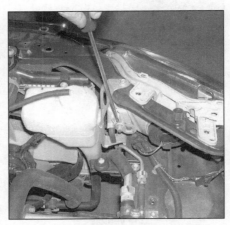

15.1a Civic vertical headlight adjuster

15.1b Civic horizontal headlight adjuster

15.1c Integra headlight adjusters

connect the electrical connector and antenna lead and withdraw the assembly.

12   Installation is the reverse of removal.

14   Headlight - replacement

Refer to illustrations 14.2, 14.3a, 14.3b and 14.4

Warning: *Halogen gas-filled bulbs are under pressure and may shatter if the surface is scratched or the bulb is dropped. Wear eye protection and handle the bulbs carefully, grasping only the base whenever possible. Do not touch the surface of the bulb with your fingers because the oil from your skin could cause it to overheat and fail prematurely. If you do touch the bulb surface, clean it with rubbing alcohol.*

1   Open the hood.

2   Reach behind the headlight assembly, unplug the electrical connector, then remove the rubber boot **(see illustration)**.

3   On Civic models, release the bulb holder retaining clip, then pull out the bulb/holder

assembly **(see illustrations)**.

4   On Integra models, rotate the bulb/holder assembly counterclockwise and remove the assembly **(see illustration)**.

5   Installation is the reverse of removal (see **Warning** above).

15   Headlights - adjustment

Refer to illustrations 15.1a, 15.1b, 15.c and 15.3

Note: *The headlights must be aimed correctly. If adjusted incorrectly they could blind the driver of an oncoming vehicle and cause a serious accident or seriously reduce your ability to see the road. The headlights should be checked for proper aim every 12 months and any time a new headlight is installed or front end body work is performed. It should be emphasized that the following procedure is only an interim step which will provide temporary adjustment until the headlights can be adjusted by a properly equipped shop.*

1   Headlights have spring-loaded adjusting screws for controlling up-and-down (inner) and left-and-right movement (outer - nearest the parking light) **(see illustrations)**.

2   There are several methods of adjusting the headlights. The simplest method requires a blank wall and a level floor.

3   Position masking tape vertically on the wall in reference to the vehicle centerline and the centerlines of both headlights **(see illustration)**.

4   Position a horizontal tape line in reference to the centerline of all the headlights.

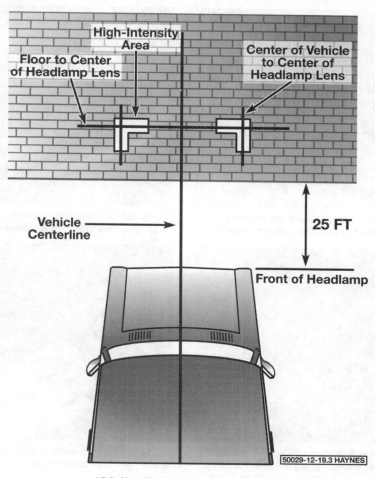

15.3 Headlight adjustment details

16.3a On Civic models, remove the bolts at the bottom center . . .

or right.

7   With the high beams on, the high intensity zone should be vertically centered with the exact center just below the horizontal line. **Note:** *It may not be possible to position the headlight aim exactly for both high and low beams. If a compromise must be made, keep in mind that the low beams are the most used and have the greatest effect on safety.*

8   Have the headlights adjusted by a dealer service department or service station at the earliest opportunity.

16 Headlight housing - replacement

Refer to illustrations 16.3a, 16.3b, 16.3c and 16.3d

1   Unplug the electrical connectors, and remove the halogen bulbs (see Section 17).

2   Remove the front bumper cover (see Chapter 11).

3   Remove the headlight housing mounting bolts/nuts and remove the housing **(see illustrations)**.

4   Installation is the reverse of removal. After you're done, adjust the headlights (see Section 15).

Note: *It may be easier to position the tape on the wall with the vehicle parked only a few inches away.*

5   Adjustment should be made with the vehicle parked 25 feet from the wall, sitting level, the gas tank half-full and no unusually heavy load in the vehicle.

6   Starting with the low beam adjustment, position the high intensity zone so it is two inches below the horizontal line and two inches to the right of the headlight vertical line. Adjustment is made by turning the vertical adjusting screw. The horizontal adjusting screw should be used to move the beam left

16.3b . . . at the left side . . .

16.3c . . . and at the top

16.3d On Integra models, remove the four headlight housing mounting bolts (arrows)

12

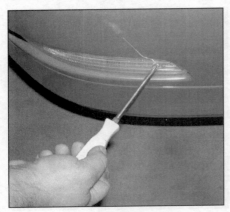

17.4a Remove the lamp housing screws . . .

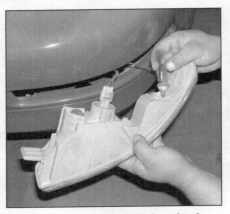

17.4b . . . and pull out the housing for access to the bulbs - Integra models

17.8a On Civic models, remove the cover from the inner panel to access the bulbs

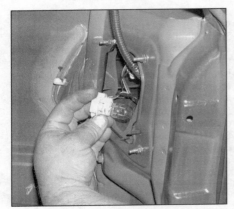

17.8b Rotate the bulb housing counterclockwise, pull it out and remove the bulb

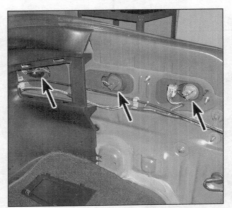

17.8c On Integra models, after removing the rear cover, rotate the bulb housings counterclockwise, pull them out and remove the bulbs

17.14 On Integra models, the high mount brake light is accessible through the trunk

17 Bulb replacement

Front turn signal/parking and side marker lights

Civic

1   If you're replacing the left (drivers side) bulb, start the engine, turn the wheels all the way to the right and stop the engine. If you're replacing the right (passengers side) bulb, start the engine, turn the wheels all the way to the left and stop the engine.
2   Pry off the clip and remove the inner fender cover.
3   Rotate the bulb holder 1/4-turn counterclockwise and remove it from the housing. Push in on the bulb and turn it counterclockwise, then pull it out of the bulb holder. Installation is the reverse of removal.

Integra

Refer to illustrations 17.4a and 17.4b

4   Remove the lamp assembly securing screws and pull it out of the fender **(see illustration)**. Turn the bulb holder 1/8-turn counterclockwise and pull it out of the housing **(see illustration)**.
5   Remove the bulb from the bulb holder.
6   Installation is the reverse of removal.

Tail light and brake light

Refer to illustrations 17.8a, 17.8b and 17.8c

7   Open the trunk or rear hatch and remove the access cover.
8   Turn the bulb holder 1/8-turn counterclockwise and pull it out of the housing **(see illustrations)**.
9   Push in on the bulb and turn it counterclockwise, then pull it out of the bulb holder.
10   Installation is the reverse of removal.

High-mounted brake light

Civic

11   Remove the screw covers (if equipped), remove the two screws and separate the housing from the body.
12   Twist the bulb holder counterclockwise, remove it from the housing and remove the bulb.
13   Installation is the reverse of removal.

Integra

Refer to illustration 17.14

14   Open the trunk to access the high-mounted brake light housing **(see illustration)**.
15   Twist the bulb holder 1/4-turn counterclockwise and pull it out of the housing.

16   Pull the bulb straight out of the bulb holder.
17   Installation is the reverse of removal.

Instrument panel lights

Refer to illustration 17.19

18   To gain access to the instrument panel lights, the instrument cluster will have to be removed first (see Section 11).
19   Rotate the bulb holder counterclockwise and remove it from the instrument cluster **(see illustration)**.
20   Pull the bulb straight out of the holder.
21   Installation is the reverse of removal.

License plate lights

Refer to illustration 17.23

22   Remove the two screws and pull out the lens.
23   Rotate the bulb holder 1/8-turn counterclockwise and detach it from the lens housing **(see illustration)**.
24   Pull the bulb straight out of the holder.
25   Installation is the reverse of removal.

Dome/cargo/trunk lights

Refer to illustration 17.26

26   Carefully pry the lens off for access to the bulb **(see illustration)**.
27   Remove the bulb from the terminals. It may be necessary to pry the bulb out - if this

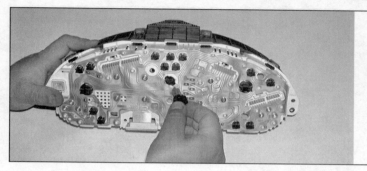

17.19 To remove an instrument cluster light bulb socket, depress it and turn it counterclockwise to release it

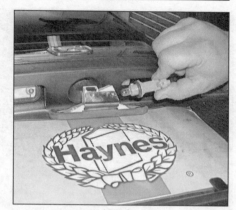

17.23 Remove the lamp housing and turn the socket counterclockwise for access to the license plate bulb

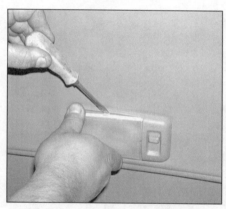

17.26 Carefully pry the interior light lens out for access to the bulb

is the case, pry only on the ends of the bulb (otherwise the glass may shatter).

28   Installation is the reverse of removal.

18 Daytime Running Lights (DRL) - general information

The Daytime Running Lights (DRL) system used on Canadian models illuminates the headlights whenever the engine is running. The only exception is with the engine running and the parking brake engaged. Once the parking brake is released, the lights will remain on as long as the ignition switch is on, even if the parking brake is later applied.

The DRL system supplies reduced power to the headlights so they won't be too bright for daytime use, while prolonging headlight life.

19 Wiper motor - check and replacement

Wiper motor circuit check

Refer to illustration 19.2
Note: *Refer to the wiring diagrams for wire colors and locations in the following checks. When checking for voltage, probe a grounded 12-volt test light to each terminal at the connector until it lights; this verifies voltage (power) at the terminal. If the following checks fail to locate the problem, have the system diagnosed by a dealer service department or other properly equipped repair facility.*

1   If the wipers work slowly, make sure the battery is in good condition and has a strong charge (see Chapter 1). If the battery is in good condition, remove the wiper motor (see below) and operate the wiper arms by hand. Check for binding linkage and pivots. Lubricate or repair the linkage or pivots as necessary. Reinstall the wiper motor. If the wipers still operate slowly, check for loose or corroded connections, especially the ground connection. If all connections look OK, replace the motor.

2   If the wipers fail to operate when activated, check the fuse. If the fuse is OK, connect a jumper wire between the wiper motor ground terminal and a good chassis ground, then retest. If the motor works now, repair the ground connection. If the motor still doesn't

work, turn the wiper switch to the HI position and check for voltage at the wiring harness connector to the motor. If there's voltage supplied to the motor, check it with fused jumper wires from the battery **(see illustration)**. If the motor now works, check for binding linkage (see Step 1 above). If the motor still doesn't work, replace it. If there's no voltage at the motor, check for voltage to the integrated control unit. If there's voltage at the integrated control unit and no voltage at the wiper motor, check the switch for continuity (see Section 7). If the switch is OK, the integrated control unit is probably bad.

3   If the interval (delay) function is inoperative, check the continuity of all the wiring between the switch and integrated control unit. If the wiring is OK, have the integrated control unit checked by a dealership or properly equipped repair facility.

4   If the wipers stop at the position they're in when the switch is turned off (fail to park), check for voltage at the park feed wire of the wiper motor connector when the wiper switch is OFF but the ignition is ON. If no voltage is present, check for an open circuit between the wiper motor and the fuse panel.

5   If the wipers won't shut off unless the ignition is OFF, disconnect the wiring from the wiper control switch. If the wipers stop, replace the switch. If the wipers keep running, there's a defective limit switch in the motor; replace the motor.

6   If the wipers won't retract below the hood line, check for mechanical obstructions in the wiper linkage or on the vehicle's body

19.2 Windshield wiper motor terminal identification - to check the motor for operation connect a fused jumper wire to the positive terminal of a 12 volt battery and terminal no. 4; the motor will operate on low speed when terminal no. 2 is grounded and high speed when terminal no. 1 is grounded

which would prevent the wipers from parking. If there are no obstructions, check the wiring between the switch and motor for continuity. If the wiring is OK, replace the wiper motor.

Wiper motor replacement
Front

Refer to illustrations 19.7, 19.10 and 19.11
7   Remove the windshield wiper arm **(see illustration)**.

19.7 To remove a wiper arm, remove the nut and pull the arm off the shaft

12

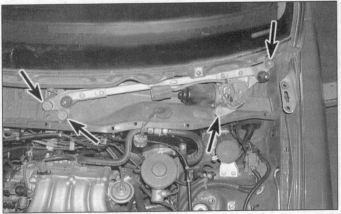

19.10 Remove the wiper-to-frame mounting bolts (arrows) and remove the complete assembly from the vehicle

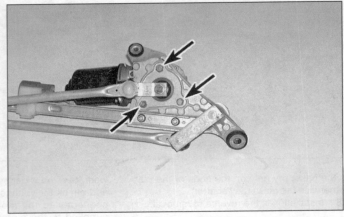

19.11 Remove the wiper motor mounting bolts and remove the motor from the linkage assembly

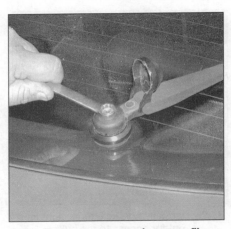

19.14 To remove a rear wiper arm, flip up the cover and remove the nut

19.17 Rear wiper motor mounting bolts (arrows)

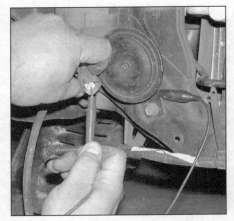

20.3 Check for voltage at the horn terminal

20.9 Horn mounting bolt (arrow)

8   Remove the cowl cover (see Chapter 11).
9   Disconnect the electrical connector from the wiper motor.
10   Detach the wiper linkage assembly from the lower cowl cover **(see illustration)**.
11   Remove the wiper motor retaining bolts **(see illustration)**.
12   Remove the wiper motor from the wiper linkage assembly.
13   Installation is the reverse of removal.

Rear

Refer to illustrations 19.14 and 19.17

14   Pull the rear wiper arm cover back to access the wiper arm retaining nut. Detach the nut and pull the wiper arm straight off the shaft to remove it **(see illustration)**.
15   Open the rear hatch and remove the trim panel (see Chapter 11).
16   Disconnect the electrical connector from the wiper motor.
17   Remove the wiper motor mounting bracket bolts and remove the motor **(see illustration)**.
18   Installation is the reverse of removal.

20   Horn - check and replacement

Check

Refer to illustration 20.3
Note: *Check the fuses before beginning electrical diagnosis.*
1   Disconnect the electrical connector from the horn.
2   To test the horn(s), connect battery voltage and ground to the horn terminals with a pair of jumper wires. If the horn doesn't sound, replace it.
3   If the horn does sound, check for voltage at the horn connector when the horn switch is depressed **(see illustration)**. If there's voltage at the connector, check for a bad ground at the horn.
4   If there's no voltage at the horn, check the relay (see Section 5).
5   If the relay is OK, check for voltage to the relay power and control circuits. If either of the circuits is not receiving voltage, inspect the wiring between the relay and the fuse panel.
6   If both relay circuits are receiving voltage, depress the horn switch and check the circuit from the relay to the horn switch for

continuity to ground. If there's no continuity, check the circuit for an open. If there's no open circuit, replace the horn switch.
7   If there's continuity to ground through the horn switch, check for an open or short in the circuit from the relay to the switch.

Replacement

Refer to illustration 20.9
8   To access the horns, the left front inner

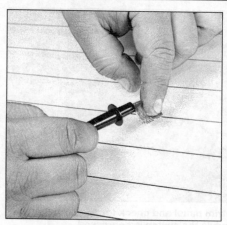

21.5 When measuring the voltage at the rear window defogger grid, wrap a piece of aluminum foil around the positive probe of the voltmeter and press the foil against the wire with your finger

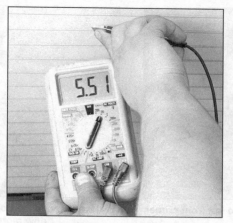

21.6 To determine if a wire has broken, check the voltage at the center of each wire. If the voltage is 5 to 6 volts, the wire is unbroken; if the voltage is 10 to 12 volts, the wire is broken between the center of the wire and the ground side; if the voltage is 0 volts, the wire is broken between the center of the wire and the power side

21.8 To find the break, place the voltmeter negative lead against the defogger ground terminal, place the voltmeter positive lead with the foil strip against the heat wire at the positive terminal end and slide it toward the negative terminal end - the point at which the voltmeter deflects from several volts to zero volts is the point at which the wire is broken

fenderwell must first be removed (see Chapter 11).

9   Disconnect the electrical connectors and remove the bracket bolt **(see illustration)**.

10   Installation is the reverse of removal.

21   Rear window defogger - check and repair

1   The rear window defogger consists of a number of horizontal heating elements baked onto the inside surface of the glass. Power is supplied through a 30-ampere fuse from the power distribution box in the engine compartment. The defogger is controlled by the instrument panel switch. On Integra models, the timer is controlled by the integrated control unit.

2   Small breaks in the element can be repaired without removing the rear window.

Check

Refer to illustrations 21.5, 21.6 and 21.8

3   Turn the ignition switch and defogger system switches to the ON position.

4   Using a voltmeter, place the positive probe against the defogger grid positive terminal and the negative probe against the ground terminal. If battery voltage is not indicated, check the fuse, defogger switch and related wiring. If voltage is indicated, but all or part of the defogger doesn't heat, proceed with the following tests.

5   When measuring voltage during the next two tests, wrap a piece of aluminum foil around the tip of the voltmeter positive probe and press the foil against the heating element with your finger **(see illustration)**. Place the negative probe on the defogger grid ground terminal.

6   Check the voltage at the center of each heating element **(see illustration)**. If the voltage is 5 to 6 volts, the element is okay (there is no break). If the voltage is 0 volts, the ele-

ment is broken between the center of the element and the positive end. If the voltage is 10 to 12 volts the element is broken between the center of the element and the ground side. Check each heating element.

7   If none of the elements are broken, connect the negative probe to a good chassis ground. The voltage reading should stay the same, if it doesn't the ground connection is bad.

8   To find the break, place the voltmeter negative probe against the defogger ground terminal. Place the voltmeter positive probe with the foil strip against the heating element at the positive side and slide it toward the negative side. The point at which the voltmeter deflects from several volts to zero is the point where the heating element is broken **(see illustration)**.

Repair

Refer to illustration 21.14

9   Repair the break in the element using a repair kit specifically for this purpose, such as Dupont paste No. 4817 (or equivalent). The kit includes plastic conductive epoxy.

10   Before repairing a break, turn off the system and allow it to cool for a few minutes.

11   Lightly buff the element area with fine steel wool; then clean it thoroughly with rubbing alcohol.

12   Use masking tape to mask off the area being repaired.

13   Thoroughly mix the epoxy, following the kit instructions.

14   Apply the epoxy material to the slit in the masking tape, overlapping the undamaged area about 3/4-inch on either end **(see illustration)**.

15   Allow the repair to cure for 24 hours before removing the tape and using the system.

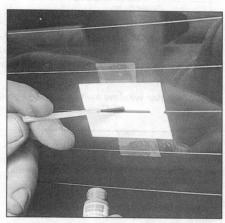

21.14 To use a defogger repair kit, apply masking tape to the inside of the window at the damaged area, then brush on the special conductive coating

22   Cruise control system - description and check

Refer to illustration 22.5

1   The cruise control system maintains vehicle speed with a servo motor located in the engine compartment on the driver's side fenderwell, which is connected to the throttle linkage by a cable. The system consists of the servo motor, brake switch, control switches, speed sensors and relays. Some features of the system require special testers and diagnostic procedures which are beyond the scope of this manual. Listed below are some general procedures that may be used to locate common problems.

2   Locate and check the fuse (see Section 3).

12

22.5 The cruise control servo is located in the left front corner of the engine compartment

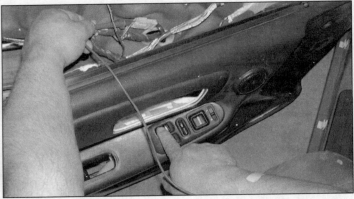

23.12a Remove the door trim panel and check for power to the window motor while the switch is depressed

CIVIC COUPE/HATCHBACK

A1	A2		A3	A4	A5
A6	A7	A8			A12

SWITCH POSITION	CONTINUITY BETWEEN
Left front (drivers switch)	The drivers switch cannot be tested for continuity
Right front	
OFF	A2, A5 and A7
UP	A2 and A5; A6 and A7
DOWN	A2 and A6; A5 and A7

TEST WITH MASTER LOCKOUT SWITCH ON

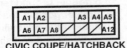

23.12b Master window switch terminal guide and continuity table - Civic coupe/hatchback

CIVIC SEDAN

C1	B1	B2	B3		B4	B5	B6	B7
	B8	B9	B10	B11		B14	B15	B16

SWITCH POSITION	CONTINUITY BETWEEN
Left front (drivers switch)	The drivers switch cannot be tested for continuity
Right front	
OFF	B1, B11 and C1
UP	B1 and B2; B11 and C1
DOWN	B2 and B11; B1 and C1
Left rear	
OFF	B14, B16 and C1
UP	B14 and B15; B16 and C1
DOWN	B15 and B16; B14 and C1
Right rear	
OFF	B9, B10 and C1
UP	B8 and B9; B10 and C1
DOWN	B8 and B10; B9 and C1

TEST WITH MASTER LOCKOUT SWITCH ON

23.12c Master window switch terminal guide and continuity table - Civic sedan

3   The brake pedal switch (or stop lamp switch) deactivates the cruise control system. Have an assistant press the brake pedal while you check the stop lamp operation.

4   If the brake lights do not operate properly, correct the problem and retest the cruise control.

5   Check the control cable between the cruise control servo/amplifier and the throttle linkage and replace as necessary **(see illustration)**.

6   The cruise control system uses a speed sensing device. The speed sensor is located in the transmission. To test the speed sensor, see Chapter 6.

7   Test drive the vehicle to determine if the cruise control is now working. If it isn't, take it to a dealer service department or an automotive electrical specialist for further diagnosis.

23 Power window system - description and check

Refer to illustrations 23.12a through 23.12h

1   The power window system operates electric motors, mounted in the doors, which lower and raise the windows. The system consists of the control switches, the motors, regulators, glass mechanisms and associated wiring.

2   The power windows can be lowered and raised from the master control switch by the driver or by remote switches located at the individual windows. Each window has a separate motor which is reversible. The position of the control switch determines the polarity and therefore the direction of operation.

3   The circuit is protected by a fuse and a circuit breaker. Each motor is also equipped with an internal circuit breaker, which prevents one stuck window from disabling the whole system.

4   The power window system will only operate when the ignition switch is ON. In addition, many models have a window lockout switch at the master control switch which, when activated, disables the switches at the rear windows and, sometimes, the switch at the passenger's window also. Always check these items before troubleshooting a window problem.

5   These procedures are general in nature, so if you can't find the problem using them, take the vehicle to a dealer service department or other properly equipped repair facility.

6   If the power windows won't operate, always check the fuse and circuit breaker first.

7   If only the rear windows are inoperative, or if the windows only operate from the master control switch, check the rear window

lockout switch for continuity in the unlocked position. Replace it if it doesn't have continuity.

8   Check the wiring between the switches and fuse panel for continuity. Repair the wiring, if necessary.

9   If only one window is inoperative from the master control switch, try the other control switch at the window. **Note:** *This doesn't apply to the driver's door window.*

10   If the same window works from one switch, but not the other, check the switch for continuity.

11   If the switch tests OK, check for a short or open in the circuit between the affected switch and the window motor.

12   If one window is inoperative from both switches, remove the trim panel from the affected door and check for voltage at the switch and at the motor while the switch is operated. If a defective switch is suspected, remove the switch and check it for continuity as indicated **(see illustrations)**.

13   If voltage is reaching the motor, disconnect the glass from the regulator (see Chapter 11). Move the window up and down by hand while checking for binding and damage. Also check for binding and damage to the regulator. If the regulator is not damaged and the window moves up and down smoothly, replace the motor. If there's binding or dam-

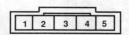

SWITCH POSITION	CONTINUITY BETWEEN
OFF	2 and 3; 4 and 5
UP	1 and 4; 2 and 3
DOWN	1 and 3; 4 and 5

24025-12-23.12D HAYNES

23.12d Passenger window switch terminal guide and continuity table - Civic (including rear window switches on sedan models)

23.12f Master window switch terminal guide and continuity table - Integra sedan

SWITCH POSITION	CONTINUITY BETWEEN
Left front (drivers switch)	The drivers switch cannot be tested for continuity
Right front	
OFF	I, J and Q
UP	H and J; I and Q
DOWN	H and I; J and Q
Left rear	
OFF	F, G and Q
UP	E and G; F and Q
DOWN	E and F; G and Q
Right rear	
OFF	O, P and Q
UP	N and P; O and Q
DOWN	N and O; P and Q

TEST WITH MASTER LOCKOUT SWITCH ON

42025-12-23.12f HAYNES

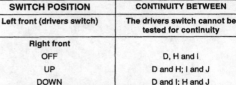

SWITCH POSITION	CONTINUITY BETWEEN
Left front (drivers switch)	The drivers switch cannot be tested for continuity
Right front	
OFF	D, H and I
UP	D and H; I and J
DOWN	D and I; H and J

TEST WITH MASTER LOCKOUT SWITCH ON

42025-12-23.12E HAYNES

23.12e Master window switch terminal guide and continuity table - Integra hatchback

SWITCH POSITION	CONTINUITY BETWEEN
OFF	A and B; D and E
UP	B and C; D and E
DOWN	A and B; C and D

42025-12-23.12G HAYNES

23.12g Passenger window switch terminal guide and continuity table - Integra hatchback and sedan

SWITCH POSITION	CONTINUITY BETWEEN
OFF	A and B; C and E
UP	A and B; D and E
DOWN	B and D; C and E

42025-12-23.12h Haynes

23.12h Rear window switch terminal guide and continuity table - Integra sedan

SWITCH POSITION	CONTINUITY BETWEEN
LOCK	1 and 2
UNLOCK	2 and 3

42025-12-24.3 HAYNES

24.3 Power door lock switch terminal guide and continuity table

age, lubricate, repair or replace parts, as necessary. **Note:** *The window motor is an integral part of the window regulator assembly. See Chapter 11 for the removal procedures.*

14 If voltage isn't reaching the motor, check the wiring in the circuit for continuity between the switches and motors. You'll need to consult the wiring diagram for the vehicle. If the circuit is equipped with a relay, check that the relay is grounded properly and receiving voltage.

15 Test the windows after you are done to confirm proper repairs.

24 Power door lock system - description and check

Refer to illustrations 24.3 and 24.6

The power door lock system operates the door lock actuators mounted in each door. The system consists of the switches, actuators, a control unit and associated wiring. Diagnosis can usually be limited to simple checks of the wiring connections and actuators for minor faults which can be easily repaired. Since this system uses an electronic control unit, in-depth diagnosis should be left to a dealership service department. The door lock control unit is located behind the instrument panel, to the right of the fuse box.

Power door lock systems are operated by bi-directional solenoids located in the doors. The lock switches have two operating positions: Lock and Unlock. When activated, the switch sends a ground signal to the door lock control unit to lock or unlock the doors. Depending on which way the switch is activated, the control unit reverses polarity to the solenoids, allowing the two sides of the circuit to be used alternately as the feed (positive) and ground side.

Some vehicles may have an anti-theft systems incorporated into the power locks. If you are unable to locate the trouble using the following general Steps, consult your a dealer service department or other qualified repair shop.

1 Always check the circuit protection first. Some vehicles use a combination of circuit breakers and fuses.

2 Operate the door lock switches in both directions (Lock and Unlock) with the engine off. Listen for the click of the solenoids operating.

3 Test the switches for continuity **(see illustration)**. Replace the switch if there's not continuity in both switch positions.

4 Check the wiring between the switches, control unit and solenoids for continuity. Repair the wiring if there's no continuity.

12

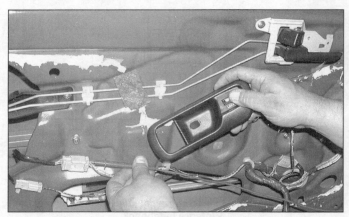

24.6 Remove the door trim panel and check for power to the door lock solenoid while the switch is depressed

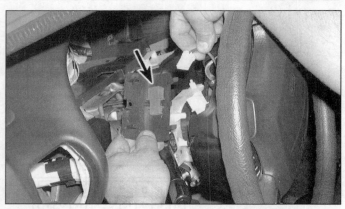

26.8 Remove the access panel, then remove the short connector (arrow) and the two-pin connector between the airbag and the cable reel

5   Check for a bad ground at the switches or the control unit.

6   If all but one lock solenoids operate, remove the trim panel from the affected door (see Chapter 11) and check for voltage at the solenoid while the lock switch is operated One of the wires should have voltage in the Lock position; the other should have voltage in the Unlock position **(see illustration)**.

7   If the inoperative solenoid is receiving voltage, replace the solenoid.

8   If the inoperative solenoid isn't receiving voltage, check for an open or short in the wire between the lock solenoid and the control unit. **Note:** *It's common for wires to break in the portion of the harness between the body and door (opening and closing the door fatigues and eventually breaks the wires).*

25 Electric rear view mirrors - description and check

1   Electric rear view mirrors use two motors to move the glass; one for up-and-down adjustments and one for left-to-right adjustments.

2   The control switch has a selector portion which sends voltage to the left or right side mirror. With the ignition ON, engine OFF, roll down the windows and operate the mirror control switch through all functions (left-right and up-down) for both the left and right side mirrors.

3   Listen carefully for the sound of the electric motors running in the mirrors.

4   If the motors can be heard but the mirror glass doesn't move, there's probably a problem with the drive mechanism inside the mirror. Remove and disassemble the mirror to locate the problem.

5   If the mirrors don't operate and no sound comes from the mirrors, check the fuse (see Section 3).

6   If the fuse is OK, remove the mirror control switch from its mounting without disconnecting the wires attached to it. Turn the ignition ON and check for voltage at the switch. There should be voltage at one terminal. If

there's no voltage at the switch, check for an opening or short in the wiring between the fuse panel and the switch.

7   If there's voltage at the switch, disconnect it. Check the switch for continuity in all its operating positions. If the switch does not have continuity, replace it.

8   Re-connect the switch. Locate the wire going from the switch to ground. Leaving the switch connected, connect a jumper wire between this wire and ground. If the mirror works normally with this wire in place, repair the faulty ground connection.

9   If the mirror still doesn't work, remove the cover and check the wires at the mirror for voltage with a test light. Check with ignition ON and the mirror selector switch on the appropriate side. Operate the mirror switch in all its positions. There should be voltage at one of the switch-to-mirror wires in each switch position (except the neutral position).

10   If there's not voltage in each switch position, check the wiring between the mirror and control switch for opens and shorts.

11   If there's voltage, remove the mirror and test it off the vehicle with jumper wires. Replace the mirror if it fails this test (see Chapter 11).

26 Airbag system - general information

Description

1   All models are equipped with a Supplemental Restraint System (SRS), more commonly known as an airbag. All models have two airbags, one for the driver and one for the front seat passenger. The SRS system is designed to protect the driver and passenger) from serious injury in the event of a head-on or frontal collision.

2   The SRS system consists of an SRS unit - which contains an impact sensor, safing sensor, self-diagnosis circuit and a back-up power circuit - located under the dash, right in front of the floor console, an airbag assembly in the center of the steering wheel and a

second airbag assembly for the front seat passenger, located in the top of the dashboard right above the glove box.

Operation

3   For the airbag(s) to deploy, the impact and safing sensors must be activated. When this condition occurs, the circuit to the airbag inflator is closed and the airbag inflates. If the battery is destroyed by the impact, or is too low to power the inflator, a back-up power unit inside the SRS unit provides power.

Self-diagnosis system

4   A self-diagnosis circuit in the SRS unit displays a light when the ignition switch is turned to the On position. If the system is operating normally, the light should go out after about six seconds. If the light doesn't come on, or doesn't go out after six seconds, or if it comes on while you're driving the vehicle, there's a malfunction in the SRS system. Have it inspected and repaired as soon as possible. Do not attempt to troubleshoot or service the SRS system yourself. Even a small mistake could cause the SRS system to malfunction when you need it.

Servicing components near the SRS system

5   Nevertheless, there are times when you need to remove the steering wheel, radio or service other components on or near the dashboard. At these times, you'll be working around components and wire harnesses for the SRS system. Do not unplug the connectors for these wires. And do not use electrical test equipment on SRS wires. *ALWAYS DISABLE THE SRS SYSTEM BEFORE WORKING NEAR THE SRS SYSTEM COMPONENTS OR RELATED WIRING.*

Disabling the SRS system

Refer to illustrations 26.8 and 26.12
Warning: *Anytime you are working in the vicinity of airbag wiring or components, DISABLE THE SRS SYSTEM.*

6   Disconnect the battery negative cable,

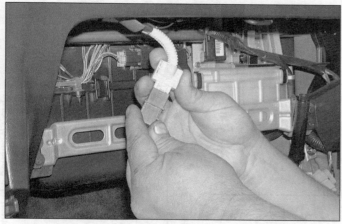

26.12 When disabling the passenger's side airbag, unplug the two-pin connector from the SRS main harness

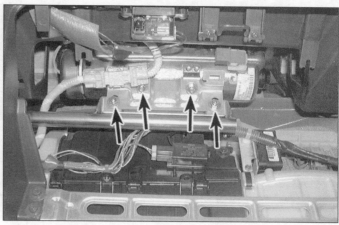

26.18 Passenger side airbag mounting screws (arrows)

then disconnect the positive cable and wait three minutes. **Caution:** *The radio in your vehicle may be equipped with an anti-theft system. Make sure you have the correct activation code before disconnecting the battery.*

7   Connect the short (red) connectors to the airbag side of the connectors as described in the following steps.

Driver's side airbag

8   Remove the access panel below the airbag and remove the short (red) connector **(see illustration)**.

9   Unplug the two-pin connector between the airbag and the cable reel.

10   Plug the short (red) connector into the airbag side of the three-pin connector.

Passenger's side airbag

11   Remove the glove box (see Chapter 11).

12   Unplug the electrical connector between the passenger side airbag and the SRS main wiring harness. Install the red short connector on the airbag side of the connector **(see illustration)**.

Enabling the SRS system

13   After you've disabled the airbag and performed the necessary service, unplug the short connector from the airbag connector and plug in the two-pin airbag connector into the two-pin cable reel connector (driver's side) or the SRS main harness (passenger's side). Attach the short connector to its holder and reinstall the lid to the underside of the steering wheel or reinstall the glove box.

14   Turn the ignition switch to the Off position.

15   Reattach the positive (first) and negative (last) battery cables (see Chapter 5).

Airbag removal and installation

Refer to illustrations 26.18

16   Disable the system (see above).

17   To remove the driver's side airbag, see Chapter 10.

18   To remove the passenger's side airbag, remove its mounting screws **(see illustration)**.

19   Installation is the reverse of removal. Enable the SRS system as described above.

---

27   Wiring diagrams - general information

Since it isn't possible to include all wiring diagrams for every year and model covered by this manual, the following diagrams are those that are typical and most commonly needed.

Prior to troubleshooting any circuits, check the fuse and circuit breakers (if equipped) to make sure they're in good condition. Make sure the battery is properly charged and check the cable connections (see Chapter 1).

When checking a circuit, make sure that all connectors are clean, with no broken or loose terminals. When unplugging a connector, do not pull on the wires. Pull only on the connector housing.

12

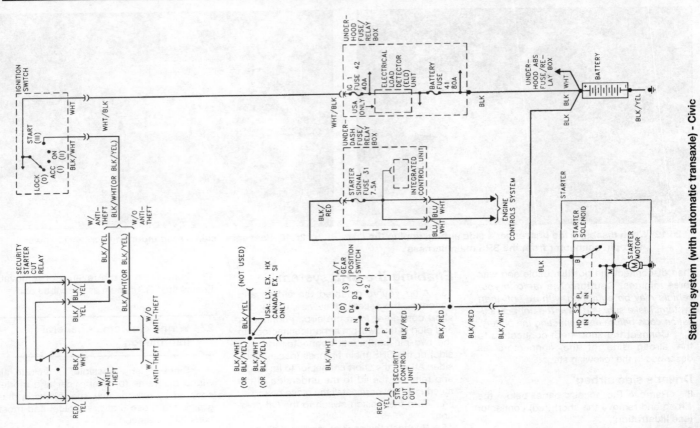

Starting system (with automatic transaxle) - Civic

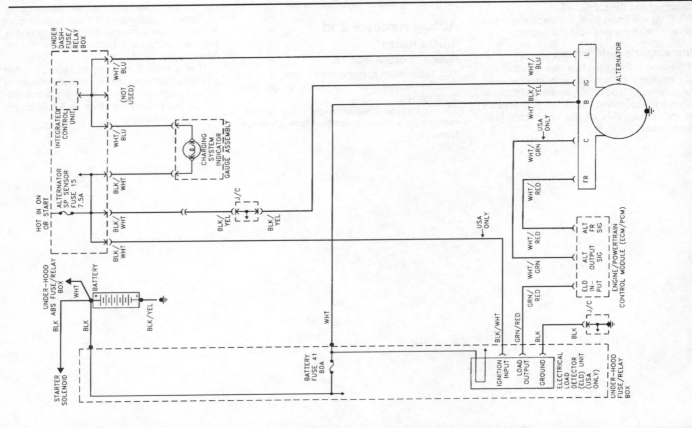

Charging system - Civic

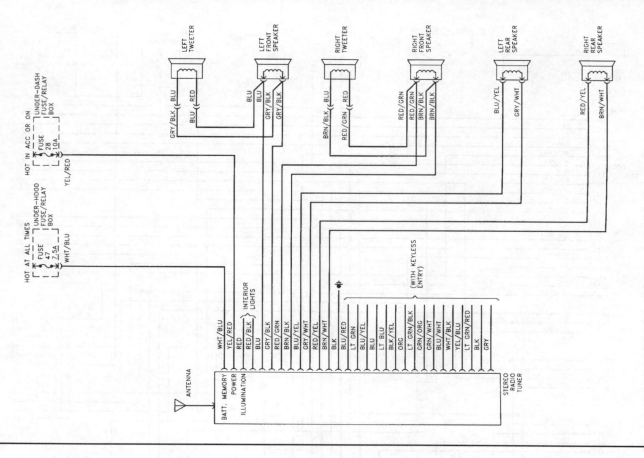

Typical stereo system - Civic

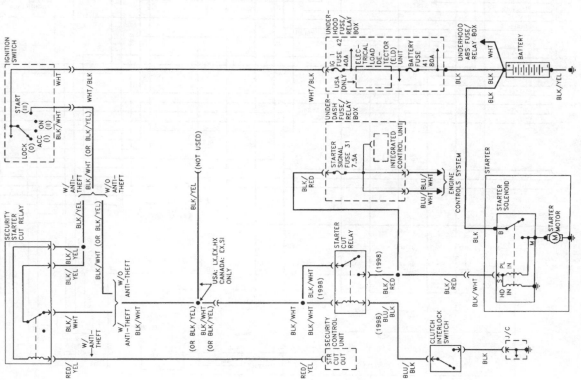

Starting system (with manual transaxle) - Civic

12

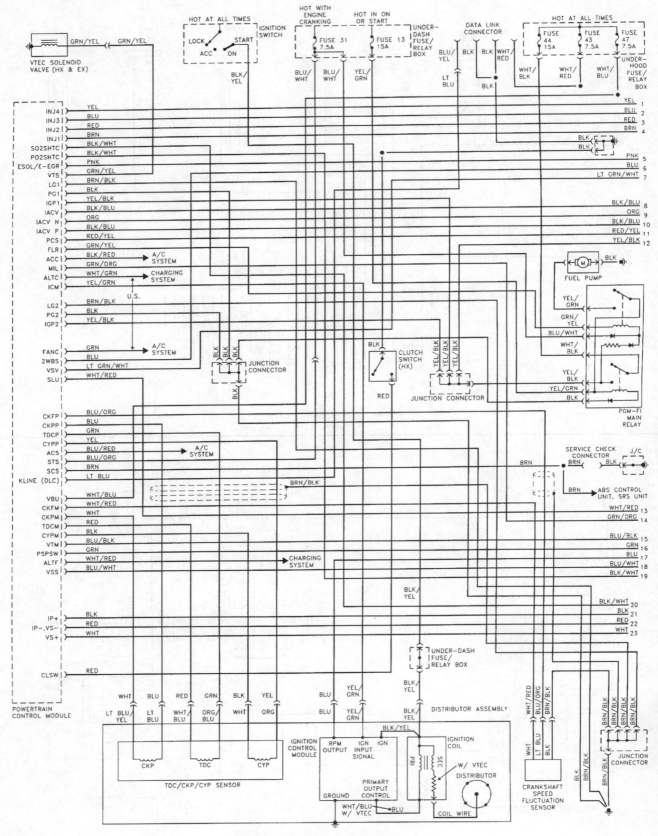

Engine control system (1 of 3) - Civic

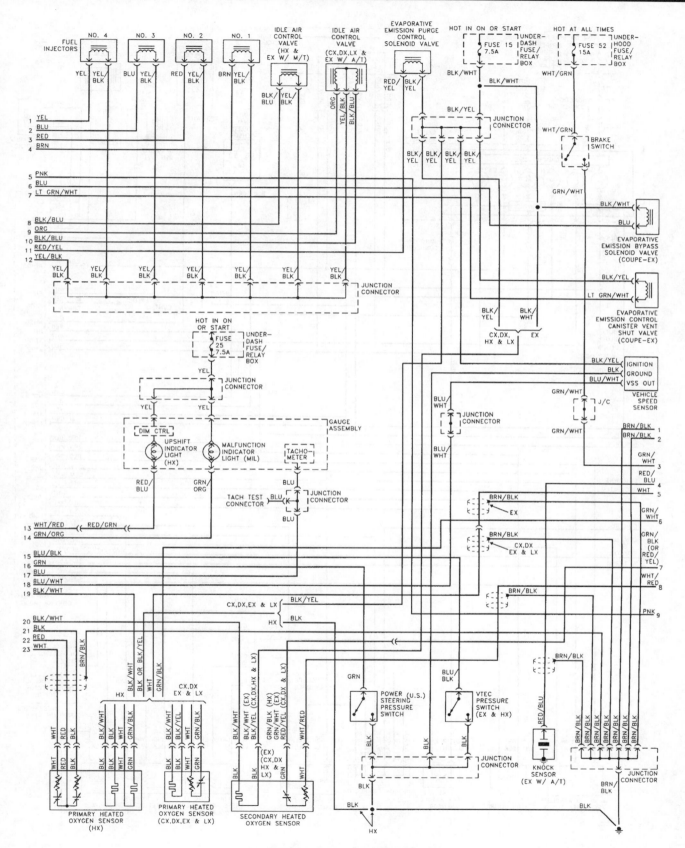

Engine control system (2 of 3) - Civic

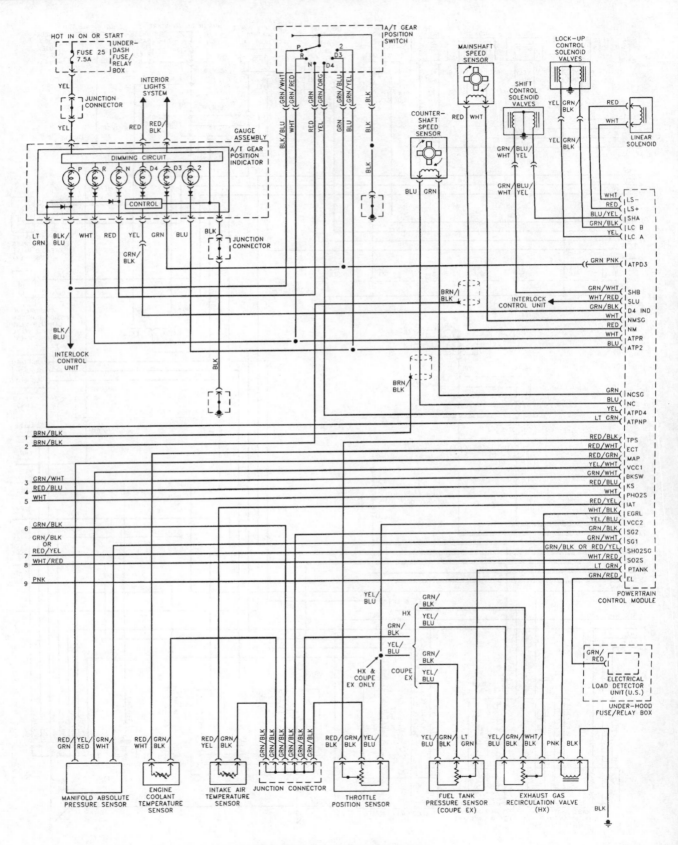

Engine control system (3 of 3) - Civic

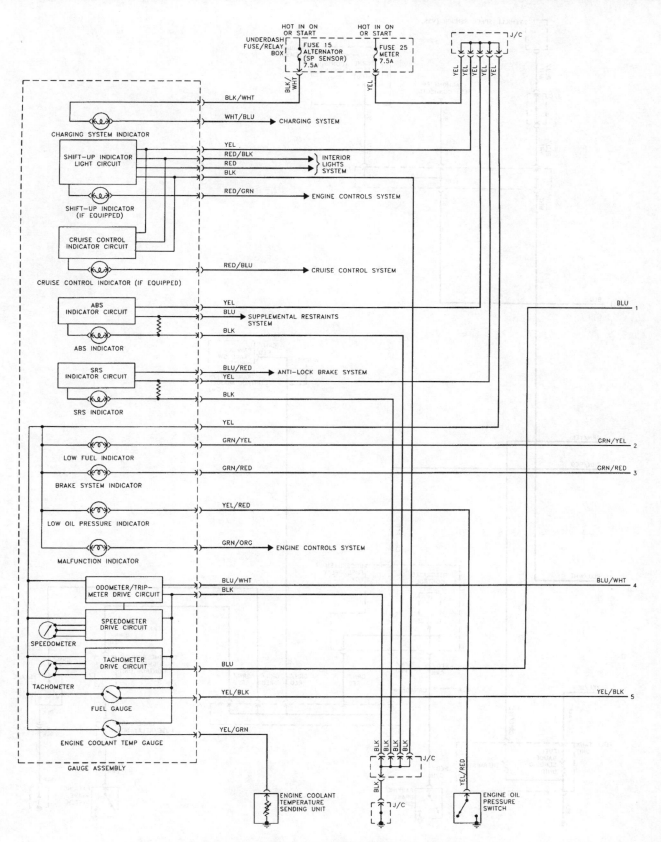

Instrument panel gauges and warning light system (1 of 2) - Civic

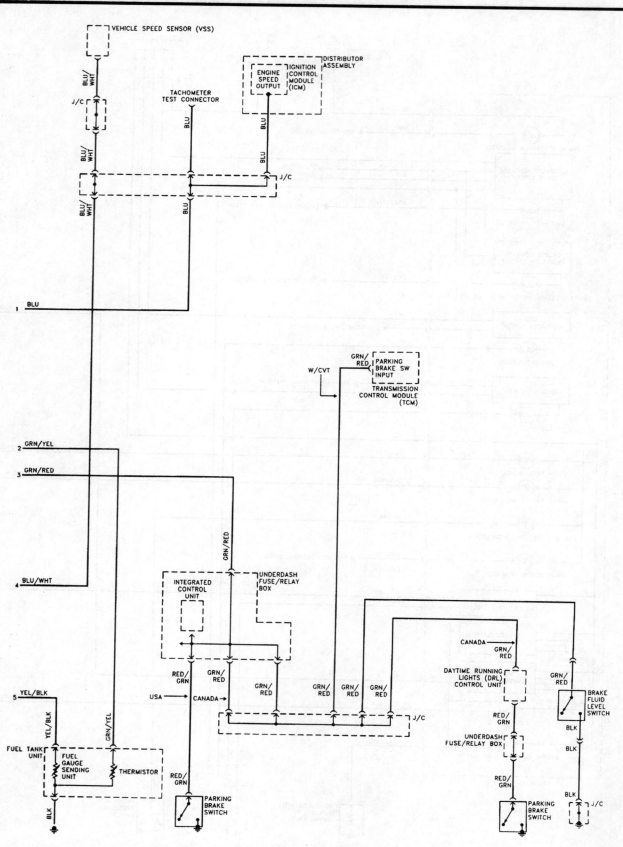

Instrument panel gauges and warning light system (2 of 2) - Civic

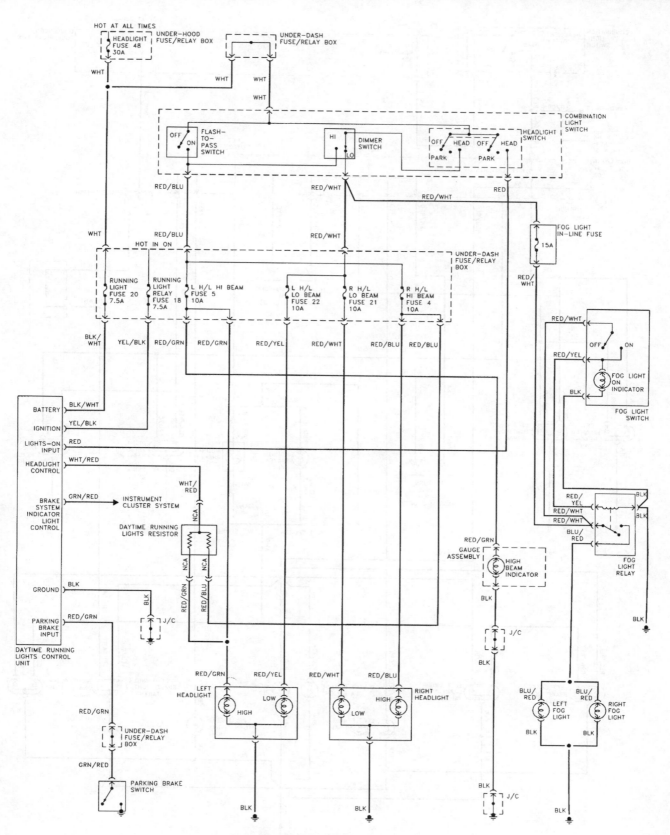

Headlight and fog light system - Civic

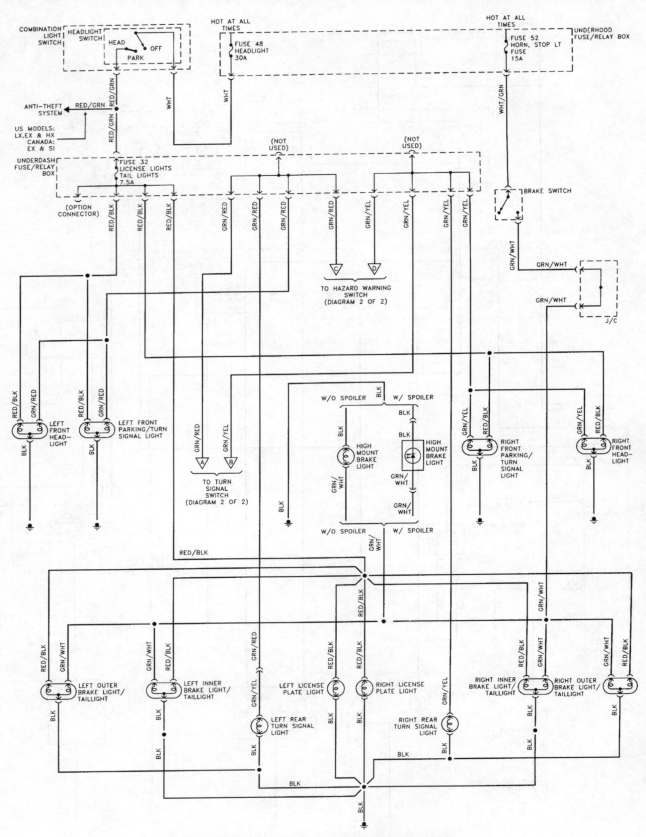

Exterior lighting system (1 of 2) - Civic coupe and sedan

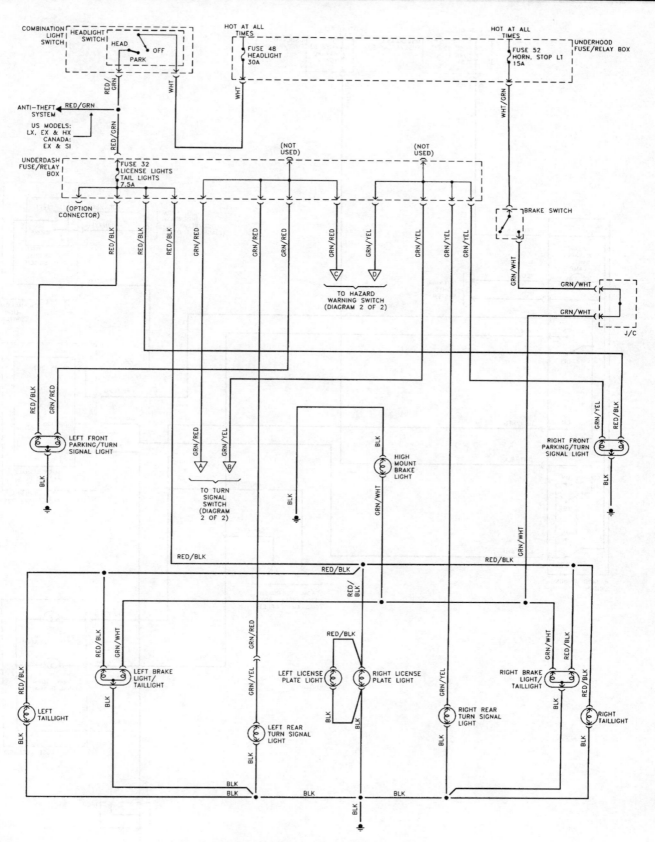

Exterior lighting system (1 of 2) - Civic hatchback

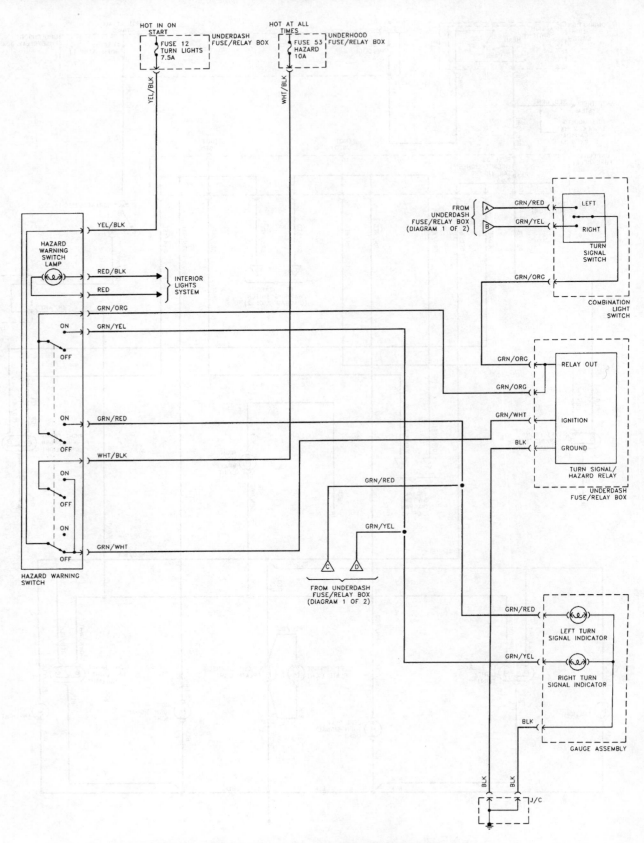

Exterior lighting system (2 of 2) - Civic coupe, sedan and hatchback

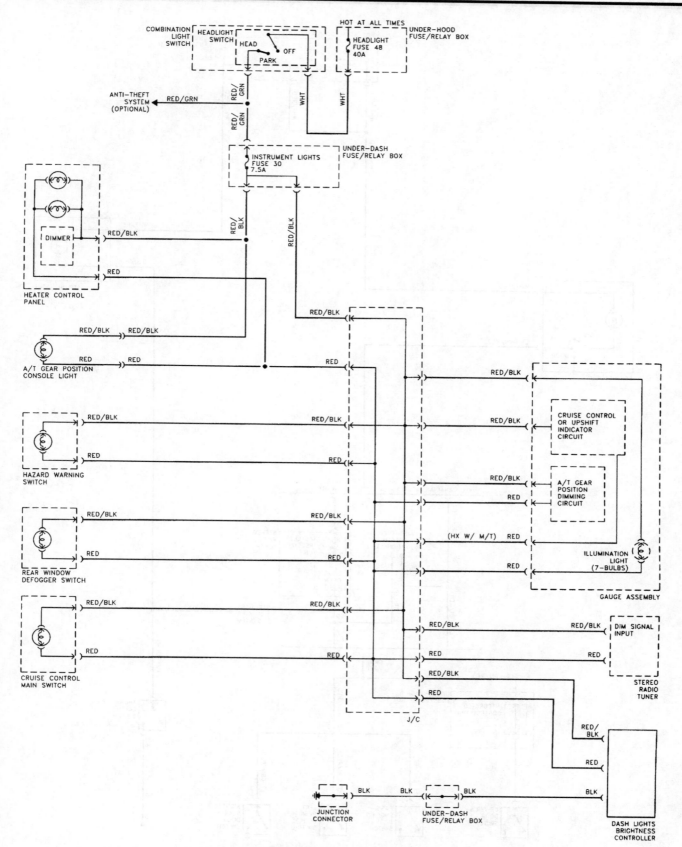

Interior lighting system (1 of 2) - Civic

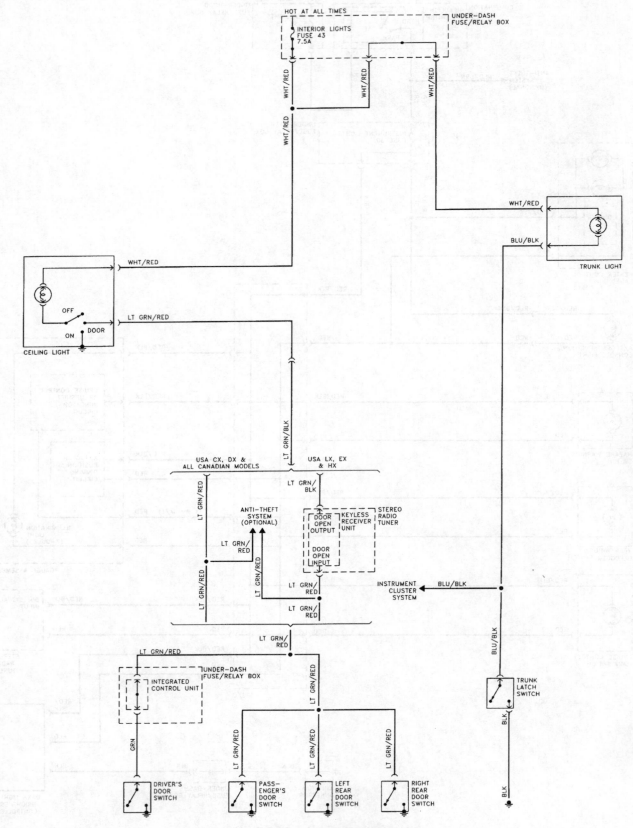

Interior lighting system (2 of 2) - Civic

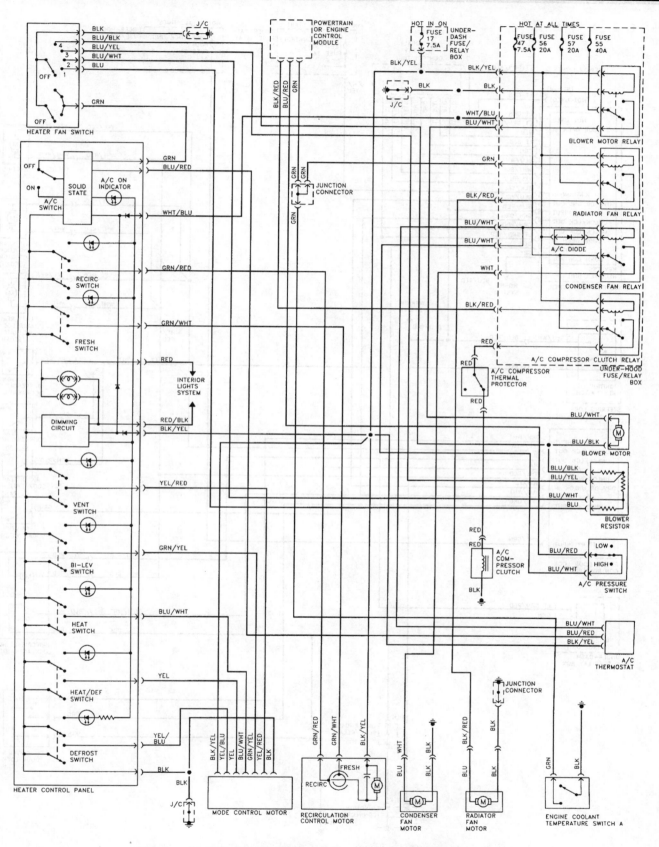

Heating and air conditioning system (including engine cooling fan) - Civic

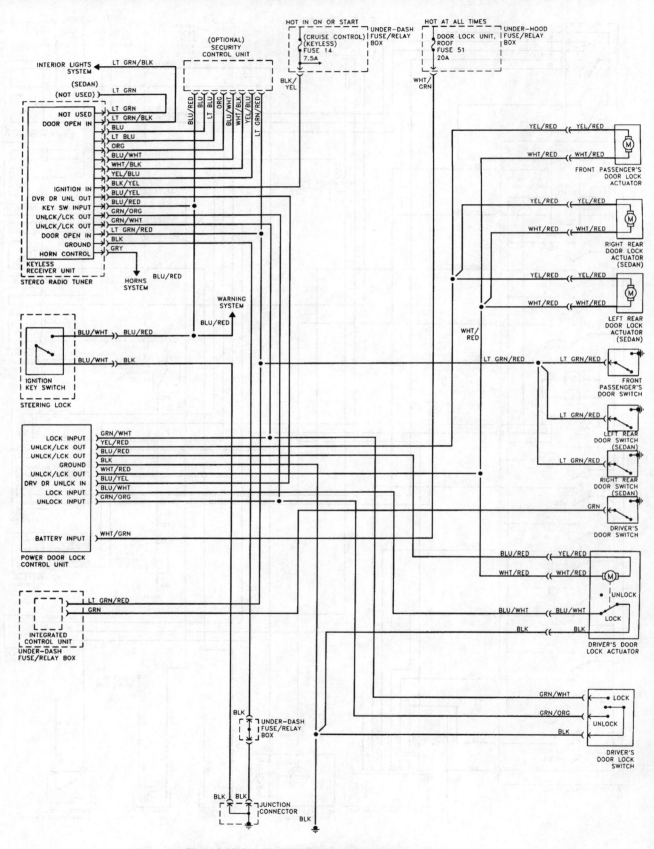

Power door lock system (with keyless entry) - Civic

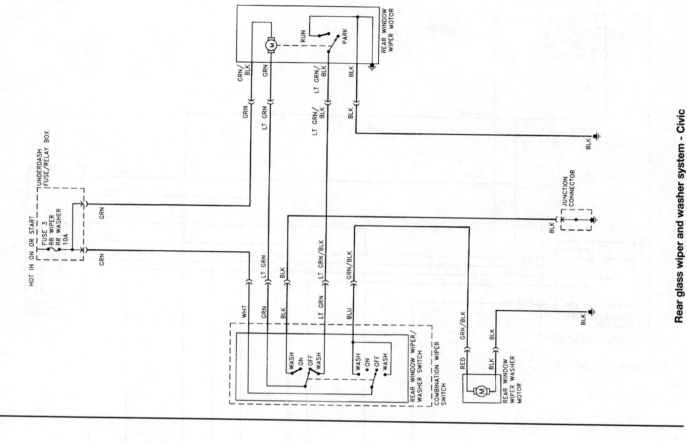

Rear glass wiper and washer system - Civic

Power door lock system (without keyless entry) - Civic

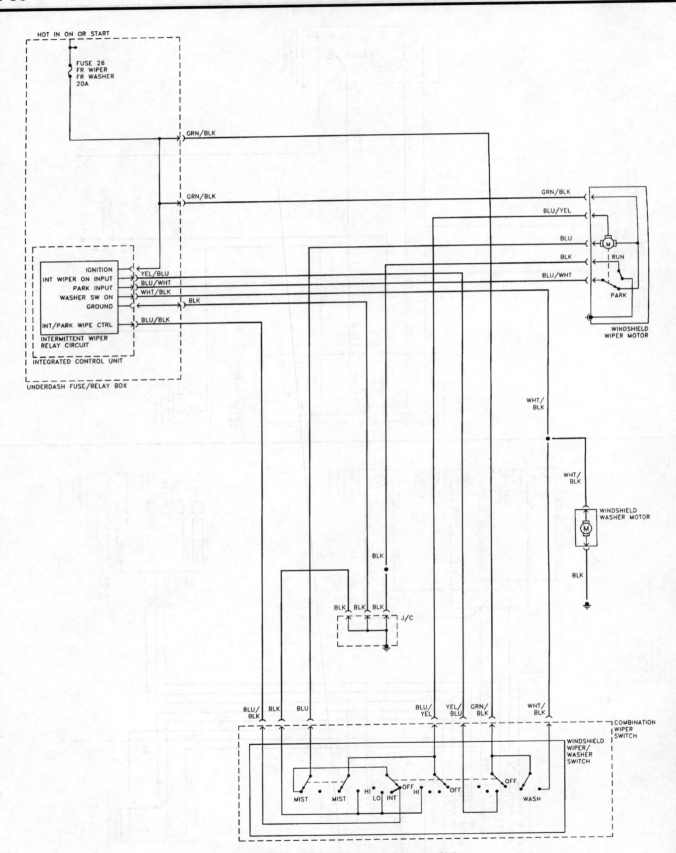

Front windshield wiper and washer system - Civic

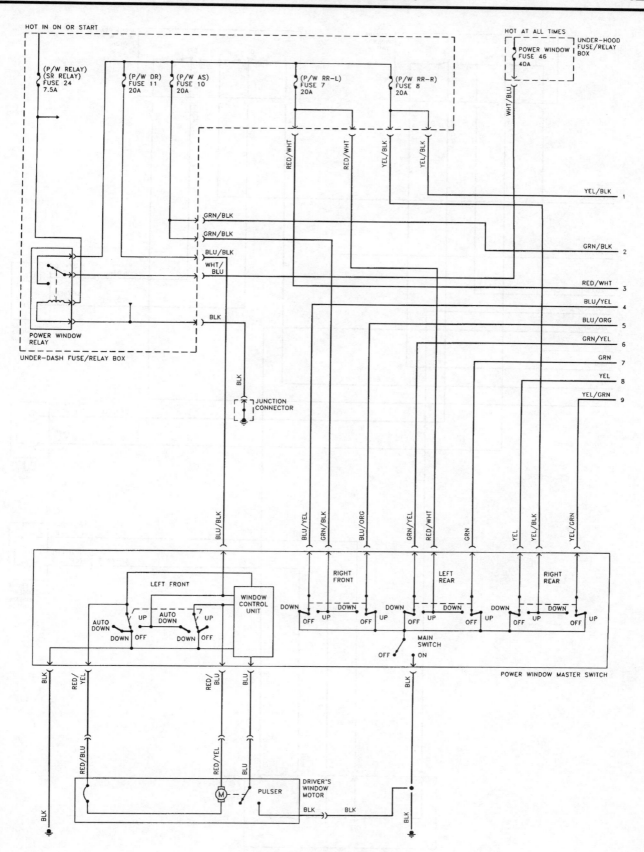

Power window system (1 of 2) - Civic

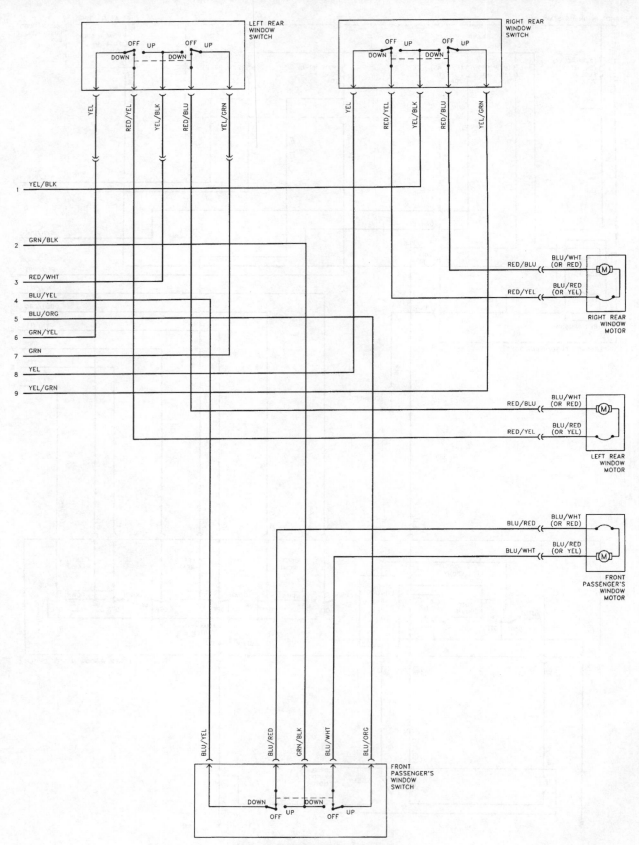

Power window system (2 of 2) - Civic

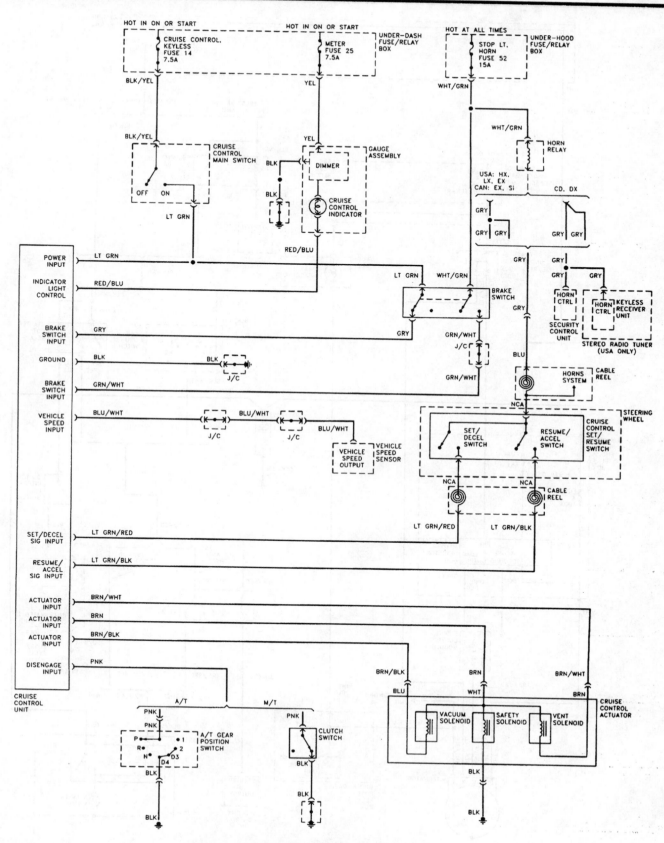

Cruise control system - Civic

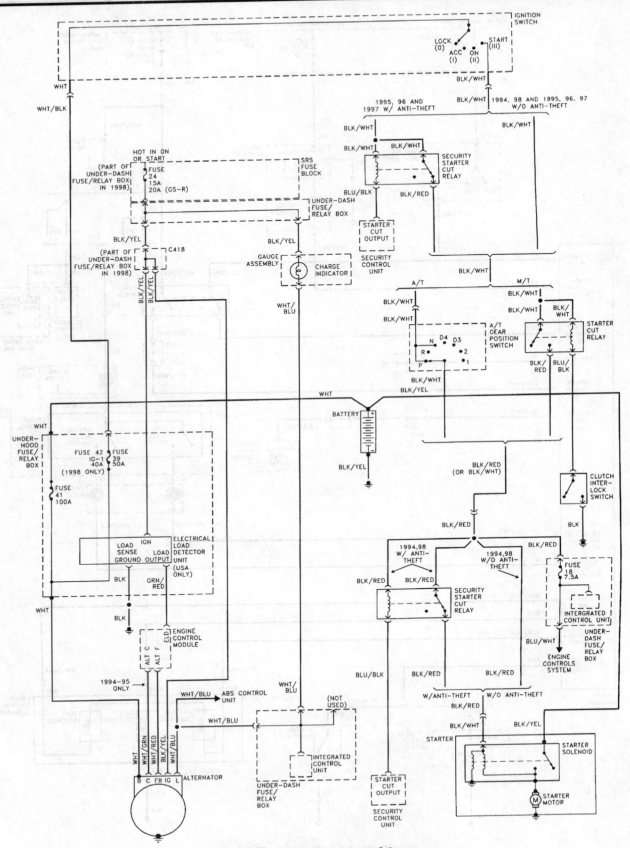

Starting and charging system - Integra

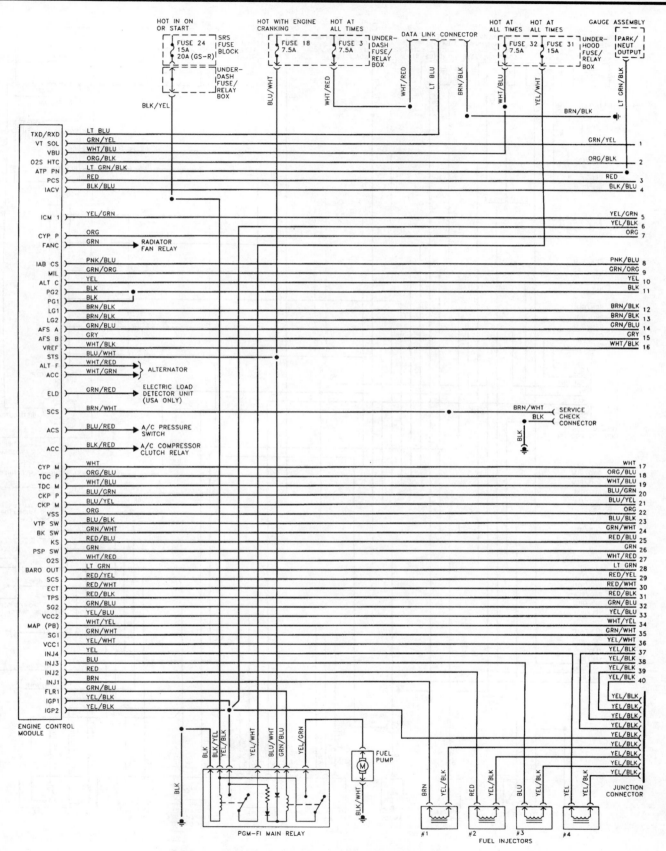

Engine control system (1 of 2) - 1994 thru 1997 Integra

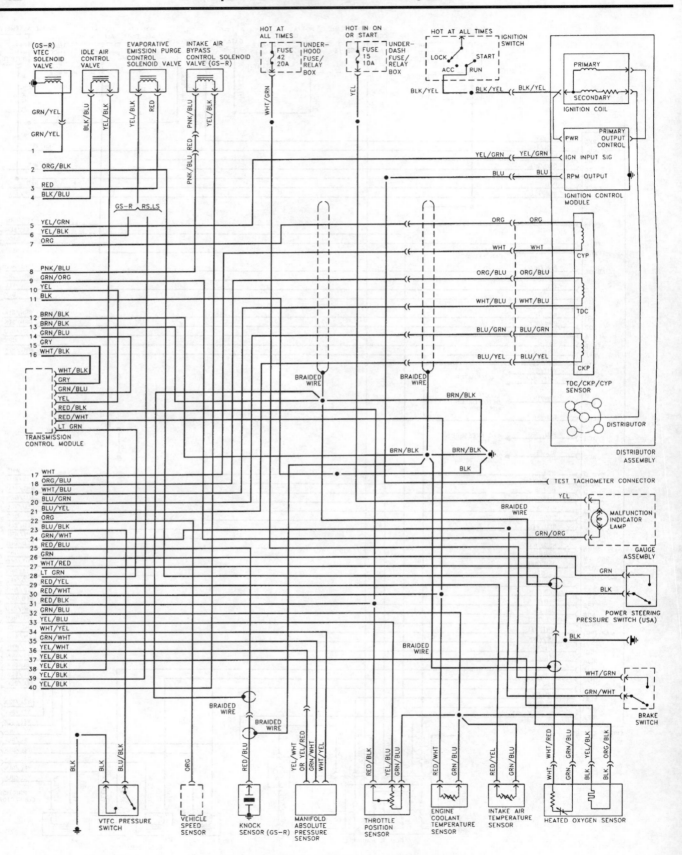

Engine control system (2 of 2) - 1994 thru 1997 Integra

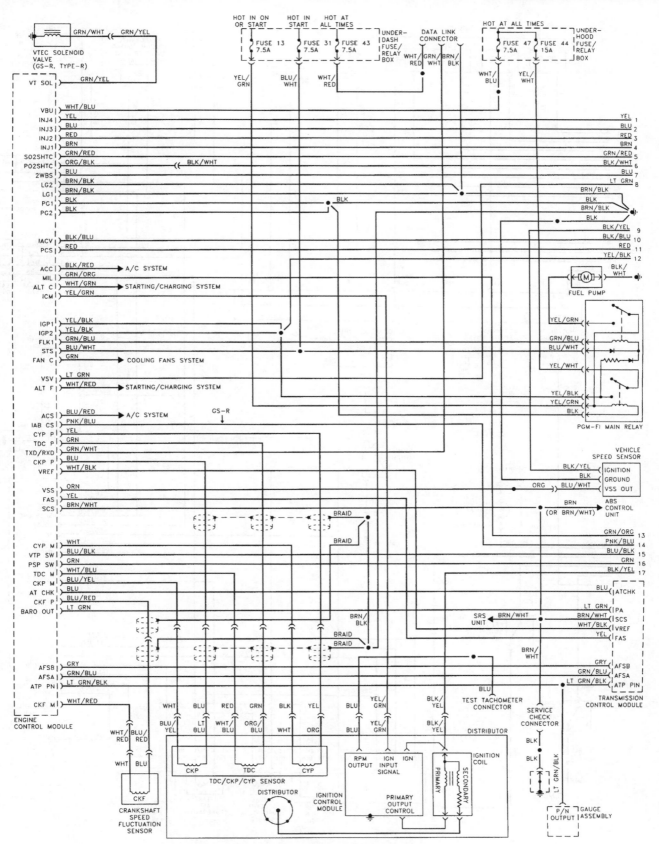

Engine control system (1 of 2) - 1998 Integra

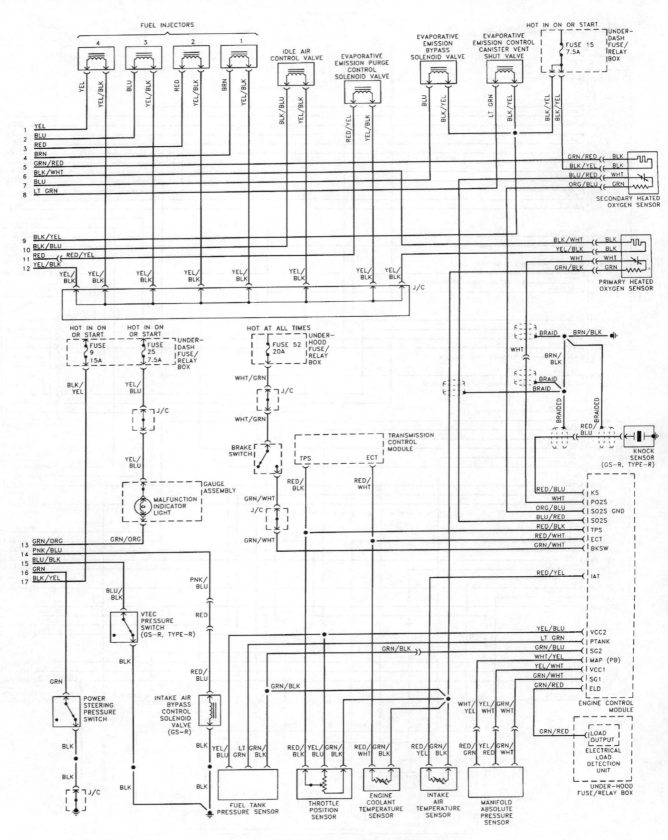

Engine control system (2 of 2) - 1998 Integra

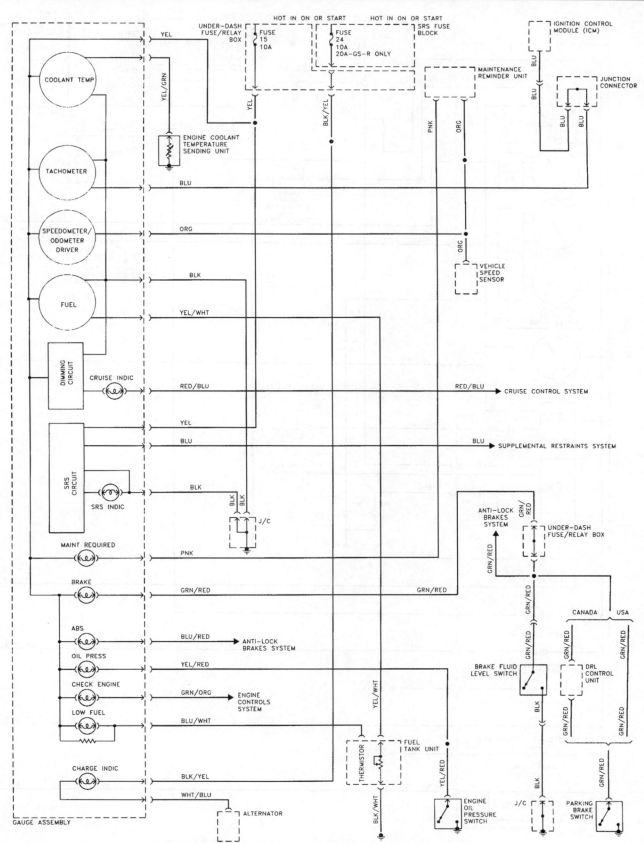

Instrument panel gauges and warning light system - 1994 Integra

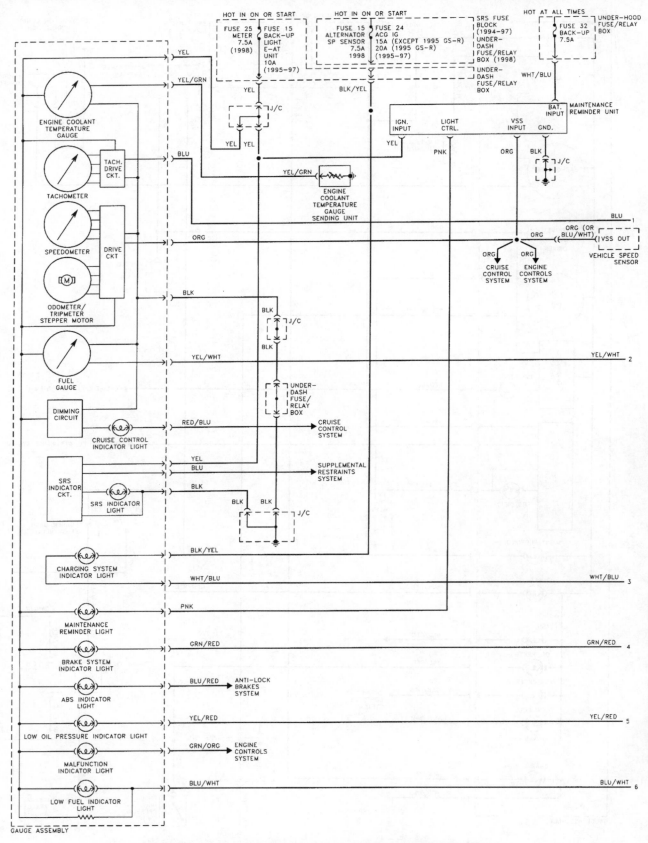

Instrument panel gauges and warning light system (1 of 2) - 1995 thru 1998 Integra

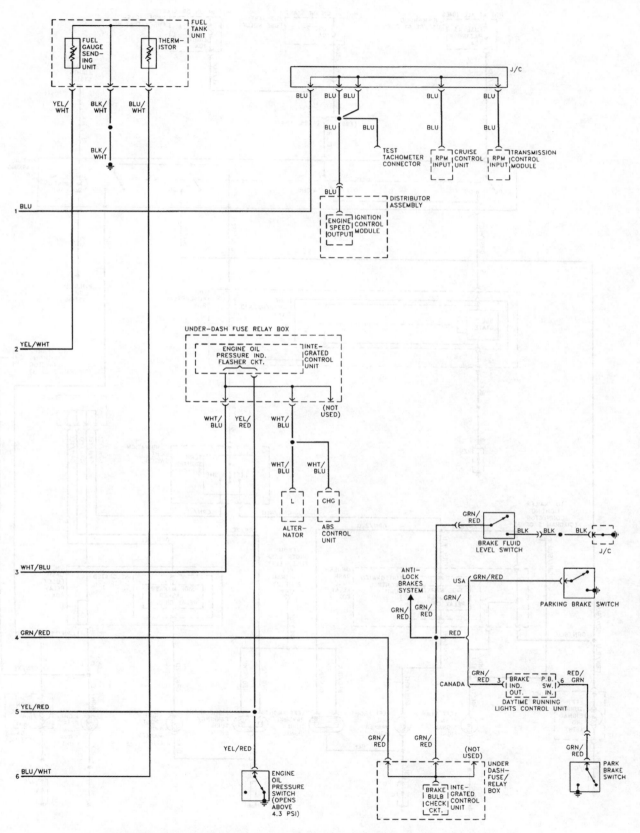

Instrument panel gauges and warning light system (2 of 2) - 1995 thru 1998 Integra

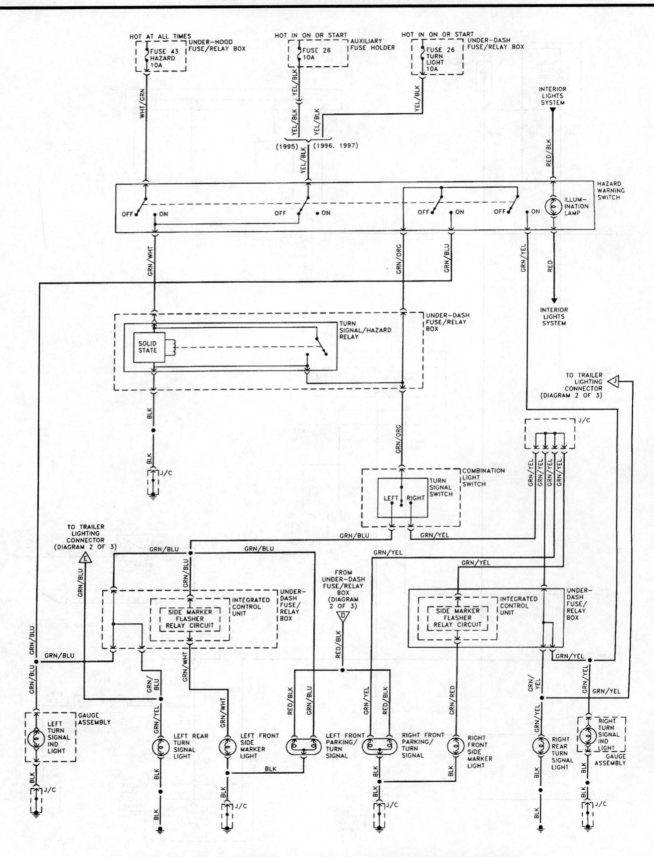

Exterior lighting system (except headlights and fog lights) (1 of 3) - 1994 thru 1997 Integra

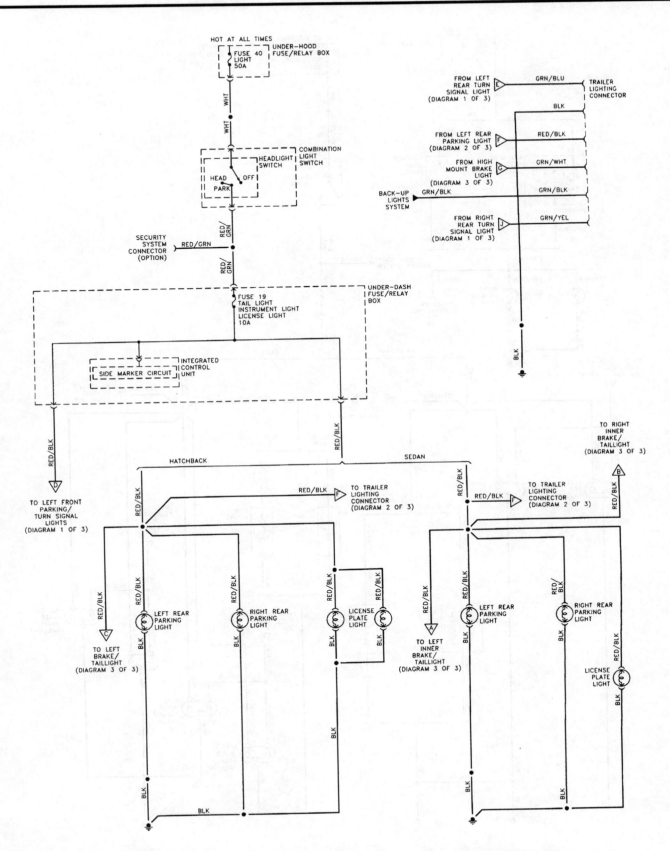

Exterior lighting system (except headlights and fog lights) (2 of 3) - 1994 thru 1997 Integra

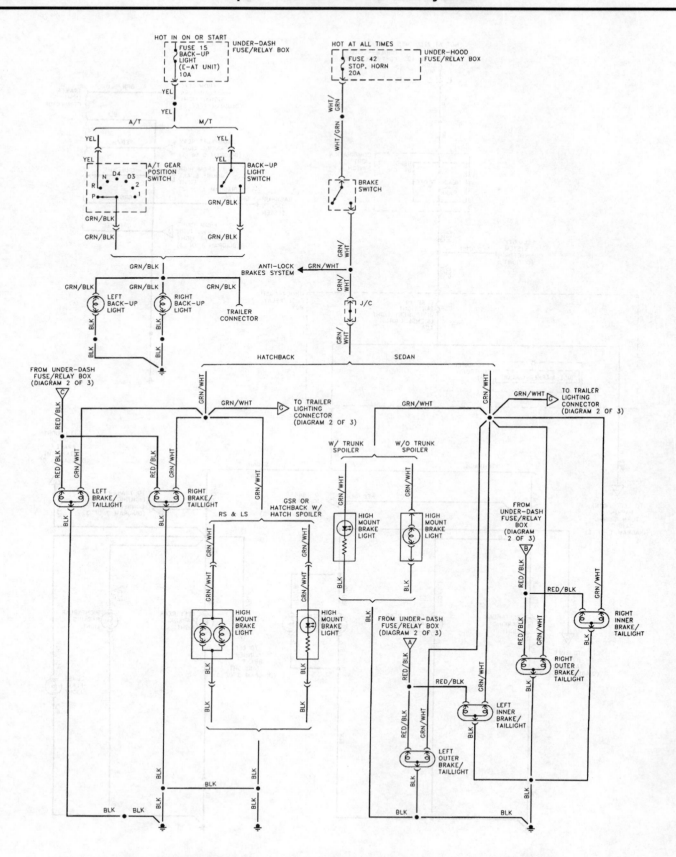

Exterior lighting system (except headlights and fog lights) (3 of 3) - 1994 thru 1997 Integra

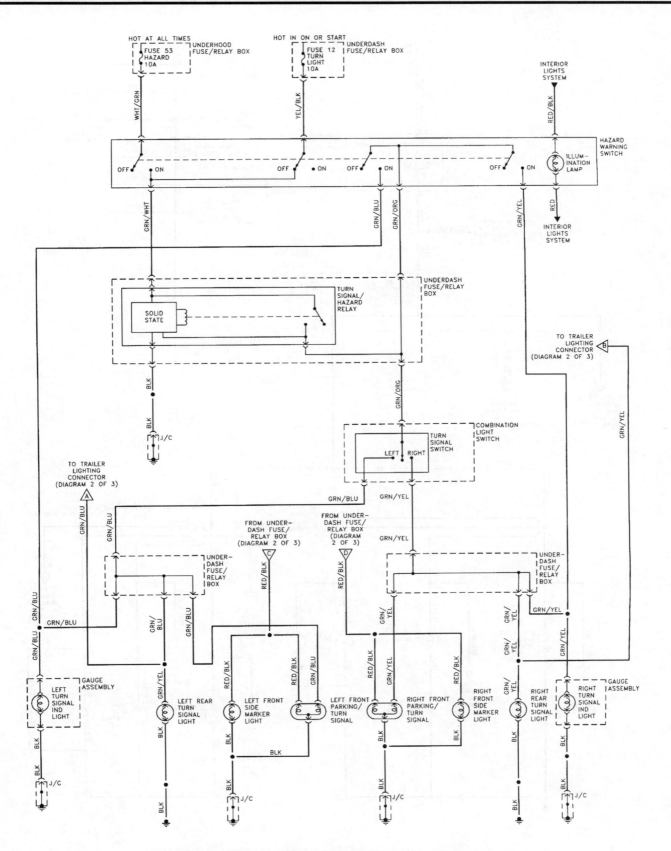

Exterior lighting system (except headlights and fog lights) (1 of 3) - 1998 Integra

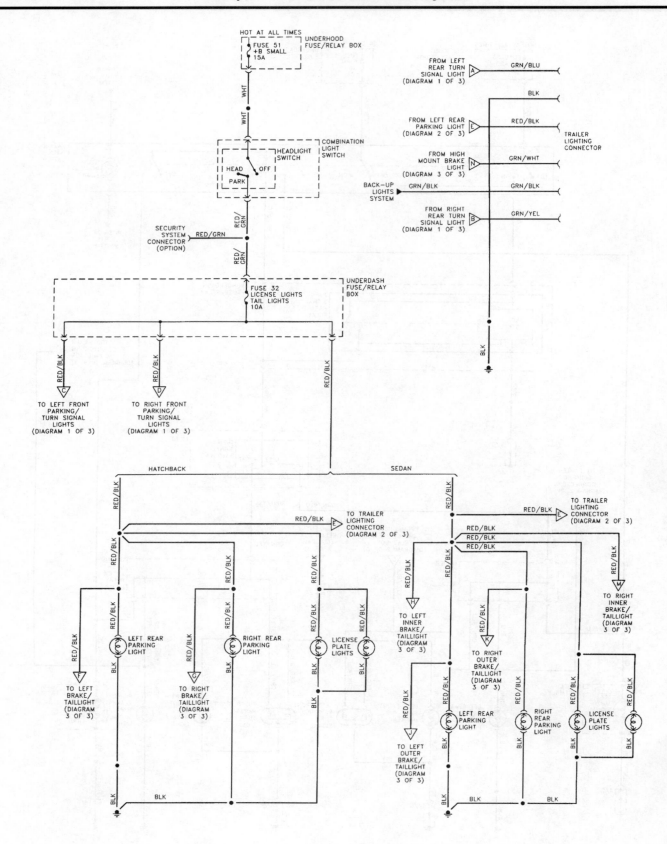

Exterior lighting system (except headlights and fog lights) (2 of 3) - 1998 Integra

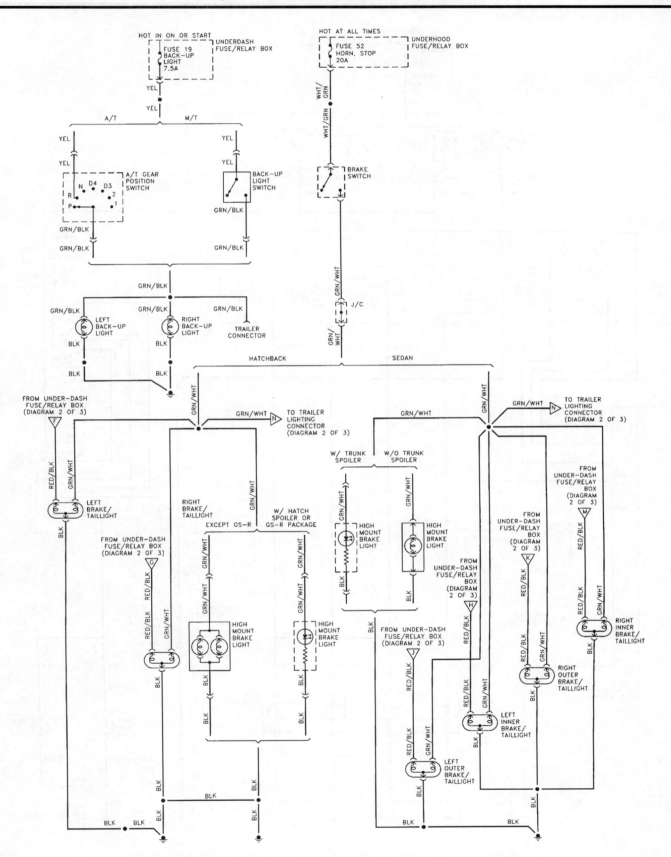

Exterior lighting system (except headlights and fog lights) (3 of 3) - 1998 Integra

12

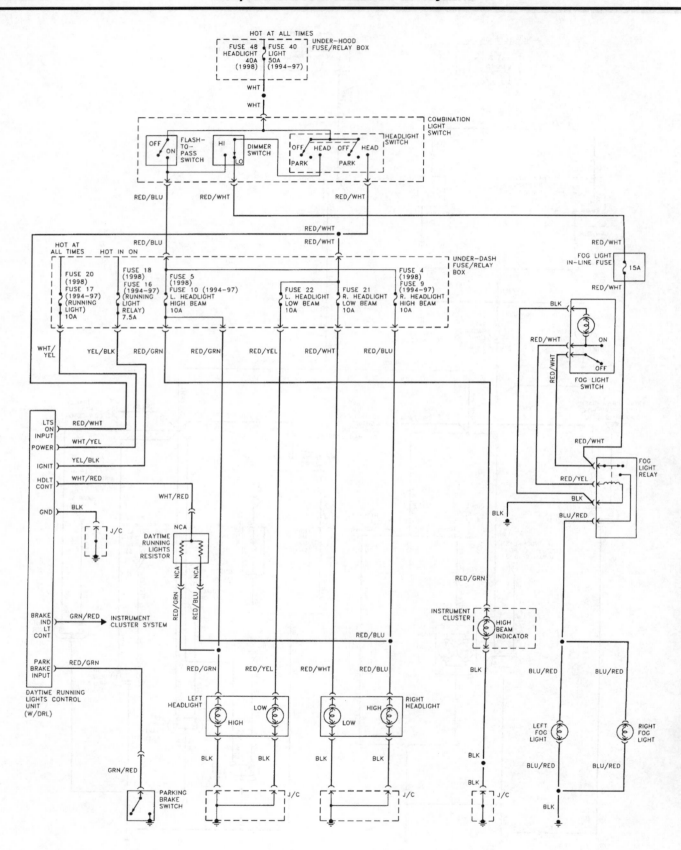

Headlight and fog light system - Integra

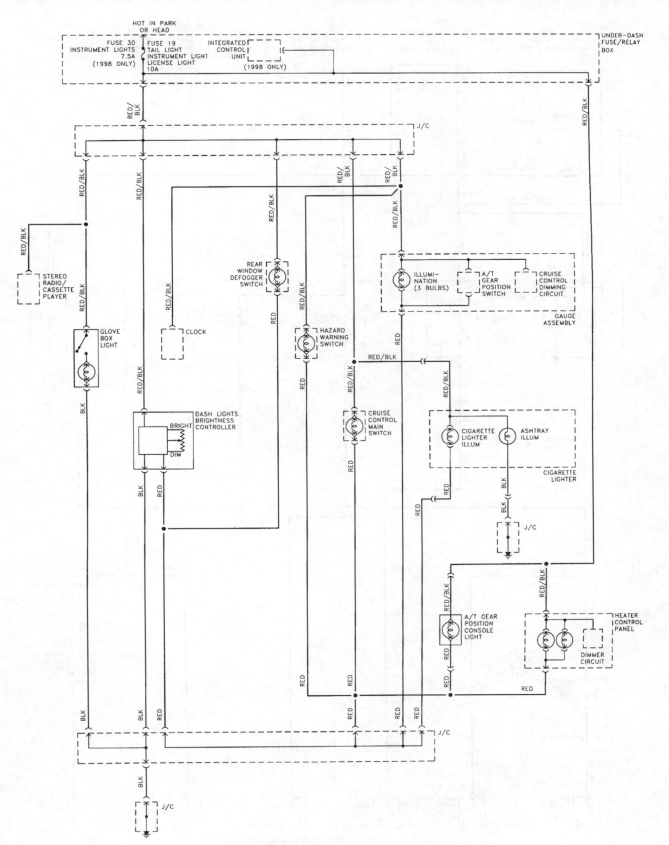

Interior lighting system (1 of 2) - Integra

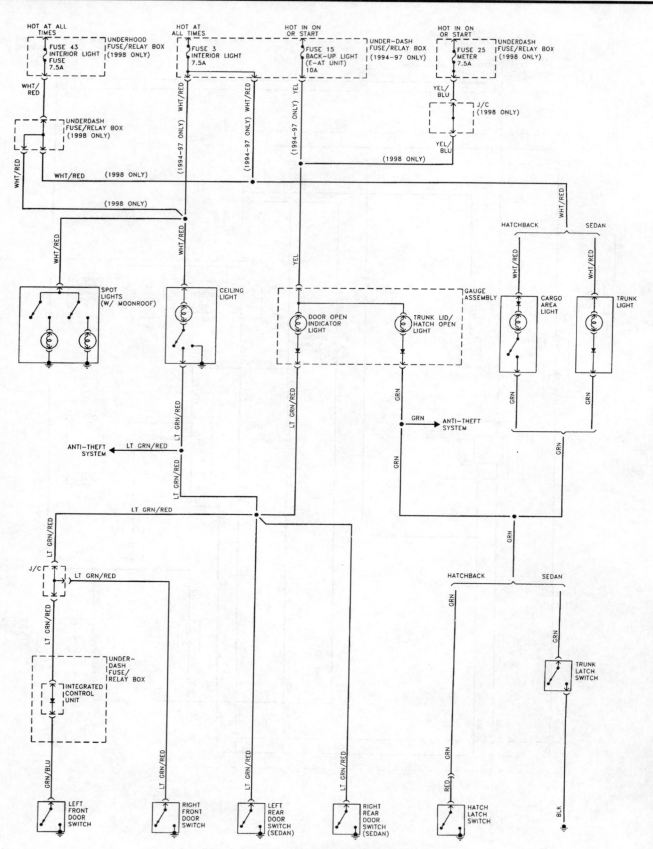

Interior lighting system (2 of 2) - Integra

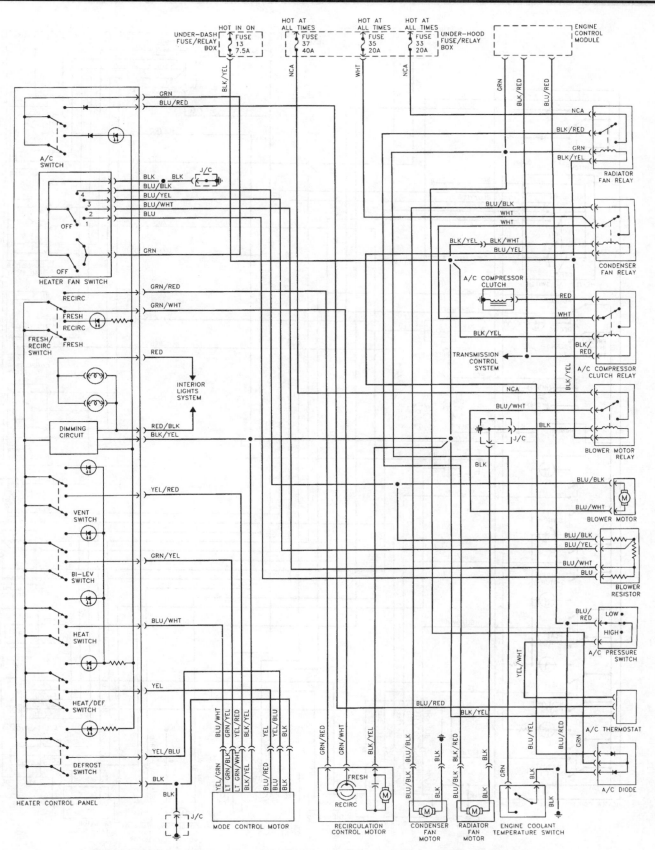

Heating and air conditioning system (including engine cooling fan) - 1994 thru 1997 Integra

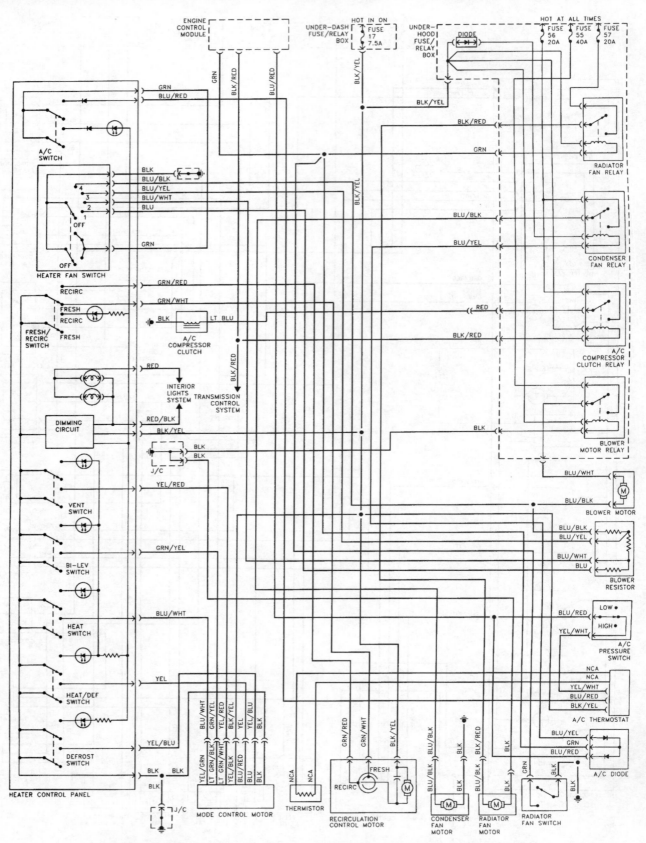

Heating and air conditioning system (including engine cooling fan) - 1998 Integra

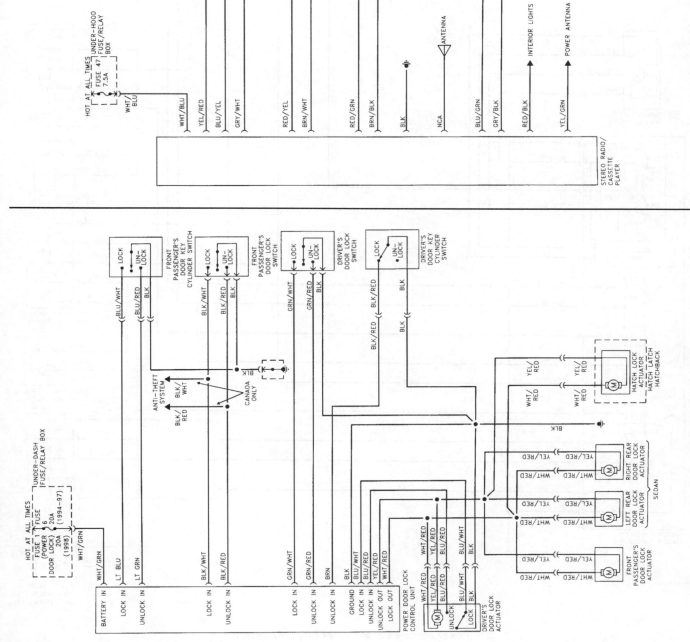

Typical stereo system - Integra

Power door lock system - Integra

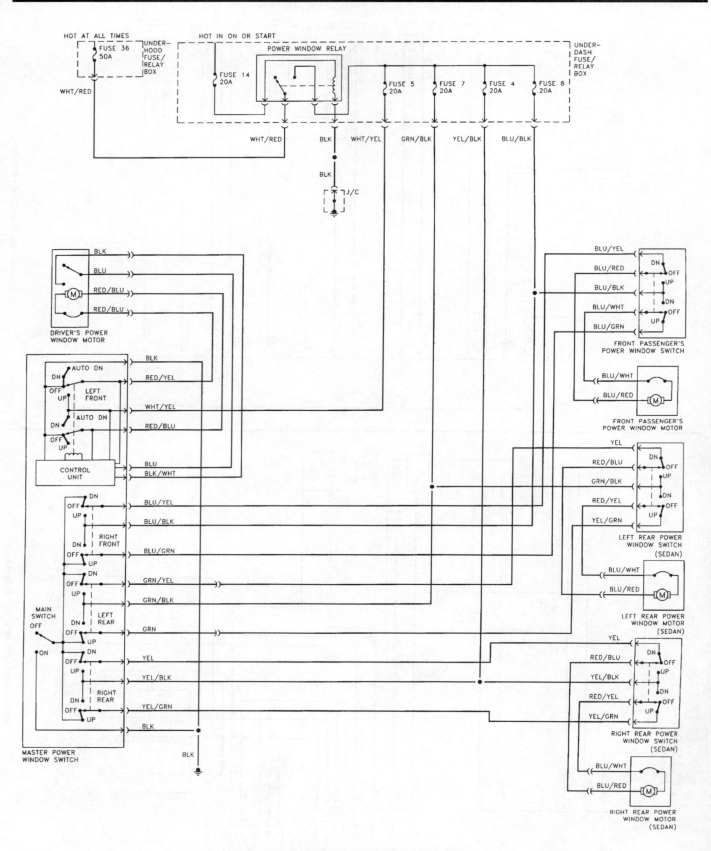

Power window system - 1994 thru 1997 Integra

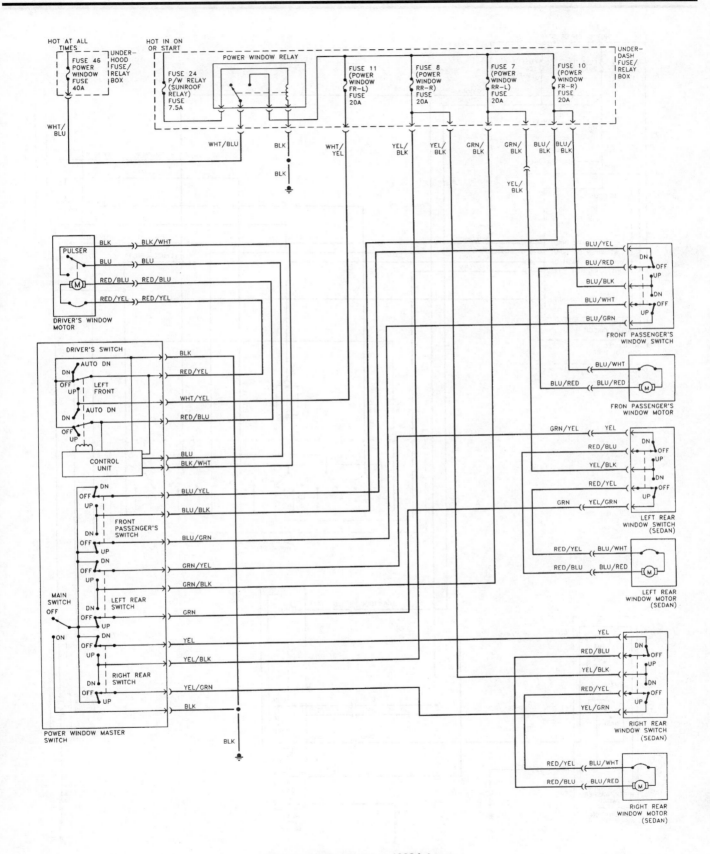

Power window system - 1998 Integra

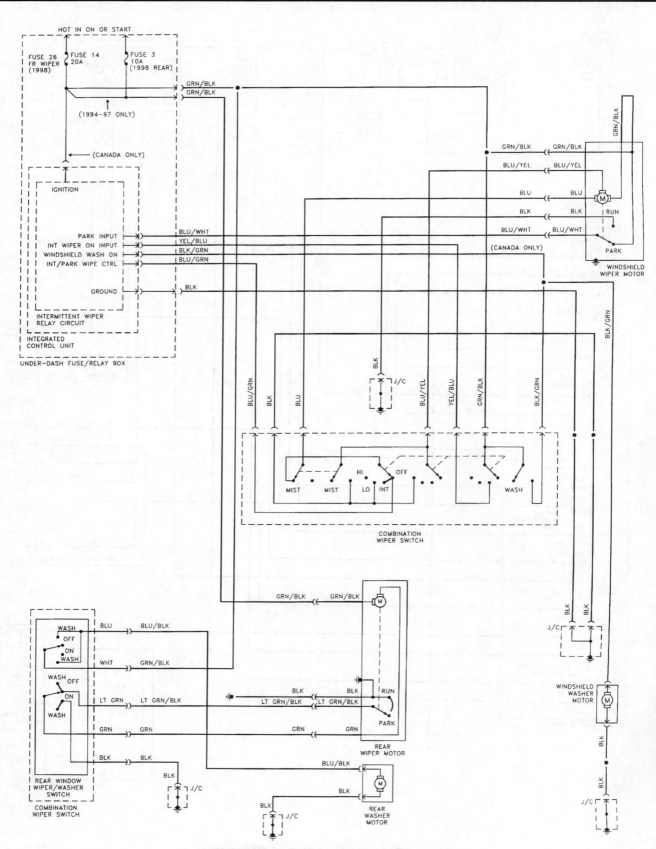

Windshield wiper and washer system - Integra

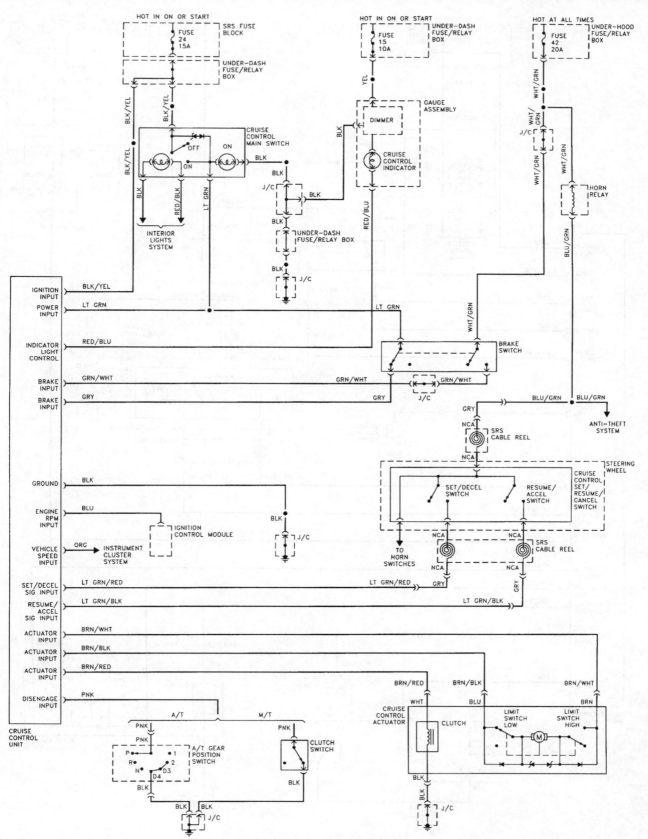

Cruise control system - 1994 thru 1997 Integra

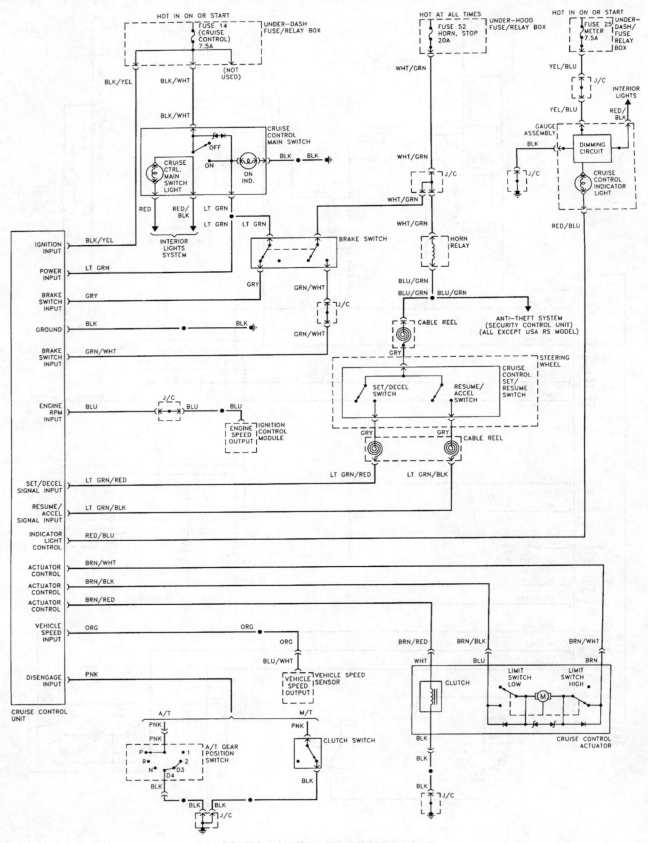

Cruise control system - 1998 Integra

Index

IND

Haynes Automotive Manuals

ACURA
*12020 Integra '86 thru '89 & Legend '86 thru '90

AMC
Jeep CJ - see JEEP (50020)
14020 Concord/Hornet/Gremlin/Spirit '70 thru '83
14025 (Renault) Alliance & Encore '83 thru '87

AUDI
15020 4000 all models '80 thru '87
15025 5000 all models '77 thru '83
15026 5000 all models '84 thru '88

AUSTIN
Healey Sprite - see MG Midget (66015)

BMW
*18020 3/5 Series '82 thru '92
*18021 3 Series except 325iX models '92 thru '98
18025 320i all 4 cyl models '75 thru '83
18035 528i & 530i all models '75 thru '80
18050 1500 thru 2002 except Turbo '59 thru '77

BUICK
Century (FWD) - see GM (38005)
*19020 Buick, Oldsmobile & Pontiac Full-size (Front wheel drive) '85 thru '98
Buick Electra, LeSabre and Park Avenue; Oldsmobile Delta 88 Royale, Ninety Eight and Regency; Pontiac Bonneville
19025 Buick Oldsmobile & Pontiac Full-size (Rear wheel drive)
Buick Estate '70 thru '90, Electra'70 thru '84, LeSabre '70 thru '85, Limited '74 thru '79
Oldsmobile Custom Cruiser '70 thru '90, Delta 88 '70 thru '85,Ninety-eight '70 thru '84
Pontiac Bonneville '70 thru '81, Catalina '70 thru '81, Grandville '70 thru '75, Parisienne '83 thru '86
19030 Mid-size Regal & Century '74 thru '87
Regal - see GENERAL MOTORS (38010)
Skyhawk - see GM (38030)
Skylark - see GM (38020, 38025)
Somerset - see GENERAL MOTORS (38025)

CADILLAC
*21030 Cadillac Rear Wheel Drive '70 thru '93
Cimarron, Eldorado & Seville - see GM (38015, 38030)

CHEVROLET
10305 Chevrolet Engine Overhaul Manual
*24010 Astro & GMC Safari Mini-vans '85 thru '93
24015 Camaro V8 all models '70 thru '81
24016 Camaro all models '82 thru '92
Cavalier - see GM (38015)
Celebrity - see GM (38005)
24017 Camaro & Firebird '93 thru '97
24020 Chevelle, Malibu, El Camino '69 thru '87
24024 Chevette & Pontiac T1000 '76 thru '87
Citation - see GENERAL MOTORS (38020)
*24032 Corsica/Beretta all models '87 thru '96
24040 Corvette all V8 models '68 thru '82
*24041 Corvette all models '84 thru '96
24045 Full-size Sedans Caprice, Impala, Biscayne, Bel Air & Wagons '69 thru '90
24046 Impala SS & Caprice and Buick Roadmaster '91 thru '96
Lumina '90 thru '94 - see GM (38010)
24048 Lumina & Monte Carlo '95 thru '98
Lumina APV - see GM (38035)
24050 Luv Pick-up all 2WD & 4WD '72 thru '82
24055 Monte Carlo all models '70 thru '88
Monte Carlo '95 thru '98 - see LUMINA
24059 Nova all V8 models '69 thru '79
*24060 Nova/Geo Prizm '85 thru '92
24064 Pick-ups '67 thru '87 - Chevrolet & GMC, all V8 & in-line 6 cyl, 2WD & 4WD '67 thru '87; Suburbans, Blazers & Jimmys '67 thru '91
*24065 Pick-ups '88 thru '98 - Chevrolet & GMC, all full-size models '88 thru '98; Blazer & Jimmy '92 thru '94; Suburban '92 thru '98; Tahoe & Yukon '95 thru '98
*24070 S-10 & GMC S-15 Pick-ups '82 thru '93
*24071 S-10, Gmc S-15 & Jimmy '94 thru '96
*24075 Sprint & Geo Metro '85 thru '94
*24080 Vans - Chevrolet & GMC '68 thru '96

CHRYSLER
10310 Chrysler Engine Overhaul Manual
*25015 Chrysler Cirrus, Dodge Stratus, Plymouth Breeze, '95 thru '98
*25020 Chrysler Full-Wheel Drive '88 thru '93
K-Cars - see DODGE Aries (30008)
Laser - see DODGE Daytona (30030)
25025 Chrysler LHS, Concorde & New Yorker, Dodge Intrepid, Eagle Vision, '93 thru '97
*25030 Chrysler/Plym. Mid-size '82 thru '95
Rear-wheel Drive - see DODGE (30050)

DATSUN
28005 200SX all models '80 thru '83
28007 B-210 all models '73 thru '78
28009 210 all models '78 thru '82
28012 240Z, 260Z & 280Z Coupe '70 thru '78
28014 280ZX Coupe & 2+2 '79 thru '83
300ZX - see NISSAN (72010)
28016 310 all models '78 thru '82
28018 510 & PL521 Pick-up '68 thru '73
28020 510 all models '78 thru '81
28022 620 Series Pick-up all models '73 thru '79
720 Series Pick-up - NISSAN (72030)
28025 810/Maxima all gas models, '77 thru '84

DODGE
400 & 600 - see CHRYSLER (25030)
*30008 Aries & Plymouth Reliant '81 thru '89
30010 Caravan & Ply. Voyager '84 thru '95
*30011 Caravan & Ply. Voyager '96 thru '98
30012 Challenger/Plymouth Saporro '78 thru '83
Challenger/'67-'76 - see DART (30025)
30016 Colt/Plymouth Champ '78 thru '87
*30020 Dakota Pick-ups all models '87 thru '96
30025 Dart, Challenger/Plymouth Barracuda & Valiant 6 cyl models '67 thru '76
*30030 Daytona & Chrysler Laser '84 thru '89
Intrepid - see Chrysler (25025)
*30034 Dodge & Plymouth Neon '95 thru '97
*30035 Omni & Plymouth Horizon '78 thru '90
30040 Pick-ups all full-size '74 thru '93
*30041 Pick-ups all full-size '94 thru '96
*30045 Ram 50/D50 Pick-ups & Raider and Plymouth Arrow Pick-ups '79 thru '93
30050 Dodge/Ply./Chrysler RWD '71 thru '89
*30055 Shadow/Plymouth Sundance '87 thru '94
*30060 Spirit & Plymouth Acclaim '89 thru '95
*30065 Vans - Dodge & Plymouth '71 thru '96

EAGLE
Talon - see MITSUBISHI Eclipse (68030)
Vision - see CHRYSLER (25025)

FIAT
34010 124 Sport Coupe & Spider '68 thru '78
34025 X1/9 all models '74 thru '80

FORD
10355 Ford Automatic Transmission Overhaul
10320 Ford Engine Overhaul Manual
*36004 Aerostar Mini-vans '86 thru '96
Aspire - see FORD Festiva (36030)
*36006 Contour/Mercury Mystique '95 thru '98
36008 Courier Pick-up all models '72 thru '82
36012 Crown Victoria & Mercury Grand Marquis '88 thru '96
36016 Escort/Mercury Lynx '81 thru '90
*36020 Escort/Mercury Tracer '91 thru '96
Exp - see FORD Pick-up (36059)
*36024 Explorer & Mazda Navajo '91 thru '95
36028 Fairmont & Mercury Zephyr '78 thru '83
36030 Festiva & Aspire '88 thru '97
36032 Fiesta all models '77 thru '80
36036 Ford & Mercury Full-size,
Ford LTD & Mercury Marquis ('75 thru '82); Ford Custom 500,Country Squire, Crown Victoria & Mercury Colony Park ('75 thru '87); Ford LTD Crown Victoria & Mercury Gran Marquis ('83 thru '87)
36040 Granada & Mercury Monarch '75 thru '82
36044 Ford & Mercury Mid-size, Ford Thunderbird & Mercury Cougar ('75 thru '82); Ford LTD & Mercury Marquis ('83 thru '86); Ford Torino,Gran Torino, Elite, Ranchero pick-up, LTD II, Mercury Montego, Comet, XR-7 & Lincoln Versailles ('75 thru '86)
36048 Mustang V8 all models '64-1/2 thru '73
36049 Mustang II all 4 cyl, V6 & V8 '74 thru '78
36050 Mustang & Mercury Capri incl. Turbo Mustang, '79 thru '93; Capri, '79 thru '86
*36051 Mustang all models '94 thru '97
36054 Pick-ups and Bronco '73 thru '79
*36058 Pick-ups and Bronco '80 thru '96
*36059 Pick-ups, Expedition &
Lincoln Navigator '97 thru '98
36062 Pinto & Mercury Bobcat '75 thru '80
36066 Probe all models '89 thru '92
*36070 Ranger/Bronco II gas models '83 thru '92
*36071 Ford Ranger '93 thru '97 &
Mazda Pick-ups '94 thru '97
*36074 Taurus & Mercury Sable '86 thru '95
*36075 Taurus & Mercury Sable '96 thru '98
*36078 Tempo & Mercury Topaz '84 thru '94
36082 Thunderbird/Mercury Cougar '83 thru '88
36086 Thunderbird/Mercury Cougar '89 and '97
36090 Vans all V8 Econoline models '69 thru '91
*36094 Vans full size '92 thru '95
*36097 Windstar Mini-van '95 thru '98

GENERAL MOTORS
*10360 GM Automatic Transmission Overhaul
*38005 Buick Century, Chevrolet Celebrity, Olds Cutlass Ciera & Pontiac 6000 all models '82 thru '96
*38010 Buick Regal, Chevrolet Lumina, Oldsmobile Cutlass Supreme & Pontiac Grand Prix front wheel drive '88 thru '95
*38015 Buick Skyhawk, Cadillac Cimarron, Chevrolet Cavalier, Oldsmobile Firenza Pontiac J-2000 & Sunbird '82 thru '94
*38016 Chevrolet Cavalier &
Pontiac Sunfire '95 thru '98
38020 Buick Skylark, Chevrolet Citation, Olds Omega, Pontiac Phoenix '80 thru '85
38025 Buick Skylark & Somerset, Olds Achieva, Calais & Pontiac Grand Am '85 thru '95
38030 Cadillac Eldorado & Oldsmobile Toronado '71 thru '85, Seville '80 thru '85, Buick Riviera '79 thru '85
*38035 Chevrolet Lumina APV, Oldsmobile Silhouette & Pontiac Trans Sport '90 thru '95
General Motors Full-size
Rear-wheel Drive - see BUICK (19025)

GEO
Metro - see CHEVROLET Sprint (24075)
Prizm - see CHEVROLET (24060) or TOYOTA (92036)
*40030 Storm all models '90 thru '93
Tracker - see SUZUKI Samurai (90010)

GMC
Safari - see CHEVROLET ASTRO (24010)
Vans & Pick-ups - see CHEVROLET

HONDA
42010 Accord CVCC all models '76 thru '83
42011 Accord all models '84 thru '89
42012 Accord all models '90 thru '93
*42013 Accord all models '94 thru '95
42020 Civic 1200 all models '73 thru '79
42021 Civic 1300 & 1500 CVCC '80 thru '83
42022 Civic 1500 CVCC all models '75 thru '79
42023 Civic all models '84 thru '91
42024 Civic & del Sol '92 thru '95
Passport - see ISUZU Rodeo (47017)
*42040 Prelude CVCC all models '79 thru '89

HYUNDAI
*43015 Excel all models '86 thru '94

ISUZU
Hombre - see CHEVROLET S-10 (24071)
*47017 Rodeo '91 thru '97, Amigo '89 thru '94, Honda Passport '95 thru '97
*47020 Trooper '84 thru '91, Pick-up '81 thru '93

JAGUAR
*49010 XJ6 all 6 cyl models '68 thru '86
*49011 XJ6 all models '88 thru '94
*49015 XJ12 & XJS all 12 cyl models '72 thru '85

JEEP
*50010 Cherokee, Comanche & Wagoneer Limited all models '84 thru '96
50020 CJ all models '49 thru '86
*50025 Grand Cherokee all models '93 thru '98
*50029 Grand Wagoneer & Pick-up '72 thru '91
*50030 Wrangler all models '87 thru '95

LINCOLN
Navigator - see FORD Pick-up (36059)
59010 Rear Wheel Drive all models '70 thru '96

MAZDA
61010 GLC (rear wheel drive) '77 thru '83
61011 GLC (front wheel drive) '81 thru '85
*61015 323 & Protegé '90 thru '97
*61016 MX-5 Miata '90 thru '97
*61020 MPV all models '89 thru '94
Navajo - see FORD Explorer (36024)
61030 Pick-ups '72 thru '93
Pick-ups '94 on - see Ford (36071)
61035 RX-7 all models '79 thru '85
*61036 RX-7 all models '86 thru '91
61040 626 (rear wheel drive) '79 thru '82
*61041 626 & MX-6 (front wheel drive) '83 thru '91

MERCEDES-BENZ
63012 123 Series Diesel '76 thru '85
*63015 190 Series 4-cyl gas models, '84 thru '88
63020 230, 250 & 280 6 cyl sohc '68 thru '72
63025 280 123 Series gas models '77 thru '81
63030 350 & 450 all models '71 thru '80

MERCURY
See FORD Listing

MG
66010 MGB Roadster & GT Coupe '62 thru '80
66015 MG Midget & Austin Healey Sprite Roadster '58 thru '80

MITSUBISHI
*68020 Cordia, Tredia, Galant, Precis & Mirage '83 thru '93
*68030 Eclipse, Eagle Talon &
Plymouth Laser '90 thru '94
*68040 Pick-up '83 thru '96, Montero '83 thru '93

NISSAN
72010 300ZX all models incl. Turbo '84 thru '89
*72015 Altima all models '93 thru '97
*72020 Maxima all models '85 thru '91
*72030 Pick-ups '80 thru '96, Pathfinder '87 thru '95
72040 Pulsar all models '83 thru '86
72050 Sentra all models '82 thru '94
*72051 Sentra & 200SX all models '95 thru '98
*72060 Stanza all models '82 thru '90

OLDSMOBILE
*73015 Cutlass '74 thru '88
For other OLDSMOBILE titles, see BUICK, CHEVROLET or GENERAL MOTORS listing.

PLYMOUTH
For PLYMOUTH titles, see DODGE.

PONTIAC
79008 Fiero all models '84 thru '88
79018 Firebird V8 models except Turbo '70 thru '81
79019 Firebird all models '82 thru '92
For other PONTIAC titles, see BUICK, CHEVROLET or GENERAL MOTORS listing.

PORSCHE
*80020 911 Coupe & Targa models '65 thru '89
80025 914 all 4 cyl models '69 thru '76
80030 924 all models incl. Turbo '76 thru '82
*80035 944 all models incl. Turbo '83 thru '89

RENAULT
Alliance, Encore - see AMC (14020)

SAAB
*84010 900 including Turbo '79 thru '88

SATURN
*87010 Saturn all models '91 thru '96

SUBARU
89002 1100, 1300, 1400 & 1600 '71 thru '79
*89003 1600 & 1800 2WD & 4WD '80 thru '94

SUZUKI
*90010 Samurai/Sidekick/Geo Tracker '86 thru '96

TOYOTA
92005 Camry all models '83 thru '91
*92006 Camry all models '92 thru '96
92015 Celica Rear Wheel Drive '71 thru '85
*92020 Celica Front Wheel Drive '86 thru '93
92025 Celica Supra all models '79 thru '92
92030 Corolla all models '75 thru '79
92032 Corolla rear wheel drive models '80 thru '87
*92035 Corolla front wheel drive models '84 thru '92
*92036 Corolla & Geo Prizm '93 thru '97
92040 Corolla Tercel all models '80 thru '82
92045 Corona all models '74 thru '82
92050 Cressida all models '78 thru '82
92055 Land Cruiser Series FJ40, 43, 45 & 55 '68 thru '82
*92056 Land Cruiser Series FJ60, 62, 80 & FZJ80 '68 thru '82
*92065 MR2 all models '85 thru '87
92070 Pick-up all models '69 thru '78
92075 Pick-up all models '79 thru '95
*92076 Tacoma '95 thru '98,
4Runner '96 thru '98, T100 '93 thru '98
92080 Previa all models '91 thru '95
92085 Tercel all models '87 thru '94

TRIUMPH
94007 Spitfire all models '62 thru '81
94010 TR7 all models '75 thru '81

VW
96008 Beetle & Karmann Ghia '54 thru '79
96012 Dasher all gasoline models '74 thru '81
*96016 Rabbit, Jetta, Scirocco, & Pick-up gas models '74 thru '91 & Convertible '80 thru '92
*96017 Golf & Jetta '93 thru '97
96020 Rabbit, Jetta, Pick-up diesel '77 thru '84
96030 Transporter 1600 all models '68 thru '79
96035 Transporter 1700, 1800, 2000 '72 thru '79
96040 Type 3 1500 & 1600 '63 thru '73
96045 Vanagon air-cooled models '80 thru '83

VOLVO
97010 120, 130 Series & 1800 Sports '61 thru '73
97015 140 Series all models '66 thru '74
*97020 240 Series all models '76 thru '93
97025 260 Series all models '75 thru '82
*97040 740 & 760 Series all models '82 thru '88

TECHBOOK MANUALS
10205 Automotive Computer Codes
10210 Automotive Emissions Control Manual
10215 Fuel Injection Manual, 1978 thru 1985
10220 Fuel Injection Manual, 1986 thru 1996
10225 Holley Carburetor Manual
10230 Rochester Carburetor Manual
10240 Weber/Zenith/Stromberg/SU Carburetor
10305 Chevrolet Engine Overhaul Manual
10310 Chrysler Engine Overhaul Manual
10320 Ford Engine Overhaul Manual
10330 GM and Ford Diesel Engine Repair
10340 Small Engine Repair Manual
10345 Suspension, Steering & Driveline
10355 Ford Automatic Transmission Overhaul
10360 GM Automatic Transmission Overhaul
10405 Automotive Body Repair & Painting
10410 Automotive Brake Manual
10415 Automotive Detailing Manual
10420 Automotive Eelectrical Manual
10425 Automotive Heating & Air Conditioning
10430 Automotive Reference Dictionary
10435 Automotive Tools Manual
10440 Used Car Buying Guide
10445 Welding Manual
10450 ATV Basics

SPANISH MANUALS
98903 Reparación de Carrocería & Pintura
98905 Códigos Automotrices de la Computadora
98910 Frenos Automotriz
98915 Inyección de Combustible 1986 al 1994
99040 Chevrolet & GMC Camionetas '67 al '87
99041 Chevrolet & GMC Camionetas '88 al '95
99042 Chevrolet Camionetas Cerradas '68 al '95
99055 Dodge Caravan/Ply. Voyager '84 al '95
99075 Ford Camionetas y Bronco '80 al '94
99077 Ford Camionetas Cerradas '69 al '91
99083 Ford Modelos de Tamaño Grande '75 al '87
99088 Ford Modelos de Tamaño Mediano '75 al '86
99091 Ford Taurus & Mercury Sable '86 al '95
99095 GM Modelos de Tamaño Grande '70 al '90
99100 GM Modelos de Tamaño Mediano '70 al '88
99110 Nissan Camionetas '80 al '96, Pathfinder '87 al '95
99118 Nissan Sentra '82 al '94
99125 Toyota Camionetas y 4-Runner '79 al '95

Haynes North America, Inc., 861 Lawrence Drive, Newbury Park, CA 91320 • (805) 498-6703